19th Linguistic Annotation Workshop (LAW-XIX-2025)

Vienna, Austria
31 July 2025

ISBN: 979-8-3313-2412-4

Printed from e-media with permission by:

Curran Associates, Inc.
57 Morehouse Lane
Red Hook, NY 12571

Some format issues inherent in the e-media version may also appear in this print version.

Association for Computational Linguistics
209 N. Eighth Street
Stroudsburg, Pennsylvania 18360

Phone: 1-570-476-8006
Fax: 1-570-476-0860

acl@aclweb.org

Additional copies of this publication are available from:

Curran Associates, Inc.
57 Morehouse Lane
Red Hook, NY 12571 USA
Phone: 845-758-0400
Fax: 845-758-2633
Email: curran@proceedings.com
Web: www.proceedings.com

LAW-XIX 2025

Proceedings of the 19th Linguistic Annotation Workshop (LAW-XIX-2025)

Proceedings of the Workshop

July 31, 2025

Order copies of this and other ACL proceedings from:

Association for Computational Linguistics (ACL)
317 Sidney Baker St. S
Suite 400 - 134
Kerrville, TX 78028
USA
Tel: +1-855-225-1962
acl@aclweb.org

The LAW-XIX organizers gratefully acknowledge the support from the following sponsors.

ELRA
LANGUAGE RESOURCES ASSOCIATION

Introduction

Linguistic annotation of natural language corpora is the backbone of supervised methods of statistical natural language processing. The Linguistic Annotation Workshop (LAW) is the annual workshop of the ACL and ELRA Special Interest Group on Annotation (SIGANN), and it provides a forum for the presentation and discussion of innovative research on all aspects of linguistic annotation, including the creation and evaluation of annotation schemes, methods for automatic and manual annotation, use and evaluation of annotation software and frameworks, representation of linguistic data and annotations, semi-supervised human in the loopmethods of annotation, crowd-sourcing approaches, and more.
As in the past, this year's LAW provides a forum for annotation researchers to work towards standardization, best practices, and interoperability of annotation information and software.
These proceedings include papers that were presented at the 19th Linguistic Annotation Workshop (LAW-XIX), co-located with ACL 2025 in Vienna, Austria, on July 31, 2025.
This edition of the workshop is the nineteenth meeting of the ACL and ELRA Special Interest Group for Annotation. The first workshop took place in 2007 at the ACL in Prague. Since then, the LAW has been held every year, consistently drawing substantial participation (both in terms of paper/poster submissions and participation in the actual workshop) providing evidence that the LAW's overall focus continues to be an important area of interest in the field, a substantial part of which relies on supervised learning from gold standard data sets and trustworthy evaluation in the era of Large Language Models. This year, we received 66 submissions, out of which 30 papers have been accepted to be presented at the workshop, as long or short papers, or as posters.
In addition, LAW-XIX features two invited talks by Junyi Jessy Li (University of Texas at Austin) and Rotem Dror (Haifa University).
The special theme of LAW-XIX is *Subjectivity and Variation in Linguistic Annotation.* As linguistic annotation increasingly supports diverse NLP applications, questions of annotator subjectivity, inter-annotator variation, and annotation uncertainty have become central to the field. Our special oral sessions aim to stimulate discussions on the challenges, methodological advances, and theoretical implications related to disagreement and subjectivity in annotation practice.
Our thanks go to SIGANN for their financial support and to our organizing committee, for their continuing organization of the LAW workshops. Most of all, we would like to thank all the authors for submitting their papers to the workshop, our program committee members for their dedication and their thoughtful reviews and our keynote speakers for sharing their insights on the topics of subjectivity, variation and social biases in linguistic annotation.

The LAW-XIX Program Co-Chairs:
Siyao Peng and Ines Rehbein

Organizing Committee

Program Chairs

Siyao Peng, LMU Munich
Ines Rehbein, University of Mannheim

SIGANN President

Amir Zeldes, Georgetown University

SIGANN Secretary

Ines Rehbein, University of Mannheim

SIGANN Officers

Claire Bonial, US Army Research Laboratory
Stefanie Dipper, Ruhr-Universität Bochum
Annemarie Friedrich, University of Augsburg
Sophie Henning, Bosch Center for Artificial Intelligence
Chu-Ren Huang, The Hong Kong Polytechnic University
Jenna D. Hwang, Allen Institute for AI
Nancy Ide, Vassar College
Sandra Kübler, Indiana University
Lori Levin, Carnegie Mellon University
Adam Meyers, New York University
Antonio Pareja-Lora, Universidad de Alcalá (UAH) / FITISPos (UAH) / ATLAS (UNED) / DMEG (UdG)
Siyao Peng, LMU Munich
Massimo Poesio, Queen Mary University of London and University of Utrecht
Sameer Pradhan, LDC, Cemantix
Jakob Prange, University of Augsburg
Ines Rehbein, University of Mannheim
Nathan Schneider, Georgetown University
Manfred Stede, University of Potsdam
Katrin Tomanek, Google
Fei Xia, University of Washington
Nianwen Xue, Brandeis University
Amir Zeldes, Georgetown University
Deniz Zeyrek, Middle East Technical University
Heike Zinsmeister, Hamburg University

Program Committee

Chairs

Siyao Peng, LMU Munich
Ines Rehbein, Mannheim University

Program Committee

Maria Becker, Heidelberg University
Verena Blaschke, LMU Munich
Claire Bonial, Army Research Lab
Miriam Butt, Konstanz University
Daniel Dakota, Indiana University
Marie-Catherine de Marneffe, FNRS - UCLouvain
Lucia Donatelli, Vrije Universiteit Amsterdam
Luise Dürlich, Uppsala University
Jonathan Dunn, University of Illinois, Urbana-Champaign
Pablo Picasso Feliciano de Faria, University of Campinas
Annemarie Friedrich, Augsburg University
Kim Gerdes, Université Paris-Saclay
Luke Gessler, Indiana University Bloomington
Ziwei Gong, Columbia University
Pingjun Hong, LMU Munich
Chengzhi Martin Hu, LMU Munich
Nancy Ide, Vassar College
Maxim Ionov, University of Cologne
Sandra Kübler, Indiana University
Ekaterina Lapshinova-Koltunski, University of Hildesheim
Ji-Ung Lee, Saarland University
Els Lefever, Ghent University
Lori Levin, Carnegie Mellon University
Lauren Levine, Georgetown University
Sebastian Loftus, LMU Munich
Abdou Mohamed Naira, SI2M Lab, INSEA
Anna Nedoluzhko, Charles University
Ercong Nie, LMU Munich
Juhyun Oh, KAIST
Teresa Paccosi, University of Trento
Alexis Palmer, University of Boulder
Antonio Pareja-Lora, University of Alcalá
Massimo Poesio, Utrecht University
Jakob Prange, Augsburg University
James Pustejovsky, Brandeis University
Sebastian Reimann, University of Jena
Josef Ruppenhofer, University of Hagen
Egil Rønningstad, University of Oslo
Tatjana Scheffler, University of Bochum
Nathan Schneider, Georgetown University
Merel Scholman, Utrecht University

Wesley Scivetti, Georgetown University
Indira Sen, Mannheim University
Soh-Eun Shim, LMU Munich
Manfred Stede, Potsdam University
Hakyung Sung, University of Oregon
Andreas Säuberli, LMU Munich
Ludovic Tanguy, CNRS, University of Toulouse
Joel Tetreault, Dataminr
Lilian Diana Awuor Wanzare, Maseno University
Bonnie Webber, University of Edinburgh
Leonie Weissweiler, UT Austin
Michael Wiegand, University of Vienna
Mohammad Yeghaneh Abkenar, Potsdam University
Karolina Zaczynska, Potsdam University
Amir Zeldes, Georgetown University
Deniz Zeyrek, Middle East Technical University
Wei Zhou, RWTH Aachen
Heike Zinsmeister, Hamburg University
Longfei Zuo, LMU Munich
Şaziye Betül Özateş, Boğaziçi University

Keynote Talk

Data Annotation in the Era of LLMs - Thoughts and Good Practices

Rotem Dror
University of Haifa
2025-07-31 09:00:00 – Room: **Room 1.15-16**

Abstract: The rise of large language models (LLMs) presents both opportunities and challenges for data annotation in NLP. In this talk, I will explore the evolving role of LLMs as annotators, particularly in tasks involving subjectivity. I will present recent work that will also be presented in the conference on how to evaluate whether an LLM is a good annotator: The Alternative Annotator Test for LLM-as-a-Judge: How to Statistically Justify Replacing Human Annotators with LLMs"—highlighting methods introduced in our paper—and discuss how LLMs compare to human annotators in consistency and reliability. I will also introduce new, unpublished research on best practices for identifying when and how LLMs can serve as reliable annotators for subjective NLP tasks. The talk aims to provide both theoretical insights and practical guidance for researchers and practitioners rethinking annotation pipelines in the LLM era.

Bio: Dr. Dror is an Assistant Professor (Senior Lecturer) at the Department of Information Systems, University of Haifa. She completed her Postdoctoral Research at the Cognitive Computation Group at the Department of Computer and Information Science, University of Pennsylvania, working with Prof. Dan Roth. She completed her Ph.D. in the Natural Language Processing Group, supervised by Prof. Roi Reichart, at the Faculty of Industrial Engineering and Management at the Technion - Israel Institute of Technology. Her research involves developing statistically sound methodologies for empirical investigation and evaluation for Data Science with a focus on Natural Language Processing applications.

Keynote Talk
Engaging experts and LLMs in corpora development

Junyi Jessy Li
University of Texas at Austin
2025-07-31 16:00:00 – Room: **Room 1.15-16**

Abstract: Large language models (LLMs) have become ever more capable, surpassing human performance on a number of tasks. Recent findings showed that LLMs can effectively replace traditional crowdsourcing to a large extent, and model training has increasingly been driven by synthetically generated data. These developments have triggered new questions about corpora development. This talk explores two of them: First, what type of human annotation can still be useful? I discuss our efforts engaging human expertise to effectively capture implicit reasoning in discourse and pragmatics, revealing weaknesses in existing models in those aspects. Second, how can we leverage LLMs to reveal task nuances that may be unknown before annotation? I present Explanation-Based Rescaling (EBR), a method that uses an LLM to rescale coarse-grained human ratings into consistent, fine-grained scores using natural language explanations from annotators, while discerning task subtleties embedded in these explanations.

Bio: Jessy Li is an Associate Professor in the Linguistics Department at the University of Texas at Austin. She received her Ph.D. (2017) from the Department of Computer and Information Science at the University of Pennsylvania. Her research interests are in computational linguistics and NLP, specifically discourse and document-level processing, natural language generation, and pragmatics. She is a recipient of an NSF CAREER Award, ACL and EMNLP Outstanding Paper Awards, an ACM SIGSOFT Distinguished Paper Award, among other honors. Jessy is the current Secretary of NAACL.

Table of Contents

Program

Thursday, July 31, 2025

08:45 - 09:00	*Opening Remarks*
09:00 - 09:45	*Keynote 1 – Rotem Dror: Data Annotation in the Era of LLMs - Thoughts and Good Practices*
09:45 - 10:30	*Oral Session 1: Disagreement and ambiguity in highly subjective tasks*
	Understanding Disagreement: An Annotation Study of Sentiment and Emotional Language in Environmental Communication Christina Barz, Melanie Siegel, Daniel Hanss and Michael Wiegand
	Measuring Label Ambiguity in Subjective Tasks using Predictive Uncertainty Estimation Richard Alies, Elena Merdjanovska and Alan Akbik
	Disagreements in analyses of rhetorical text structure: A new dataset and first analyses Freya Hewett and Manfred Stede
10:30 - 11:00	*Coffee*
11:00 - 11:30	*Oral Session 2: Subjectivity in linguistic annotation*
	Subjectivity in the Annotation of Bridging Anaphora Lauren Levine and Amir Zeldes
	The revision of linguistic annotation in the Universal Dependencies framework: a look at the annotators' behavior Magali Sanches Duran, Lucelene Lopes and Thiago Alexandre Salgueiro Pardo
11:30 - 12:30	*Poster Session 1*
	Forbidden FRUIT is the Sweetest: An Annotated Tweets Corpus for French Unfrozen Idioms Identification Julien Bezançon, Gaël Lejeune, Antoine Gautier, Marceau Hernandez and Félix Alié
	Another Approach to Agreement Measurement and Prediction with Emotion Annotations Quanqi Du and Veronique Hoste

Thursday, July 31, 2025 (continued)

Harmonizing Divergent Lemmatization and Part-of-Speech Tagging Practices for Latin Participles through the LiLa Knowledge Base
Marco Passarotti, Federica Iurescia and Paolo Ruffolo

UD-KSL Treebank v1.3: A semi-automated framework for aligning XPOS-extracted units with UPOS tags
Hakyung Sung, Gyu-Ho Shin, Chanyoung Lee, You Kyung Sung and Boo Kyung Jung

Bootstrapping UMRs from Universal Dependencies for Scalable Multilingual Annotation
Federica Gamba, Alexis Palmer and Daniel Zeman

Classifying TEI Encoding for DutchDraCor with Transformer Models
Florian Debaene and Veronique Hoste

Label Bias in Symbolic Representation of Meaning
Marie Mikulová, Jan Štěpánek and Jan Hajič

An Annotation Protocol for Diachronic Evaluation of Semantic Drift in Disability Sources
Nitisha Jain, Chiara Di Bonaventura, Albert Merono Penuela and Barbara McGillivray

Pre-annotation Matters: A Comparative Study on POS and Dependency Annotation for an Alsatian Dialect
Delphine Bernhard, Nathanaël Beiner and Barbara Hoff

Where it's at: Annotating Verb Placement Types in Learner Language
Josef Ruppenhofer, Annette Annette Portmann, Christine Renker, Matthias Schwendemann, Katrin Wisniewski and Torsten Zesch

ICLE-RC: International Corpus of Learner English for Relative Clauses
Debopam Das, Izabela Czerniak and Peter Bourgonje

ExpLay: A new Corpus Resource for the Research on Expertise as an Influential Factor on Language Production
Carmen Schacht and Renate Delucchi Danhier

12:30 - 14:00 *Lunch*

Thursday, July 31, 2025 (continued)

	Enhancing an Annotation Scheme for Clinical Narratives in Portuguese through Human Variation Analysis Ana Luisa Fernandes, Purificação Silvano, António Leal, Nuno Guimarães, Rita Rb-Silva, Luís Filipe Cunha and Alípio Jorge
15:00 - 15:30	*Oral Session 3: Datasets*
	Expanding the UNSC Conflicts Corpus by Incorporating Domain Expert Annotations and LLM Experiments Karolina Zaczynska
	Guidelines for Fine-grained Sentence-level Arabic Readability Annotation Nizar Habash, Hanada Taha-Thomure, Khalid Elmadani, Zeina Zeino and Abdallah Abushmaes
15:30 - 16:00	*Coffee*
16:00 - 16:45	*Keynote 2 – Junyi Jessy Li: Engaging experts and LLMs in corpora development*
16:45 - 17:00	*Wrap-up*

Understanding Disagreement: An Annotation Study of Sentiment and Emotional Language in Environmental Communication

Christina S. Barz
Faculty of Social Sciences
Darmstadt University
of Applied Sciences
Schöfferstraße 3
64295 Darmstadt
Germany
christina.barz@h-da.de

Melanie Siegel
Faculty of Computer Science
Darmstadt University
of Applied Sciences
Schöfferstraße 3
64295 Darmstadt
Germany
melanie.siegel@h-da.de

Daniel Hanss
Faculty of Social Sciences
Darmstadt University
of Applied Sciences
Schöfferstraße 3
64295 Darmstadt
Germany
daniel.hanss@h-da.de

Michael Wiegand
Digital Philology
Faculty of Philological and
Cultural Studies
University of Vienna
AT-1010 Vienna, Austria
michael.wiegand@univie.ac.at

Abstract

Emotional language is central to how environmental issues are communicated and received by the public. To better understand how such language is interpreted, we conducted an annotation study on sentiment and emotional language in texts from the environmental activist group Extinction Rebellion. The annotation process revealed substantial disagreement among annotators, highlighting the complexity and subjectivity involved in interpreting emotional language. In this paper, we analyze the sources of these disagreements, offering insights into how individual perspectives shape annotation outcomes. Our work contributes to ongoing discussions on perspectivism in NLP and emphasizes the importance of human-centered approaches and citizen science in analyzing environmental communication.

1 Introduction

Addressing the escalating environmental crises requires coordinated global action (IPCC, 2022; Fritsche and Masson, 2021). Emotions play a key role in motivating such action, shaping a range of behaviors from policy support to civil disobedience (Brosch, 2025; Schneider et al., 2021; Van Valkengoed and Steg, 2019).

Although there has been limited interdisciplinary research on the role of emotional language in environmental communication, existing studies suggest that such language can play a key role in mobilizing individuals for collective action (Salas Reyes et al., 2021; Kaushal et al., 2022; Zaremba et al., 2024). In this context, we define *emotional language* as the use of words or expressions that convey affective states. Importantly, we use the term *emotional language* - rather than emotion - to emphasize that our focus is on the strategic use of emotion-related expressions in group communication, rather than on measuring the actual felt emotions of individual speakers or writers. This distinction is particularly relevant when analyzing collective actors such as environmental groups, whose language is often shaped by strategic communication goals. However, the outcome of using emotional language in different socio-political contexts - especially in the discourse of groups with different ideologies, identities and thematic priorities - is still poorly researched and not well understood (Salas Reyes et al., 2021; Zaremba et al., 2024; Lehrer et al., 2023; Berger et al., 2019).

This paper is part of a broader project examining emotional language in environmental communication by highly visible and polarizing activist groups, and analyzing the emotional reactions such language provokes among the public (Barz et al., 2025). While the larger dataset includes multiple organizations, this study focuses on tweets from **Extinction Rebellion** (XR), a global activist group using nonviolent civil disobedience to demand urgent climate action. Our overarching goal is to develop a comprehensive, annotated dataset tai-

Proceedings of the 19th Linguistic Annotation Workshop (LAW-XIX-2025), pages 1–20
July 31, 2025

lored to environment-related communication, with applications in both environmental communication research and Natural Language Processing (NLP).

For this paper, we annotated sentiment and emotional language in XR's X (formerly Twitter) discourse, revealing substantial annotator disagreement. We analyze the factors driving this disagreement and explore how these insights can refine future annotation efforts in NLP and environmental communication research. Our findings highlight challenges in creating reliable annotated datasets and contribute to the broader debate on **perspectivism** in NLP, which recognizes that multiple valid interpretations of a text can coexist due to annotators' diverse backgrounds, experiences, and perspectives—challenging the notion of a single *ground truth* (Frenda et al., 2024; Uma et al., 2021; Rodríguez-Barroso et al., 2024).

To guide our investigation of these challenges and the implications of annotator subjectivity, our current work is structured around the following **research questions**:

RQ1 What factors may contribute to variation and disagreement in annotator labeling behavior?

RQ2 What insights can be gained from the observed disagreement, and how can they inform future annotation efforts?

The **main contributions** of this paper are as follows:

- We provide the first annotated and publicly available dataset of emotional language in XR's X discourse, contributing to the study of environmental communication.
- We perform analyses to systematically examine annotator disagreement, providing methodological insights into the influence of perspective in text annotation.
- We highlight the implications of perspectivism in annotation, demonstrating its relevance for both NLP applications and environmental communication research.

2 Related Work

This section reviews relevant literature on environmental communication as well as sentiment and emotion analysis.

2.1 Environmental Communication Studies

Environmental communication examines how humans perceive, discuss, and respond to environmental issues, with increasing attention to climate change communication (Carvalho and Peterson, 2024).

The study of environmental communication has gained prominence, particularly with social media's role in discourse and mobilization (Carvalho and Peterson, 2024; Schäfer, 2024; Lee et al., 2024; Amangeldi et al., 2024). Recent studies increasingly use computational methods, focusing on automated framing, discourse analysis, and translation studies (Hirsbrunner, 2024; Schäfer and Hase, 2023; Bird et al., 2024; Yasmin et al., 2024). However, NLP approaches beyond framing—such as sentiment, and emotion analysis—remain underexplored, despite emotional language's well-documented role in motivating collective action (Kaushal et al., 2022; Zaremba et al., 2024).

Research in this area has also predominantly analyzed news media (Anderson, 2024; Lahsen, 2022), prompting calls for broader investigations into the communication strategies of environmental groups and activist movements (Anderson, 2024).

2.2 Sentiment and Emotion Analysis, and Available Datasets

Emotion analysis is rarely applied to environmental communication, leading to a shortage of dedicated models and human-labeled datasets. Existing climate-related datasets primarily address sentiment, climate change denial, misinformation, or public opinion rather than emotional language (Stede and Patz, 2021). For instance, the *ClimaConvo* dataset includes 15,309 tweets from 2022 labeled for sentiment, climate change denial, hate speech, and humor (Shiwakoti et al., 2024). Similarly, the *Twitter Climate Change Sentiment Dataset* (Qian, 2021) comprises 43,943 tweets (2015–2018) labeled as news, pro (supporting anthropogenic climate change), neutral, or anti (rejecting anthropogenic climate change). A few datasets include emotional language, such as a collection of speeches by environmental activists, including Greta Thunberg, which focuses on anger (Ponton and Raimo, 2024). The *Emotional Climate Change Stories* (ECCS) dataset explores climate change storytelling and readers' emotional reactions, containing 180 short stories designed to evoke five emotions—anger, fear, com-

Climate Change and Sentiment Categories

Category	Example
CLIMATE DETECTION	
About Climate Change	*Climate change is one of the greatest threats of our time.*
CLIMATE SENTIMENT	
Positive/Opportunity	*Switching to renewable energy helps fight the climate crisis and creates new jobs.*
Negative/Risk	*Rising sea levels are threatening coastal cities around the world as average temperatures rise.*

Emotion Categories

Category	Example
ANGER	*It's infuriating to see politicians ignore climate science!*
CONCERN	*Today we are disappointed and worried: The Supreme Court of Norway has chosen to back oil over our rights to a liveable future.*
FEAR	*The alarming state of nature in the UK is a matter that should concern everyone.*
HOPE	*Every tree planted is a step towards a healthier planet.*
JOY	*We're celebrating today as more cities commit to 100% renewable energy!*
PRIDE	*Proud of our community for coming together to reduce plastic waste!*
SADNESS	*It's heartbreaking to witness the destruction of the Amazon rainforest.*
SOLIDARITY	*In unity with our brothers and sisters across the globe, let's stand united for climate justice.*

Table 1: Annotation categories for multi-label document-level annotations and example tweets.

passion, guilt, and hope—as well as neutral stories (Zaremba et al., 2024).

To our knowledge, no dataset or study exclusively analyzes environmental organizations' or activist groups' communication. Most datasets capture individual opinions or personal expressions of sentiment and emotion within broader discourse (Dahal et al., 2019; El Barachi et al., 2021).

A key challenge in sentiment and emotion analysis is the inherent subjectivity of emotion recognition, especially in social media, where tone, context, and audience interpretation vary widely (Pozzi et al., 2016; Almeida et al., 2018). To address this, researchers have employed multi-label annotation approaches to allow overlapping emotional categories and dataset creation methods beyond majority voting to incorporate diverse perspectives (Mostafazadeh Davani et al., 2022; Alhuzali and Ananiadou, 2021).

3 Data and Annotation

This section outlines the dataset and annotation process used in our study.

3.1 Data

The dataset used in this study consists of 2,199 English-language tweets from the international activist group *Extinction Rebellion*, extracted in September 2024. The tweets were published between 2022 and 2024. The dataset includes the following metadata: group name, timestamp, retweet count, reply count, like count, and tweet ID. The complete dataset, including annotations, is provided in the supplementary materials and is publicly available to the research community at Hugging Face Datasets.

3.2 Annotation Process and Annotators

Our project employs **multi-label annotation**, where each tweet can be assigned multiple labels simultaneously from a predefined set of categories, reflecting the complex emotions and sentiments expressed. The annotations are made at the **document level**, meaning labels are applied to the entire tweet rather than single segments or sentences. This approach provides a compact and interpretable representation of each tweet. The dataset of 2,199 tweets was independently annotated by three experienced annotators. None of the annotators were involved in the authorship of this paper. To ensure consistency and clarity, we developed comprehensive annotation guidelines that provided clear definitions for each category, along with illustrative examples. The full guidelines are available in the supplementary material.

The annotation process was organized as follows: Initially, annotators labeled a small set of 10 tweets to familiarize themselves with the data format and task. Following this, each annotator participated in individual feedback sessions to address ambiguities and ensure alignment on labeling criteria. These sessions were conducted by one of the co-authors, who provided detailed guidance and clarification as needed. Periodic feedback sessions were held after every 500 tweets, allowing annotators to ask questions and resolve any issues that arose. While these sessions were conducted individually, all annotators received the same clar-

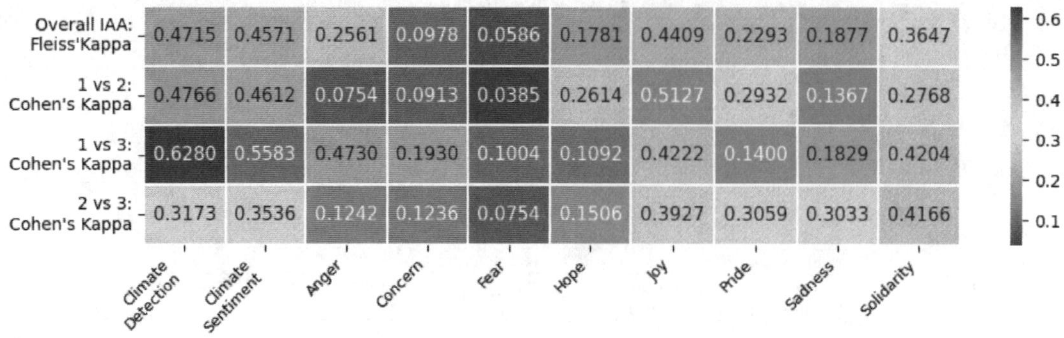

Figure 1: Heatmap displaying Fleiss' Kappa (Fleiss, 1971) and pairwise Cohen's Kappa coefficients (Cohen, 1960) to evaluate **overall and pairwise IAA** across all annotation categories.

ifications to maintain consistency across annotations. Any uncertainty raised by one annotator was systematically addressed with the others.

The annotators consisted of three paid research assistants, all proficient in English, female, and residing in Germany. Their academic backgrounds were as follows: Annotator 1 (A1) and Annotator 3 (A3) were students in *Business Psychology*, while Annotator 2 (A2) was a student in *Expanded Media*. Annotators were instructed to label tweets based on several categories: CLIMATE DETECTION (indicating whether a tweet relates to climate change), CLIMATE SENTIMENT (categorized as *risk*, *opportunity*, or *neutral*), and a set of emotion labels including ANGER, CONCERN, FEAR, HOPE, JOY, PRIDE, SADNESS, and SOLIDARITY, as outlined in Table 1. The climate detection and sentiment categories were adapted from prior annotation tasks and language models (Webersinke et al., 2021; Shiwakoti et al., 2024), while the emotional categories were refined through an in-depth qualitative analysis of a random sample from the larger dataset of several activist organizations in our project, identifying the most relevant emotions for the context. Annotators were instructed to assess **sentiment and emotion from the writer's perspective**.

Our dataset retains all annotations provided by the three annotators. This approach allows for the preservation of individual annotations, as they are central to our research focus.

4 Understanding Annotator Disagreement

To better understand the sources and implications of annotator disagreement in our dataset, we address our two research questions in two parts. First, we conduct a set of quantitative and qualitative analyses to identify factors that may contribute to variation in labeling behavior. Then, we reflect on the insights gained from these observations and how they can guide future annotation practices and research design.

4.1 Data Analysis

To address the factors that contribute to variation and disagreement in annotator labeling behavior (**RQ1**), we perform a number of analyses. In this section, we describe the approaches we use and the results we obtain for each of these analyses to answer **RQ1**.

Category	**Annotator**		
	1	**2**	**3**
CLIMATE DETECTION			
About Climate Change	647	461	805
CLIMATE SENTIMENT			
Risk	447	353	614
Opportunity	71	8	31
Emotions			
ANGER	269	55	184
CONCERN	566	54	151
FEAR	125	8	17
HOPE	150	74	33
JOY	32	22	33
PRIDE	38	9	4
SADNESS	61	9	30
SOLIDARITY	97	21	45

Table 2: **Absolute frequency distribution** per annotator for 2,199 tweets.

Label Distribution. We first examine individual annotation tendencies by counting the absolute frequencies of assigned labels. This allows us to identify differences in the annotators' labeling

ANGER			CONCERN			HOPE		
A1	A2	A3	A1	A2	A3	A1	A2	A3
murdering	tree	murdering	massively	corruption	warned	equitable	comments	**hope**
allow	hundred	**angry**	ongoing	threatening	massively	gather	expiration	touch
protested	immediate	denounce	escalating	reached	widely	preserve	helping	bit
false	helping	sleepwalking	allow	problems	horrific	joined	allowing	reasonable
lobbyists	training	address	twice	changing	suffer	motorway	degree	planning
sentence	lethal	hands	cultural	trust	deal	threats	faster	conference
murderous	claims	murderous	describes	result	ignore	achieve	linked	civilization
sleepwalking	politician	escalating	poorest	trees	positive	expiration	date	greed
polluting	camp	failure	tool	develop	propaganda	positive	ourselves	firm
exposing	release	behind	horrific	produce	further	voice	prevent	glass

Table 3: 10 words with the **highest PMI values** (listed from highest to lowest) for each annotator (A1, A2, A3) and the most frequent emotions, i.e., ANGER, CONCERN, and HOPE.

patterns and to assess the overall prevalence of categories in the dataset. Analysis of the label distributions across the three annotators (Table 2) reveals considerable variation in annotation choices. In particular, A2 assigns the fewest labels, indicating a more conservative approach, except for the category HOPE. In contrast, A1 and A3 tend to assign more labels, with A1 generally assigning the highest frequency. In addition, the categories PRIDE and JOY are the least frequently assigned across the dataset. The variation in the distribution of labels suggests that annotators may use different thresholds for identifying sentiment and emotional content.

Inter-Annotator Agreement. To assess the degree of agreement across categories, we compute both overall and pairwise IAA. The computed **Fleiss' Kappa** (Fleiss, 1971) values for all three annotators range from moderate agreement (0.4715 for CLIMATE DETECTION) to slight agreement (0.0586 for FEAR), with higher agreement observed for CLIMATE DETECTION, CLIMATE SENTIMENT, and JOY, as shown in Figure 1.
Low prevalence of categories generally results in lower IAA scores, as rare categories increase the likelihood of discrepancies between annotators (Artstein and Poesio, 2008). However, in our case, JOY-despite being one of the least frequently labeled emotions-has relatively high agreement. This suggests that while annotators identify JOY less frequently, when they do, they are more consistent in their judgments compared to other emotions. Notably, we do not find a clear relationship between category prevalence and IAA across the dataset.

To explore whether disagreement is linked to specific annotator pairs, we calculate **pairwise Cohen's Kappa** scores (Cohen, 1960), as shown in Figure 1. The results indicate that disagreement is not systematic, as no two annotators consistently exhibit a higher level of agreement while the third annotator deviates as an outlier across all categories. However, disagreement varies across pairs and categories; for example, A1 and A3 agree on ANGER with a score of 0.4730, while A1 and A2's agreement is only 0.0754. This variability suggests that subjectivity influences annotation, with more subjective categories showing lower agreement, and more objective categories like CLIMATE DETECTION and CLIMATE SENTIMENT showing higher agreement.

Pointwise Mutual Information. To address potential *lexical biases*—where certain words may lead annotators to consistently assign specific labels—we conducted a Pointwise Mutual Information (PMI) analysis for the most prevalent emotion categories (HOPE, ANGER, and CONCERN). PMI quantifies the strength of association between a word and a category by comparing their co-occurrence probability to what would be expected under independence, with higher PMI values indicating a stronger, non-random relationship (Church and Hanks, 1990). However, it is not appropriate for categories that are not frequently labeled. For infrequently labeled categories, the statistical reliability of the PMI is reduced because the occurrences of these categories are too sparse to yield meaningful associations.

Through our analysis, it became clear that A3 showed a lexical bias, paying close attention to words explicitly mentioning emotions, such as *hope* for HOPE and *angry* for ANGER (see Table 3). Our PMI analysis generally shows that annotations are not random, reflecting diverse associations for specific emotions. For example, A3 often assigns labels based on explicit emotional terms, while A1 links more indirect words such as *equitable* or

Topic ID	Topic Size	Topic Name
0	470	Global Fossil Fuel Protests
1	234	Extreme Weather and Climate Change
2	144	XR Decentralized Climate Advocacy
3	184	Climate Crisis and Health Responses
4	104	Climate Activism and Donations
5	88	Extreme Global Heat Events
6	89	Nonviolent Civil Disobedience in Movements
7	104	Climate Action and Sustainability
8	87	Plant-Based Diet and Agriculture
9	130	Peaceful Protest and Arrests
10	83	Citizens' Assemblies for Climate Action
11	94	Environmental Policy and Advocacy
12	99	Climate Change and Fascism Concerns
13	110	Climate and Resource Conflict in Congo
14	91	Critique of Economic Growth Models
15	45	Connecting with Local XR Groups
16	43	Environmental Pollution and Resource Extraction

Table 4: Topic modeling results from BERTopic including names generated by ChatGPT-4o and number of tweets categorized with this topic (OpenAI et al., 2024; Grootendorst, 2022).

achieve with HOPE, and *murdering* or *sentence* with ANGER. A2, in contrast, associates words like *comments* and *expiration* with HOPE, or *tree* and *hundred* with ANGER, indicating a stronger focus on context over specific words. For instance, A2 labeled the following tweet as expressing HOPE:

> That's an understandable doubt, Donald. However, the science isn't telling us a better world isn't possible. Surpassing 1.5C is a blow to everything we've been working towards, but there is no expiration on climate action. Every fraction of a degree saved counts.

Overall, the PMI analysis highlights distinct emotional associations and annotation strategies among annotators, as shown in Table 3.

Clustering-Based Topic Modeling. We applied **BERTopic** (Grootendorst, 2022) to examine potential *topic biases* in labeling the most prevalent emotion categories (i.e., HOPE, ANGER, and CONCERN). This clustering method leverages semantic embeddings and hierarchical density-based clustering (**HDBSCAN**) to automatically determine the number of clusters based on parameters such as *min_cluster_size*. To enhance interpretability, we used **ChatGPT-4o** to generate cluster names based on representative words (OpenAI et al., 2024). Our full parameter settings are provided in Table 5 in Appendix B. We clustered the dataset into 17 distinct topics (see Figure 2 for the resulted topics). Subsequently, we analyzed the most prevalent topics within tweets labeled with specific emotions for each annotator. The results indicate that annotators associated emotions with different topics, particularly in the case of HOPE (see Figure 2). In contrast, the emotions ANGER and CONCERN show greater overlap in their most frequently assigned topics; these results are included for completeness in Figures 5 and 6 in Appendix B.

Additionally, we computed **pairwise Cohen's Kappa scores** (Cohen, 1960) for each topic, revealing substantial variation in agreement across topics. This suggests that annotator disagreement is topic-dependent rather than systematic (see Figures 7, 8, and 9, Appendix B).

Temporal Analysis. We conducted a temporal analysis by calculating the mean labels for every set of 100 annotated tweets per annotator to track shifts in annotation patterns over time. The trends show that A1 assigned more emotion labels at the beginning of the annotation process compared to later stages, and also more than the other annotators (see Figure 4 in Appendix A). This could be due to the familiarization process, where annotators typically experience fluctuations at the start of the task, potentially influenced by feedback discussions during the initial phase. Other factors, such as annotators' daily moods or emotional states, and external influences like media exposure to environmental issues, could also have biased annotation patterns (Gautam and Srinath, 2024; Bodenhausen et al., 2000; Englich and Soder, 2009; Vrselja et al., 2024).

Spearman Correlations. To assess co-labeling

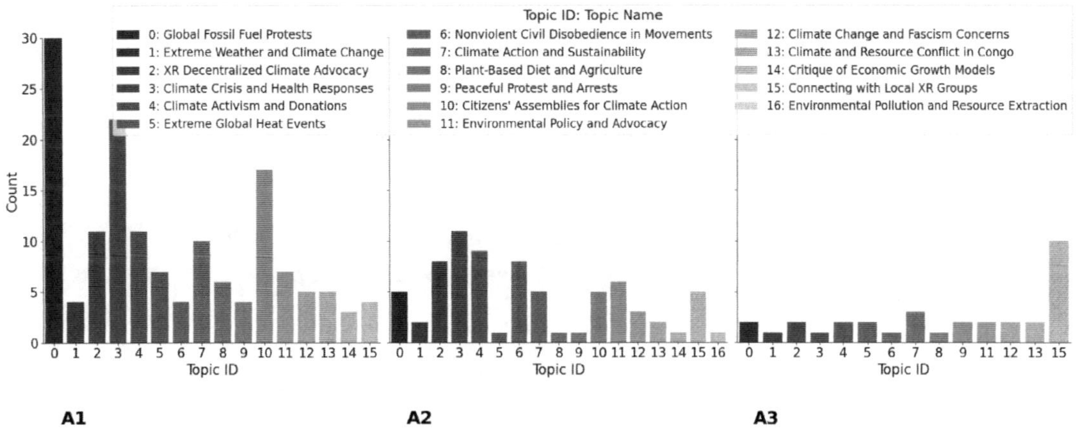

Figure 2: Plots showing the **count of tweets by topic** labeled with the emotion HOPE per annotator (A1, A2, A3).

frequency and potential difficulties in distinguishing categories, we calculated Spearman correlations (Spearman, 1904) for all label pairs separately for each annotator. With correlations of up to 0.33 between most positive emotions, we observe that A1 and A2 have higher correlations in some cases, reflecting a higher number of co-labels (see Figure 3 for the correlation patterns associated with A1). Conversely, correlations for A3 labels are predominantly near to zero. This suggests varying interpretations of emotions, particularly in their differentiation. For A1 and A2, positive emotions appear to be more closely related than for A3. Additionally, a topic bias was clearly observed, as A1 showed a correlation of 0.28 between CLIMATE DETECTION and CONCERN, indicating that tweets on climate change were more often labeled with CONCERN. Correlation matrices for all annotators are included in Figures 10, and 11 in Appendix C for completeness and detailed reference.

Qualitative Interviews. To explore sources of disagreement, we conducted qualitative interviews with all three annotators. These aimed at understanding individual perspectives rather than drawing statistical inferences.

All annotators reported following the same procedure that had been instructed, feeling confident in their understanding of the task, and recognizing that they should label emotions from the writer's perspective. However, they differed in their **emotional responses to environmental crises**. A1 primarily experiences *concern*, while also labeling CONCERN the most. A2's response is dominated by *anger*, which is also their most frequently assigned negative emotion. A3, despite reporting *fear* as their dominant reaction, labeled it the least. These differences may hint at subtle personal tendencies, as A1 and A2 more frequently assigned emotion labels that align with their own reported emotional reactions. We also explored annotators' **mental imagery or immediate associations with environmental groups**. A1 mentioned groups such as *Extinction Rebellion* and *Last Generation* and labeled more emotions overall, which might suggest a perceived link between radical activism and emotional expressiveness (Ostarek et al., 2024). In contrast, A2 and A3 associated environmental groups with *Fridays for Future* and *Greenpeace* and labeled fewer emotions, possibly reflecting differences in how they perceive the emotional tone of these groups.

Another key factor was **personal affectedness**. A1 did not consider themselves personally affected, while A2 described their perceived affectedness in their home country of Nigeria and A3 reported an indirect sense of affectedness, emphasizing empathy for strongly affected populations worldwide. Notably, A1, despite feeling the least affected, labeled the highest number of emotions.

External factors may have also played a significant role. A3 **engaged with climate news** daily, A1 consumed little, and A2 had difficulty engaging with environmental news due to emotional reactions, often avoiding such content. However, no clear link emerged between news consumption and annotation behavior. Procedural influences, such as annotation guidelines and feedback discussions, may have shaped interpretations, along with

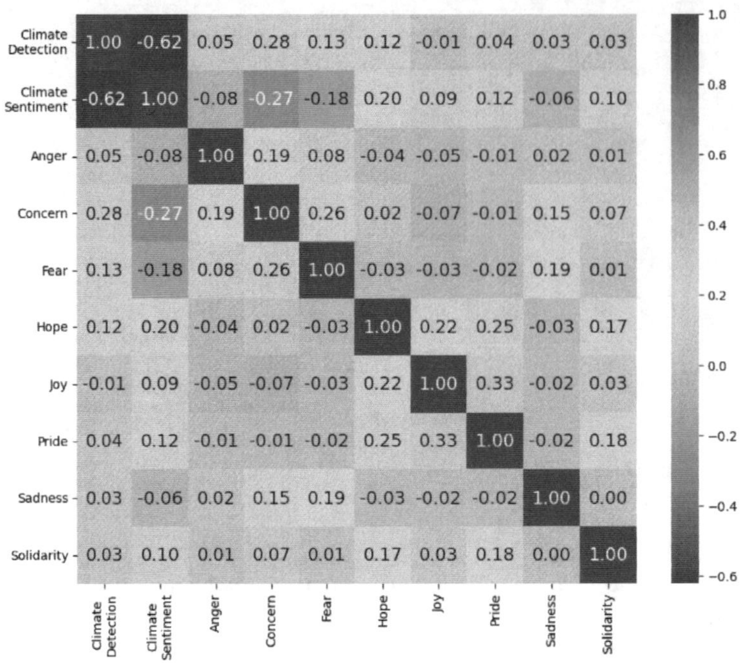

Figure 3: Spearman correlation (Spearman, 1904) matrix of the categories labeled by A1, showing the common occurrences of the labels.

differences in prior knowledge and familiarity with environmental discourse.

Final Considerations. Previous research has shown that distinguishing between annotation errors and perspectivism can be challenging (Weber-Genzel et al., 2024). However, given our research focus on understanding how individuals interpret environmental communication, we argue that variation in annotation tendencies is meaningful rather than problematic. Our study assumes that reading and interpreting environmental texts is inherently subjective, with recipient perspectives playing a crucial role in annotation outcomes. While factors such as annotation guidelines, feedback discussions, and annotator expertise may influence annotation subjectivity, they do not invalidate the presence of diverse and valuable perspectives in the data. This assumption aligns with prior research showing that emotion labeling is inherently subjective (Buechel and Hahn, 2022; Du et al., 2023), a tendency that is likely amplified in highly visible and polarized topics such as environmental activism (Ostarek et al., 2024).

4.2 Insights gained from Analysis

In this section, we discuss the valuable insights that can be gained from the observed disagreement in our annotations and how these insights can help inform future annotation efforts, addressing **RQ2**. While our analyses provide an initial understanding of the variability in annotation outcomes, the conclusions drawn are specific to our dataset and annotation context, and may not be easily generalized beyond this study.

The diversity in perspectives reflected in our annotations may be influenced by both internal and external factors. To improve the quality and reliability of future annotation efforts, it is crucial to systematically account for these influences. We acknowledge that high-quality annotations, as well as our proposed strategies to enhance them, come with increased resource demands, which are constrained by available research funding. Nevertheless, we aim to propose best practices that can be adapted based on available resources.

One potential approach is to collect **annotator-specific metadata** prior to annotation, including sociodemographic variables, domain expertise, prior engagement with the topic, personal stance, and emotional disposition toward the subject matter.

Additionally, intra-annotator variability should be considered by incorporating **daily self-reports** on factors such as recent exposure to the topic through media consumption, current emotional states, and subjective attitudes on the day of annotation. Furthermore, **external contextual variables**, such as ongoing political events or environmental incidents (e.g., natural disasters), should be tracked on a daily or weekly basis. Controlling for these factors would enable a more nuanced understanding of annotator subjectivity and facilitate structured dataset curation, allowing for more interpretable and representative NLP models. This approach aligns with the principles of **human-centered NLP**, which advocate for the explicit modeling of annotator subjectivity and diversity to enhance the interpretability and fairness of computational models (Soni et al., 2024; Kotnis et al., 2022).

Ideally, annotations should either be **representative of diverse perspectives or fully stratified into distinct target audience segments**. A potential implementation of this perspective-aware annotation strategy could involve weak perspectivism, where separate datasets are curated for different audience segments, with majority voting applied within each segment to create internally consistent annotations (Cabitza et al., 2023; Holovenko, 2024). Given that our research focuses on environmental communication, integrating author perspectives into the annotation process—akin to **citizen science**—could be highly beneficial when feasible (Paramonov and Poletaev, 2024; Bono et al., 2023; Klie et al., 2023). For instance, members of XR could annotate texts to better capture the writer's perspective, while non-members could provide annotations reflecting the reader's perspective. Alternatively, Large Language Models (LLMs) could be leveraged to infer writer intentions based on linguistic cues, while reader perceptions could be analyzed separately through annotations segmented by audience groups.

5 Conclusions and Future Work

This study examines disagreement in environmental communication annotation, particularly within activist group discourse. Our findings highlight the impact of internal factors, such as sociodemographic backgrounds and emotions, and external factors like the annotation process. These challenges hinder achieving high IAA in subjective language assessment, especially in emotionally charged topics like environmental activism. Our results align with previous research questioning the idea of a single ground truth in annotation tasks (Cabitza et al., 2023; Uma et al., 2021; Rodríguez-Barroso et al., 2024; Valette, 2024). Perspectivism in NLP tasks, such as hate speech detection and emotion recognition, underscores the role of individual annotators' perspectives on labeling outcomes (Abercrombie et al., 2024; Larimore et al., 2021; Frenda et al., 2024; Fleisig et al., 2023; Xu et al., 2024; Abercrombie et al., 2023; Du et al., 2023). This subjectivity is critical in environmental communication, where diverse reactions provide valuable insights into audience perceptions. Importantly, disagreements among annotators reveal the varied emotional engagement with environmental issues (Cabitza et al., 2023; Zaremba et al., 2024).

Future research should improve annotation methods to better address subjectivity. Adopting perspectivist frameworks, using pre-annotation surveys to capture annotators' backgrounds, and integrating LLMs to complement human labeling are promising approaches. Expanding our dataset to include more environmental groups and studying the temporal aspects of annotation subjectivity, such as emotions or external events, could offer further insights. Ultimately, applying these findings to tailor environmental communication strategies for diverse audiences will be crucial in bridging NLP and environmental communication.

Limitations

While our study provides valuable insights, it is imperative to acknowledge its limitations. First, the analysis is based on a relatively small group of annotators (n=3), all of whom are female students residing in Germany. While this approach is useful for an in-depth exploration of subjectivity, it limits the generalizability of our findings. Despite these limitations, our study is a first attempt to understand perspectivism in environmental communication. To enhance the range of perspectives that can be captured, future studies should aim to recruit a more diverse and larger pool of annotators. Second, the dataset consists solely of tweets from XR, a highly visible and polarizing activist group. While this allows for a focused analysis, it does not account for the full diversity of environmental communication used by different organizations. While we assume a higher likelihood that this group employs more radical and emotionally charged language, other groups may exhibit significantly less emotional language in their communication. Expanding the dataset to include posts from a wider range of environmental groups would enhance the robustness of the findings.

Third, part of our study relies on qualitative interviews conducted after the annotation process to infer annotator subjectivity. While these interviews provide valuable self-reported insights, they do not allow for real-time tracking of changes in annotation tendencies over time. Furthermore, it is not clear whether the results of the interviews depend on the previous annotations. For example, an annotator may have reported more concern about environmental crises simply because they labeled it more frequently in the tweets.

Additionally, we did not check reliability by giving our annotators the same tweets a second time. Implementing daily or real-time self-assessments during the annotation process would provide a more precise and accurate measurement of fluctuating annotator subjectivity.

Ethical Considerations

The annotation process involved reading environmental and climate-related texts, some of which addressed extreme weather events or broader environmental crises. Such content may evoke strong emotional responses, including feelings of eco- or climate anxiety, which can impact annotators' well-being. All annotators were financially compensated for their work, which involved engaging with potentially repetitive and emotionally challenging content.

To address these concerns, we took steps to protect the annotators' mental well-being. Annotators were informed that they could pause or discontinue the task at any time without providing a reason. We regularly checked in with them about their well-being during the annotation process and provided contact information for support services in case of psychological distress. Additionally, the annotators were fully informed about the purpose of their work, including the creation of a dataset for research purposes.

We also treated annotators' personal information with care. All sociodemographic data and mentions of individual annotators included in this paper were disclosed with their explicit consent.

Regarding the dataset, the collection and planned publication of tweet IDs were reviewed and approved in consultation with the university's data protection officer. The dataset does not contain personal data, as we only worked with group-level content (i.e., tweets published by the environmental activist group *Extinction Rebellion*). All usernames appearing in the dataset were anonymized, except for public figures such as politicians, in accordance with established ethical guidelines for working with social media data.

Acknowledgments

We would like to thank our student assistants, who preferred to remain anonymous, for their valuable contributions to the annotation work. This research was funded by the Office of Equal Opportunities at Darmstadt University of Applied Sciences, as well as by additional internal university funding.

References

Gavin Abercrombie, Dirk Hovy, and Vinodkumar Prabhakaran. 2023. Temporal and second language influence on intra-annotator agreement and stability in hate speech labelling. In *Proceedings of the 17th Linguistic Annotation Workshop (LAW-XVII)*, pages 96–103, Toronto, Canada. Association for Computational Linguistics.

Gavin Abercrombie, Nikolas Vitsakis, Aiqi Jiang, and Ioannis Konstas. 2024. Revisiting annotation of online gender-based violence. In *Joint International Conference on Computational Linguistics, Language Resources and Evaluation 2024*, pages 31–41. ELRA Language Resources Association.

Hassan Alhuzali and Sophia Ananiadou. 2021. SpanEmo: Casting multi-label emotion classification as span-prediction. In *Proceedings of the 16th Conference of the European Chapter of the Association for Computational Linguistics: Main Volume*, pages 1573–1584, Online. Association for Computational Linguistics.

Alex MG Almeida, Ricardo Cerri, Emerson Cabrera Paraiso, Rafael Gomes Mantovani, and Sylvio Barbon Junior. 2018. Applying multi-label techniques in emotion identification of short texts. *Neurocomputing*, 320:35–46.

Daniyar Amangeldi, Aida Usmanova, and Pakizar Shamoi. 2024. Understanding environmental posts: Sentiment and emotion analysis of social media data. *IEEE Access*.

Alison Anderson. 2024. *Advancing the environmental communication field: A research agenda*, pages 47–68. De Gruyter Mouton, Berlin, Boston.

Ron Artstein and Massimo Poesio. 2008. Inter-coder agreement for computational linguistics. *Computational Linguistics*, 34(4):555–596.

Christina Barz, Melanie Siegel, and Daniel Hanss. 2025. Analyzing the online communication of environmental movement organizations: NLP approaches to topics, sentiment, and emotions. In *1st Workshop on Ecology, Environment, and Natural Language Processing*.

Natalie Berger, Ann-Kathrin Lindemann, and Gaby-Fleur Böl. 2019. Wahrnehmung des Klimawandels durch die Bevölkerung und Konsequenzen für die Risikokommunikation. *Bundesgesundheitsblatt-Gesundheitsforschung-Gesundheitsschutz*, 62(5):612–619.

Steven Bird, Angelina Aquino, and Ian Gumbula. 2024. Envisioning NLP for intercultural climate communication. In *Proceedings of the 1st Workshop on Natural Language Processing Meets Climate Change (ClimateNLP 2024)*, pages 111–122, Bangkok, Thailand. Association for Computational Linguistics.

Galen V Bodenhausen, Shira Gabriel, and Megan Lineberger. 2000. Sadness and susceptibility to judgmental bias: The case of anchoring. *Psychological Science*, 11(4):320–323.

Carlo Bono, Mehmet Oğuz Mülâyim, Cinzia Cappiello, Mark James Carman, Jesus Cerquides, Jose Luis Fernandez-Marquez, Maria Rosa Mondardini, Edoardo Ramalli, and Barbara Pernici. 2023. A citizen science approach for analyzing social media with crowdsourcing. *IEEE Access*, 11:15329–15347.

Tobias Brosch. 2025. From individual to collective climate emotions and actions: A review. *Current Opinion in Behavioral Sciences*, 61:101466.

Sven Buechel and Udo Hahn. 2022. Emobank: Studying the impact of annotation perspective and representation format on dimensional emotion analysis. *arXiv preprint arXiv:2205.01996*.

Federico Cabitza, Andrea Campagner, and Valerio Basile. 2023. Toward a perspectivist turn in ground truthing for predictive computing. In *Proceedings of the AAAI Conference on Artificial Intelligence*, volume 37, pages 6860–6868.

Anabela Carvalho and Tarla Rai Peterson. 2024. *Rethinking environmental communication scholarship*, pages 3–6. De Gruyter Mouton, Berlin, Boston.

Kenneth W. Church and Patrick Hanks. 1990. Word association norms, mutual information, and lexicography. *Computational Linguistics*, 16(1):22–29.

Jacob Cohen. 1960. A coefficient of agreement for nominal scales. *Educational and Psychological Measurement*, 20(1):37–46.

Biraj Dahal, Sathish AP Kumar, and Zhenlong Li. 2019. Topic modeling and sentiment analysis of global climate change tweets. *Social Network Analysis and Mining*, 9:1–20.

Quanqi Du, Sofie Labat, Thomas Demeester, and Veronique Hoste. 2023. Unimodalities count as perspectives in multimodal emotion annotation. In *2nd Workshop on Perspectivist Approaches to NLP (NLPerspectives 2023), co-located with the 26th European Conference on Artificial Intelligence (ECAI 2023)*, volume 3494. CEUR-WS. org.

May El Barachi, Manar AlKhatib, Sujith Mathew, and Farhad Oroumchian. 2021. A novel sentiment analysis framework for monitoring the evolving public opinion in real-time: Case study on climate change. *Journal of Cleaner Production*, 312:127820.

Birte Englich and Kirsten Soder. 2009. Moody experts—how mood and expertise influence judgmental anchoring. *Judgment and Decision Making*, 4(1):41–50.

Eve Fleisig, Rediet Abebe, and Dan Klein. 2023. When the majority is wrong: Modeling annotator disagreement for subjective tasks. *arXiv preprint arXiv:2305.06626*.

Joseph L Fleiss. 1971. Measuring nominal scale agreement among many raters. *Psychological Bulletin*, 76(5):378.

Simona Frenda, Gavin Abercrombie, Valerio Basile, Alessandro Pedrani, Raffaella Panizzon, Alessandra Teresa Cignarella, Cristina Marco, and Davide Bernardi. 2024. Perspectivist approaches to natural language processing: A survey. *Language Resources and Evaluation*, pages 1–28.

Immo Fritsche and Torsten Masson. 2021. Collective climate action: When do people turn into collective environmental agents? *Current Opinion in Psychology*, 42:114–119.

Sanjana Gautam and Mukund Srinath. 2024. Blind spots and biases: Exploring the role of annotator cognitive biases in NLP. *arXiv preprint arXiv:2404.19071*.

Maarten Grootendorst. 2022. Bertopic: Neural topic modeling with a class-based tf-idf procedure. *arXiv preprint arXiv:2203.05794*.

Simon David Hirsbrunner. 2024. Computational methods for climate change frame analysis: Techniques, critiques, and cautious ways forward. *Wiley Interdisciplinary Reviews: Climate Change*, 15(5):e902.

Anastasia Holovenko. 2024. What are your triggers? Context-dependent detection of emotional triggers in influence campaigns. Master's thesis, Ukrainian Catholic University.

IPCC. 2022. Climate change 2022: Impacts, adaptation, and vulnerability. *Intergovernmental Panel on Climate Change*.

Sanjay Kaushal, Sarvsureshth Dhammi, and Anamita Guha. 2022. Climate crisis and language–a constructivist ecolinguistic approach. *Materials Today: Proceedings*, 49:3581–3584.

Jan-Christoph Klie, Ji-Ung Lee, Kevin Stowe, Gözde Gül Şahin, Nafise Sadat Moosavi, Luke Bates, Dominic Petrak, Richard Eckart De Castilho, and Iryna Gurevych. 2023. Lessons learned from a citizen science project for natural language processing. *arXiv preprint arXiv:2304.12836*.

Bhushan Kotnis, Kiril Gashteovski, Julia Gastinger, Giuseppe Serra, Francesco Alesiani, Timo Sztyler, Ammar Shaker, Na Gong, Carolin Lawrence, and Zhao Xu. 2022. Human-centric research for NLP: Towards a definition and guiding questions. *arXiv preprint arXiv:2207.04447*.

Myanna Lahsen. 2022. Evaluating the computational ("big data") turn in studies of media coverage of climate change. *Wiley Interdisciplinary Reviews: Climate Change*, 13(2):e752.

Savannah Larimore, Ian Kennedy, Breon Haskett, and Alina Arseniev-Koehler. 2021. Reconsidering annotator disagreement about racist language: Noise or signal? In *Proceedings of the Ninth International Workshop on Natural Language Processing for Social Media*, pages 81–90.

Bruce Y Lee, Brian Pavilonis, Danielle C John, Jessie Heneghan, Sarah M Bartsch, and Ilias Kavouras. 2024. The need to focus more on climate change communication and incorporate more systems approaches. *Journal of Health Communication*, 29(sup1):1–10.

Lena Lehrer, Lennart Hellmann, Hellen Temme, Leonie Otten, Johanna Hübenthal, Mattis Geiger, Mirjam A Jenny, and Cornelia Betsch. 2023. Communicating climate change and health to specific target groups. *Journal of Health Monitoring*, 8(Suppl 6):36.

Aida Mostafazadeh Davani, Mark Díaz, and Vinodkumar Prabhakaran. 2022. Dealing with disagreements: Looking beyond the majority vote in subjective annotations. *Transactions of the Association for Computational Linguistics*, 10:92–110.

Aaron OpenAI, Hurst, Adam Lerer, Adam P Goucher, Adam Perelman, Aditya Ramesh, Aidan Clark, AJ Ostrow, Akila Welihinda, Alan Hayes, Alec Radford, et al. 2024. Gpt-4o system card. *arXiv preprint arXiv:2410.21276*.

Markus Ostarek, Brent Simpson, Cathy Rogers, and James Ozden. 2024. Radical climate protests linked to increases in public support for moderate organizations. *Nature Sustainability*, pages 1–7.

IV Paramonov and A Yu Poletaev. 2024. Annotation of text corpora by sentiment and irony in a project of citizen science. *Automatic Control and Computer Sciences*, 58(7):797–807.

Douglas Mark Ponton and Anna Raimo. 2024. Comparative discourse strategies in environmental advocacy: Analysing the rhetoric of Greta Thunberg and Chris Packham. *Languages*, 9(9):307.

Federico Alberto Pozzi, Elisabetta Fersini, Enza Messina, and Bing Liu. 2016. *Sentiment analysis in social networks*. Morgan Kaufmann.

Ed Qian. 2021. Twitter climate change sentiment dataset. Accessed: 2024-12-30.

Nuria Rodríguez-Barroso, Eugenio Martínez Cámara, Jose Camacho Collados, M Victoria Luzón, and Francisco Herrera. 2024. Federated learning for exploiting annotators' disagreements in natural language processing. *Transactions of the Association for Computational Linguistics*, 12:630–648.

Raúl Salas Reyes, Vivian M Nguyen, Stephan Schott, Valerie Berseth, Jenna Hutchen, Jennifer Taylor, and Nicole Klenk. 2021. A research agenda for affective dimensions in climate change risk perception and risk communication. *Frontiers in Climate*, 3:751310.

Mike S Schäfer. 2024. Social media in climate change communication: State of the field, new developments and the emergence of generative AI. *Dialogues on Climate Change*, page 29768659241300666.

Mike S Schäfer and Valerie Hase. 2023. Computational methods for the analysis of climate change communication: Towards an integrative and reflexive approach. *Wiley Interdisciplinary Reviews: Climate Change*, 14(2):e806.

Claudia R Schneider, Lisa Zaval, and Ezra M Markowitz. 2021. Positive emotions and climate change. *Current Opinion in Behavioral Sciences*, 42:114–120.

Shuvam Shiwakoti, Surendrabikram Thapa, Kritesh Rauniyar, Akshyat Shah, Aashish Bhandari, and Usman Naseem. 2024. Analyzing the dynamics of climate change discourse on twitter: A new annotated corpus and multi-aspect classification. In *Proceedings of the 2024 Joint International Conference on Computational Linguistics, Language Resources and Evaluation (LREC-COLING 2024)*, pages 984–994.

Nikita Soni, H. Andrew Schwartz, João Sedoc, and Niranjan Balasubramanian. 2024. Large human language models: A need and the challenges. In *Proceedings of the 2024 Conference of the North American Chapter of the Association for Computational Linguistics: Human Language Technologies (Volume 1: Long Papers)*, pages 8631–8646, Mexico City, Mexico. Association for Computational Linguistics.

Charles Spearman. 1904. The proof and measurement of association between two things. *The American Journal of Psychology*, 15(1):72–101.

Manfred Stede and Ronny Patz. 2021. The climate change debate and natural language processing. In *Proceedings of the 1st Workshop on NLP for Positive Impact*, pages 8–18.

Alexandra N Uma, Tommaso Fornaciari, Dirk Hovy, Silviu Paun, Barbara Plank, and Massimo Poesio. 2021. Learning from disagreement: A survey. *Journal of Artificial Intelligence Research*, 72:1385–1470.

Mathieu Valette. 2024. What does perspectivism mean? An ethical and methodological countercriticism. In *Proceedings of the 3rd Workshop on Perspectivist Approaches to NLP (NLPerspectives) @ LREC-COLING 2024*, pages 111–115, Torino, Italia. ELRA and ICCL.

Anne M Van Valkengoed and Linda Steg. 2019. Meta-analyses of factors motivating climate change adaptation behaviour. *Nature Climate Change*, 9(2):158–163.

Ivana Vrselja, Mario Pandžić, Martina Lotar Rihtarić, and Maria Ojala. 2024. Media exposure to climate change information and pro-environmental behavior: The role of climate change risk judgment. *BMC Psychology*, 12(1):262.

Leon Weber-Genzel, Siyao Peng, Marie-Catherine De Marneffe, and Barbara Plank. 2024. VariErr NLI: Separating annotation error from human label variation. *arXiv preprint arXiv:2403.01931*.

Nicolas Webersinke, Mathias Kraus, Julia Anna Bingler, and Markus Leippold. 2021. Climatebert: A pretrained language model for climate-related text. *arXiv preprint arXiv:2110.12010*.

Jin Xu, Mariët Theune, and Daniel Braun. 2024. Leveraging annotator disagreement for text classification. *arXiv preprint arXiv:2409.17577*.

Musarat Yasmin et al. 2024. Framing vulnerability: An ecolinguistic analysis of gender and climate change discourse. *Current Research in Environmental Sustainability*, 7:100258.

Dominika Zaremba, Jarosław M Michałowski, Christian A Klöckner, Artur Marchewka, and Małgorzata Wierzba. 2024. Correction: Development and validation of the emotional climate change stories (eccs) stimuli set. *Behavior Research Methods*, 56(7):8158.

A Temporal Analysis

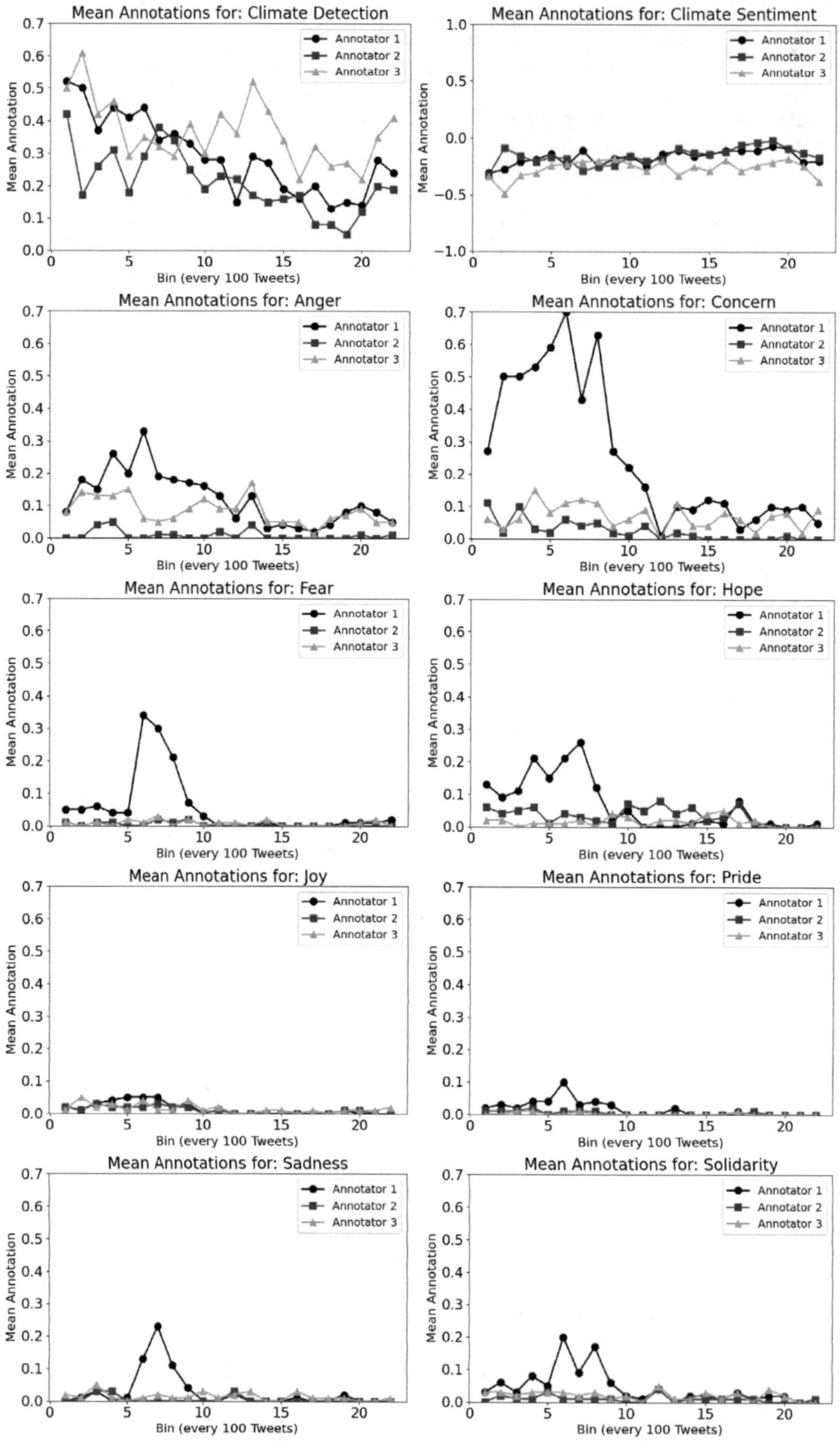

Figure 4: Set of plots showing the **distribution of true labels** assigned by each annotator across specific categories, illustrating the amount of labels given per category **over time**.

B Clustering-Based Topic Modeling

Component	Setting
Embedding Model	SentenceTransformer("all-MiniLM-L6-v2")
UMAP Configuration	random_state=777, n_neighbors=29
HDBSCAN Configuration	metric='euclidean', min_cluster_size=31, cluster_selection_method='eom', prediction_data=True, min_samples=5

Table 5: Parameter settings used for BERTopic modeling (Grootendorst, 2022).

B.1 Topics for Anger and Concern

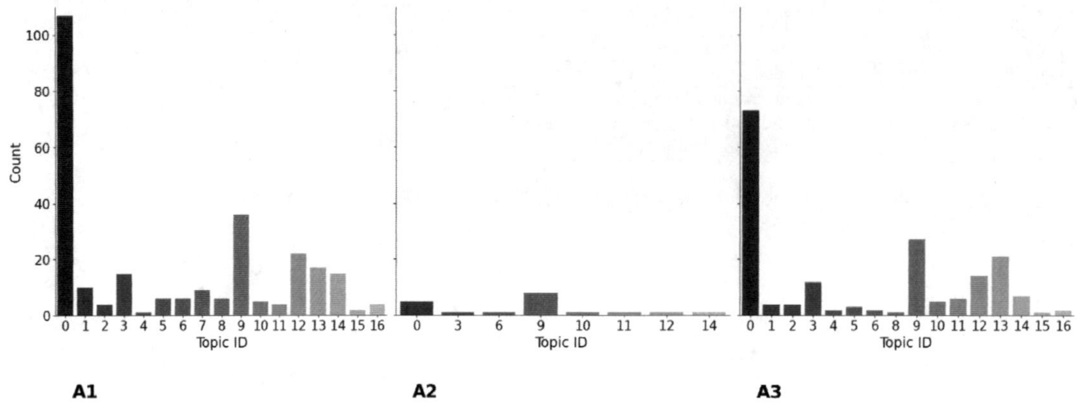

Figure 5: Plots showing the **count of tweets by topic** labeled with the emotion ANGER per annotator (A1, A2, A3).

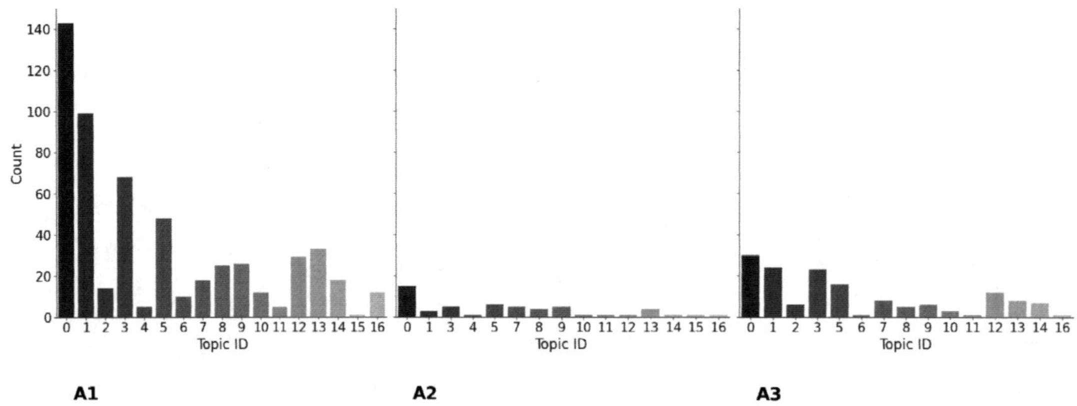

Figure 6: Plots showing the **count of tweets by topic** labeled with the emotion CONCERN per annotator (A1, A2, A3).

B.2 Inter-Annotator Agreement for A1 and A2 by Topics

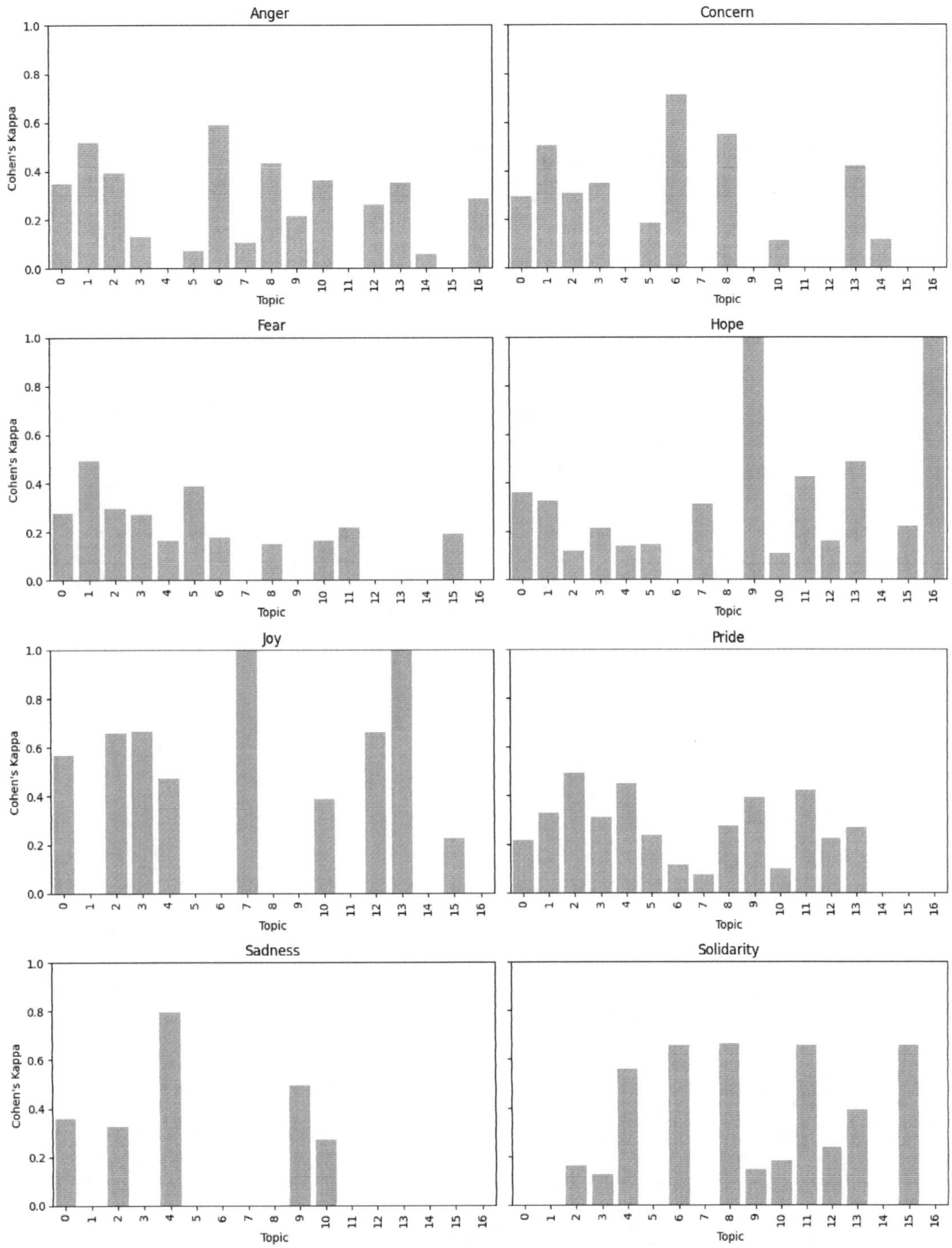

Figure 7: Set of plots showing the calculated **Cohen's Kappa** (Cohen, 1960) **values per topic** for annotator pair A1 and A2.

B.3 Inter-Annotator Agreement for A1 and A3 by Topics

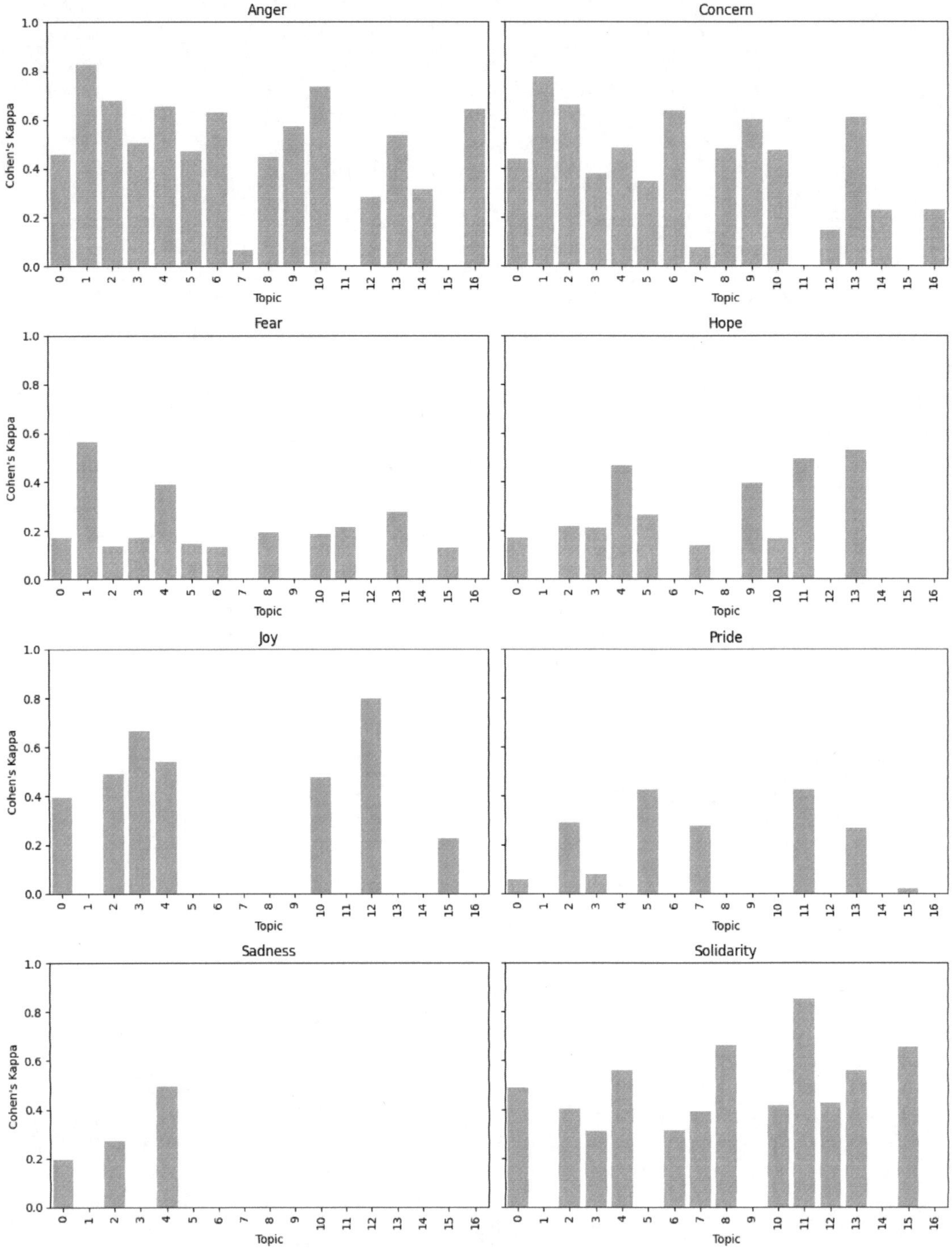

Figure 8: Set of plots showing the calculated **Cohen's Kappa** (Cohen, 1960) **values per topic** for annotator pair A1 and A3.

B.4 Inter-Annotator Agreement for A2 and A3 by Topics

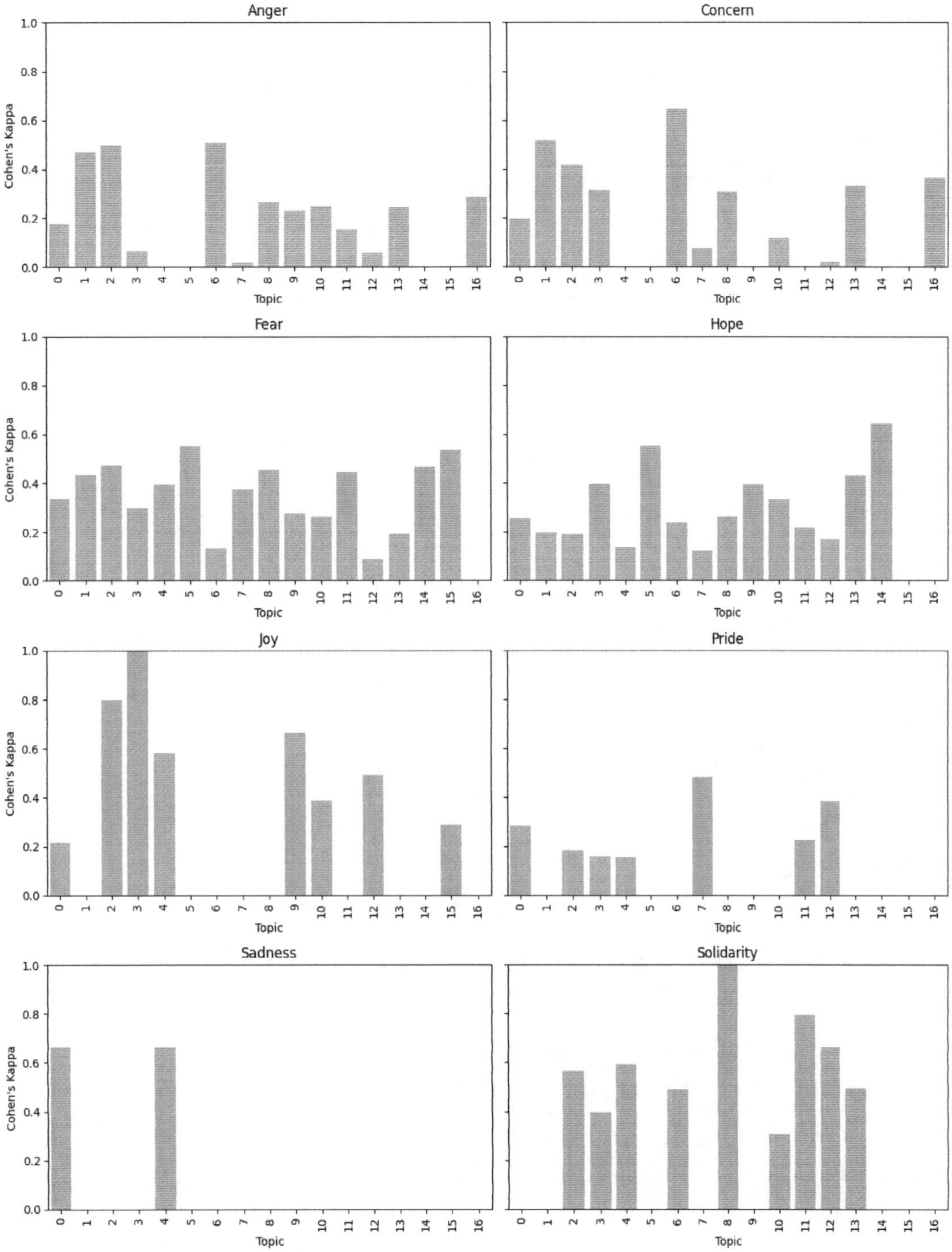

Figure 9: Set of plots showing the calculated **Cohen's Kappa** (Cohen, 1960) **values per topic** for annotator pair A2 and A3.

C Label Spearman Correlation Matrices

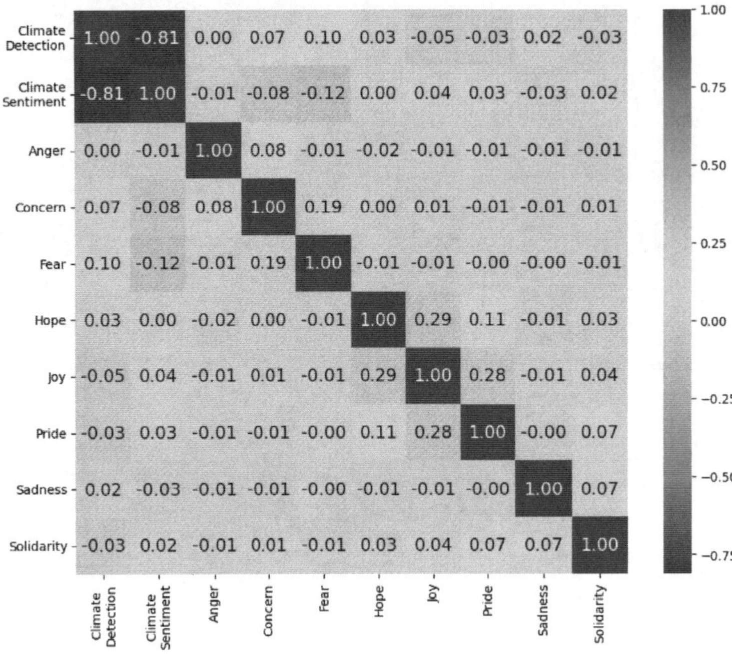

Figure 10: Spearman correlation (Spearman, 1904) matrix of the categories labeled by A2, showing the common occurrences of the labels.

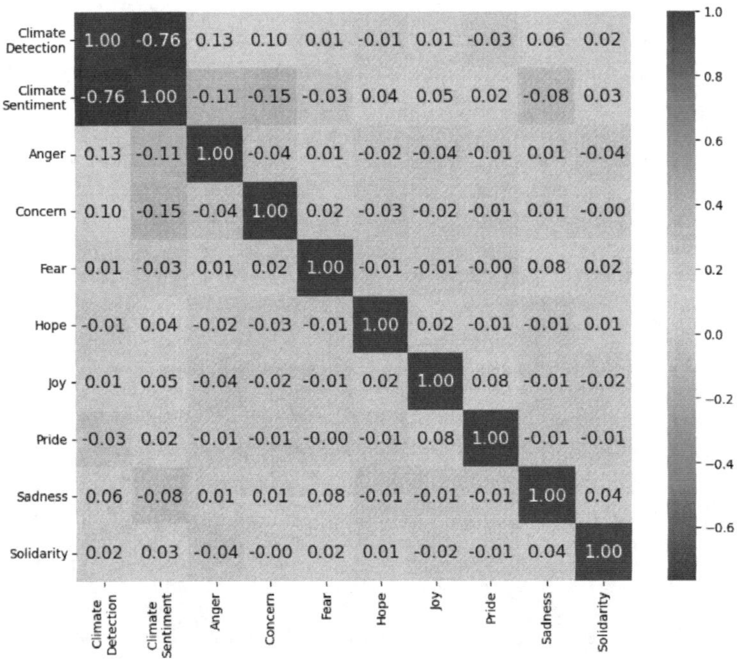

Figure 11: Spearman correlation (Spearman, 1904) matrix of the categories labeled by A3, showing the common occurrences of the labels.

Measuring Label Ambiguity in Subjective Tasks using Predictive Uncertainty Estimation

Richard Alies[1], Elena Merdjanovska[1,2] and Alan Akbik[1,2]
[1]Humboldt-Universität zu Berlin
[2]Science of Intelligence
rarichn@gmail.com, {elena.merdjanovska, alan.akbik}@hu-berlin.de

Abstract

Human annotations in natural language corpora vary due to differing human perspectives. This is especially prevalent in subjective tasks. In these datasets, certain data samples, i.e. annotatable instances, are more prone to label variation and can be indicated as ambiguous. This paper investigates methodologies for quantifying such label ambiguity by leveraging uncertainty estimation techniques when fine-tuning transformer-based models. We conducted experiments on three tasks characterized by subjective content and inherent label ambiguity: classifying sentiment, emotions and hate speech. The selected datasets include multi-annotator labels, which we use to derive a label ambiguity score for each data sample. This score is the entropy of the empirical probability distribution of annotator labels. The results indicate that uncertainty estimation techniques can measure label ambiguity to some extent. Deep Ensembles consistently outperform other techniques, increasing the correlation coefficients between model uncertainty and annotator disagreement, but the observed correlations are low. When comparing the annotator label distributions with the predicted class distributions, we see that Label Smoothing is able to notably reduce this difference, however a discrepancy still exists. This suggests that uncertainty estimation techniques improve the quantification of label ambiguity, however their ability remains limited, highlighting the need for further research [1].

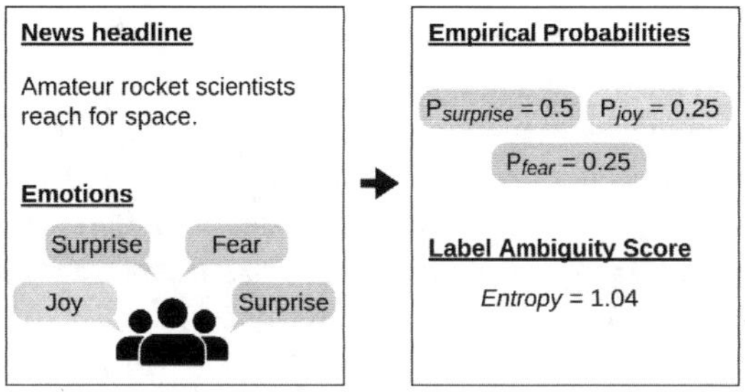

Figure 1: Example text snippet for emotion classification, showing the diverse emotion labels assigned by a group of annotators. Given these labels, we calculate the empirical probability distribution over classes. We use the characteristics of this distribution to define the *label ambiguity score* for the given text snippet.

1 Introduction

Natural language processing often relies on annotated corpora. Due to the subjective nature of language (Mohammad, 2016), annotation tasks often involve subjective judgments, where the meaning of text can be open to multiple interpretations due to personal perceptions, cultural backgrounds or contextual nuances. This subjectivity leads to label ambiguity, a phenomenon where different annotators assign different labels to the same piece of text, reflecting the inherent uncertainty in human language understanding (Mostafazadeh Davani et al., 2022; Khurana et al., 2025). This issue is particularly pronounced in applications requiring nuanced understanding of human emotions or opinions. For example, consider a movie review stating:

> *"The film was surprisingly unconventional and thought-provoking."*

Some annotators might label this as *positive* due to its praise of originality, while others might perceive it as *negative* if they prefer traditional narratives. Such discrepancies highlight the difficulty in assigning definitive labels to subjective content (Plank et al., 2014b).

Current models excel in well-defined tasks with clear, objective labels, such as spam detection, where the distinction between spam and not-spam is relatively straightforward. However, they often underperform in subjective tasks due to their inability to account for label ambiguity (Pavlick and Kwiatkowski, 2019). These models tend to pro-

[1]Code available at: https://github.com/halra/raala

Proceedings of the 19th Linguistic Annotation Workshop (LAW-XIX-2025), pages 21–34
July 31, 2025

vide overconfident predictions even on inherently ambiguous samples, lacking mechanisms to reflect uncertainty in their outputs (Guo et al., 2017). This overconfidence can lead to misguided trust in the model's predictions and obscure the identification of samples, i.e. annotatable items, that require further human review or special attention (Zhang and Yang, 2021).

Furthermore, traditional evaluation metrics and training methodologies do not address the challenges posed by label ambiguity sufficiently (Beigman and Klebanov, 2009). Models are usually trained to minimize error, based on the assumption that there is a single correct label for each sample, which is not always the case in subjective tasks (Uma et al., 2021). This can result in models that are ill-equipped to handle the variability present in real-world data (Aroyo and Welty, 2015).

The core problem addressed in this paper is the lack of effective methodologies for detecting and quantifying label ambiguity in text classification models. Without proper identification and handling of ambiguous samples, models cannot differentiate between confidently correct predictions and those that are uncertain due to inherent ambiguity in the data. This limitation may hinder the development of reliable NLP systems capable of managing the complexities of human language interpretation, particularly in applications where understanding nuance and subjectivity is crucial.

To address this problem, the paper investigates whether techniques for estimating uncertainty in model predictions can serve as a means to measure label ambiguity.

Label ambiguity is often demonstrated in datasets with crowd-sourced annotations, which exhibiti varying degrees of annotator agreement. For instance, in the GoEmotions dataset — a corpus for fine-grained emotion classification (Demszky et al., 2020) — some text samples receive unanimous labels, while others have annotations spread across multiple emotion categories. The variance in annotations indicates the level of ambiguity for each sample. Traditional models might still assign high confidence to a single label, disregarding the underlying uncertainty reflected in the annotators' disagreement (Mostafazadeh Davani et al., 2022).

Given many annotators for each sample, we frame the *empirical probability distribution* over classes as a ground truth measure for sample-level ambiguity, as shown in Figure 1. This allows us to evaluate how well the sample-level uncertainty scores from various techniques align with ambiguity, by comparing them against the empirical probability distribution. In an additional ambiguity detection experiment, we define a threshold and have the models, equipped with stated uncertainty estimation techniques, predict which samples are ambiguous; samples with uncertainty scores within the threshold are marked as ambiguous.

Our contributions can be summarized as follows:

- We propose an empirical label ambiguity measure. This includes framing the annotator label distribution over classes as a ground truth measure for sample-level ambiguity.

- We evaluate uncertainty estimation techniques for measuring label ambiguity. These techniques are trained using a single label, and not a distribution, and we evaluate how well their output class distributions capture the inherent label ambiguity. We see that the techniques successfully improve over the Baseline Softmax in quantifying label ambiguity, but their performance is limited.

- We present an ambiguity detection task and evaluate the methods. We conduct experiments that classify samples as ambiguous based on defined uncertainty thresholds, demonstrating modest improvements over standard fine-tuning and random baselines.

2 Evaluation Data for Label Ambiguity

In this section, we outline the evaluation data and metrics employed to investigate label ambiguity in subjective tasks. We utilize publicly available datasets with inherent annotation ambiguity, each annotated with multi-annotator labels, described in Section 2.1. We define the *label ambiguity score* as the entropy of the empirical probability distribution over annotator labels, explained in Section 2.2.

2.1 Datasets

We employ publicly available datasets with multi-annotator labels, which demonstrate annotator disagreements. In our experiments, we utilize GoEmotions (Demszky et al., 2020), Rotten Tomatoes Reviews (Pang and Lee, 2005), and the GAB Hate Speech Corpus (Kennedy et al., 2020). For each dataset we used 70% for training, 15% as validation and 15% as a holdout test set.

Table 1 summarizes the dataset characteristics. This includes the original characteristics of each

		Samples	Classes	Annotators
GoEmotions	*orig.*	58,009	28	4.3
	modif.	23,990	9	2.8
Rotten Tomatoes	*orig.*	4,999	2	5.55
	modif.	4,999	2	5.55
GAB Hate Speech	*orig.*	27,665	13[1]	3+
	modif.	4,674	2	3.12

Table 1: Overview of the three datasets. The columns show the total number of samples, number of classes and average number of annotators per sample.

dataset, as well as the modified ones used in this paper. Following are the modifications we applied:
GoEmotions: We reduced the label set to 9 primary emotions: sadness, neutral, love, gratitude, disapproval, amusement, adminration, annoyance, approaval. We also removed examples with only one annotator vote, and balanced the dataset across classes.
GAB Hate Speech: We consolidated the multiple hate categories into a binary hate label and balanced the resulting subset. Merging all hate categories into one class brings more variety into the hate class, which induces more disagreements than according to the original label set.

2.2 Label Ambiguity Score

We define the label ambiguity score using empirical probability distributions. These distributions consist of empirical probabilities for each class computed using labels from multiple human annotators. The empirical probabilities are computed as the proportion of annotators who choose that class relative to the total number of annotators. This distribution reflects annotator consensus and allows us to compute the label ambiguity score, given that ambiguous samples exhibit higher disagreement among annotators.

We use the entropy of this distribution as a *label ambiguity score*, calculated for each dataset example. Higher entropy indicates greater disagreement among annotators and ambiguity, whereas lower entropy corresponds to stronger consensus.

We analyse the distribution of label ambiguity scores for each dataset in Figure 2. We can see that the GoEmotions and Rotten Tomatoes datasets have wide distributions, with the data samples exhibiting either total agreement (label ambiguity score close to zero), or different levels of ambiguity. The high label ambiguity scores in GoEmotions overall, larger than 1, are due to the larger number of classes, whereas Rotten Tomatoes and GAB Hate Speech have only two classes. For GAB Hate Speech, we see a bimodal histogram with two very narrow peaks, indicating two very distinct groups of samples - low ambiguity around 0 or high ambiguity around 0.6.

[2]Total number including various types of hate speech.

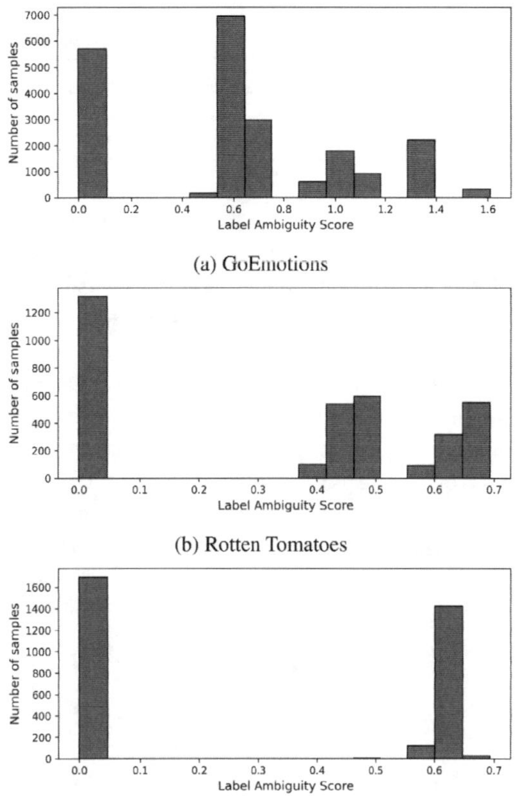

(a) GoEmotions

(b) Rotten Tomatoes

(c) GAB Hate Speech

Figure 2: Distribution of label ambiguity scores

3 Methods

We describe our methodology for uncertainty estimation to assess label ambiguity. Our goal is to use uncertainty estimation either to directly predict the label ambiguity score or to approximate the full label distribution across classes. We detail the uncertainty estimation techniques employed in Section 3.2, and explain how we derive an uncertainty score from the model outputs in Section 3.3.

3.1 Baseline Softmax and Oracle Softmax Distribution

First, we will briefly explain the standard finetuning approach for classification, used as a baseline in our paper.

Baseline Softmax. In this approach, the target labels used are the *majority vote* of the multi-annotator labels. This means that the model is trained on one-hot encoded labels where each sample is assigned exactly one class - the most frequent one of the crowd annotations. The model outputs a softmax distribution (Bridle, 1990) over the classes, which can be interpreted as a probability distribution. This predicted distribution is used to later calculate the uncertainty score.

Additionally, we include another standard approach, that is common when dealing with multi-annotator datasets (Plank et al., 2014a).

Oracle Softmax. Instead of the majority vote, this approach uses soft training labels, obtained from the *full distribution of annotations*. The frequency of annotator votes for each class is used as a corresponding soft label. This represents an ideal scenario where the distribution of human annotator labels for the training samples is known. Again, the softmax distribution is used to calculate the uncertainty score.

The goal of this paper is to measure label ambiguity when annotator distributions are in fact not available and all of our evaluated approaches train with a single label for each sample. This makes the *Oracle Softmax* approach infeasible, however we include it as an upper performance bound, because it could inform us on the potential of ambiguity quantification when richer labels are available.

3.2 Uncertainty Estimation Techniques

We focus on three techniques: *Monte Carlo Dropout*, *Deep Ensembles* and *Label Smoothing*. These techniques all involve fine-tuning models for classification, using the majority vote of the multi-annotator labels and no additional information about the annotator distribution.

Deep Ensemble (DE) involves training multiple neural networks independently, each initialized differently (Lakshminarayanan et al., 2017). In our case, we use multiple instances of the same model architecture, which are just multiple instances of the previously explained *Baseline Softmax*. Each of these models outputs a predicted distribution over classes. We use the average of these distributions to calculate the uncertainty score.

Monte Carlo Dropout (MCD) is a method used for estimating uncertainty in neural network predictions (Gal and Ghahramani, 2016). By randomly disabling neurons during inference, it provides multiple stochastic predictions that help measure model uncertainty. We use the average of these predicted distributions to calculate the uncertainty score.

Label Smoothing (LS) is a technique that modifies the target labels to reduce model overconfidence by assigning soft probabilities to non-target labels (Szegedy et al., 2015). Instead of using hard one-hot encoded labels, we uniformly distribute a fraction of the label probability mass across other classes which helps mitigate overfitting. Similar to the other methods, the output softmax distribution is used to calculate the uncertainty score.

3.3 Uncertainty Score

Each uncertainty estimation technique outputs a predicted probability distribution over the classes. Given this probability distribution, we calculate its entropy as an *uncertainty score*. Entropy quantifies the amount of uncertainty or randomness in a probability distribution (Namdari and Li, 2019).

In addition to the entropy, we can calculate other uncertainty metrics, such as variance and the Jensen-Shannon divergence (JSD). We initially experimented with all three of them, however our results showed that they perform very similarly. The comparison of the three uncertainty metrics for the task of ambiguity detection can be found in Appendix A. Due to this, we only use entropy in the remainder of this paper.

4 Experiment: Measuring Label Ambiguity

In the first experiment, we evaluate the effectiveness of the uncertainty estimation techniques in measuring label ambiguity. Here, we compare how correlated the ambiguity and uncertainty scores are, as well as how close the empirical and predicted distributions are.

4.1 Experimental Setup

We compare the three uncertainty estimation techniques (Section 3.2) with the *Baseline Softmax* and *Oracle Softmax* fine-tuning. We perform the experiment using three datasets, listed in Section 2.1.

We selected well-known models that have consistently demonstrated robust performance across natural language processing tasks. Namely BERT (Devlin et al., 2019), RoBERTa (Liu et al., 2019) and XLNet (Yang et al., 2020). Table 2 provides a high-level overview of the key specifications for BERT, RoBERTa, and XLNet. Despite differences in training strategies and data volumes, all three models share a transformer-based architecture. By employing three different models we can verify the generalizability of our findings.

	BERT	RoBERTa	XLNet
Vocab. size	30,522	50,265	32,000
Max. seq. length	512	512	512
Training data	16GB	160GB+	158GB+
Pre-train object.	MLM, NSP	MLM	Permut. LM

Table 2: Comparison of Architectural Specifications

All experiments were ran for 3 random seeds and tables show the mean scores and standard deviations. Further implementation details can be found in Appendix C.

We calculate multiple metrics to evaluate how well the techniques measure ambiguity. To compare the scores themselves, we calculate the Pearson correlation coefficient between the predictive entropies (uncertainty scores) and the empirical entropies (label ambiguity scores). A high correlation indicates that the model's uncertainty estimates align with human perceptions of ambiguity, suggesting that the model can effectively identify ambiguous samples.

To compare the empirical and predicted distributions directly, we calculate the Jensen-Shannon divergence (JSD), Kullback–Leibler divergence (KLD) and mean squared error - averaged over all classes (MSE). With this, for each sample, we evaluate how close the distribution of predicted class probabilities is to the empirical distribution of the annotator labels. These metrics are calculated for each sample independently, and then averaged over samples.

4.2 Results - Baseline Softmax

The classification metrics for the *Baseline Softmax* model can be found in Appendix B. We see that the three tasks have different difficulty levels. The F1 score for sentiment classification (Rotten Tomatoes) is the highest - 0.87, followed by hate speech classification (GAB Hate Speech) with 0.77 and emotion classification (GoEmotions) with 0.64. Additionally, we see that the scores on each dataset are consistent across the three transformer models.

Additionally, we compare the most common cases of disagreements in the models' predictions and the human annotations. On the GoEmotions dataset we compare the classifier's confusion matrix with human annotation co-occurence counts. Half of the ten most frequent pairs *neutral* ↔ *approval*, *neutral* ↔ *disapproval*, *neutral* ↔ *sadness*, and *annoyance* ↔ *disapproval* appear in *both* rankings, giving a 50% overlap. This shows that the models often make prediction mistakes exactly where annotators tend to attribute multiple emotions, which means these mistakes can be attributed to annotator disagreement and label variation. On another hand, the remaining pairs in Table 3a) are class distinctions genuinely difficult for the model.

The complete confusion and co-occurrence heatmaps are shown in Figure 6 in Appendix E.

4.3 Results - Measuring Label Ambiguity

Table 4 shows our aggregated results—averaged over the three model architectures.

As expected, *Oracle Softmax* has the highest correlation and lowest JSD, KLD and MSE out of all the methods. The average correlations for *Oracle Softmax* are in the range 0.290 - 0.375 across all datasets and models, indicating moderate correlation (Hopkins, 2000). This is expected, since it incorporates annotator distribution information during training, while the other techniques do not. A minor exception is the GoEmotions dataset, where even though the *Oracle Softmax* method achieves the lowest MSE and highest correlation, its relatively higher JSD and KLD suggest that, while it minimizes squared differences, it does not fully capture the distribution. One reason for this could be the larger number of classes in GoEmotions, compared to the other two datasets.

In all cases, all uncertainty estimation techniques improve over *Baseline Softmax*. The *Deep Ensemble* technique achieves the highest mean correlation coefficients of 0.218 and 0.212 for GoEmotions and Rotten Tomatoes. *Monte Carlo Dropout* also shows substantial improvement, with average correlations of 0.216 and 0.167 for GoEmotions and Rotten Tomatoes.

On the GAB Hate Corpus, we generally observe much lower correlations than for the other two datasets. One potential reason for this could be the very narrow peaks in the histogram of this dataset (see Figure 2) when compared to the other two, which means that this dataset includes a very limited variety of label ambiguity scores. Additionally, for this dataset we applied the most significant modification, which was changing the target into binary classification (hate or no hate), by merging all various hate classes into one.

Overall, our results suggest that using uncer-

Rank	Pair	Count
1	neutral ↔ approval	74
2	annoyance ↔ disapproval	62
3	approval ↔ neutral	56
4	neutral ↔ disapproval	55
5	annoyance ↔ neutral	47
6	neutral ↔ annoyance	47
7	disapproval ↔ neutral	46
8	approval ↔ admiration	45
9	neutral ↔ sadness	41
10	disapproval ↔ annoyance	38

(a) Classifier confusion pairs.

Rank	Pair	Count
1	neutral ↔ approval	226
2	approval ↔ neutral	226
3	sadness ↔ neutral	159
4	neutral ↔ sadness	159
5	neutral ↔ disapproval	151
6	disapproval ↔ neutral	151
7	annoyance ↔ neutral	143
8	neutral ↔ annoyance	143
9	annoyance ↔ disapproval	116
10	disapproval ↔ annoyance	116

(b) Human co-occurrence pairs.

Table 3: Most frequent emotion pairs in the misclassifications of the baseline classifier (left) and in the human co-annotations (right) on the 9-class GoEmotions dataset.

tainty scores derived from uncertainty estimation techniques, particularly *Deep Ensembles* and *MC Dropout*, enhance the model's ability to detect ambiguous samples. However, it is important to note that the correlation coefficients between the uncertainty and ambiguity scores are low, with values close to 0.2, indicating that while there is a positive relationship, it is small (Hopkins, 2000). This suggests that the techniques' ability to detect ambiguity is limited and there is room for improvement.

When comparing the distributions, *Label Smoothing* significantly reduces the discrepancy between the predicted and annotator distributions, much better than *Deep Ensemble* and *Monte Carlo Dropout*. This is opposite from the correlation analysis, where in terms of overall correlation of entropies, *Label Smoothing* scores much lower than the other methods. With this, we see that training with soft labels significantly improves the predicted class distributions and makes them more ambiguity-aware, even when the soft labels are only in the form of a uniform smoothing factor.

Figure 3 showcases the improvement the *Deep Ensemble* brings over the *Baseline Softmax*, by visualizing the correlation across all data samples on the GoEmotions dataset. The scatter plots show that the *Deep Ensemble* technique results in a stronger positive correlation, with data points more closely following an upward trend compared to the baseline. This highlights the finding that the uncertainty score derived from ensembles of models improves the measuring of label ambiguity, as opposed to using a single model.

As an additional insight, for BERT on Rotten Tomatoes we selected the top-100 most-uncertain sentences for MC Dropout, Deep Ensemble, and Label-Smoothing. Eighteen sentences (18 %) occur in *all* three lists, and the pair-wise Jaccard overlaps average 0.24 ± 0.01. Across the entire score vectors the mean Spearman correlation is 0.50 ± 0.20 (after aligning on common IDs). Each estimator nonetheless brings novel evidence: 39%, 43%, and 40% of their respective top-100 sentences are unique to MC, Smoothing, and DE.

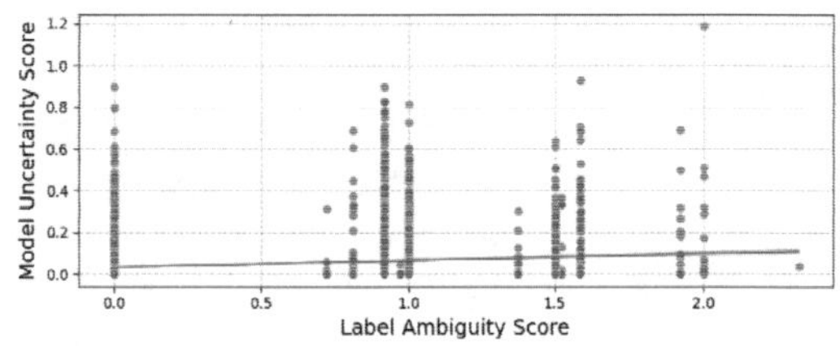

(a) *Baseline*: Correlation 0.095

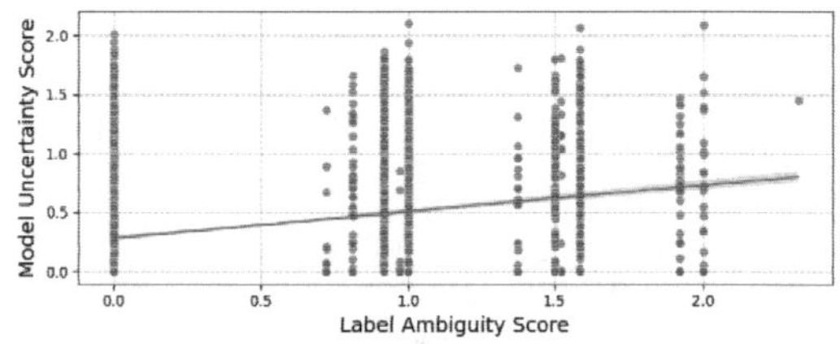

(b) *Deep Ensemble*: Correlation 0.226

Figure 3: Correlation between label ambiguity scores and uncertainty scores across all data samples. Results for the GoEmotions dataset using XLNet.

5 Experiment: Detecting Ambiguous Samples

This experiment demonstrates our methodology for detecting ambiguous samples in text classification using model uncertainty estimates. We apply percentile-based thresholds and flag samples that exceed these thresholds. With this, we assess the overlap between model-identified and annotator-identified ambiguous samples and evaluate how

		Distribution			Ambiguity Score	
Dataset	**Technique**	**Mean JSD ↓**	**Mean KLD ↓**	**Mean MSE ↓**	**Correlation ↑**	**% Improv. ↑**
GoEmotions	Baseline Softmax	0.342 ± 0.005	5.303 ± 0.440	0.0608 ± 0.0009	0.084 ± 0.007	-
	Deep Ensemble	**0.285 ± 0.002**	3.271 ± 0.050	0.0443 ± 0.0003	0.218 ± 0.007	163%
	MC Dropout	0.294 ± 0.002	2.799 ± 0.039	0.0478 ± 0.0003	0.216 ± 0.003	161%
	Label Smoothing	0.340 ± 0.002	**1.115 ± 0.007**	0.0407 ± 0.0004	0.155 ± 0.012	87%
	Oracle Softmax	0.382 ± 0.006	1.489 ± 0.042	**0.0125 ± 0.0003**	**0.375 ± 0.009**	**354%**
Rotten Tomatoes	Baseline Softmax	0.150 ± 0.002	2.662 ± 0.102	0.1174 ± 0.0027	0.081 ± 0.015	-
	Deep Ensemble	0.115 ± 0.002	1.788 ± 0.051	0.0880 ± 0.0017	0.212 ± 0.009	174%
	MC Dropout	0.125 ± 0.005	1.754 ± 0.093	0.0989 ± 0.0045	0.167 ± 0.020	122%
	Label Smoothing	0.084 ± 0.003	0.245 ± 0.009	0.0745 ± 0.0033	0.135 ± 0.010	78%
	Oracle Softmax	**0.070 ± 0.003**	**0.208 ± 0.013**	**0.0543 ± 0.0024**	**0.290 ± 0.020**	**279%**
GAB Hate Speech	Baseline Softmax	0.208 ± 0.003	3.262 ± 0.224	0.1794 ± 0.0032	0.036 ± 0.043	-
	Deep Ensemble	0.165 ± 0.002	1.922 ± 0.078	0.1390 ± 0.0019	0.073 ± 0.013	185%
	MC Dropout	0.176 ± 0.004	1.970 ± 0.107	0.1536 ± 0.0036	0.084 ± 0.033	173%
	Label Smoothing	0.132 ± 0.003	0.381 ± 0.009	0.1205 ± 0.0039	0.046 ± 0.033	65%
	Oracle Softmax	**0.104 ± 0.010**	**0.355 ± 0.048**	**0.0916 ± 0.0109**	**0.375 ± 0.031**	**1075%**

Table 4: Evaluation of the experiment of measuring label ambiguity. Three distribution metrics: Jensen-Shannon divergence (JSD), Kullback–Leibler divergence (KLD) and mean squared error (MSE) are shown. The Pearson correlation coefficients of the uncertainty and ambiguity scores are also shown, together with percentage improvement over the *Baseline Softmax* (%Improv.), in terms of the correlations. The scores are averaged over all test set samples, and then averaged over the three models. The table shows mean ± std., where the standard deviation is calculated over the models. In each column, the best scores are **bolded**, and the second-best are underlined.

Metric	Value
Common to all three	18 / 100 (18%)
Mean Jaccard	0.24 ± 0.01
Mean Spearman ρ	0.50 ± 0.20
Unique to MC Dropout	39 %
Unique to Label Smoothing	43 %
Unique to Deep Ensemble	40 %

Table 5: Overlap statistics for the top–100 most-uncertain Rotten-Tomatoes items.

well our model-derived uncertainty works for detecting human ambiguity.

The first experiment, gives us correlation coefficients which are positive, but low. This does not tell us what these values imply for the practical use of these methods. With this second experiment, we hope to get better insights into whether these correlation values are sufficient to guide downstream filtering of ambiguous samples.

5.1 Task Setup

With this experiment, we transform the task into a binary classification task, where the two classes are *ambiguous* and *non-ambiguous*. We refer to this setup as ambiguity detection. We assign ground truth labels based on the label ambiguity scores. A sample is labeled as *ambiguous* if its label ambiguity score exceeds a pre-defined threshold.

We set this threshold dynamically, to always match the 60th percentile of the ambiguity scores. We chose this threshold as it has been adopted in some prior works with limited backing (Dumitrache et al., 2015). Intuitively, in Figure 2, we see that applying a dataset-specific threshold using the 60th percentile, would result in a large number of samples flagged as ambiguous. This is confirmed in Table 6, where we see that the shares of ambiguous samples are close to 50%[3]. In other words, we flag as ambiguous almost all samples that do not have perfect agreement among the annotators.

This is one way to separate samples into two classes according to their annotator agreement scores. In reality, determining this threshold and defining the difference between ambiguous and non-ambiguous samples is a very significant question, but also challenging to answer and out of the scope of this paper.

During inference, we apply the same type of thresholding using the 60th percentile to the model-

[3]The 60th percentile threshold implies that 40% of the samples will be flagged. However, with 2–5 annotators per item, ambiguity scores are limited to a few possible values. For some datasets, like GAB Hate Speech, this includes a lot of ties, which raises the ambiguous shares to over 40%, but avoids arbitrarily splitting items with identical agreement.

derived uncertainty scores. This determines the predicted label for each sample: if the uncertainty score is above the threshold the sample is predicted as ambiguous.

5.2 Random Baseline

For this task, we also include a random baseline in the evaluations. Here, instead of calculating an uncertainty score, we randomly generate a number between 0 and 1 for each sample. Then, on these random scores we apply the same threshold as explained in the previous section: if the random score is above the threshold the sample is predicted as ambiguous. This helps us assess the practical effectiveness of the uncertainty techniques in detecting ambiguous samples.[4]

5.3 Results

The main results of this experiment, in terms of error rates, are shown in Table 6. We can see that all methods consistently outperform the *Random baseline*, which has error rates of around 50%. This indicates that all methods are helpful in flagging ambiguous samples.

Out of the techniques, and consistent with our previous experiments, *Deep Ensemble* achieved the lowest error rates, with average of 41.19%. Notably, these rates are promising when compared to a *Random Baseline*, indicating that our techniques capture meaningful predictive information. We obtained comparable scores across the three datasets. On the GoEmotions dataset, all three techniques outperformed the *Baseline Softmax*, whereas on the Rotten Tomatoes and GAB Hate Speech datasets, *Label Smoothing* and *Monte Carlo Dropout* performed worse than the *Baseline Softmax*. The *Oracle Softmax* approach again provided an advantage by reducing the average error rate to around 37%.

In Figure 4, we present the ROC curves of the ambiguity detection task. The ROC curves illustrate the trade-off between the true positive rate and the false positive rate at various threshold settings.

Out of the methods, the *Deep Ensemble* exhibits the highest area under the curve (AUC) of 0.61, indicating the best overall performance where *Monte Carlo Dropout* performs slightly below Deep Ensemble but still surpasses the *Baseline Softmax* and

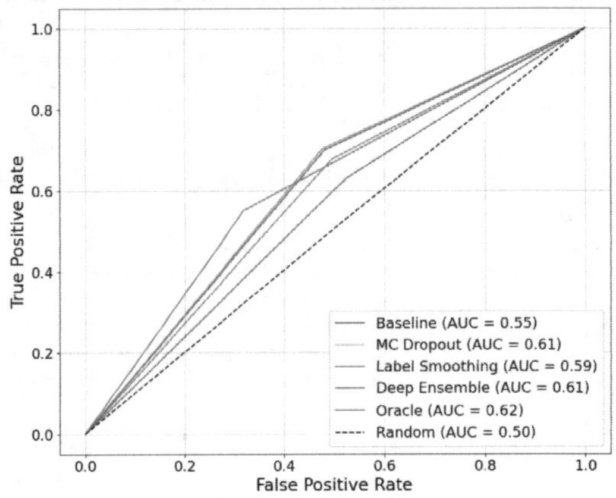

Figure 4: ROC curves for ambiguity detection, on the GoEmotions dataset with RoBERTa. Each sample is annotated as ambiguous if the empirical entropy (label ambiguity score) is over 60% of the maximum value.

Label Smoothing techniques. All four methods outperform the Random baseline.

These results are consistent with our previous analysis, reinforcing the conclusion that the *Deep Ensemble* technique is more adept at capturing label ambiguity.

6 Related Work

There have been numerous studies addressing human label variation and label ambiguity. Snow et al. (2008) highlighted the variability in annotations obtained from non-expert annotators and the impact of this variability on NLP tasks. They demonstrated that aggregating multiple annotations can improve the quality of labels.

Another study proposed leveraging annotator disagreement instead of resolving it, suggesting that disagreement can provide valuable information.They advocated for models that learn from soft labels reflecting annotator probabilities rather than hard labels (Plank et al., 2014a). We include this as our Oracle Softmax approach.

Uncertainty estimation techniques have gained attention as a means to quantify model confidence (Gal and Ghahramani, 2016; Lakshminarayanan et al., 2017). In the context of deep learning, methods such as Monte Carlo Dropout (Gal and Ghahramani, 2016) approximate Bayesian inference by performing dropout at inference time, enabling models to estimate predictive uncertainty. Similarly, Deep Ensembles (Gal and Ghahramani, 2016) improve uncertainty estimation by training multiple models with different initializations and aggregat-

[4]An alternative random baseline is to always output the majority class (non-ambiguous). This will result in error rates equal to the share of ambiguous samples, which are sometimes better than the random baseline we use. However, this would also give us a zero precision and recall scores of the class of interest, making it unusable for this task.

	GoEmotions	Rotten Tomatoes	GAB Hate Speech	Average
%Ambiguous	53.81	42.80	45.93	-
Error Rate (%)				
Random	51.52 ± 0.61	52.34 ± 0.77	50.21 ± 0.25	51.36
Baseline Softmax	45.01 ± 1.75	41.64 ± 1.23	44.13 ± 2.84	43.59
Deep Ensemble	40.90 ± 0.29	39.75 ± 0.57	42.91 ± 3.57	41.19
Monte Carlo Dropout	40.73 ± 0.37	42.79 ± 0.68	45.76 ± 2.91	43.09
Label Smoothing	42.83 ± 0.68	45.73 ± 1.78	47.99 ± 2.95	46.18
Oracle Softmax	**37.62 ± 0.49**	**37.13 ± 1.10**	**37.39 ± 1.09**	**37.38**

Table 6: Ambiguity rates and error rates (mean ± std) for ambiguity detection. The results are averaged over the three models. In each column, the best scores are **bolded**, and the second-best are underlined.

ing their predictions.

These techniques have shown effectiveness in improving model calibration and detecting out-of-distribution samples. Bley et al. (2024) evaluated various uncertainty estimation methods under dataset shift and found that ensembles generally provide better calibration and uncertainty estimates compared to single models.

Malinin and Gales (2018) introduced Prior Networks to model predictive uncertainty, distinguishing between data uncertainty and model uncertainty in text classification tasks.

Recent research has begun to explore the relationship between model uncertainty and label ambiguity. Braiek and Khomh (2024) studied how incorporating human-like uncertainty into models can improve robustness in image classification tasks. They showed that models trained with uncertain labels can better handle ambiguous inputs.

Despite these advancements, there is limited work specifically focusing on leveraging uncertainty estimation techniques to detect label ambiguity arising from annotator disagreement in subjective text classification.

7 Conclusion

In this paper, we focused on three subjective tasks of great interest: sentiment, emotion, and hate speech classification. For each task, we used public datasets with published multi-annotator labels. For every sample in these datasets, we defined a label ambiguity score as the entropy of the annotator label distribution, which measures the inherent randomness in the labeling process.

We assessed the effectiveness of uncertainty estimation in quantifying label ambiguity. Our evaluation included three techniques—Deep Ensemble, Monte Carlo Dropout, and Label Smoothing—which we compared with both a Baseline Softmax model and an Oracle Softmax approach, the latter serving as an upper performance bound. For each method, we computed an uncertainty score defined as the entropy of the predicted label distribution.

First, we evaluated whether predictive uncertainty techniques could effectively capture label ambiguity by calculating the correlation between uncertainty scores and label ambiguity scores. Our findings indicate that these techniques—most notably Deep Ensembles—outperform the Baseline Softmax approach, with both Deep Ensembles and Monte Carlo Dropout showing a low positive correlation with label ambiguity. Additionally, we assessed the alignment between predicted class distributions and annotator class distributions. Here, the Label Smoothing approach was successful in reducing the discrepancy between the distributions, making the predictions more ambiguity-aware.

Next, we applied the uncertainty estimation techniques to an ambiguity detection task, classifying each sample as either ambiguous or non-ambiguous using a fixed threshold. Under these conditions, the Deep Ensemble approach achieved an error rate of about 40%, reducing it when compared to the Baseline Softmax approach.

Our results indicate that when fully leveraging annotator labels, as in the Oracle Softmax finetuning, the models' ability to quantify ambiguity improves, but the performance improvements remain modest. Although the current uncertainty estimation techniques do not perfectly capture all aspects of label ambiguity, the findings are promising and indicate further research in this direction is needed. We believe this paper can provide a foundation for future research into more robust and effective methods for quantifying label ambiguity.

Limitations

Several limitations of our study should be acknowledged. First, our experiments were primarily conducted on the GoEmotions, Rotten Tomatoes and GAB Hate Corpus datasets, which, while extensive and diverse, may not capture all nuances of subjective expressions across different cultures, languages or contexts.

Second, uncertainty estimation techniques like Deep Ensembles require training multiple models, increasing computational complexity and resource requirements. This may limit their practicality in environments with constrained resources or real-time processing needs. While uncertainty estimation techniques provide valuable information about model confidence, interpreting these estimates in a meaningful way for end-users remains a challenge.

And third, we focus on single-label classification which has inherent limitations as opposed to multi-label classification and may not be the most suitable for tasks such as emotion classification.

Acknowledgments

Elena Merdjanovska and Alan Akbik are supported by the Deutsche Forschungsgemeinschaft (DFG, German Research Foundation) under Germany's Excellence Strategy – EXC 2002/1 "Science of Intelligence" – project number 390523135. Alan Akbik is supported by the Deutsche Forschungsgemeinschaft (DFG, German Research Foundation) under Emmy Noether grant "Eidetic Representations of Natural Language" (project number 448414230).

References

Lora Aroyo and Chris Welty. 2015. Truth is a lie: Crowd truth and the seven myths of human annotation. *AI Magazine*, 36(1):15–24.

Eyal Beigman and Beata Beigman Klebanov. 2009. Learning with annotation noise. In *ACL-IJCNLP*.

Florian Bley, Sebastian Lapuschkin, Wojciech Samek, and Grégoire Montavon. 2024. Explaining predictive uncertainty by exposing second-order effects. *Preprint*, arXiv:2401.17441.

Houssem Ben Braiek and Foutse Khomh. 2024. Machine learning robustness: A primer. *Preprint*, arXiv:2404.00897.

John S Bridle. 1990. Probabilistic interpretation of feedforward classification network outputs, with relationships to statistical pattern recognition. In *Neurocomputing: Algorithms, architectures and applications*, pages 227–236. Springer.

Dorottya Demszky, Dana Movshovitz-Attias, Jeongwoo Ko, Alan Cowen, Gaurav Nemade, and Sujith Ravi. 2020. GoEmotions: A dataset of fine-grained emotions. In *Proceedings of the 58th Annual Meeting of the Association for Computational Linguistics*, pages 4040–4054, Online. Association for Computational Linguistics.

Jacob Devlin, Ming-Wei Chang, Kenton Lee, and Kristina Toutanova. 2019. Bert: Pre-training of deep bidirectional transformers for language understanding. *Preprint*, arXiv:1810.04805.

Anca Dumitrache, Lora Aroyo, and Chris Welty. 2015. Crowdtruth measures for language ambiguity: The case of medical relation extraction. In *LD4IE@ISWC*.

Yarin Gal and Zoubin Ghahramani. 2016. Dropout as a bayesian approximation: Representing model uncertainty in deep learning. *Preprint*, arXiv:1506.02142.

Chuan Guo, Geoff Pleiss, Yu Sun, and Kilian Q. Weinberger. 2017. On calibration of modern neural networks. *Preprint*, arXiv:1706.04599.

W.G. Hopkins. 2000. *A New View of Statistics*. Internet Society for Sport Science.

Brendan Kennedy, Mohammad Atari, Aida Mostafazadeh Davani, Leigh Yeh, Ali Omrani, Yehsong Kim, Kris Koombs, Shreya Havaldar, G J Portillo-Wightman, Elaine Gonzalez, Joe Hoover, Aida Azatian, Alyzeh Hussain, Austin Lara, Gabriel Olmos, Adam Omary, Christina Park, Clarisa Wang, Xin Wang, and Morteza Dehghani. 2020. The gab hate corpus: A collection of 27k posts annotated for hate speech.

Urja Khurana, Eric Nalisnick, and Antske Fokkens. 2025. DefVerify: Do hate speech models reflect their dataset's definition? In *Proceedings of the 31st International Conference on Computational Linguistics*, pages 4341–4358, Abu Dhabi, UAE. Association for Computational Linguistics.

Balaji Lakshminarayanan, Alexander Pritzel, and Charles Blundell. 2017. Simple and scalable predictive uncertainty estimation using deep ensembles. *Preprint*, arXiv:1612.01474.

Yinhan Liu, Myle Ott, Naman Goyal, Jingfei Du, Mandar Joshi, Danqi Chen, Omer Levy, Mike Lewis, Luke Zettlemoyer, and Veselin Stoyanov. 2019. Roberta: A robustly optimized bert pretraining approach. *Preprint*, arXiv:1907.11692.

Ilya Loshchilov and Frank Hutter. 2019. Decoupled weight decay regularization. *Preprint*, arXiv:1711.05101.

Andrey Malinin and Mark Gales. 2018. Predictive uncertainty estimation via prior networks. *Preprint*, arXiv:1802.10501.

Saif Mohammad. 2016. A practical guide to sentiment annotation: Challenges and solutions. In *Proceedings of the 7th Workshop on Computational Approaches to Subjectivity, Sentiment and Social Media Analysis*, pages 174–179, San Diego, California. Association for Computational Linguistics.

Aida Mostafazadeh Davani, Mark Díaz, and Vinodkumar Prabhakaran. 2022. Dealing with disagreements: Looking beyond the majority vote in subjective annotations. *Transactions of the Association for Computational Linguistics*, 10:92–110.

Alireza Namdari and Zhaojun (Steven) Li. 2019. A review of entropy measures for uncertainty quantification of stochastic processes. *Advances in Mechanical Engineering*, 11(6):1687814019857350.

Bo Pang and Lillian Lee. 2005. Seeing stars: Exploiting class relationships for sentiment categorization with respect to rating scales. In *Proceedings of the ACL*.

Ellie Pavlick and Tom Kwiatkowski. 2019. Inherent disagreements in human textual inferences. *Transactions of the Association for Computational Linguistics*, 7:677–694.

Barbara Plank, Dirk Hovy, and Anders Søgaard. 2014a. Learning part-of-speech taggers with inter-annotator agreement loss. In *Proceedings of the 14th Conference of the European Chapter of the Association for Computational Linguistics*, pages 742–751, Gothenburg, Sweden. Association for Computational Linguistics.

Barbara Plank, Dirk Hovy, and Anders Søgaard. 2014b. Linguistically debatable or just plain wrong? In *Proceedings of the 52nd Annual Meeting of the Association for Computational Linguistics (Volume 2: Short Papers)*, pages 507–511, Baltimore, Maryland. Association for Computational Linguistics.

Rion Snow, Brendan O'Connor, Daniel Jurafsky, and Andrew Ng. 2008. Cheap and fast – but is it good? evaluating non-expert annotations for natural language tasks. In *Proceedings of the 2008 Conference on Empirical Methods in Natural Language Processing*, pages 254–263, Honolulu, Hawaii. Association for Computational Linguistics.

Christian Szegedy, Vincent Vanhoucke, Sergey Ioffe, Jonathon Shlens, and Zbigniew Wojna. 2015. Rethinking the inception architecture for computer vision. *Preprint*, arXiv:1512.00567.

Alexandra Uma, Tommaso Fornaciari, Anca Dumitrache, Tristan Miller, Jon Chamberlain, Barbara Plank, Edwin Simpson, and Massimo Poesio. 2021. SemEval-2021 task 12: Learning with disagreements. In *Proceedings of the 15th International Workshop on Semantic Evaluation (SemEval-2021)*, pages 338–347, Online. Association for Computational Linguistics.

Zhilin Yang, Zihang Dai, Yiming Yang, Jaime Carbonell, Ruslan Salakhutdinov, and Quoc V. Le. 2020. Xlnet: Generalized autoregressive pretraining for language understanding. *Preprint*, arXiv:1906.08237.

Yu Zhang and Qiang Yang. 2021. A survey on multitask learning. *Preprint*, arXiv:1707.08114.

A Comparison of Uncertainty Metrics - Ambiguity Detection

In this paper we use entropy as an uncertainty score, however, we experimented with variance and JSD (Jensen-Shannon divergence between uniform and a given distribution). Figure 5 shows ROC curves for different techniques, for the ambiguity detection task. For MC Dropout and Deep Ensemble, we also see different variants of the uncertainty score. We see that all three variants (JSD, variance and entropy) behave similarly across all thresholds, which is why we chose to use one of them throughout the paper.

B Baseline Softmax Results

Table 7 shows the classification metrics of the Baseline Softmax fine-tuning runs.

C Implementation Details

We fine-tuned three transformer-based models: BERT (`bert-base-uncased`) (Devlin et al., 2019), RoBERTa (`roberta-base`) (Liu et al., 2019) and XLNet (`xlnet-base-cased`) (Yang et al., 2020).

Consistent hyperparameters were used across all experiments to ensure fair comparisons and isolate the effects of the uncertainty estimation techniques:

- Seeds: [42, 13, 815]
- Seeds for Deep Ensamble: [[42, 13, 815, 142, 113], [142, 113, 1815, 1142, 1113], [242, 213, 2815, 2142, 2113]]
- Optimizer: AdamW (Loshchilov and Hutter, 2019)
- Learning Rate: 5×10^{-5}
- Batch Size: 8
- Number of Epochs:
  - 14 epochs for Baseline Softmax, MC Dropout and Label Smoothing experiments
  - And [10, 11, 13, 14, 15] epochs for Deep Ensembles to introduce diversity among ensemble members

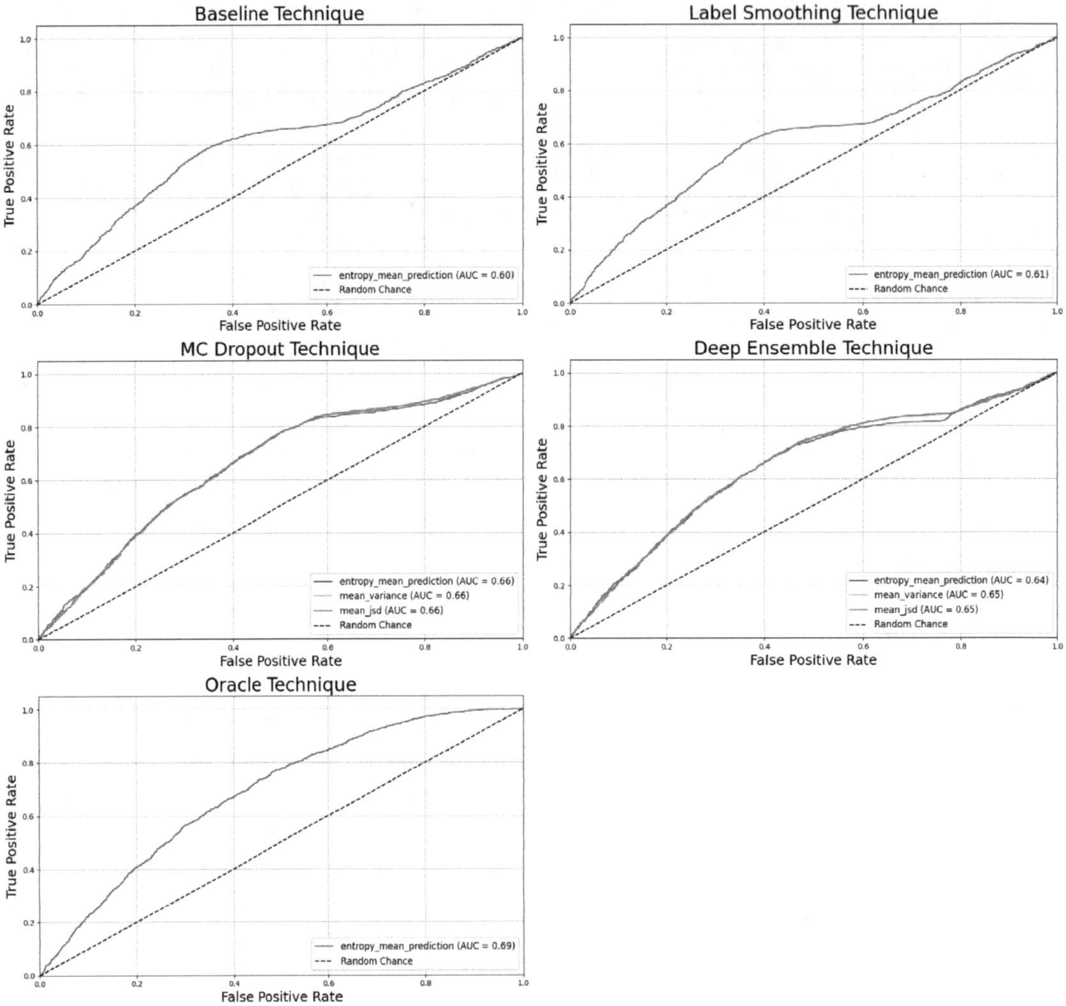

Figure 5: XLNet with GoEmotions ROC/AUC

Model	Dataset	Precision	Recall	F1 Score	Accuracy
RoBERTa	Rotten Tomatoes	0.87	0.87	0.87	0.87
	GoEmotions	0.64	0.64	0.64	0.64
	GAB Hate Corpus	0.78	0.78	0.78	0.78
BERT	Rotten Tomatoes	0.85	0.85	0.85	0.85
	GoEmotions	0.64	0.65	0.64	0.65
	GAB Hate Corpus	0.77	0.77	0.77	0.77
XLNet	Rotten Tomatoes	0.88	0.87	0.87	0.87
	GoEmotions	0.64	0.64	0.64	0.64
	GAB Hate Corpus	0.77	0.77	0.77	0.77

Table 7: Classification Metrics for the Baseline Softmax Models

- Dropout Rate: 0.1

Specific parameters for each uncertainty estimation technique were:

- Monte Carlo Dropout:
  - Number of Stochastic Forward Passes during inference: 100
  - Dropout enabled during inference
  - Dropout during inference: 0.5
- Deep Ensembles:
  - Ensemble Size: 5 models
  - Different random seeds and epochs for each ensemble member
- Label Smoothing:
  - Smoothing Factor: $\epsilon = 0.3$

We split each dataset into training, validation and test sets using a 70/15/15 stratified split to maintain class distribution.

D Correlation between Ambiguity and Uncertainty Scores

Table 8 shows the correlation coefficients and percentage improvement over baseline, averaged over all data samples. The rightmost column shows the average correlation over the 3 datasets.

As expected, *Oracle Softmax* has the highest correlation out of all the methods, with average correlations around 0.35 across all datasets and models, indicating moderate correlation (Hopkins, 2000).

In most cases, all uncertainty estimation techniques improve over *Baseline Softmax*. The *Deep Ensemble* technique achieves the highest mean correlation coefficients ranging between 0.204 and 0.226 for GoEmotions and RottenTomatoes, across the three models. *Monte Carlo Dropout* also shows substantial improvement, with correlations ranging between 0.126 and 0.229 for GoEmotions and RottenTomatoes across models.

On the GAB Hate Corpus, especially in combination with XLNet the results do not align with the patterns observed in the other datasets and models. For this dataset, we even see lower correlations than the baseline, when using *Monte Carlo Dropout* and *Label Smoothing*.

E Class-Level Analysis - Heatmaps

Figure 6 shows the heatmaps comparing the disagreements in the model (baseline BERT) and in human annotations.

Model	Method	GoEmotions Corr.	GoEmotions % Improv.	Rotten Tomatoes Corr.	Rotten Tomatoes % Improv.	GAB Hate Speech Corr.	GAB Hate Speech % Improv.	Average Corr.
BERT	Baseli.	0.081 $\pm$ 0.002	-	0.101 $\pm$ 0.009	-	0.024 $\pm$ 0.042	-	0.069
	DE	0.204 $\pm$ 0.008	152%	0.207 $\pm$ 0.004	105%	0.078 $\pm$ 0.016	225%	0.163
	MCD	0.196 $\pm$ 0.003	142%	0.126 $\pm$ 0.030	25%	0.087 $\pm$ 0.031	262%	0.136
	LS	0.141 $\pm$ 0.011	74%	0.123 $\pm$ 0.013	22%	0.070 $\pm$ 0.038	192%	0.111
	Oracle	**0.372 $\pm$ 0.013**	**359%**	**0.264 $\pm$ 0.012**	**161%**	**0.399 $\pm$ 0.014**	**1562%**	**0.345**
RoBERTa	Baseli.	0.075 $\pm$ 0.007	-	0.083 $\pm$ 0.009	-	0.031 $\pm$ 0.037	-	0.063
	DE	0.224 $\pm$ 0.005	199%	0.224 $\pm$ 0.013	170%	0.076 $\pm$ 0.009	145%	0.175
	MCD	0.229 $\pm$ 0.006	205%	0.191 $\pm$ 0.024	130%	0.112 $\pm$ 0.039	261%	0.177
	LS	0.169 $\pm$ 0.019	125%	0.131 $\pm$ 0.009	58%	0.056 $\pm$ 0.041	81%	0.119
	Oracle	**0.383 $\pm$ 0.008**	**411%**	**0.303 $\pm$ 0.030**	**265%**	**0.379 $\pm$ 0.010**	**1123%**	**0.355**
XLNet	Baseli.	0.095 $\pm$ 0.011	-	0.059 $\pm$ 0.028	-	0.054 $\pm$ 0.049	-	0.069
	DE	0.226 $\pm$ 0.008	138%	0.204 $\pm$ 0.010	246%	0.065 $\pm$ 0.013	20%	0.165
	MCD	0.223 $\pm$ 0.001	135%	0.183 $\pm$ 0.005	210%	0.052 $\pm$ 0.029	-4%	0.153
	LS	0.155 $\pm$ 0.007	63%	0.150 $\pm$ 0.009	154%	0.012 $\pm$ 0.020	-78%	0.106
	Oracle	**0.371 $\pm$ 0.006**	**291%**	**0.302 $\pm$ 0.019**	**412%**	**0.346 $\pm$ 0.069**	**541%**	**0.340**

Table 8: Correlation coefficients (mean $\pm$ std.) and percentage improvement over *Baseline* for each model. In each column, per model, the best scores are **bolded**, and the second-best are underlined.

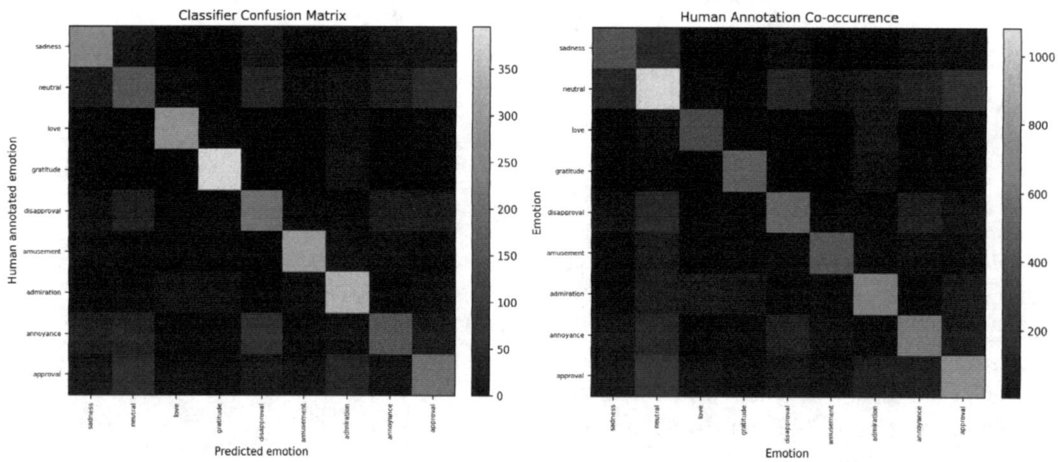

Figure 6: Heat-maps of model confusions (left) and human co-occurrences (right) on GoEmotions.

Disagreements in analyses of rhetorical text structure: A new dataset and first analyses

Freya Hewett and Manfred Stede
Applied Computational Linguistics
University of Potsdam
Germany
lastname at uni-potsdam.de

Abstract

Discourse structure annotation is known to involve a high level of subjectivity, which often results in low inter-annotator agreement. In this paper, we focus on 'legitimate disagreements', by which we refer to multiple valid annotations for a text or text segment. We provide a new dataset of English and German texts, where each text comes with two parallel analyses (both done by well-trained annotators) in the framework of Rhetorical Structure Theory. Using the *RST-Tace* tool, we build a list of all conflicting annotation decisions and present some statistics for the corpus. Thereafter, we undertake a qualitative analysis of the disagreements and propose a typology of underlying reasons. From this we derive the need to differentiate two kinds of ambiguities in RST annotation: those that result from inherent linguistic ambiguity, and those that arise from specifications in the theory and/or the annotation schemes.

1 Introduction

Natural language contains many ambiguities with varied possible interpretations, especially in the domains of pragmatics and discourse. The differences and similarities of annotations from individual coders, the inter-annotator agreement (IAA), is often used to demonstrate that annotation guidelines are effective, the annotators have worked in a precise way, and that overall, the annotations are of a high quality. In recent years, however, the instances of disagreement have gained interest as a resource for more informative models of the underlying task, often under the heading of 'perspectivism' (Uma et al., 2021).

In this study, we focus on the annotation of discourse structure using Rhetorical Structure Theory (RST; Mann and Thompson, 1988). RST annotations provide information about how segments in a text are related to each other with semantic or pragmatic relations such as `cause`, `background`, or `contrast`; we give a brief overview in Sct. 2.1.

With its focus on pragmatic aspects of language use, RST annotation is generally considered to be highly subjective, and as discussed by Marchal et al. (2022), disagreement in alternative annotations can reflect either incorrect annotations or – more interestingly – instances of item ambiguity or of inherent task subjectivity. So far, empirical studies on annotator disagreement in RST (and also for similar frameworks) have been scarce, as we show in Sct. 2.2; one reason is probably the fact that comparing entire tree structures as alternative analyses is a relatively complicated undertaking. To make it more effective, in this paper, we utilise the RST-Tace software (Wan et al., 2019) to compute the individual points of disagreement between two annotators, which we then analyse further.

We use a dataset of English and German corpora that have recently been made available and partly were extended by us with a secondary annotation (see Sct. 3), and we add to this the double-annotated part of the English RST Discourse Treebank (Carlson et al., 2003), which to our knowledge has so far not been analysed for the reasons of the disagreements. For these corpora, we manually inspect a motivated subset of the points of disagreement and build a typology of categories for legitimate alternative analyses.

Our results have multiple implications. Firstly, they provide insights into the variability of discourse structure, as it is comprehended by different annotators. Secondly, our results can lead to improvements on the RST annotation process, with guidelines being made more precise and annotators being made aware of areas of particular difficulty. Thirdly, our disagreement data and typology can be used to improve evaluation methods of discourse parsers and provide inspiration for evaluation of other similarly subjective tasks.

In Sct. 2 we give a brief overview of RST and

Proceedings of the 19th Linguistic Annotation Workshop (LAW-XIX-2025), pages 35–47

outline previous work that has looked at annotation disagreement, and in Sct. 3 we introduce the composition of our dataset. Sct. 4 explains RST-Tace (henceforth: Tace), which provides us with the starting point for our analyses that we present in Sct. 5. In Sct. 6 we discuss these results, before Sct. 7 concludes and outlines possible avenues for future work.

2 Background and Related Work

2.1 A brief overview of RST

Idea. According to Mann and Thompson (1988), an analysis in Rhetorical Structure Theory is conducted by first breaking the text into its Elementary Discourse Units (either simple sentences, or certain types of clauses), which we henceforth call 'EDUs', and then recursively combine adjacent EDUs to form larger units (henceforth: 'spans'). We will use the term 'unit' to refer to a portion of text that is either an EDU or a span. Each combination of adjacent units is labelled with a coherence relation; Mann and Thompson proposed a set of ca. 25 relations. Most of them join one unit that is "more important for the author's purposes" – the 'nucleus' – with a unit that is less important – the 'satellite'. The result is a projective tree where units are marked for their nuclearity status. An example in the original notation proposed by Mann and Thompson (but with actual text removed for brevity) can be seen in Figure 1. Nucleus units have an incoming arrow and a vertical line connecting it to the next upper level.

Corpora. For English, the RST Discourse Treebank (RST-DT; Carlson et al., 2003) was introduced in 2003; it is based on annotation guidelines by Carlson and Marcu (2001), where the size of the relation set has been increased to 78. A part of the corpus comes with two annotations and will be part of our dataset (see Sct. 3). A second important English corpus is GUM (Zeldes, 2017), which is being continuously extended with new data and also with new annotation layers. The annotation guidelines of RST-DT and GUM differ in terms of EDU characterisation and relation set, so that the corpora are not immediately comparable. A smaller English corpus that was recently released contains speeches from the UN Security Council (Zaczynska and Stede, 2024). A part of that has two distinct RST analyses, and these will also be used in our study.

For German, a collection of RST data was recently made available by Shahmohammadi and Stede (2024). A part of that material is double-annotated and will be used in our analyses. This data, as well as the UNSC data, were annotated according to the guidelines by Stede et al. (2017).

2.2 Earlier research: disagreement in discourse structure

Annotation projects in all areas of NLP feature some level of disagreement, with possible sources of disagreement at the level of the annotator, the data, or the context (Basile et al., 2021). In the case of RST, disagreements can arise at the annotator level due to ambiguous EDUs being interpreted differently or genuine errors being made (Mann and Thompson, 1988). At the context level, the same annotator can acknowledge that multiple annotations are reasonable – but in traditional annotation practice has to select one of them. At the data level, text spans (whether they are ambiguous or not) can belong to multiple categories simultaneously.[1]

This final aspect of multiple concurrent relations is included in the proposal by Zeldes et al. (2024) for eRST, which aims to provide solutions for some of the limitations of RST. It allows for so-called 'secondary relations' to be annotated on a unit, which breaks the tree property of the overall structure. Zeldes et al. (2024) mention that allowing for multiple relations could also help in providing more information on RST parser 'errors', which in fact constitute legitimate predictions. Liu et al. (2023) explore the types of errors that RST parsers make, finding that implicit discourse relations and long-distance relations are difficult to identify. They use the double annotated English-language RST-DT corpus subset and find that some of the 'errors' found when comparing a parsers' output to a gold annotation, do actually correspond to plausible relations in alternative trees produced by other annotators.

In a recent study, Zikánová (2024), using the Prague Dependency Treebank in addition to a small set of five Czech texts with RST annotations, outlines seven factors which lead to different interpretations of coherence. These include the interpretation of relations due to polysemous or under-

[1]A discussion on the systematicity of many such ambiguities, due to RST's supplying both 'intentional' and 'informational' relations, originated shortly after RST was originally published; see, e.g., (Moore and Pollack, 1992). Correspondingly, ambiguities arising from the multi-faceted notion of nuclearity were dissected by (Stede, 2008).

specified nature of discourse connectives, or the interpretation of scope due to abstract coreferential expressions.

In the context of discourse parsing, Huber et al. (2021) propose using nuclearity distributions rather than a binary nucleus-satellite distinction, for the benefit of nuclearity-sensitive downstream applications. They create 'silver-standard' trees using summarisation and sentiment analysis data, which feature nuclearity distributions and compare these to the doubly annotated section of the RST-DT. They find that these distributions capture disagreement more than the binary assignment.

3 The corpus

Overall, the corpus used in this study consists of 156 texts in English and German, coming from four sources. All texts have two annotations that were produced by well-trained annotators, and the pair always features identical EDU segmentation. This makes a systematic disagreement analysis much easier, and it reflects an annotation procedure convention to separate the segmentation process from the tree building step. (But see our remark in the Limitations section at the end.)

The English texts are from the RST-DT (Carlson et al., 2003) and the UNSC-RST corpus (Zaczynska and Stede, 2024). The texts in the RST-DT are articles from the Wall Street Journal from the late 1980s. We use a subset of the corpus which consists of texts having two annotations that are based on identical segmentation. The UNSC-RST corpus contains transcripts of speeches from the UN Security Council in the years 2014/15, and we work with its doubly-annotated subset.

The German-language data consist of the doubly-annotated subsets of the APA-RST corpus, which are newspaper articles and their manual simplifications into 'easy language' (Hewett, 2023), and of the Potsdam Commentary Corpus (PCC), which collects commentaries from local newspapers (Shahmohammadi and Stede, 2024).

Five different trained annotators created the analyses of the APA-RST texts, and there was a follow-up step that corrected obvious errors or violations of the schema. The same procedure was applied in UNSC-RST, with a team of four annotators. Two well-trained annotators were involved in building the PCC subset, and also at the time in producing the RST-DT.

Since the two German corpora are based on the same annotation guidelines, we fuse them into a single set that we call APA+PCC. UNSC-RST had the same guidelines but is in English; the RST-DT features a much more fine-grained relation set and hence different guidelines. We thus have three subcorpora for which disagreements can be analysed, but cross-corpus comparisons have to keep in mind the differences. For instance, the PCC/UNSC-RST guidelines were conceived for opinionated text, with the goal of supporting argumentation analysis. Hence they distinguish between the relations `Evidence`, `Reason` and `Cause` with different constellations of objective/subjective material. The RST-DT uses many relations that are absent in the PCC/UNSC-RST, such as six fine-grained versions of `Elaboration`, or the relations `Topic-Shift` and `Example`. (A proposal for mapping between the relations sets was made as part of a shared task on RST parsing (Braud et al., 2023).)

Statistics on our corpus size can be found in Table 1. We make available the parallel APA+PCC and UNSC data as XML files in the customary `rs3` format, and as a `csv` that builds on the output of Tace (see below).[2] The RST-DT data is licensed from the LDC[3]; therefore, only the list of IDs of the texts that we used is part of the repository.

4 Mapping out the disagreements: RST-Tace

We use Tace (Wan et al., 2019) on our corpus to compare the pairs of plausible annotations. Tace takes two RST annotated texts as input, which have identical segmentation, and produces a table comparing the two annotations. Tace calculates IAA using four different aspects: nuclearity (N), relations (R), constituents (C) and attachment points (A), based on a proposal by Iruskieta et al. (2015). A constituent is the satellite span, the attachment point is the span which the constituent is linked to. Pairs of annotated units are matched according to the overlap between central subconstituents (CS); the nuclear units of the satellite of the relation above, or the satellite if the relation is between two EDUs. In Figure 1a, for the `e-elaboration` relation spanning the EDUs 1 and 2, the constituent is 2, the attachment point is 1, and the CS is 2.

Based on the type of mis/match between the two annotators, we create five bins of "annotation deci-

[2]The repository can be found at `https://github.com/discourse-lab/RSTmulti/`.

[3]`https://www.ldc.upenn.edu`

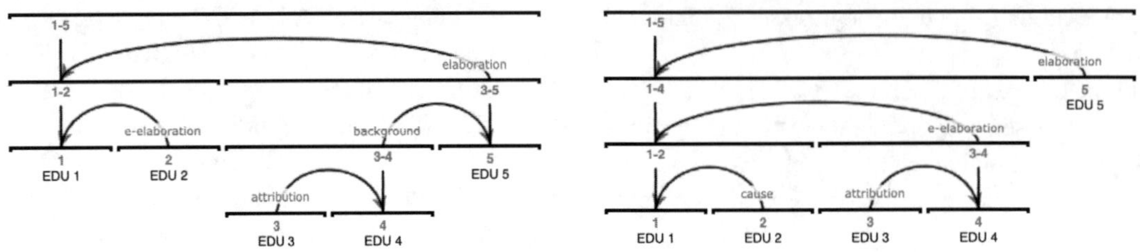

(a) Annotator 1

(b) Annotator 2

Figure 1: Two parallel example annotations.

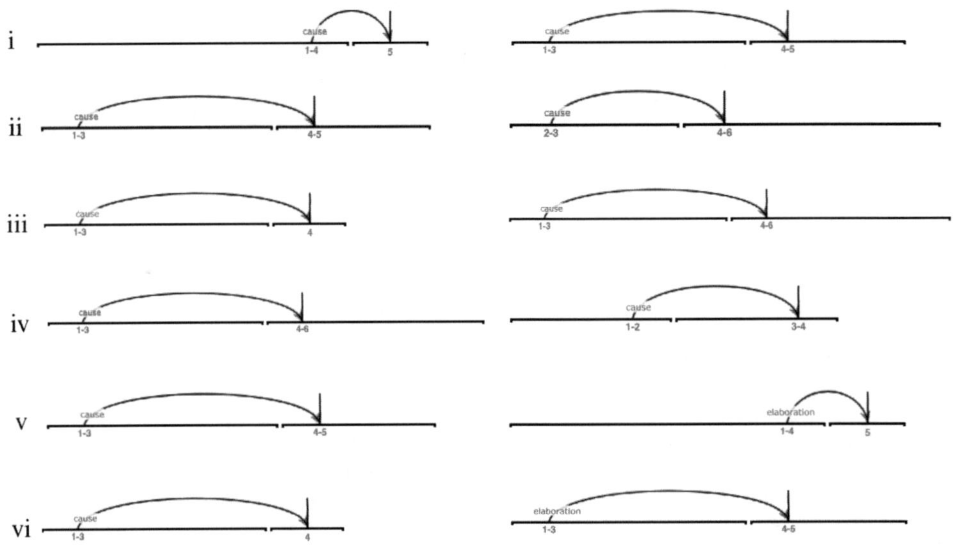

Figure 2: Two parallel extracts from example annotations to illustrate different versions of 'scope mismatch'.

sions" that can be extracted from Tace's output[4], in the form of a spreadsheet where each row contains inter alia the EDU numbers participating in the annotation decision, the actual text spans, and the relations assigned by the annotators. We illustrate the bins with examples from Figures 1a, 1b and 2:

1: Perfect match – Annotators analysed two units in the same way. Example: The `attribution` relation in Fig. 1 constitutes a perfect match.

2: Relation mismatch – Annotators identified the same pair of units but chose a different relation. We can distinguish (i) two mononuclear relations with the same N/S distribution, (ii) one mono- and one multinuclear relation, and (iii) the same units but the N/S distribution is reversed. Example: The different relations between EDUs 1 and 2 (`cause` versus `e-elaboration`) in Fig. 1 belong to category 2(i).

3: Scope mismatch – Annotators disagree on the scope of a relation. This comprises six different constellations: (i) identical overall span; identical relation; different split points; (ii) different overall spans; identical relation; identical split point; different argument spans; (iii) different overall spans; identical relation; one identical argument span; (iv) different overall spans but one common end point; identical relation; different split point, different argument spans; (v) identical overall span, different relations, different split points; (vi) different over-

[4]Details on how we convert the output from Tace to these annotation decisions can be found in Appendix A.2.

all spans, different relations, identical split point, one identical argument span. Example: The `elaboration` relation that encompasses the EDUs 1 to 5 in Fig. 1 belongs to the category 3(i). All cases of scope mismatch can be seen in ascending order from top to bottom in Fig. 2.

4: Left/right priority mismatch – Annotators identified one identical unit, but one attaches it to the left context and one to the right context. Example: The span 3-4 in Fig. 1.

5: No match – Decisions of the first annotator that are not matched at all by the second annotator.

5 Analysis

Table 1 provides some corpus statistics and the distributions of the five bins and the average unit lengths for our three corpora.[5]

In this Section, we cover the three biggest (ignoring "no match") mismatch groups: We will make observations on the perfect matches and then give the results of a qualitative analysis of all relation and scope matches in the corpora APA+PCC and RST-DT. (Analysis of the UNSC corpus and of the remaining bins for the other corpora is left for future work.) For this qualitative analysis, we approach the task from the perspective of a third trained annotator who, however, does not add a third annotation but instead makes a qualitative judgement on the existing two annotations, for each individual mismatch. Section 5.1 discusses the statuses of mismatch and judgement, while in Section 5.2, we present a categorization of underlying *reasons* for the disagreements.

5.1 Status of mismatches

For the *status* of a mismatch, we distinguish four types of judgement that the third annotator can make on a mismatch:

- **Dis**agree: One of the annotations does not seem agreeable, but the other does.[6]

- **Both** are correct and important: A "good" annotation would actually use both relations to do full justice to the text unit (this is the situation that is captured by eRST, as mentioned above).

- **Vague**: One could see things either way, depending on some factors that are to be analysed further (see below).

- Either/**Or**: One can see things either way, but the two ways are actually mutually exclusive.

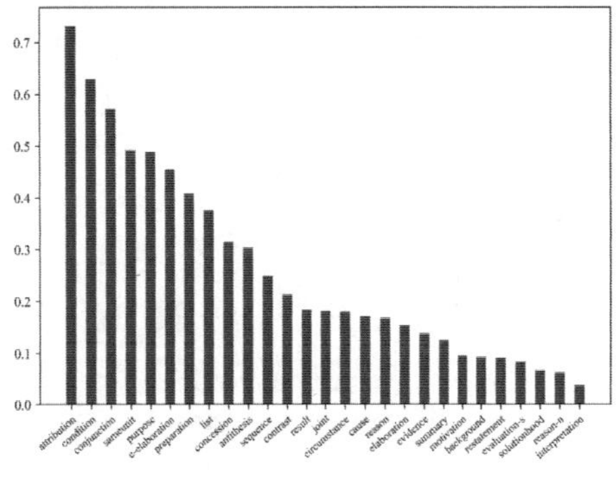

Figure 3: Corpus APA+PCC combined with UNSC-RST: The proportion of relations that occur in a 'perfect match': i.e. the constituent, attachment point, nuclearity and relation are the same.

5.1.1 Perfect match

Fig. 4 shows the confusion matrix for APA+PCC, bins 1 and 2 combined.[7] The diagonal corresponds to perfect matches, which make up between 26% and 49% of all decisions – see Table 1. The avg. number of involved EDUs shows that perfect matches have a clear tendency to occur at the leaf nodes of the trees. Figure 3 shows the relations that occur in a perfect match in the UNSC and the APA+PCC subcorpora combined.[8] `Attribution`, `condition`, and `conjunction` occur frequently in perfect matches, which are relations that often have a clear signal.

For our present purposes, we decided to not analyse the perfect matches; i.e., no status labels were assigned.

5.1.2 Relation mismatch

According to Table 1, this is the largest group of mismatches, and similar to the perfect matches it occurs predominantly at the leaf nodes. When two annotators link the same units but use different

[5]We note that all matches consist of two annotated spans, except for 'no matches', which are counted individually. Therefore the counts for no matches are inflated.

[6]In principle, the situation of disagreeing with both annotations could also arise, but we did not encounter this.

[7]The confusion matrices for the UNSC (Fig. 5) and for the RST-DT (Fig. 6) can be found in Appendix A.1.

[8]We do not include RST-DT in this plot, as it uses a different relation set.

Subcorpus	APA+PCC				UNSC				RST-DT			
Size	46 texts		640 EDUs		84 texts		1346 EDUs		26 texts		768 EDUs	
Agreement	N	R	C	A	N	R	C	A	N	R	C	A
	.50	.33	.46	.42	.60	.38	.55	.51	.56	.37	.53	.49
Tace output bin	n		Span length		n		Span length		n		Span length	
Perfect match	183 (26%)		3.1		410 (29%)		4.4		397 (49%)		5.9	
Relation mismatch	135 (20%)		3.7		288 (20%)		4.2		165 (20%)		4.9	
Scope mismatch	152 (22%)		7.1		301 (21%)		5.9		125 (15%)		11.3	
Left/right mismatch	25 (4%)		3.2		49 (3%)		3.2		8 (1%)		4.4	
No match	197 (28%)		7.4		369 (26%)		7.6		115 (14%)		13.6	

Table 1: Statistics on the corpora and the six bins from Tace output. The average span length is the average number of EDUs contained in the overall relation span. Agreeement values are calculated by Tace and represent F1 values.

relations, this provides the clearest indications for problems with the relation set or with individual definitions provided in the annotation guidelines.

For the 135 instances in APA+PCC, we limit the scope of our analysis to the relation text span that we extracted, i.e., we do not study them in their surrounding context. We find 25 cases of **Dis**, many of which are mismatches between `elaboration` and `entity-elaboration`, where only one appears to actually apply. In 15 cases, no judgement seemed possible because of the missing context; the vast majority are from group 2(ii), involving a mononuclear relation and a `list`, where it is not clear whether other `list` members would warrant the analysis. Of the 28 **Both** cases, many involve a `conjunction` relation, where the other annotator opted for a more informative relation (which points to a guideline problem; see Sct. 6). Roughly half of the **Both** cases do not exhibit a clear linguistic signal and thus would not be annotated in the eRST approach. We find 72 **Vague** cases, and their two biggest subgroups are (i) those where annotators use one of the contrastive relations `contrast`, `antithesis`, `concession`; and (ii) those involving one or two causal relations. When both annotators chose a causal relation, the mismatch is due to different decisions on subjectivity (e.g., `cause` vs. `reason`), while cases with one annotator using a causal relation it is not clear whether a causal connection should be inferred or not (these cases all have no explicit connective).

Within the 165 instances of relation mismatches in the RST-DT, approximately 90 were **Vague**, with a large subset of these (around 50) involving relations that seem to be very similar, such as `analogy` and `comparison`. The second largest subset involved a causal relation in one annotation. Overall, around half of the **Vague** category have some kind of `elaboration` relation in at least one annotation. Around 50 of the relation mismatches represented cases where one annotation does not seem agreeable (**Dis**). The RST-DT has a larger relation set with more fine-grained relations, which has several implications, particularly for this **Dis** category. 12 **Dis** cases involved the same relation, where one relation had the additional suffix '-e' to signify an embedded unit, 19 cases involved a mismatch between `elaboration-object-attribute` and `elaboration-additional`, which mostly differ due to the elaboration being restrictive or non-restrictive. We note that the majority of the **Dis** cases were of this nature and therefore represented negligible 'errors'.

5.1.3 Scope mismatch

In APA+PCC, of the various subcategories listed for (3) at the end of Sct. 4, (i), (ii) and (iv) each occur at most eight times in the data, so that we ignore them here. (iii) has 50 instances and is actually quite close to a 'perfect match', the only difference being that one of the arguments of the relation is of different length in the two annotations. Since this can only be evaluated in context, we studied the 50 instances in their full tree context. In 8 cases (16%), the judgement was **Dis**, as the underlying 'logic' in one of the two analyses seemed implausible. We found a single instance of **EO**, where the different scopes of a `background` relation actually lead to different implications in the surrounding context. The vast majority is **Vague**, usually involving an EDU or very short span being attached to the tree one level lower/higher in the two analyses. One example is a sequence 'If A, then B. Then C.'[9] which can be analysed by first linking B and C into a `list` that forms the satellite of the `condition`, or by stacking two separate `conditions`.

[9]This sounds somewhat uncommon in English, but in German, it is a way of deriving two conclusions from the same antecedent.

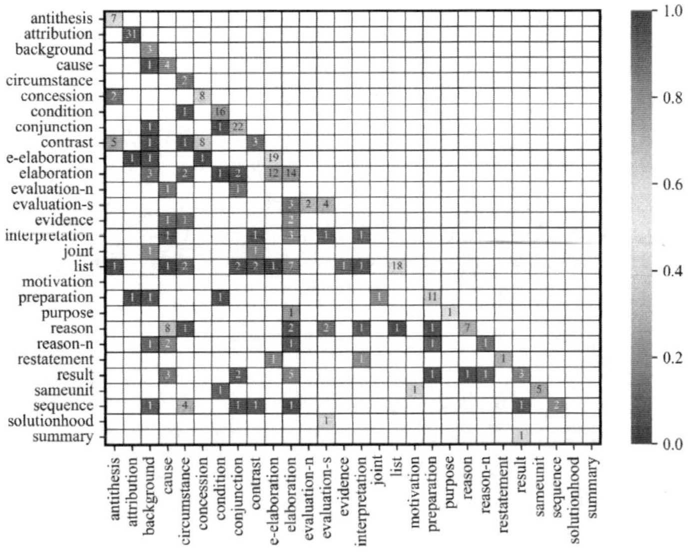

Figure 4: Relations in the categories 'Perfect match' or 'Relation mismatch' in the double annotated subsets of the German-language subcorpora (APA+PCC).

For longer spans, one recurring pattern stems from annotators applying the "strong nuclearity principle".[10] In one example, annotator A sees span 8-13 as evaluating the preceding span 1-7; for annotator B, EDU 13 evaluates span 1-12, but therein, span 1-7 is the central nucleus. Both analyses are plausible, the preference depends on the "weight" one gives to the strong nuclearity principle in the decision process.

Another prominent group of disagreements results from ambiguous contrastive/concessive adverbials such as *aber* and *dabei* (which in English are best rendered by the conjunction 'but') or *stattdessen* ('instead'). When they appear sentence-initial, their scope is not restricted by syntax, and their function can be a "strong" contrast between propositions or merely a "weak" signal of topic change, which can lead to different assignments of the boundary of the preceding span (and sometimes of the following span).

Regarding (v) (16 instances) and (vi) (68 instances), they are by their definition rather different, sharing only the overall span (v) or only one argument span (vi). Thus they are the closest constellations to "no match", and for now we leave their investigation to future work.

The same patterns can be found in our RST-DT subcorpus within the subcategory 3(iii), which consists of 49 cases (of a total of 125 scope mismatches). We note that of these 49, the relation `elaboration-additional` is present in 19 of these cases (almost 40%), compared to its presence in the whole corpus at 17%. The over-proportional presence of this relation makes it clear that it is difficult to pinpoint boundaries between what is being elaborated upon and what constitutes an elaboration, particularly at a higher level in an RST tree. `Attribution` also occurs frequently within 3(iii), and whilst some cases were judged to be **Dis**, i.e. the scope of the attribution did not seem plausible, other cases were ambiguous, with it being difficult to tell how much of the information can be attributed to a source. Examples of this include citing a report or statement without direct quotes. Overall, as the RST-DT has segmentation rules that result in more EDUs per text, and generally more embedded segments, other scope mismatches involved relations such as `sameunit`, and both annotations are equally correct. We also note that the RST-DT texts are mostly longer than those in the German subcorpora and often consist of multiple paragraphs; this formal aspect leads to some annotations which follow these text boundaries, and others which do not, resulting in scope mismatches or left/right mismatches. The RST-DT texts also represent different types of text that can be found in a newspaper; some feature multiple

[10]This principle states that when a relation holds between two spans, it also holds between the central nuclei of the spans (Marcu, 2000).

different topics which each have a lead sentence. An annotator can choose to include the lead sentence directly in the block of text related to the lead, or can separate the lead with a relation such as `summary`. The nature of this relation, as well as, e.g., `comment` or `circumstance`, combined with the mention of specific entities, can make it difficult to pin down exactly what is being commented on or summarised. We also have three cases which we classified as **EO**: These were all due to decisions higher up in the tree, where more specific relations were used, which then limit the scope of elaborations in a specific way. One example of this involved the relation `Topic-Drift` at the highest level in the tree, which meant that an elaboration was limited to the left-hand side of this relation.

5.2 Reasons for disagreement

Following the categorization of mismatches in the Tace-induced five "formal" bins (step 1) and our judgements on the statuses for a large subset of the mismatches in APA+PCC and RST-DT (step 2) in the previous subsection, we now propose categories of the underlying reasons of the disagreements; they resulted from our observations while conducting the status judgements that we just discussed above.

Formal structural alternatives. When a sequence of EDUs plays the same rhetorical role toward a common nucleus, this can be represented either by stacking the same relation, or by first linking the EDUs into a `List`, which is then attached to the nucleus. Annotation guidelines should provide guidance for these situations. Likewise, they should specify whether multinuclear relations with more than two nuclei should be binarized or not. (The GUM guidelines[11] do this; others do not.)

Relation definition overlap. As RST definitions operate with different notions, they are by no means mutually exclusive. `Elaboration`, for example, applies to many EDU pairs where another relation (causal or other) is also appropriate, as our mismatch data shows. Guidelines can suggest to prefer relations that are more informative over very general ones. Another domain where annotators struggle to distinguish similar relations is `Antithesis/Concession/Contrast`, as our confusion matrices show.

Epistemic status of propositions. `Evidence`, `reason` and `cause` differ in whether the satellite is presented as a factual or as a subjective statement. In many of our corpus instances this is a case of vagueness, where two analyses are equally plausible.

Presupposed knowledge, subjective bias. We found many cases where the decision on non/indentity of referents (e.g., two names of local geolocations) entails topic continuity or switch and hence different coherence relations. Besides such factual knowledge, other mismatches result from subjective interpretation. One example from a corpus text about raising children is the coherence relation depending on whether the expression *all families* includes single parents with their children, or not.

Assignment of 'importance'. When annotators apply the aforementioned strong nuclearity principle, they assign degrees of importance to spans and recursively to EDUs. This can be done by using relations with a 'good' nucleus/satellite assignment (e.g., choosing between Background and Elaboration, or between Cause and Result) or preferring a multinuclear relation like Joint. Perception of relative importance can be highly subjective, however, and the interdependencies between relation/nuclearity decisions on low and high levels of the tree lead to ensuing annotator disagreements.

Text structure. Attachment decisions on higher levels can be influenced by the tension between accounting either for common text structure patterns (in editorials: opening—core—conclusion) or for topic shift, which can run across the borders of the structure blocks. Similarly, in the RST-DT we found examples where the format of the article, esp. paragraph breaks, seems to affect annotation decisions.

Scope of adverbial connectives etc. This is not as much an underlying reason but rather a surface phenomenon that facilitates disagreements. We mentioned examples of ambiguous connectives in Sct. 5; other cases concern demonstratives (*Due to this, ..*) and also ambiguous boundaries of indirect speech: *A said that B. C.* Sometimes it is not clear whether C is in the scope of *said*.

6 Discussion

Our findings on disagreements confirm and extend those of Zikánová (2024), and provide a much larger dataset for further study. We also find that the ambiguity of coreferential expressions or attributive verbs lead to scope mismatches in parallel

[11] https://wiki.gucorpling.org/gum/rst

annotations, while on the annotator level the perception of importance can lead to relation mismatches. These sources of ambiguities are not specific to RST annotation but a fact of language use, and they connect to earlier findings that implicitness – the lack of an overt signal clearly associated with a specific relation – leads to more disagreement (Liu et al., 2023; Pastor and Oostdijk, 2024). This is of particular relevance to automatic discourse parsing and led to the emphasis on signal annotation in eRST (Zeldes et al., 2024).

Ambiguity that is inherent in language, however, needs to be kept distinct from aspects of the theory and the annotation guidelines that create some undesirable choice points for annotators. Our observations on the interaction between perception of importance and nuclearity assignments on all levels of the tree reinforces the concerns stated by Morey et al. (2018), who pointed out that the strong nuclearity principle – and the degree to which annotators rely on it – leads to an inherently unclear notion of the *argument* of a coherence relation in an analysis. 'Perception of importance' is inherently subjective, like the ambiguities discussed above, but it should not propagate to an array of other annotation decisions and cause additional variability in the structures of longer texts. A large number of disagreements that we classified as due to **Vague**ness result from this.

The second important source for them is the routine applicability of multiple relation definitions to a given text span. Our 'status' categories distinguish **Vague** from **Both**, where the former may to some extent be curable by clearer relation definitions, while the latter corresponds to the situation where an annotator should have the option to in the first place assign two relations rather than one. The eRST approach offers this, though only in the presence of overt signals; it can be worthwhile to investigate annotators' behaviour if it would also be allowed in implicit contexts. In addition, other forms of underspecification (of the scopes of certain relations) could be a way of reflecting actual vagueness from the viewpoint of an annotator.

Offering annotators the means to make their uncertainties transparent requires a revised model of discourse structure, and still we will usually work with multiple annotators, so that their potentially-underspecified representations need to be compared in systematic ways to one another. In addition, the consequences for machine learning in discourse parsers and for their evaluation need to be considered – all aspects of perspectivism need to be attended to.

7 Conclusions

This is the first study of RST annotation disagreement that uses a sizeable English/German dataset with two alternative trees, which (except for the RST-DT) we also make publicly available. We have proposed a method for systematically studying the disagreements in three steps of analysis: (i) A formal analysis that extends the output of Tace and builds a list of individual points of disagreement between the annotators. (ii) An evaluation of the status of these disagreements. (iii) A typology of reasons for these disagreements. Using parts of our corpus – 480 instances of disagreements in total – we undertook a first qualitative analysis in this way, and then discussed some implications for potential improvements of annotation guidelines and for incorporating uncertainty into the annotation process.

Limitations

Our study started out with alternative RST analyses that are built on identical EDU segmentations. We believe this is a good decision when first embarking on the empirical analysis of RST structures, but ultimately, segmentation needs to be included into the overall picture.

The judgements made from the perspective of the 'third annotator' in Sct. 5 are the decisions of one of the authors of this paper; from a methodological perspective they can be strengthened by adding a second expert and determining agreement.

Our approach makes inspecting many types of agreement more efficient, but removing the context from the material that is being judged obviously creates some limitations. For scope mismatches, we consulted the full text, but for relation mismatches on identical spans we did not. This might lead to some inaccurate judgements.

Finally, using Tace limits the approach to handling concurrent annotations pairwise; if more than two are available, they cannot be immediately integrated into the present workflow.

Acknowledgments

This work was funded by the Deutsche Forschungsgemeinschaft (DFG, German Research Foundation) – Project-ID 317633480 – SFB 1287.

References

Valerio Basile, Michael Fell, Tommaso Fornaciari, Dirk Hovy, Silviu Paun, Barbara Plank, Massimo Poesio, and Alexandra Uma. 2021. We need to consider disagreement in evaluation. In *Proceedings of the 1st Workshop on Benchmarking: Past, Present and Future*, pages 15–21, Online. Association for Computational Linguistics.

Chloé Braud, Yang Janet Liu, Eleni Metheniti, Philippe Muller, Laura Rivière, Attapol Rutherford, and Amir Zeldes, editors. 2023. *Proceedings of the 3rd Shared Task on Discourse Relation Parsing and Treebanking (DISRPT 2023)*. The Association for Computational Linguistics, Toronto, Canada.

Lynn Carlson and Daniel Marcu. 2001. Discourse tagging reference manual. Technical report, Univ. of Southern California/ISI. Unpublished manuscript.

Lynn Carlson, Daniel Marcu, and Mary Ellen Okurowski. 2003. Building a discourse-tagged corpus in the framework of Rhetorical Structure Theory. In Jan van Kuppevelt and Ronnie Smith, editors, *Current Directions in Discourse and Dialogue*. Kluwer, Dordrecht.

Freya Hewett. 2023. APA-RST: A text simplification corpus with RST annotations. In *Proceedings of the 4th Workshop on Computational Approaches to Discourse (CODI 2023)*, pages 173–179, Toronto, Canada. Association for Computational Linguistics.

Patrick Huber, Wen Xiao, and Giuseppe Carenini. 2021. W-RST: Towards a weighted RST-style discourse framework. In *Proceedings of the 59th Annual Meeting of the Association for Computational Linguistics and the 11th International Joint Conference on Natural Language Processing (Volume 1: Long Papers)*, pages 3908–3918, Online. Association for Computational Linguistics.

Mikel Iruskieta, Iria da Cunha, and Maite Taboada. 2015. A qualitative comparison method for rhetorical structures: identifying different discourse structures in multilingual corpora. *Language Resources and Evaluation*, 49(2):263–309.

Yang Janet Liu, Tatsuya Aoyama, and Amir Zeldes. 2023. What's Hard in English RST Parsing? Predictive Models for Error Analysis. In *Proceedings of the 24th Annual Meeting of the Special Interest Group on Discourse and Dialogue*, pages 31–42, Prague, Czechia. Association for Computational Linguistics.

William C. Mann and Sandra A. Thompson. 1988. Rhetorical Structure Theory: Toward a functional theory of text organization. *Text - Interdisciplinary Journal for the Study of Discourse*, 8(3):243–281.

Marian Marchal, Merel Scholman, Frances Yung, and Vera Demberg. 2022. Establishing annotation quality in multi-label annotations. In *Proceedings of the 29th International Conference on Computational Linguistics*, pages 3659–3668, Gyeongju, Republic of Korea. International Committee on Computational Linguistics.

Daniel Marcu. 2000. The Rhetorical Parsing of Unrestricted Texts: A Surface-based Approach. *Computational Linguistics*, 26(3):395–448.

Johanna D. Moore and Martha E. Pollack. 1992. A problem for RST: The need for multi-level discourse analysis. *Computational Linguistics*, 18(4):537–544.

Mathieu Morey, Philippe Muller, and Nicholas Asher. 2018. A dependency perspective on RST discourse parsing and evaluation. *Computational Linguistics*, 44(2):197–235.

Martial Pastor and Nelleke Oostdijk. 2024. Signals as Features: Predicting Error/Success in Rhetorical Structure Parsing. In *Proceedings of the 5th Workshop on Computational Approaches to Discourse (CODI 2024)*, pages 139–148, St. Julians, Malta. Association for Computational Linguistics.

Sara Shahmohammadi and Manfred Stede. 2024. Discourse parsing for German with new RST corpora. In *Proceedings of the 20th Conference on Natural Language Processing (KONVENS 2024)*, pages 65–74, Vienna, Austria. Association for Computational Linguistics.

Manfred Stede. 2008. RST revisited: Disentangling nuclearity. In Cathrine Fabricius-Hansen and Wiebke Ramm, editors, *'Subordination' versus 'coordination' in sentence and text*. John Benjamins, Amsterdam.

Manfred Stede, Maite Taboada, and Debopam Das. 2017. Annotation Guidelines for Rhetorical Structure. Unpublished manuscript.

Alexandra N. Uma, Tommaso Fornaciari, Dirk Hovy, Silviu Paun, Barbara Plank, and Massimo Poesio. 2021. Learning from Disagreement: A Survey. *Journal of Artificial Intelligence Research*, 72:1385–1470.

Shujun Wan, Tino Kutschbach, Anke Lüdeling, and Manfred Stede. 2019. RST-Tace A tool for automatic comparison and evaluation of RST trees. In *Proceedings of the Workshop on Discourse Relation Parsing and Treebanking 2019*, pages 88–96, Minneapolis, MN. Association for Computational Linguistics.

Karolina Zaczynska and Manfred Stede. 2024. Rhetorical strategies in the UN security council: Rhetorical Structure Theory and conflicts. In *Proceedings of the 25th Annual Meeting of the Special Interest Group on Discourse and Dialogue*, pages 15–28, Kyoto, Japan. Association for Computational Linguistics.

Amir Zeldes. 2017. The GUM corpus: Creating multilayer resources in the classroom. *Language Resources and Evaluation*, 51(3):581–612.

Amir Zeldes, Tatsuya Aoyama, Yang Janet Liu, Siyao Peng, Debopam Das, and Luke Gessler. 2024. eRST: A Signaled Graph Theory of Discourse Relations and Organization. *Computational Linguistics*, pages 1–47.

Šárka Zikánová. 2024. Text Structure and Its Ambiguities: Corpus Annotation as a Helpful Guide. In *Proceedings of the 24th Conference Information Technologies – Applications and Theory (ITAT 2024)*, pages 2–12, Drienica, Slovakia.

A Appendix

A.1 Confusion matrices

Figures 5 and 6 show the confusion matrices for perfect matches and relation mismatches in the UNSC and the RST-DT, respectively.

A.2 Tace categories

Table 2 shows how we produced our annotation labels using the output from Tace.[12] In a first step, we used all the matches from Tace. Tace distinguishes between three different categories when comparing two RST trees: 'no matching', 'partially identical CS' and 'completely identical CS'. For each category, it is further specified which of the four aspects match (nuclearity, relations, constituents, and attachment points). More information on what constitutes a match can be found in Wan et al. (2019). We used the categories outlined in Table 2. We then went through the 'no matches' category, according to Tace, and applied simple rules to find further members of our categories. We did this as we are interested in all cases of e.g. relation mismatch, regardless of whether the central subconstituent is the same (which is the method Tace uses to classify matches). We applied the rules in the following order: relation mismatch, relation mismatch with nuclearity switched, left/right mismatch, scope mismatch. An annotated unit can only occur once in our categorisation.

[12] More information can be found in our script: `https://github.com/discourse-lab/RSTmulti/`. Tace is available here: `https://github.com/tkutschbach/RST-Tace`.

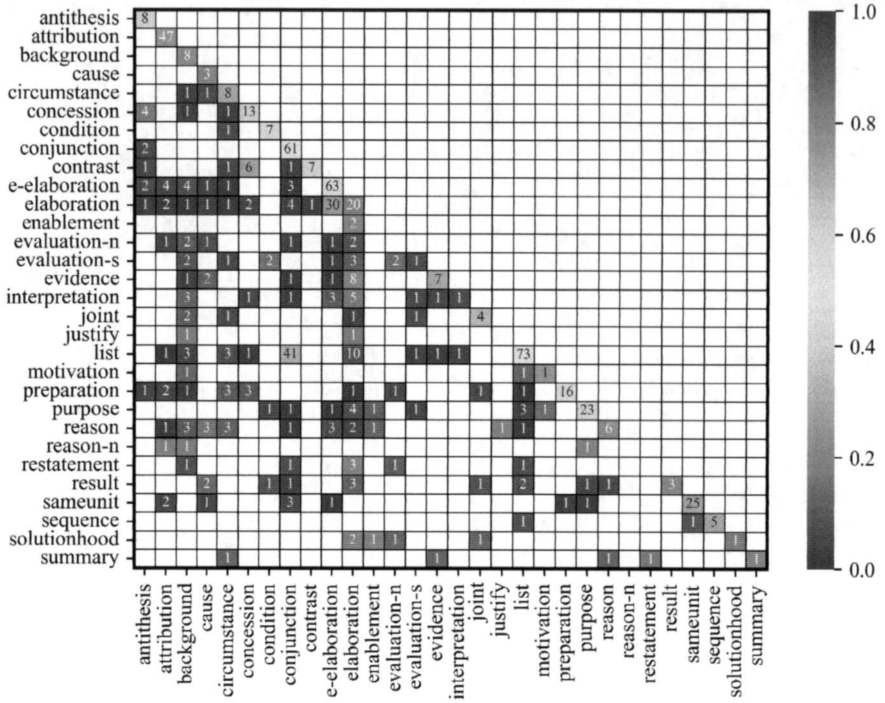

Figure 5: Relations in the categories 'Perfect match' or 'Relation mismatch' in the double annotated subset of the UNSC (Zaczynska and Stede, 2024).

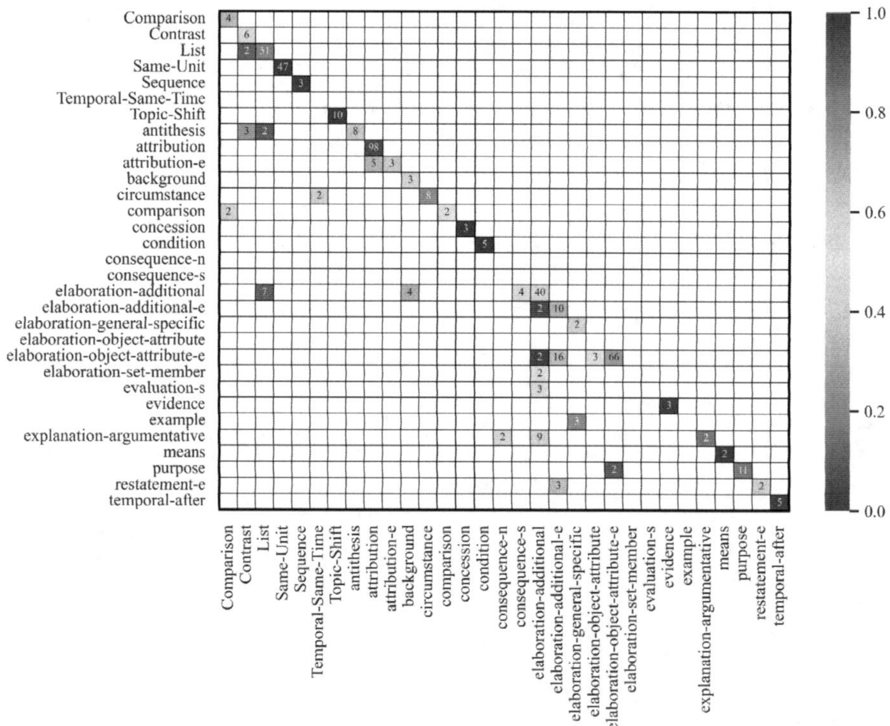

Figure 6: Relations in the categories 'Perfect match' or 'Relation mismatch' in the double annotated subset of RST-DT. Relation pairs which only occur once are not shown, for readability reasons.

Tace output	Matching	Agreement	Disagreement	Other conditions
Perfect match		*NRCA*		
Relation mismatch		*NCA*		
	C1=*C2* *and* *A1*=*A2* or *C1*=*A2* *and A1*=*C2*		*N/N-N/S*, ≠ *R*	
	C1=*C2* *and* *A1*=*A2*	*A*	*N/N-N/S*, ≠ *R*	
	C1=*A2* *and* *A1*=*C2*		*N/S*, ≠ *R*	
Left/right mismatch	Completely identical CS	*C*	*N/S*, ≠ *R*	
	Partially identical CS		*N/N-N/S*, ≠ *R*	One span identical, the non-identical span on left in first annotation and on right in second annotation
Scope mismatch		*NR*		
		NRC		
		NRA		
				Not in any of the above categories, other conditions are outlined in Section 4
No match				Not in any of the above categories

Table 2: Information on how our categories were derived using Tace's (Wan et al., 2019) output.

Subjectivity in the Annotation of Bridging Anaphora

Lauren Levine and **Amir Zeldes**
Georgetown University
Department of Linguistics
{lel76, amir.zeldes}@georgetown.edu

Abstract

Bridging refers to the associative relationship between inferable entities in a discourse and the antecedents which allow us to understand them, such as understanding what "the door" means with respect to an aforementioned "house". As identifying associative relations between entities is an inherently subjective task, it is difficult to achieve consistent agreement in the annotation of bridging anaphora and their antecedents. In this paper, we explore the subjectivity involved in the annotation of bridging instances at three levels: anaphor recognition, antecedent resolution, and bridging subtype selection. To do this, we conduct an annotation pilot on the test set of the existing GUM corpus, and propose a newly developed classification system for bridging subtypes, which we compare to previously proposed schemes. Our results suggest that some previous resources are likely to be severely under-annotated. We also find that while agreement on the bridging subtype category was moderate, annotator overlap for exhaustively identifying instances of bridging is low, and that many disagreements resulted from subjective understanding of the entities involved.

1 Introduction

Bridging is an anaphoric phenomenon where a newly introduced discourse entity is dependent on an associated, non-identical antecedent entity for interpretation. The term "bridging" refers to a discourse participant's construction of an implicature from the entity they are currently processing back to an antecedent entity (Clark, 1975). This associative relation can be triggered by a broad variety of linguistic mechanisms, including lexical part-whole relations (*a house - the door*) and implicit arguments (*a murder - the victim*). Since the phenomenon was first commented on by Clark (1975), it has received a variety of theoretical treatments, including Prince (1981)'s closely related notion of *Inferrables* which centers information status as the key component in identifying anaphoric bridging relations. Such theoretical divides have resulted in a number of different annotation formalisms varying in their definitions of bridging, as well as in their delineations of sub-varieties of bridging (Kobayashi and Ng, 2020). While there has recently been some effort to harmonize bridging annotations across different corpora (Levine and Zeldes, 2024), the current landscape of bridging resources remains heterogeneous. The lack of consistency in and across bridging resources largely stems from their differing definitions for bridging, as well as the subjective annotator judgments that go into identifying instances of bridging.

In this paper, we explore subjectivity in the annotation of bridging anaphora in order to understand how to account for that subjectivity and create more consistent annotations in future efforts. We examine three stages in the annotation process where annotators must make subjective judgments: (1) recognition of the bridging anaphor, (2) resolving back to its associated antecedent, and (3) identifying the subtype category of the bridging pair. To this end, we conduct an annotation pilot on the test set of an existing English corpus, GUM (v10) (Zeldes, 2017). While the GUM corpus includes bridging annotations, the annotation guidelines are underspecified and do not include bridging subtype annotations. This annotation pilot is a preliminary phase in the development a new bridging resource, GUMBridge. For this effort, we develop a new classification system for bridging subtypes organized under 3 relation types: COMPARISON relations, ENTITY relations, and SET relations, as well as an additional OTHER category. We also create annotation guidelines for how to identify instances of bridging anaphor-antecedent pairs and how to classify them into subtypes.

Analyzing the results of this pilot, we find on the one hand that we are able to identify substantially

Proceedings of the 19th Linguistic Annotation Workshop (LAW-XIX-2025), pages 48–59
July 31, 2025

more and denser attestation of bridging than suggested by several previous resources. In terms of subjectivity, we find moderate agreement for the selection of the bridging subtype category and for the selection of an antecedent for a given anaphor. However, the annotator overlap in the recognition of bridging anaphora is considerably lower, despite mostly plausible precision. We conduct a qualitative evaluation of the annotations from the pilot, and we find that subjectivity plays a role in each of the three annotator judgment stages listed above, especially for recall. We explore this role for each stage, and then give recommendations on how to structure the annotation of bridging anaphora in order to account for subjectivity in annotator judgment.

2 Background

As mentioned above, there are a number of different annotation formalisms for bridging, all with somewhat different definitions of bridging as a phenomenon. In English, the evaluation of bridging resolution systems (systems which aim to automatically identify bridging anaphora and resolve back to their associative antecedents) is commonly conducted using the following three corpora: ISNotes (Markert et al., 2012), BASHI (Rösiger, 2018), and ARRAU RST (Poesio and Artstein, 2008; Uryupina et al., 2019). While ARRAU RST annotates bridging instances by identifying mention pairs that establish cohesion in text and then classifies then via a set of predefined semantic relations, ISNotes and BASHI annotate bridging anaphora based on the information status of entities, considering bridging to be a sub-variety of mediated information.

The information status (IS) of an entity refers to the extent to which the entity is accessible to the reader/hearer of a discourse (Nissim et al., 2004). Generally speaking, "New" information is unrecognized by the reader/hearer, while "Given" information is recognized. "Given" entities may be recognized by the reader/hearer for various reasons: the entity may have been previously introduced in the discourse (coreference), the entity may be accessible via generics/world knowledge, or, in the case of bridging, the referent of the entity may be inferred from a previous entity in the discourse. Instances of bridging and generics/world knowledge are both considered "Accessible" in that they are recognized by the reader/hearer when they are first introduced to the discourse, but only instances of bridging depend on an associative antecedent for comprehension.

	Tokens	Bridging Instances	Bridging per 1k Tokens
ARRAU RST	229k	3.7k	16.5
ISNotes	40k	663	16.6
BASHI	58k	459	7.9
GUM (v10; full)	228k	1.9k	8.3
GUM (v10; test only)	26k	222	8.5
GUMBridge (v0.1)	26k	401	15.4

Table 1: Frequency of bridging instances several English bridging resources.

There are also a number of other existing bridging resources: in English, GUM, SciCorp (Roesiger, 2016), corefpro (Grishina, 2016), RED (Richer Event Descriptions, O'Gorman et al. 2016); as well as in other languages: GRAIN (Schweitzer et al., 2018) and DIRNDL (Eckart et al., 2012) in German, PDT (Nedoluzhko et al., 2009) in Czech, and PCC (Ogrodniczuk and Zawisławska, 2016) in Polish, to name a few. There have additional been efforts in areas closely related to bridging, such as Recasens et al. (2010), which puts forward a typology for classifying near-identity relations (NIDENT) for coreference, and Modjeska (2004)'s work on other-anaphora, which we now consider a subtype of bridging. We provide background on ISNotes, BASHI, and ARRAU RST, as they are commonly used in bridging resolution evaluation (Yu et al., 2022; Kobayashi et al., 2023), and they illustrate diverging perspectives on identifying bridging instances. Table 1 shows comparative statistics for these three resources, the original GUM bridging annotations, and the bridging annotations produced in the GUMBridge annotation pilot described in this paper.

ISNotes is a corpus of 50 Wall Street Journal (WSJ) documents from the OntoNotes corpus (Weischedel et al., 2011) annotated for fine-grained information status. ISNotes distinguishes three main categories of IS: `New`, `Old`, and `Mediated`. `Old` information is that which known to the hearer and/or has been refereed to previously, while `New` information is introduced for the first time. `Mediated` information has not been introduced before, but is not independently comprehensible, requiring either an inference from a previous mention or from general/real-world knowledge. Within the `Mediated` category, there are six subcategories, including `bridging`. The corpus contains 663 instances of bridging in the mediated/bridging category, and there are an additional 253 instances of comparative anaphora in the mediated/comparison category, which is considered a variety of bridging (~16.6 bridging instances per 1k tokens). Markert et al. (2012) report Cohen's κ for annotator pairs, ranging ~0.6-0.7 for mediated/bridging, and ~0.8 for mediated/comparison. They note that the agreement for mediated/bridging is more annotator dependent relative to the other IS categories.

The BASHI corpus is also annotated on top of 50 WSJ documents from the OntoNotes corpus, and it includes a total of 459 bridging pairs (~7.9 bridging instances per 1k tokens). Rösiger (2018) introduces the contrast between referential bridging and lexical bridging, where referential bridging is a properly anaphoric relation (antecedent is required for the interpretation of the anaphor) and lexical bridging is a non-anaphoric semantic relation between two entities. The corpus specifically contains annotations only for referential bridging, not lexical bridging. The bridging instances in BASHI have the subtypes definite, indefinite, and comparative anaphora. Annotator agreement is reported for these categories individually and together. The joint agreement for identifying bridging pairs is 59.3%, with a higher rate for comparative anaphora at 71.4% and lower agreement for definite at 63.8% and indefinite at 42.3%.

ARRAU is a multi-genre corpus covering a variety of anaphoric phenomena, composed of 4 subcorpora, each with its own annotation specifications. ARRAU RST is the largest sub-corpus, and also the one most used in evaluation for bridging resolution. It is composed of WSJ news data, and it includes 3,777 bridging annotations (~16.5 bridging instances per 1k tokens). ARRAU's bridging annotation connects related mentions which establish "entity coherence" via non-identity relations, but as this casts a very broad scope, annotation is limited to a fixed set of semantic relations. The corpus uses an inventory of 9 bridging subtypes for annotation: possession, element-set, subset-set, anaphora marked with 'other', along with accompanying inverse relations of the previous, and an additional under-specified relation. The annotation schema and guidelines for bridging in ARRAU were extended from the GNOME project (Poesio, 2004). Coders in the GNOME project displayed high agreement (95.2%) in the choice of bridging subtype labels from its fixed set of relations, but low recall (22%) in unanimously identifying instances of bridging.

Limiting annotation to a predefined set of relations restricts the scope of bridging as a phenomenon, but also aims to increase consistency in the annotation. However, as has been noted in Rösiger (2018), annotating from predefined relations can also introduce false positives, in the case that an instance of a semantic relation is not actually a case of associative anaphoric reference that would constitute referential bridging. For instance, the case of *Europe - Spain* displays a meronomy relation, but it is not anaphoric because *Spain* can be interpreted without reference to *Europe*. Annotating from an information status informed perspective aims to avoid such false positives, providing a more concrete linguistic criteria for identifying instances of bridging when compared to the notion of "entity coherence", and eliminating the need to only annotate a predefined set of relations for scoping reasons. However, this information status based approach also greatly widens the scope of what should be considered bridging, which in turn increases the influence of subjective judgment by annotators. As such, in order to forward an information status informed annotation perspective, we must develop means of dealing with additional subjectivity it produces.

As we can see in Table 1, there has been considerable variation in the frequency of bridging annotations in previous resources, with ARRAU RST (counting both lexical and referential bridging) and ISNotes identifying bridging instances with approximately twice the rate per 1k tokens as the annotations in BASHI and GUM v10. This suggests that some previous bridging resources, such as BASHI and GUM, have likely been under-annotated for bridging instances and prompts a need for the reexamination of bridging annotation procedures.

3 Annotation Pilot

The analysis on subjectivity in the annotation of bridging instances in this paper is conducted using the results of an annotation pilot for the creation of a new bridging resource called GUMBridge. Built on top of GUM, an existing multi-genre corpus of English, GUMBridge aims to unite aspects of currently existing formalisms: using an information status-informed view of identifying bridging instances (as in ISNotes and BASHI), followed by subtype categorization using a taxonomy of semantic relations (as in ARRAU). Additionally,

GUMBridge aims to add genre diversity to the core English bridging resources, as ISNotes, BASHI, and ARRAU RST are all composed of WSJ news data from more than 30 years ago, offering little to analyze in terms on genre diversity. While the development of this resource is still underway, an adjudicated version of the bridging annotations for the GUMBridge test set (version 0.1) is released with this paper[1]. The details of this adjudication process are described in Section 3.5. The guidelines for identifying instances of bridging (v0.1) are described in Section 3.1, and the classification system for bridging subtypes (v0.1) is described in Section 3.2.

3.1 Identifying Bridging Instances

In the GUMBridge annotation effort, we adopt an information status-informed perspective on identifying instances of bridging anaphora. As stated in Section 2, the information status of an entity refers to the extent to which an entity is accessible to the reader/hearer of a discourse upon its introduction. We say that an entity is "Accessible" if it has not been mentioned before but its reference is inferable for a reader/header. Bridging occurs when the first mention of an entity is "Accessible" via an inference from a previous, non-identical entity in the discourse. In contrast with entities which are accessible due to being generic, or being part of world knowledge or the discourse situation, the bridging anaphor is not accessible by itself, but dependent on the previous entity for interpretation. Annotators are provided with an overview of this definition of bridging and accessibility and are instructed to consider the following when deciding whether a particular entity is a bridging anaphor:

1. Do you judge this entity to be to some degree accessible in the discourse?

2. Does that accessibility rely on the understanding of a previous entity in the discourse? If so, identify that previous entity's most recent mention.

If the entity passes the above criteria, it is a bridging anaphor and the previous entity is its associative antecedent. Once identified, a bridging pair can then be assigned a subtype category as described in the following section.

3.2 Classification of Bridging Subtypes

In order to categorize the varieties of bridging present in GUMBridge, we create a new classification system for bridging subtypes. The classification system is composed of 11 categories, 10 of which are organized under 3 relation types: COMPARISON relations, ENTITY relations, and SET relations, and an additional OTHER category. The bridging subtype classification system developed for GUMBridge (v0.1) is shown in Figure 1. A brief description of each of the bridging subtypes follows below. A brief comparison to the bridging subtypes of ARRAU is included in Appendix C.

COMPARISON-RELATIVE The anaphor is preceded by a comparative marker (other, another, same, more, etc.), ordinal (second, third, etc.), or comparative adjective (larger, smaller, etc.), which implies a comparison to the antecedent (or vice versa).

(1) Several women walked into the room. **Other women** soon followed.

COMPARISON-TIME The anaphor refers to a specific time/time frame which is understandable with reference to the time/time frame expressed by the antecedent (or vice versa).

(2) I went shopping Wednesday, March 3rd. I will go again **the following Wednesday**.

COMPARISON-SENSE The type of the anaphor is omitted but inferable via comparison to the antecedent (or vice versa).

(3) I've been to the Chinese restaurant. I want to go to **the Italian one**.

ENTITY-ASSOCIATIVE The anaphor is an attribute or closely associated entity of the antecedent (or vice versa). This frequently manifests as implicit arguments of a predicate as in example (4), relational nouns as in example (5), and prototypical associations as in example (6):

(4) There was a murder last night. **The victim** has yet to be identified.

(5) There is a child in the park. **The parent** must be nearby.

(6) I went to a wedding last week. **The reception** was really fun.

[1] https://github.com/lauren-lizzy-levine/gumbridge

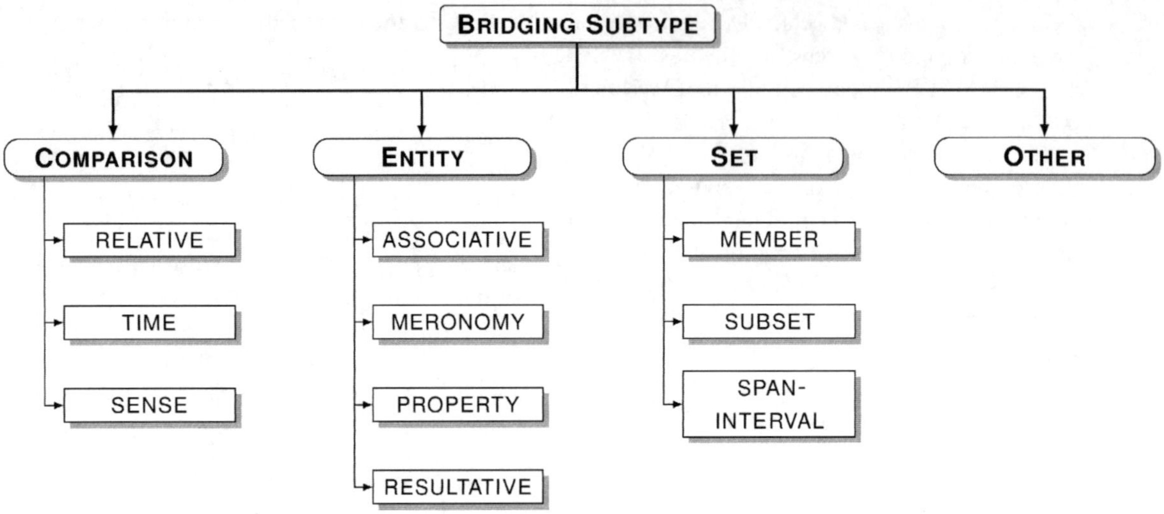

Figure 1: Bridging Subtype Classification in GUMBridge v0.1.

ENTITY-MERONOMY The anaphor is a subunit of the antecedent (or vice versa), i.e., there is some part-whole relation between the anaphor and the antecedent.

(7) I saw a large house by the lake. **The door** was red.

ENTITY-PROPERTY The anaphor is a physical or intangible property of the antecedent (or vice versa). For example: smell, length, style, etc.

(8) I picked up a bouquet of roses. **The scent** was lovely.

ENTITY-RESULTATIVE The anaphor is logically inferable from the antecedent (or vice versa). This is typically the result of a transformative or product producing process, such as cooking.[2]

(9) Though my flour was a strange texture, **the bread** came out perfectly.

SET-MEMBER The anaphor is an element of the antecedent set (or vice versa).

(10) I got several books for my birthday. **The mystery novel** was my favorite.

SET-SUBSET The anaphor is a subset of the antecedent set (or vice versa).

(11) A group of students entered the hall. **The boys** wore neckties with their uniforms.

[2]This subtype subsumes the TRANSFORMED type proposed by Fang et al. (2022) specifically for recipe outcomes.

SET-SPAN-INTERVAL The anaphor is a sub-span of the spatial or temporal antecedent interval (or vice versa).

(12) If you want to meet up on Sunday, I will be free in **the morning**.

OTHER The anaphor and antecedent fit the criteria for identifying a bridging pair, but do not fall into any of the bridging subtypes detailed above. For instance, Ogrodniczuk and Zawisławska (2016) give examples of metareference:

(13) I went to Sensational Cakes yesterday, but I didn't think **the cakes** were very good.

Metareference allows for reference back to a name or label, as in example (13). Such instances are unique and interesting enough to wish not to shoehorn them into another category, but are not common enough to warrant a separate category in the subtype classification.

As stated in Section 3.1, the criterion for identifying instances of bridging is anaphoric, relying on information status and resolution back to an associative antecedent. The subtype labels primarily allow us to understand how the phenomenon manifests in a discourse, and, as such, there is no theoretical reason to limit the number of subtypes that can apply to an instance of bridging to just one. Indeed, there are cases of bridging where multiple subtypes may apply:

(14) Several women walked into the room. **One** left immediately.

(15) I will come to visit <u>this week</u>, as I could not come **the previous week**.

Example (14) shows an instance for which COMPARISON-SENSE and SET-MEMBER both apply, while example (15) show a case where COMPARISON-RELATIVE and COMPARISON-TIME apply. In this annotation pilot, annotators where instructed to select a single bridging subtype, prioritizing certain categories over others if they occurred together. However, in principle, all applicable subtypes could be annotated. In our subsequent efforts to annotate the remaining data in GUM and produce a full version of GUMBridge, we intend to support the annotation of multiple bridging subtypes for a single bridging pair for the entire corpus.

3.3 Annotation Procedure

The GUMBridge annotation pilot was conducted on the test set of the existing GUM (v10) corpus, which consists of 26 documents (~26k tokens) across 16 genres (academic writing, biographies, courtroom transcripts, essays, fiction, how-to guides, interviews, letters, news, online forum discussions, podcasts, political speeches, spontaneous face to face conversations, textbooks, travel guides, and vlogs). The GUM corpus already includes annotations for entity spans, coreference,[3] and information status, i.e., "New", "Given", and "Accessible" (not including accessibility from instances of bridging).

The documents of the test set were double annotated, with one author of this paper acting as Annotator A and various linguistics graduate students acting as Annotator B for different documents in the test set. Each of the 8 annotators acting as Annotator B was assigned between 2 and 4 documents of the test set. The annotation was completed using the GitDox annotation interface (Zhang and Zeldes, 2017). For the existing entity annotations in the document, the annotator was instructed to identify whether the entity is a bridging anaphor, and, if so, create a link between the anaphor and its associative antecedent. The annotator was instructed to also update the IS of the bridging anaphor to "Accessible" and select a bridging subtype annotation for the anaphor. The full annotation guidelines provided to the annotators are included as supplementary materials.

[3]The coreference scheme considers all mentions eligible for bridging, including indefinite anaphors, discourse deixis to non-nominal antecedents and more, see Zeldes (2022) for a detailed discussion.

3.4 Agreement Study

In Table 2, we provide agreement numbers for three stages of the bridging annotation process: anaphor recognition, antecedent resolution, and subtype categorization.

	Precision	Recall	F1 Score
Anaphor Recognition	0.44	0.34	0.38
Anaphor+Antecedent Recognition	0.32	0.25	0.28
		Accuracy	
Antecedent Resolution		0.72	
		Cohen's κ	
Bridging Subtype		0.58	

Table 2: GUMBridge pilot inter-annotator agreement.

For the recognition of bridging pairs (anaphor+antecedent) and recognition of the bridging anaphor alone, we give the PRF of Annotator B relative to Annotator A. We see that the F1 for bridging anaphor recognition is 0.38, and the F1 for bridging pair recognition is only 0.28. As the recognition of bridging pairs is inherently limited by the recognition of the anaphor, we also give the accuracy of Annotator B selecting the antecedent entity when both annotators agree on the bridging anaphor, which is 72% of a total of 133 cases. Finally, for the 96 instances where both annotators agreed on the anaphor and antecedent of a bridging pair, the Cohen's Kappa for the bridging subtype annotation is 0.58, which indicates moderate agreement. These numbers suggest that the key hurdle is in anaphor recognition, though antecedent resolution and subtype labeling are also non-trivial.

In Figure 2, we show a confusion matrix of the bridging subtype labels assigned by Annotator A and Annotator B to the overlapping bridging pairs. We see that the subtypes with the most overlap are the COMPARISON categories and ENTITY-ASSOCIATIVE. And while there are some categories for which the disagreement is spread among a number of categories, we see that the categories of ENTITY-MERONOMY and SET-MEMBER are particularly confusable, which indicates how part-whole and set-member relations can be quite similar. The categories of ENTITY-ASSOCIATIVE and OTHER are also particularly confusable, which

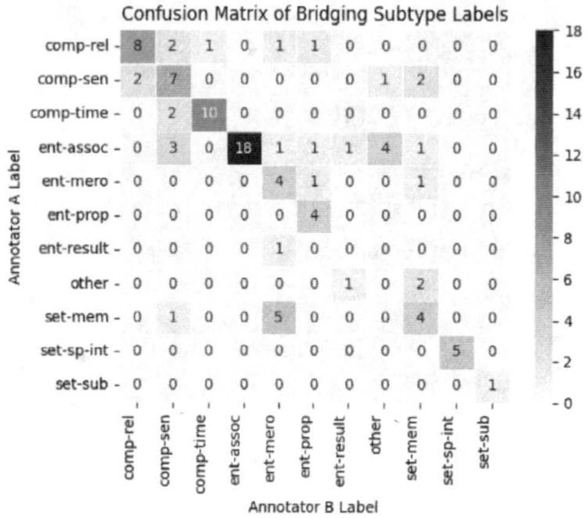

Figure 2: Confusion matrix of bridging subtypes for bridging instances with matching anaphor and antecedent annotations.

speaks to how ENTITY-ASSOCIATIVE may be an overly broad category. Although agreement on bridging subtype annotation is moderate, it is clear that refinement in the guidelines for the categories is still needed. However, as agreement on the identification of bridging instances is substantially lower, recognition of bridging anaphora forms the limiting point in the annotation process.

3.5 Data Adjudication

As shown in the previous section, the results of the annotation pilot had low annotator agreement, necessitating a qualitative analysis of annotations to determine the cause of the disagreements. As a part of this process, the annotations from the pilot were adjudicated to produce a single set of reference bridging annotations for the test set of GUMBridge (v0.1), available with the release of this paper under the Creative Commons Attribution (CC-BY) version 4.0 license. The composition of the GUMBridge test set by bridging subtype after the adjudication is shown in Appendix A. The test set of GUMBridge has a total of 401 bridging annotations, with an average of 15.4 bridging instances per 1k tokens. This is on par with the higher rate of bridging instances per 1k tokens found in IS-Notes and ARRAU RST as shown in in Table 1. While the limited size of the data set annotated in this pilot limits our ability to make observations on genre effects, for completeness, a breakdown of the bridging relation types observed in each genre is included in Appendix B .

Notably, the number of instances in the test set of the GUM (v10) annotations nearly doubles, going from 222 instances of bridging to 401 in GUMBridge test, suggesting a significant improvement in coverage of bridging instances in this new annotation effort. Even though there is less consistency in this annotation effort compared to some of those discussed in Section 2, numbers suggest higher recall, which allows us to capture a greater scope of bridging instances. As bridging is generally a sparse phenomenon, the annotations can be manually reviewed and validated in the adjudication process even if initial agreement is low. As such, we believe it is preferable to favor a high recall method of annotation and eliminate false positives upon review, rather than risk many interesting cases that will remain unidentified.

Completely Matching	61
Different Subtype	35
Different Antecedent	37
Annotator B Only	172
Annotator A Only	257
Total	562

Table 3: Counts of annotator agreement/disagreement types in GUMBridge pilot annotations.

The adjudication process involved comparing all of the diverging judgments from Annotator A and Annotator B at the level of anaphor, antecedent, and subtype. Table 3 shows the proportion of such disagreements in the pilot annotations. Of the 172 instances that Annotator B labeled as bridging which Annotator A initially did not label as bridging at all, upon reevaluation, it was concluded that 64 (37%) could reasonably be considered a form of bridging. Many of these judgments relied on subjective understanding of the discourse entities involved. In the following section, we provide an analysis of the impact of subjectivity in this annotation pilot and how it may be better handled in the future.

4 Subjectivity in Bridging Annotation

Previous work on subjectivity in the development of linguistic data has heavily featured areas where annotator judgments can be highly variable, such as hate speech detection and sentiment analysis (e.g., Waseem (2016); Kenyon-Dean et al. (2018)), though attention has also been given to tasks which seem more objective, such as part of speech annotation (e.g., Plank et al. (2014)). Several works discuss the paradigms for and implications of including subjective judgments in annotation efforts, rather than trying to eliminate all ambiguity (Ovesdotter Alm, 2011; Röttger et al., 2022). Ultimately, the appropriate approach depends on the linguistic task at hand and what the researchers are hoping to achieve with the annotation effort.

Although detailed guidelines are provided to annotators in this paper's annotation pilot, subjective judgment is still an inherent part of the annotation of bridging instances, as annotators are making decisions based off their understanding of the implicit relationships that exist between entities in a discourse. As previously noted, there are three decision points in the annotating of bridging instances that can introduce subjective judgment: (1) recognition of the bridging anaphor, (2) identifying the corresponding associative antecedent, and (3) selecting the bridging subtype category of the pair. The sections below give examples to illustrate the unique considerations regarding subjectivity that are present at each of these annotation stages.

4.1 Subtype Categorization

Selecting a bridging subtype category relies on understanding the relationship between the anaphor and the antecedent in a bridging pair. The exact nature of the relationship between two entities is dependent on the annotator's subjective conception of the two entities. It is possible that a lack of familiarity with related entities may cause annotation errors:

(16) the cuttings → **the first pad**

In example (16), "the cuttings" refer to cactus cuttings, each of which is a whole pad. Without this particular knowledge, it would be reasonable for an annotator to assume that a pad is a portion of a cutting or that a cutting is a portion of a pad.

There may be additional uncertainty in interpreting an entity based on the context of the discourse:

(17) peppermint plants → **the mint**

In the discourse context of example (17), it is unclear whether "the mint" is referring back to a specific part of the peppermint plant (e.g. the leaves), or whether it is an instance of synecdoche, referring to the plant as a whole.

There are also instances where multiple subtypes are possible in the context of the discourse:

(18) some basil → **seed**

In the discourse context of example (18), a question is being posed whether "some basil" can be grown from "seed". As such, it is reasonable to say that the basil comes from the seed in which case the subtype would be ENTITY-RESULTATIVE. However, it is also reasonable to say that seed is a part of the basil plant, in which case the subtype would be ENTITY-MERONOMY. In such cases, it is necessary to have a priority hierarchy for deciding which bridging subtype category should be assigned, or we must allow for multiple subtype annotations. In future work, we intend to support the annotation of multiple bridging subtypes for the entire GUMBridge corpus.

4.2 Antecedent Selection

When an annotator is selecting the associative antecedent of a bridging anaphor, there are also opportunities for subjective judgments to be made. In some cases, it is possible that multiple preceding entities could be reasonable candidates for a bridging antecedent:

(19) your mouth → **other body parts...**
teeth → **other body parts...**

The example (19) refers to a case where a dental cast is being made and the narrator wonders what other body parts can be given the same treatment. It is not clear whether "the other body parts" are more appropriately in contrast with the "mouth" or "teeth", or even both, if we accept both teeth and mouths as body parts.

There is also the possibility for disagreement on the denotation of the anaphor:

(20) the bridge → **the edge**
the upper levels → **the edge**

In example (20), the narrator considers looking over "the edge", and it is unclear whether it is the edge of a particular bridge, or if it is the edge of some general upper level. In such cases, it may be beneficial to impose an easy to execute heuristic, such as selecting the option nearer to the bridging anaphor, assuming we are aiming for a single reference decision. Note that this is different from cases in which multiple labels apply, since the two interpretations, while both possible, are mutually exclusive.

4.3 Anaphor Identification

When identifying a bridging anaphor, annotators must make subjective judgments on whether an entity is accessible due to world knowledge (and hence not bridging) or whether the accessibility can be attributed to an antecedent entity. For instance, one annotator had "Leucippus and Democritus" bridge from "ancient Greek philosophers", but not "Aristotle" who is more widely known. This illustrates how an annotator's world knowledge may influence what they consider to be "Accessible" in a manner that is undesirable as it will lead to inconsistencies among annotators. We recommend that concrete criteria for generic/world knowledge accessibility should be tied to a knowledge base, such as Wikipedia, rather than left up to individual annotator judgment. For named entities, this type of linking or Wikification is already available for GUM (Lin and Zeldes, 2021) and will be integrated in future annotation efforts.

5 Conclusion

In this paper, we examine the influence of subjectivity in annotator judgment on the various stages of annotating instances of bridging. We make this examination using the resulting annotations from a pilot to create a new resource for bridging annotations, GUMBridge. We also release an adjudicated version of the bridging annotations for the preliminary test set of GUMBridge (v0.1). In subsequent work, we plan to refine the guidelines and annotation procedure used in this pilot, which we will then use to annotate the remainder of the GUM corpus (dev and train) to produce a full version of GUMBridge, as well as extending our annotations to GUM's out-of-domain challenge test set, GENTLE (GEnre Tests for Linguistic Evaluation, Aoyama et al. 2023). As the time and effort required to manually annotate bridging limits the scalability of the annotation process, we will also investigate incorporating semi-automated methods, such as combining LLMs or other systems for bridging resolution with human correction in order to improve the efficiency of the process.

In our development of GUMBridge test (v0.1), we found that annotators' agreement on selecting the subtype of a bridging pair was moderate, but that it was more difficult to get the annotators to align on the identification of bridging anaphora. This indicates that recognition of bridging anaphora is the stage in the annotation process that is most vulnerable to the subjective judgment of annotators, and that should be given the most consideration when trying to account for annotator subjectivity. While some subjectivity arises from the inherent ambiguity of language in context, other aspects of subjectivity can be accounted for by providing guidelines on how to decide on preferable judgments when multiple options are available.

Limitations

The analysis presented in this paper on subjectivity in the annotation of bridging anaphora is based on a pilot annotation study for a new resource that is still in development. This limits the amount of data available for analysis to a test set of 26k tokens. The reliability of the annotation schema is also a limitation, as the results of the annotation pilot showed agreement on identification of bridging anaphora to be undesirably low, and the annotation schema/instructions will need to undergo revision in future work.

References

Tatsuya Aoyama, Shabnam Behzad, Luke Gessler, Lauren Levine, Jessica Lin, Yang Janet Liu, Siyao Peng, Yilun Zhu, and Amir Zeldes. 2023. GENTLE: A genre-diverse multilayer challenge set for English NLP and linguistic evaluation. In *Proceedings of the 17th Linguistic Annotation Workshop (LAW-XVII)*, pages 166–178, Toronto, Canada. Association for Computational Linguistics.

Herbert H. Clark. 1975. Bridging. In *Theoretical Issues in Natural Language Processing*.

Kerstin Eckart, Arndt Riester, and Katrin Schweitzer. 2012. *A Discourse Information Radio News Database for Linguistic Analysis*, pages 65–76. Springer Berlin Heidelberg, Berlin, Heidelberg.

Biaoyan Fang, Timothy Baldwin, and Karin Verspoor. 2022. What does it take to bake a cake? the RecipeRef corpus and anaphora resolution in procedural text. In *Findings of the Association for Computational Linguistics: ACL 2022*, pages 3481–3495, Dublin, Ireland. Association for Computational Linguistics.

Yulia Grishina. 2016. Experiments on bridging across languages and genres. In *Proceedings of the Workshop on Coreference Resolution Beyond OntoNotes (CORBON 2016)*, pages 7–15, San Diego, California. Association for Computational Linguistics.

Kian Kenyon-Dean, Eisha Ahmed, Scott Fujimoto, Jeremy Georges-Filteau, Christopher Glasz, Barleen Kaur, Auguste Lalande, Shruti Bhanderi, Robert Belfer, Nirmal Kanagasabai, Roman Sarrazingendron, Rohit Verma, and Derek Ruths. 2018. Sentiment analysis: It's complicated! In *Proceedings of the 2018 Conference of the North American Chapter of the Association for Computational Linguistics:*

Human Language Technologies, Volume 1 (Long Papers), pages 1886–1895, New Orleans, Louisiana. Association for Computational Linguistics.

Hideo Kobayashi, Yufang Hou, and Vincent Ng. 2023. PairSpanBERT: An enhanced language model for bridging resolution. In *Proceedings of the 61st Annual Meeting of the Association for Computational Linguistics (Volume 1: Long Papers)*, pages 6931–6946, Toronto, Canada. Association for Computational Linguistics.

Hideo Kobayashi and Vincent Ng. 2020. Bridging resolution: A survey of the state of the art. In *Proceedings of the 28th International Conference on Computational Linguistics*, pages 3708–3721, Barcelona, Spain (Online). International Committee on Computational Linguistics.

Lauren Levine and Amir Zeldes. 2024. Unifying the scope of bridging anaphora types in English: Bridging annotations in ARRAU and GUM. In *Proceedings of The Seventh Workshop on Computational Models of Reference, Anaphora and Coreference*, pages 41–51, Miami. Association for Computational Linguistics.

Jessica Lin and Amir Zeldes. 2021. WikiGUM: Exhaustive entity linking for wikification in 12 genres. In *Proceedings of the Joint 15th Linguistic Annotation Workshop (LAW) and 3rd Designing Meaning Representations (DMR) Workshop*, pages 170–175, Punta Cana, Dominican Republic. Association for Computational Linguistics.

Katja Markert, Yufang Hou, and Michael Strube. 2012. Collective classification for fine-grained information status. In *Proceedings of the 50th Annual Meeting of the Association for Computational Linguistics (Volume 1: Long Papers)*, pages 795–804, Jeju Island, Korea. Association for Computational Linguistics.

Natalia N Modjeska. 2004. Resolving other-anaphora.

Anna Nedoluzhko, Jiří Mírovský, and Petr Pajas. 2009. The coding scheme for annotating extended nominal coreference and bridging anaphora in the Prague dependency treebank. In *Proceedings of the Third Linguistic Annotation Workshop (LAW III)*, pages 108–111, Suntec, Singapore. Association for Computational Linguistics.

Malvina Nissim, Shipra Dingare, Jean Carletta, and Mark Steedman. 2004. An annotation scheme for information status in dialogue. In *Proceedings of the Fourth International Conference on Language Resources and Evaluation (LREC'04)*, Lisbon, Portugal. European Language Resources Association (ELRA).

Tim O'Gorman, Kristin Wright-Bettner, and Martha Palmer. 2016. Richer Event Description: Integrating event coreference with temporal, causal and bridging annotation. In *Proceedings of the 2nd Workshop on Computing News Storylines (CNS 2016)*, pages 47–56, Austin, Texas. Association for Computational Linguistics.

Maciej Ogrodniczuk and Magdalena Zawisławska. 2016. Bridging relations in Polish: Adaptation of existing typologies. In *Proceedings of the Workshop on Coreference Resolution Beyond OntoNotes (CORBON 2016)*, pages 16–22, San Diego, California. Association for Computational Linguistics.

Cecilia Ovesdotter Alm. 2011. Subjective natural language problems: Motivations, applications, characterizations, and implications. In *Proceedings of the 49th Annual Meeting of the Association for Computational Linguistics: Human Language Technologies*, pages 107–112, Portland, Oregon, USA. Association for Computational Linguistics.

Barbara Plank, Dirk Hovy, and Anders Søgaard. 2014. Linguistically debatable or just plain wrong? In *Proceedings of the 52nd Annual Meeting of the Association for Computational Linguistics (Volume 2: Short Papers)*, pages 507–511, Baltimore, Maryland. Association for Computational Linguistics.

Massimo Poesio. 2004. Discourse annotation and semantic annotation in the GNOME corpus. In *Proceedings of the Workshop on Discourse Annotation*, pages 72–79, Barcelona, Spain. Association for Computational Linguistics.

Massimo Poesio and Ron Artstein. 2008. Anaphoric annotation in the ARRAU corpus. In *Proceedings of the Sixth International Conference on Language Resources and Evaluation (LREC'08)*, Marrakech, Morocco. European Language Resources Association (ELRA).

Ellen F. Prince. 1981. Toward a taxonomy of given-new information. *Radical pragmatics*, pages 223–255.

Marta Recasens, Eduard Hovy, and M. Antònia Martí. 2010. A typology of near-identity relations for coreference (NIDENT). In *Proceedings of the Seventh International Conference on Language Resources and Evaluation (LREC'10)*, Valletta, Malta. European Language Resources Association (ELRA).

Ina Roesiger. 2016. SciCorp: A corpus of English scientific articles annotated for information status analysis. In *Proceedings of the Tenth International Conference on Language Resources and Evaluation (LREC'16)*, pages 1743–1749, Portorož, Slovenia. European Language Resources Association (ELRA).

Ina Rösiger. 2018. BASHI: A corpus of Wall Street Journal articles annotated with bridging links. In *Proceedings of the Eleventh International Conference on Language Resources and Evaluation (LREC 2018)*, Miyazaki, Japan. European Language Resources Association (ELRA).

Paul Röttger, Bertie Vidgen, Dirk Hovy, and Janet Pierrehumbert. 2022. Two contrasting data annotation paradigms for subjective NLP tasks. In *Proceedings of the 2022 Conference of the North American Chapter of the Association for Computational Linguistics: Human Language Technologies*, pages 175–190, Seattle, United States. Association for Computational Linguistics.

Katrin Schweitzer, Kerstin Eckart, Markus Gärtner, Agnieszka Falenska, Arndt Riester, Ina Rösiger, Antje Schweitzer, Sabrina Stehwien, and Jonas Kuhn. 2018. German radio interviews: The GRAIN release of the SFB732 silver standard collection. In *Proceedings of the Eleventh International Conference on Language Resources and Evaluation (LREC 2018)*, Miyazaki, Japan. European Language Resources Association (ELRA).

Olga Uryupina, Ron Artstein, Antonella Bristot, Federica Cavicchio, Francesca Delogu, Kepa Joseba Rodríguez, and Massimo Poesio. 2019. Annotating a broad range of anaphoric phenomena, in a variety of genres: the ARRAU corpus. *Natural Language Engineering*, 26:95 – 128.

Zeerak Waseem. 2016. Are you a racist or am I seeing things? annotator influence on hate speech detection on Twitter. In *Proceedings of the First Workshop on NLP and Computational Social Science*, pages 138–142, Austin, Texas. Association for Computational Linguistics.

Ralph Weischedel, Sameer Pradhan, Lance Ramshaw, Martha Palmer, Nianwen Xue, Mitchell Marcus, Ann Taylor, Craig Greenberg, Eduard Hovy, Robert Belvin, et al. 2011. Ontonotes release 4.0. *LDC2011T03, Philadelphia, Penn.: Linguistic Data Consortium*, 17.

Juntao Yu, Sopan Khosla, Ramesh Manuvinakurike, Lori Levin, Vincent Ng, Massimo Poesio, Michael Strube, and Carolyn Rosé. 2022. The CODI-CRAC 2022 shared task on anaphora, bridging, and discourse deixis in dialogue. In *Proceedings of the CODI-CRAC 2022 Shared Task on Anaphora, Bridging, and Discourse Deixis in Dialogue*, pages 1–14, Gyeongju, Republic of Korea. Association for Computational Linguistics.

Amir Zeldes. 2017. The GUM corpus: Creating multilayer resources in the classroom. *Language Resources and Evaluation*, 51(3):581–612.

Amir Zeldes. 2022. Can we fix the scope for coreference? Problems and solutions for benchmarks beyond OntoNotes. *Dialogue & Discourse*, 13(1):41–62.

Shuo Zhang and Amir Zeldes. 2017. GitDOX: A linked version controlled online XML editor for manuscript transcription. In *Proceedings of the Thirtieth International Florida Artificial Intelligence Research Society Conference (FLAIRS 2017)*, pages 619–623.

A Subtypes in GUMBridge Test

Table 4 shows the counts of the bridging subtypes in the adjudicated version of GUMBridge test v0.1.

B Subtypes by Genre in GUMBridge Test

Figure 3 shows the number of bridging instances per 1k tokens of each bridging relation type (COMPARISON, SET, ENTITY, and OTHER) in each of the 16 genres in GUMBridge test (v0.1).

COMPARISON	
RELATIVE	59
TIME	27
SENSE	45
Subtotal	131
ENTITY	
ASSOCIATIVE	124
MERONOMY	37
PROPERTY	9
RESULTATIVE	21
Subtotal	191
SET	
MEMBER	31
SUBSET	14
SPAN-INTERVAL	18
Subtotal	63
OTHER	16
Total	401

Table 4: Counts of bridging subtypes in adjudicated GUMBridge data.

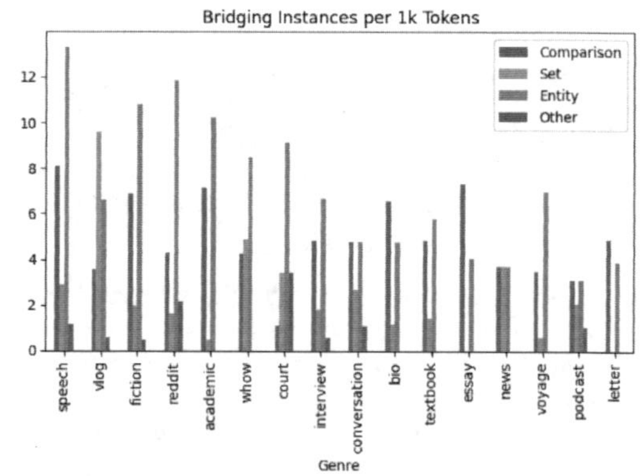

Figure 3: Counts of bridging relation types by genre in adjudicated GUMBridge data.

C Comparison with ARRAU Bridging Subtypes

In order to allow for better comparison between the resources of GUMBridge and ARRAU, we include a brief comparison of how ARRAU's bridging subtypes[4] map onto the proposed schema for GUMBridge:

[4]As the GUMBridge schema does not differentiate the relative roles of the anaphor and antecedent in the subtype relation, ARRAU's inverse subtypes map the same as their regular subtypes.

possession → Part-of relations that will mostly fall under ENTITY-MERONOMY or ENTITY-PROPERTY.

element-set → Maps to SET-MEMBER.

subset-set → Maps to SET-SUBSET.

'other' anaphora → Maps to COMPARISON-RELATIVE, which encompasses additional comparative markers not covered in ARRAU, including ordinals and comparative adjectives.

under-specified → ENTITY-ASSOCIATIVE unless one of the other ENTITY subtypes is a better fit based on the context. However, sense anaphora (green shirt → **red one**) should be mapped to COMPARATIVE-SENSE.

The revision of linguistic annotation in the Universal Dependencies framework: a look at the annotators' behavior

Magali S. Duran and **Lucelene Lopes** and **Thiago A. S. Pardo**
Núcleo Interinstitucional de Linguística Computacional, Universidade de São Paulo – Brazil
magali.duran@gmail.com lucelene@gmail.com taspardo@icmc.usp.br

Abstract

This paper presents strategies to revise an automatically annotated corpus according to the Universal Dependencies framework and discusses the learned lessons, mainly regarding the annotators' behavior. The revision strategies are not relying on examples from any specific language and, because they are language-independent, can be adopted in any language and corpus annotation initiative.

1 Introduction

The construction of annotated datasets is a challenging task, especially for low-resource languages. In order to take advantage of the experience of high-resource languages, projects in other languages have adopted successful annotation models, "skipping" the steps of instantiating a theory (i.e., the linguistic model to be used) and creating tag sets, which are steps discussed by Hovy and Lavid, 2010 and Pustejovsky et al., 2017. Reutilizing annotation models is important, but is also key to have information on how to design an annotation task. It has become clear to the scientific community that sharing the know-how to building annotated corpora can encourage other research groups to undertake their own annotation projects. For this reason, over the last two decades, discussion on the corpus annotation process has been gaining prominence in the Natural Language Processing (NLP) scene.

Seminal works laid the foundations of "annotation science" (Ide, 2007; Hovy and Lavid, 2010; Ide and Pustejovsky, 2017). The availability of new technologies has brought new possibilities, such as crowdsourcing the annotation (Snow et al., 2008; Hovy et al., 2013) and using LLMs as annotators (Pavlovic and Poesio, 2024; Weissweiler et al., 2023; Torrent et al., 2024). In addition, annotation has expanded its purposes, as shown by the case of perspectivism (Leonardelli et al., 2023; Akhtar et al., 2021), which takes into account annotation disagreements. However, perspectivism hardly applies to the traditional prescriptive paradigm, which is the case of the annotation discussed here (see Röttger et al., 2022 for a comparison between prescriptive and descriptive annotation paradigms).

Depending on the annotation model, different annotation formats and standards are adopted. For the Universal Dependencies (UD) framework (de Marneffe et al., 2021) – the focus of this paper – the CoNLL-U format is the standard. This format is an evolution of CoNLL-X (Buchholz and Marsi, 2006) and was developed to annotate datasets used in the shared tasks of 2017 and 2018 (Hajič and Zeman, 2017; and Zeman et al., 2018).

To get an idea of the scope of the UD, its current version (May, 2025) has 319 treebanks and 179 languages, representing a valuable resource for training multilingual models and developing cross-language studies. Thanks to this resource, several multilingual parsers have been trained, such as UDPipe 2 (Straka, 2018), UDify (Kondratyuk and Straka, 2019) and Stanza (Qi et al., 2020), which makes it possible to start a new annotation project by automatically pre-annotating the corpus and posteriorly manually revising it, which is another well established annotation method.

The revision of a pre-annotated corpus is significantly different from annotating from scratch. Correcting an entire corpus in order to improve the performance in some NLP task is a big challenge. It is not evident which sentences contain errors or how many errors there are. In particular, when the tool used for pre-annotation already has good accuracy, the annotators need to be very good judges in order to analyze the sentences, identify errors and propose corrections. In the particular case of CoNLL-U, annotators have to deal with dozens of labels and a multilayered annotation.

Drawing on five years of experience with annotation, this paper presents adopted (language

Proceedings of the 19th Linguistic Annotation Workshop (LAW-XIX-2025), pages 60–69
July 31, 2025 ©2025 Association for Computational Linguistics

agnostic) annotation strategies and discusses the lessons learned – mainly those regarding annotator behavior – for a corpus of news texts in Portuguese, following the UD framework. We believe that the fundamental lessons can provide insights for similar projects in other languages, and, for this reason, we have purposely not presented any examples in Portuguese, and, where we considered important to provide an example, we have given it in English to increase its usefulness.

Basically, we decided to adopt a "divide-and-conquer" strategy, which consisted of revising linguistic layers (in some of the 10 CoNLL-U columns) separately and sequentially, as the information of one layer benefits from the corrections made in the others. This strategy allowed us to learn during the process and inspired us to develop resources to improve consistency, a fundamental requirement for building a gold standard corpus.

This paper is organized as follows. In Section 2, we comment on our project and on the reasons that led us to choose the UD annotation. Section 3 presents our approach to annotation revision and the strategies developed to iteratively combine the best of human annotation skills with the best of computational power, doing our best to ensure consistency and to save time. Section 4 comments on related work, and Section 5 draws some conclusions and presents insights for future work.

2 The Porttinari Project

The aim of the Porttinari (Pardo et al., 2021) project is to annotate corpora from different genres according to UD, with a view to train robust and multigenre parsers in Portuguese that benefit downstream applications.

The idea of choosing language-dependent theories, instantiating them, and creating our own annotation model was soon discarded, as this would limit the future use of our parsers in multilingual tasks. The reasons that led us to choose the UD "universal" annotation model were:

- it is a model that has come a long way in refining tag sets applicable to different languages;
- 179 languages have already been annotated with UD tag sets (UD v2.16, May, 2025);
- the maintainers are speakers of different languages, constituting a multilingual initiative;
- the community is active and open to discussion, taking into account problems from different language families;
- the set of annotated corpora has already proven results both in multilingual applications and in typological studies;
- although the tag sets of Universal Part-of-Speech tags (UPOS, hereafter) and dependency relations (DEPRELs, hereafter) are fixed and do not allow changes, the CoNLL-U model reserves a column for annotating language-specific Part-of-Speech tags and allows DEPRELs to have subtypes, which gives some flexibility for language-specific phenomena to be covered (the CoNLL-U format is described in Table 1 and exemplified in Table 2);

In what follows, we describe and comment on the main steps of the annotation effort carried out on our initial corpus, called Porttinari-base, composed of news texts, containing 168,080 tokens and 8,418 sentences.

2.1 Tokenization and sentence segmentation

It is important to note that the minimum scope of UD annotation is the token (which almost always coincides with the concept of a word) and the maximum scope is the sentence. Therefore, the segmentation into sentences and tokenization processes need to be carried out carefully so that the CoNLL-U files are well formed. Errors on these levels may result in structural changes to the CoNLL-U files and affect the entire annotation.

2.2 Selection of parser and annotation tool

We opted for UDPipe 2 (Straka, 2018) to pre-annotate our data because it was already widely adopted in the international research community, reaching state-of-the-art results. We also previously evaluated annotation tools and chose Arborator-Grew (Guibon et al., 2020) because it has a very user-friendly graphic interface and allows several annotators to work at the same time, both in blind and visible modes. Moreover, in Arborator-Grew we can choose which layers to exhibit. Fig. 1 shows the graphic interface used for human revisions, with all layers exhibited.

2.3 Drawing up guidelines in Portuguese

When we started our annotation project following the UD model, there were already annotated UD

1	2	3	4	5	6	7	8	9	10
ID	**FORM**	**LEMMA**	**UPOS**	**XPOS**	**FEATS**	**HEAD**	**DEPREL**	**DEPS**	**MISC**
Token identifier (numeric)	Token form (word or symbol)	Lemma of the token form	PoS tag in the UD tag set	Optional extended (language-specific) PoS tag	List of morphological features associated to the token	ID of the token's head for the dependency tree	Dependency relation tag of the token towards the token's head	HEAD-DEPREL pairs for the enhanced dependency graph	Any additional annotation

Table 1: CoNLL-U 10-columns format to each token of a sentence (official UD abbreviation and content description).

<table>
<tr><th>ID</th><th>FORM</th><th>LEMMA</th><th>UPOS</th><th>XPOS</th><th>FEATS</th><th>HEAD</th><th>DEPREL</th><th>DEPS</th><th>MISC</th></tr>
<tr><td>1-2</td><td>I'd</td><td>_</td><td>_</td><td>_</td><td>_</td><td>_</td><td>_</td><td>_</td><td>_</td></tr>
<tr><td>1</td><td>I</td><td>I</td><td>PRON</td><td>_</td><td>Case=Nom|Number=Sing|Person=1|PronType=Prs</td><td>3</td><td>nsubj</td><td>_</td><td>_</td></tr>
<tr><td>2</td><td>would</td><td>would</td><td>AUX</td><td>_</td><td>VerbForm=Fin</td><td>3</td><td>aux</td><td>_</td><td>_</td></tr>
<tr><td>3</td><td>love</td><td>love</td><td>VERB</td><td>_</td><td>VerbForm=Inf</td><td>0</td><td>root</td><td>_</td><td>_</td></tr>
<tr><td>4</td><td>to</td><td>to</td><td>PART</td><td>_</td><td>_</td><td>5</td><td>mark</td><td>_</td><td>_</td></tr>
<tr><td>5</td><td>set</td><td>set</td><td>VERB</td><td>_</td><td>VerbForm=Inf</td><td>3</td><td>xcomp</td><td>_</td><td>_</td></tr>
<tr><td>6</td><td>them</td><td>they</td><td>PRON</td><td>_</td><td>Case=Acc|Number=Plur|Person=3|PronType=Prs</td><td>5</td><td>obj</td><td>_</td><td>_</td></tr>
<tr><td>7</td><td>free</td><td>free</td><td>ADJ</td><td>_</td><td>Degree=Pos</td><td>5</td><td>xcomp</td><td>_</td><td>SpaceAfter=No</td></tr>
<tr><td>8</td><td>.</td><td>.</td><td>PUNCT</td><td>_</td><td>_</td><td>3</td><td>punct</td><td>_</td><td>_</td></tr>
</table>

Table 2: Example of CoNLL-U annotation for the sentence "I'd love to set them free.".

corpora in Portuguese, but they had only used the generic UD guidelines. As Röttger et al. (2022) argue, annotation for training models needs to be prescriptive and accompanied by very clear guidelines, so that annotators can consult them during the annotation process, improving the annotation consistency. For this reason, our first step was to produce two manuals explaining and exemplifying, in Portuguese, the use of the two UD tag sets: UPOS and DEPREL, bridging the gap between general UD guidelines and observable phenomena in Portuguese (Duran, 2021; and Duran, 2022). The first versions of both manuals were enriched throughout the process, adding examples of not-so-frequent constructions found in the corpus (currently the UPOS manual has 55 pages, and the DEPREL manual has 166 pages with 308 annotated examples).

3 The annotation strategy: divide-and-conquer

Differentiating among 17 UPOS and 37 DEPREL labels is a complex task, even for experienced linguists. For this reason, we divided the revision task into four steps, based on CoNLL-U columns:

- Step 1 - column 4: UPOS;
- Step 2 - column 3: LEMMA;
- Step 3 - column 6: FEATS;
- Step 4 - columns 7 and 8: HEAD/DEPREL.

This revision strategy was adopted with the belief that it would create a cascade effect, yielding the following outcomes:

- gradual accumulation of expertise in the tasks;
- the mitigation of error propagation across annotation layers, as errors corrected in initial columns reduce the likelihood of inconsistencies in later ones;
- the ability to select and train annotators for the tasks, starting with those deemed simpler;
- the opportunity to retrain the parser at the conclusion of each step and to apply it to the portion of the corpus yet to be revised.

Although we did not anticipate a cyclical nature, any decision that affected the entire corpus was followed by a punctual revision of the already annotated sentences, in order to maintain consistency.

The remaining columns of CoNLL-U were not revised: columns 1, 2, and 10 (ID, FORM, and MISC) were only changed when we corrected segmentation and tokenization problems; column 5 (XPOS) was left blank because we had no need to use another PoS tag set; column 9 (DEPS) was left blank because multilingual parsers were not (and are not at the time of writing this paper) prepared to simultaneously annotate enhanced dependencies. In the following, we comment on lessons learned during each of the four revision steps.

3.1 STEP 1 - Revising UPOS

We started with UPOS because it constitutes the smallest and simplest set of UD labels with great equivalence to the set of labels of the Brazilian grammatical nomenclature. Furthermore, this

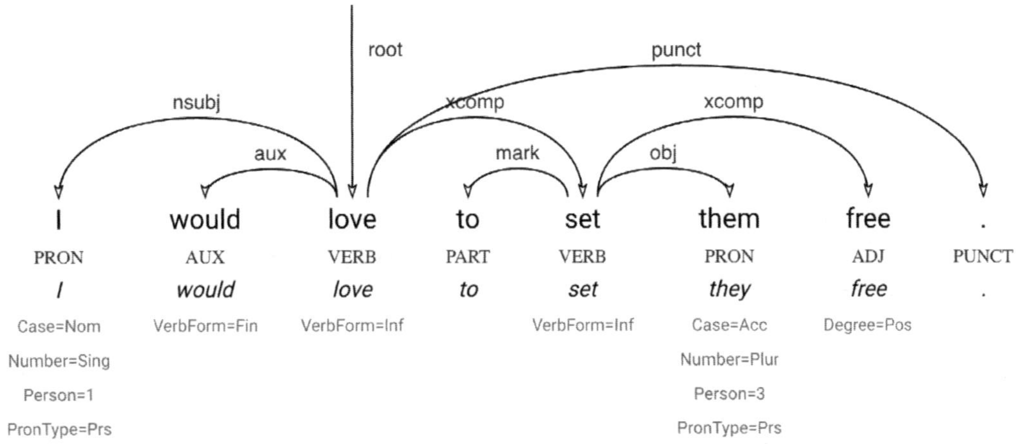

Figure 1: Example of the tree representation of a sentence – codified in CoNLL-U – using Arborator-Grew.

nomenclature is a background that annotators already had and which could facilitate their training. Additionally, from the UPOS, we can restrict the FEATS and DEPREL accepted, making the next steps easier.

The task of UPOS revision proved to be more laborious than we first imagined. As the parser we used had a good performance[1], finding errors required an "eagle eye" and the ability to stay focused. Not all annotators had this ability and this step helped us to identify annotators with best performance in revision tasks, whom we invited to the next steps.

The task involves two sub-tasks: identifying the error and suggesting the correct UPOS label. In each package, all disagreement cases were analyzed by an experienced linguist who made the adjudication and used what she learned during this experience to give feedback to the annotators. The assessment of the annotators' work, therefore, was based on the adjucator's analysis of the disagreements. This does not guarantee that all errors in the corpus have been corrected. In fact, the maintenance of the corpus always brings some corrections to errors identified after the first annotation has been completed.

In some cases, annotators overlooked errors and made no changes (a). When corrections were made, three scenarios emerged: the error was correctly identified and appropriately corrected (b); the error was detected, but an incorrect correction was applied (c); or, more rarely, a non-existent error was mistakenly introduced (d). Fig. 2 shows the results of UPOS correction for the first 2,177 sentences from a total of 8,418 sentences in the corpus and the learning curve during this initial phase. It is very interesting to note that:

- the proportion of tokens that needed correction but were missed by annotators decreases as the annotation process runs (probably due to acquired annotation experience);
- the proportion of tokens that should be and were corrected increased (same reason above);
- in the last week, there are still 2.38% of tokens that showed annotation problems (cases (a), (c) and (d)), but this value is almost half of what occurred in the first week (4.48%).

In the first four weeks, the sentences were shorter (around 14 tokens per sentence) than in the last week (29 tokens per sentence). Following this revision, these sentences were used to retrain the parser, and the remaining sentences were re-annotated and manually revised until all UPOS were corrected.

We selected ten annotators for this step (undergraduate linguistics students) because we wanted to speed up the task without overburdening the annotators. That expectation, however, did not materialize. There were many disagreements, both in the errors detected and in the proposed corrections, which required a lot of adjudication. As the errors detected were distributed among the sentences, in the first weeks almost 50% of the sentences needed adjudication. However, these disagreements in errors detected and corrected do not stand out when we used Kappa (Carletta, 1996), as the unchanged PoS

[1] UPOS: 92%, LEMMA: 90%, FEATS: 76%, UAS (correct HEAD): 88%; LAS (correct HEAD and DEPREL): 87%.

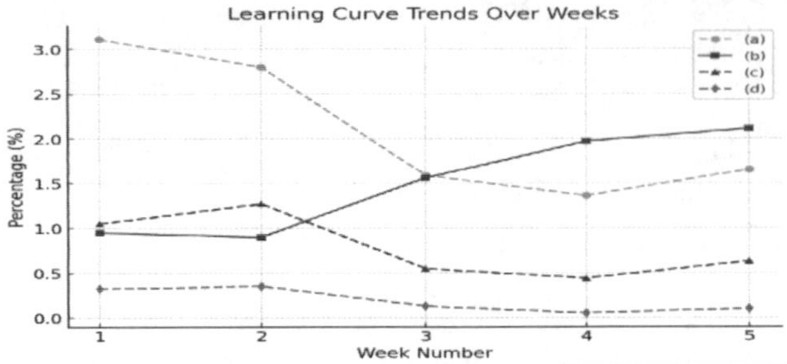

week number	total number of sentences	total number of tokens	(a) tokens needing correction that were missed		(b) tokens that should and were corrected		(c) tokens that should be corrected, but were changed to an incorrect tag		(d) tokens already correct, but changed (error insertion)	
1	481	6,857	213	3.11%	65	0.95%	72	1.05%	22	0.32%
2	492	6,919	194	2.80%	62	0.90%	88	1.27%	24	0.35%
3	482	6,787	108	1.59%	106	1.56%	37	0.55%	9	0.13%
4	480	6,553	89	1.36%	129	1.95%	29	0.44%	3	0.05%
5	242	7,104	117	1.65%	150	2.11%	45	0.63%	7	0.10%
total	2,177	34,220	721	2.11%	512	1.50%	271	0.79%	64	0.19%

Figure 2: Manual revision outcomes for the first five weeks of UPOS revision.

tags (more than 90%) counted as agreements (and they really should be counted, because, although it may not seem obvious, all the tokens were actually revised, even those left unchanged). During the analysis of disagreements, we learned that the majority was not always right, which means that a majority voting strategy would not be a good solution to substitute adjudication.

Dealing with remote annotators was underestimated (in 2021 we were in isolation due to Covid-19). We even implemented a log in the annotation tool to study the behavior of annotators who missed many errors. This was important to identify undesirable behaviors, such as annotators who checked sentences a few seconds after opening them for annotation, without enough time to at least read them. Then we realized an important feature of the revision task: as there is no blank space to fill in, it is difficult to distinguish an annotator who has agreed with the automatic annotation from an annotator who has barely read the sentence.

3.1.1 Splitting the workload into packages

We made packages of 20 sentences, starting with the smallest sentences in the corpus, and when we learned something recurrent, we systematized the automatic revision of what had already been annotated, ensuring homogeneity. Every 200 sentences, we automated the correction of recurring errors in the next packages. Every 2,000 sentences, we retrained the parser, so that the number of errors in the packages to be revised gradually decreased.

In the final count, 168.080 UPOS (one per token) were human revised, of which 6,437 (3.83%) were manually corrected. In addition to correcting the errors, the most important thing is that we confirmed the accuracy of the unedited UPOS, which led us to obtain a corpus with 100% of the revised UPOS, as far as we could tell, correct.

3.1.2 New lexical resources

Within this step, we developed lists of non-ambiguous single tokens and non-ambiguous co-occurring tokens (regardless of whether they constitute multiword expressions or not) and used them to automatically annotate the respective UPOS (Lopes et al., 2021).

These lists mainly contain function words (conjunctions, adpositions, determiners, etc.) and crystallized constructions.

3.2 STEP 2 - Revising LEMMA

Our initial plan was to make a fully automatic revision of the lemmas, using a lexicon. We thought that, by providing the token form and its UPOS as input, we would obtain a unique possible lemma, so that only out-of-vocabulary tokens would require human revision. This is true in most cases, but we found exceptions: in Portuguese, there are identical forms of nouns and verbs, with the same UPOS (NOUN or VERB), with different lemmas. For example, "fui", "foi", "fomos", "foram" are verbal forms of both verbs "ir" (to go) and "ser" (to be), both in the present tense, requiring humans in the loop to "disambiguate" the lemma in context.

We employed a single annotator (with lexicographical expertise) for the whole task: revision of the lemmas of 1,825 tokens (out of the 168,080 tokens), being 1,708 of them disambiguated and 117 annotated (out-of-vocabulary words).

When searching for a lexicon to correct the lemmas, we found one that contained all possible PoS tags for each form, with all possible lemmas and morphological features such as: gender (used for nouns, adjectives and pronouns), tense, mode, person (used for verbs), and number (used for various categories). We saw the opportunity to map the tag set used by the resource to the UD tag set, which allowed us to automatically check the lemma and feature annotations. This mapping proved to be more complex than expected, and we ended up having to make several improvements in the process, but the resulting lexicon (Lopes et al., 2022) has helped us automate several tasks ever since.

This step turned out to be the shortest (excluding the time spent on building the lexicon), since 98.91% of the lemmas were automatically revised using the lexicon and only 1.09% required manual revision.

3.3 STEP 3 - Revising FEATS

Unlike the UPOS and LEMMA columns, which have a label and a lemma for each token respectively, the FEATS column does not have a one-to-one relationship with the tokens. In fact, 42.8% of the 168,080 tokens in the corpus did not require any feature, and 57.2% required one or more features, depending on their UPOS. The corpus has a total of 281,970 features unequally distributed among the 96,134 tokens that require them. Given a token, plus its LEMMA and UPOS, we expected to automatically solve the FEATS revision, using the lexicon we customized in the previous step. However, even with this triple data input, there were tokens that admit more than one possible set of features in Portuguese. In this step, human intervention was required to resolve 8,050 cases (7,933 ambiguities and 117 out-of-vocabulary words). These ambiguous tokens pertain to the VERB (7,543 cases), PRON (3,822) and NOUN (132) classes, while the out-of-vocabulary words pertain to NOUN (93), ADJ (22), VERB (1), and ADP (1).

Therefore, the FEATS revision was predominantly automatic, with only 4.79% of the tokens requiring human revision, as described in more detail in Lopes et al. (2024).

3.4 STEP 4 - Revising HEAD-DEPREL

The task of revising dependency relations involves several operations: identifying HEAD errors, detecting DEPREL errors, and suggesting both a corrected HEAD and an appropriate DEPREL label to replace the incorrect annotation. Furthermore, when the error affects the annotation of the sentence root, a series of additional modifications is required, making this step the most complex in the entire process. Just like in the UPOS step, in some instances annotators overlooked errors and made no changes. However, when corrections were made, several scenarios occurred:

- the error was correctly identified and appropriately corrected;
- the error was correctly identified, and the DEPREL was correctly changed, but a necessary change of HEAD had not been made;
- the error was correctly identified, but an incorrect correction was applied to HEAD or DEPREL or both;
- the error was incorrectly identified and the correction introduced a HEAD or DEPREL error or both.

In this phase, our team consisted of four annotators and one adjudicator. The best annotators from the UPOS step were hired for the DEPREL step. However, not all of them repeated their good performance, perhaps because DEPRELs are harder and require more in-depth logical thinking, which is not always the case with the UPOS revision.

At the beginning of this step, 400 sentences received double-blind annotation from two annotators (200 of each pair) and, after calculating the inter-annotator agreement, all the sentences were analyzed by a more experienced linguist, in order to check the complexity of the task as a whole.

The inter-annotator agreement (Table 3) combines relations that were revised and considered correct and relations that were changed in the same way by both annotators (which we refer by pairs of annotators A1-A2 and A3-A4), but does not reflect all possible scenarios. When analyzing the results of the first 400 sentences, we noticed that in most cases one annotator saw an error and another annotator saw another, both of which were relevant. In several cases, both annotators missed an error. In addition, we noticed some cases of intra-annotator disagreement (when annotators deviated from the guidelines and disagreed with their own earlier decisions for similar cases).

Annotators	DEPREL (%)	HEAD (%)	HEAD+DEPREL (%)
A1-A2	96.92	97.21	95.96
A3-A4	97.67	97.79	96.62
average	97.50	97.29	96.29

Table 3: Human annotators agreement for HEAD-DEPREL revision.

To overcome these problems, instead of using double-blind annotation and inter-annotator agreement to guide the adjudication, we adopted in this step the double non-blind revision: the annotators checked each other's work (each package received a first and a second revision sequentially) and they were allowed to communicate to discuss disagreements. This proved to be an appropriate decision, as we combined the revision capacities, generating synergy. Moreover, we noticed greater motivation on the part of the annotators when the task was no longer totally solitary. The cases in which the annotators were unable to reach a consensus were revised by an experienced linguist. These cases sometimes required study before a decision was adopted and became part of our annotation manual. Problems for which we could not find a clear solution were discussed via issues on UD's github.

At this step, we verified two facts that probably occur in other languages: a) there is not always a direct correlation between sentence length and annotation complexity (many long sentences are a combination of very simple clause patterns); b) nominal predicates presented more difficult constructions to annotate than verbal ones.

During DEPREL revision, we noticed correlations between UPOS and DEPREL, as well as correlations between some features and DEPREL, which could be used to identify recurring errors. These findings inspired the construction of an error checker (Lopes et al., 2023), which played a crucial role in improving the consistency of the annotation.

The HEAD and DEPREL of the 168,080 tokens (100% of the corpus) were fully revised by humans. Of this total, 15,358 (9.14%) had a HEAD change and 13,816 (8.22%) had a DEPREL change. Of these, a total of 6,542 (3.89%) tokens had their HEAD and DEPREL changed simultaneously.

The DEPREL revision provides a very suitable scenario for doing what Pandey et al. (2020) proposed: studying annotation as a psychological process. Building on that, we observed these interesting things on our psychological process analysis:

- when annotators realize that the parser makes few mistakes, they begin to "trust" the parser and start to question the annotation less, missing the errors;
- annotators believe that, if the parser gets difficult things right, it will not get easy things wrong; therefore, things that are considered "easy" are taken out of the focus of the revision and "silly" mistakes are no longer corrected (for example, in Portuguese, as in English, the copula verb is also a passive auxiliary (to be), but this is so often well distinguished by the parser that a label mistake goes unnoticed);
- annotators also believe that the "lightning does not strike the same tree twice" and, when they find an error in a sentence, they sometimes are blind to other errors in the same sentence;
- annotators often do not recognize patterns in less frequent constructions, separated by a long time interval (3 days or more); this leads them to annotate similar constructions in different ways, what seems to be a case of slip, that is, an error type caused by reasons different from absence of knowledge, probably due to memory decay (with specific regard to memory decay in human annotation, see Pandey et al. 2020);
- annotators miss most frequently errors regarding functional words, as they naturally tend to engage in a "skimming and scanning" reading process, focusing more on content words.

3.5 Overview of the process

We gained valuable insights throughout the process. Primarily, we learned that each annotation layer requires different linguistic knowledge and different annotator profiles. The cascade approach required human annotators at all steps, including STEPS 2 and 3, where the automation of most cases relieved the workload. Although both STEPS 1 and 4 heavily employed human resources, STEP 1 required annotators focused on pattern recognition with some

step	CoNLL-U column	human revision		tool to revise	performed tasks	required knowledge	automatic revision		tokens changed		tokens unchanged	
1	UPOS	168,080	100.0%	Arborator-Grew	revision	morphosyntax	–	0%	6,440	3.83%	161,640	96.17%
2	LEMMA	1,825	1.09%	spreadsheet	disamb./annot.	morphology	166,255	98.91%	3,649	2.17%	164,431	97.83%
3	FEATS	8,050	4.79%	spreadsheet	disamb./annot.	lexicography	160,030	95.21%	29,274	17.42%	138,806	82.58%
4	HEAD	168,080	100.0%	Arborator-Grew	revision	syntax	–	0%	15,358	9.14%	152,722	90.86%
	DEPREL	168,080	100.0%	Arborator-Grew	revision	syntax	–	0%	13,816	8.22%	154,264	91.78%

Table 4: Summary of revision steps.

knowledge of morphosyntax, while STEP 4 required annotators with in-depth logical reasoning and solid knowledge of syntax. As the learning curve is long, we should avoid hiring a workforce with high turnover and, ideally, multitasking annotators should be trained. People with knowledge of Computational Linguistics are essential both for designing the tasks and for spotting opportunities to optimize them. Likewise, computer support is essential at all stages of the process. Table 4 summarizes the results of each step.

4 Related work

The lack of a parser was a barrier for low-resource languages to start annotation for the morphosyntactic and syntactic layers. However, with datasets and multilingual models, the barrier is no longer the lack of a parser, but the lack of resources and systematic procedures to efficiently revise the pre-annotated corpus. In recent years, various proposals have been put forward to save effort in human revision. The following are some of them.

Hovy et al. (2014) adopt crowd-sourced lay annotators to annotate PoS tags, putting the target word in bold, one context token on the left and one on the right, and presenting multiple choice questions, abridging the process of annotating from scratch. They used majority voting to decide disagreements. The model trained on the resulting data achieved slightly less than an expert in the task (82.6% and 86.8%, respectively). Using a lexicon, they performed a new task, only restricting the labels available for a given token, achieving 83.7%.

Weissweiler et al. (2023) examined the morphological capabilities of ChatGPT in 4 languages (English, German, Turkish and Tamil) and found that in none of them did LLM achieve human-level performance in the proposed tasks, nor did it match the state-of-the-art models.

Freitas and de Souza (2024) used two different models to annotate the corpus (UDPipe 2 and Stanza) and performed a human revision of all cases of disagreement between the two automatic annotations, adopting the heuristic that the agreement of the systems would be indicative of the correct annotation.

Machado and Ruiz (2024) evaluated 3 LLMs in PoS tag assignment using UD tag set in texts written in Brazilian Portuguese and showed that the best performance was achieved by ChatGPT-3, with 90% of accuracy.

None of them, however, covers the complete revision of the corpus.

5 Final remarks

Porttinari-base was launched in 2023 (Duran et al., 2023) and has been used to train a state-of-the-art parser (Lopes and Pardo, 2024), reaching over 96% of accuracy. We have been using this parser to pre-annotate corpora of new genres within the larger multi-genre project Porttinari.

The divide-and-conquer strategy was very successful: the expected cascade effect was achieved, leading to an increasing reduction in errors. We hypothesize that, just as one annotation layer benefits greatly from improvements in another layer, small improvements in the performance of a tagger or parser can significantly impact the performance of downstream applications.

For the interested reader, all the resources and tools that we mentioned are freely available on the POeTiSA project website: `https://sites.google.com/icmc.usp.br/poetisa`

Acknowledgments

This work was carried out at the Center for Artificial Intelligence of the University of São Paulo (C4AI - http://c4ai.inova.usp.br/), with support by the São Paulo Research Foundation (FAPESP grant #2019/07665-4) and by IBM Corporation. The project was also supported by the Ministry of Science, Technology and Innovation, with resources of Law n. 8.248, of October 23, 1991, within the scope of PPI-SOFTEX, coordinated by Softex and published as Residence in TIC 13, DOU 01245.010222/2022-44.

References

Sohail Akhtar, Valerio Basile, and Viviana Patti. 2021. Whose opinions matter? perspective-aware models to identify opinions of hate speech victims in abusive language detection. *CoRR*, abs/2106.15896.

Sabine Buchholz and Erwin Marsi. 2006. CoNLL-X shared task on multilingual dependency parsing. In *Proceedings of the Tenth Conference on Computational Natural Language Learning*, CoNLL-X '06, pages 149–164, USA. Association for Computational Linguistics.

Jean Carletta. 1996. Assessing agreement on classification tasks: The kappa statistic. *Computational Linguistics*, 22(2):249–254.

Marie-Catherine de Marneffe, Christopher D. Manning, Joakim Nivre, and Daniel Zeman. 2021. Universal Dependencies. *Computational Linguistics*, 47(2):255–308.

Magali Duran, Lucelene Lopes, Maria das Graças Nunes, and Thiago Pardo. 2023. The dawn of the Porttinari multigenre treebank: Introducing its journalistic portion. In *Anais do XIV Simpósio Brasileiro de Tecnologia da Informação e da Linguagem Humana*, pages 115–124, Porto Alegre, RS, Brasil. SBC.

Magali Sanches Duran. 2021. Manual de anotação de PoS tags: Orientações para anotação de etiquetas morfossintáticas em língua portuguesa, seguindo as diretrizes da abordagem Universal Dependencies (UD). Technical Report 434, ICMC-USP.

Magali Sanches Duran. 2022. Manual de anotação de relações de dependência: Orientações para anotação de relações de dependência em língua portuguesa, seguindo as diretrizes da abordagem Universal Dependencies (UD). Technical Report 440, ICMC-USP.

Cláudia Freitas and Elvis de Souza. 2024. A study on methods for revising dependency treebanks: in search of gold. *Language Resources and Evaluation*, 58(1):111–131.

Gaël Guibon, Marine Courtin, Kim Gerdes, and Bruno Guillaume. 2020. When collaborative treebank curation meets graph grammars. In *Proceedings of the Twelfth Language Resources and Evaluation Conference*, pages 5291–5300, Marseille, France. European Language Resources Association.

Jan Hajič and Dan Zeman, editors. 2017. *Proceedings of the CoNLL 2017 Shared Task: Multilingual Parsing from Raw Text to Universal Dependencies*. Association for Computational Linguistics, Vancouver, Canada.

Dirk Hovy, Taylor Berg-Kirkpatrick, Ashish Vaswani, and Eduard Hovy. 2013. Learning whom to trust with MACE. In *Proceedings of the 2013 Conference of the North American Chapter of the Association for Computational Linguistics: Human Language Technologies*, pages 1120–1130, Atlanta, Georgia. Association for Computational Linguistics.

Dirk Hovy, Barbara Plank, and Anders Søgaard. 2014. Experiments with crowdsourced re-annotation of a POS tagging data set. In *Proceedings of the 52nd Annual Meeting of the Association for Computational Linguistics (Volume 2: Short Papers)*, pages 377–382, Baltimore, Maryland. Association for Computational Linguistics.

Eduard Hovy and Julia Lavid. 2010. Towards a science of corpus annotation: a new methodological challenge for corpus linguistics. *International Journal of Translation*, 22:13–36.

Nancy Ide. 2007. Annotation science: From theory to practice and use (invited talk). In *Data Structures for Linguistic Resources and Applications. Proceedings of the Biennial GLDV Conference 2007, 11.–13. April, Universität Tübingen*, pages 1–5, Tübingen. Narr.

Nancy Ide and James Pustejovsky, editors. 2017. *Handbook of Linguistic Annotation*. Springer, Dordrecht.

Dan Kondratyuk and Milan Straka. 2019. 75 languages, 1 model: Parsing Universal Dependencies universally. In *Proceedings of the 2019 Conference on Empirical Methods in Natural Language Processing and the 9th International Joint Conference on Natural Language Processing (EMNLP-IJCNLP)*, pages 2779–2795, Hong Kong, China. Association for Computational Linguistics.

Elisa Leonardelli, Gavin Abercrombie, Dina Almanea, Valerio Basile, Tommaso Fornaciari, Barbara Plank, Verena Rieser, Alexandra Uma, and Massimo Poesio. 2023. SemEval-2023 task 11: Learning with disagreements (LeWiDi). In *Proceedings of the 17th International Workshop on Semantic Evaluation (SemEval-2023)*, pages 2304–2318, Toronto, Canada. Association for Computational Linguistics.

Lucelene Lopes, Magali Duran, Paulo Fernandes, and Thiago Pardo. 2022. PortiLexicon-UD: a portuguese lexical resource according to Universal Dependencies model. In *Proceedings of the Language Resources and Evaluation Conference*, pages 6635–6643, Marseille, France. European Language Resources Association.

Lucelene Lopes, Magali Duran, and Thiago Pardo. 2024. Desambiguação de lema e atributos morfológicos na anotação do córpus Porttinari-base. In *Anais do XV Simpósio Brasileiro de Tecnologia da Informação e da Linguagem Humana*, pages 336–345, Porto Alegre, RS, Brasil. SBC.

Lucelene Lopes, Magali S. Duran, and Thiago A. S. Pardo. 2021. Universal dependencies-based pos tagging refinement through linguistic resources. In *Intelligent Systems*, pages 601–615, Cham. Springer International Publishing.

Lucelene Lopes, Magali S. Duran, and Thiago A. S. Pardo. 2023. Verifica UD - a verifier for Universal Dependencies annotation in Portuguese'. In *Proc. of the UDFest-BR 2023*, UDFest-BR, pages 1–8.

Lucelene Lopes and Thiago Pardo. 2024. Towards Portparser - a highly accurate parsing system for Brazilian Portuguese following the Universal Dependencies framework. In *Proceedings of the 16th International Conference on Computational Processing of Portuguese - Vol. 1*, pages 401–410, Santiago de Compostela, Galicia/Spain. Association for Computational Lingustics.

Mateus Machado and Evandro Ruiz. 2024. Evaluating large language models for the tasks of PoS tagging within the Universal Dependency framework. In *Proceedings of the 16th International Conference on Computational Processing of Portuguese - Vol. 1*, pages 454–460, Santiago de Compostela, Galicia/Spain. Association for Computational Lingustics.

Rahul Pandey, Carlos Castillo, and Hemant Purohit. 2020. Modeling human annotation errors to design bias-aware systems for social stream processing. In *Proceedings of the 2019 IEEE/ACM International Conference on Advances in Social Networks Analysis and Mining*, ASONAM '19, pages 374–377, New York, NY, USA. Association for Computing Machinery.

Thiago Pardo, Magali Duran, Lucelene Lopes, Ariani Felippo, Norton Roman, and Maria Nunes. 2021. Porttinari - a large multi-genre treebank for Brazilian Portuguese. In *Anais do XIII Simpósio Brasileiro de Tecnologia da Informação e da Linguagem Humana*, pages 1–10, Porto Alegre, RS, Brasil. SBC.

Maja Pavlovic and Massimo Poesio. 2024. The effectiveness of llms as annotators: A comparative overview and empirical analysis of direct representation. In *3rd Workshop on Perspectivist Approaches to NLP, NLPerspectives 2024 at LREC-COLING 2024 - Workshop Proceedings*, 3rd Workshop on Perspectivist Approaches to NLP, NLPerspectives 2024 at LREC-COLING 2024 - Workshop Proceedings, pages 100–110. European Language Resources Association (ELRA). Publisher Copyright: © 2024 ELRA Language Resource Association.; 3rd Workshop on Perspectivist Approaches to NLP, NLPerspectives 2024 ; Conference date: 21-05-2024.

James Pustejovsky, Harry Bunt, and Annie Zaenen. 2017. *Designing Annotation Schemes: From Theory to Model*, pages 21–72. Springer Netherlands, Dordrecht.

Peng Qi, Yuhao Zhang, Yuhui Zhang, Jason Bolton, and Christopher D. Manning. 2020. Stanza: A python natural language processing toolkit for many human languages. *CoRR*, abs/2003.07082.

Paul Röttger, Bertie Vidgen, Dirk Hovy, and Janet Pierrehumbert. 2022. Two contrasting data annotation paradigms for subjective NLP tasks. In *Proceedings of the 2022 Conference of the North American Chapter of the Association for Computational Linguistics: Human Language Technologies*, pages 175–190, Seattle, United States. Association for Computational Linguistics.

Rion Snow, Brendan O'Connor, Daniel Jurafsky, and Andrew Ng. 2008. Cheap and fast – but is it good? evaluating non-expert annotations for natural language tasks. In *Proceedings of the 2008 Conference on Empirical Methods in Natural Language Processing*, pages 254–263, Honolulu, Hawaii. Association for Computational Linguistics.

Milan Straka. 2018. UDPipe 2.0 prototype at CoNLL 2018 UD shared task. In *Proceedings of the CoNLL 2018 Shared Task: Multilingual Parsing from Raw Text to Universal Dependencies*, pages 197–207.

Tiago Timponi Torrent, Thomas Hoffmann, Arthur Lorenzi Almeida, and Mark Turner. 2024. *Copilots for Linguists: AI, Constructions, and Frames*. Elements in Construction Grammar. Cambridge University Press.

Leonie Weissweiler, Valentin Hofmann, Anjali Kantharuban, Anna Cai, Ritam Dutt, Amey Hengle, Anubha Kabra, Atharva Kulkarni, Abhishek Vijayakumar, Haofei Yu, Hinrich Schuetze, Kemal Oflazer, and David Mortensen. 2023. Counting the bugs in ChatGPT's wugs: A multilingual investigation into the morphological capabilities of a large language model. In *Proceedings of the 2023 Conference on Empirical Methods in Natural Language Processing*, pages 6508–6524, Singapore. Association for Computational Linguistics.

Daniel Zeman, Jan Hajič, Martin Popel, Martin Potthast, Milan Straka, Filip Ginter, Joakim Nivre, and Slav Petrov. 2018. CoNLL 2018 shared task: Multilingual parsing from raw text to Universal Dependencies. In *Proceedings of the CoNLL 2018 Shared Task: Multilingual Parsing from Raw Text to Universal Dependencies*, pages 1–21, Brussels, Belgium. Association for Computational Linguistics.

Forbidden FRUIT is the Sweetest: An Annotated Tweet Corpus for French Unfrozen Idioms Identification

Julien Bezançon[1,2], **Félix Alié**[2], **Antoine Gautier**[1], **Marceau Hernandez**[1,2], **Gaël Lejeune**[1,2]
[1]STIH, Sorbonne Université, Paris, France
[2]CERES, Sorbonne Université, Paris, France
firstname.lastname@sorbonne-universite.fr

Abstract

Multiword expressions (MWEs) are a key area of interest in NLP, studied across various languages and inspiring the creation of dedicated datasets and shared tasks such as PARSEME. Puns in multiword expressions (PMWEs) can be described as MWEs that have been "unfrozen" to acquire a new meaning or create wordplay. Unlike MWEs, they have received little attention in NLP, mainly due to the lack of resources available for their study. In this context, we introduce the French Unfrozen Idioms in Tweets (FRUIT) corpus, a dataset of tweets spanning three years and comprising 60,617 tweets containing both MWEs and PMWE candidates. We first describe the process of constructing this corpus, followed by an overview of the manual annotation task performed by three experts on 600 tweets, achieving an inter-annotator agreement score α up to 0.83. Insights from this manual annotation process were then used to develop a Game With A Purpose (GWAP) to annotate more tweets from the FRUIT corpus. This GWAP aims to enhance players' understanding of MWEs and PMWEs. Currently, 13 players made 2,206 annotations on 931 tweets, reaching an α score of 0.70. In total, 1,531 tweets from the FRUIT corpus have been annotated.

1 Introduction

Multiword Expressions (MWEs) have long posed a significant challenge in Natural Language Processing, sometimes referred to as a "pain in the neck" (Sag et al., 2002). The term MWE corresponds to a large span of linguistic objects, more or less subject to variations and with a certain degree of idiomaticity at the lexical, syntactic, semantic, pragmatic and/or statistical levels (Baldwin and Kim, 2010). Constant et al. (2017) describe them as both idiosyncratic and pervasive across different languages. MWEs are valuable not only for linguistic analysis but also for improving NLP tasks such as Machine Translation.

Wordplays and puns created from MWEs (hereafter PMWEs) can be described as MWEs that have undergone lexical, syntactic, semantic and/or pragmatic changes to create a wordplay. Their idiomatic status has been broken, leading to the emergence of a new meaning (Eline and Zhu, 2014). In linguistics, this phenomenon is often referred to as "*défigement*" (FR, "unfreezing"), which is often found in French linguistic literature. Mejri (2013) claims that the underlying MWE should always remain identifiable in a PMWE. Therefore, the MWE (1) is still recognisable in the PMWE (2).

1. *Tu quoque mi **fili*** (Latin, you too, my **son**)
2. *Tu quoque mi **chili*** (Latin, you too, my **chili**)

PMWE studies in NLP present several interests: (I) it can help to characterise MWEs by their productivity in wordplay (Lecler, 2006), (II) it allows the real-time detection of wordplays and even MWEs (Haßler and Hümmer, 2005; Cusimano, 2015) and (III) they shed light on the cognitive processes that allow human speakers to recognise these particular MWEs. We argue that such a study could also benefit MWEs recognition in NLP as PMWEs share the same linguistic challenges, such as idiomaticity across multiple levels, making them particularly challenging for NLP tasks like Machine Translation.

In this paper, we introduce the French Unfrozen Idioms in Tweets corpus (FRUIT), which consists of 60,617 tweets collected for the identification of French PMWEs. To our knowledge, no previous effort has been made to annotate PMWEs or create a dedicated corpus for them. The FRUIT corpus builds upon and expands an existing Twitter (now X) dataset (Bezançon and Lejeune, 2023). Section 3 details the corpus construction and the methodology for identifying PMWEs. We then introduce two annotation tasks:

Proceedings of the 19th Linguistic Annotation Workshop (LAW-XIX-2025), pages 70–86
July 31, 2025 ©2025 Association for Computational Linguistics

Manual Annotation Task Three experts in NLP and linguistics annotated 600 tweets containing potential MWEs and PMWEs, highlighting challenges in the identification of these entities, which we discuss in Section 6. The results of this annotation are available on GITHUB[1].

Annotation through a GWAP Using insights from the manual annotation task, we designed a GWAP to facilitate large-scale annotation of MWEs and PMWEs by a broader audience. The source code of this GWAP is available on GITHUB[2].

Through these annotation tasks, we aim to assess the difficulty of identifying both MWEs and PMWEs in tweets, combining expert knowledge with a gamified approach to enable non-expert contributors to participate in the annotation process. We provide the scripts used for tweet collection, along with all tweet IDs, in a dedicated GITHUB repository[3].

2 Related Work

MWE Identification As explained by Constant et al. (2017), MWE processing involves two main tasks: (i) discovery (ii) identification. Discovery involves detecting and adding MWEs to a lexicon, whereas identification focuses on automatically annotating MWEs in text. MWE identification is made very difficult by the evasive nature of MWEs (Geeraert et al., 2018). Savary et al. (2019) claims that without the creation of syntactic lexicons and at least some morphosyntactic information, we will not make significant progress on this task. Various approaches have been explored to build such lexicons, including crowdsourcing (Ramisch et al., 2016) and gamified platforms (Krstev and Savary, 2017; Fort et al., 2018, 2020). The PARSEME shared tasks (Savary et al., 2017) further demonstrate the community's commitment to improving MWE processing. As with MWEs, we believe that the creation of dedicated resources is a major challenge for identifying PMWEs.

GWAPs GWAPs (Games With A Purpose) correspond to games designed to let the machine learn from human inputs (Lafourcade et al., 2015). They have been widely used in NLP, particularly for resource creation (Lafourcade, 2007) and annotation (Hiebel et al., 2024; Madge et al., 2019). GWAPs offer several advantages: (i) they attract different types of players, such as the ones identified by Bartle (1996) and (ii) they provide an efficient alternative to traditional crowdsourcing methods (Fort et al., 2011; Fort, 2022). GWAPs have been successfully applied to MWE annotation, as demonstrated by RIGORMORTIS (Fort et al., 2020).

Wordplays While wordplay has been studied to some extent in NLP — particularly through shared tasks such as JOKER-CLEF (Ermakova et al., 2022, 2023, 2024) or the SEMEVAL tasks (Miller et al., 2017) — PMWEs remain largely unexplored. However, like Wordplays, PMWEs present unique challenges, both in terms of understanding linguistic creativity (Partington, 2009) and generating computationally creative text (Valitutti et al., 2013).

3 Building a French Tweets Corpus Containing PMWEs

3.1 Getting PMWEs Candidates

We compiled a list of 216 French MWEs to query the TWITTER API over a three-years period (from 2020 to 2023), yielding a dataset of 3,369,636 tweets. These MWEs were manually selected by four researchers specializing in NLP or linguistics. The only selection criterion was the conventionality of a MWE. Conventionalized MWEs tend to have a non-compositional meaning and are commonly recognized by speakers of a given language (Nunberg et al., 1994). Among these MWEs, we find (i) advertising slogans, (ii) famous quotes, (iii) movie catchphrases and (iv) other types of MWEs:

- (i) "*C'est le second effet Kisscool*" ("it's the second Kisscool effect", French advertising slogan for a chewing-gum brand)
- (ii) "*Travailler plus pour gagner plus*" ("work more to earn more", Nicolas Sarkozy, 2007)
- (iii) "*Dans l'espace, personne ne vous entend crier*" ("in space, no one will hear you scream", Alien movie catchphrase, 1979)
- (iv) "*Au bout du rouleau*" ("At the end of the rope")

Each tweet of this corpus is linked to the MWE that prompted its extraction (hereafter *seed*). Consequently, every tweet has some likelihood of con-

[1] https://github.com/JulienBez/ForbiddenFrUIT
[2] https://github.com/CERES-Sorbonne/Defricheur
[3] https://github.com/JulienBez/FrUIT

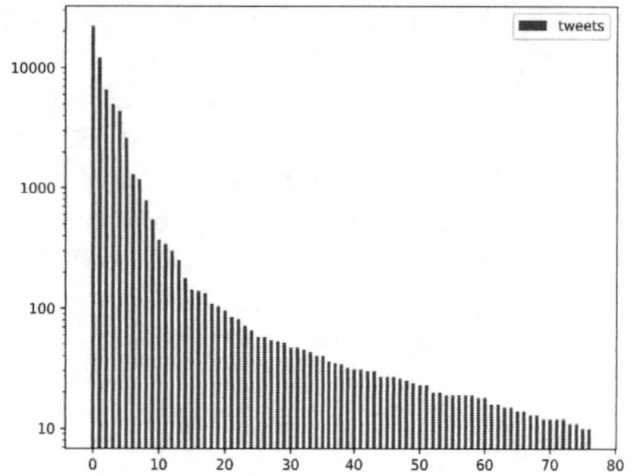

Figure 1: Logscale Zipf-like distribution of tweets per *seeds* in our corpus.

taining either a MWE or a PMWE, as it shares at least one word with its *seed*.

3.2 Filtering Steps

To retain only the most relevant tweets, we applied a three-step filtering process: (i) we discarded any tweet containing less than 50 % of the words of its corresponding *seed* (without preprocessing), (ii) we filtered out duplicates (tweets with identical IDs or texts) and (iii) we excluded tweets associated with *seeds* that appeared in fewer than ten tweets. This final step ensured that we retained only the most productive seeds.

After filtering, 60,617 tweets and 77 *seeds* remained. Figure 1 shows that the top ten *seeds* generated 86.51 % (56,769 tweets) of our dataset.

3.3 Asserting the Presence of PMWE Candidates

To complete the corpus creation, we aimed to verify the presence of PMWE candidates. To achieve this goal, we applied the algorithm introduced in (Bezançon and Lejeune, 2023). This algorithm uses token-level alignments between a MWE and a sentence to extract PMWE candidates, as illustrated in Table 1. It then ranks candidates for each MWE according to a cosine similarity score, measuring how closely a candidate resembles the original MWE. The higher the score, the closer a candidate is to a MWE (see Appendix A.1).

When comparing the MWE "*que la force soit avec toi*" ("May the force be with you", Stars Wars franchise) with the sequence "*que la force* ***ouvrière*** *soit avec toi*" ("May the **worker** force be with you"), found in a tweet, we observe the insertion of the word "*ouvrière*", creating the term "*Force Ouvrière*" ("worker force"), which is the name of a labor union in France. This change is captured in the alignment. Table 2 shows an example of the ranking obtained with this algorithm with the MWE "*que la force soit avec toi*". We used this algorithm to prioritize tweets most likely to contain PMWEs for annotation in Section 4.

que	*la*	*force*	-	*soit*	*avec*	*toi*
que	*la*	*force*	***ouvrière***	*soit*	*avec*	*toi*

Table 1: Token level alignment between the MWE "*que la force soit avec toi*" (may the force be with you) and a PMWE candidate.

Candidate							Score
que la	-	force	du ×2	soit	-	avec toi	0.85
que la	-	force	-	soit	tjrs	avec toi	0.83
que la	-	force	update	soit	-	avec toi	0.83
que la	-	force	rhétorique	soit	-	avec toi	0.83
que la	-	force	tranquille	soit	-	avec toi	0.83
que la	-	force	-	soit	toujours	avec toi	0.83
que la	-	force	marocaine	soit	-	avec toi	0.83
que la	vraie	force	-	soit	-	avec toi	0.83
que la	tri	force	-	soit	-	avec toi	0.81
que la	-	force	ouvrière	soit	-	avec toi	0.78

Table 2: Examples of aligned segments found with our methodology. For each candidate, we give its cosine score.

4 Setting up the Annotation Tasks

4.1 Creating Annotation Samples

To generate annotation samples, we applied the algorithm presented in Section 3. First, we filtered tweets based on their similarity scores, removing those with a score below 0.5 under the assumption that such candidates were unlikely to contain PMWEs. This process excluded 10,605 tweets.

Additionally, we removed tweets with a similarity score exceeding 0.99, eliminating another 29,960 tweets, as these were highly likely to contain only MWEs without modifications. Following this filtering, 25,052 tweets remained for annotation.

4.2 Annotation Guidelines

Defining both MWEs and PMWEs from a linguistic and a NLP perspective can be challenging. While linguistic literature does not always agree on all aspects of MWEs (Lamiroy, 2008), PMWEs have been scarcely studied in NLP. For annotation purposes, we adopted the following definitions:

Multiword expression A multiword expression is a fixed sequence of words, either in statistical terms (the words frequently appear next to each other) or in semantic ones (the sequence has a global, non-compositional meaning).

Pun in multiword expression Wordplays or puns created from multiword expressions can be described as multiword expressions that have been unfrozen. To formally identify a wordplay or a pun created from a multiword expression, we must be able to recognise the multiword expression from which it is derived.

Unfreezing Process by which a multiword expression becomes a wordplay or a pun. It involves a formal modification, usually paired with a semantic shift within the multiword expression. This process must not be misjudged for a tense or a number variation, for instance.

We bear in mind that, in the long term, these definitions are intended for non-expert individuals who will learn about these concepts during the annotation process. In addition to these definitions, we give some examples of PMWEs, such as (2), (4) and (6):

1. "*Mangez cinq fruits et légumes par jour*"
("eat five fruits and vegetables a day")

2. "*Mangez cinq **riches** et légumes par jour*"
("eat five **rich** and vegetables a day")

3. "*Repris de justice*"
("convicted")

4. "*Repris de **justesse***"
("narrowly recovered")

5. "*C'est le deuxième effet Kisscool*"
("it's the second Kisscool effect")

6. "*C'est le deuxième effet **confinement***"
("it's the second **lockdown** effect")

(1) becomes (2) (seen at a demonstration in Paris) and (3) becomes (4) (Le Canard Enchaîné, 2017) by word substitution and are well-known MWEs in French. (4) also has a phonetic dimension (ʒys + tɛs VS ʒys + tis). (5) becomes (6) (seen in our corpus) by word substitution as well, but is an older MWE dating from the 80's, so that it may be hard to recognise for some younger speakers. We also introduced true counter-examples found in our corpus, which show variations that do not create a PMWE from a MWE. For instance:

7. "*Max a cassé sa pipe*"
("Max kicked the bucket")

8. "*Max avait cassé sa pipe*"
("Max kicked the bucket")

9. "*Pierre qui roule n'amasse pas mousse*"
("a rolling stone gathers no moss")

10. "*Pierres qui roulent n'amassent pas mousse*"
("rolling stones gather no moss")

(8) shows a tense change and (9) a number change. Nevertheless, these 2 examples do not contain any PMWE. They show minor variations of MWEs that mustn't be confused with unfreezing processes, as specified in our PMWE definition.

5 Manual Annotation Task

The annotation task was performed by 3 annotators, A_1, A_2, and A_3, who are also authors of this paper. All had prior experience working with MWEs and PMWEs and had participated in previous annotation tasks. A_3 specializes in linguistics while A_1 and A_2 work in NLP and computer science. The participants were asked to answer two binary questions:

- Does the tweet contain a PMWE ?
- Do you recognize a MWE, unfrozen or not ?

The goal was to directly identify PMWEs without requiring further analysis. After each annotation phase, adjudication sessions were conducted to review the annotations, discuss encountered issues, and resolve disagreements.

5.1 Annotation Phase I: Pilot

Initially, 100 tweets were provided to all three annotators without additional information (such as guidelines or the seed used to fetch them). This sample aimed to assess the difficulty of the annotation task and the annotators' intuition. Krippendorff's (Krippendorff, 2013) α score was 0.19, indicating a significant lack of agreement and highlighting the complexity of identifying PMWEs. An adjudication session followed, where annotators reviewed each tweet and collaboratively established the first set of annotation guidelines.

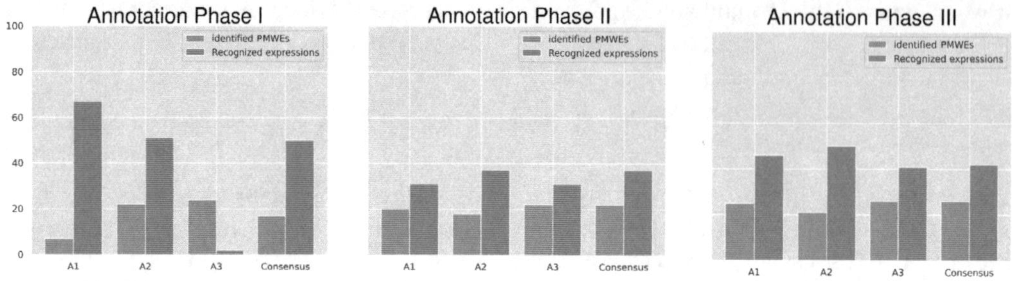

Figure 2: Number of identified PMWEs and recognised MWEs for each annotator and consensus on our three annotation samples.

5.2 Annotation Phase II: First Consolidation

A second set of 100 tweets was provided to the annotators using the newly established guidelines. The resulting Krippendorff's α score improved significantly to 0.77. However, the adjudication session revealed that this sample was easier to annotate due to the high recognizability of PMWEs, leading to fewer disagreements.

5.3 Annotation Phase III: Second Consolidation

A final common sample of 100 tweets was provided. The initial Krippendorff's α score was 0.67, lower than in Phase II but still an improvement over the pilot study.

Discrepancies in annotation strategies emerged: A_1 and A_2 focused on formal changes in MWEs, while A_3 placed greater emphasis on contextual influences. Additionally, A_3 was stricter about variations in quotations and MWEs involving word order changes. Based on these observations, we corrected our annotation guidelines, as explained in Section 6 and each annotator revised its annotations for this sample. The α score for this phase increased to 0.83.

5.4 Annotation Phase IV: Individual Annotations

Beyond the three annotation phases, we proceeded to an individual annotation phase in which each annotator was allocated an additional 100 tweets to annotate.

5.5 Manual Annotation Overview

In total, we annotated 600 tweets. Table 3 shows the frequency of each annotation type across the steps of our annotation process. Of the 600 annotated tweets, 137 (22.83 % of the annotated tweets) were identified as containing a PMWE, whereas 251 (41.83 %) contain only a MWE and 212 (35.33 %) contain nothing. Notably, all identified PMWEs were consistently paired with a recognised MWE. This is expected, as a PMWE should always be linked to an underlying MWE.

Figure 2 presents the number of identified PMWEs and recognised MWEs by each annotator across each annotation phase. We included a consensus column that reflects the final annotations after adjudication. Figure 3 displays the merged confusion matrix for all three annotators.

PMWE	MWE	I	II	III	IV	Total
+	+	17	22	26	72	137
+	-	0	0	0	0	0
-	+	50	37	42	122	251
-	-	33	41	32	106	212
		100	100	100	300	600

Table 3: Frequency of annotations at each step of the manual annotation process : Pilot (I), First consolidation (II), Second consolidation (III) and Individual (IV).

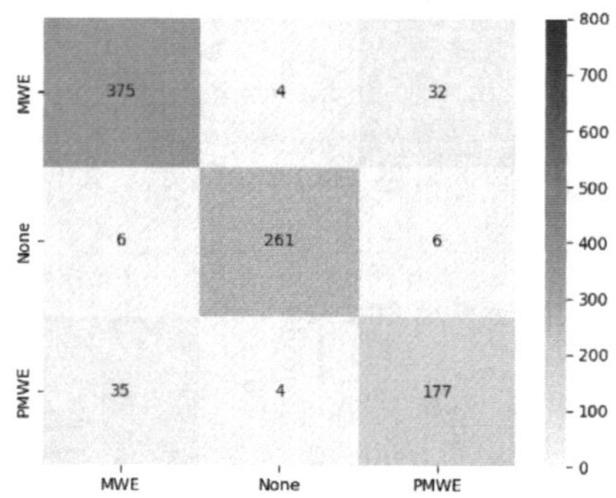

Figure 3: Merged confusion Matrix for the 3 annotators on the 300 tweets they annotated in common.

6 Issues Encountered During the Manual Annotation Task

Throughout the manual annotation process, we identified three major discrepancies between annotator A_3 and the other two annotators: (i) A_3 considered contextual influences more heavily, (ii) applied a stricter approach when annotating MWEs derived from quotations, and (iii) exhibited a different stance on MWEs with word order changes. These differences may stem from A_3's linguistic background, whereas A_1 and A_2 specialise in NLP. Below, we explain how we addressed these discrepancies and refined our annotation guidelines to minimise ambiguity in future PMWE-related annotation tasks.

(i) Contextual influences Although this is a rare scenario, a MWE can unfreeze itself without undergoing a formal modification (Eline and Zhu, 2014). In such cases, only the surrounding context signals the presence of a PMWE. Following the adjudication mentioned in Section 5.3, we decided not to annotate as PMWE any MWE where contextual influences alone reveal a PMWE. This type of PMWE is both infrequent and challenging to identify, introducing significant complexity and inconsistency to the annotation task.

(ii) MWEs corresponding to quotations A_1 and A_2 allowed for minor variations in MWEs originating from well-known quotations. For example, the meme-derived phrase "*Moi je trouve la question elle est vite répondue*" ("I think the question is quickly answered") was frequently truncated to "*La question elle est vite répondue*" ("The question is quickly answered"). While A_3 annotated this as a PMWE, A_1 and A_2 did not. To maintain consistency, we opted for a more flexible approach, permitting slight modifications in MWEs originating from quotations.

(iii) MWEs with word order changes Some PMWEs closely resemble their base MWEs, differing only by slight shifts in word order. The most notable example in our dataset was "*Maurice, tu pousses le bouchon un peu trop loin*" ("Maurice, you're pushing things a little too far"), sometimes reordered as "*Tu pousses le bouchon un peu trop loin, Maurice*" ("You're pushing things a little too far, Maurice"). Since this variation does not appear to involve intentional wordplay, but rather an ignorance of the original quote, we chose not to classify it as a PMWE. However, we encountered a case where the MWE "*Que la force soit avec toi*" ("May the force be with you") became "*avec toi la Force est*"("with you the force is") in a tweet. In this case, the unfreezing process deliberately played with the original word order, so we decided to annotate it as a PMWE.

We also noticed that annotators sometimes repeated the same mistakes from previous annotation phases. To minimise this, we decided to share all consensus annotations among annotators. This way, whenever an annotator encounters a previously discussed case, they can easily refer to our established decision. Moving forward, we plan to leverage our manual annotation findings to develop a GWAP for annotating both MWEs and PMWEs in tweets. This approach will allow us to collect a larger number of annotations efficiently and is presented in the next section.

7 Expanding Annotations with a GWAP

To scale up the annotations of the FRUIT corpus, we developed a participatory science task in the form of a Game With a Purpose (GWAP). This initiative incorporates lessons from our manual annotation task to improve both accuracy and participant engagement.

7.1 Annotation Task Design

Players assume the role of investigators tracking a criminal organisation that manipulates MWEs to conceal hidden messages. Their mission is to identify tweets containing disguised MWEs (PMWEs), following the guidelines established in Section 4. For each tweet, the game highlights a potential MWE and players have to determine (i) if they can identify the indicated MWE and (ii) if this MWE corresponds to a hidden message (i.e. a PMWE). Figure 4 provides a screenshot of the annotation interface.

To encourage engagement, the game features a scoring system and badge collection: players earn points when they annotate a tweet and receive badges when they annotate multiple tweets sharing the same MWE (see Figure 8). Each badge has a design associated with its corresponding MWE. By gamifying this annotation task, we aim to attract different types of players, such as the ones described in Bartle (1996).

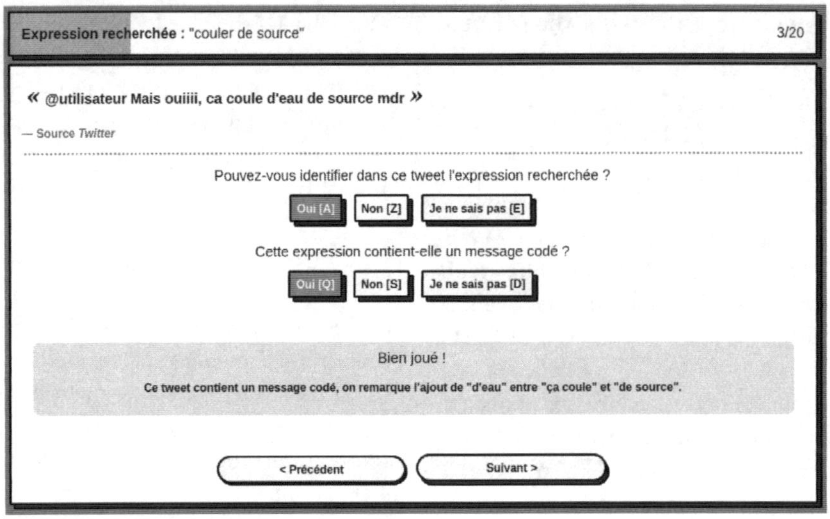

Figure 4: Instance of a tweet to annotate in our GWAP. The upper box contains the indicated MWE, while the lower box contains the tweet and the questions we ask the players to answer. The green box contains the correction given for this tweet.

7.2 Progressive Learning

As shown in Section 6, identifying PMWE and even MWE can be ambiguous. To address this challenge, we incorporated several features into our GWAP to help players gradually learn key concepts related to MWE and PMWEs. Figure 9 illustrate this GWAP annotation process.

Guidelines Players receive a simplified version of the guidelines from Section 4. Prior research shows that clear instructions significantly improve annotation accuracy (Nédellec et al., 2006; Hiebel et al., 2022).

Training set Previous studies suggest that training annotators enhances their performances (Dandapat et al., 2009). To this end, we created a training set of 20 tweets, which players must complete before proceeding to the real annotation task. We selected 20 representative tweets from our previous annotation task, illustrating various MWEs and PMWEs to train the players. After the annotation of each of these tweets, we give feedback and corrections, helping them refine their understanding of the task.

Redundant MWE We dynamically generate random sets for each player, with each set containing up to 20 tweets for annotation. All tweets in a set share the same indicated MWE, allowing players to become more familiar with it and produce more consistent annotations. Once a set is completed, a new one is generated. Players can always revisit previous annotation sets to review or revise their work, fostering continuous learning.

Control Tweets To ensure annotation quality, we randomly distribute 80 of the 600 annotated tweets in Section 5 as control tweets. These tweets have been selected because of their unambiguous annotations. Players receive immediate feedback on these tweets, reinforcing learning and improving consistency. Control tweets can be annotated more than once by a player, allowing us to assess the player's consistency over time.

7.3 Playerbase

As for now, our GWAP has been tested with a limited number of researchers with varying degrees of familiarity with both MWEs and PMWEs. We count 13 players, including A_2, who had not worked on the annotation of PMWEs for over a year at that time. All players speak fluent French and work either in linguistics, computer science or literature. We plan to expand the annotation task available to a wider audience soon.

7.4 Annotation Results

2,206 annotations were made by the 13 players, with an average of 169.7 annotations per player. In total, 931 unique tweets were annotated (1,031 by taking into account training and control tweets). Figure 5 shows the distribution of tweets per number of annotations. We computed an α score of 0.70

Figure 5: Discrete distribution of tweets per number of annotations for every tweet annotated at least once.

PMWE	MWE	N	R	P	F
+	+	61	92.14	93.14	92.63
+	-	0	/	/	/
-	+	29	85.43	84.61	85.02
-	-	10	76.59	81.81	79.12
Mean			84.72	86.52	85.59

Table 4: Recall (R), precision (P) and F-score (F) obtained by comparing annotations made by the players with annotations made by the experts for each possible annotation made.

by taking into account every tweet which were annotated more than once (595 tweets, training and control tweets included). We compared our crowd-sourced annotations on the training and control tweets with the annotations made by the experts in Section 5. All the 80 control tweets and the 20 training tweets were annotated more than once, therefore, we include them all in this comparison. Table 4 summarises the results we obtained for each annotation category.

We observe that the mean F-score is high (85.59), indicating a high level of agreement between players and experts. Surprisingly, PMWE identification has a better F-score than MWE recognition (92.63 against 85.02). This can likely be attributed to the fact that our guidelines are more focused on PMWEs. No annotator has identified a PMWE without recognising a MWE, which is why we do not report metrics for this particular scenario. Table 7, 8, 9 and 10 in the Appendix show the 100 tweets (control + training) given to our players.

8 Discussion

In this paper, we introduced the FRUIT corpus, containing 60,617 tweets among which 1,531 have been manually annotated through (i) an expert review and (ii) a GWAP. The results of the manual annotation task show that both MWE and PMWE identification tasks are challenging, even for experts with substantial experience in these two notions. We argue that the low inter-annotator score of 0.19 obtained during our pilot annotation (Section 5.1), alongside the discussion presented in Section 5.3, may be attributed to differences in the interpretation of MWEs and PMWEs between NLP experts and linguistics experts. Despite these challenges, by developing clearer guidelines and organising adjudication sessions, we improved our understanding of both MWEs and PMWEs, which likely contributed to an increase in our inter-annotator score to 0.83.

The GWAP demonstrates that it is possible to teach non-expert individuals how to recognise and identify both MWEs and PMWEs. To achieve this, we leveraged the guidelines developed during the manual annotation task. We also allowed our players to improve their understanding of the key notions through progressive learning (Section 7.2). The results exhibit a high level of agreement between players, with an inter-annotator score of 0.70. Furthermore, we unveil that our players tend to agree with the reference annotation made by our three experts, with an observed mean F-score of 85.59 for every type of annotation (92.63 for PMWE identification).

This result might be influenced by the fact that our players are primarily from the research area, and some of them having already basic knowledge on MWEs and occasionally PMWEs. Despite this potential bias, the insights obtained from this annotation task will inform future improvements to the GWAP and the annotation process.

Looking ahead, we intend to continue annotating the FRUIT corpus through the GWAP presented here. In particular, we want to make this GWAP available to a wider non-expert audience so that we can observe the quality of our progressive learning. We also plan to create a second annotation task, whose goal will be to annotate found PMWEs at different levels.

We plan to assemble a multilingual dataset containing MWEs and PMWEs from films and article titles (media and scientific). Such a dataset could help us analyse differences in PMWE construction across languages. This future work could benefit from a participatory annotation task, such as the one described here.

Ethical Considerations

We have ensured that our annotators remain anonymous. To sign up for GWAP, we only ask for a username and password, without collecting any additional data. We have also anonymised every tweet in the FRUIT corpus. Finally, we inform players of the potential presence of offensive content in tweets (violence, hatred, inappropriate content, etc.). If a player identifies an offensive tweet, we invite them to contact us so that we can deal with it.

Acknowledgments

We would like to thank Karën Fort for her suggestions, including the addition of collectable badges, and her help while designing the annotation by sets used in our GWAP. Finally, we thank all the players who participated in our GWAP.

References

Timothy Baldwin and Su Nam Kim. 2010. Multiword Expressions. In Nitin Indurkhya and Fred J. Damerau, editors, *Handbook of Natural Language Processing*, 2 edition. Chapman and Hall/CRC.

Richard Bartle. 1996. Hearts, clubs, diamonds, spades: Players who suit muds. *The Journal of Virtual Environments, 1*.

Julien Bezançon and Gaël Lejeune. 2023. Reconnaissance de défigements dans des tweets en français par des mesures de similarité sur des alignements textuels. In *30e Conférence sur le Traitement Automatique des Langues Naturelles, TALN*, pages 56–67, Paris, France. ATALA.

Mathieu Constant, Gülşen Eryiğit, Johanna Monti, Lonneke van der Plas, Carlos Ramisch, Michael Rosner, and Amalia Todirascu. 2017. Survey: Multiword Expression Processing: A Survey. *Computational Linguistics*, 43(4):837–892. Place: Cambridge, MA Publisher: MIT Press.

Christophe Cusimano. 2015. Figement de séquences défigées. *Pratiques*, (159-160):69 78.

Sandipan Dandapat, Priyanka Biswas, Monojit Choudhury, and Kalika Bali. 2009. Complex linguistic annotation – no easy way out! a case from Bangla and Hindi POS labeling tasks. In *Proceedings of the Third Linguistic Annotation Workshop (LAW III)*, pages 10–18, Suntec, Singapore. Association for Computational Linguistics.

Joël Eline and Lichao Zhu. 2014. Défigement et inférence - cas d'études du Canard enchaîné. *SHS Web of Conferences*, 8:681 695. 1 citations (Crossref) [2023-11-09] 0 citations (Semantic Scholar/DOI) [2022-11-14].

Liana Ermakova, Anne-Gwenn Bosser, Tristan Miller, Victor Preciado, Grigori Sidorov, and Adam Jatowt. 2024. *Overview of the CLEF 2024 JOKER Track: Automatic Humour Analysis*, pages 165–182.

Liana Ermakova, Tristan Miller, Julien Boccou, Albin Digue, Aurianne Damoy, and Paul Campen. 2022. Overview of the clef 2022 joker task 2: translate wordplay in named entities. *Proceedings of the Working Notes of CLEF*, pages 1666–1680.

Liana Ermakova, Tristan Miller, Anne-Gwenn Bosser, Victor Manuel Palma Preciado, Grigori Sidorov, and Adam Jatowt. 2023. Overview of joker–clef-2023 track on automatic wordplay analysis. In *International Conference of the Cross-Language Evaluation Forum for European Languages*, pages 397–415. Springer.

Karën Fort. 2022. *Myriadisation et éthique pour le traitement automatique des langues*. Accreditation to supervise research, ED n°77 : Informatique - Automatique - Électronique - Électrotechnique - Mathématiques de Lorraine (IAEM-Lorraine).

Karën Fort, Gilles Adda, and K. Bretonnel Cohen. 2011. Last words: Amazon Mechanical Turk: Gold mine or coal mine? *Computational Linguistics*, 37(2):413–420.

Karën Fort, Bruno Guillaume, Matthieu Constant, Nicolas Lefèbvre, and Yann-Alan Pilatte. 2018. "Fingers in the Nose": Evaluating Speakers' Identification of Multi-Word Expressions Using a Slightly Gamified Crowdsourcing Platform. In *Proceedings of the Joint Workshop on Linguistic Annotation, Multiword Expressions and Constructions (LAW-MWE-CxG-2018)*, pages 207–213, Santa Fe, New Mexico, USA. Association for Computational Linguistics.

Karën Fort, Bruno Guillaume, Yann-Alan Pilatte, Mathieu Constant, and Nicolas Lefèbvre. 2020. Rigor Mortis: Annotating MWEs with a Gamified Platform. In *Proceedings of the Twelfth Language Resources and Evaluation Conference*, pages 4395–4401, Marseille, France. European Language Resources Association.

Kristina Geeraert, R. Harald Baayen, and John Newman. 2018. *"Spilling the bag" on idiomatic variation*, pages 1–33. Number 2 in Phraseology and Multiword Expressions. Language Science Press.

Gerda Haßler and Christiane Hümmer. 2005. Figement et défigement polylexical : l'effet des modifications dans des locutions figées. *Linx. Revue des linguistes de l'université Paris X Nanterre*, (53):103–119.

Nicolas Hiebel, Olivier Ferret, Karën Fort, and Aurélie Névéol. 2022. CLISTER : A corpus for semantic textual similarity in French clinical narratives. In *Proceedings of the Thirteenth Language Resources and Evaluation Conference*, pages 4306–4315, Marseille, France. European Language Resources Association.

Nicolas Hiebel, Bertrand Remy, Bruno Guillaume, Olivier Ferret, Aurélie Névéol, and Karen Fort. 2024. Hostomytho: A GWAP for synthetic clinical texts evaluation and annotation. In *Proceedings of the 10th Workshop on Games and Natural Language Processing @ LREC-COLING 2024*, pages 14–20, Torino, Italia. ELRA and ICCL.

Klaus Krippendorff. 2013. *Content Analysis: An Introduction to Its Methodology*. SAGE.

Cvetana Krstev and Agata Savary. 2017. Games on Multiword Expressions for Community Building. *Infotheca*, 17(2):7–25.

Mathieu Lafourcade. 2007. Making people play for Lexical Acquisition with the JeuxDeMots prototype. In *SNLP'07: 7th International Symposium on Natural Language Processing*, page 7, Pattaya, Chonburi, Thailand.

Mathieu Lafourcade, Alain Joubert, and Nathalie Le Brun. 2015. *Games with a Purpose (GWAPS)*. John Wiley & Sons.

Béatrice Lamiroy. 2008. Le figement: à la recherche d'une définition. *ZFSL, Zeitschrift für französische Sprache und Literatur*, 36:85–99.

Aude Lecler. 2006. Le défigement : un nouvel indicateur des marques du figement ? *Cahiers de praxématique*, (46).

Chris Madge, Richard Bartle, Jon Chamberlain, Udo Kruschwitz, and Massimo Poesio. 2019. Making text annotation fun with a clicker game. In *Proceedings of the 14th International Conference on the Foundations of Digital Games*, FDG '19, New York, NY, USA. Association for Computing Machinery.

Salah Mejri. 2013. Figement et défigement : problématique théorique. *Pratiques. Linguistique, littérature, didactique*, (159-160):79–97. 3 citations (Crossref) [2023-11-09] 2 citations (Semantic Scholar/DOI) [2022-11-15] Number: 159-160 Publisher: Association CRESEF.

Tristan Miller, Christian Hempelmann, and Iryna Gurevych. 2017. SemEval-2017 task 7: Detection and interpretation of English puns. In *Proceedings of the 11th International Workshop on Semantic Evaluation (SemEval-2017)*, pages 58–68, Vancouver, Canada. Association for Computational Linguistics.

Claire Nédellec, Philippe Bessières, Robert R. Bossy, Alain Kotoujansky, and Alain-Pierre Manine. 2006. Annotation guidelines for machine learning-based named entity recognition in microbiology. In *Proceeding of Data and Text Mining for Integrative Biology Workshop 17. European Conference on Machine Learning 10. European Conference on Principles and Practice of Knowledge Discovery in Databases*, Workshop on data and text mining for integrative biology, Berlin, Germany. Springer - Verlag. ON LINE.

Geoffrey Nunberg, Ivan A. Sag, and Thomas Wasow. 1994. Idioms. *Language*, 70:491–538.

Alan Scott Partington. 2009. A linguistic account of wordplay: The lexical grammar of punning. *Journal of Pragmatics*, 41(9):1794–1809.

Carlos Ramisch, Silvio Cordeiro, Leonardo Zilio, Marco Idiart, and Aline Villavicencio. 2016. How Naked is the Naked Truth? A Multilingual Lexicon of Nominal Compound Compositionality. In *Proceedings of the 54th Annual Meeting of the Association for Computational Linguistics (Volume 2: Short Papers)*, pages 156–161, Berlin, Germany. Association for Computational Linguistics.

Ivan A. Sag, Timothy Baldwin, Francis Bond, Ann Copestake, and Dan Flickinger. 2002. Multiword Expressions: A Pain in the Neck for NLP. In *Computational Linguistics and Intelligent Text Processing*, Lecture Notes in Computer Science, pages 1–15, Berlin, Heidelberg. Springer.

Agata Savary, Silvio Cordeiro, and Carlos Ramisch. 2019. Without lexicons, multiword expression identification will never fly: A position statement. In *Proceedings of the Joint Workshop on Multiword Expressions and WordNet (MWE-WN 2019)*, pages 79–91, Florence, Italy. Association for Computational Linguistics.

Agata Savary, Carlos Ramisch, Silvio Cordeiro, Federico Sangati, Veronika Vincze, Behrang QasemiZadeh, Marie Candito, Fabienne Cap, Voula Giouli, Ivelina Stoyanova, and Antoine Doucet. 2017. The PARSEME Shared Task on Automatic Identification of Verbal Multiword Expressions. In *Proceedings of the 13th Workshop on Multiword Expressions (MWE 2017)*, pages 31–47, Valencia, Spain. Association for Computational Linguistics.

Alessandro Valitutti, Hannu Toivonen, Antoine Doucet, and Jukka M Toivanen. 2013. "let everything turn well in your wife": generation of adult humor using lexical constraints. In *Proceedings of the 51st Annual Meeting of the Association for Computational Linguistics (Volume 2: Short Papers)*, pages 243–248.

A Appendix

Table 5 shows the number of tweets of the FRUIT corpus filtered at each step. Figure 6 shows the confusion matrices obtained at the end of our manual annotation task. We discuss several aspects regarding our methodology for building the FRUIT corpus in Section A.1. In Section A.2, we further describe our GWAP.

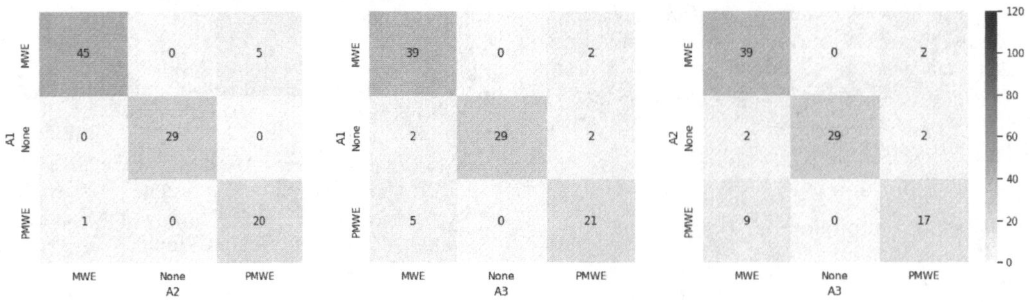

Figure 6: Confusion matrix for each annotation pair for the 300 tweets annotated in common by the 3 annotators.

	Initial	< 50 %	Dup.	By seeds
Filtered	/	3,268,394	15,381	20,244
Total	3,369,636	101,242	85,861	60,617

Table 5: Statistics on each filtering step. **< 50 %** corresponds to the number of tweets with less than 50 % of the words of their *seed*, **Dup.** to filtered duplicate tweets and **By seeds** to tweets filtered according to their *seed*.

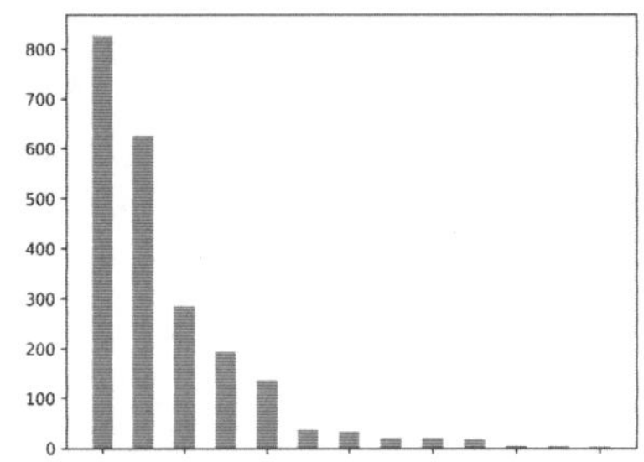

Figure 7: Number of annotations produced by each player.

A.1 Corpus Building Details

Each query made on Twitter consisted of one of our MWEs. We queried Twitter daily, issuing one query per MWE. Among the returned tweets, we only retained those that contained more than half of the words in the corresponding MWE, filtering out the rest.

These MWEs were primarily selected for their conventional nature, which mean that they must remain recognisable to a broad audience. We adopt a broad definition of MWE, encompassing verbal MWEs, phrasemes, collocations, idioms, and even citations, especially well-known ones, as they tend to be conventionalised. For example, we consider a citation such as "*travailler plus pour gagner plus*" a MWE because (i) it is conventionalised, and (ii) it carries an additional meaning, making it somewhat non-compositional. This particular citation, used by Nicolas Sarkozy in 2007, is now often referenced satirically as a symbol of capitalism.

To compute similarity scores, we vectorised each candidate and seed expression using the TFIDFVECTORIZER feature from the SCIKIT-LEARN library. We used word bigrams and trigrams. This process was repeated across multiple linguistic representation layers obtained with the SPACY library, incorporating POS tags and lemmas in addition to tokens.

A.2 Annotation Tasks Details

We take into account the fact that the FRUIT corpus is imbalanced (86.51 % of the tweets were found with the top 10 first *seeds*) when creating our annotation samples. For the manual annotation task, each sample was created using a maximum of 5 tweets related to the same *seed* to ensure diversity. For our GWAP, we limited to 500 the maximum number of tweets for a *seed*, randomly selecting 500 tweets if a *seed* has more than this number. We plan to add more tweets over time.

Figure 9 summarises the annotation process we implemented in our GWAP. Figure 7 shows the number of annotations made by each player, while Figure 8 shows the top four players in our ranking system. More annotations were made during the redaction of this paper, which is why the scores shown here are higher than the number of annotated tweets we indicate. Table 6 contains every tweet used for the training phase of our GWAP, alongside with the consensus annotation made during the manual annotation task. We also show our control tweets in Table 7, Table 8 and Table 9.

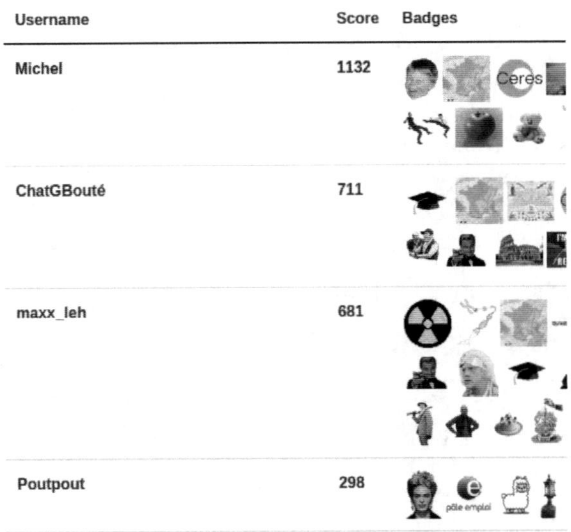

Username	Score	Badges
Michel	1132	
ChatGBouté	711	
maxx_leh	681	
Poutpout	298	

Figure 8: Top 4 players in our ranking.

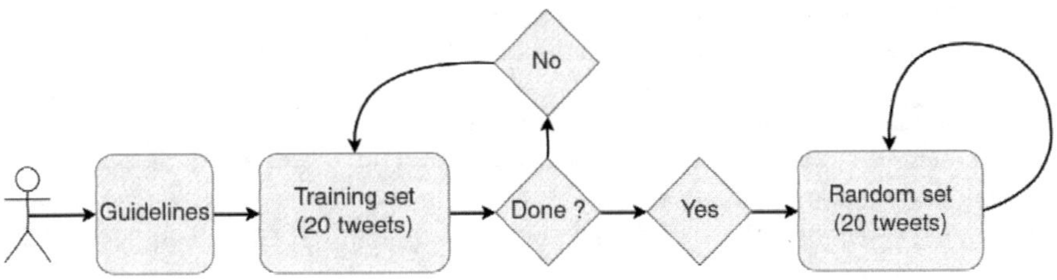

Figure 9: Summary of the annotation process we implemented in our GWAP.

Tweet	MWE	PMWE
« Pourquoi ils n'ont pas de programme ? Parce que le programme de Giscard et de Macron c'est le même : **travailler plus pour même plus gagner plus** et réduire les impôts des riches. Ca fait 50 ans qu'il existe ce programme, vaut mieux pas qu'il l'énonce ! » https://t.co/m28301zbZJ	+	+
@utilisateur @utilisateur **Travailler plus pour gagner moins** !!!	+	+
@utilisateur Sans oublier qu'il s'agit de salariés ayant un niveau de vie "confortable" (euphémisme) sans difficultés à boucler leurs fins de mois, donc absolument pas motivés à "**travailler plus pour gagner autant**".	+	+
@utilisateur **C'est le deuxième effet covid**	+	+
@utilisateur_Danaos C'était peut être pas son intention mais c'est le résultat. Le deuxième effet étant une réserve de voix au second tour ...	-	-
@utilisateur Mais ouiiii, **ca coule d'eau de source mdr**	+	+
@utilisateur ça coule de source après donc bon	+	-
Tant qu'il y a de l'amour il y a de la vie! https://t.co/AU0mrWeGJa	+	+
J'aime mon pays France mondial j'aime la planète Terre l'eau le vent le gel le froid le soleil la lune la nuit l'hiver l'été l'automne et le printemps quand je vois tout cela **tant qu'il y a la vie il y a de l'amour il y a de l'espoir** j'aime la planète Terre	+	+
Travailler pour plus tard la gâter c'est mon objectif	-	-
@utilisateur **Casse toi en Espagne pauvre con**	+	+
@utilisateur_pic @utilisateur Et pour compléter, tous les profs du secondaire ne l'ont pas mais tous font de l'orientation etc. Alors oui c'est injuste. Mais ce que tu décris ce sont des missions liées à des primes. **Travailler plus pour gagner à peine plus** n'était pas le sujet initial. Bonne journée.	+	+
La question, elle est vite et parfaitement répondue ce samedi par Eric Neuhoff (qui a regardé les #Cesar2021 jusqu'au bout, lui...) sur le site du @utilisateur_Figaro. C'est oui. https://t.co/10cBkZXMFe	+	+
@utilisateur C'était un beau pays la France. Mais elle n'est plus. Plus aucune valeur, plus rien. Le combat de certains derniers irréductibles est vain, perdu d'avance. **Égalité , fraternité , liberté=confiné**.	+	+
@utilisateur__anton Nn toi en ce moment tu fais l'aigri, **ma France tu l'aimes ou tu l'as quittes** fin .	+	+
Mohamed SALAH **que la force de l'Égypte Antique soit avec toi** Ouvre le chapitre vengeance face au RÉAL MADRID https://t.co/Pp9trT29WF	+	+
@utilisateur **Que la Force (du Droit) soit avec toi** alors ! En souhaitant qu'en plus vous trouviez un meilleur appart' !	+	+
@utilisateur @utilisateur @utilisateur Mais bon faire autrement ce serait discriminatoire... . Le patriarcat... C'est fini ou pas ? A un moment faut prendre position ! **Le beurre l'argent du beurre et les glawis du crémier**... Ca va 5mn!	+	+
@utilisateur @utilisateur @utilisateur_ alors là Maurice tu pousses le bouchon un peu trop loin	+	-
@utilisateur Ce dossier survient au plus mauvais moment pour Emmanuel Macron dans la mesure où celui-ci fournit des armes de destruction massive à son(a) futur(e) adversaire du second tour. L'épilogue de ce scrutin présidentiel devient désormais indécis.	+	-

Table 6: Training tweets given to our players, with the consensus annotations from the manual annotation phase. We highlight PMWEs in bold and underline MWEs.

Tweet	MWE	PMWE
Allez on inaugure ces perles en beauté ! **Que la force d'Apoula Edel soit avec toi** champion https://t.co/xkpU2JOAtm	oui	oui
@utilisateur_blond Regard au delà doit porter, **que la force de découverte avec toi, soit**	oui	oui
@utilisateur aller ryzeuh **que la force du cookie monster soit avec toi**	oui	oui
Rien ne les obligent a travailler a la SNCF. Il y a plein de jobs ouverts pour lequels les horaires sont plus souples. Vous voulez **la vache, le lait, le beurre et l'argent de la cremiere**. Ne plus céder aux methodes marxistes de la CGT, c'est la seule solution. https://t.co/iu01c3VOFG	oui	oui
@utilisateur_BLITZERS Ils font le tour du monde en ce moment ou quoi ? J'ai raté un épisode ?	non	non
@utilisateur_Lol Maurice tu pousses le bouchon un peu trop loin	oui	non
@utilisateur Là j'avoue tu pousses le bouchon un petit peu trop loin Maurice!	oui	non
@utilisateur **Jean tu pousses le bouchon un peu trop loin et T es pas Maurice**	oui	oui
@utilisateur **C'est le deuxième effet coupe du monde**	oui	oui
@utilisateur C'est le deuxième effet kiss cool	oui	non
@utilisateur **C'est le deuxième effet qui se coule** de la politique de Biden: balkaniser l'UE quand les victimes de l'ultra libéralisme vont commencer à être déstabilisés donc livrés aux mafias!	oui	oui
Il y a bien longtemps, dans une galaxie très lointaine… @utilisateur_LiT_Sand	oui	non
Il y a bien longtemps, dans une galaxie très lointaine…	oui	non
La question est vite répondue : le public vote à l'unanimité pour @utilisateur. https://t.co/c33004Zyuk	oui	non
@utilisateur Pour **gagner plus et travailler moins** pardi. Ça ne va pas aider les gens à trouver facilement un médecin.	oui	oui
@utilisateur **C'est le deuxième effet grumpy** lol	oui	oui
C'est plus le deuxième effet kisscool, **c'est le deuxième effet médiapart**: y a toujours une deuxième révélation après la première pour enfoncer le clou https://t.co/4ZAHfWRQEK	oui	oui
La vie n'essaie pas de la prévoir La vie c'est la pluie, le beau temps C'est une larme, des souvenirs Des espoirs de l'amour C'est un sourire a tes lèvres. https://t.co/zqGRxkrX8m	non	non
@utilisateur **Que la force du #digital soit avec toi** ! https://t.co/4BOoO2Qlgj	oui	oui
@_clemparker_ **Que la fibre.. euuuh la force soit avec toi**..! Et là-bas, tu auras un nouveau chez toi.	oui	oui
Il y aura deux grands choix de société en 2022 : **travailler plus pour gagner pareil** ou **travailler moins pour gagner pareil**. Les innombrables candidats se répartissent dans ces deux catégories. #Presidentielle2022 https://t.co/28M1LA1WnA	oui	oui
@utilisateur @utilisateur @utilisateur @utilisateur Ah oui si on est contre une immigration non contrôlée on est raciste. Je m'en fout de la couleur de peau ou de la provenance des immigrés. Ce que je souhaite c'est préserver notre mode et niveau de vie. **On ne peut pas et ne veut pas accueillir toute la misère du monde**!	oui	oui

Table 7: Control tweets given to our players, with the consensus annotations from the manual annotation phase. We highlight PMWEs in bold and underline MWEs.

Tweet	MWE	PMWE
Tu préfères être suivi(e) par Christine Lagarde dans ton sommeil comme une personne de basse classe sociale ou bien épiler des maîtres chiens à chaque fois que tu rencontres une nouvelle personne ? Moi je pense la question elle est vite répondue. Bisous.	oui	non
@utilisateur_Opin @utilisateur L'ourse est morte à cause d'un type venu chez elle, armé jusqu'aux dents et avec l'intention de tuer. Pour moi la question est vite répondue !	oui	non
TRAVAILLER PLUS POUR GAGNER MOINS L'accord pour la modernisation des ressources humaines de la police nationale 2022/2027 signé par les syndicats « maison » est historique... POUR LA 1RE FOIS ILS ONT ACTÉ LA FUTURE BAISSE DE SALAIRE ! Lire en ligne https://t.co/P3BMuAp1Xp https://t.co/jz2YdfDZ2n	oui	oui
Nous ne sommes pas les seuls êtres vivants sur terre. Quand nous gérons mal nos déchets, c'est les animaux qui en souffrent ! #StopPollution https://t.co/Jq2oqHTuQo	non	non
@utilisateur Et nous ne sommes pas les seuls, j'en suis convaincu...	non	non
@utilisateur @utilisateur @utilisateur @utilisateur La thrombose c'est la protéine Spike en revanche. L'oxyde de graphène c'est pour plus tard, c'est le deuxième effet kiss cool. Bon rétablissement à lui	oui	non
@utilisateur Ça coule de source hehe	oui	non
@utilisateur Çà coule de source	oui	non
@utilisateur Comment faire pour discréditer une personne, et bien tous les coups sont permis. Pauvre France, c'est ça qu'on appelle liberté, égalité, fraternité. Vive Reconquête, vive Eric Zemmour et vive la France	oui	non
@utilisateur @utilisateur_Danaos @utilisateur On se connait ? Non. Alors faut s'en tenir à ce que vous connaissez. Dès le moment où on avoue que tous les coups sont permis car "c'est la campagne" vous discréditez le politique. Un cirque. Pas plus. Et tout ce qui sera dit pourra être remis en cause à travers ce prisme.	oui	non
@utilisateur_morel Ces gens utilisent un vocabulaire complexe qui demande d'avoir étudié et pratiqué. Mais là l'éducation qu'ils ont reçue ne semble pas soutenue par de l'intelligence. On a donné de la confiture aux cochons...	oui	non
@utilisateur_Desouche @utilisateur Bravo pour l'initiative de toute façon c'est donner de la confiture à des cochons quand on voit ce qu'ils font des quartiers, dommage car il y'a certainement des gens bien qui vont en pâtir à cause de ces raclures	oui	non
@utilisateur_ Non tkt ça va aller on y croit que la force soit avec toi	oui	non
@utilisateur_Ringo Ouai enfin tu comprends rien visiblement x) Pas grave, bonne journée mon brave et que la force soit avec toi	oui	non
Le plus grand chagrin d'amour c'est quand la mort s'en mêle. Tant qu'il y a la vie, il y a de l'espoir. As long as you live, fight for what you love	oui	non
Je ne sais pas ce qu'il reste de ces 3 mots : Liberté, égalité et fraternité !	oui	non
@utilisateur **Travailler moins pour gagner plus** donc voilà votre solution ? heureusement vous serez jamais au pouvoir	oui	oui
@utilisateur @utilisateur Il m'est arrivé la même chose ; nous ne sommes pas les seuls, malheureusement... de plus en plus de censure !!!	non	non
Ça va coulé de source #adp2020 https://t.co/nRga33whi6	oui	non
@_NdRoussel @utilisateur_steiger Ça fait grave penser à "la France tu l'aimes ou tu la quitte" de Sarko. Y'a des moods chelou au PCF en ce moment.	oui	non

Table 8: Control tweets given to our players, with the consensus annotations from the manual annotation phase. We highlight PMWEs in bold and underline MWEs.

Tweet	MWE	PMWE
@utilisateur Euh je ne trouve pas c'est un tweet qui reflète malheureusement une triste réalité. Mais bon Zazou tu dois faire partie de ces gens qui pensent que l'**on peut et doit accueillir toute la misère du monde**. J'ai hâte qu'ils frappent à ta porte	oui	oui
En "douce France de l'omerta", n'aurais été victime d'agressions crapuleuses, frappes répétées, LGBTI Phobies caractérisées homophobes, d'humiliation, d'harcèlement & bénéficié d'aucune hospitalisation! **Liberté égalité dignité fraternité justice**?! > https://t.co/Q6C6cb5ihd https://t.co/2tAz9NA6Kt	oui	oui
@utilisateur_C_O_N_S **Tu pousses le bouchon un peu trop loin Farid pour ne pas t'appeler Maurice** grrrrrr	oui	oui
@utilisateur Le mec a peur que les grands méchants patrons utilisent le pied dans la porte pour faire travailler les pauvres employés plus, mais diminuer les salaires unilatéralement par le saccage monétaire c'est OK	non	non
@utilisateur @utilisateur_liberal On est en train de toujours s'occuper à travailler plus pour l'occupation et l'agitation de nos démarches au niveau de. Point.	non	non
@utilisateur **c'est le deuxième effet du décolleté d'hier**? (soignes toi bien)	oui	oui
@utilisateur @utilisateur @utilisateur @utilisateur_ Bonne chance ! **Que la force d'Eren soit avec toi**	oui	oui
Bon vent @utilisateur. **Que la force du panda soit avec toi**. https://t.co/AAAPfSJTKd	oui	oui
@utilisateur Merci pour l'info et **que la Force de guérir soit avec toi** !	oui	oui
@utilisateur_ghostz @utilisateur **À défaut de la Force, que la chance soit avec toi** @utilisateur Comme on dit: Fingers crossed	oui	oui
@utilisateur_canna Looooool **que la force de la weed soit avec toi** !	oui	oui
@utilisateur_ "Alors, tu préfères **le beurre, l'argent du beurre ou le cul de la crémière** ? Pour moi, la question elle est vite répondue" https://t.co/CgyZcXgKMj	oui	oui
@utilisateur On ne sait pas mais **peut on encore se permettre d'accueillir toute la misère du monde ?**	oui	oui
@utilisateur Hé **Maurice macron tu pousses le bouchon un peu trop loin** tout va te péter à la G.... (en 6 lettres) Achtung achtung ... Pour que cette folie s'arrête je sais ce qu'il faut faire mais j'vous l'dirai pas ou du moins pas tout suite ! Tout arrive à celui qui sait attendre ...	oui	oui
J'ai encore lu que Macron veut «augmenter les profs qui travailleront plus». Ça a été dit 100 fois mais rappelons quand même que çá n'a aucun sens. Une augmentation c'est **gagner plus sans travailler plus**. **Gagner plus en travaillant plus** c'est juste normal.	oui	oui
@utilisateur, Conseiller Regional @utilisateur, soutient les salarié•es de #BREGAMS en lutte contre un Accord de Performance Collective (APC) qui les fait **travailler plus pour gagner beaucoup moins**! https://t.co/19ANl3MAZo https://t.co/kfalDVFJRE	oui	oui
@utilisateur @utilisateur @utilisateur Ça nous coûtera notre maison et tout nos biens, même nos enfants et notre corps, quand il faudra payer l'addition de l'argent magique dans quelques années. C'est le deuxième effet kisscool, le plan pour installer une société comme en Chine et justifier l'injustifiable.	oui	non
@utilisateur **C'est le deuxième effet du coup de coeur vaccin**	oui	oui
@utilisateur_Stream **Que la force du requin soit avec toi**	oui	oui
@utilisateur **Que la force de l'amour soit avec toi** pour vaincre cette saloperie !	oui	oui

Table 9: Control tweets given to our players, with the consensus annotations from the manual annotation phase. We highlight PMWEs in bold and underline MWEs.

Tweet	MWE	PMWE
@utilisateur **Que la (Tri)force soit avec toi** !	oui	oui
@utilisateur_philippot Gros con qui se la joue plus français que tout le monde. La devise c'est liberté, égalité, fraternité. Le reste n'est pas français. Traître.	non	non
@utilisateur_dufour Ils se vengent de votre position. Assumez	non	non
@utilisateur_trading @utilisateur @utilisateur @utilisateur Vous n'avez toujours pas compris que votre position est nauséabonde parce qu'elle se défile/cache derrière une notion juridique qui n'a pas de sens d'être utilisée, au lieu de tout simplement assumer le fait de dire "je ne crois pas les victimes". Dites le, allez, assumez un peu.	non	non
jusqu'ici tout va bien	oui	non
@utilisateur Et ces gens qui soutiennent Macron vont eux-aussi impactés par cette **politique de destruction massive** du modèle économique et social issu du CNR, des idéaux républicains etc.	oui	oui
@utilisateur_1ere Mais qu'attendent donc la #NUPES et toutes ces **ONG de destruction massive** pour enfin revendiquer le droit de cuissage, ou une dotation de quelques vierges, pour tout migrant illégal qui arriverait en #France? Un accueil digne pour ces pauvres gens, serait la moindre des choses.	oui	oui
Terrible !Ces gens là sont nos pires ennemis : cette oligarchie mondialiste qui se trouve dans tous ces pays qui ont participé à cette mascarade criminelle. Ceux-ci ont utilisé les pays à leur solde comme **instrument de destruction massive** contre les peuples d'y trouvant:tromperie https://t.co/7G5U6x8QXP	oui	oui
NOUVEAUTE / Sinaïve, Dasein EP (Buddy Records) / Reprise Party (Langue Pendue) **Il y a bien longtemps, dans une très petite galaxie fort lointaine**, nous nous battions au sujet de l'usage de la langue française dans un contexte noisy pop. Par @utilisateur https://t.co/e4QHjnWGqS	oui	oui
Rappel : la seule "nouvelle mission" qui intéresse Macron sera les remplacements bouche-trous. Soit, compte tenu de l'inflation, **travailler plus pour gagner aussi peu qu'avant**. Et ça passera, parce que la profession est désormais dépolitisée. #Cassandre https://t.co/GSwCFTlZgX	oui	oui
@utilisateur_morel Cette photo montre aussi, qu'hormis la petite foule de "journalistes" qui se pressent autour de la Raclure néo nazie, la salle, qu'on aperçoit à l'arrière plan, est déserte Ça, **c'est le deuxième effet "grand angle"**	oui	oui
@utilisateur_man_one **Le futur est déjà derrière nous**	oui	oui
@utilisateur_delb Putain mais j'ai honte pour lui... **À genoux en rampant devant les racistes pseudo-damnés de la terre**	oui	oui
@utilisateur Mes excuses et courage ! **Que la force des dieux soit avec toi** toujours en ta faveur ! https://t.co/fFDyUl75Sc	oui	oui
Go mon #Bilou ! **Que la force du champs de lin soit avec toi** ! @utilisateur @utilisateur @utilisateur @utilisateur https://t.co/LONjqVzRRi	oui	oui
On ne peut pas et accueillir toute la misère du monde en prendre soin à grands coups de milliards et s'occuper de nos bébés placés qui EUX sont notre futur. L'État a clairement fait son choix! https://t.co/bbDFXivU26	oui	non
@utilisateur **Président momo "Maurice" tu pousses le bouchon un peu trop loin** et Il n'y a pas de musulmans modérés.	oui	oui
@utilisateur Qui a été formé à Bordeaux, joue en principauté et sera le futur joueur du PSG ? La question elle est vite repondue	oui	non

Table 10: Control tweets given to our players, with the consensus annotations from the manual annotation phase. We highlight PMWEs in bold and underline MWEs.

Another Approach to Agreement Measurement and Prediction with Emotion Annotations

Quanqi Du, Véronique Hoste
LT3, Language and Translation Technology Team, Ghent University, Belgium
Groot-Brittanniëlaan 45, 9000 Ghent, Belgium
firstname.lastname@ugent.be

Abstract

Emotion annotation, as an inherently subjective task, often suffers from significant inter-annotator disagreement when evaluated using traditional metrics like kappa or alpha. These metrics often fall short of capturing the nuanced nature of disagreement, especially in multimodal settings. This study introduces Absolute Annotation Difference (AAD), a novel metric offering a complementary perspective on inter- and intra-annotator agreement across different modalities. Our analysis reveals that AAD not only identifies overall agreement levels but also uncovers fine-grained disagreement patterns across modalities often overlooked by conventional metrics. Furthermore, we propose an AAD-based RMSE variant for predicting annotation disagreement. Through extensive experiments on the large-scale DynaSent corpus, we demonstrate that our approach significantly improves disagreement prediction accuracy, rising from 41.71% to 51.64% and outperforming existing methods. Cross-dataset prediction results suggest good generalization. These findings underscore AAD's potential to enhance annotation agreement analysis and provide deeper insights into subjective NLP tasks. Future work will investigate its applicability to broader emotion-related tasks and other subjective annotation scenarios.

1 Introduction

Despite the significant progress in multi-modal NLP (Garg et al., 2022), such as GPT-4o[1], accurately recognizing and interpreting human emotions across different modalities (Zhang et al., 2024) remains a substantial challenge. This difficulty primarily arises from the complexity and variability of emotional expressions (Lindquist and Barrett, 2008; Barrett, 2009), which often manifest themselves differently across modalities. Consequently, there is a growing demand for fine-grained and reliable datasets to support the training and evaluation of emotion recognition systems (Yang et al., 2023; Ridley et al., 2024).

As a common and popular practice, the use of evaluation metrics like the kappa/alpha family has almost become a standard step in dataset construction (Zhao et al., 2018). However, even with careful dataset design, many annotated (multimodal) emotion datasets exhibit low kappa/alpha scores (Busso et al., 2008, 2016; Zadeh et al., 2018; Zhao et al., 2022; Du et al., 2025), and few studies have explored the reason behind these low scores. Given that the interpretation of kappa/alpha values can be significantly influenced by factors such as the numbers of annotators and categories(Antoine et al., 2014), and considering the inherently subjective nature of emotion annotation (Chou et al., 2024; Plaza-del Arco et al., 2024; Maladry et al., 2024), we propose the complementary use of the Absolute Annotation Difference (AAD) as an intuitive metric to better measure and examine agreement and disagreement patterns, particularly in datasets with low kappa/alpha scores.

To validate this proposal, we conducted two experiments. The first is a pilot study on a small multimodal emotion dataset, where (dis)agreement was assessed using both kappa/alpha and AAD. The findings suggest that AAD provides a distinct perspective on (dis)agreement and effectively uncovers annotation patterns. Building on these insights, the second experiment applied AAD to (dis)agreement modelling and prediction, achieving an accuracy improvement of nearly 10%. Together, these experiments highlight the added value of AAD in enhancing the analysis and prediction of (dis)agreement in emotion annotation tasks.

By offering a complementary view to conventional metrics, our work contributes to a more nuanced understanding of annotation reliability. We hope this research can inspire further methodological innovation in dataset evaluation and design.

[1]https://openai.com/index/hello-gpt-4o/

Proceedings of the 19th Linguistic Annotation Workshop (LAW-XIX-2025), pages 87–102
July 31, 2025

2 Related Work

Many tasks in natural language processing and computer vision sometimes suffer from disagreement (Basile, 2020; Uma et al., 2021; Mostafazadeh Davani et al., 2022), as they involve tasks (e.g. emotion detection, hate speech detection) which are difficult to define and influenced by an annotator's cultural, social, ethnic, and other backgrounds. In addition, annotation differences might also just be caused by attention slips (Beigman Klebanov et al., 2008). In their survey paper, Uma et al. (2021) identified several sources of disagreement, including annotator errors, annotation schemes, ambiguity, subjectivity and item difficulty. Although disagreement is sometimes undesirable, there are also scholars embracing disagreement and proposing to preserve disagreement as different perspectives to the same stimuli (Akhtar et al., 2020; Plepi et al., 2022; Cabitza et al., 2023).

2.1 Disagreement Measurement

Irrespective of the provenance of this disagreement, annotation disagreement is usually measured with statistical approaches, such as Cohen's kappa (1960), Fleiss' kappa (1971) or Krippendorff's alpha (2007). According to Landis and Koch (1977), for categorical data, kappa values smaller than 0 are regarded as poor agreement, and these values can increase from slight (0.01 to 0.20), fair (0.21 to 0.40), moderate (0.41 to 0.60) and substantial agreement (0.61 to 0.80), up until 0.81 to 1.00 as almost perfect agreement. Kappa is usually used for categorical ratings, while Krippendorff's alpha is more adaptive with different levels of measurement (Stevens, 1946), able to measure agreement in nominal, ordinal, interval and ratio data (Krippendorff, 2011). As for Krippendorff's alpha, it is suggested to rely on data when the alpha is greater than 0.8, discard data when the alpha is smaller than 0.667, and only draw tentative conclusions when the alpha is in-between (Krippendorff, 2004).

Although the use of such metrics has become the de facto standard for agreement measurement – offering a single, comprehensive score to summarize overall agreement across a dataset – these metrics have notable shortcomings. For Kappa, the primary concerns are the prevalence problem and the bias problem (Di Eugenio and Glass, 2004), two major paradoxes that complicate its interpretation (Wang and Xia, 2019). Specifically, kappa values fluctuate significantly when category distributions are imbalanced or when annotators favour certain categories. Similarly, Krippendorff's alpha is not only affected by skewed category distributions but it is also highly sensitive to the choice of distance function and levels of measurement (Krippendorff, 2011).

In emotion annotation tasks, these limitations are even more pronounced. Emotion datasets often exhibit a natural skew toward more frequently used categories (Zadeh et al., 2018), and defining the appropriate levels of measurement for emotion annotations poses additional challenges. Emotions are commonly annotated using both categorical and dimensional labels (Busso et al., 2016; Labat et al., 2024), which can be interconverted under specific conditions(Park et al., 2021). While Antoine et al. (2014) advocate for the use of weighted Krippendorff's alpha as a more reliable metric for ordinal annotations, achieving the commonly accepted threshold of 0.667 (Landis and Koch, 1977) in emotion annotation remains elusive in empirical studies (Antoine et al., 2014; Wood et al., 2018). This difficulty has led to increased scrutiny of these metrics, particularly in subjective domains such as emotion annotation, where the interpretation of scores often comes into question(Wong et al., 2021).

To address these challenges, we propose the use of the intuitive Absolute Annotation Difference (AAD) method as a complementary approach to measure agreement and examine (dis)agreement patterns in emotion annotation tasks. As the name suggests, AAD refers to the absolute difference between two or more sets of annotations. For dimensional annotations, AAD can be straightforwardly calculated as the absolute difference between two annotations, which can be formulated as

$$D^i = |x_i - y_i|, \quad i \in \mathcal{M} \tag{1}$$

whereby x_i and y_i represent the assigned dimensional labels (i.e., valence values) respectively for the instance i in the dataset $\mathcal{M}$. For categorical annotations, we propose converting them into two- or multi-dimensional representations and computing Euclidean differences, as suggested by Antoine et al. (2014). For example, when categorical annotations are projected into the valence-arousal space, the absolute difference will be formulated as

$$D^i = \sqrt{(x_{i1} - x_{i2})^2 + (y_{i1} - y_{i2})^2}, \quad i \in \mathcal{M} \tag{2}$$

whereby x_{i1} and x_{i2} correspond to the projected valence values and y_{i1} and y_{i2} denote the projected arousal values for the instance i in the dataset $\mathcal{M}$, respectively. This ADD approach offers another perspective on agreement and provides deeper insights into (dis)agreement patterns, particularly in datasets with low kappa or alpha scores.

2.2 Disagreement Prediction

In addition to measuring agreement after emotion annotation, an equally compelling question is whether, and to what extent, it is possible to predict disagreement before the annotation process. While previous studies have focused on predicting individual annotators' ratings or the label distributions within a group (Fleisig et al., 2023; Weerasooriya et al., 2023), these approaches address disagreement only indirectly. To the best of our knowledge, direct disagreement prediction has been explored in only one prior study, specifically on sentiment analysis, conducted by Wan et al. (2023).

In their work, Wan et al. (2023) fine-tuned a RoBERTa model (Liu et al., 2019) on the DynaSent dataset (Potts et al., 2021) to predict disagreement using both binary disagreement labels and continuous disagreement rates. Additionally, they incorporated demographic information, such as age, gender, and ethnicity, to enhance the model's predictive performance. However, the inclusion of demographic data raises significant concerns related to annotator privacy and the potential for misrepresentation or underrepresentation of diverse social values and opinions (Weerasooriya et al., 2023).

We propose an alternative approach that leverages AAD to quantify disagreement and predict annotator disagreement based solely on textual features within the task, without relying on additional demographic information. This approach ensures privacy preservation and avoids biases associated with demographic-based selection, while providing an effective framework for disagreement prediction.

3 Data

To thoroughly investigate annotator disagreement within and across modalities and identify factors that make certain data types (textual, audio, silent video, or multimodal) challenging to annotate, we designed a two-session annotation study.

In the first session, four annotators independently annotated a small dataset across four modality setups: text, audio, silent video, and multimodal, providing distinct sets of annotations for each modality to assess inter-annotator agreement.

In the second session, one annotator re-annotated the dataset twice – 114 and 290 days later. These additional annotations enabled intra-annotator agreement analysis by comparing the three sets over time. The annotator reported vaguely remembering the content of some instances but stated not to have a recollection of the previous annotations.

Data collection and annotators Following Du et al. (2025), we use a subset of their Unic dataset, consisting of 94 YouTube video clips featuring authentic emotional expressions, unlike the exaggerated portrayals common in movies or TV series. Each video clip spans about 10 seconds, which was deemed sufficient in preliminary tests for identifying emotional states across modalities (Du et al., 2025). Four annotators (two male, two female college students proficient in English) participated after training on the annotation method and tools, ensuring consistent and informed annotations.

Annotation method All 94 video clips were annotated across three separate modalities – text, audio, and silent video – and also received a holistic multimodal emotion annotation. To capture emotional states as comprehensively as possible, both categorical and dimensional approaches were employed. For the categorical framework, we adopted the same labels as Du et al. (2025): *disgust*, *disappointment*, *confusion*, *surprise*, *contentment*, *joy*, and *neutral*. These categories were curated by clustering a larger set of emotions to reduce potential noise. For example, *love* is grouped under *joy* due to its lower frequency and closely related meaning. In the dimensional framework, emotional states were rated based on *valence* and *arousal*, using a 5-point scale ranging from very negative or very calm (1) to very positive or very excited (5), respectively. The dataset is available upon request.

4 Annotation Difference Analysis

To evaluate the annotations across annotators and modalities, we performed significance tests using the four sets of annotations from the first annotation session. Chi-Square test results suggest that both the categorical and dimensional emotion annotations are significantly influenced by the modality ($p = 6.068e^{-6}$, $p = 0.002$), and the annotators ($p = 3.669e^{-25}$, $p = 2.660e^{-42}$).

		text	audio	video	all
	e_4	.32	.27	.19	.29
κ	v_4	.33	.23	.21	.27
	a_4	.04	.06	.11	.09
α	$v_4 - nominal/unweight$	.33	.23	.22	.27
	$v_4 - ordinal/weight$	.64	.48	.46	.52
	$v_4 - interval/weight$	.64	.48	.46	.52
	$v_4 - ratio/weight$	.59	.42	.38	.46
	$a_4 - nominal/unweight$	.05	. 07	.12	.09
	$a_4 - ordinal/weight$	.01	.21	.32	.23
	$a_4 - interval/weight$	.01	.17	.30	.21
	$a_4 - ratio/weight$	<.01	.08	.19	.12

Table 1: Agreement with Fleiss' kappa and Krippendorff's alpha for the 4 annotation setups and in which *all* refers to the multimodal setup. v_4, a_4,and e_4 refer to the agreement of valence, arousal and emotion across 4 annotators.

As a common practice in dataset construction, we calculated both Fleiss' kappa and (weighted) Krippendorff's alpha. For emotion and valence, the kappa results, ranging from 0.19 to 0.33, suggest low agreement in the annotations, and similarly, the Krippendorff's alpha results, ranging from 0.22 and 0.64, reflect the same conclusion. This holds true even when considering different levels of measurement (e.g., ordinal and interval, etc.) or using weighted versus unweighted approaches valence annotations. Note that in our experiments, valence is scaled as integers from 1 to 5, which can be interpreted as very negative, negative, neutral, positive and very positive, making it a hybrid of multiple data types (Stevens, 1946). Default weights were applied in the calculation across these data types. For arousal, the results indicate less agreement.

The results in Table 1, along with similarly low agreement scores from other datasets, such as $\kappa = 0.27$ in IEMOCAP (Busso et al., 2008) or $\alpha = 0.25$ in CMU-MOSEI (Zadeh et al., 2018), prompted us to further investigate emotion annotation differences in the following sections.

4.1 Inter-annotator agreement across modalities

In addition to the common agreement statistics used to evaluate inter-annotator agreement among the four annotators, we also calculated the absolute annotation difference (AAD) between each pair of annotators. This approach allowed us to gain deeper insights into the specific areas where annotators agreed or disagreed, and to investigate whether any systematicity could be identified in these disagreements.

We begin with the valence annotations. Recall that valence was annotated on a scale of 1 to 5, ranging from very negative, weakly negative, neutral, over weakly positive to very positive. A valence difference of 0 or 1 between a pair of annotators indicates that they share the same or a similar assessment of the valence of a given fragment. However, when the valence difference is 2 or greater, it suggests that annotators hold a significantly different interpretation of the polarity (i.e., weakly negative versus weakly positive, neutral versus positive) expressed in the fragment.

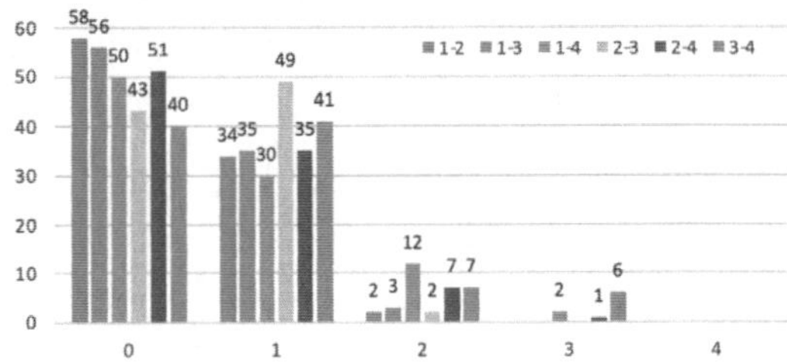

Figure 1: Absolute valence difference in texts between each pair of annotators (represented with different colours). The X-axis and Y-axis stand for valence difference and frequency respectively. Results for the other modalities are available in Figure 7 in Appendix B.

Diff	Text/%	Audio/%	Video/%	All/%
0	52.84	50.35	45.74	49.65
1	39.72	39.36	42.91	38.48
2	5.85	8.33	10.28	10.46
3	1.60	1.77	1.06	1.06
4	0.00	0.18	0.00	0.35

Table 2: Valence difference distribution in percentage across modalities, averaged from the six pairs of annotators.

As shown in Figure 1 and Table 2, the valence difference highlights (dis)agreement patterns among annotators. Figure 1 indicates that most of the valence differences between the six pairs of annotators are indeed limited to 0 or 1, with this tendency being consistent across the text, audio, video and multimodality setups. Table 2 confirms this, showing that in 52.84%, 50.35%, 45.74% and 49.65% of the text, audio, video and multimodality annotations, respectively, annotators selected the same valence score. Additionally, in around 40% of the cases, annotators chose a valence score in the nearest neighbouring category. This suggests that approximately 90% of the annotations show a strong agreement, with annotators consistently selecting the same or similar sentiment labels.

An interesting observation is that, according to

the kappa scores for valence, the agreement in the multimodal setup (0.52) is higher than in the audio setup (0.48). However, based on the results in Table 2, fewer annotators choose the same or similar labels in the multimodal setup (49.65% and 38.48%) compared to the audio setup (50.35% and 39.36%). One possible explanation is that the same or similar choices (diff = 0, 1) focus solely on agreement, whereas kappa combines both agreement and disagreement (diff > 1) into a single score. This suggests that while there is a greater degree of overall agreement in the multimodal setup, the higher kappa/alpha score may reflect less frequent or less severe disagreement compared to the audio setup.

Diff	Text/%	Audio/%	Video/%	All/%
0	33.51	37.41	41.67	35.28
1	38.65	45.39	44.50	43.44
2	22.34	15.07	13.12	18.26
3	4.96	2.13	0.71	2.84
4	0.53	0.00	0.00	0.18

Table 3: Arousal difference distribution in percentage acorss modalities, averaged from the six pairs of annotators.

Similarly, the absolute arousal differences, as presented in Table 3, suggest that annotators generally select the same or similar arousal labels with consistency. However, the frequency of identical choices is lower compared to valence.

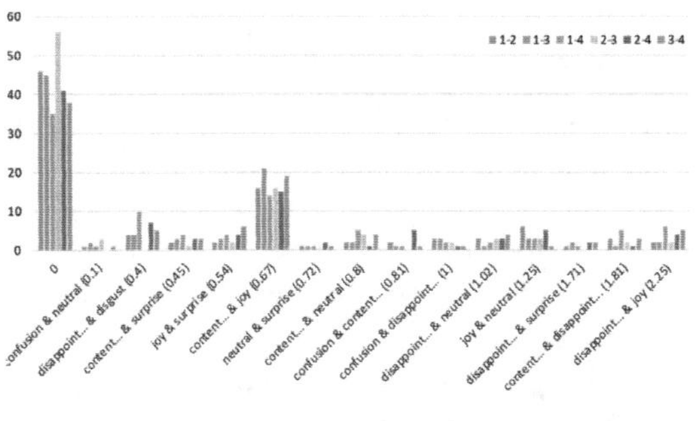

Figure 2: Emotion difference on the text modality between each pair of annotators. The X-axis and Y-axis stand for emotion (Euclidean) difference and frequency respectively. Results for the other modalities are available in Figure 8 in Appendix B.

As for the emotion annotations, we projected the different categorical emotion labels into a two-dimensional space as a vector, using their averaged valence and arousal scores (Table 8 in Appendix A). The Euclidean distance between the two vectors is the difference between two emotions. Then we plotted the distribution of emotion differences among the four annotators for the same instance.

Diff	Text/%	Audio/%	Video/%	All/%
0	46.28	44.68	35.46	43.62
0.1	1.42	0.35	1.95	2.13
0.4	5.32	1.06	2.3	5.67

Table 4: Distribution of top 3 minimum differences in percentage for different modalities, averaged from the six pairs of annotators. *Diff* stands for the absolute difference value in ascending order, ranging from 0 to 2.25.

As expected, the results in Figure 2 and Table 4 suggest a relatively high inter-annotator agreement. About 46.28%, 44.68%, 35.46% and 43.62% of the instances in the text, audio, video and multimodality setups, respectively, are annotated with identical emotions. Meanwhile, the most common confusing emotion pairs were *contentment* and *joy*, accounting for more than 10% of the instances in all modality setups. This indicates that it is more challenging to differentiate emotions with similar valence values.

Based on the results of the valence, arousal and emotion analysis across modality, we can conclude that rather than relying solely on a single and comprehensive score provided by kappa/alpha, the absolute annotation difference (AAD) reveals valuable and insightful phenomena in emotion annotation. For instance, we found that most of the disagreement occurs between labels in the nearest neighbouring categories. Specifically, for valence, confusion frequently arose between labels with the same polarity but varying intensity. In the case of emotion annotations, disagreement often stemmed from emotions with similar valence but different arousal levels.

4.2 Intra-annotator agreement across modalities

Given the complexity of emotion annotation, we also calculated the absolute valence, arousal and emotion differences between three sets of annotations from the same annotator, who annotated the same dataset 114 days and 290 days after the initial annotation. The results as shown in Figure 3 confirm our earlier insights with respect to inter-annotator agreement. However, as expected, since inter-annotator differences in cultural and emotional background were minimized, the number of instances with identical annotation between the two annotation rounds was higher.

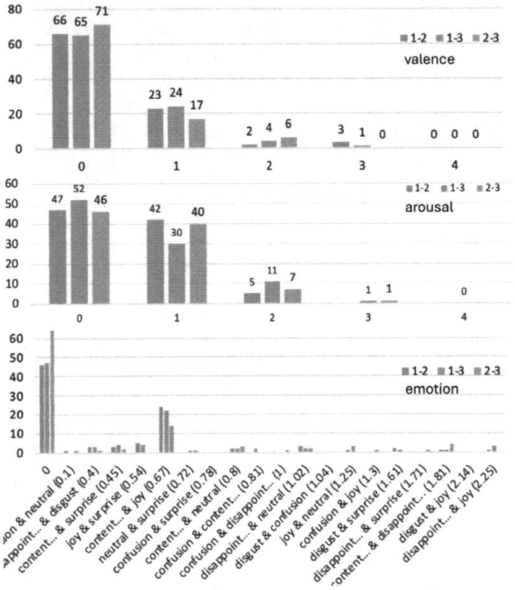

Figure 3: Absolute valence, arousal difference and emotion difference in text from three sets of annotations from the same annotator. Results of other modalities are available in Figure 9 and Figure 10 in Appendix B.

4.3 Qualitative analysis

The previous analysis focused on each modality setup individually, but it is also valuable to examine all setups together. Therefore, we further investigated the annotations with the most and least inter-annotator agreement on valence across all modality setups. This allowed us to gain a broader understanding of the patterns of (dis)agreement when considering all modalities simultaneously.

No.	text	audio	video	all
12	0,50	0,50	1,17	0,50
13	0,50	0,67	0,67	0,50
14	1,50	1,00	1,17	0,50
15	0,67	1,17	1,00	1,17
16	0,00	0,50	0,00	0,00
17	0,67	0,00	1,17	0,50
18	0,00	0,00	0,00	0,50

Figure 4: Part of the valence difference heatmap across modalities. Adequate agreement (≤ 0.5) is in blue while poor agreement (> 0.5) is in orange.

To identify the annotations with the most and least inter-annotator agreement, we first calculated the averaged valence difference score for each instance across all modality setups, ranging from 0 to 2.5, as shown in Figure 4. Since no instance has a full agreement (diff = 0) across all modality setups, we set a difference score of 0.5 (e.g. at most two annotator pairs showing a minimal annotation difference of 1) as the cut-off between adequate and poor agreement. As a result, weobserved that, 19% of the 94 instances exhibit adequate agreement across all four modality setups, 8.5% show poor agreement, while the large majority of the instances reside in between. Therefore, the top 19% (18 instances) and the bottom 8.5% (8 instances) were selected for further analysis as the high-agreement and high-disagreement annotations, respectively.

Although there is no actual gold standard annotation for the dataset, we assumed the emotion annotations obtained in the second annotation session (114 days after the first annotation) as silver standard to match the averaged valence difference score of each instance with a corresponding categorical emotion label.

With the emotion labels attached to the instances, it is found that for the 18 instances with adequate agreement in all four modality setups, only 2 negative emotion labels (two *disappointment*) appeared out of 72 labels, accounting for 2.8%. In contrast, for the 8 instances with poor agreement across all four modality setups, 12 negative emotion labels were recorded (11 *disappointment* and 1 *disgust*) out of 32 labels. This trend was also observed in the instances with adequate/poor agreement in three out of four modality setups (27 and 21 instances respectively), where the negative labels account for 22.2% and 40.5%, respectively.

This interesting finding suggests that, in our dataset, annotators tend to agree more on non-negative emotion states, but exhibit greater disagreement on negative emotions. One possible explanation for this phenomenon is that people tend to express positive emotions more openly, while they may feel less inclined to fully reveal negative emotions (Du et al., 2023).

5 Disagreement Prediction

Based on the insights from our agreement analysis, we also explored the potential of using AAD to model and predict disagreement, with the goal of identifying instances where annotators exhibit diverse interpretations, which can reveal valuable insights into the data. However, there are only a few studies on disagreement prediction, particularly concerning modalities such as audio or video. One recent research that caught our attention is the work of Wan et al. (2023) who performed disagreement prediction on a dataset of over 100,000 textual instances (Potts et al., 2021). Given the constraints of data availability and computation cost, we conducted our initial investigation on texts, taking the research of Wan et al. (2023) as a starting point.

5.1 A novel rating strategy

We began by defining and scaling disagreement, as there are varying degrees of disagreement that we intend to investigate in greater detail. In the experiment of Wan et al. (2023), labels agreed by more than half of the annotators are considered the majority labels, while labels different from the majority are viewed as minority labels without looking at the nature of the underlying label. Since 5 annotators were involved in the annotation, Wan et al. (2023) calculated their disagreement rate as the number of minority labels divided by 3, where 3 is the borderline of minority labels in case of a majority, as formulated in the following:

$$D = \frac{\frac{n_{minority}}{N_{total}}}{\frac{3}{N_{total}}} = \frac{n_{minority}}{3} \quad (3)$$

Annotation distribution	Binary label	Wan's	Ours
🙂🙂🙂😐😐	disagree	0.67	0.77
🙂🙂🙂😐☹️	disagree	0.67	1.26
🙂🙂🙂😕☹️	disagree	0.67	N/A
☹️-negative 😐-neutral 🙂-positve 😕-mixed			

Figure 5: Comparison of two disagreement rating strategies on the same annotation distributions.

For example, as shown in Figure 5, there are three sets of annotations where the majority labels share the same sentiment *positive*, but the minority labels differ. The first minority labels are both *neutral*, and while the second are *neutral* and *negative*, both sets of annotations are assigned with a disagreement rate of 0.67. Considering the fact that the distance between *positive* and *negative* is much greater than that between *positive* and *neutral*, it is not appropriate to assign them the same level of disagreement.

As an alternative to the disagreement rating method of Wan et al. (2023), we propose to utilize the information from the absolute annotation difference (AAD) to evaluate the disagreement rate. Specifically, we take a variant of the root mean square error (RMSE) of the label distribution, which compares the differences between every two annotations (of an annotation set) that may vary. This approach is useful because, in practice, there are no "truth" annotations and aggregated annotations should not be considered as the "truth" (Cabitza et al., 2023). The variant is formulated as:

$$D^i = \sqrt{\frac{1}{\binom{n}{2}} \sum_{(x,y)\in\mathcal{N}} (x_i - y_i)^2}, \quad i \in \mathcal{M} \quad (4)$$

whereby n is the annotator number of the annotator set $\mathcal{N}$, $\binom{n}{2}$ is the number of different ways to select two annotators from the annotator set $\mathcal{N}$, $x, y \in \mathcal{N}$ are the considered annotators, and x_i and y_i represent the assigned sentiment labels respectively for the instance i in the dataset $\mathcal{M}$. Figure 5 provides further examples of the formula's application.

Our rating strategy considers sentiment annotation more like ordinal/interval variables rather than nominal ones. If we assign different sentiments with distinctive values, for example, {*negative* : -1, *neutral* : 0 and *positive* : 1}, we would derive more fine-grained disagreement rate scores, as shown in Figure 5, which effectively represent the sentiment distance among all the labels. Since it is difficult to assign a value to the *mixed* label and our evaluation dataset does not contain the *mixed* label, we excluded the instances with this label from the original DynaSent (Potts et al., 2021) dataset. The remaining instances, annotated with *negative*, *neutral* and *positive* labels, were mapped to -1, 0, and 1, respectively. The final reduced DynaSent dataset contained 75,127 instances, which was split into training, validation and test datasets with a ratio of about 6:2:2.

5.2 Experiment and results

Following the study of Wan et al. (2023), disagreement prediction was framed as both a binary classification task and a regression task, to represent different levels of disagreement. The experiments were conducted by fine-tuning a RoBERTa-base model (Liu et al., 2019) with a fixed learning rate 1e-5, and batch size 8 for 10 epochs, using NVIDIA Tesla V100-SXM2-16GB GPUs. Also, a DeBERTa-base (He et al., 2020) and DeBERTaV3-base (He et al., 2022) were investigated for the sake of comparison. Since Wan et al. (2023) used 4 scales for the regression task, we mapped the input RMSE scores into 4 scales. Additionally, to evaluate the accuracy and f1 score for the regression task, we also mapped the regression output into 4 scales based on their absolute distance, leading to the disparity compared with the binary classification task as shown in Table 5 and Table 6.

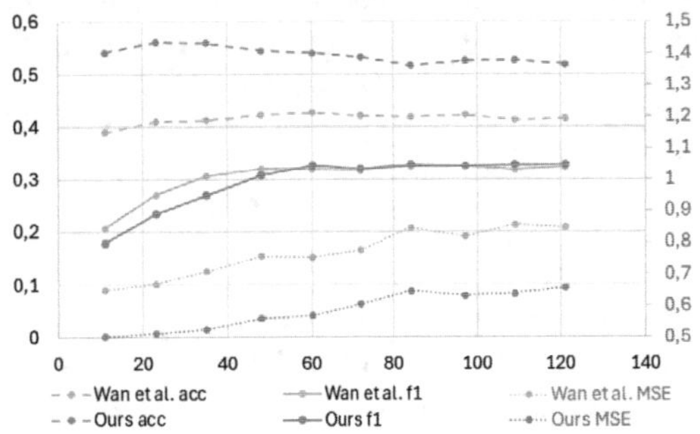

Figure 6: Comparison of two disagreement rating strategies during the training process of regression models with 4-scale outputs. Accuracy and f1 are plotted against the primary axis in black on the left, while MSE is plotted against the secondary axis in red on the right.

Task	Source	DynaSent	**acc (↑)**	**f1 (↑)**	**MSE (↓)**
Bin.	Wan et al.	original	N/A	74.9	0.361
Reg.	Wan et al.	original	N/A	11.8	0.114
Bin.	Reproduced	original	73.89	57.7	0.261
Reg_4	Reproduced	original	37.46	31.4	0.111
Reg_4	Reproduced	reduced	**41.71**	32.1	**0.097**

Table 5: Results based on the rating strategy of Wan et al. reported in Wan et al. (2023) (upper) and reproduced by us (bottom) on the test dataset of the original and reduced DynaSent. Reg_4 refers to the regression output evaluated on a scale of 4.

Task	Model	Lr	**acc (↑)**	**f1 (↑)**	**MSE (↓)**
Bin.	RoBERTa-base	1e-5	69.37	60.9	0.306
Reg_4	RoBERTa-base	1e-5	**51.64**	32.3	**0.072**
Reg_4	RoBERTa-base	5e-6	51.55	32.0	0.067
Reg_4	RoBERTa-base	1e-6	55.98	25.4	0.055
Reg_4	DeBERTa-base	1e-5	52.55	33.2	0.071
Reg_4	DeBERTaV3-base	1e-5	51.11	31.5	0.074

Table 6: Results based on the RMSE rating strategy with different models and learning rates on the test dataset of the reduced DynaSent. Reg_4 refers to the regression output evaluated on a scale of 4.

Figure 6 shows the RoBERTa-base model performance during the training process (10 epochs) on the validation dataset of the reduced DynaSent. During training, our disagreement rating strategy outperformed the other in terms of accuracy and MSE. For accuracy, higher values are better, while for MSE, lower values are preferred. Despite an overfitting warning during the 10 epochs training, it does not matter significantly when our main focus is the comparison of the two disagreement rating strategies.

The increase from 41.71% to 51.64% in accuracy and the drop from 0.097 to 0.072 in MSE in the final results on the test dataset, as shown in Table 5. and Table 6, reaffirms the better model performance based on our disagreement rating strategy. This suggests that using the AAD-based RMSE for rating disagreement yields improved performance in the task of sentiment annotation disagreement prediction. Additional experiments with other setups, as shown in Table 6, confirm these results.

5.3 Cross-dataset generalization

To test the model on our 94 instances of video subtitles, a fifth annotator was invited to independently annotate the subtitles, allowing for a similar experiment as in the previous section. We applied the AAD-based RMSE regression model, and the results are shown in Table 7.

	Instances	acc	f1	precision	recall
Reg_2	94	60.64	58.57	64.26	61.14
Reg_4	94	45.74	30.97	34.07	32.89
label-1	31	N/A	50.57	39.29	70.97
label-2	13	N/A	24.00	25.00	23.08
label-3	2	N/A	0	0	0

Table 7: Results of the regression task when the predictions are evaluated on a scale of 2 and 4, respectively, and the result breakdown, with label 1 to 3 for increasing disagreement.

In general, the results indicate the feasibility of predicting annotator (dis)agreement before annotation, even when the model was transferred to a new test dataset. Specifically, when evaluated with two polarities, i.e., agreement and disagreement, the models showed an accuracy of 60.64% and an f1 of 58.57%. When further breaking down the disagreement into three levels (label 1-3), unbalanced performance across levels of disagreement was observed, which might be caused by the imbalance of the label distribution in the training dataset with a ratio of 54:17:2.

6 Conclusion

While traditional IAA measures are favoured for providing a single comprehensive score that summarizes overall agreement across a dataset, they often complicate the interpretation of low scores and fail to capture finer (dis)agreement patterns. Prior research (e.g., Basile et al. (2021)) has highlighted these limitations, but effective solutions remain an open area of research. Our study contributes a systematic exploration of AAD as a more interpretable measure of annotation variations, particularly in subjective tasks like emotion recognition. Rather than presenting AAD as a completely novel metric, we demonstrate its potential to complement existing agreement measures by providing richer insights into (dis)agreement.

We first applied AAD to analyze both inter- and intra-annotator (dis)agreement with a multimodal dataset, which enables us to observe how these (dis)agreements manifest differently depending on the input channel, proving a more comprehensive understanding of (dis)agreement across modalities. Furthermore, a nearly 10% increase in accuracy in the disagreement prediction task demonstrates the advantages of our AAD-based approach.

Due to the scarcity of available (multimodal) emotion datasets with sets of annotations for agreement study, we conducted our study on the most suitable dataset currently accessible. While a larger dataset could further validate our findings, our dataset is representative of real-world annotation challenges, and the observed improvements in disagreement prediction align with prior work. We would extend this research when new datasets become available, but the current results already demonstrate the effectiveness and potential impact of AAD.

7 Limitations

Although the database used in this study is relatively small, it provides valuable insights and lays a foundation for future research with larger datasets.

8 Acknowledgments

This research received funding from the Flemish Government under the Flanders Artificial Intelligence Research program (FAIR) (174K02325). We are grateful to Professor Thomas Demeester for his valuable guidance and support throughout the development of this work. We also extend our thanks the anonymous reviewers for their insightful and constructive feedback.

References

Sohail Akhtar, Valerio Basile, and Viviana Patti. 2020. Modeling annotator perspective and polarized opinions to improve hate speech detection. In *Proceedings of the AAAI conference on human computation and crowdsourcing*, volume 8, pages 151–154.

Jean-Yves Antoine, Jeanne Villaneau, and Anaïs Lefeuvre. 2014. Weighted krippendorff's alpha is a more reliable metrics for multi-coders ordinal annotations: experimental studies on emotion, opinion and coreference annotation. In *Proceedings of the 14th Conference of the European Chapter of the Association for Computational Linguistics*, pages 550–559.

Lisa Feldman Barrett. 2009. Variety is the spice of life: A psychological construction approach to understanding variability in emotion. *Cognition and emotion*, 23(7):1284–1306.

Valerio Basile. 2020. It's the end of the gold standard as we know it. on the impact of pre-aggregation on the evaluation of highly subjective tasks. In *CEUR WORKSHOP PROCEEDINGS*, volume 2776, pages 31–40. CEUR-WS.

Valerio Basile, Michael Fell, Tommaso Fornaciari, Dirk Hovy, Silviu Paun, Barbara Plank, Massimo Poesio, and Alexandra Uma. 2021. We need to consider disagreement in evaluation. In *Proceedings of the 1st Workshop on Benchmarking: Past, Present and Future*, pages 15–21, Online. Association for Computational Linguistics.

Beata Beigman Klebanov, Eyal Beigman, and Daniel Diermeier. 2008. Analyzing disagreements. In *Coling 2008: Proceedings of the workshop on Human Judgements in Computational Linguistics*, pages 2–7, Manchester, UK. Coling 2008 Organizing Committee.

Carlos Busso, Murtaza Bulut, Chi-Chun Lee, Abe Kazemzadeh, Emily Mower, Samuel Kim, Jeannette N Chang, Sungbok Lee, and Shrikanth S Narayanan. 2008. Iemocap: Interactive emotional dyadic motion capture database. *Language resources and evaluation*, 42:335–359.

Carlos Busso, Srinivas Parthasarathy, Alec Burmania, Mohammed AbdelWahab, Najmeh Sadoughi, and Emily Mower Provost. 2016. MSP-IMPROV: An acted corpus of dyadic interactions to study emotion perception. *IEEE Transactions on Affective Computing*, 8:67–80.

Federico Cabitza, Andrea Campagner, and Valerio Basile. 2023. Toward a perspectivist turn in ground truthing for predictive computing. In *Proceedings of the AAAI Conference on Artificial Intelligence*, volume 37, pages 6860–6868.

Huang-Cheng Chou, Lucas Goncalves, Seong-Gyun Leem, Ali N Salman, Chi-Chun Lee, and Carlos Busso. 2024. Minority views matter: Evaluating speech emotion classifiers with human subjective annotations by an all-inclusive aggregation rule. *IEEE Transactions on Affective Computing*.

Jacob Cohen. 1960. A coefficient of agreement for nominal scales. *Educational and psychological measurement*, 20(1):37–46.

Barbara Di Eugenio and Michael Glass. 2004. Squibs and discussions: The kappa statistic: A second look. *Computational Linguistics*, 30(1):95–101.

Quanqi Du, Sofie Labat, Thomas Demeester, and Veronique Hoste. 2023. Unimodalities count as perspectives in multimodal emotion annotation. In *Proceedings of the 2nd Workshop on Perspectivist Approaches to NLP co-located with 26th European Conference on Artificial Intelligence (ECAI 2023)*. CEUR Workshop Proceedings.

Quanqi Du, Sofie Labat, Thomas Demeester, and Veronique Hoste. 2025. Unic: a dataset for emotion analysis of videos with multimodal and unimodal labels. *Language resources and evaluation*.

Eve Fleisig, Rediet Abebe, and Dan Klein. 2023. When the majority is wrong: Modeling annotator disagreement for subjective tasks. In *Proceedings of the 2023 Conference on Empirical Methods in Natural Language Processing*, pages 6715–6726.

Joseph L Fleiss. 1971. Measuring nominal scale agreement among many raters. *Psychological bulletin*, 76(5):378.

Muskan Garg, Seema Wazarkar, Muskaan Singh, and Ondřej Bojar. 2022. Multimodality for NLP-centered applications: Resources, advances and frontiers. In *Proceedings of the Thirteenth Language Resources and Evaluation Conference*, pages 6837–6847, Marseille, France. European Language Resources Association.

Andrew F Hayes and Klaus Krippendorff. 2007. Answering the call for a standard reliability measure for coding data. *Communication methods and measures*, 1(1):77–89.

Pengcheng He, Jianfeng Gao, and Weizhu Chen. 2022. DeBERTaV3: Improving DeBERTa using ELECTRA-style pre-training with gradient-disentangled embedding sharing. In *The Eleventh International Conference on Learning Representations*.

Pengcheng He, Xiaodong Liu, Jianfeng Gao, and Weizhu Chen. 2020. DeBERTa: Decoding-enhanced BERT with disentangled attention. In *International Conference on Learning Representations*.

Klaus Krippendorff. 2004. *Content analysis: An introduction to its methodology*. Sage publications.

Klaus Krippendorff. 2011. Computing krippendorff's alpha-reliability.

Sofie Labat, Thomas Demeester, and Véronique Hoste. 2024. EmoTwiCS: A corpus for modelling emotion trajectories in dutch customer service dialogues on twitter. *Language Resources and Evaluation*, 58(2):505–546.

J Richard Landis and Gary G Koch. 1977. The measurement of observer agreement for categorical data. *biometrics*, pages 159–174.

Kristen A Lindquist and Lisa Feldman Barrett. 2008. Emotional complexity. *Handbook of emotions*, 4:513–530.

Yinhan Liu, Myle Ott, Naman Goyal, Jingfei Du, Mandar Joshi, Danqi Chen, Omer Levy, Mike Lewis, Luke Zettlemoyer, and Veselin Stoyanov. 2019. Roberta: A robustly optimized bert pretraining approach. *arXiv preprint arXiv:1907.11692*.

Aaron Maladry, Alessandra Teresa Cignarella, Els Lefever, Cynthia van Hee, and Veronique Hoste. 2024. Human and system perspectives on the expression of irony: An analysis of likelihood labels and rationales. In *Proceedings of the 2024 Joint International Conference on Computational Linguistics, Language Resources and Evaluation (LREC-COLING 2024)*, pages 8372–8382, Torino, Italia. ELRA and ICCL.

Aida Mostafazadeh Davani, Mark Díaz, and Vinodkumar Prabhakaran. 2022. Dealing with disagreements: Looking beyond the majority vote in subjective annotations. *Transactions of the Association for Computational Linguistics*, 10:92–110.

Sungjoon Park, Jiseon Kim, Seonghyeon Ye, Jaeyeol Jeon, Hee Young Park, and Alice Oh. 2021. Dimensional emotion detection from categorical emotion. In *Proceedings of the 2021 Conference on Empirical Methods in Natural Language Processing*, pages 4367–4380, Online and Punta Cana, Dominican Republic. Association for Computational Linguistics.

Flor Miriam Plaza-del Arco, Alba A. Cercas Curry, Amanda Cercas Curry, and Dirk Hovy. 2024. Emotion analysis in NLP: Trends, gaps and roadmap for future directions. In *Proceedings of the 2024 Joint International Conference on Computational Linguistics, Language Resources and Evaluation (LREC-COLING 2024)*, pages 5696–5710, Torino, Italia. ELRA and ICCL.

Joan Plepi, Béla Neuendorf, Lucie Flek, and Charles Welch. 2022. Unifying data perspectivism and personalization: An application to social norms. In *Proceedings of the 2022 Conference on Empirical Methods in Natural Language Processing*, pages 7391–7402.

Christopher Potts, Zhengxuan Wu, Atticus Geiger, and Douwe Kiela. 2021. Dynasent: A dynamic benchmark for sentiment analysis. In *Proceedings of the 59th Annual Meeting of the Association for Computational Linguistics and the 11th International Joint Conference on Natural Language Processing (Volume 1: Long Papers)*, pages 2388–2404. Association for Computational Linguistics.

Harrison Ridley, Stuart Cunningham, John Darby, John Henry, and Richard Stocker. 2024. The affective audio dataset (aad) for non-musical, non-vocalized, audio emotion research. *IEEE Transactions on Affective Computing*.

Stanley Smith Stevens. 1946. On the theory of scales of measurement. *Science*, 103(2684):677–680.

Alexandra N Uma, Tommaso Fornaciari, Dirk Hovy, Silviu Paun, Barbara Plank, and Massimo Poesio. 2021. Learning from disagreement: A survey. *Journal of Artificial Intelligence Research*, 72:1385–1470.

Ruyuan Wan, Jaehyung Kim, and Dongyeop Kang. 2023. Everyone's voice matters: Quantifying annotation disagreement using demographic information. In *Proceedings of the AAAI Conference on Artificial Intelligence*, volume 37, pages 14523–14530.

Juan Wang and Bin Xia. 2019. Relationships of cohen's kappa, sensitivity, and specificity for unbiased annotations. In *Proceedings of the 4th International Conference on Biomedical Signal and Image Processing*, pages 98–101.

Tharindu Cyril Weerasooriya, Alexander Ororbia, Raj Bhensadadia, Ashiqur KhudaBukhsh, and Christopher Homan. 2023. Disagreement matters: Preserving label diversity by jointly modeling item and annotator label distributions with disco. In *Findings of the Association for Computational Linguistics: ACL 2023*, pages 4679–4695. Association for Computational Linguistics.

Ka Wong, Praveen Paritosh, and Lora Aroyo. 2021. Cross-replication reliability - an empirical approach to interpreting inter-rater reliability. In *Proceedings of the 59th Annual Meeting of the Association for Computational Linguistics and the 11th International Joint Conference on Natural Language Processing (Volume 1: Long Papers)*, pages 7053–7065, Online. Association for Computational Linguistics.

Ian Wood, John P. McCrae, Vladimir Andryushechkin, and Paul Buitelaar. 2018. A comparison of emotion annotation schemes and a new annotated data set. In *Proceedings of the Eleventh International Conference on Language Resources and Evaluation (LREC 2018)*, Miyazaki, Japan. European Language Resources Association (ELRA).

Jingyuan Yang, Qirui Huang, Tingting Ding, Dani Lischinski, Danny Cohen-Or, and Hui Huang. 2023. Emoset: A large-scale visual emotion dataset with rich attributes. In *Proceedings of the IEEE/CVF International Conference on Computer Vision*, pages 20383–20394.

AmirAli Bagher Zadeh, Paul Pu Liang, Soujanya Poria, Erik Cambria, and Louis-Philippe Morency. 2018. Multimodal language analysis in the wild: CMU-MOSEI dataset and interpretable dynamic fusion graph. In *Proceedings of the 56th Annual Meeting of the Association for Computational Linguistics (Volume 1: Long Papers)*, pages 2236–2246.

Shiqing Zhang, Yijiao Yang, Chen Chen, Xingnan Zhang, Qingming Leng, and Xiaoming Zhao. 2024. Deep learning-based multimodal emotion recognition from audio, visual, and text modalities: A systematic review of recent advancements and future prospects. *Expert Systems with Applications*, 237:121692.

Jinming Zhao, Tenggan Zhang, Jingwen Hu, Yuchen Liu, Qin Jin, Xinchao Wang, and Haizhou Li. 2022. M3ED: Multi-modal multi-scene multi-label emotional dialogue database. In *Proceedings of the 60th Annual Meeting of the Association for Computational Linguistics*, pages 5699–5710.

Xinshu Zhao, Guangchao Charles Feng, Jun S Liu, and Ke Deng. 2018. We agreed to measure agreement–redefining reliability de-justifies krippendorff s alpha. *China Media Research*, 14(2):1–16.

A Categorical emotion labels and their averaged valence and arousal scores

Emotion	valence	arousal	vector
confusion	3.0	2.9	(3.0, 2.9)
contentment	3.8	3.0	(3.8, 3.0)
disappointment	2.0	2.8	(2.0, 2.8)
disgust	2.0	3.2	(2.0, 3.2)
joy	4.1	3.6	(4.1, 3.6)
neutral	3.0	3.0	(3.0, 3.0)
surprise	3.6	3.4	(3.6, 3.4)

Table 8: Categorical emotion labels and their averaged valence and arousal scores.

B Valence and Emotion Difference in Three Other Modality Setups

Figures 7 through 10 present the results of valence and emotion differences across audio, (silent) video and multimodal setups.

C Distribution of Disagreement

As shown in Figure 11, the distribution of disagreement rate changes with the rating strategies. One notable change is that more instances, regardless of sentiment polarity, are labelled as weak disagreement (0.33) instead of the stronger one (0.67). In both rating strategies, a larger proportion of negative instances receive strong disagreement (0.67) than neutral and positive ones, aligning with our findings in Section 4.3 that disagreement tends to happen more in negative instances.

D Discrepancy between Original and Reproduced Results

As shown in Table 5, there is quite some discrepancy between the F1 scores reported in Wan et al. (2023) and those of our reproduced experiments, while the MSE scores remain in the same range. For the sake of comparison, we believe that the results on the reduced dataset are better compared to our reproduced experiments following the same experimental set-up.

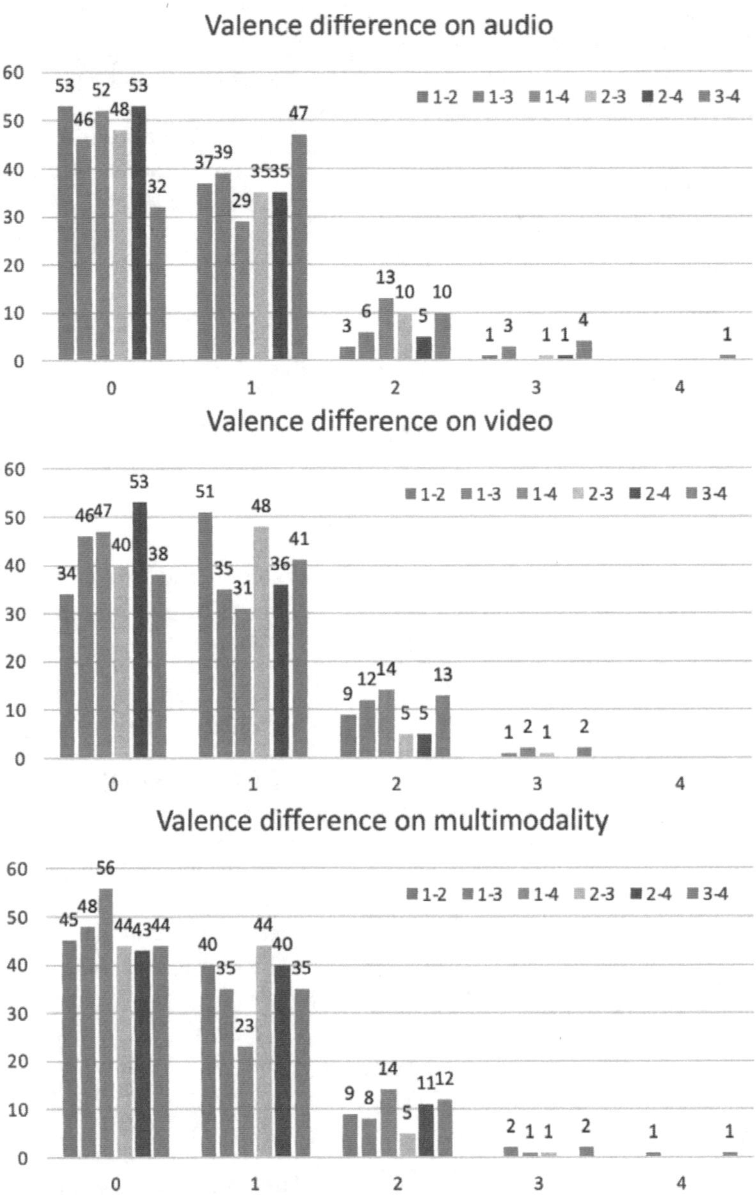

Figure 7: Absolute valence difference in audio, video and multimodal setups between each pair of annotators (represented with different colours). The X-axis is the absolute difference in valence; the Y-axis stands for the frequency of the difference values in the data.

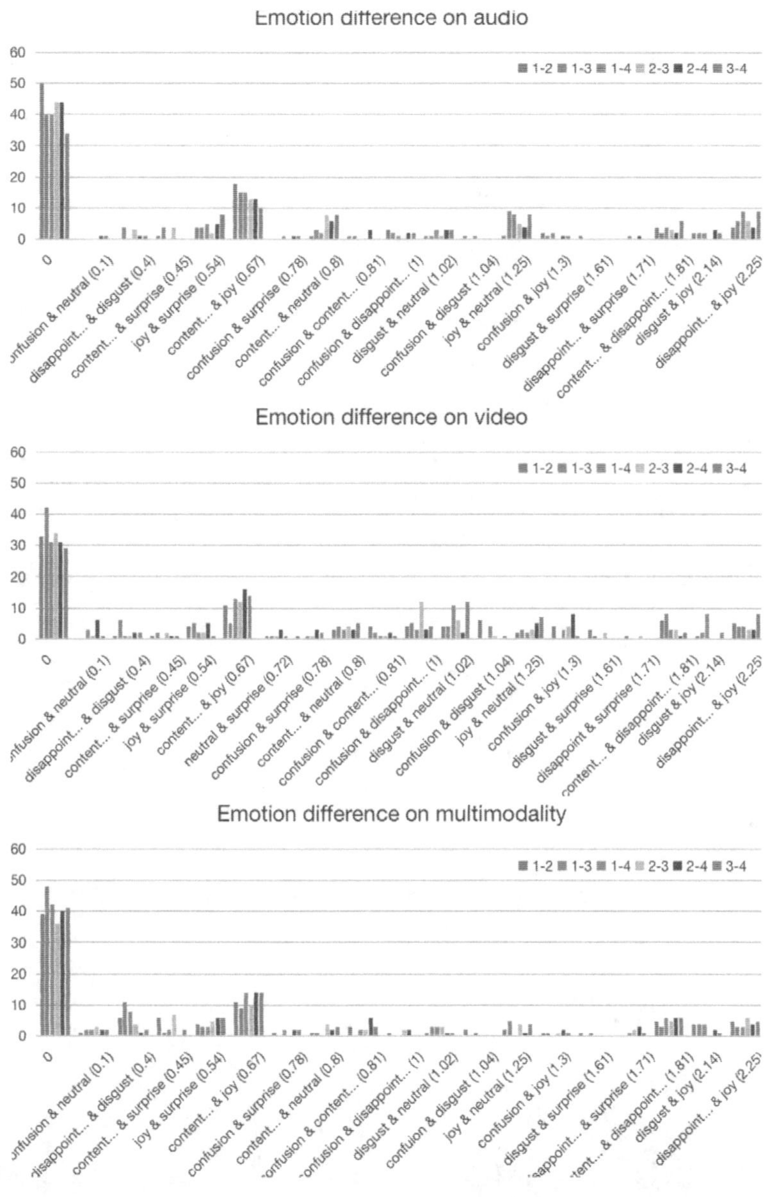

Figure 8: Emotion difference in audio, video and multimodal setups between each pair of annotators. The X-axis is the Euclidean distance between emotion vectors, while the Y-axis stands for the frequency of the difference values in the data.

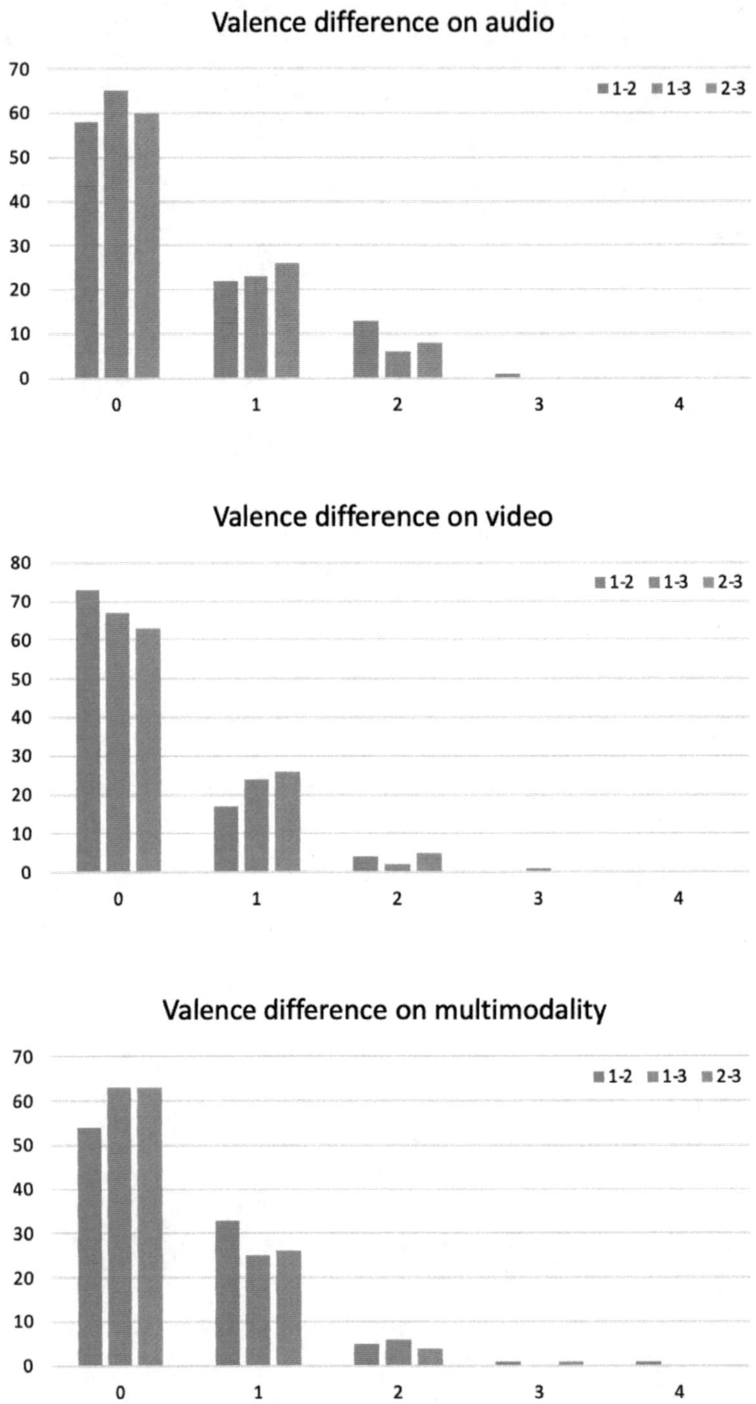

Figure 9: Absolute valence difference in audio, video and multimodal setups from three sets of annotations from the same annotator. The X-axis is the absolute difference in valence; the Y-axis stands for the frequency of the difference values in the data.

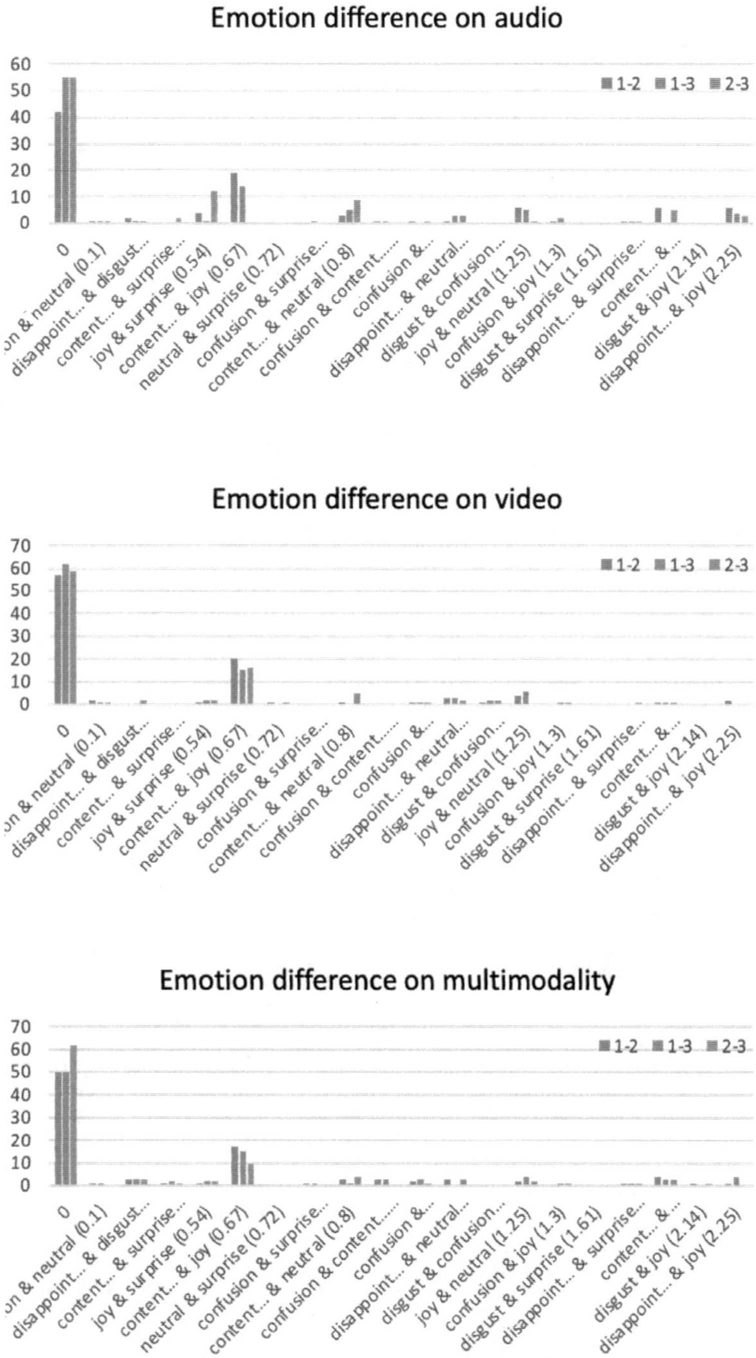

Figure 10: Absolute valence difference in audio, video and multimodal setups from three sets of annotations from the same annotator. The X-axis is the absolute difference in valence; the Y-axis stands for the frequency of the difference values in the data.

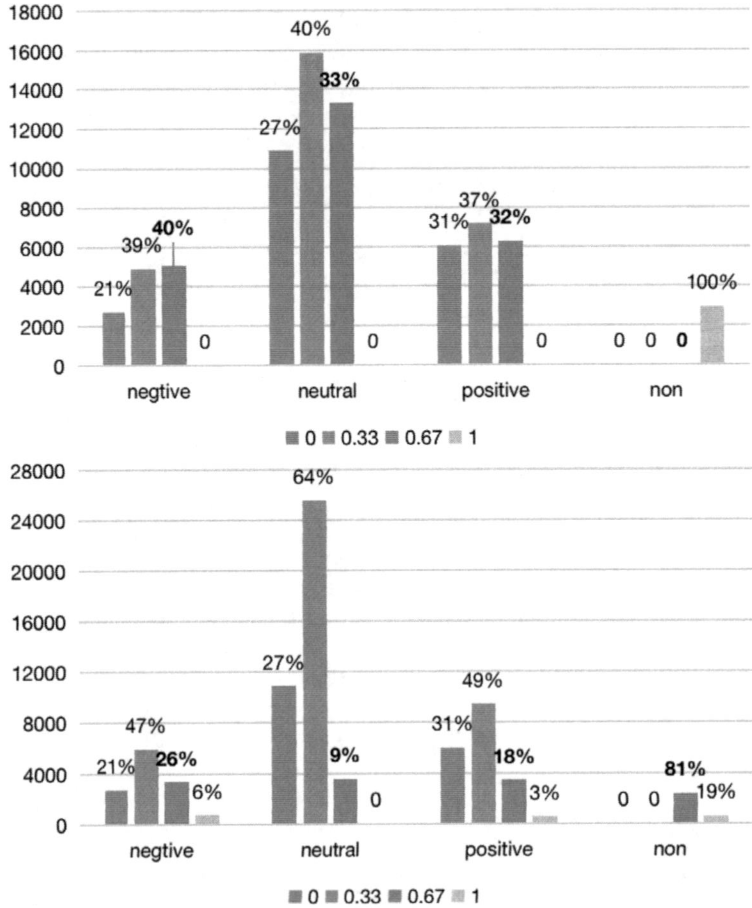

Figure 11: Distribution of disagreement rate across sentiment polarities in the reduced DynaSent dataset with different rating strategies. The first is based on the number of disagreement labels, while the second is mapped with RMSE scores. The X-axis represents the major sentiment polarities, with *non* referring to no majority.

Harmonizing Divergent Lemmatization and Part-of-Speech Tagging Practices for Latin Participles through the LiLa Knowledge Base

Marco Passarotti and Federica Iurescia and Paolo Ruffolo
Università Cattolica del Sacro Cuore
CIRCSE Research Centre
Largo Gemelli, 1, 20123 Milan, Italy
{marco.passarotti,federica.iurescia,paolo.ruffolo}@unicatt.it

Abstract

This paper addresses the challenge of divergent lemmatization and part-of-speech (PoS) tagging practices for Latin participles in annotated corpora. We propose a solution through the LiLa Knowledge Base, a Linked Open Data framework designed to unify lexical and textual data for Latin. Using lemmas as the point of connection between distributed textual and lexical resources, LiLa introduces hypolemmas — secondary citation forms belonging to a word's inflectional paradigm — as a means of reconciling divergent annotations for participles. Rather than advocating a single uniform annotation scheme, LiLa preserves each resource's native guidelines while ensuring that users can retrieve and analyze participial data seamlessly. Via empirical assessments of multiple Latin corpora, we show how the LiLa's integration of lemmas and hypolemmas enables consistent retrieval of participle forms regardless of whether they are categorized as verbal or adjectival.

1 Introduction

Lemmatization and part-of-speech (PoS) tagging constitute fundamental steps in many natural language processing (NLP) workflows, including information retrieval, machine translation, and sentiment analysis (Manning and Schutze, 1999; Jurafsky and Martin, 2025). Lemmatization is the process of reducing a word to its canonical form (or lemma), while PoS tagging entails assigning discrete grammatical categories (e.g., Verb, Noun, Adjective) to tokens in a text. Together, these tasks provide a structured linguistic representation that enables downstream algorithms to handle lexical variation systematically.

Despite the apparent straightforwardness of these tasks, significant variability arises when moving across different annotation schemes and corpora. One source of variability is the choice of annotation guidelines for morphological categories such as participles. In some corpora, participles – morphologically derived verb forms that can function as adjectives (e.g., *broken window*), nouns (e.g., *the breaking of the law*), or as parts of periphrastic verb tenses (e.g., *has broken*) – are consistently lemmatized under the corresponding verb root (e.g., *break*) (see, for Latin, Busa (1974–1980)). Other corpora treat such forms as belonging to the adjective category when they occur in attributive or predicative positions, lemmatizing them separately (e.g., *broken*) (see, for English, Marcus et al. (1993). These divergent lemmatization practices stem from different theoretical perspectives on morphological and syntactic categories, as well as from the practical goals of corpus designers.

A similar issue affects PoS tagging decisions. For instance, the Penn Treebank guidelines (Marcus et al., 1993) tend to annotate verb-derived adjectives such as *broken* or *burnt* as adjectives (with tag: JJ) when used attributively (*broken glass*, *burnt toast*), whereas the Universal Dependencies framework (De Marneffe et al., 2021) may tag these forms as VERB with the accompanying feature for participles (`VerbForm=Part`), or as ADJ depending on their syntactic function.

These differences can significantly impact the consistency of corpora used in training NLP systems. Models trained on one annotation scheme may struggle to generalize effectively to data labeled under a different scheme (Atwell et al., 2000). In the context of lemmatization, inconsistent treatment of participles can complicate tasks such as vocabulary alignment and cross-lingual transfer (McDonald et al., 2011). Moreover, variations in lemmatization and PoS tagging guidelines impede the comparability of results across distinct corpora, thereby influencing empirical linguistic research.

Such annotation discrepancies underscore the need for clear and consistent guidelines in lemmatization and PoS tagging. Nevertheless, accomplishing this task is not straightforward. Even within

Proceedings of the 19th Linguistic Annotation Workshop (LAW-XIX-2025), pages 103–114
July 31, 2025

the same language, deciding whether a participial form should be considered purely verbal or adjectival can depend on its syntactic position, degree of lexicalization, and the morphological tradition followed by linguists or corpus designers (Aronoff and Fudeman, 2022). In highly inflected languages, such as Czech, or Latin, these decisions become even more complex because participial forms often carry additional morphological information related to gender, number, and case. The ongoing development of universal annotation frameworks like Universal Dependencies seeks to mitigate some of these inconsistencies by promoting cross-linguistic standards (De Marneffe et al., 2021). However, adapting such frameworks to diverse linguistic phenomena remains a non-trivial undertaking, and the tension between theoretical adequacy and practical utility persists.

Addressing these challenges demands the development and adoption of more harmonized annotation frameworks, to integrate heterogeneous resources while preserving their unique annotation guidelines. In this paper, the divergent criteria employed for lemmatization and PoS tagging of participles in multiple Latin corpora are empirically examined in a few corpora and a solution to harmonize the divergent annotation practices is proposed.

After presenting some issues of divergent lemmatization and PoS tagging in Latin corpora (Section 2), the paper introduces the corpora under consideration as part of the LiLa Knowledge Base of interoperable resources for Latin (Section 3). By exploiting the interoperability among the corpora facilitated by their publication in LiLa, an empirical assessment is conducted to determine the extent of divergence in lemmatization and PoS tagging of participles across the corpora under investigation (Section 4). Section 5 demonstrates how the modeling based upon an extensive collection of Latin lemmas employed by LiLa enables the harmonization of diverse annotation practices for participles without enforcing a single, uniform approach. Finally, Section 6 concludes the paper, sketching the future work.

2 Lemmatization and PoS Tagging in Latin Corpora

Latin, as a highly inflected language, presents numerous challenges for the design and implementation of lemmatization and PoS tagging schemes in annotated corpora. Available Latin resources often diverge in how they treat morphological categories, leading to inconsistencies and reduced interoperability across corpora. A primary source of variation lies in the criteria for determining both the lemma and the PoS of morphologically complex forms.

Like for many other languages, one notable point of discrepancy in Latin corpora is the treatment of participles. Depending on the corpus or annotation scheme, participles may be categorized as adjectives or verbal forms.

In certain corpora, like for instance the *Index Thomisticus* corpus (Busa, 1974–1980) and Treebank (Passarotti et al., 2019), participles are mostly lemmatized under their verbal dictionary entry (e.g., *laudo* for any participial forms of 'to praise'), reflecting the view that participles are primarily verbal derivatives.[1]

Conversely, other resources, including the *Opera Latina* corpus by LASLA (Denooz, 2004) and the large repository *Corpus Corporum*[2] treat participles as distinct lemmas when they exhibit syntactic properties characteristic of adjectives, thereby assigning them an independent lemma (e.g., *laudatus* - perfect participle of *laudo* - as a standalone entry when functioning attributively). Nonetheless, the boundary between verbal and adjectival functions often remains subtle.

These differing conventions can yield inconsistent lexical representations and hamper comparative analyses across datasets.

3 The LiLa Knowledge Base

LiLa (Linking Latin) is a Linked Open Data (LOD) Knowledge Base (KB) developed to promote interoperability across a broad spectrum of textual and lexical resources for Latin (Passarotti et al., 2020).[3] Its conceptual model revolves around two primary components:

1. the Lemma Bank,[4] a collection of approximately 200,000 Latin lemmas (canonical citation forms of lexical items) published as LOD

[1]The *Index Thomisticus* corpus lemmatizes participles always under the verb and never under the adjective. Only a limited set of fully lexicalized nominalized participles are lemmatized under the noun, like *aduentus* 'arrival'. Instead, the *Index Thomisticus* Treebank includes a few participle forms lemmatized under the adjective, mostly when technical terms of Thomas Aquinas's philosophy are concerned, like *efficiens* 'efficient', lit. 'executing, accomplishing'.

[2]https://mlat.uzh.ch/home

[3]http://lila-erc.eu

[4]http://lila-erc.eu/data/id/lemma/LemmaBank

and originating from the LEMLAT 3.0 morphological analyzer (Passarotti et al., 2017);

2. a set of linguistic resources for Latin published as LOD and interconnected through the Lemma Bank, including corpora, lexica, and dictionaries.[5]

As new resources are integrated, the Lemma Bank is continually expanded, while resources link back to the Lemma Bank by connecting their lexical entries in lexical resources and individual word occurrences (tokens) in textual resources to the corresponding lemma in the LiLa Lemma Bank.

The LiLa KB leverages several established ontologies to represent the (meta)data of interlinked linguistic resources. Chief among these are POWLA for corpus data (Chiarcos, 2012), OLiA for linguistic annotation (Chiarcos and Sukhareva, 2015), and Ontolex-Lemon for lexical data (McCrae et al., 2017). In addition, LiLa employs its own ontology[6] to model lemmas in the Lemma Bank as instances of the class `lila:Lemma`,[7] defined as a subclass of `ontolex:Form`.[8] The class `lila:Lemma` has a specific subclass `lila:Hypolemma`,[9] whose instances are citation forms that belong to a word's regular inflectional paradigm but receive a different PoS tag or degree of comparison than their 'most canonical' lemma, including participles, gerundives, deadjectival adverbs, and comparatives (see Section 5).

For lexical resources, each lexical entry, modeled using the class `ontolex:LexicalEntry`,[10] is connected to its corresponding lemma in the Lemma Bank through the property `ontolex:canonicalForm`.[11] With respect to textual resources, tokens are represented as instances of the class `Terminal`[12] in the POWLA ontology and linked to their corresponding lemma in the Lemma Bank via the property `lila:hasLemma`.[13]

Among the textual resources currently interlinked in the LiLa KB are those examined in this study, selected for their manually verified lemmatization and PoS tagging. Specifically, they include:

- the corpus *Opera Latina* by LASLA, which collects approximately 1.7M tokens from Classical Latin texts (Fantoli et al., 2024);[14]
- the *Index Thomisticus* Treebank (ITTB) (Passarotti et al., 2019), which features the entire text of Thomas Aquinas' *Summa contra Gentiles* for a total of more than 375K tokens enhanced with syntactic annotation according to two styles (Mambrini et al., 2022):[15] the Universal Dependencies one and another resembling that of the analytical layer of the Prague Dependency Treebank (Bamman et al., 2008);
- the UDante treebank, which includes the Latin texts of Dante Alighieri annotated according to the Universal Dependencies style (55K) (Passarotti et al., 2021);[16]
- the CIRCSE Latin Library,[17] a collection of a few Classical and Medieval Latin texts for a total of more than 900K tokens, namely: *Pharsalia* (approx. 67K tokens)[18] by Lucan, the autobiography *Vita Caroli* of the emperor of the Holy Roman Empire Charles IV (18K) (Gamba et al., 2024),[19] *Epistulae ex Ponto* (25K)[20] and *Tristia* (28K)[21] by Ovid (Alagni et al., 2024), *Confessiones* (92K),[22] *De Trinitate* (131K)[23] and *De Civitate Dei* (330K)[24] by Augustine;

[5]The full list of resources currently interlinked in LiLa is available at `https://lila-erc.eu/data-page/`.

[6]`http://lila-erc.eu/ontologies/lila/`

[7]`http://lila-erc.eu/ontologies/lila/Lemma`

[8]`http://www.w3.org/ns/lemon/ontolex#Form`

[9]`http://lila-erc.eu/ontologies/lila/Hypolemma`

[10]`http://www.w3.org/ns/lemon/ontolex#LexicalEntry`

[11]`http://www.w3.org/ns/lemon/ontolex#canonicalForm`

[12]`http://purl.org/powla/powla.owl#Terminal`

[13]`http://lila-erc.eu/ontologies/lila/hasLemma`

[14]`http://lila-erc.eu/data/corpora/Lasla/id/corpus`

[15]`http://lila-erc.eu/data/corpora/ITTB/id/corpus`

[16]`http://lila-erc.eu/data/corpora/UDante/id/corpus`

[17]`http://lila-erc.eu/data/corpora/CIRCSELatinLibrary/id/corpus`

[18]`http://lila-erc.eu/data/corpora/CIRCSELatinLibrary/id/corpus/Pharsalia`

[19]`http://lila-erc.eu/data/corpora/CIRCSELatinLibrary/id/corpus/Vita%20Caroli`

[20]`http://lila-erc.eu/data/corpora/CIRCSELatinLibrary/id/corpus/P.%20Ovidii%20Epistulae%20ex%20Ponto`

[21]`http://lila-erc.eu/data/corpora/CIRCSELatinLibrary/id/corpus/P.%20Ovidii%20Tristia`

[22]`http://lila-erc.eu/data/corpora/CIRCSELatinLibrary/id/corpus/Confessiones`

[23]`http://lila-erc.eu/data/corpora/CIRCSELatinLibrary/id/corpus/De%20Trinitate`

[24]`http://lila-erc.eu/data/corpora/CIRCSELatinLibrary/id/corpus/De%20Ciuitate%20Dei`

- the corpus CLaSSES, a digital resource which gathers non-literary Latin texts (inscriptions, writing tablets, letters) of different periods and provinces of the Roman Empire (47K) (De Felice et al., 2023);[25]

- chapter VII of *Liber Abbaci*, a historic treaty on arithmetic written in 1202 by Leonardo Fibonacci (30K) (Grotto et al., 2021).[26]

4 Assessing Divergences through LiLa

To investigate lemmatization divergences among the six corpora under examination, we begin by selecting relevant tokens using LiLa[27] — namely, those linked via the property `lila:hasLemma` to a lemma in the Lemma Bank with PoS = VERB or to a hypolemma with PoS = ADJ.[28] We then perform minimal preprocessing, removing tokens that are linked to an ADJ hypolemma but are not participles, specifically gerundives (hypolemmas ending in .**ndus*, e.g., *laudandus* 'to be praised'), and comparatives (hypolemmas ending in .**-or*), e.g., *citerior* 'further' (see Section 5). Conversely, we retain tokens lemmatized as participles, regardless of their grade or PoS features. For instance, we include comparative and superlative forms of both present and perfect participles (e.g., *promptiores* 'the more attentive (ones)',[29] *abstrusior* 'more recondite',[30] *diligentissimo* '(to) the most attentive (one)',[31] *desideratissima* 'the most desired'),[32] and adverbs derived from participles (e.g., *affluenter* 'abundantly',[33] or *fortunate* 'fortunately').[34]

Next, tokens are normalized by lowercasing, removing diacritics, and replacing *j* with *i*, and *v* with *u*. We also remove enclitics by leveraging the lemmatization available in LiLa; for instance, any token listing *que* 'and'[35] among its lemmas has the enclitic *-que* removed.

From these preprocessed items, two lists of normalized types are compiled: (i) types linked to a lemma with PoS = VERB, and (ii) types linked to a hypolemma with PoS = ADJ. Types linked to a VERB lemma require further preprocessing, as they may include verb forms that are not participles. To filter out these non-participial forms, these types are processed with the LEMLAT morphological analyzer for Latin (Passarotti et al., 2017). Only forms recognized as participles are retained, and any remaining homographs (e.g., *amatis*, which can be either a perfect participle form or the first-person plural present active indicative of *amo* 'to love') are resolved through manual verification.

For each type, we record the total number of tokens across the six corpora and the distribution within each corpus.

These lists are compared to identify shared types, representing participles that exhibit divergent lemmatization strategies in the corpora. An illustrative example is *abundans*, the present participle of the first-conjugation verb *abundo* 'to overflow', which appears under the hypolemma *abundans* (ADJ) in nine occurrences from the *Opera Latina* corpus, and under the lemma *abundo* (VERB) in one occurrence from *Opera Latina*, one from the UDante Treebank, and one from the CIRCSE Latin Library.

Types linked to an ADJ hypolemma that do not appear in the VERB-linked type list are participles consistently associated with a participle hypolemma across all corpora. Conversely, types linked to a VERB lemma that do not appear in the ADJ-linked type list are participles always lemmatized with a verbal lemma.

As an initial overview of the data, Table 1 reports the number of participle tokens (both overall and per corpus) associated with a VERB lemma or an ADJ hypolemma. In all corpora, the majority of participle tokens are lemmatized under the VERB lemma, although the relative proportion of ADJ lemmas varies — from approximately 15:1 in the CIRCSE Latin Library to about 3:1 in the ITTB. Looking at the total of participle tokens lemmatized as VERB versus those as ADJ, the proportion is 5:1 (128,325 vs 26,162). However, this figure may be misleading because the presence of a few participle tokens with exceptionally high frequencies

[25] `http://lila-erc.eu/data/corpora/CLaSSES/id/corpus`

[26] `http://lila-erc.eu/data/corpora/CorpusFibonacci/id/corpus`

[27] See the SPARQL queries (1) and (2) in the Appendix.

[28] The LiLa Lemma Bank uses the Universal PoS tagset (Petrov et al., 2011).

[29] Lemmatized under *promptus* (`http://lila-erc.eu/data/id/hypolemma/35758`) in the *Liber Abbaci*.

[30] Lemmatized under *abstrudo* (`http://lila-erc.eu/data/id/lemma/87036`) in the CIRCSE Latin Library.

[31] Lemmatized under *diligens* (`http://lila-erc.eu/data/id/hypolemma/12447`) in the *Opera Latina* corpus.

[32] Lemmatized under *desidero* (`http://lila-erc.eu/data/id/lemma/98900`) in CLaSSES.

[33] Lemmatized under *affluo* (`http://lila-erc.eu/data/id/lemma/88030`) in the ITTB.

[34] Lemmatized under *fortunatus* (`http://lila-erc.eu/data/id/hypolemma/17176`) in UDante.

[35] `http://lila-erc.eu/data/id/lemma/131416`

	TOTAL	LASLA	ITTB	UDante	CIRCSE	CLaSSES	Fibonacci
VERB	128,325	79,086	15,888	1,564	30,975	667	145
ADJ	26,162	17,603	5,715	425	2,236	168	15

Table 1: Number of participle tokens by PoS assignment.

can skew the interpretation of the results.

To provide a more nuanced perspective, Table 2 presents a type-based distribution of lemmatization of participles by PoS. In particular, it lists the total number of participle types and tokens consistently assigned to the same PoS (either ADJ or VERB) across all corpora, as well as those that are sometimes lemmatized as VERB and sometimes as an ADJ hypolemma. The number of hapax forms is also reported.

Focusing on types, Table 2 confirms that most participles are consistently lemmatized as VERB in the corpora, but it additionally reveals a sizable number of types (and tokens) with inconsistent PoS assignment. Among the 22,851 total types, 2,202 exhibit inconsistent PoS, corresponding to 41,173 tokens. It should be noted that many types that are consistently assigned to a given PoS (either VERB or ADJ) are hapax forms, which necessarily excludes them from the inconsistent VERB/ADJ category because at least two tokens are required for a type to show inconsistent assignment.

For the participle types t that fall under the category VERB/ADJ in Table 2, we calculate the entropy of PoS assignment:

$$H(t) = -log_2(p_V(t)) - log_2(p_A(t))$$

where:

$$p_V(t) = \frac{f_V(t)}{f_V(t) + f_A(t)}$$

$$p_A(t) = \frac{f_A(t)}{f_V(t) + f_A(t)}$$

$f_V(t)$ and $f_A(t)$ are the number of tokens lemmatized as VERB or ADJ respectively for the type t. We estimate an overall *index of homogeneity* as the average of $H(t)$. $H(t)$ is normalized with values in the range of the interval [0,1], where $H(t) = 1$ is maximum entropy, i.e., 50% VERB and 50% ADJ, and $H(t) = 0$ is minimum entropy, i.e., 100% VERB and 0% ADJ, or 0% VERB and 100% ADJ.[36]

Using the values reported in Table 2, the average entropy of PoS assignment to participle tokens in the examined corpora is $H(t) = 0.76$. This moderately high value indicates that, for tokens whose types belong to the VERB/ADJ category, no single PoS assignment clearly predominates. Specifically, these VERB/ADJ types account for 23,136 tokens labeled as VERB and 18,037 tokens labeled as ADJ.

Having established the overall extent of inconsistent PoS assignment for participle types across the investigated corpora, Tables 3 and 4 present the distribution of participle types, tokens and hapax per corpus according to (in)consistent PoS assignment. These tables illustrate the degree of (in)consistency in participle PoS assignment within each individual corpus.

An examination of the data in Tables 3 and 4 indicates that no Latin corpus under consideration exhibits completely consistent PoS assignment for participle forms. Apart from the Fibonacci corpus — which, due to its limited size, exerts minimal influence on the overall findings — ITTB and CIRCSE yield the smallest proportions of participle types that are invariably assigned the ADJ category. The proportion of participle types that fall within the VERB/ADJ category varies among corpora: it is approximately 2% in ITTB, 4% in CIRCSE and 8% in LASLA. Table 5 provides the average entropy, $H(t)$, of PoS assignment for participle tokens in each corpus. Consistent with the proportions described above, the ITTB and CIRCSE corpora exhibit the lowest average entropy values, indicating the lowest degree of uncertainty in PoS assignment for participles.

This variability in PoS assignment (and by extension, lemmatization) for participles is unsurprising, given the inherently hybrid nature of participles, which can function as both nominal and verbal forms. The Universal Dependencies documentation about the `VerbForm` feature (i.e., form of verb or deverbative)[37] states that "some verb forms in some languages actually form a gray zone between

[36] Since the word types considered are those whose tokens show different PoS assignment, maximum and minimum entropy is never found.

[37] `https://universaldependencies.org/u/feat/VerbForm.html`

Category	No. Types [No. Hapax]	No. Tokens
VERB only	18,623 [13,497]	105,189
ADJ only	2,026 [1,320]	8,125
VERB/ADJ	2,202 [0]	41,173
TOTAL	22,851 [14,799]	154,487
VERB/ADJ (VERB)		23,136
VERB/ADJ (ADJ)		18,037

Table 2: Number of participle types [hapax] and tokens by (in)consistency of PoS assignment.

Category	CLaSSES	LASLA	CIRCSE
VERB only	343 (660) [267]	14,853 (69,160) [7,166]	8,412 (27,433) [4,716]
ADJ only	87 (161) [63]	2,207 (9,272) [1,123]	392 (1,317) [256]
VERB/ADJ	4 (14) [0]	1,472 (18,257) [0]	346 (4,461) [0]
VERB/ADJ (VERB)	(7)	(9,926)	(3,542)
VERB/ADJ (ADJ)	(7)	(8,331)	(919)

Table 3: Number of participle types (tokens) [hapax] by (in)consistency of PoS assignment per corpus. First set.

verbs and other parts of speech (nouns, adjectives and adverbs). For instance, participles may be either classified as verbs or as adjectives, depending on language and context".[38]

As shown by the data presented in the preceding tables, the presence of such a gray zone in PoS assignment considerably complicates information retrieval from annotated corpora, as different lemmas and PoS tags must be queried to capture all forms within a verb's inflectional paradigm. A potential solution would be to enforce highly stringent annotation guidelines. For instance, one might mandate that all participles be assigned exclusively the verbal lemma and VERB PoS, irrespective of their syntactic function. In practice, however, no corpus under investigation adopts such an approach, as demonstrated, because it conflicts with the fact that PoS labels tend to reflect the function of a word in discourse — that is, its contextual rather than purely lexical or morphological properties. As an illustrative example, consider the type *confusa* 'mingled', a perfect participle form of the third conjugation verb *confundo* 'to mingle', which exhibits an entropy value of $H(\textit{confusa}) = 0.99$. This value is derived from the following distribution: out of 43 total tokens, 20 are assigned PoS ADJ (1 in CIRCSE, 19 in LASLA), whereas 23 are assigned PoS VERB (1 in ITTB, 10 in CIRCSE, and 12 in LASLA).

[38]For one of the most recent pieces of evidence on the challenges presented by this gray zone, see `https://github.com/UniversalDependencies/docs/issues/1088#issuecomment-2722358950`.

To address the challenges of PoS assignment for participles in Latin corpora, the LiLa KB has developed a strategy that harmonizes the various criteria followed by these corpora without introducing a new annotation framework. Although designed for Latin corpora, this solution is language-independent and can be applied to any language for which a LOD collection of lemmas and hypolemmas is made available.

5 Harmonizing Divergences through LiLa

This Section describes the methodology used in the LiLa Knowledge Base to reconcile discrepancies in the annotation of participles, which may be labeled as either adjectives or verbs in different textual resources.

To address this issue, the Lemma Bank makes use of the class `lila:Hypolemma`, a subclass of `lila:Lemma` (see Section 3), to represent citation forms that belong to a word's regular inflectional paradigm but receive a different PoS tag or degree of comparison than their 'most canonical' lemma.

Typical examples of hypolemmas include participles and gerundives (assigned PoS ADJ but linked to lemmas with PoS VERB) as well as deadjectival adverbs (assigned PoS ADV but linked to lemmas with PoS ADJ). A limited set of comparative adjectives (e.g., *exterior* from *exter* 'external', or *posterior* from *posterus* 'next') is also recorded as hypolemmas with PoS ADJ linked to lemmas with the same PoS. These forms are typically treated as canonical citation forms in Latin corpora, rather

Category	ITTB	UDante	Fibonacci
VERB only	2,506 (15,576) [1,276]	1,086 (1,554) [862]	77 (145) [48]
ADJ only	211 (4,280) [51]	216 (392) [148]	9 (15) [7]
VERB/ADJ	59 (1,747) [0]	7 (43) [0]	0 (0) [0]
VERB/ADJ (VERB)	(312)	(10)	(0)
VERB/ADJ (ADJ)	(1,435)	(33)	(0)

Table 4: Number of participle types (tokens) [hapax] by (in)consistency of PoS assignment per corpus. Second set.

Corpus	avg H(t)
CLaSSES	0.94
UDante	0.88
LASLA	0.78
CIRCSE	0.76
ITTB	0.7

Table 5: Average entropy of PoS assignment to participles tokens by corpus.

than being lemmatized under their positive-degree forms.

In the Lemma Bank, hypolemmas are connected to their corresponding lemmas via the symmetric properties `lila:hasHypolemma`[39] and `lila:isHypolemma`.[40]

For example, the lemma *armo* 'to furnish with weapons' (VERB)[41] is linked via the properties `lila:hasHypolemma/lila:isHypolemma` to three hypolemmas (ADJ): the participles *armans* (present tense), *armatus* (perfect tense), and *armaturus* (future tense).

In the textual resources examined in this study, there are currently 76 occurrences of the different inflected forms of the perfect participle *armatus* (e.g., *armatas*, *armati*, *armato*) linked to the lemma *armo*, and 265 occurrences linked to the hypolemma *armatus*. The modeling approach employed in LiLa facilitates the reconciliation of these divergent lemmatization practices across multiple corpora by linking the participle forms to the Lemma Bank. Regardless of whether a perfect participle form of *armo* is treated as an adjective (lemma *armatus*) or a verb (lemma *armo*) in individual corpora, its occurrences can be uniformly retrieved and integrated via a SPARQL query that traverses the LiLa knowledge graph. This query identifies tokens from different corpora linked, via the property `lila:hasLemma`, either to a lemma with PoS VERB or to a hypolemma with PoS ADJ, which are in turn connected through the properties `lila:hasHypolemma/lila:isHypolemma`.[42]

Figure 1 provides a graphical representation of how a textual occurrence of the plural accusative feminine form *armatas* is linked to the hypolemma *armatus*, which, in turn, is connected to the lemma *armo*. This arrangement parallels the linking of future and present participles to the same lemma. The token *armatas*[43] is drawn from Vergil's *Georgica*, as indicated in the figure by the link between the token and the Document Layer of this text via the property `powla:hasLayer`.[44]

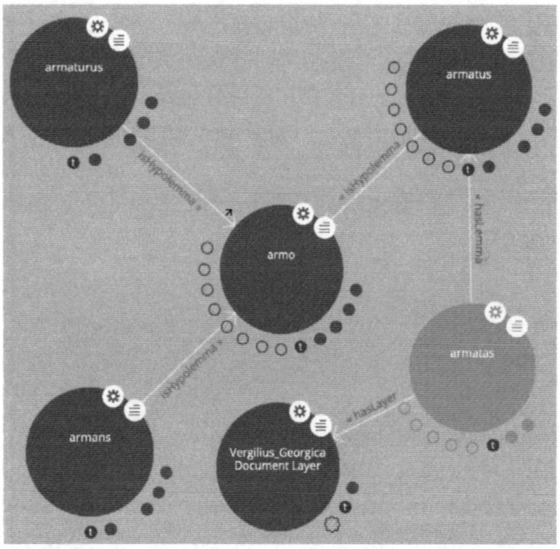

Figure 1: A token (*armatas*) linked to a participle hypolemma (*armatus*) in the LiLa Lemma Bank.

The LiLa Lemma Bank modeling does not include the harmonization of nominalized participle

[39]http://lila-erc.eu/ontologies/lila/hasHypolemma

[40]http://lila-erc.eu/ontologies/lila/isHypolemma

[41]http://lila-erc.eu/data/id/lemma/90036

[42]The SPARQL query (3) reported in the Appendix generalizes this search, retrieving word types by harmonized lemmatization, i.e., regardless of whether a token is lemmatized to a lemma with PoS VERB, or to one of its hypolemmas with PoS ADJ.

[43]http://lila-erc.eu/data/corpora/Lasla/id/corpus/VergiliusGeorgica/Vergilius_Georgica_VerGeor1.BPN_t_0001719

[44]http://purl.org/powla/powla.owl#hasLayer

forms with their corresponding base verbs. Instead, these forms are recorded as separate lemmas, independent of the verbal lemma from which they originate. For example, in the Lemma Bank *intellectus* 'intellect' is listed as a lemma with PoS NOUN, distinct from its base verb *intelligo* 'to understand'. This decision reflects the fact that fully lexicalized nominalizations typically appear as independent entries in dictionaries and, in most cases, receive PoS tag NOUN in corpus annotation.

However, challenges may arise when PoS and lemma assignment in a corpus are determined on a contextual basis rather than a strictly lexical one. Such challenges occur, for instance, when a participle form is used as a noun in a given context, but this nominalization is not sufficiently lexicalized to warrant its own dictionary entry. In these scenarios, the LiLa approach typically links such occurrences with their corresponding participle, recorded as a hypolemma with PoS ADJ, rather than creating a distinct lemma for the nominalization in the Lemma Bank. This is the case of a token like *mendicantem* 'beggar' (present participle of *mendico* 'to go begging') in the following sentence drawn from Plautus' *The Captives*:[45] [...] *ne patri,* [...] *decere uideatur magis, me saturum seruire apud te* [...] *potius quam illi* [...] *mendicantem uiuere* '[...] otherwise it might seem more appropriate to my father that I should be a well-fed slave at your place, [...] rather than [...] live as a beggar back there'.[46]

6 Conclusion

This study has highlighted the challenges posed by divergent lemmatization and PoS tagging schemes for Latin participles in annotated corpora. By demonstrating how these discrepancies can be addressed via the LiLa Knowledge Base, we show that heterogeneous annotation practices — whether stemming from theoretical approaches or from the practical aims of corpus designers — hinder interoperability among resources. Through LiLa's Lemma Bank and the notion of hypolemma, it is possible to unify tokens annotated as either verbal or adjectival participles under a shared representational framework, preserving corpus-specific practices while enabling cross-resource integration.

Rather than enforcing a single "correct" solution, LiLa's graph-based design allows researchers to explore and compare multiple annotation strategies across corpora with minimal manual intervention. In so doing, it promotes data interoperability, and provides a robust platform for linguistic research and NLP applications. Ultimately, this approach underscores the value of LOD methodologies in bridging divergent annotation practices and advancing the broader goal of accessible and reusable linguistic resources.

In future research, we aim to extend our analysis to include nominalized participle forms, which may be documented as independent entries and lemmas in both lexical and textual resources, as well as in the Lemma Bank. After collecting the set of nominalized participle tokens from corpora and corresponding entries from the lexical resources published in LiLa, we will apply the same analytical methodology outlined in this study. This will allow us to assess the degree of consistency in the treatment of nominalized participles across different linguistic resources.

Finally, given the language-independent nature of LiLa's strategy for harmonizing PoS assignment divergences in participles, we hope that other languages will adopt the same architecture. In particular, building and publishing collections of lemmas and hypolemmas as LOD for different languages is crucial for enabling distributed linguistic resources to interoperate in the Semantic Web. A pertinent example is offered by the LiITA Knowledge Base, which has recently implemented a Lemma Bank to enhance LOD-based interoperability across Italian linguistic resources (Litta et al., 2024).[47]

Acknowledgments

The "LiLa - Linking Latin" project has received funding from the European Research Council (ERC) under the European Union's Horizon 2020 research and innovation programme – Grant Agreement No. 769994.

References

Aurora Alagni, Francesco Mambrini, and Marco Passarotti. 2024. Lifeless winter without break: Ovid's exile works and the LiLa knowledge base. In *Proceedings of the 10th Italian Conference on Computational Linguistics (CLiC-it 2024)*, pages 4–12, Pisa, Italy. CEUR Workshop Proceedings.

[45] `https://lila-erc.eu/data/corpora/Lasla/id/corpus/PlautusCaptiui/Plautus_Captiui_PlCapt.BPN_t_0002418`

[46] Text and translation of this excerpt are drawn from De Melo (2011).

[47] `https://www.liita.it`

Mark Aronoff and Kirsten Fudeman. 2022. *What is Morphology?* John Wiley & Sons.

ES Atwell, George Demetriou, John Hughes, Amanda Schiffrin, Clive Souter, and Sean Wilcock. 2000. A comparative evaluation of modern English corpus grammatical annotation schemes. *ICAME Journal: International Computer Archive of Modern and Medieval English Journal*, 24:7–23.

David Bamman, Marco Passarotti, Roberto Busa, Gregory R Crane, et al. 2008. The Annotation Guidelines of the Latin Dependency Treebank and Index Thomisticus Treebank: the Treatment of some specific Syntactic Constructions in Latin. In *Proceedings of the Sixth International Conference on Language Resources and Evaluation (LREC 2008). May 28-30, 2008, Marrakech, Morocco*, pages 71–76.

Roberto Busa. 1974–1980. *Index Thomisticus*. Frommann-Holzboog, Stuttgart - Bad Cannstatt, Germany.

Christian Chiarcos. 2012. POWLA: Modeling Linguistic Corpora in OWL/DL. In *The Semantic Web: Research and Applications. 9th Extended Semantic Web Conference, ESWC 2012, Heraklion, Crete, Greece, May 27–31, 2012, Proceedings*, number 7295 in Lecture Notes in Computer Science, pages 225–239, Berlin/Heidelberg, Germany. Springer.

Christian Chiarcos and Maria Sukhareva. 2015. OLiA – Ontologies of Linguistic Annotation. *Semantic Web*, 6(4):379–386.

Irene De Felice, Lucia Tamponi, Federica Iurescia, and Marco Passarotti. 2023. Linking the Corpus CLaSSES to the LiLa Knowledge Base of Interoperable Linguistic Resources for Latin. In *Proceedings of CLiC-it 2023: 9th Italian Conference on Computational Linguistics, Nov 30 — Dec 02, 2023, Venice, Italy*, pages 1–7.

Marie-Catherine De Marneffe, Christopher D Manning, Joakim Nivre, and Daniel Zeman. 2021. Universal Dependencies. *Computational linguistics*, 47(2):255–308.

Wolfgang David Cirilo De Melo. 2011. *Amphitryon ; The Comedy of Asses ; The Pot of Gold ; The Two Bacchises ; The Captives*. Plautus 1, Ed. 2011. Harvard University Press, Cambridge, Mass.

Joseph Denooz. 2004. Opera Latina : une base de données sur internet. *Euphrosyne*, 32:79–88.

Margherita Fantoli, Marco Passarotti, Dominique Longrée, et al. 2024. Lemmas in Dialogue: Linking the LASLA Corpus to the LiLa Knowledge Base. *Recent Trends and Findings in Latin Linguistics: Volume I: Syntax, Semantics and Pragmatics. Volume II: Semantics and Lexicography. Discourse and Dialogue*, pages 297–314.

Federica Gamba, Marco Passarotti, and Paolo Ruffolo. 2024. Publishing the Dictionary of Medieval Latin in the Czech Lands as Linked Data in the LiLa Knowledge Base. *Italian Journal of Computational Linguistics*, 10(1):95–116.

Francesco Grotto, Rachele Sprugnoli, Margherita Fantoli, Maria Simi, Flavio Massimiliano Cecchini, and Marco Passarotti. 2021. The Annotation of Liber Abbaci, a Domain-Specific Latin Resource. In *Proceedings of the Eighth Italian Conference on Computational Linguistics (CLiC-it 2021). Milan, Italy, January 26-28, 2022*, pages 176–183. Accademia University Press.

Daniel Jurafsky and James H. Martin. 2025. *Speech and Language Processing: An Introduction to Natural Language Processing, Computational Linguistics, and Speech Recognition with Language Models*, 3rd edition. Online manuscript released January 12, 2025.

Eleonora Litta, Marco Passarotti, Paolo Brasolin, Giovanni Moretti, Valerio Basile, Andrea Di Fabio, and Cristina Bosco. 2024. The Lemma Bank of the LiITA Knowledge Base of Interoperable Resources for Italian. In *Proceedings of the 10th Italian Conference on Computational Linguistics (CLiC-it 2024)*, pages 517–522, Pisa, Italy. CEUR Workshop Proceedings.

Francesco Mambrini, Marco Passarotti, Giovanni Moretti, and Matteo Pellegrini. 2022. The Index Thomisticus Treebank as Linked Data in the LiLa Knowledge Base. In *Proceedings of the Thirteenth Language Resources and Evaluation Conference*, pages 4022–4029.

Christopher Manning and Hinrich Schutze. 1999. *Foundations of Statistical Natural Language Processing*. MIT press.

Mitch Marcus, Beatrice Santorini, and Mary Ann Marcinkiewicz. 1993. Building a Large Annotated Corpus of English: The Penn Treebank. *Computational linguistics*, 19(2):313–330.

John P McCrae, Julia Bosque-Gil, Jorge Gracia, Paul Buitelaar, and Philipp Cimiano. 2017. The OntoLex-Lemon Model: Development and Applications. In *Electronic lexicography in the 21st century. Proceedings of eLex 2017 conference*, pages 587–597, Brno, Czech Republic. Lexical Computing CZ s.r.o.

Ryan McDonald, Slav Petrov, and Keith Hall. 2011. Multi-source Transfer of Delexicalized Dependency Parsers. In *Proceedings of the 2011 conference on empirical methods in natural language processing*, pages 62–72.

Marco Passarotti, Marco Budassi, Eleonora Litta, and Paolo Ruffolo. 2017. The Lemlat 3.0 Package for Morphological Analysis of Latin. In *Proceedings of the NoDaLiDa 2017 Workshop on Processing Historical Language*, volume 133, pages 24–31, Gothenburg. Linköping University Electronic Press.

Marco Passarotti, Flavio Massimiliano Cecchini, Rachele Sprugnoli, Giovanni Moretti, et al. 2021. UDante. L'annotazione sintattica dei testi latini di Dante. *Studi Danteschi*, 86:309–338.

Marco Passarotti, Francesco Mambrini, Greta Franzini, Flavio Massimiliano Cecchini, Eleonora Litta, Giovanni Moretti, Paolo Ruffolo, and Rachele Sprugnoli. 2020. Interlinking through Lemmas. The Lexical Collection of the LiLa Knowledge Base of Linguistic Resources for Latin. *Studi e Saggi Linguistici*, LVIII(1):177–212.

Marco Passarotti et al. 2019. The Project of the Index Thomisticus Treebank. *Digital classical philology. Ancient Greek and Latin in the digital revolution*, 10:299–319.

Slav Petrov, Dipanjan Das, and Ryan McDonald. 2011. A Universal Part-of-Speech Tagset. *arXiv preprint arXiv:1104.2086*.

A Appendix

(1)

SPARQL query to retrieve types lemmatized to lemmas with PoS VERB (endpoint: https://lila-erc.eu/sparql/):

```
PREFIX rdfs: <http://www.w3.org
   /2000/01/rdf-schema#>
PREFIX lila: <http://lila-erc.eu/
   ontologies/lila/>
PREFIX dc: <http://purl.org/dc/
   elements/1.1/>
PREFIX rdf: <http://www.w3.org
   /1999/02/22-rdf-syntax-ns#>
PREFIX powla: <http://purl.org/
   powla/powla.owl#>

SELECT distinct ?corpora_title ?
   token1_label ?lemma1_label (
   count(?token1) as ?nToken1)
WHERE
{
  VALUES ?corpora {
    <http://lila-erc.eu/data/
       corpora/CIRCSELatinLibrary
       /id/corpus>
    <http://lila-erc.eu/data/
       corpora/UDante/id/corpus>
    <http://lila-erc.eu/data/
       corpora/Lasla/id/corpus>
    <http://lila-erc.eu/data/
       corpora/CorpusFibonacci/id
       /corpus>
    <http://lila-erc.eu/data/
       corpora/CLaSSES/id/corpus>
    <http://lila-erc.eu/data/
       corpora/ITTB/id/corpus>
  }
  ?lemma1 rdf:type lila:Lemma ;
     lila:hasPOS lila:verb ;
     rdfs:label ?lemma1_label .
     ?token1 lila:hasLemma ?
        lemma1 ;
     rdf:type powla:Terminal ;
     powla:hasLayer ?
        DocumentLayer1 ;
     rdfs:label ?token1_label .
  ?DocumentLayer1 powla:
     hasDocument ?Document1 .
  ?Document1 ^powla:
     hasSubDocument ?corpora .
  ?corpora dc:title ?
     corpora_title .
    }
order by ?token1_label
```

(2)

SPARQL query to retrieve types lemmatized to hypolemmas with PoS ADJ (endpoint: https://lila-erc.eu/sparql/):

```
PREFIX rdfs: <http://www.w3.org
   /2000/01/rdf-schema#>
PREFIX lila: <http://lila-erc.eu/
   ontologies/lila/>
PREFIX dc: <http://purl.org/dc/
   elements/1.1/>
PREFIX rdf: <http://www.w3.org
   /1999/02/22-rdf-syntax-ns#>
PREFIX powla: <http://purl.org/
   powla/powla.owl#>

SELECT distinct ?corpora2_title ?
   token2_label ?lemma2_label (
   count(?token2) as ?nToken2)
    WHERE
    {
      VALUES ?corpora2 {
    <http://lila-erc.eu/data/
       corpora/CIRCSELatinLibrary
       /id/corpus>
    <http://lila-erc.eu/data/
       corpora/UDante/id/corpus>
    <http://lila-erc.eu/data/
       corpora/Lasla/id/corpus>
    <http://lila-erc.eu/data/
       corpora/CorpusFibonacci/id
       /corpus>
```

```
    <http://lila-erc.eu/data/
       corpora/CLaSSES/id/corpus>
    <http://lila-erc.eu/data/
       corpora/ITTB/id/corpus>
  }
  ?lemma2 rdf:type lila:Hypolemma
      ;
      lila:hasPOS lila:adjective
         ;
      rdfs:label ?lemma2_label .
      ?token2 lila:hasLemma ?
         lemma2 ;
      rdf:type powla:Terminal ;
      powla:hasLayer ?
         DocumentLayer2 ;
      rdfs:label ?token2_label .
  ?DocumentLayer2 powla:
     hasDocument ?Document2 .
  ?Document2 ^powla:
     hasSubDocument ?corpora2 .
  ?corpora2 dc:title ?
     corpora2_title .
}
order by ?token2_label
```

(3)

SPARQL query to retrieve types by harmonized lemmatization, i.e, either lemmatized to a lemma with PoS VERB, or to one of its hypolemmas with PoS ADJ (endpoint: https://lila-erc.eu/sparql/):

```
PREFIX lila: <http://lila-erc.eu/
   ontologies/lila/>
PREFIX rdfs: <http://www.w3.org
   /2000/01/rdf-schema#>
PREFIX dc: <http://purl.org/dc/
   elements/1.1/>
PREFIX rdf: <http://www.w3.org
   /1999/02/22-rdf-syntax-ns#>
PREFIX powla: <http://purl.org/
   powla/powla.owl#>
SELECT ?token_label ?lemma_label
   ?lemma ?pos_label (count(?
   token) as ?nToken) WHERE {
  VALUES ?corpora {
    <http://lila-erc.eu/data/
       corpora/CIRCSELatinLibrary
       /id/corpus>
    <http://lila-erc.eu/data/
       corpora/UDante/id/corpus>
    <http://lila-erc.eu/data/
       corpora/Lasla/id/corpus>
  <http://lila-erc.eu/data/
     corpora/CorpusFibonacci/id
     /corpus>
  <http://lila-erc.eu/data/
     corpora/CLaSSES/id/corpus>
  <http://lila-erc.eu/data/
     corpora/ITTB/id/corpus>
}
{
  ?pos rdf:type lila:Verb;
       rdfs:label ?pos_label.
  ?lemma rdf:type lila:Lemma ;
         lila:hasPOS ?pos ;
         rdfs:label ?
            lemma_label .
  ?token lila:hasLemma ?lemma ;
         rdf:type powla:
            Terminal ;
         powla:hasLayer ?
            DocumentLayer ;
         rdfs:label ?
            token_label .
  ?DocumentLayer powla:
     hasDocument ?Document .
  ?Document ^powla:
     hasSubDocument ?corpora .
}
UNION{
  ?pos rdf:type lila:Adjective;
       rdfs:label ?pos_label.
  ?hypolemma rdf:type lila:
     Hypolemma ;
            lila:hasPOS ?pos ;
            rdfs:label ?
               lemma_label .

  ?hypolemma  lila:isHypolemma
     ?lemma.

  ?token lila:hasLemma ?
     hypolemma ;
         rdf:type powla:
            Terminal ;
         powla:hasLayer ?
            DocumentLayer ;
         rdfs:label ?
            token_label .
  ?DocumentLayer powla:
     hasDocument ?Document .
  ?Document ^powla:
     hasSubDocument ?corpora .
}
```

```
} group by ?token_label ?lemma  ?
   lemma_label ?pos_label
```

UD-KSL Treebank v1.3: A semi-automated framework for aligning XPOS-extracted units with UPOS tags

Hakyung Sung[1] Gyu-Ho Shin[2]
Chanyoung Lee[3] You Kyung Sung[4] Boo Kyung Jung[5]
[1]Linguistics, University of Oregon
[2]Linguistics, University of Illinois Chicago
[3]Korean Language and Literature, Konkuk University
[4]Library and Information Science, Chung-Ang University
[5]East Asian Languages and Literatures, Yale University

Abstract

The present study extends recent work on Universal Dependencies annotations for second-language (L2) Korean by introducing a semi-automated framework that identifies morphosyntactic constructions from XPOS sequences and aligns those constructions with corresponding UPOS categories. We also broaden the existing L2-Korean corpus by annotating 2,998 new sentences from argumentative essays. To evaluate the impact of XPOS-UPOS alignments, we fine-tune L2-Korean morphosyntactic analysis models on datasets both with and without these alignments, using two NLP toolkits. Our results indicate that the aligned dataset not only improves consistency across annotation layers but also enhances morphosyntactic tagging and dependency-parsing accuracy, particularly in cases of limited annotated data.

1 Introduction

Ongoing efforts to develop linguistic annotations for learner corpora have produced valuable resources that support quantitative, targeted analyses of specific linguistic features (e.g., argument structure constructions: Sung and Kyle, 2024, stance-taking features: Eguchi and Kyle, 2023, grammatical errors: Dahlmeier et al., 2013, sign language: Mesch and Schönström, 2018). One such initiative focuses on morphosyntactic features, including part-of-speech (POS) categories and dependency relations, thereby allowing for more fine-grained investigations on linguistic structures produced by learners (Gries and Berez, 2017). These investigations can inform theoretical models of language development and improve empirical approaches to evaluating learner performance. In parallel, many learner corpora follow the Universal Dependencies (UD) framework, providing cross-linguistic consistency in grammatical structures via universal POS and dependency tags (Berzak et al., 2016; Di Nuovo et al., 2019; Lee et al., 2017; Kyle et al., 2022; Rozovskaya, 2024).

Notably, second language (L2) Korean has recently been incorporated into this growing body of UD-annotated learner corpora (Sung and Shin, 2023, 2024, 2025). Previous research on UD annotations for L2 Korean has produced expert-curated resources with detailed XPOS tags from the Korean-specific Sejong set, enabling fine-grained morphosyntactic feature extraction. In contrast, the corresponding universal POS (UPOS) tags in these corpora were typically generated automatically—using a domain-general Korean analysis package (e.g., Stanza-GSD; Qi et al., 2020)—with minimal human validation (Sung and Shin, 2025). This disparity in annotation procedures may lead to inconsistencies, potentially undermining the dataset's internal reliability and reducing the accuracy of downstream applications.[1]

To address this gap, this study extends recent L2-Korean UD work (Sung and Shin, 2025) by introducing a semi-automated framework that aligns XPOS tags with UPOS categories, combining automation with targeted human validation. This framework is informed by the structure of Korean *eojeol*—a morphosyntactic unit defined by whitespace segmentation—and explains how different morphemes combine to form specific morphosyntactic categories.We also expand the L2-Korean corpus with 2,998 newly annotated sentences from argumentative essays. To assess the benefits of XPOS–UPOS alignment on model performance, we fine-tune L2-Korean morphosyntactic analysis models on datasets with and without this alignment using two NLP toolkits. Results show that alignment improves tagging and dependency parsing accuracy, particularly in low-resource settings—likely due to greater consistency

[1]According to Kanayama et al., 2017 (p. 270), UPOS tagging errors can negatively impact dependency parsing, one of the downstream tasks sensitive to annotation inconsistencies.

Proceedings of the 19th Linguistic Annotation Workshop (LAW-XIX-2025), pages 115–125
July 31, 2025 ©2025 Association for Computational Linguistics

between UPOS tags and syntactic dependencies.

2 Datasets

2.1 L2-Korean UD treebank v1.2

We built upon the latest L2-Korean UD treebank (UD-KSL v1.2; Sung and Shin, 2025), which contains 12,984 manually annotated sentences. In its previous iterations, each sentence was annotated by trained linguists across three annotation layers: (1) Each eojeol was segmented into individual morphemes—the minimal meaning-bearing units, including both lexical roots and grammatical affixes (e.g., case particles, verbal morphology); (2) Each morpheme was tagged with its lexical or grammatical category using XPOS tags based on the Sejong tag set (Appendix A); (3) Dependency relations between eojeols indicating grammatical functions (e.g., subject, object) were annotated according to the UD framework (de Marneffe et al., 2021).

2.2 Data collection

Participant profiles and essay prompts We collected argumentative essays from 153 L2-Korean learners with diverse linguistic backgrounds, including Czech (n = 40; mean age = 24.3, SD = 2.8), English (n = 49; mean age = 23.7, SD = 4.5), Mandarin Chinese (n = 36; mean age = 25.5, SD = 3.2), and Korean as a heritage language (n = 28; mean age = 24.0, SD = 2.0). All texts were elicited through a genre-controlled writing tasks designed to assess learners' linguistic ability to construct and support claims in Korean.[2] Essay prompts were adapted from the official Test of Proficiency in Korean. For Mandarin Chinese-speaking learners, two prompts were used: (1) "Which do you think is more important, conservation of nature or development of nature?" (2) "Which do you prefer, competition or cooperation?"; for the other learner groups, three prompts were used (1) "Is early language education necessary for children?", (2) "Do we need to learn history?", (3) "Which do you prefer, competition or cooperation?".

Data elicitation and transcription Participants wrote argumentative essays by hand during individual Zoom sessions, with 20 minutes allocated per topic. Prompts were presented on the spot in both Korean and the participant's native language, and reference materials were not allowed. Handwritten

[2]The texts included in UD-KSL v1.2, which lacked genre control, consisted primarily of descriptive or narrative texts.

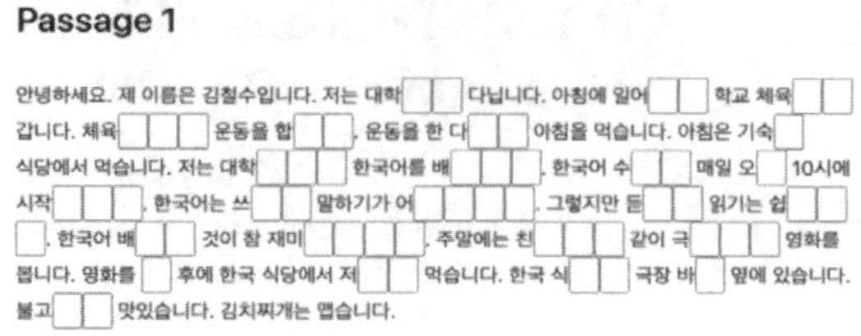

Figure 1: Example of the Korean C-test (Lee-Ellis, 2009)

essays were submitted as image files and manually transcribed into machine-readable texts by native Korean speakers with advanced linguistic expertise, preserving all original errors (i.e., no *a priori* corrections were made, nor was technical assistance applied, during manual transcription). All personally identifying information was anonymized.

Proficiency evaluation While collecting the samples, we measured participants' general Korean language proficiency using the Korean C-test (Lee-Ellis, 2009), which serves as a proxy for overall language ability by assessing comprehension of Korean sentences of varying lengths and complexity. The test comprises five passages with blanks inserted at the syllable level (Figure 1); each blank corresponds to a syllable and may appear in various positions within an eojeol. For testing efficiency, only the first four passages were used, as recommended by Lee-Ellis (2009). Participants received one point for each correctly restored blank, with a maximum possible score of 188. The test took approximately 20 minutes to complete, and participants' scores ranged from 37 to 181 (M = 114, SD = 32.9). These proficiency scores were included as metadata in the dataset. Although they were not used in the current analysis, we believe they may serve as a valuable resource for future studies.

2.3 Manual annotations: XPOS & deprel

Following the UD-KSL treebank v1.2 annotation procedure, we manually lemmatized eojeols, annotated XPOS tags, and marked dependency relations, using the three-layer approach described in Section 2.1. Four native Korean speakers served as annotators. Raw data were first auto-tagged using a *Stanza* Korean (GSD) model (Qi et al., 2020) fine-tuned on UD-KSL, and then reviewed and corrected by two primary annotators. Disagreements were resolved by a third annotator, with a fourth intervening if no consensus was reached. In total, 2,998 sentences were annotated and updated.

Annotation guideline Alongside the annotations, we developed an open-source annotation guideline covering 43 XPOS tags and 31 UD tags used in constructing the UD-KSL treebank.[3] Each tag was described in four categories: (1) Definition provided a brief explanation of the tag's core meaning; (2) Characteristics outlined its syntactic roles and functions in Korean, along with tagging guidelines; (3) Clarifications addressed ambiguous instances, distinctions from similar tags, exceptions, and rules for compound or derived forms (for XPOS only); and (4) Examples illustrated usage through representative examples drawn from the treebank.

3 XPOS-UPOS alignment

3.1 Motivation

The alignment between XPOS and UPOS tags is essential for capturing Korean's morphological richness while preserving the UD framework's cross-linguistic consistency. UPOS tags are intentionally coarse-grained to support cross-linguistic comparison by abstracting away from language-specific details (de Marneffe et al., 2021). While this abstraction serves the goals of universality, it also introduces challenges for morphologically rich languages such as Korean, where multiple grammatical elements are often agglutinated within a single spacing unit (Sohn, 1999). In such cases, the coarse granularity of UPOS may obscure important morphosyntactic information that is relevant for fine-grained linguistic analysis or learner language annotation (Han et al., 2020).

To illustrate this issue, consider the eojeol 학생이 (glossed as student.NOM), which consists of two morphemes: (1) 학생 'student,' a lexical morpheme tagged as NNG (common noun), corresponding to the UPOS category NOUN; and (2) -이, a grammatical morpheme tagged as JKS (nominative case marker), which could map to the UPOS category PART. However, in the UD framework, UPOS tagging in Korean is applied at the eojeol level, requiring a single UPOS tag for the entire unit. In this case, it is typically labeled as NOUN, since the lexical noun functions as the syntactic head (cf. Noh et al., 2018).

When XPOS annotations are available, identifying the head morpheme within an eojeol enables more accurate and consistent mapping from XPOS to UPOS categories. This alignment preserves the syntactic abstraction offered by UPOS while retaining key morphological details from the XPOS layer (e.g., Kanayama et al., 2018, Figure 3).[4]

3.2 Process and rationale

To construct reliable alignments between XPOS and UPOS tags, we used the gold-standard XPOS annotations from the UD-KSL v1.2. We first extracted all eojeol-level constructions,[5] each annotated with a sequence of XPOS tags. This yielded 2,080 unique constructions in the latest treebank, each representing a distinct morphological structure within an eojeol. We also recorded their frequencies to identify recurring patterns.

To focus manual review on common constructions, we applied a frequency threshold of five. Constructions that appeared more than five times were manually examined for XPOS–UPOS alignment, while those with five or fewer occurrences were assigned UPOS tags using default mapping heuristics. Notably, the manually reviewed constructions accounted for 96.41% (64,583 out of 66,989) of all eojeols in the treebank.

Using this frequency-screened dataset, we aligned each XPOS sequence with a corresponding UPOS tag. For example, NNG+JKO was mapped to NOUN, as it includes a common noun followed by an accusative case marker. Similarly, VA+EF was mapped to ADJ, reflecting a descriptive adjective followed by a sentence-final ending. Two Korean linguists independently performed the initial alignment using a double-blind procedure. Disagreements were adjudicated by a third linguist with relevant expertise. Table 1 presents representative constructions, their UPOS mappings, and corpus frequency counts.

3.3 Challenges

While direct alignment from XPOS to UPOS is currently the most practical approach, it inevitably sacrifices the rich, language-specific distinctions that XPOS encodes in favor of UPOS's universal categories (Lee et al., 2019). In Korean, where a single eojeol can encapsulate multiple morphemes

[3] https://nlpxl2korean.github.io/UD-KSL/

[4] To our knowledge, no fixed standard exists for mapping XPOS to UPOS in existing Korean UD treebanks. According to official UD guidelines, if an XPOS field is included, the treebank's README must specify how each XPOS tag maps to a UPOS value. This mapping may depend on additional contextual or annotated information (cf. https://universaldependencies.org/format.html).

[5] Drawing on a usage-based constructionist approach, we define *constructions* as morphosyntactic sequences within an eojeol that instantiate dedicated form-function mappings.

Eojeol	Composition	Gloss	XPOS tag	UPOS tag	Frequency
학교에	학교+에	school+LOC	NNG+JKB	ADP	2706
곳에	곳+에	place+LOC	NNB+JKB	ADP	284
이	이	DEM.PROX	MM	DET	176
정말	정말	really	MAG	ADV	4077
빠르게	빠르+게	be.fast+ADV	VA+EC	ADV	326
예쁘다	예쁘+다	be.pretty+DECL	VA+EF	ADJ	615
예쁜	예쁘+ㄴ	be.pretty+ADN	VA+ETM	ADJ	589
책을	책+을	book+ACC	NNG+JKO	NOUN	3679
책	책	book	NNG	NOUN	2546
학생이	학생+이	student+NOM	NNG+JKS	NOUN	2536
내가	나+가	I+NOM	NP+JKS	PRON	326
나도	나+도	I+FOC	NP+JX	PRON	759
먹고	먹+고	eat+CNJ	VV+EC	VERB	3553
먹는	먹+는	eat+RL	VV+ETM	VERB	2553
싶다	싶+다	want+DECL	VX+EF	AUX	639
싶어서	싶+어서	want+CNJ	VX+EC	AUX	303

Table 1: Examples of XPOS-to-UPOS alignment within Korean eojeols. Glosses follow the Leipzig Glossing Rules (see Appendix B for detailed descriptions).

with different syntactic functions, this one-to-one mapping cannot fully preserve grammatical nuance. Below, we list the UPOS labels that lacked direct XPOS equivalents during alignment; such labels are more likely to require case-by-case evaluation to ensure annotation accuracy.

Adverbial construction (ADV) Adverbial functions in Korean arise in two main ways: (1) through inflectional suffixes that attach to adjectival or verbal stems (e.g., the adverbializing suffix -게), and (2) through adverbial postpositions attached to nominal forms (e.g., the adverbial postpositions -에게). In our alignment scheme, the UPOS tag ADV is assigned only when explicit adverbial morphology is present. For example, 빠르게 (parsed_XPOS tagged as 빠르_VA+게_EC; 'fast' + adverbial suffix) is tagged ADV because -게 makes the stem function adverbially. Likewise, nominal forms with adverbial postpositions, such as 학교에서 (parsed as 학교_NNG+에서_JKB; 'school' + adverbial postposition), receive the ADV tag only if the XPOS sequence explicitly includes a recognized adverbial postposition.

Auxiliary verb construction (AUX) In Korean, auxiliary predicates, including both auxiliary verbs (e.g., 하려고 하다 and auxiliary adjectives (e.g., 예뻐 보이다), convey rich grammatical meanings and differ significantly from their Indo-European counterparts (Cho and Whitman, 2022). Under the UD framework, AUX typically denotes a closed class of verbs expressing tense, aspect, or modality.[6] However, many auxiliary verbs in Korean—tagged as VX under the XPOS scheme—retain substantial lexical meaning, complicating a purely functional classification. For example, in 먹어보다 (parsed as 먹_VV+어_EC+보_VX+다_EF; 'eat' + connective ending + 'try' + sentence-final ending), the auxiliary 보다 ('try') manifests its own lexical nuance rather than simply marking aspect or modality.

Auxiliary constructions can appear either within a single eojeol (e.g., 먹어보다) or split across multiple eojeols (e.g., 먹어 보았다). This variation depends on factors such as orthographic convention, formality, and speaker preference. When the construction appears as a single eojeol, our alignment process poses no difficulty: all morphemes are housed within one spacing unit, and the UPOS tag is determined by the syntactic head (typically the main verb) resulting in a VERB tag.

However, when the main and auxiliary verbs are split across two eojeols, additional analysis is needed to determine their syntactic roles. Predicate constructions were tagged as VERB or ADJ based on the lexical root, while accompanying auxiliaries were labeled AUX, following a predefined list (cf. Sung and Shin, 2025, Section 3.1.2). For example:

[6] https://universaldependencies.org/ko/index.html

- 가고 싶다 (가_VV+고_EC 싶_VX+다_EF, 'want to go'), the lexical verb 가고 ('to go') is tagged as VERB, and the auxiliary 싶다 ('to want') is tagged as AUX.

- 좋지 않다 (좋_VA+지_EC 않_VX+다_EF, 'to not be good'), the adjectival verb 좋지 ('to be good') is tagged as ADJ, and the negation expression 않다 ('not') is tagged as AUX.

While we followed UD guidelines for auxiliary constructions as closely as possible, the following cases required annotation adjustments due to syntactic constraints or gaps in the existing auxiliary inventories:

- 먹을 수 있다 (먹_VV+을_ETM 수_NNB 있_VX+다_EF, 'can eat'): In this construction, the main verb 먹다 ('to eat') is tagged as VERB, and the modal auxiliary 있다 ('can/be able to') ideally fits AUX. However, because 있다 functions as the clausal-level predicate, it was annotated as the syntactic root. As AUX cannot serve as a clause root under UD guidelines,[7] we tagged 있다 as ADJ—a compromise that preserves its predicative role while conforming to UD constraints.

- One exception to the AUX tagging scheme involved the verb 되다 ('to become'), which occurs in various clausal types including passive, aspectual, and modal constructions (e.g., 하게 되다, 'end up doing'). While 되다 functions grammatically as an auxiliary, it is not included in the closed list of auxiliaries under the current UD Korean guidelines. We thus annotated the entire construction as VERB. Nevertheless, based on its auxiliary-like morphosyntactic behavior, we suggest that 되다 in such contexts should be reconsidered as AUX for future annotation consistency.

Determinative ending for predicate (VERB, ADJ) In Korean, predicates (including verbs and adjectives) can combine with ETM morphemes to form noun-modifying clauses, serving a similar function to English participial or relative clauses. For instance, in 책을 읽은 사람 'the person who read a book', the verb 읽다 'to read' takes the ETM ending -은 to modify the noun 사람 'person.'

[7]https://universaldependencies.org/bm/pos/AUX_.html

We assigned UPOS tags based on the lexical categories of predicates: forms derived from verbal stems (VV) were tagged as VERB, and those from adjectival stems (VA) were tagged as ADJ. For instance, in (책을) 읽은 사람 (parsed as 읽_VV+은_ETM 사람_NNG, 'who read the [book]'), the predicate 읽은 was tagged as VERB; in 예쁜 꽃 (parsed as 예쁘_VA+ㄴ_ETM 꽃_NNG 'a pretty flower'), the predicate 예쁘 was tagged as ADJ.

Case particle (NOUN, ADP) Case particles, attached morphologically to noun stems, play a crucial role in indicating grammatical functions such as subject, object, or adverbial modifiers. However, the UPOS tag set provides only a limited range of functional categories (e.g., ADP, PART), which cannot fully capture the morphosyntactic diversity found in Korean particles. In earlier UD annotations, noun phrases with different case particles were uniformly tagged as NOUN, masking their syntactic roles. In our alignment, we addressed this limitation by utilizing XPOS information to differentiate noun phrases based on particle type. For instance, noun phrases ending in topic markers (e.g., -은/는) or nominative case markers (e.g., -이/가) were retained as NOUN, as in 학생은 (학생_NNG+은_JX) ('the student [topic]') or 고양이가 (고양이_NNG+가_JKS) ('the cat [subject]'). In contrast, phrases marked with adverbial postpositions, such as -에서 ('at/from') or -로 ('by/with'), were classified as ADP where appropriate, as in 학교에서 (학교_NNG+에서_JKB) ('at school') or 버스로 (버스_NNG+로_JKB) ('by bus').

3.4 Semi-automatic alignment

We aligned XPOS and UPOS through a semi-automatic, two-phase process that combined rule-based alignment with manual validation and iterative refinement. First, we developed an automatic alignment script by using a predefined lookup table that mapped each Sejong XPOS tag to its corresponding UPOS tag. This step corrected 3,063 UPOS tags in the annotated texts of the current work (Section 2.2) and 11,691 tags in the existing UD dataset (Section 2.1). Next, a principal annotator conducted three rounds of manual verification. In the first round, a random 10% of corrected tokens were reviewed to flag mismatches and ambiguous cases. In the second round, the lookup table was modified based on common errors (e.g., auxiliary versus main predicates, adverbial postpo-

UPOS tag	UD-KSL v1.2 Unaligned	Aligned	Δ (A–U)	UD-KSL working set Unaligned	Aligned	Δ (A–U)
ADJ	4952	9267	+4315	2580	3810	+1230
ADP	1176	1015	-161	290	106	-184
ADV	19545	18864	-681	6332	6237	-95
AUX	1993	1968	-25	754	747	-7
CCONJ	9	7	-2	—	—	—
DET	1265	1421	+156	589	596	+7
NOUN	29481	29835	+354	9669	9720	+51
NUM	418	453	+35	95	104	+9
PART	1	1	0	2	1	-1
PRON	2771	3107	+336	713	747	+34
PROPN	19	—	-19	—	—	—
PUNCT	13032	13030	-2	3342	3342	—
SYM	2	—	-2	—	—	—
VERB	26117	21822	-4295	7825	6787	-1038
X	189	180	-9	79	73	-6

Table 2: Changes in UPOS tag frequencies before and after the alignment process applied to the UD-KSL v1.2 and UD-KSL working set.

sitions) and the script was re-run. In the final round, spot checks were performed on all remaining corrected tokens, and any remaining issues were resolved by consensus.

Table 2 presents the distribution of UPOS tags after completing the entire process across two datasets: (1) the original dataset from the previous L2-Korean UD treebank project (*UD-KSL-v1.2*), and (2) the annotated dataset developed in the current work (*UD-KSL working set*).

4 Experiments

We conducted experiments to assess the impact XPOS-UPOS alignment on model performance using a 2×2×2 design. The factors were: dataset type (*UD-KSL v1.2* vs. *UD-KSL working set*); refinement type (*aligned* [a dataset in which UPOS tags were aligned with corresponding XPOS tags] vs. *unaligned*); and toolkit type (*spaCy* vs. *Trankit*). L2-Korean morphosyntactic analysis models were fine-tuned on both dataset versions with both toolkits to determine whether the XPOS-UPOS alignment enhance the accuracy of morphosyntactic parsing and tagging in L2-Korean data.

4.1 Model training and evaluation

We used two open-source NLP toolkits—*spaCy* (Honnibal et al., 2020) and *Trankit* (Van Nguyen et al., 2021)—to train morphosyntactic analysis models. Both toolkits support fine-tuning on local machines, offer robust performance, and provide user-friendly interfaces suitable even for users with minimal programming experience.

Each parser was trained and evaluated on two datasets: *UD-KSL v1.2* and the *UD-KSL working set*. These datasets include gold-standard UPOS, XPOS, and dependency labels, and were divided into training, validation, and test sets using an 8:1:1 split. The larger *UD-KSL v1.2* set comprised 10,323 training, 1,327 validation, and 1,327 test sentences, while the smaller *UD-KSL working set* contained 2,386 training, 311 validation, and 301 test sentences. Both datasets were provided in fixed and unfixed versions to evaluate the impact of data refinement on model performance.

During training, the toolkits were provided with full morphosyntactic input: lemmatized (i.e., all morphemes parsed in an eojeol text along with UPOS tags, XPOS tags, and dependency labels. During evaluation, the models predicted lemma, UPOS, XPOS, and dependency relations from raw text input. Performance was assessed using standard linguistic metrics: F1-scores for UPOS and XPOS tagging, lemma accuracy for base form identification, and Labeled and Unlabeled Attachment Scores (LAS/UAS) for dependency parsing.

To ensure consistency and isolate the effect of our aligned training data, we used default hyperparameter settings for both toolkits. This allowed us to evaluate model performance under standardized

Dataset	Metric	*spaCy*			*Trankit*		
		Unaligned	Aligned	Δ (A–U)	Unaligned	Aligned	Δ (A–U)
UD-KSL v1.2	UPOS	84.55	**90.86**	+6.31	95.74	**96.21**	+0.47
	XPOS	82.54	**82.78**	+0.24	90.25	**90.41**	+0.16
	LEMMA	87.53	87.53	0.00	84.50	**84.51**	+0.01
	UAS	**81.53**	81.29	-0.24	**91.06**	90.83	-0.23
	LAS	**75.08**	74.79	-0.29	88.24	88.24	0.00
UD-KSL working set	UPOS	89.05	**89.28**	+0.23	92.02	**96.06**	+4.04
	XPOS	81.21	**81.68**	+0.47	87.43	**90.94**	+3.51
	LEMMA	86.35	**86.38**	+0.03	76.41	**81.63**	+5.22
	UAS	**79.99**	79.43	-0.56	83.14	**87.81**	+4.67
	LAS	**72.21**	72.02	-0.19	80.07	**84.99**	+4.92

Table 3: Performance metrics from unfixed to fixed configurations. The Δ column indicates the performance change from the unfixed to the fixed configurations for each model.

configurations without introducing optimization-related variance. Neither model was trained on additional data beyond our manually annotated UD-KSL working set. While Trankit leverages multilingual representations from `XLM-RoBERTa` (Conneau et al., 2020), spaCy's `tok2vec` model was trained from scratch using only the subword features extracted from our Korean dataset.

4.2 Results

Table 3 summarizes model performance of each toolkit on the two datasets. Our current work mainly inquired into the benefits of UPOS alignments. In the following discussions, we explore the improvements brought by this alignment.

Performance on UPOS tagging Aligning UPOS tags improved the accuracy of both spaCy and Trankit, although the degree of improvement varied across datasets and models. For spaCy, alignments led to a substantial improvement on UD-KSL v1.2 ($\Delta = +6.31$) and a slight increase on the UD-KSL working set ($\Delta = +0.23$). Trankit also benefited from alignments, showing a modest gain in accuracy on UD-KSL v1.2 ($\Delta = +0.47$) and a more notable improvement on the UD-KSL working set ($\Delta = +3.51$). These results suggest that alignment contributes to more accurate UPOS predictions across models and datasets.

Performance on XPOS tagging Similar patterns were observed for XPOS tagging, although improvements varied by model. For spaCy, aligning UPOS tags resulted in marginal gains on both UD-KSL v1.2 ($\Delta = +0.24$) and the UD-KSL working set ($\Delta = +0.47$). In contrast, Trankit showed clearer benefits for the UD-KSL working set ($\Delta = +3.51$) compared to UD-KSL v1.2 ($\Delta = +0.16$). These results suggest that UPOS alignment may be especially beneficial for XPOS tagging in low-resource settings, where training data is limited, as in the UD-KSL working set.

Performance on dependency parsing The impact of UPOS alignment on dependency parsing varied by model. For spaCy, alignment did not lead to improvements; parsing accuracy slightly declined on both UD-KSL v1.2 (UAS: $\Delta = -0.24$, LAS: $\Delta = -0.29$) and the UD-KSL working set (UAS: $\Delta = -0.56$, LAS: $\Delta = -0.19$). In contrast, Trankit showed clear gains on the working set, with increases in UAS ($\Delta = +4.67$) and LAS ($\Delta = +4.92$), while the effect on UD-KSL v1.2 was negligible (UAS: $\Delta = -0.23$, LAS: $\Delta = 0.00$). These findings indicate that the influence of UPOS alignment on parsing performance was asymmetric, likely shaped by both model architecture and data characteristics. Further research is needed to identify the underlying factors and assess their relative contributions to dependency parsing performance.

Performance by toolkit Clear differences emerged between spaCy and Trankit in terms of the benefits gained from UPOS alignment. Trankit consistently showed greater improvements across tasks, particularly in low-resource settings. This may reflect architectural differences: Trankit leverages a transformer-based model capable of capturing long-distance dependencies and contextual information, while spaCy's tok2vec model relies on subword-level features and more localized lexical representations.

Performance by dataset size Data size appeared to influence the effectiveness of the alignment. The smaller dataset benefited substantially more from the alignment, particularly when trained on *Trankit*. This suggests that alignment can serve as a compensatory strategy in low-resource settings by enhancing label consistency. In contrast, the larger dataset—likely benefiting from stronger baseline performance due to more training data—showed smaller gains, indicating diminishing returns from alignment as data availability increases.

Additional finding: Discrepancies in lemmatization performance Although lemmatization was not a primary focus of this study, our results reinforce Trankit's relatively low lemmatization accuracy, as previously reported by Sung and Shin (2025). We tested whether UPOS alignment might mitigate this issue, but observed no substantial improvement, suggesting that architectural refinements are still needed.

spaCy, which integrates the rule-based morphological analyzer *MeCab* (Kudo, 2005) for Korean, leverages token-level embeddings from its tok2vec layer to capture local morphological patterns while minimizing interference from broader context. In contrast, Trankit's transformer-based seq2seq lemmatizer, adapted from Stanza (Qi et al., 2020), may place undue emphasis on long-distance dependencies, potentially introducing irrelevant context or overfitting—especially when data are limited. Further investigation is needed to validate these hypotheses and explore strategies for improving transformer-based lemmatization for L2 Korean.

5 Conclusion

Building upon prior L2-Korean UD annotation efforts (Sung and Shin, 2023, 2024, 2025), the present work introduced a semi-automatic framework for aligning fine-grained XPOS tags with UPOS tags for (L2-)Korean treebanks. We also augmented the UD-KSL treebank by annotating 2,998 new sentences from an argumentative writing domain. To support reproducibility and promote further research in L2 Korean NLP, all relevant resources have been made publicly available via the UD-KSL treebank: `https://github.com/UniversalDependencies/UD_Korean-KSL/tree/dev`.

We evaluated the effect of XPOS-UPOS alignment by training models both with and without alignment across two open-access NLP toolkits. Alignment consistently improved tagging accuracy for UPOS, XPOS, and LEMMA. However, dependency-parsing gains varied by toolkit and dataset size: on the smaller annotated dataset, the transformer-based Trankit showed more pronounced improvements than spaCy; on the larger dataset, alignment yielded minimal parsing gains for both toolkits, although Trankit still outperformed spaCy overall. These results suggest that the alignment enhances tagging robustness, while transformer architectures strengthen contextual parsing. Conversely, spaCy's dictionary-driven hybrid lemmatizer outperformed Trankit in lemma generation, suggesting that integrating lexicon-based methods could further improve lemmatization accuracy. Overall, this semi-automated alignment supports more consistent UPOS annotations and robust morphosyntactic analysis in L2 Korean NLP research.

Limitations

One limitation of the current approach may lie in its level of granularity. While the proposed method adopts a linguistically informed alignment strategy, more nuanced or hierarchical frameworks may be better suited to capturing the full complexity of Korean morphosyntax. In particular, certain constructions that did not lend themselves to straightforward mapping between XPOS and UPOS tags remain underexplored. Additional edge cases beyond those discussed in Section 3.3 warrant further investigation to enhance alignment consistency and coverage.

Another limitation is the continued reliance on human annotators despite the use of automated tools for initial tagging. Variability in annotator expertise and training may affect the consistency and accuracy of annotation outputs.

Acknowledgments

This study was supported by the 2024 Korean Studies Grant Program of the Academy of Korean Studies (AKS-2024-R-012).

References

Yevgeni Berzak, Jessica Kenney, Carolyn Spadine, Jing Xian Wang, Lucia Lam, Keiko Sophie Mori, Sebastian Garza, and Boris Katz. 2016. Universal dependencies for learner english. In *Proceedings of the 54th Annual Meeting of the Association for Computational Linguistics (Volume 1: Long Papers)*, pages 737–746.

Sungdai Cho and John Whitman. 2022. *The Cambridge handbook of Korean linguistics*. Cambridge University Press.

Alexis Conneau, Alexei Baevski, Ronan Collobert, Abdelrahman Mohamed, and Michael Auli. 2020. Unsupervised cross-lingual representation learning for speech recognition. *arXiv preprint arXiv:2006.13979*.

Daniel Dahlmeier, Hwee Tou Ng, and Siew Mei Wu. 2013. Building a large annotated corpus of learner english: The nus corpus of learner english. In *Proceedings of the eighth workshop on innovative use of NLP for building educational applications*, pages 22–31.

Marie-Catherine de Marneffe, Christopher D Manning, Joakim Nivre, and Daniel Zeman. 2021. Universal dependencies. *Computational linguistics*, 47(2):255–308.

Elisa Di Nuovo, Cristina Bosco, Alessandro Mazzei, Manuela Sanguinetti, and 1 others. 2019. Towards an italian learner treebank in universal dependencies. In *CEUR workshop proceedings*, volume 2481, pages 1–6. CEUR-WS.

Masaki Eguchi and Kristopher Kyle. 2023. Span identification of epistemic stance-taking in academic written english. In *Proceedings of the 18th Workshop on Innovative Use of NLP for Building Educational Applications (BEA 2023)*, pages 429–442. Association for Computational Linguistics.

Stefan Th Gries and Andrea L Berez. 2017. Linguistic annotation in/for corpus linguistics. *Handbook of linguistic annotation*, pages 379–409.

Ji Yoon Han, Tae Hwan Oh, Lee Jin, and Hansaem Kim. 2020. Annotation issues in universal dependencies for korean and japanese. In *Proceedings of the Fourth Workshop on Universal Dependencies (UDW 2020)*, pages 99–108.

Matthew Honnibal, Ines Montani, Sofie Van Landeghem, and Adriane Boyd. 2020. spacy: Industrial-strength natural language processing in python.

Hiroshi Kanayama, Na-Rae Han, Masayuki Asahara, Jena D Hwang, Yusuke Miyao, Jinho D Choi, and Yuji Matsumoto. 2018. Coordinate structures in universal dependencies for head-final languages. In *Proceedings of the Second Workshop on Universal Dependencies (UDW 2018)*, pages 75–84.

Hiroshi Kanayama, Masayasu Muraoka, and Katsumasa Yoshikawa. 2017. A semi-universal pipelined approach to the conll 2017 ud shared task. In *Proceedings of the CoNLL 2017 Shared Task: Multilingual Parsing from Raw Text to Universal Dependencies*, pages 265–273.

Taku Kudo. 2005. Mecab: Yet another part-of-speech and morphological analyzer. *http://mecab. sourceforge. net/*.

Kristopher Kyle, Masaki Eguchi, Aaron Miller, and Theodore Sither. 2022. A dependency treebank of spoken second language english. In *Proceedings of the 17th Workshop on Innovative Use of NLP for Building Educational Applications (BEA 2022)*, pages 39–45.

Chanyoung Lee, Tae hwan Oh, and Hansam Kim. 2019. ㅎ국어 보ㅍ 의존구ㅁ 뉴섬 (universal dependencies) ㅂ 바ㅋ읍 ㄱ [a study on universal dependency annotation for korean]. *ㅇ 예산ㅅ 길ㅛ 젠 [Language Facts and Perspectives]*, 47:141–175.

John Lee, Herman Leung, and Keying Li. 2017. Towards universal dependencies for learner chinese. In *Proceedings of the NoDaLiDa 2017 Workshop on Universal Dependencies (UDW 2017)*, pages 67–71.

Sunyoung Lee-Ellis. 2009. The development and validation of a korean c-test using rasch analysis. *Language Testing*, 26(2):245–274.

Johanna Mesch and Krister Schönström. 2018. From design and collection to annotation of a learner corpus of sign language. In *8th Workshop on the Representation and Processing of Sign Languages, Miyazaki, Japan, 12 May, 2018*, pages 121–126. European Language Resources Association.

Youngbin Noh, Jiyoon Han, Tae Hwan Oh, and Hansaem Kim. 2018. Enhancing universal dependencies for korean. In *Proceedings of the second Workshop on Universal Dependencies (UDW 2018)*, pages 108–116.

Peng Qi, Yuhao Zhang, Yuhui Zhang, Jason Bolton, and Christopher D Manning. 2020. Stanza: A python natural language processing toolkit for many human languages. In *Proceedings of the 58th Annual Meeting of the Association for Computational Linguistics: System Demonstrations*, pages 101–108.

Alla Rozovskaya. 2024. Universal dependencies for learner russian. In *Proceedings of the 2024 Joint International Conference on Computational Linguistics, Language Resources and Evaluation (LREC-COLING 2024)*, pages 17112–17119.

Ho-Min Sohn. 1999. *The Korean language*. New York, NY: Cambridge University Cambridge University Press.

Hakyung Sung and Kristopher Kyle. 2024. Annotation scheme for english argument structure constructions treebank. In *Proceedings of The 18th Linguistic Annotation Workshop (LAW-XVIII)*, pages 12–18.

Hakyung Sung and Gyu-Ho Shin. 2023. Towards l2-friendly pipelines for learner corpora: A case of written production by l2-korean learners. In *Proceedings of the 18th Workshop on Innovative Use of NLP for Building Educational Applications (BEA 2023)*, pages 72–82.

Hakyung Sung and Gyu-Ho Shin. 2024. Constructing a dependency treebank for second language learners of korean. In *Proceedings of the 2024 Joint International Conference on Computational Linguistics, Language Resources and Evaluation (LREC-COLING 2024)*, pages 3747–3758.

Hakyung Sung and Gyu-Ho Shin. 2025. Second language korean universal dependency treebank v1.2: Focus on data augmentation and annotation scheme refinement. In *Proceedings of the Workshop on Resources and Representations for Under-Resourced Languages and Domains (RESOURCEFUL-2025)*.

Minh Van Nguyen, Viet Dac Lai, Amir Pouran Ben Veyseh, and Thien Huu Nguyen. 2021. Trankit: A light-weight transformer-based toolkit for multilingual natural language processing. In *Proceedings of the 16th Conference of the European Chapter of the Association for Computational Linguistics: System Demonstrations*, pages 80–90.

A Sejong tagset

Tag	Description	Tag	Description
NNG	Noun, common	EP	Ending, prefinal
NNP	Noun, proper	EF	Ending, closing
NNB	Noun, bound	EC	Ending, connecting
NR	Numeral	ETN	Ending, nounal
NP	Pronoun	ETM	Ending, determinative
VV	Verb, main	XPN	Prefix, nounal
VA	Adjective	XSN	Suffix, noun derivative
VX	Verb, auxiliary	XSV	Suffix, verb derivative
VCP	Copular, positive	XSA	Suffix, adjective derivative
VCN	Copular, negative	XR	Root
MM	Determiner	NF	Undecided (considered as a noun)
MAG	Adverb, common	NV	Undecided (considered as a predicate)
MAJ	Adverb, conjunctive	NA	Undecided
IC	Exclamation	SF	Period, Question, Exclamation
JKS	Case particle, nominative	SE	Ellipsis
JKG	Case particle, prenominal	SP	Comma, Colon, Slash
JKO	Case particle, objectival	SO	Hyphen, Swung Dash
JKB	Case particle, adverbial	SW	Symbol
JKC	Case particle, complement	SS	Quotation, Bracket, Dash
JKV	Case particle, vocative	SH	Chinese characters
JKQ	Case particle, conjunctive	SL	Foreign characters
JX	Case particle, auxiliary	SN	Number

B Gloss

Gloss tags and their definitions are taken from the Leipzig Glossing Rules.[8]

Gloss	Description
ACC	accusative case
ADN	attributive modifier
ADV	adverbial
CNJ	conjunctive suffix
DECL	declarative ending
DEM	demonstrative
FOC	focus particle
LOC	locative case
NOM	nominative
PROX	proximal demonstrative
RL	relativizer

[8] https://www.eva.mpg.de/lingua/pdf/Glossing-Rules.pdf

Bootstrapping UMRs from Universal Dependencies for Scalable Multilingual Annotation

Federica Gamba[1*] and **Alexis Palmer**[2] and **Daniel Zeman**[1]

[1]Charles University, Faculty of Mathematics and Physics
[2]University of Colorado Boulder
{gamba,zeman}@ufal.mff.cuni.cz alexis.palmer@colorado.edu

Abstract

Uniform Meaning Representation (UMR) is a semantic annotation framework designed to be applicable across typologically diverse languages. However, UMR annotation is a labor-intensive task, requiring significant effort and time especially when no prior annotations are available. In this paper, we present a method for bootstrapping UMR graphs by leveraging Universal Dependencies (UD), one of the most comprehensive multilingual resources, encompassing languages across a wide range of language families. Given UMR's strong typological and cross-linguistic orientation, UD serves as a particularly suitable starting point for the conversion. We describe and evaluate an approach that automatically derives partial UMR graphs from UD trees, providing annotators with an initial representation to build upon. While UD is not a semantic resource, our method extracts useful structural information that aligns with the UMR formalism, thereby facilitating the annotation process. By leveraging UD's broad typological coverage, this approach offers a scalable way to support UMR annotation across different languages.

1 Introduction

Uniform Meaning Representation (UMR) (Van Gysel et al., 2021) is a graph-based meaning representation framework primarily grounded in Abstract Meaning Representation (AMR) (Banarescu et al., 2013). Unlike AMR, which is mainly designed for English, UMR was specifically developed with a cross-linguistic scope, focusing particularly on morphologically complex and low-resource languages. UMR provides a sentence-level representation that captures core elements of meaning such as predicate-argument structure and word senses. Compared to AMR, it also introduces features to better handle tense, aspect, modality, and quantification in a way that generalizes across languages. Beyond the sentence level, UMR supports document-level annotation, which defines strategies to represent coreference among entities and events, temporal relations, and modal relations. All these features make UMR a rich, flexible framework for modeling meaning in cross-lingual contexts. UMR graphs are directed graphs, mostly acyclic, with each concept represented as a node and edges encoding semantic relations. Through the use of re-entrancies, a single node can participate in multiple relations, supporting the expression of shared arguments and anaphoric reference.

As is often the case with deep semantic annotations, annotating data according to the UMR formalism has proven to be extremely time-consuming, highlighting the need for alternative solutions and partial automation of the annotation process. This issue is particularly relevant for languages which lack the same resources and annotators as widely spoken languages like English. In this paper, we present a method for converting Universal Dependencies (UD) (de Marneffe et al., 2021) trees into (partial) UMRs. UD is one of the most comprehensive multilingual resources, covering a wide range of typologically diverse languages – 179 in total as of version 2.16. In light of the typologically motivated nature of UMR, UD's broad typological coverage is particularly valuable for this task. At the same time, while UMR abstracts away from the morpho-syntactic representation of language properties, UD is primarily concerned with representing morpho-syntax. Since UD is not a semantic resource, a full UMR graph cannot be expected from this conversion. However, generating reasonably accurate partial graphs is already highly beneficial, as it provides annotators with a structured starting point, reducing the effort required for manual annotation.

Our contributions include: a) a language-independent UD-to-UMR converter; b) a manually

[*]Work partially done while visiting the University of Colorado Boulder.

Proceedings of the 19th Linguistic Annotation Workshop (LAW-XIX-2025), pages 126–136
July 31, 2025 ©2025 Association for Computational Linguistics

annotated test set comprising 100 parallel sentences in three languages (Czech, English, and Italian), for a total of 300 sentences;[1] c) two-fold evaluation of the conversion, aimed at providing insights into the interaction between syntax and semantics.

The remainder of the paper is structured as follows. We first provide background on conversion strategies to UMR (Section 2), followed by the presentation (Section 3) and evaluation (Section 4) of the UD-to-UMR converter. Finally, we conclude with a discussion of future directions (Section 5).

2 Related Work

Like other forms of semantic representation, UMR annotation is a time-consuming and labor-intensive task, highlighting the need for automatization methods that could streamline the process. Converting AMR corpora to UMR (Bonn et al., 2023) is undoubtedly a promising and valid approach. However, due to UMR's inherent emphasis on multilinguality, restricting UMRs to languages with existing AMRs is not sufficient. Instead, it is crucial to develop strategies that leverage other available corpora to generate UMRs.

Buchholz et al. (2024) address this challenge by proposing a method to bootstrap UMRs from interlinear glossed text (IGT), providing annotators with a preliminary structure rather than requiring them to annotate from scratch – an objective that aligns with our UD-to-UMR conversion efforts. While their approach is applied exclusively to Arapaho, its potential for broader applicability is demonstrated with Quechua data. Their method generates subgraphs centered around individual verbs, leaving it to the annotator to integrate them into a cohesive structure for complex constructions, such as subordinate clauses. In contrast, our approach builds a single, comprehensive graph that directly incorporates subordination.

Another line of research involves converting the Prague Dependency Treebank (PDT) to UMR (Lopatková et al., 2024). The tectogrammatical layer in PDT (Hajič et al., 2020) captures deep syntactic-semantic properties of language; while maintaining the dependency structure used at the surface-syntactic level, it encodes semantic features such as argument (valency) structure, predicate senses, and semantic attributes of nodes. PDT trees share structural similarities with UD trees, but the presence of rich semantic annotations facilitates a more comprehensive conversion to UMR, including elements such as coreference. PDT is a Czech resource, so its conversion process remains language-specific. However, a similar PDT-style annotation exists for Latin,[2] and efforts are underway to convert it as well.

A prior attempt to generate meaning representations from dependency syntax was made by Han and Pavlova (2019), who focused on developing a system to convert UD trees into AMRs. This approach utilizes a rewriting system supported by a lexical resource containing predicates from the PropBank dataset. While this work serves as an important precedent, it differs from our approach in at least three key aspects: it converts to AMR rather than UMR, it is language-specific (English only), and it is highly lexicalized, relying on PropBank to disambiguate concepts.

In addition to efforts to generate complete or partial UMRs, there have also been attempts to automatically extract specific elements of the graph, such as verbal aspect (Chen et al., 2021) and word senses (Gamba, 2024).

3 UD-to-UMR Approach

In our work, we focus exclusively on generating the sentence-level UMR graph and alignments for each sentence, whereas a full UMR annotation typically includes a document-level block. Our approach involves iterating over all nodes in each UD tree and processing them sequentially. For each node, we determine its position in the sentence graph being generated and produce alignments by extracting token indices. To handle UMR graphs and UD trees, we use the Penman (Goodman, 2020) and Udapi (Popel et al., 2017) Python libraries, respectively.

Concept nodes are defined as lemmas. Since we do not rely on language-specific frame files, we extract UD lemmas to label concepts. This approach occasionally leads to a literal interpretation of the sentence, which may not always align perfectly with the intended UMR representation. However, in most cases, it provides a sufficient approximation for our purposes.

Participant roles are defined through a set of linguistically informed rules that map UD annotations to UMR structures. These mappings go beyond

[1] The converter and the annotated test set are openly available at `https://github.com/fjambe/UD2UMR`.

[2] The texts annotated in the PDT style are the Index Thomisticus Treebank (ITTB) (Passarotti, 2019) and a portion of the Latin Dependency Treebank (LDT) (Bamman and Crane, 2006).

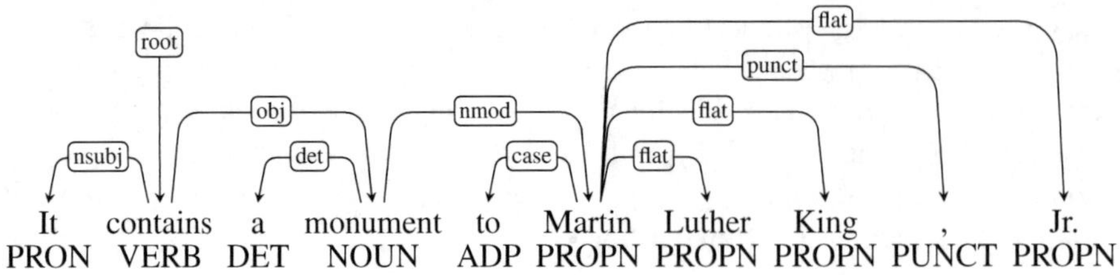

Figure 1: UD tree for the sentence *It contains a monument to Martin Luther King, Jr.* (English PUD, w02005029).

a simple one-to-one correspondence between UD syntactic relations and UMR semantic roles; they combine syntactic labels with morphological features (e.g., Case, Polarity) to infer appropriate semantic roles. For instance, nsubj, csubj, and obl:agent are mapped to the semantic role actor, while obj, nsubj:pass, and csubj:pass are interpreted as undergoer. Morphological cues play a key role in disambiguation: for example, a dependent labeled obl with Case=Dat is treated as a recipient. In some cases, the mapping introduces abstract predicates rather than roles. For instance, appositions (appos) are not merely mapped to a role label; instead, they are converted to the abstract predicate identity-91, following UMR conventions. Similarly, copular constructions (cop) are also converted to a set of of abstract predicate structures. Since UD relations are not as semantically fine-grained as UMR roles require, exact alignment is not always possible. Our goal is to approximate semantic roles in a principled way using available syntactic and morphological cues, rather than striving for exhaustive and exact coverage. The participant roles in our generated UMRs correspond to non-lexicalized semantic roles[3] typically used in what UMR guidelines call 'Stage 0 annotation', where no PropBank-style frame files are available. Incorporating frame files would introduce language-specific dependencies, and our goal is to develop a broadly applicable approach.

Hereafter, we use the English sentence "It contains a monument to Martin Luther King, Jr." as an example and present the corresponding human-annotated graph, the converted UMR graph, and its UD tree (Figure 1).

[3]For example, *actor*, *theme*, *recipient*, rather than frame-specific arguments like ARG0 or ARG1.

Gold UMR graph:

```
(s1c / contain
    :actor (s1t / thing
        :refer-number singular)
    :undergoer (s1m / monument
        :mod (s1p / person
            :name (s1n / name
                :op1 "Martin"
                :op2 "Luther"
                :op3 "King"
                :op4 "Jr."))
        :refer-number singular)
    :modal-strength full-affirmative
    :aspect state)
```

Generated UMR graph:

```
(s1c / contain
    :actor (s1t2 / thing
        :refer-number singular)
    :undergoer (s1m / monument
        :mod (s1t / type-NE
            :name (s1n / name
                :op1 "Martin"
                :op2 "Luther"
                :op3 "King"
                :op4 "Jr."))
        :refer-number singular)
    :modal-strength full-affirmative
    :aspect ASP)
```

In this example, the graphs diverge in the aspect attribute and type-NE element present in the converted graph. The aspect attribute is generated during conversion whenever a predicate is identified, even if no specific value can be assigned. In such cases, it is represented by the placeholder string ASP, ready for annotators to fill in. This approach is necessary because UD morphological features do not consistently provide aspect information, and can prove helpful as the objective is not to automatically produce perfect UMRs, but rather to streamline the annotation process. Similarly, for Named Entities, UD does not provide sufficient information to determine the correct type (e.g., person, place, or other values from the provided UMR hierarchy). Therefore, we assign a default placeholder (type-NE) to be refined during annotation. The same approach is applied to handle several relations that cannot be extracted from a syntactic tree, but where we can at least identify the broader category (e.g., the placeholder `OBLIQUE`, encompassing various UMR relations such as `temporal`, `place`, `goal`, `source`, and others).

3.1 Syntax-Semantics Mismatches

Mapping syntax to semantics becomes particularly challenging when linguistic structure does not directly align with conceptual meaning. Szubert et al. (2018) observed that, while much of the semantics in English AMRs can be mapped to the lexical and syntactic structure of a sentence, substantial structural differences between AMR and dependency syntax often lead to non-isomorphic mappings between syntactic and semantic representations.

One key issue involves eventive concepts, which do not always correspond to verbal predicates. While verbs are prototypical carriers of event meaning, many events are expressed through nominal constructions (so-called event nominals) that lack explicit grammatical markers of aspect (e.g., *his arrival* vs. *he arrived*). Since UD relies on syntactic categories, such nominal events are difficult to identify automatically.[4]

Syntax and semantics also diverge in the case of abstract concepts, defined as concepts that are identified and annotated even though they do not consistently correspond to any overt word in the sentence. Among those, UMR introduces a set of abstract predicates to account for core non-verbal clause functions, such as `identity-91` (equational) and `have-mod-91` (property predication). In copula-using languages, these often align with copular constructions. While some heuristics can help disambiguate such structures, assigning these predicates automatically based on syntax alone remains highly challenging.

Another problematic phenomenon is re-entrancies, where the same participant appears multiple times in a sentence. Since UD trees do not encode repeated participants, extracting this information is not trivial.[5] Moreover, re-entrancies represent a form of coreference, which is typically handled at the discourse level rather than within sentence-level annotation, and is outside our current scope.

Finally, aspectual categories in UMR introduce additional complexity. UMR provides fine-grained aspectual distinctions, but these often rely more on lexical semantics and human interpretation than on overt morphosyntactic markers. For instance, in languages like Czech or Italian, the distinction between states and activities (in UMR annotated as aspect) relies primarily on lexical meaning rather than explicit grammatical cues. As a result, UD-based approaches struggle to capture such differences effectively.

3.2 Lexical Resources

Syntactic information alone is often inadequate for capturing semantic distinctions. In certain cases, lexical information can provide valuable insights, though it tends to be language-specific. To account for this, we adopt a modular approach, designing our converter to allow for the integration of language-specific lexical resources while ensuring that the code operates independently of them.

As of the current implementation, we have created lexical resources to cover interpersonal terms (used to assign the abstract predicate `have-rel-role-92`), conjunctions, verbs associated with specific `modal-strength` values, and subordinate conjunctions that help disambiguate adverbial clauses to assign the appropriate UMR relation. This set of lexical phenomena could be further expanded —- for example, by incorporating adverbials that signal specific `modal-strength` values —- but we leave this for future work. Lexical resources are available for Czech, English, French, Italian, and Latin, and it is straightforward to extend this to additional languages.

3.3 Impact of UD Annotation on Conversion

We have observed that variations in the consistency of the UD annotation have a significant impact on conversion. As in parsing (Gamba and Zeman, 2023a,b), a lack of harmonization in treebanks leads to error propagation, affecting the overall quality of the conversion.

The granularity of UD annotation also influences conversion outcomes. For example, when converting from the Italian Parallel UD Treebank (PUD) (Zeman et al., 2017), unwanted articles appear in the UMR graphs because the feature

[4] One possible approach is leveraging derivational lexicons, but this is only feasible for high-resource languages where such lexicons exist.

[5] Enhanced UD (Nivre et al., 2020) could be leveraged to extract this type of information; however, full annotation across all enhancement types is available for only 19 treebanks to date. Some of the missing enhancements can be extracted heuristically from basic UD trees, though the heuristics are partially language-specific.

PronType=Art is not annotated in the treebank.[6] Without this feature, distinguishing articles from other determiners (tagged as DET)—which do belong in UMR[7]—is not possible.

Similarly, the UD subtypes tmod and lmod, which mark temporal and locative obl and advmod modifiers, are not widely used across treebanks. If consistently available, they could help disambiguate UMR relations such as temporal and place.[8] However, their usefulness is limited, as these labels may also correspond to roles like start[9] or goal.[10] This highlights a structural limitation of UD, where syntactic distinctions are often less fine-grained than those required by UMR.

Additionally, some specific phenomena vary too much across languages to be handled uniformly in conversion. A notable example is date and time expressions, which differ widely in format, preventing a systematic conversion to the standardized UMR date-entity structure. This challenge is reflected by the difficulty of establishing a language-agnostic UD annotation strategy for these expressions, as noted by Zeman (2021). Even when semantically equivalent, their syntactic structures are not always compatible across languages, making it difficult to establish universal annotation rules.

4 Evaluation

Evaluating the performance of our UD-to-UMR conversion system is crucial for understanding its strengths and limitations. To this end, we propose a two-fold evaluation aimed at addressing two key questions: (a) How accurate is the conversion? That is, to what extent are the partial graphs constructed from UD syntactic information correct? and (b) How useful is the conversion for annotators? Specifically, does providing converted graphs as a starting point help streamline annotation?

To answer the first question, we design a quantitative evaluation to assess the converter's performance. However, evaluating converted UMR graphs poses challenges, as these graphs are often incomplete due to the inherent difficulty of capturing certain semantic phenomena solely from syntax. While tools like AnCast (Sun and Xue, 2024) and metrics like Smatch (Cai and Knight, 2013; Opitz, 2023) exist for evaluating graph-based meaning representations, relying solely on the metrics they provide would be insufficient. A more insightful approach involves focusing on specific challenging phenomena rather than just general scores. For example, examining how well the converter handles abstract predicates offers a clearer understanding of its performance with complex structures. Our approach is inspired by Groschwitz et al. (2023), who developed the GrAPES evaluation suite to assess not only the overall performance of AMR parsers but also their ability to handle specific linguistic and structural phenomena. Similarly, we aim to complement overall F_1 scores with targeted evaluations of key challenges in UMR conversion.
Another factor affecting evaluation is graph connectivity. To prevent the generation of disconnected subgraphs, some converted triples[11] are discarded before finalizing the graph. This happens when the parent node cannot be converted, leaving the subgraph unattached to the main structure. Such trade-off ensures structural integrity, while slightly affecting overall conversion scores and adding complexity to interpretation of the evaluation results.

In addition to the quantitative evaluation, we address the second question by conducting a time-based evaluation. Our goal is to measure whether, and to what extent, providing annotators with a graph backbone (the converted UD graph) helps them complete their annotations more efficiently.

4.1 Test Set

Our test set consists of 100 sentences per language,[12] covering Italian, English, and Czech. Each set is composed of 30 sentences annotated manually from scratch, and 70 automatically converted graphs that were then manually corrected. The decision to include more converted sentences than fully manual ones stems from the fact that

[6] As of UD v2.16.

[7] Some determiners, like *some* and *all* in English, are included in UMR graphs because they contribute meaning – for example, by indicating quantity. In contrast, articles are left out, since they typically do not add any semantic content.

[8] Defined in the UMR guidelines as the location at which the action takes place.

[9] Location at which a motion event begins.

[10] Location at which the action ends.

[11] A UMR graph is essentially a collection of triples, where triples can be of three types: 1) instances (g, instance, 'graph'), 2) edges (r, actor, g), and 3) attributes (g, refer-number, plural).

[12] However, for one sentence in Czech and English our approach did not output any graph; therefore only 99 sentences are actually evaluated for these languages. This occurred because the conversion process discards certain triples to prevent disconnected subgraphs. In these cases, the issue stemmed from the top node, i.e. the root of the syntactic tree, being a copular construction, which typically requires mapping to an abstract predicate and is often challenging to convert. Consequently, all triples became disconnected and were discarded, preventing the generation of a graph for these sentences.

annotation from scratch is highly time-consuming and labor-intensive. Additionally, starting from a converted backbone ensures greater comparability across UMRs, as multiple UMR structures can be equally valid.

The Italian and English test sets were each annotated by one annotator, whereas the 100 Czech sentences were evenly split among three annotators, both for manually annotated and converted sets. The sentences are sourced from PUD treebanks (Zeman et al., 2017), containing texts from two genres (Wikipedia and news) and five original languages, from which translations were made.[13] We randomly select our test set from the complete PUD treebank, in order to sample across both genres and original languages.

4.2 Quantitative Evaluation

The evaluation proposed here aims to measure the extent to which UD-converted UMRs align with their manually annotated counterparts, providing a measure of the conversion process's effectiveness. To structure our evaluation, we use AnCast (Sun and Xue, 2024) to process graphs. While its built-in metrics are insufficient for our specific needs (Section 4), its evaluation framework remains valuable and can be partially leveraged.

A key challenge in the evaluation is identifying which nodes to compare between the converted and gold-standard graphs. Typically, this task is handled by the alignment block, which maps UMR nodes to surface tokens. However, since the UMR guidelines do not formally regulate alignment annotation, inconsistencies arise in the data, making the parsing process more complex than expected. Specifically, a major limitation we encounter is that AnCast does not support discontinuous alignment ranges, which are common in UMR annotations. For instance, in a sentence like *He had already arrived*, the alignment for the predicate *arrive* would be discontinuous (aligning to *had* at position 2 and *arrived* at position 4, i.e. `2-2, 4-4`). Due to this limitation, we are unable to use manually provided alignment blocks and instead adopt AnCast's automated anchor extraction method. This method identifies a subset of highly similar node pairs between the two graphs and iteratively refines the anchor matrix through the anchor broadcast process. For a detailed explanation of this approach, see Sun and Xue (2024).

Table 1 presents evaluation results for Czech, English, and Italian across several linguistic categories. It includes both dependency-style evaluations and the phenomenon-specific evaluations described earlier. English generally has the highest performance, while Czech and Italian exhibit greater variability. Performance varies significantly across semantic categories. For example, relatively high scores are achieved for the assignment of `refer-person` and `refer-number` to newly generated entities,[14] or for annotation of operands (`op1`, `op2`, ...). It indicates that these categories are relatively straightforward to map to syntax, despite structural divergences between the annotation frameworks. In contrast, phenomena that tend not to be overtly encoded at the syntactic level, such as modal strength, or phenomena with very specific structures, such as inverted relations, present significant challenges for automatic extraction.

A consistent trend across all languages is the higher precision compared to recall; this is not surprising, particularly considering that, as mentioned in Section 4, some correct triples are discarded to prevent graph disconnection.

A key consideration is that we adopt a strict evaluation approach. Specifically, there are instances where we are unable to extract a UMR relation from the UD tree but can at least assign a placeholder indicating the broader category (e.g., `OBLIQUE`, Section 3). In the proposed evaluation, these cases have been counted as incorrect; however, there are instances where this annotation could be considered (partially) correct, as it corresponds to a group of UMR relations that we have defined as falling under the broader label. Another significant limitation stems from the alignment strategy, as only nodes that are successfully aligned following the anchor broadcast process are evaluated, meaning that a number of triples are excluded from assessment. As a result, the scores may be affected by the fact that not all nodes are compared.

[13] The first 750 sentences in PUD were originally written in English, while the remaining 250 sentences originated in German, French, Italian, or Spanish and were translated into other languages via English.

[14] The UMR representation of these attributes differs from their representation in morphosyntax. E.g., the English pronoun *he* is not represented as a lexicalized concept, but it is converted to an abstract concept `person` with `refer-number singular` and `refer-person 3rd`. Moreover, in pro-drop languages the equivalent pronoun (such as *on* 'he' in Czech) may be omitted at the syntactic level, while it is explicitly included in the corresponding UMR graph.

	Subtype	Czech Precision	Czech Recall	Czech F1	English Precision	English Recall	English F1	Italian Precision	Italian Recall	Italian F1
					Overall					
parent-label		0.666	0.622	0.643	0.718	0.668	0.692	0.712	0.704	0.708
					Edges					
LAS		0.276	0.234	0.253	0.366	0.331	0.347	0.311	0.317	0.314*
UAS		0.516	0.437	0.473	0.582	0.527	0.553	0.493	0.503	0.498*
child-label		0.374	0.317	0.343	0.449	0.407	0.427	0.401	0.409	0.405
LAS	manual**	0.234	0.257	0.245	0.168	0.219	0.190	0.237	0.260	0.248
					Participants					
LAS		0.222	0.203	0.212	0.362	0.303	0.330	0.304	0.269	0.285
UAS		0.380	0.348	0.364	0.502	0.420	0.457	0.432	0.383	0.406
					Non-participants					
LAS		0.240	0.443	0.311	0.351	0.447	0.393	0.256	0.535	0.346
UAS		0.309	0.571	0.401	0.427	0.543	0.478	0.306	0.641	0.346
					Arguments					
LAS		0.378	0.138	0.202	0.457	0.286	0.351	0.500	0.152	0.233
UAS		0.449	0.164	0.240	0.543	0.340	0.418	0.516	0.156	0.240
					Operands					
LAS		0.658	0.453	0.536	0.613	0.575	0.594	0.714	0.533	0.610
UAS		0.671	0.462	0.547	0.642	0.602	0.621	0.725	0.541	0.620
					Entities					
LAS	`refer-number`	0.862	0.403	0.549	0.952	0.385	0.548	0.875	0.167	0.280
LAS	`refer-person`	0.889	0.706	0.787	0.900	0.281	0.429	1.000	0.241	0.389
					Modal strength					
LAS	polarity	0.704	0.605	0.651	0.813	0.688	0.745	0.870	0.637	0.735
LAS	strength	0.180	0.155	0.166	0.224	0.189	0.205	0.235	0.172	0.199
					Inverted relations					
UAS		0.364	0.112	0.171	0.426	0.294	0.348	0.667	0.184	0.288
child-label		0.250	0.077	0.118	0.277	0.191	0.226	0.417	0.115	0.180
					Abstract predicates					
parent-label	predicate	0.410	0.211	0.278	0.581	0.340	0.429	0.548	0.274	0.366
UAS	dependents	0.487	0.447	0.466	0.565	0.565	0.565	0.500	0.500	0.500
LAS	ARG nodes	0.397	0.437	0.416	0.500	0.620	0.554	0.500	0.633	0.559

Table 1: **Evaluation results on the test set** for Czech, English, and Italian.
Inspired by dependency syntax (Buchholz and Marsi, 2006), LAS (Labeled Attachment Score) requires all three components of a dependency triple to be correct (`parent, edge, child`), whereas UAS (Unlabeled Attachment Score) evaluates the correctness of the child-parent relation, disregarding the edge label (`parent, child`). We extend these metrics by introducing *child-label* (`edge, child`) and *parent-label* (`parent, edge`). The *Overall* category includes all triples, since the *parent-label* metric is relevant for more than just edges. *Edges* considers only Edge triples, while the subsequent italicized lines correspond to particular subtasks. Specifically, for *Participants*, *Non-participants*, *Arguments*, and *Operands*, Edge triples are filtered based on whether the edge belongs to one of these four categories. More fine-grained phenomena are then evaluated, as described below.
Entities: we evaluate how correctly `refer-number` and `refer-person` are assigned to newly-generated abstract concepts representing entities (see 4.2).
Modal strength: we separately assess if the polarity (`positive`, `negative`) and strength (`full`, `partial`, `neutral`) values are correctly assigned.
Inverted relations: we evaluate the reported metrics exclusively for inverted triples (e.g., `actor-of`).
Abstract predicates (AP): the *predicate* subcategory measures how accurately predicate labels of APs representing core non-verbal clause functions (e.g., `identity-91`) are assigned, considering only Instance triples; *dependents* evaluates how correctly the child nodes of an AP are assigned to it; *ARG nodes* refers to the correct assignment of arguments to the parent, that is the AP.
* To assess the influence of automatic alignment on evaluation metrics, we manually aligned 10 Italian sentences. On this manually aligned sample, we achieved a LAS of 0.277 and a UAS of 0.569.
** LAS measured on the 30 fully manual sentences only.

	Manual		Converted		Time Reduction
	sentence length	time (min)	sentence length	time (min)	
Czech	17.13	31.57	15.29	17.62	44.24%
English	20.13	10.17	18.40	9.35	8.07%
English (2)	16.90	*20.20*	17.50	*10.48*	*48.12%*
Italian	21.23	11.07	19.51	7.66	30.78%

Table 2: Average annotation time (in minutes per sentence) and sentence length (in number of tokens, excluding punctuation) for each language and annotation approach, and observed time reduction from conversion. Italics indicate the less experienced annotator of the English subset.

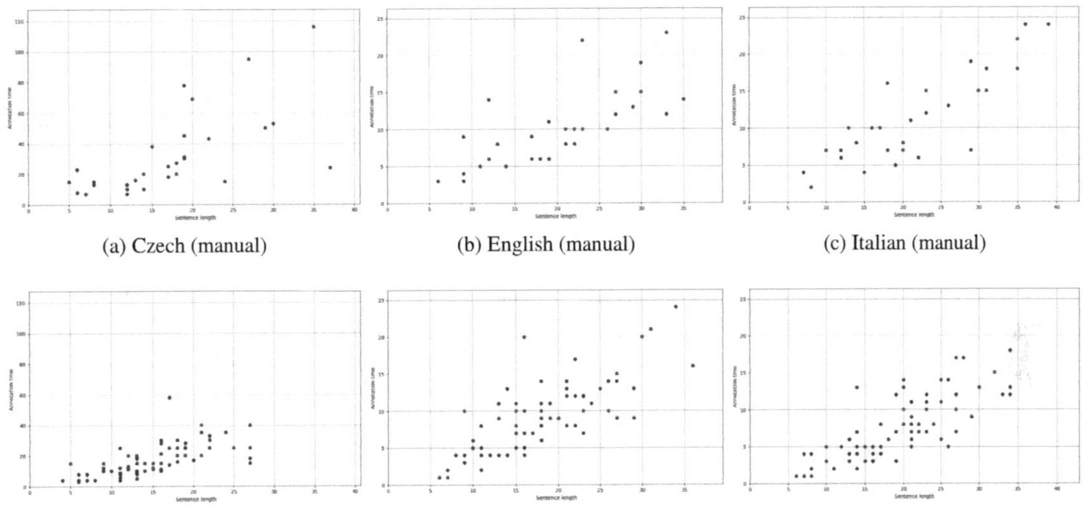

(a) Czech (manual) (b) English (manual) (c) Italian (manual)

(d) Czech (converted) (e) English (converted) (f) Italian (converted)

Figure 2: Correlation between sentence length and annotation time for Czech, Italian, and English. The x-axis shows the sentence length (number of tokens, excluding punctuation); the y-axis represents the time taken to annotate each sentence in minutes. Each point corresponds to a specific sentence.

Language	Type	Score	
		Pearson	Spearman
Czech	manual	0.660	0.773
	converted	0.658	0.760
English	manual	0.728	0.797
	converted	0.754	0.737
Italian	manual	0.858	0.808
	converted	0.770	0.782

Table 3: Pearson's correlation and Spearman's rank for sentence length (in tokens) *vs.* annotation time.

4.3 Time-based Evaluation

The second evaluation assesses the impact of bootstrapping UMRs from UD on the efficiency of the annotation process, specifically measuring whether converted graphs help annotators work faster. To this end, we compare the annotation time required under two conditions (see Subsection 4.1): (1) 30 sentences are manually annotated from scratch and (2) for 70 sentences, annotators are given the conversion-generated graph and asked to make corrections. For each condition, the annotation time per sentence is recorded and the results are averaged within each group (Table 2). These average times are then analyzed in relation to the sentence length, measured by the number of tokens (Table 3, Figure 2). This approach allows us to assess the effectiveness of the conversion in streamlining the annotation process, particularly as it scales with sentence complexity.

The results confirm that automatic conversion substantially reduces annotation time, though the extent of improvement varies across languages. As shown in Table 2, Czech benefits the most from conversion, with a 44.24% reduction in annotation time, followed by Italian (30.78%) and English (8.07%). These differences suggest that language-specific factors may influence conversion efficiency; some languages might inherently benefit more from pre-annotated structures, while others appear to gain less. A key factor is annotator expertise: since the English annotator is the most experienced, the conversion process may have provided limited time savings. In contrast, less experienced annotators may benefit more from pre-converted graphs, as they reduce the need for extensive manual work; this is likely part of the explanation of the longer times and greater time reduction in Czech. To test the role of experience, a less experienced annotator annotated a subset of English sentences.[15] The observed reduction in annotation time (48.12%) supports our hypothesis that experience plays a crucial role in benefiting from converted graphs.

Table 3 investigates the correlation between sentence length and annotation time for both manual and converted approaches. The results confirm that sentence length is a strong predictor of annotation time, with generally high correlations observed across all languages. In most cases, manual annotation exhibits slightly stronger correlations than converted annotation. This suggests that sentence length influences manual annotation time more directly, whereas the conversion approach introduces additional variability, possibly due to errors that require corrections. Despite these differences, the correlations for the converted method remain relatively close to those for the manual method, implying that conversion does not fundamentally alter the relationship between sentence length and annotation time. Instead, it mainly accelerates the process while maintaining a similar complexity pattern.

5 Conclusion and Future Work

In this paper, we introduced an approach to bootstrap UMR graphs from UD trees. The approach was evaluated from two angles: the accuracy (LAS) of generated graphs, and the relative speedup of manual work. Multiple UD-related factors were discussed as possible obstacles for better results (but we cannot measure the impact of each such factor separately). And even if some semantic relations cannot be accurately extracted from syntax, the proposed conversion method has proven to be a valuable tool for annotation. By automating part of the process, it helps to make the annotation workflow faster, reducing the time and effort needed for annotators to complete their tasks. Given the broad availability of syntactic parsers, the potential of this approach is significant. In principle, a dependency parser can be applied to any dataset to generate the syntactic tree, which can then be converted to UMR. This makes the method highly accessible and scalable for a wide range of linguistic datasets.

Future work includes extending evaluation to a broader range of typologically diverse languages to further assess the robustness of the proposed approach. While the current results already demonstrate cross-linguistic applicability, additional testing on languages with different syntactic structures and morphologies will provide deeper insight into the generalizability and limitations of the conversion process. Additionally, refining specific conversion choices—such as improving aspect annotation and integrating named entity recognition (via dedicated NER tools or the Universal NER project (Mayhew et al., 2024)) could enhance semantic accuracy. To maximize the scalability of this approach, we also plan to develop a comprehensive guide to complement the existing technical documentation, making it easier for new users to apply the converter to additional languages.

Acknowledgments

The work described herein has been supported by the grant *Language Understanding: from Syntax to Discourse* of the Czech Science Foundation (Project No. 20-16819X) and by the grants *LINDAT/CLARIAH-CZ* (Project No. LM2023062) and *UMR* (Project No. LUAUS23283) of the Ministry of Education, Youth, and Sports of the Czech Republic. It has also been partially supported by the Charles University, GAUK project No. 104924, UNCE24/SSH/009, and SVV project No. 260 821. Finally, the second author is supported in part by a grant from the CNS Division of National Science Foundation (Award no: NSF_2213805) entitled *Building a Broad Infrastructure for Uniform Meaning Representations*.

References

David Bamman and Gregory Crane. 2006. The design and use of a Latin dependency treebank. In *Proceedings of the Fifth Workshop on Treebanks and*

[15]10 sentences were annotated manually from scratch, while for 20 sentences the annotator had to correct generated graphs.

Linguistic Theories (TLT2006), pages 67–78. Citeseer.

Laura Banarescu, Claire Bonial, Shu Cai, Madalina Georgescu, Kira Griffitt, Ulf Hermjakob, Kevin Knight, Philipp Koehn, Martha Palmer, and Nathan Schneider. 2013. Abstract Meaning Representation for sembanking. In *Proceedings of the 7th Linguistic Annotation Workshop and Interoperability with Discourse*, pages 178–186, Sofia, Bulgaria. Association for Computational Linguistics.

Julia Bonn, Skatje Myers, Jens E. L. Van Gysel, Lukas Denk, Meagan Vigus, Jin Zhao, Andrew Cowell, William Croft, Jan Hajič, James H. Martin, Alexis Palmer, Martha Palmer, James Pustejovsky, Zdenka Urešová, Rosa Vallejos, and Nianwen Xue. 2023. Mapping AMR to UMR: Resources for adapting existing corpora for cross-lingual compatibility. In *Proceedings of the 21st International Workshop on Treebanks and Linguistic Theories (TLT, GURT/SyntaxFest 2023)*, pages 74–95, Washington, D.C. Association for Computational Linguistics.

Matthew J. Buchholz, Julia Bonn, Claire Benet Post, Andrew Cowell, and Alexis Palmer. 2024. Bootstrapping UMR annotations for Arapaho from language documentation resources. In *Proceedings of the 2024 Joint International Conference on Computational Linguistics, Language Resources and Evaluation (LREC-COLING 2024)*, pages 2447–2457, Torino, Italia. ELRA and ICCL.

Sabine Buchholz and Erwin Marsi. 2006. CoNLL-X shared task on multilingual dependency parsing. In *Proceedings of the Tenth Conference on Computational Natural Language Learning (CoNLL-X)*, pages 149–164, New York City. Association for Computational Linguistics.

Shu Cai and Kevin Knight. 2013. Smatch: an evaluation metric for semantic feature structures. In *Proceedings of the 51st Annual Meeting of the Association for Computational Linguistics (Volume 2: Short Papers)*, pages 748–752, Sofia, Bulgaria. Association for Computational Linguistics.

Daniel Chen, Martha Palmer, and Meagan Vigus. 2021. AutoAspect: Automatic annotation of tense and aspect for uniform meaning representations. In *Proceedings of the Joint 15th Linguistic Annotation Workshop (LAW) and 3rd Designing Meaning Representations (DMR) Workshop*, pages 36–45, Punta Cana, Dominican Republic. Association for Computational Linguistics.

Marie-Catherine de Marneffe, Christopher D. Manning, Joakim Nivre, and Daniel Zeman. 2021. Universal Dependencies. *Computational Linguistics*, 47(2):255–308.

Federica Gamba. 2024. Predicate sense disambiguation for UMR annotation of Latin: Challenges and insights. In *Proceedings of the 1st Workshop on Machine Learning for Ancient Languages (ML4AL 2024)*, pages 19–29, Hybrid in Bangkok, Thailand and online. Association for Computational Linguistics.

Federica Gamba and Daniel Zeman. 2023a. Latin morphology through the centuries: Ensuring consistency for better language processing. In *Proceedings of the Ancient Language Processing Workshop*, pages 59–67, Varna, Bulgaria. INCOMA Ltd., Shoumen, Bulgaria.

Federica Gamba and Daniel Zeman. 2023b. Universalising Latin Universal Dependencies: a harmonisation of Latin treebanks in UD. In *Proceedings of the Sixth Workshop on Universal Dependencies (UDW, GURT/SyntaxFest 2023)*, pages 7–16, Washington, D.C. Association for Computational Linguistics.

Michael Wayne Goodman. 2020. Penman: An open-source library and tool for AMR graphs. In *Proceedings of the 58th Annual Meeting of the Association for Computational Linguistics: System Demonstrations*, pages 312–319, Online. Association for Computational Linguistics.

Jonas Groschwitz, Shay Cohen, Lucia Donatelli, and Meaghan Fowlie. 2023. AMR parsing is far from solved: GrAPES, the granular AMR parsing evaluation suite. In *Proceedings of the 2023 Conference on Empirical Methods in Natural Language Processing*, pages 10728–10752, Singapore. Association for Computational Linguistics.

Jan Hajič, Eduard Bejček, Jaroslava Hlavacova, Marie Mikulová, Milan Straka, Jan Štěpánek, and Barbora Štěpánková. 2020. Prague dependency treebank - consolidated 1.0. In *Proceedings of the Twelfth Language Resources and Evaluation Conference*, pages 5208–5218, Marseille, France. European Language Resources Association.

Kelvin Han and Siyana Pavlova. 2019. Going from UD towards AMR.

Markéta Lopatková, Eva Fučíková, Federica Gamba, Jan Štěpánek, Daniel Zeman, and Šárka Zikánová. 2024. Towards a conversion of the Prague Dependency Treebank data to the Uniform Meaning Representation. In *Proceedings of the 24th Conference Information Technologies–Applications and Theory (ITAT 2024)*, pages 62–76, Košice, Slovakia. CEUR-WS.org.

Stephen Mayhew, Terra Blevins, Shuheng Liu, Marek Suppa, Hila Gonen, Joseph Marvin Imperial, Börje Karlsson, Peiqin Lin, Nikola Ljubešić, Lester James Miranda, Barbara Plank, Arij Riabi, and Yuval Pinter. 2024. Universal NER: A gold-standard multilingual named entity recognition benchmark. In *Proceedings of the 2024 Conference of the North American Chapter of the Association for Computational Linguistics: Human Language Technologies (Volume 1: Long Papers)*, pages 4322–4337, Mexico City, Mexico. Association for Computational Linguistics.

Joakim Nivre, Marie-Catherine de Marneffe, Filip Ginter, Jan Hajič, Christopher D. Manning, Sampo Pyysalo, Sebastian Schuster, Francis Tyers, and Daniel Zeman. 2020. Universal Dependencies v2: An evergrowing multilingual treebank collection. In *Proceedings of the Twelfth Language Resources and Evaluation Conference*, pages 4034–4043, Marseille, France. European Language Resources Association.

Juri Opitz. 2023. SMATCH++: Standardized and extended evaluation of semantic graphs. In *Findings of the Association for Computational Linguistics: EACL 2023*, pages 1595–1607, Dubrovnik, Croatia. Association for Computational Linguistics.

Marco Passarotti. 2019. The Project of the Index Thomisticus Treebank. *Digital Classical Philology*, 10:299–320.

Martin Popel, Zdeněk Žabokrtský, and Martin Vojtek. 2017. Udapi: Universal API for Universal Dependencies. In *Proceedings of the NoDaLiDa 2017 Workshop on Universal Dependencies (UDW 2017)*, pages 96–101, Gothenburg, Sweden. Association for Computational Linguistics.

Haibo Sun and Nianwen Xue. 2024. Anchor and broadcast: An efficient concept alignment approach for evaluation of semantic graphs. In *Proceedings of the 2024 Joint International Conference on Computational Linguistics, Language Resources and Evaluation (LREC-COLING 2024)*, pages 1052–1062, Torino, Italia. ELRA and ICCL.

Ida Szubert, Adam Lopez, and Nathan Schneider. 2018. A structured syntax-semantics interface for English-AMR alignment. In *Proceedings of the 2018 Conference of the North American Chapter of the Association for Computational Linguistics: Human Language Technologies, Volume 1 (Long Papers)*, pages 1169–1180, New Orleans, Louisiana. Association for Computational Linguistics.

Jens EL Van Gysel, Meagan Vigus, Jayeol Chun, Kenneth Lai, Sarah Moeller, Jiarui Yao, Tim O'Gorman, Andrew Cowell, William Croft, Chu-Ren Huang, and 1 others. 2021. Designing a uniform meaning representation for natural language processing. *KI-Künstliche Intelligenz*, 35(3):343–360.

Daniel Zeman. 2021. Date and time in Universal Dependencies. In *Proceedings of the Fifth Workshop on Universal Dependencies (UDW, SyntaxFest 2021)*, pages 173–193, Sofia, Bulgaria. Association for Computational Linguistics.

Daniel Zeman, Martin Popel, Milan Straka, Jan Hajič, Joakim Nivre, Filip Ginter, Juhani Luotolahti, Sampo Pyysalo, Slav Petrov, Martin Potthast, Francis Tyers, Elena Badmaeva, Memduh Gokirmak, Anna Nedoluzhko, Silvie Cinková, Jan Hajič jr., Jaroslava Hlaváčová, Václava Kettnerová, Zdeňka Urešová, and 43 others. 2017. CoNLL 2017 shared task: Multilingual parsing from raw text to Universal Dependencies. In *Proceedings of the CoNLL 2017 Shared Task: Multilingual Parsing from Raw Text to Universal Dependencies*, pages 1–19, Vancouver, Canada. Association for Computational Linguistics.

Classifying TEI Encoding for DutchDraCor with Transformer Models

Florian Debaene, Véronique Hoste
LT[3], Language and Translation Technology Team, Ghent University
Groot-Brittanniëlaan 45, 9000 Ghent, Belgium
firstname.lastname@ugent.be

Abstract

Computational Drama Analysis relies on well-structured textual data, yet many dramatic works remain in need of encoding. The Dutch dramatic tradition is one such an example, with currently 180 plays available in the DraCor database, while many more plays await integration still. To facilitate this process, we propose a semi-automated TEI encoding annotation methodology using transformer encoder language models to classify structural elements in Dutch drama. We fine-tune 4 Dutch models on the DutchDraCor dataset to predict the 9 most relevant labels used in the DraCor TEI encoding, experimenting with 2 model input settings. Our results show that incorporating additional context through beginning-of-sequence (BOS) and end-of-sequence (EOS) tokens greatly improves performance, increasing the average macro F1 score across models from 0.717 to 0.923 (+0.206). Using the best-performing model, we generate silver-standard DraCor labels for EmDComF, an unstructured corpus of early modern Dutch comedies and farces, paving the way for its integration into DutchDraCor after validation.

1 Introduction & Related Work

The Drama Corpora Project (DraCor) is a rapidly growing open database that employs TEI XML encoding to standardize language-independent, digitally readable formatting of dramatic texts (Fischer et al., 2019). This encoding facilitates computational and comparative research on drama across historical periods, languages, and cultures. However, manually encoding texts according to the Text Encoding Initiative (TEI Consortium, 2025) is a labor-intensive and time-consuming process, which presents a major bottleneck in the expansion and scalability of DraCor. This challenge is evident for the Dutch dramatic tradition among others, which has only recently been incorporated into DraCor. Currently, DutchDraCor contains 180 encoded plays, while hundreds of historical Dutch plays remain unencoded (Debaene et al., 2024), which complicates further structural and comparative analysis. Accelerating the structural encoding of these plays would not only advance research in Dutch literary studies but also support the emerging field of Computational Drama Analysis (Andresen and Reiter, 2024), enabling large-scale, cross-linguistic, and diachronic comparisons of dramatic traditions.

To address this bottleneck, recent research has explored the use of Machine Learning (ML) to support or automate aspects of TEI annotation in digital literary corpora. Pagel et al. (2021) investigate the automatic enrichment of German dramatic text with structural TEI elements. Using fine-tuned BERT-based models, they predict 5 elements (*"act"*, *"scene"*, *"stage"*, *"speaker"*, *"speech"*) and achieve promising results in identifying these structural features from plain text after sentence tokenization. Similarly, Schneider and Fabo (2024) focus on the fine-grained classification of stage directions in French theater. They propose a detailed 13-class typology of stage directions and fine-tune transformers to classify these, demonstrating that even with limited training data, transfer learning techniques can support the structural annotation tasks relevant for computational literary studies.

Building on these approaches, this work aims to automatically annotate historical Dutch drama with structural DraCor labels by leveraging the existing DutchDraCor as a dataset. Assigning a label from the most fundamental set of TEI elements to each line of text from DutchDraCor, we model this task as a multiclass classification problem. Innovatively, we experiment with incorporating additional contextual information as adjacent lines in the model input, introducing beginning-of-sequence (BOS) and end-of-sequence (EOS) tokens, to operationalize the structurally repetitive nature of dramatic texts. To our knowledge, this feature of drama has not been put to use in similar classification

Proceedings of the 19th Linguistic Annotation Workshop (LAW-XIX-2025), pages 137–141
July 31, 2025

contexts, as related work focuses on classifying individual textual instances, often sentences. We hypothesize, however, that expanding the context will improve models' performance for this task, as it might help models to classify speakers, spoken text, act divisions and stage directions when the immediately preceding and subsequent context is given. The ultimate aim of this research is to support the semi-automated annotation of unstructured dramatic texts for DutchDraCor, reducing the manual workload for human annotators. After validation, the automatically annotated labels following from this work in other unstructured plays can serve as gold-standard TEI markup and facilitate DraCor integration. This work presents a methodology that offers scalable solutions to support the incorporation of dramatic literary traditions into DraCor, even if no specifically historically adapted language models exist, as we expect it to be transferable to encoding drama in other languages and contexts. Our contributions to automatically encode drama therefore include:

1. **Operationalizing DutchDraCor for ML:** We create and release the DutchDraCor4ML dataset, enabling supervised learning for TEI encoding classification in historical Dutch.

2. **Fine-tuning Dutch transformer models for TEI encoding classification:** We apply 4 Dutch transformer-based encoder models, both historical and contemporary, to classify TEI elements in historical Dutch drama. We release the best performing fine-tuned model, GysBERT4DutchDraCor.

3. **Improving classification by increasing context:** We enhance classification performance by increasing the model input context and by introducing BOS and EOS tokens, improving the average macro F1 score from 0.717 to 0.923 (+0.206) across models.

4. **Application on EmDComF corpus:** We apply GysBERT4DutchDracor to EmDComF (Debaene et al., 2024), an unstructured corpus of early modern Dutch comedies and farces, generating silver-standard TEI labels, and release EmDComF4DutchDraCor.

2 Operationalizing DutchDraCor

Given that DutchDraCor contains 180 manually annotated plays with TEI encoding, we can operationalize these annotations to create a fine-tuning dataset for TEI encoding classification. In total, TEI files in DutchDraCor contain 52 unique labels. However, predicting all 52 labels is unnecessary, as rule-based approaches can help create some of the umbrella TEI elements, such as speaker turns containing a speaker and their spoken text, or the list of characters containing all roles of the play. We therefore focus on extracting the most relevant labels from the DutchDraCor plays on the condition that a label contains text. After manual inspection, the following 9 labels seemed to encode all textual instances of a play: *"line"*, for spoken lines by each *"speaker"*; *"stage"* for stage directions; *"head"* for structural indications such as act and scene divisions; *"persName"* for author names and the list of characters, which is in some plays annotated with *"role"*; *"paragraph"* elements indicating legal clauses regarding ownership, dedications, or other prefaces; and *"title"* and *"titlePart"* elements, which marks statements from the title page regarding place of publishing and the editor. Creating random 70-20-10% splits based on the 180 DutchDraCor plays, all text contained in the aforementioned labels was extracted per split for training, testing and development respectively (Section 3), resulting in the label distribution showed in Table 1.

	Train	Test	Dev
line	175,807	64,175	24,857
speaker	40,395	12,986	6,357
stage	3,819	1,304	601
head	2,044	904	316
persName	1,453	444	219
role	1,323	436	203
paragraph	1,211	385	167
titlePart	327	147	63
title	310	97	42

Table 1: Label distribution of the DutchDraCor dataset.

3 Model Fine-Tuning

We leverage the operationalized DutchDraCor dataset to fine-tune existing language models for classification. For this, we choose language models trained on Dutch. These include GysBERT (Manjavacas Arevalo and Fonteyn, 2022), fine-tuned on historical Dutch, RobBERT (Delobelle et al., 2020) and BERTje (de Vries et al., 2019), both fine-tuned on contemporary Dutch, and finally GysDRAMA, a GysBERT model fine-tuned by continuing full-model pre-training on Dutch dramatic texts (Debaene et al., Forthcoming). Each of these models are given the dataset for fine-tuning in 2 model input settings. In setting T, extracted text is given and the model is tasked to predict the correct label. In setting T+C, extracted text is contextualized with adjacent lines, namely the preceding and subsequent line, and delimited with beginning-of-sequence (BOS) and end-of-sequence (EOS) tokens. The model is then tasked to predict the correct label. An example from the opening scene of Vondel's Gysbreght van Aemstel (1637), with both model input settings:

model input	**label**
1T. Gysbreght van Aemstel.	*head*
2T. Het eerste bedryf.	*head*
3T. Gysbreght van Aemstel	*speaker*
4T. Het hemelsche gerecht heeft zich...	*line*
1T+C. [BOS] Gysbreght van Aemstel. [EOS] Het eerste bedryf.	*head*
2T+C. Gysbreght van Aemstel. [BOS] Het eerste bedryf. [EOS] Gysbreght van Aemstel	*head*
3T+C. Het eerste bedryf. [BOS] Gysbreght van Aemstel [EOS] Het hemelsche gerecht heeft zich...	*speaker*

Using both input settings, the models were fine-tuned using the transformers library (Wolf et al., 2020) on 4x NVIDIA A100-SXM4 (40 GB GPU memory) GPUs for 5 epochs with batchsize 8. To prevent overfitting, we implemented early stopping if the eval_F1 did not increase after 3 evaluations on the dev set. We evaluated every 2000 steps, which coincided with a quarter epoch roughly. After training, model performance was evaluated on the test set.

4 Results

Table 2 presents the F1 scores of the 4 fine-tuned transformer encoder models (BERTje, GysBERT, GysDRAMA, and RobBERT) for predicting the 9 labels in the DutchDraCor dataset. Each model was evaluated with the 2 input settings: (1) using only the extracted text (T), and (2) incorporating additional context from adjacent lines with BOS and EOS tokens (T+C).

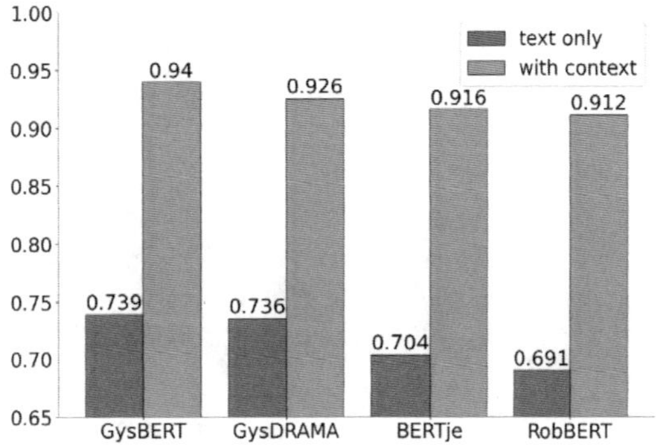

Figure 1: Macro averaged F1 scores on test set.

4.1 Performance Improvement with Context

Across all models, providing contextual information (T+C) greatly improves classification performance for almost all labels. The average macro F1 score increases from 0.717 to 0.923 (+0.206), demonstrating the importance of contextualization in TEI encoding classification. This increase is particularly pronounced for labels that are often ambiguous without additional textual cues, such as *"persName"* and *"role"*, and *"title"* and *"titlePart"*, where classifiers in the text-only setting struggle due to limited information. By explicitly marking the sequence boundaries and incorporating surrounding lines, models gain a better understanding of which textual cues lead to the correct TEI label, resulting in more accurate predictions. Figure 1 visualizes these improvements, showing a consistent trend where contextualization benefits all models, regardless of whether they were initially pre-trained on historical or contemporary Dutch. This suggests that the improvement is not merely due to domain adaptation but rather an inherent advantage of the structurally repetitive nature of dramatic texts.

4.2 Model Comparisons

GysBERT consistently performs best when using contextualized input (T+C), achieving the highest F1 scores for 7 of the 9 labels, including *"head"* (0.951), *"line"* (0.997), *"paragraph"* (0.813), *"persName"* (0.966), *"speaker"* (0.986), *"stage"* (0.918), and *"titlePart"* (0.906). GysDRAMA, which was specifically pre-trained on Dutch dramatic texts, follows closely behind, especially for *"role"* (0.950), *"title"* (0.984) on par with GysBERT, and *"speaker"* (0.979). BERTje and RobBERT also show strong improvement with context but slightly trail behind GysBERT and GysDRAMA in

	BERTje		GysBERT		GysDRAMA		RobBERT	
	T	T+C	T	T+C	T	T+C	T	T+C
line	0.992	0.996	0.991	**0.997**	0.993	0.995	0.992	0.996
speaker	0.940	0.983	0.852	**0.986**	0.882	0.979	0.909	0.985
stage	0.757	0.898	0.838	**0.918**	0.831	0.894	0.821	0.900
head	0.932	0.904	0.936	**0.951**	0.936	0.921	0.913	0.925
persName	0.362	0.939	0.176	**0.966**	0.172	0.956	0.237	0.940
role	0.661	0.913	0.680	0.936	0.697	**0.950**	0.668	0.904
paragraph	0.608	0.774	0.644	**0.813**	0.716	0.756	0.687	0.779
titlePart	0.647	0.848	0.451	**0.906**	0.702	0.896	0.488	0.801
title	0.723	**0.990**	0.646	0.985	0.723	0.984	0.623	0.974

Table 2: Detailed F1 scores on test set after fine-tuning on text only (T) and text with context (T+C).

several categories, as the latter are domain-adapted to historical Dutch. However, BERTje achieves the highest score for *"title"* (0.990), and RobBERT maintains competitive performance across labels but does not outperform GysBERT or GysDRAMA in any class. These results emphasize the benefit of domain-specific model fine-tuning for TEI encoding classification, as models like GysBERT and GysDRAMA demonstrate a stronger ability to capture the textual patterns inherent in historical Dutch dramatic texts leading to the correct TEI label. Nevertheless, the fact that even the contemporary Dutch language models BERTje and RobBERT benefit from the added context suggests the generalizability of our approach.

4.3 Label-Specific Insights

"Line" is classified with near-perfect accuracy by all models, with scores reaching up to 0.997. By far the largest class, spoken text follows easily discernible patterns in Dutch drama. Structural elements (*"head"*, *"stage"*, *"speaker"*) show strong classification improvements when context is provided, particularly *"speaker"*, where model performance improves from 0.852 (GysBERT, T) to 0.986 (T+C). Less frequent labels (*"persName"*, *"role"*, *"paragraph"*, *"titlePart"*) benefit the most from context. For example, the classification performance for *"persName"* improves dramatically in GysBERT (from 0.176 to 0.966), suggesting that surrounding textual cues help identify named entities. Finally, while performance improves notably with context to predict *"paragraph"* (GysBERT, 0.813), it remains one of the weaker classes. This suggests that legal clauses, dedications, and prefaces in historical Dutch drama may vary significantly in structure, making them harder to classify.

5 Conclusion & Future Work

This work suggests that incorporating contextual information substantially enhances TEI encoding classification in historical Dutch drama, improving performance across both historical Dutch models (GysBERT, GysDRAMA) and general-purpose Dutch models (BERTje, RobBERT). By expanding the input beyond isolated text segments, transformer-based encoder models achieve a deeper understanding of dramatic structures, leading to more accurate predictions. Notably, even models not pre-trained on historical language successfully classify TEI labels when given additional context, highlighting fine-tuning and contextualization as effective strategies for adapting modern NLP techniques to this specific annotation task for historical and literary corpora. Beyond Dutch drama, these findings suggest broader applications for Machine Learning and deep learning techniques in TEI encoding, particularly in other dramatic traditions facing similar challenges in encoding standardization and accessibility. Transformer encoder models, with contextualized input, offer a scalable approach to facilitating Computational Drama Analysis across languages and periods, even when domain-specific language models are not readily available. Future work should explore cross-linguistic adaptations and deeper integration with TEI workflows, advancing the intersection of NLP and digital humanities for more comprehensive literary and theater studies.

Limitations

In this work, we researched whether context improves TEI encoding classification, but did not investigate the impact of context quantity on model performance. Although we found that adding contextual input improves classification performance, transformer models have a fixed context window, which may limit their ability to capture distant dependencies beyond the three-sample input. We base our findings on fine-tuning with a single random seed. This means that the observed performance differences between models, such as GysDRAMA performing slightly worse than GysBERT, may be due to randomness rather than inherent model differences. Given that these differences are small, it is possible that they are not statistically significant. Future work should investigate this more systematically. However, model comparison was not the main focus of this study; rather, our goal was to explore how to effectively structure an automatic annotation task for TEI encoding historical drama with existing resources, making detailed benchmarking somewhat beyond our current scope. Furthermore, since our experiments focus exclusively on Dutch drama, the generalizability of this approach to other dramatic traditions or languages with perhaps different structural conventions seems feasible, but remains untested. Inconsistencies in TEI annotations across historical texts, including variations in editorial practices and incomplete markup, pose additional challenges that may introduce noise and affect model reliability. Future research should address these limitations by exploring multilingual validation, improving long-text processing, and refining TEI standardization to support broader applications in Computational Drama Analysis.

Acknowledgments

The computational resources (Stevin Supercomputer Infrastructure) and services used in this work were provided by the VSC (Flemish Supercomputer Center), funded by Ghent University, FWO and the Flemish Government – department EWI. This work was supported by the Research Foundation Flanders (FWO) under grant G032123N.

References

Melanie Andresen and Nils Reiter. 2024. *Computational Drama Analysis: Reflecting on Methods and Interpretations*. De Gruyter.

Wietse de Vries, Andreas van Cranenburgh, Arianna Bisazza, Tommaso Caselli, Gertjan van Noord, and Malvina Nissim. 2019. BERTje: A Dutch BERT Model. arXiv:1912.09582.

Florian Debaene, Aaron Maladry, Pranaydeep Singh, Els Lefever, and Véronique Hoste. Forthcoming. Unlocking domain knowledge: Model adaptation for non-normative dutch. *Computational Linguistics in the Netherlands Journal*, 14.

Florian Debaene, Kornee van der Haven, and Veronique Hoste. 2024. Early Modern Dutch comedies and farces in the spotlight: Introducing EmDComF and its emotion framework. In *Proceedings of the Third Workshop on Language Technologies for Historical and Ancient Languages (LT4HALA) @ LREC-COLING-2024*, pages 144–155, Torino, Italia. ELRA and ICCL.

Pieter Delobelle, Thomas Winters, and Bettina Berendt. 2020. RobBERT: a Dutch RoBERTa-based Language Model. In *Findings of the Association for Computational Linguistics: EMNLP 2020*, pages 3255–3265, Online. Association for Computational Linguistics.

Frank Fischer, Ingo Börner, Mathias Göbel, Angelika Hechtl, Christopher Kittel, Carsten Milling, and Peer Trilcke. 2019. Programmable Corpora: Introducing DraCor, an Infrastructure for the Research on European Drama. Zenodo.

Enrique Manjavacas Arevalo and Lauren Fonteyn. 2022. Non-parametric word sense disambiguation for historical languages. In *Proceedings of the 2nd International Workshop on Natural Language Processing for Digital Humanities*, pages 123–134, Taipei, Taiwan. Association for Computational Linguistics.

Janis Pagel, Nidhi Sihag, and Nils Reiter. 2021. Predicting Structural Elements in German Drama. In *Proceedings of the Second Conference on Computational Humanities Research*, volume 1613, page 0073.

Alexia Schneider and Pablo Ruiz Fabo. 2024. Stage direction classification in french theater: Transfer learning experiments. In *Proceedings of the 8th Joint SIGHUM Workshop on Computational Linguistics for Cultural Heritage, Social Sciences, Humanities and Literature (LaTeCH-CLfL 2024)*, pages 278–286.

TEI Consortium. 2025. Tei p5: Guidelines for electronic text encoding and interchange. 4.9.0.

Thomas Wolf, Lysandre Debut, Victor Sanh, Julien Chaumond, Clement Delangue, Anthony Moi, Pierric Cistac, Tim Rault, Rémi Louf, Morgan Funtowicz, and 1 others. 2020. Transformers: State-of-the-art natural language processing. In *Proceedings of the 2020 conference on empirical methods in natural language processing: system demonstrations*, pages 38–45.

Label Bias in Symbolic Representation of Meaning

Marie Mikulová and **Jan Štěpánek** and **Jan Hajič**
Charles University, Faculty of Mathematics and Physics
Institute of Formal and Applied Linguistics
Malostranské náměstí 25, 118 00 Prague 1, Czech Republic
{mikulova,stepanek,hajic}@ufal.mff.cuni.cz

Abstract

This paper contributes to the trend of building semantic representations and exploring the relations between a language and the world it represents. We analyse alternative approaches to semantic representation, focusing on methodology of determining meaning categories, their arrangement and granularity, and annotation consistency and reliability. Using the task of semantic classification of circumstantial meanings within the Prague Dependency Treebank framework, we present our principles for analyzing meaning categories. Compared with the discussed projects, the unique aspect of our approach is its focus on how a language, in its structure, reflects reality. We employ a two-level classification: a higher, coarse-grained set of general semantic concepts (defined by questions: where, how, why, etc.) and a fine-grained set of circumstantial meanings based on data-driven analysis, reflecting meanings fixed in the language. We highlight that the inherent vagueness of linguistic meaning is crucial for capturing the limitless variety of the world but it can lead to label biases in datasets. Therefore, besides semantically clear categories, we also use fuzzy meaning categories. We support this position with a brief annotation experiment.

1 Motivation

Natural language is a very powerful way of describing the world. Communication using natural language is remarkably efficient because it allows the use of a finite grammar and lexicon to describe a potentially infinite set of situations, knowledge, emotions (i.e. *content*, as we will simplistically refer to the communicated reality in this paper). The means of language have many meanings. The meanings expressed may be relatively vague in relation to the content being described. The properties of natural language, such as ambiguity or vagueness, therefore pose challenging problems for symbolic representations of meaning.

The research question we tackle in this contribution can be illustrated by the examples (1)–(7).

(1) John worked **quickly**.
(2) John worked **with a chisel**.
(3) John worked **with a wood**.
(4) John worked **with a colleague**.
(5) John worked **with / without a smile**.
(6) **With his skills** John worked **with success**.
(7) John worked **behind the house**.

How can we describe the meanings of the highlighted expressions in examples (1)–(7)? One may simply state that, in all examples, some circumstance of John's working is expressed and to use one very coarse-grained category "circumstance" for all expressions (cf. a single label *Adverbial* in the Universal Conceptual Cognitive Annotation project (Abend and Rappoport, 2013)). However, it is clear that the circumstance in (7) is semantically considerably distinct from the circumstances expressed in (1)–(6). It seems that a finer distinction into spatial and, let's say, "broad manner-related" circumstances would be more appropriate. But it is also evident that the circumstances in (1)–(6) differ. Some more significantly, some less so. Are *to work with a chisel* and *with wood* the same semantic category? Should a semantic classification distinguish between *with a smile* and *without a smile*? The question posed in this paper is: what granularity should semantic classification have, and, more importantly, what should determine this granularity? This also raises a question for linguistic annotation: On how fine-grained categories can human annotators agree?

2 Introduction

Meaning representation has long been an important task in computational linguistics, yet it remains challenging for both machines and human annotators. New or extended symbolic representations of meaning are continuously being proposed (e.g., Uniform Meaning Representation (UMR; Van Gy-

Proceedings of the 19th Linguistic Annotation Workshop (LAW-XIX-2025), pages 142–159

sel et al., 2021), Abstract Meaning Representation (AMR; Banarescu et al., 2013), Universal Conceptual Cognitive Annotation (UCCA; Abend and Rappoport, 2013), Deep Universal Dependencies (Droganova and Zeman, 2019), Parallel Meaning Bank (Abzianidze et al., 2017)).

Meaning representation (semantic role labelling, word sense disambiguation) is typically modelled by means of a dictionary or pre-defined set of meaning categories, and a meaning is then captured through the best-fitting label from this set. Most of these approaches have a primary focus on verbs with varying degree of elaborate classification of the verb participant semantic roles (e.g., VerbNet (Kipper et al., 2008), FrameNet (Baker et al., 1998), PropBank (Palmer et al., 2005), PDT-Vallex (Urešová et al., 2024b), SynSemClass (Urešová et al., 2024a)), and there are also broader databases for word senses in general, such as WordNet (Miller, 1995), OntoNotes (Hovy et al., 2006).

Relatively few frameworks have focused on comprehensive accounts of non-participant (adjuncts, adverbials, circumstants) roles, though they are very frequent and contribute crucial semantics to sentences. In this respect, we have to mention the Xposition project (or SNACS - Semantic Network of Adposition and Case Supersenses; Schneider et al., 2018; Gessler et al., 2022), which focuses on the semantics of prepositions and it is relatively close to our project. In this project, 52 so-called supersenses are distinguished and organized into a multi-level hierarchy. At the highest level, circumstances, participants, and configurations (noun attributes) are differentiated. The set of labels is partially up to three levels deep, but in terms of expressed meaning, it is relatively coarse-grained.

This contribution aims to critically consider the trend of building semantic representations, highlighting its challenges, and limitations in addressing the following issues in the task of semantic classification of circumstances (outlined in Sect. 1):

(i) The arrangement and granularity of meaning categories, principles upon which a semantic classification can be built to ensure its credibility, explainability, broadness in coverage, and suitability for consistent manual annotation of real texts;

(ii) The relation between language and the world it describes, the boundaries of linguistic meaning and the role of context and knowledge in determining semantic categories for linguistic annotation – arguably one of the most challenging questions in current computational linguistics.

Our semantic classification is developed within the Prague Dependency Treebank (PDT) framework (Hajič et al., 2020). The description of circumstantial meanings is based on a large volume of real examples that PDT corpora provide and the proposal is subsequently used to enrich the semantic annotation in these corpora (for the upcoming release in 2026). We support our approach with a pilot annotation and evaluate the results.

The paper is organized as follows: In Sect. 3, based on the analysis of recent projects dealing with semantic annotation, we discuss key points of meaning representation: description models (Sect. 3.1), granularity of semantic roles (Sect. 3.2), and consistency and reliability of annotation (Sect. 3.3). In Sect. 4, we describe our project on the semantic classification of circumstants within the PDT framework, applying these key points. The annotation experiment is presented in Sect. 5. Our position and findings are summarized in Sect. 6. Supportive material is provided in Appendix A.

3 Meaning Representation Key Points

In the semantic representation projects, labels are determined more or less intuitively (often without any apparent underlying theory), which results in varying granularity both within a single classification and across different semantic representation systems. Different degrees of granularity and (dis)arrangement of categories, as well as their (un)clear definition, influence the reliability and consistency of annotated data. We are aware of the complexity (and unresolvability) of these issues, but we believe that it is important to raise and explore them, seeking guidance toward their solution.

3.1 Linguistic Meaning and what is Beyond

Regarding semantics, questions about the relation between (extra-linguistic) content and linguistic meaning, which have been repeatedly raised in philosophy, logic, and linguistics (Frege, 1892; Saussure, 1916; Wittgenstein, 1953), are now relevant again. In the proposals of semantic representations, the distinction between these two domains is not always clearly made, which leads to unclear principles in the design of the representations. Resolving this issue should be an integral part of defining any semantic representation, especially given its direct implications for portability to other languages.

Languages differ significantly in the meaning categories they express and the formal means they use to do so (cf. Comrie, 1989; Croft, 2003; Haspelmath, 2010 in general; Levinson and Wilkins, 2006 for spatial circumstants). A cross-language semantic representation cannot simply be proposed in the domain of linguistic meaning. However, the representation in the content domain is a task of a completely different nature, mainly in two aspects (cf. Hajičová and Sgall, 1980):

(i) while there is a clear support in the form of analysed language for the representation of linguistic meaning, it is difficult, if not impossible, to find the principles and criteria by which semantic categories in the content domain are determined;

(ii) while a representation of linguistic meaning is one of the levels of the language system, a representation of the content is beyond language itself and is the object of interdisciplinary study.

The language-independent semantic representation has to be approached by trial and error (cf. the development of semantic categories from a complicated multi-layer hierarchy (Schneider et al., 2015) to a simpler hierarchy (Schneider et al., 2018) in the SNACS project) or refined with the incorporation of any new language (cf. interesting comparison of English, Chinese, and Czech in the AMR framework; Xue et al., 2014). The language-independent representation may lead to a small number of very general categories (in UCCA, only one category (*Adverbial*), later 7 (Wang et al., 2021), were established for circumstants), or, on the contrary, to the postulation of more and more subtle structuring (cf. several hundred semantic categories for prepositional phrases in the Preposition Project, Litkowski and Hargraves, 2021). Intuitively designed, language-independent categories vary in granularity even within a single framework. E.g., according to the UMR guidelines (Bonn and et al., 2022), both the circumstants in the sentences *He decorated the room in a creative way* and *Lindbergh crossed the Atlantic in the Spirit of St. Louis* are labelled with the same *Manner* category. In contrast, the circumstant in *I read it in the newspaper* is labelled with the subtle category *Medium*.

We argue that the level of linguistic meaning (the meaning of a sentence is determined by its structure and the meanings of its constituents; cf. also the notion of compositionality (Partee, 2004; Szabó, 2022) or literal meaning (Searle, 1978)) should be considered as starting point for further semantic-pragmatic interpretation of the sentence semantics in which knowledge of the context and general knowledge of the world are applied; cf. ideas postulated in Function Generative Description (Sgall et al., 1986; Sgall, 1995); these questions were reopened by Bender et al., 2015 (cf. also Dinu et al., 2018; Li et al., 2021).[1]

3.2 Arrangement and Granularity

The concept of semantic categories is a widely accepted practice for labelling the meanings of both core and non-core participants. However, as we already mentioned, there is no consensus among linguists on how to define and delimit these categories, which results in considerably diverse set of labels – varying both in quantity and in level of semantic granularity (the verb-oriented projects PropBank, FrameNet, and VerbNet are compared in Petukhova and Bunt, 2008, for an interesting comparative research for prepositional phrases, see O'Hara and Wiebe, 2009).[2]

The repertoire of semantic categories is closely related to their interrelations. Traditionally, semantic categories are organized (if they are organized at all) in a hierarchy (WordNet, FrameNet and partially in OntoNotes and SNACS). In the UMR project, it is proposed to organize semantic categories not through a strict hierarchy, but rather in a lattice-like architecture, in which categories can also divide the semantic space into overlapping domains (Van Gysel et al., 2019).

However, is a hierarchy or lattice a good solution for organizing meanings for the linguistic annotation tasks? The assumption of semantic categories that are mutually disjoint and have clear boundaries

[1]The idea of distinguishing between formally expressed meaning and "real" meaning is also applied in the SNACS project (Hwang et al., 2017): each prepositional phrase is assigned two labels, both selected from the same set of 52 supersenses. One label represents the meaning conveyed by the preposition itself (approximately the domain of linguistic meaning), while the other represents the semantic role that would be expected based on the predicate or the situation (approximately the domain of content).

[2]In SNACS, the set of 52 supersenses is roughly the same granularity as the functors in PDT (cf. Sect. 4; Scivetti and Schneider, 2023). For example, three labels are distinguished within spatial meanings: `GOAL`, `SOURCE`, and the hierarchically superior category `LOCUS`. These categories correspond approximately to the PDT functors `DIR3`, `DIR1`, and `LOC` respectively (see Table 1). The aim of the current project is to achieve a more fine-grained classification within these broad categories. For example, we intend to describe the various locations of the cat in relation to the dog in instances such as this one (taken from the SNACS documentation to illustrate the `LOCUS` category): *The cat is on top of / off / beside / near the dog* via the fine-grained subfunctors `surface`, `outside`, `beside` (cf. Table 4). SNACS's supersenses make no such fine distinctions.

has already been questioned many times (see Kilgarriff, 1997; Hanks, 2000; Tuggy, 1993). While some form of arrangement can serve as a helpful tool, at the same time, it leads to inconsistencies in cases where very different meanings are combined. A lattice structure seems to be more appropriate, but it does not resolve semantically complex cases (e.g., *at his party* is an answer to the questions *When?* and *Where did he laugh?* and merges location and time; the example is from Clematide and Klenner, 2013 study on (coarse-grained) meanings of German prepositions).

We argue that the distinction between the centre of language and its periphery (well known in linguistics throughout its modern development; Daneš, 1966) should also be applied on the semantic level. The meaning disambiguation is either straightforward – making category selection (even fine-grained) clear – or the meaning is more or less complex and vague (where none of the categories fits completely, or more than one fits partially; Mani, 1998; Hanks, 2000; Sgall, 2002; Erk et al., 2013). In such cases, determining the appropriate category is always debatable, regardless of the arrangement approach (none, hierarchy, lattice). Inter-annotator agreement in such instances tends to be low. This notion also matches results in cognitive linguistics: mental categories show "fuzzy boundaries" and different levels of granularity in the course of reasoning (see Rosch, 1975; Hobbs, 1985; Hampton, 2007).

As Sgall (2002) points out, without a certain degree of indistinctness of meaning it would not be possible to capture with limited means the unlimited range of the world we perceive and speak of. The fuzzy meanings are not only a precondition of the natural language universality but also one of its consequences (cf. also Mani, 1998). These properties of natural language communication – vagueness and underspecification – pose challenges for semantic representation. As computational linguists, how can we address this issue? We need a flexible annotation scheme that enables annotators to capture and articulate their interpretations of ambiguous or fuzzy cases, facilitating subsequent analysis and generalization.

3.3 Reliability and Consistency

Reliable and accurate labels are crucial for classification models. While it is a common practice to collect multiple annotations to ensure high-quality labels, these are often condensed into a single "gold" label through majority voting. However, this approach leads to significant information loss and uncertain ground truth labels in applications with high label variance (cf. Uma et al., 2021). Many NLU tasks provide evidence of annotator disagreement (e.g., Pavlick and Kwiatkowski, 2019; Nie et al., 2020; Zhang and de Marneffe, 2021; Jiang et al., 2023 investigate disagreement in NLI tasks; Erk et al., 2013 provide a summary and discussion of inter-annotator agreement in WSD tasks;[3] Wein, 2025 examine disagreement in AMR framework),[4] and a growing body of research aims to develop learning methods that do not rely on the single gold-label assumption (cf. Erk et al., 2013; Dumitrache et al., 2019; Plank, 2022; Gruber et al., 2024).

Spatial functors		**Temporal functors**	
LOC	where	TWHEN	when
DIR1	where from	TSIN	since when
DIR2	which way	TTILL	till when
DIR3	where to	THL	how long
Causal functors		TFHL	for how long
CAUS	why	THO	how often
AIM	for what purpose	TFHRW	from when
CNCS	despite what	TOWH	to when
COND	under what conditions		
INTT	with what intention		
Manner and other functors			
MANN	how	EXT	how much
ACMP	accompanied by	MEANS	by means of
BEN	benefit of	REG	with regard to
CPR	comparison with	RESL	what result
CRIT	according to	RESTR	except for
DIFF	with what difference	SUBS	on behalf of
CONTRD	against what	HER	inheritance

Table 1: PDT functors for circumstants

4 Prague Dependency Treebank

We develop our semantic classification of circumstants within the Prague Dependency Treebank (PDT) project. The PDT framework is unique in its attempt to systematically include and link different layers of language including a semantic representation at deep syntactic annotation layer called tectogrammatical. Regarding the current trend in the development of semantic representations in the field of computational linguistics, it

[3]IAA is generally relatively low (66.5% to 86%) in corpora that use fine-grained sense distinctions (WordNet, FrameNet) and higher (more than 90 %) in those with more coarse-grained categories (OntoNotes).

[4]The SNACS 52-label set was used to annotate *The Little Prince* novel in English (Schneider et al., 2018), Hindi (Arora et al., 2021), Korean (Hwang et al., 2020), and Mandarin Chinese (Peng et al., 2020). IAA ranges from 75% to 93%. The results from the annotation of the SNACS project show higher agreement on linguistic meaning than on content domain.

should be highlighted that in the latest version PDT-C 2.0 (Hajič et al., 2024), there is a large amount of genre-diversified data (more than 3 million tokens) manually annotated with an interlinked semantic, syntactic, and morphological annotation. The annotation scenario of PDT is based on the original, well-developed theory of language description, so-called Functional Generative Description (FGD; Sgall et al., 1986) and was reflected in several detailed annotation manuals available from the project web site.[5]

4.1 Linguistic Meaning Layer

In Sect. 3.1, we stated that semantic representation requires distinguishing between the domain of linguistic meaning and the domain of (extra-linguistic) content. The highest tectogrammatical layer in the multi-layer PDT scheme is conceived as a layer of linguistic meaning. It captures complex semantic annotations of a sentence: predicate-argument structure, fine-grained classification of semantic roles, semantic counterparts of morphological categories, topic-focus articulation, information structure, grammatical coreference, ellipsis. Later, annotations extending beyond the level of linguistic meaning – such as coreference, bridging, or discourse relations were added.

Figure 1: Same linguistic meaning and different content
A *There is a cross* **on** *the church tower.*
B *There is a cross* **on** *the church tower.*

In the PDT framework, we now focus on fine-grained classification of circumstances. We illustrate the semantic level at which our semantic classification operates using Fig. 1 and 2 and the examples below them. Our goal is to describe how a given language (in our case, Czech) reflects reality through its form and structure – that is, we describe linguistic meaning rather than content or reality itself. Therefore, our categories for spatial meanings do not distinguish the difference in the placement of the cross in images A and B (in Fig. 1) because the language itself does not make this distinction

[5]https://ufal.mff.cuni.cz/pdt-c

Figure 2: Different linguistic meaning and same content
A tree grows **beside** *the house.*
A tree grows **near** *the house.*

(the same preposition is used for both placements). On the other hand (cf. Fig. 2), we differentiate between placement "beside" something and placement "near" something, as these meanings are formally differentiated: the prepositions *beside* and *near* are not interchangeable in all contexts (cf. the proposal of spatial meaning labels in Table 4 in Appendix A). The tectogrammatical representations of sentences capture language specific patterning of the extra-linguistic content.

4.2 Two-level Semantic Classification

Regarding the arrangement and granularity of semantic categories (Sect. 3.2), we employ a two-level semantic classification of circumstants: a coarse-grained classification into *functors* (see Table 1) and a fine-grained into *subfunctors* (based on the FGD theory and first described in Panevová, 1980). While functor labelling has already been completed in the PDT corpora, the set of subfunctors is currently the focus of our research.

Functors are language-independent concepts defined by questions we ask about specific circumstances. This means that the way someone may ask (*how*, *when*, *where*, *why*, etc.), determines the granularity of the functor classification (see Table 1). Functors (although several dozen are distinguished) describe circumstantial meanings only as generalized categories and, from the perspective of linguistic meaning, they reflect only a rough classification.

A fine-grained subcategorization of circumstants into *subfunctors* involves delimiting subtle semantic distinctions within a single functor while sharing the basic semantics of that functor (answer the same question on the circumstance). The circumstants assigned different functors are not substitutable when answering a question about particular circumstance, i.e. the question "How did he work?" cannot be answered by a spatial circumstant as in (7); this question is answered by a manner circumstant (as in (1)–(6)), which may have different sub-meanings (subfunctors). The fine-grained classification of circumstants is language-specific and based on the notion of linguistic meaning. We aim to create a set of meaning categories that have formal support in the language (see description of our methodology in Mikulová, 2024).

4.3 Fuzzy Meanings

In Sect. 3.2, we indicated that we need a set of labels that account for the high degree of vagueness in language. It becomes evident (see also Sect. 5.3) that in addition to clear, well-differentiated meanings, there are fuzzy cases, both at the level of functors and subfunctors, and that the situation is not uniform across all circumstants. While in spatial and temporal domains, the system of questions (*where*, *where from*, *where to*, etc.) is instructive and divides the conceptual time-space straightforwardly into discrete subdomains (see Table 1; ambiguous cases include the aforementioned example *at his party*, in which temporal and spatial localizations are expressed at the same time), in the manner-related domain, the basic question *how* yields diverse responses as we outlined by (1)–(6). Moreover, not all manner-related circumstants can be questioned by *how* (in (6), the only response to the question *How did John work?* is the circumstant *with success*, while the response *with his skills* is less suitable, even impossible). Therefore, we do not treat all variable manner-related circumstants as representatives of a single functor. To divide this heterogeneous group of meanings, we formulate specific questions: *with regard to what* (`REG`; for *with his skills* in (6)), *by means of what* (`MEANS`; (2)), *accompanied by what* (`ACMP`; (4)); see Table 1.

A similar situation arises at the level of subfunctors. While spatial and temporal meanings are typically expressed through formal means in Czech (and other languages; e.g., *before* vs. *after*, *above* vs. *below*; see the proposal of subfunctors for the `LOC` functor in Table 4), languages generally lack special formal means for distinguishing fine-grained subtypes within manner-related and other meanings. An exception is, e.g., the expression of +/- opposition (as in (5)). In the manner-related domain, a limited number of forms are used for various meanings (see the same form *with* used for various meanings in (2)–(6)). To distinguish subtle meaning categories, we look for other linguistic criteria. We mainly apply the principle of form substitutability (see more in Mikulová, 2024). E.g., the Czech preposition *s* 'with' in the `MEANS-tool` meaning (2) can be replaced by the preposition *pomocí* 'with the help of', whereas for the `MEANS-material` meaning (3) this substitution is not possible; in the `ACMP-community` meaning (4), the preposition *s* 'with' can be replaced by *společně s* 'together with', etc.

However, there are still a relatively large number of cases whose meaning is difficult to describe, where none of the well-defined labels fit well, or some overlap, even though the content described may be quite simple and clear. How can we describe the meaning of the circumstant in (8)?

(8) *Šel do kampaně* ***s*** *novou* ***iniciativou.***
'He went into the campaign **with** a new **initiative**.'

To account for this situation, we introduce:
– special labels to capture generalizable fuzzy cases; e.g., we introduce the `event` label (see Table 4 in Appendix A) for the cases where the meanings of place and time overlap.
– special labels for distinction between central, clear meanings and complex ones (such as in (8)); cf. `CIRC` and `side-effect` labels in Table 5.

We also allow annotators to select more than one category from a list. When using a fuzzy category, annotators are required to provide a description of the meaning, thereby collecting material for further research.

5 Label Bias Experiment

The position described in Sect. 4 is supported here by a brief annotation experiment.[6]

5.1 Design

In line with the research questions that we want to address, and the annotators that we have available, we choose the following experiment design.

We examine two annotation tasks:

Task 1: Annotation of fine-grained meanings (subfunctors) within the spatial functor `LOC` (*where*). The spatial meanings are well-definable and formally distinguished. The proposed set of 24 labels used for the experiment is in Table 4 in Appendix A. A high inter-annotator agreement is expected.

Task 2: Annotation of meanings (both functors and subfunctors) for circumstants expressed by the polyfunctional preposition *s* 'with'. In addition to several clear meanings, the preposition

[6]Input data and experimental annotations are freely available at `https://github.com/ufal/Subfunctor-annotation-experiment-2025`.

Annotator	2 options (%)		Not shared (%)	
	Task 1	Task 2	Task 1	Task 2
A	11.25	13.3	6.50	17.6
B	6.25	17.6	3.75	15.2
C	9.25	13.0	2.50	13.8
D	1.25	4.0	2.50	11.3

Table 2: Percentage of sentences where each annotator selected two options or did not share the selected labels with any other annotator.

also expresses a range of less clear-cut, difficult-to-describe meanings. The proposed set of 26 labels is in Table 5.[7] In this experiment, we aim to evaluate the reliability of the taxonomy and the complexity of the task compared to Task 1.

For Task 1, 400 sentences were randomly selected from the PDT-C dataset, ensuring proportional representation of all forms in the sample. For Task 2, 500 sentences were randomly selected, ensuring proportional representation of all original functors. Each task was annotated by the same 4 annotators (A, B, C, D). In both tasks, if annotators were uncertain about the label choice, they could provide one alternative label and add an explanatory comment.

5.2 Results

To assess the complexity of the tasks and the reliability of the proposed sets of labels for consistent annotation, we evaluated both tasks from different perspectives. To compare the annotators, we measured how often they selected two options and how often the labels they proposed were not shared by any other annotator (see Table 2). In Task 1, the annotators were more confident and the choice of an option not shared by others was much rarer.

Giving the annotators the possibility to select an alternative label in the annotation made measuring inter-annotator agreement more complex than usually. For an initial estimation, we calculated Cohen's κ (Cohen, 1960) for each pair of annotators ignoring the alternative labels (see Table 3). With the exception of the pair A–B, all other pairs surpassed 0.8 in Task 1 and 0.6 in Task 2 (see Table 6 in Appendix A for more details). Also note that with the exception of annotators B and C (who agreed less in the second task, rank 2 versus 4) the pairs would be ranked the same by κ.

We also calculated Krippendorff's coefficient α (Krippendorff, 1980) to get a single number incorporating all the annotators. We removed the label `other` from the data prior to the calculation, as there could be different reasons why two annotators selected it for a given sentence; the second option was considered if `other` was the first option. The coefficient for Task 1 was calculated as $\alpha_1 = \mathbf{0.865}$, which shows a high degree of agreement, while $\alpha_2 = \mathbf{0.648}$ for Task 2 indicates poor agreement. However, we have not taken the second choice into account.[8]

A_i	A_j	κ	
		Task 1	Task 2
A	B	0.787	0.548
A	C	0.803	0.603
A	D	0.813	0.636
B	C	0.877	0.629
B	D	0.872	0.641
C	D	0.893	0.668

Table 3: Cohen's κ for each pair of annotators (considering the 1st label only) in both the tasks.

To show which subfunctors competed against each other most of the time we plotted a confusion matrix. We did not have golden data for comparison, so we created them: we used the data as "votes" for the correct subfunctor for each sentence.[9] There were still 6 sentences in Task 1 and 29 sentences in Task 2 that did not have a clear winner, so we let a fifth annotator break the ties. When populating the matrix, we considered each option separately, so we can understand the experiment as having 8 annotators, from whom only one half annotates all the data. Normalizing the matrix per rows clearly shows which subfunctors were confused most of the time or behaved similarly (see Fig. 3).[10] The numbers on the diagonal of the confusion matrix normalized per rows show the precision of the annotators, in the matrix normalized per columns, they show the recall. These two numbers are also shown together with the frequency of each subfunctor in Fig. 7 in Appendix A. We can observe how precision and recall differ in the two tasks: in Task 1, both values are relatively high and only drop around the middle of the graph, i.e., for less frequent subfunctors. In Task 2, the values are scattered almost from the beginning.

[7]The annotators assigned both functors and subfunctors in Task 2, but we used only subfunctors in the following calculations (functor is always implied by the subfunctor).

[8]Finding a satisfactory measure of agreement in this situation exceeds the scope of this paper.

[9]The first option had 1 vote, the second option had 0.95 votes, and the special value `other` had a penalty of 0.03.

[10]The other matrices are in Appendix A.

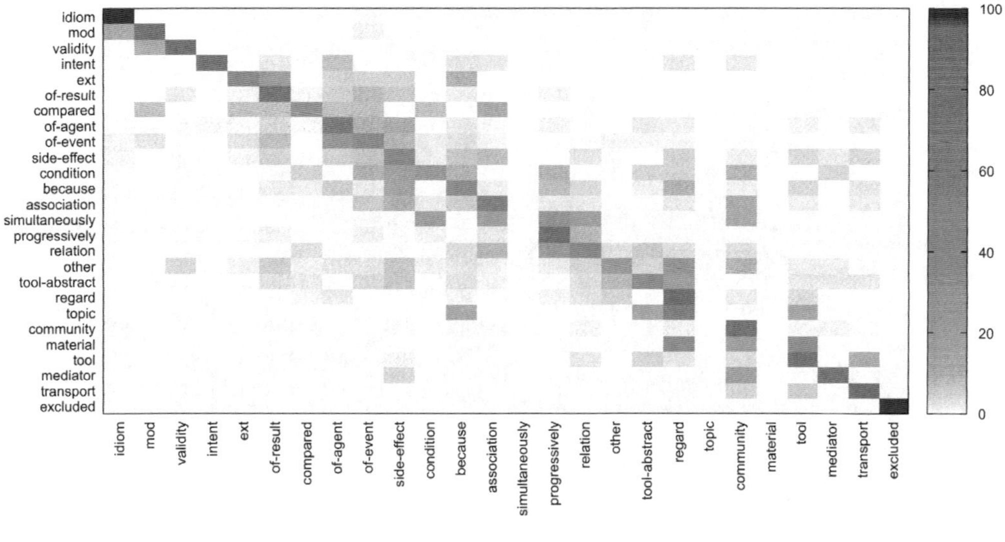

Figure 3: Confusion matrix for Task 2. It is calculated for each annotator against the created "golden data" and the values are summed for each pair of subfunctors. The matrix is normalized per rows, values are sorted to move the large values towards the diagonal as described in (Thoma, 2017) to group similarly behaving labels together.

5.3 Data Analysis

As expected, the experiment confirmed (in all measured aspects) that the annotation of fine-grained meanings in the (more manageable and formally fixed) spatial domain (Task 1) leads to more consistent annotation than the annotation of formally less distinct manner-related meanings (Task 2). In both tasks, some labels show high IAA, while others are frequently confused. Data analysis reveals competing labels.

In Task 1, there are significantly more cases with high IAA (e.g., in (9), there was 100% agreement on the meaning of `front`, in (10) on `near`), and groups of labels that were confused with each other are less common. A detailed analysis shows that cases where the form cannot be relied upon unambiguously exhibit the most hesitation and disagreement. E.g., in (11), the annotators disagreed on whether the polyfunctional preposition *u* 'beside/at' expresses the localization "beside a given place" (`adjacency`, *u divadla je škola* 'there is a school beside the theater') or a more general localization "within a given place" (`within`, *pracuje u divadla* 'he works at theater'). Disagreements typically occur with meanings of localization within a given place (`within`, `surface`, `area`), where several basic forms (*v*, *na*, *u* 'in/at/on') compete and the nature of the given place is also important (whether it has an interior and a surface); cf. (12) with competition of `area` and `inside` meanings.

(9) *Stará paní stála **před statkem**.*
'The old lady stood **in front of a farm**.'

(10) *Bydlí **blízko závodu**.*
'She lives **near a factory**.'

(11) *Dělala **u plničky** kostkového cukru.*
'She worked **at** [lit. by, beside] a sugar cube **filler**.'

(12) *Cvičila **na louce**.*
'She was exercising **in** [lit. on] **a meadow**.'

(13) ***S** psacím **strojem** se nedalo psát.*
'It was impossible to write **with the typewriter**.'

(14) ***S přibývajícím věkem** zjišťuje, že už nemá kamarády.*
'**With increasing age**, he finds out he has no friend.'

(15) ***S** velkými **oběťmi** zde udržují bezpečnost.*
'They maintain safety here **with** great **sacrifices**.'

(16) *Společnost nemá s těmito **akciemi** žádné plány.*
'The company has no plans **with** these **shares**.'

In Task 2, we observe high agreement only for a few clearly and narrowly semantically defined meanings, such as `community` (4), `transport`, or `tool` (13). Regarding less concrete and more abstract meanings, the label for the mutual conditionality of two events (`progressively`, (14)) shows high agreement. For other cases, the confusion matrices show which labels are closely related, and the IAA of these cases decreases. Although in the literature (Fillmore, 1994; Bonami et al., 2004) manner circumstants are usually distinguished according to their relation to an agent (5), event (1), or result (6), in real examples these distinctions are often difficult to make. E.g., in (15) all three subfunctors (of-agent, of-event, and of-result) were assigned, and no single label prevailed.

The high variability of labels in many examples leads to low values of both precision and recall. E.g., the tool-abstract label shows very low precision. Often, when this label was used, the final agreement was on a different label. On the other hand, regard label has a low recall (below 60%), meaning that annotators mostly disagreed on it, however when this label was used, it was mostly in cases where there was majority agreement (e.g., in (16), regard label won over tool-abstract). The tool-abstract label was also assigned as an alternative label in (8). This example showed zero agreement among the 4 annotators, other assigned labels were: mediator, association, community, side-effect and the fifth annotator chose mediator and side-effect.

For further annotation, it is necessary to evaluate in which cases the disagreements occurred due to insufficient guidelines, and their improvement will lead to greater consistency. Annotators used the special fuzzy labels less than expected and tended to assign a specific meaning. This seems to be a good practice, as the merging of various labels into a fuzzy one can always be done afterwards; on the contrary, different perspectives are valuable for further investigation.

6 Conclusion

This paper puts under scrutiny the annotation of circumstantial meanings in the Prague Dependency Treebank, addressing challenges in meaning representation. Our approach centres attention on the intricate relation between language and the world it describes, emphasizing the need for a classification system that accommodates both clear-cut and vague meanings. Our two-level classification balances broad semantic concepts with fine-grained distinctions, reflecting linguistic meaning. We introduce fuzzy meaning labels for cases where rigid classification fails. An annotation experiment confirms this perspective, showing varying levels of annotator agreement, from unanimous to none. By incorporating fuzzy labels and multiple annotations, we enhance the precision and explanatory power of semantic descriptions. Ongoing development within the Prague Dependency Treebank will further refine and extend this framework.
Description of language is far from complete.

Limitation

Our experiment has several limitations. We are aware that the two tasks are not fully comparable – in the Task 1, the selected circumstants varied in form but belonged to the same semantic domain, while in the Task 2, the circumstants had the same form but differed in semantic domain. More importantly, the possibility to select a second alternative label prevented the use of standard evaluation methods, making it difficult to apply conventional metrics for assessing annotation reliability. In addition, the lack of gold standard data poses a challenge. Due to the nature of the task, such data cannot exist. Our study serves as a basis for future efforts to establish a gold standard rather than relying on one from the outset.

Acknowledgments

The research reported in the paper was supported by the Czech Science Foundation under the projects GA23-05238S and GX20-16819X. The work described herein has also been using data and tools provided by the LINDAT/CLARIAH-CZ Research Infrastructure (https://lindat.cz), supported by the Ministry of Education, Youth and Sports of the Czech Republic (Project No. LM2023062).

We would also like to thank all our outstanding annotators for not working like machines, but for thinking critically during annotation and pointing out the shortcomings of the annotation guidelines. Without their efforts, this contribution would not have been possible.

References

Omri Abend and Ari Rappoport. 2013. Universal Conceptual Cognitive Annotation (UCCA). In *Proceedings of the 51st Annual Meeting of the Association for Computational Linguistics*, pages 228–238, Sofia, Bulgaria. Association for Computational Linguistics.

Lasha Abzianidze, Johannes Bjerva, Kilian Evang, Hessel Haagsma, Rik van Noord, Pierre Ludmann, Duc-Duy Nguyen, and Johan Bos. 2017. The Parallel Meaning Bank: Towards a Multilingual Corpus of Translations Annotated with Compositional Meaning Representations. In *Proceedings of the 15th Conference of the European Chapter of the Association for Computational Linguistics*, pages 242–247, Valencia, Spain. Association for Computational Linguistics.

Aryaman Arora, Nitin Venkateswaran, and Nathan Schneider. 2021. SNACS Annotation of Case Markers and Adpositions in Hindi. In *Proceedings of the Society for Computation in Linguistics 2021*, pages

454–458, Online. Association for Computational Linguistics.

Collin F. Baker, Charles J. Fillmore, and John B. Lowe. 1998. The Berkeley FrameNet Project. In *36th Annual Meeting of the Association for Computational Linguistics and 17th International Conference on Computational Linguistics*, pages 86–90, Montreal, Quebec, Canada. Association for Computational Linguistics.

Laura Banarescu, Claire Bonial, Shu Cai, Madalina Georgescu, Kira Griffitt, Ulf Hermjakob, Kevin Knight, Philipp Koehn, Martha Palmer, and Nathan Schneider. 2013. Abstract Meaning Representation for Sembanking. In *Proceedings of the 7th Linguistic Annotation Workshop and Interoperability with Discourse*, pages 178–186, Sofia, Bulgaria. Association for Computational Linguistics.

Emily M. Bender, Dan Flickinger, Stephan Oepen, Woodley Packard, and Ann Copestake. 2015. Layers of Interpretation: On Grammar and Compositionality. In *Proceedings of the 11th International Conference on Computational Semantics*, pages 239–249, London, UK. Association for Computational Linguistics.

Olivier Bonami, Danièle Godard, and Brigitte Kampers-Manhe. 2004. Adverb classification. In *Handbook of French Semantics*, pages 143–184, Stanford, California. Center for the Study of Language and Information.

Julia Bonn and et al. 2022. Uniform Meaning Representation (UMR) 0.9 Specification.

Simon Clematide and Manfred Klenner. 2013. A pilot study on the semantic classification of two German prepositions: Combining monolingual and multilingual evidence. In *Proceedings of the International Conference Recent Advances in Natural Language Processing*, pages 148–155, Hissar, Bulgaria.

Jacob Cohen. 1960. A Coefficient of Agreement for Nominal Scales. *Educational and Psychological Measurement*, 20(1):37–46.

Bernard Comrie. 1989. *Language universals and linguistic typology: Syntax and morphology*. University of Chicago press.

William Croft. 2003. *Typology and universals*. Cambridge University Press.

František Daneš. 1966. The relation of centre and periphery as a language universal. *Travaux linguistiques de Prague*, 2:9–21.

Georgiana Dinu, Miguel Ballesteros, Avirup Sil, Sam Bowman, Wael Hamza, Anders Sogaard, Tahira Naseem, and Yoav Goldberg, editors. 2018. *Proceedings of the Workshop on the Relevance of Linguistic Structure in Neural Architectures for NLP*. Association for Computational Linguistics, Melbourne, Australia.

Kira Droganova and Daniel Zeman. 2019. Towards deep Universal Dependencies. In *Proceedings of the Fifth International Conference on Dependency Linguistics*, pages 144–152, Paris, France. Association for Computational Linguistics.

Anca Dumitrache, Lora Aroyo, and Chris Welty. 2019. A Crowdsourced Frame Disambiguation Corpus with Ambiguity. In *Proceedings of the 2019 Conference of the North American Chapter of the Association for Computational Linguistics: Human Language Technologies*, pages 2164–2170, Minneapolis, Minnesota. Association for Computational Linguistics.

Katrin Erk, Diana McCarthy, and Nicholas Gaylord. 2013. Measuring Word Meaning in Context. *Computational Linguistics*, 39(3):511–554.

Charles J Fillmore. 1994. Under the circumstances (place, time, manner, etc.). In *Proceedings of the Twentieth Annual Meeting of the Berkeley Linguistics Society: General Session Dedicated to the Contributions of Charles J. Fillmore (1994)*, pages 158–172.

Gottlob Frege. 1892. On sense and reference.

Luke Gessler, Austin Blodgett, Joseph C. Ledford, and Nathan Schneider. 2022. Xposition: An Online Multilingual Database of Adpositional Semantics. In *Proceedings of the Thirteenth Language Resources and Evaluation Conference*, pages 1824–1830, Marseille, France. European Language Resources Association.

Cornelia Gruber, Katharina Hechinger, Matthias Assenmacher, Göran Kauermann, and Barbara Plank. 2024. More Labels or Cases? Assessing Label Variation in Natural Language Inference. In *Proceedings of the Third Workshop on Understanding Implicit and Underspecified Language*, pages 22–32, Malta. Association for Computational Linguistics.

Jan Hajič, Eduard Bejček, Alevtina Bémová, Eva Buráňová, Eva Fučíková, Eva Hajičová, Jiří Havelka, Jaroslava Hlaváčová, Petr Homola, Pavel Ircing, Jiří Kárník, Václava Kettnerová, Natalia Klyueva, Veronika Kolářová, Lucie Kučová, Markéta Lopatková, David Mareček, Marie Mikulová, Jiří Mírovský, Anna Nedoluzhko, Michal Novák, Petr Pajas, Jarmila Panevová, Nino Peterek, Lucie Poláková, Martin Popel, Jan Popelka, Jan Romportl, Magdaléna Rysová, Jiří Semecký, Petr Sgall, Johanka Spoustová, Milan Straka, Pavel Straňák, Pavlína Synková, Magda Ševčíková, Jana Šindlerová, Jan Štěpánek, Barbora Štěpánková, Josef Toman, Zdeňka Urešová, Barbora Vidová Hladká, Daniel Zeman, Šárka Zikánová, and Zdeněk Žabokrtský. 2024. Prague Dependency Treebank - Consolidated 2.0 (PDT-C 2.0). LINDAT/CLARIAH-CZ digital library at the Institute of Formal and Applied Linguistics, Faculty of Mathematics and Physics, Charles University, Prague, Czech Republic, http://hdl.handle.net/11234/1-5813.

Jan Hajič, Eduard Bejček, Jaroslava Hlaváčová, Marie Mikulová, Milan Straka, Jan Štěpánek, and Barbora Štěpánková. 2020. Prague Dependency Treebank -

Consolidated 1.0. In *Proceedings of the Twelfth Language Resources and Evaluation Conference*, pages 5208–5218, Marseille, France. European Language Resources Association.

Eva Hajičová and Petr Sgall. 1980. Linguistic Meaning and Knowledge Representation in Automatic Understanding of Natural Language. In *Proceedings of the 8th International Conference on Computational Linguistics*, pages 67–75, Tokyo, Japan. International Committee on Computational Linguistics.

James A Hampton. 2007. Typicality, graded membership, and vagueness. *Cognitive science*, 31(3):355–384.

Patrick Hanks. 2000. Do word meanings exist? *Computers and the Humanities*, 34(1/2):205–215.

Martin Haspelmath. 2010. Comparative concepts and descriptive categories in crosslinguistic studies. *Language*, 86(3):663–687.

Jerry R Hobbs. 1985. Granularity. In *Proceedings of the Ninth International Joint Conference on Artificial Intelligence*. Elsevier.

Eduard Hovy, Mitchell Marcus, Martha Palmer, Lance Ramshaw, and Ralph Weischedel. 2006. OntoNotes: The 90% Solution. In *Proceedings of the Human Language Technology Conference of the NAACL*, pages 57–60, New York City, USA. Association for Computational Linguistics.

Jena D. Hwang, Archna Bhatia, Na-Rae Han, Tim O'Gorman, Vivek Srikumar, and Nathan Schneider. 2017. Double Trouble: The Problem of Construal in Semantic Annotation of Adpositions. In *Proceedings of the 6th Joint Conference on Lexical and Computational Semantics*, pages 178–188, Vancouver, Canada. Association for Computational Linguistics.

Jena D. Hwang, Hanwool Choe, Na-Rae Han, and Nathan Schneider. 2020. K-SNACS: Annotating Korean Adposition Semantics. In *Proceedings of the Second International Workshop on Designing Meaning Representations*, pages 53–66, Barcelona Spain (online). Association for Computational Linguistics.

Nan-Jiang Jiang, Chenhao Tan, and Marie-Catherine de Marneffe. 2023. Ecologically Valid Explanations for Label Variation in NLI. In *Findings of the Association for Computational Linguistics: EMNLP 2023*, pages 10622–10633, Singapore. Association for Computational Linguistics.

Adam Kilgarriff. 1997. I don't believe in word senses. *Computers and the Humanities*, 31:91–113.

Karin Kipper, Anna Korhonen, Neville Ryant, and Martha Palmer. 2008. A large-scale classification of English verbs. *Language Resources and Evaluation*, 42:21–40.

Klaus Krippendorff. 1980. *Content Analysis*. Sage Publications, Newbury Park, CA.

Stephen C Levinson and David P Wilkins. 2006. *Grammars of space: Explorations in cognitive diversity*, volume 6. Cambridge University Press.

Zuchao Li, Hai Zhao, Shexia He, and Jiaxun Cai. 2021. Syntax Role for Neural Semantic Role Labeling. *Computational Linguistics*, 47(3):529–574.

Ken Litkowski and Orin Hargraves. 2021. The Preposition Project. *arXiv:2104.08922*.

Inderjeet Mani. 1998. A theory of granularity and its application to problems of polysemy and underspecification of meaning. In *Proceedings of the Sixth International Conference on Principles of Knowledge Representation and Reasoning*, pages 245–257, San Francisco, CA, USA. Morgan Kaufmann Publishers Inc.

Marie Mikulová. 2024. Fine-grained Classification of Circumstantial Meanings within the Prague Dependency Treebank Annotation Scheme. In *Proceedings of the 2024 Joint International Conference on Computational Linguistics, Language Resources and Evaluation*, pages 7314–7323, Torino, Italia. European Language Resources Association and International Committee on Computational Linguistics.

George A Miller. 1995. WordNet: a lexical database for English. *Communications of the ACM*, 38(11):39–41.

Yixin Nie, Xiang Zhou, and Mohit Bansal. 2020. What Can We Learn from Collective Human Opinions on Natural Language Inference Data? *Preprint*, arXiv:2010.03532.

Tom O'Hara and Janyce Wiebe. 2009. Exploiting Semantic Role Resources for Preposition Disambiguation. *Computational Linguistics*, 35(2):151–184.

Martha Palmer, Daniel Gildea, and Paul Kingsbury. 2005. The Proposition Bank: An Annotated Corpus of Semantic Roles. *Computational Linguistics*, 31(1).

Jarmila Panevová. 1980. *Formy a funkce ve stavbě české věty*. [Forms and Functions in Czech Sentence Construction]. Academia, Prague, Czech Republic.

Barbara Hall Partee. 2004. *Compositionality in Formal Semantics: Selected Papers of Barbara H. Partee*. Blackwell, Hoboken, USA, Malden, MA.

Ellie Pavlick and Tom Kwiatkowski. 2019. Inherent disagreements in human textual inferences. *Transactions of the Association for Computational Linguistics*, 7:677–694.

Siyao Peng, Yang Liu, Yilun Zhu, Austin Blodgett, Yushi Zhao, and Nathan Schneider. 2020. A Corpus of Adpositional Supersenses for Mandarin Chinese. In *Proceedings of the Twelfth Language Resources and Evaluation Conference*, pages 5986–5994, Marseille, France. European Language Resources Association.

Volha Petukhova and Harry Bunt. 2008. LIRICS Semantic Role Annotation: Design and Evaluation of a Set of Data Categories. In *Proceedings of the Sixth International Conference on Language Resources and Evaluation*, Marrakech, Morocco. European Language Resources Association.

Barbara Plank. 2022. The "Problem" of Human Label Variation: On Ground Truth in Data, Modeling and Evaluation. In *Proceedings of the 2022 Conference on Empirical Methods in Natural Language Processing*, pages 10671–10682, Abu Dhabi, United Arab Emirates. Association for Computational Linguistics.

Eleanor Rosch. 1975. Cognitive representations of semantic categories. *Journal of experimental psychology: General*, 104(3):192.

Ferdinand de Saussure. 1916. Cours de linguistique générale, ed. *C. Bally and A. Sechehaye, with the collaboration of A. Riedlinger, Lausanne and Paris: Payot*.

Nathan Schneider, Jena D. Hwang, Vivek Srikumar, Jakob Prange, Austin Blodgett, Sarah R. Moeller, Aviram Stern, Adi Bitan, and Omri Abend. 2018. Comprehensive Supersense Disambiguation of English Prepositions and Possessives. In *Proceedings of the 56th Annual Meeting of the Association for Computational Linguistics*, pages 185–196, Melbourne, Australia. Association for Computational Linguistics.

Nathan Schneider, Vivek Srikumar, Jena D. Hwang, and Martha Palmer. 2015. A Hierarchy with, of, and for Preposition Supersenses. In *Proceedings of the 9th Linguistic Annotation Workshop*, pages 112–123, Denver, Colorado, USA. Association for Computational Linguistics.

Wesley Scivetti and Nathan Schneider. 2023. Meaning Representation of English Prepositional Phrase Roles: SNACS Supersenses vs. Tectogrammatical Functors. In *Proceedings of the Fourth International Workshop on Designing Meaning Representations*, pages 68–73, Nancy, France. Association for Computational Linguistics.

John R. Searle. 1978. Literal Meaning. *Erkenntnis*, 13(1):207–224.

Petr Sgall. 1995. From Meaning via Reference to Content. In *Karlovy Vary studies in reference and meaning*, pages 172–183. Filosofia Publications, Prague, Czech Republic.

Petr Sgall. 2002. Freedom of language: its nature, its sources, and its consequences. In *Prague Linguistic Circle Papers: Travaux du cercle linguistique de Prague nouvelle série. Volume 4*, pages 309–329. John Benjamins Publishing Company.

Petr Sgall, Eva Hajičová, and Jarmila Panevová. 1986. *The Meaning of the Sentence and Its Semantic and Pragmatic Aspects*. Academia/Reidel Publishing Company, Prague/Dordrecht.

Zoltán Gendler Szabó. 2022. Compositionality. In Edward N. Zalta and Uri Nodelman, editors, *The Stanford Encyclopedia of Philosophy*. Metaphysics Research Lab, Stanford University, Standford, USA.

Martin Thoma. 2017. Analysis and Optimization of Convolutional Neural Network Architectures. Master's thesis, KIT – University of the State of Baden-Wuerttemberg and National Research Center of the Helmholtz Association.

David Tuggy. 1993. Ambiguity, polysemy, and vagueness. *Cognitive Linguistics*, 4(2):273–290.

Alexandra N Uma, Tommaso Fornaciari, Dirk Hovy, Silviu Paun, Barbara Plank, and Massimo Poesio. 2021. Learning from disagreement: A survey. *Journal of Artificial Intelligence Research*, 72:1385–1470.

Zdeňka Urešová, Cristina Fernández Alcaina, Peter Bourgonje, Eva Fučíková, Jan Hajič, Eva Hajičová, Georg Rehm, Kateřina Rysová, and Karolina Zaczynska. 2024a. SynSemClass 5.1. LINDAT/CLARIAH-CZ digital library at the Institute of Formal and Applied Linguistics), Faculty of Mathematics and Physics, Charles University, Prague, Czech Republic, http://hdl.handle.net/11234/1-5808.

Zdeňka Urešová, Alevtina Bémová, Eva Fučíková, Jan Hajič, Veronika Kolářová, Marie Mikulová, Petr Pajas, Jarmila Panevová, and Jan Štěpánek. 2024b. PDT-Vallex: Czech valency lexicon linked to treebanks 4.5 (PDT-Vallex 4.5). LINDAT/CLARIAH-CZ digital library at the Institute of Formal and Applied Linguistics, Faculty of Mathematics and Physics, Charles University, Prague, Czech Republic, http://hdl.handle.net/11234/1-5814.

Jens E. L. Van Gysel, Meagan Vigus, Pavlina Kalm, Sook-kyung Lee, Michael Regan, and William Croft. 2019. Cross-Linguistic Semantic Annotation: Reconciling the Language-Specific and the Universal. In *Proceedings of the First International Workshop on Designing Meaning Representations*, pages 1–14, Florence, Italy. Association for Computational Linguistics.

Jens EL Van Gysel, Meagan Vigus, Jayeol Chun, Kenneth Lai, Sarah Moeller, Jiarui Yao, Tim O'Gorman, Andrew Cowell, William Croft, Chu-Ren Huang, Jan Hajič, James H. Martin, Stephan Oepen, Martha Palmer, James Pustejovsky, Rosa Vallejos, and Nianwen Xue. 2021. Designing a Uniform Meaning Representation for Natural Language Processing. *KI-Künstliche Intelligenz*, 35(3-4):343–360.

Zhuxin Wang, Jakob Prange, and Nathan Schneider. 2021. Subcategorizing Adverbials in Universal Conceptual Cognitive Annotation. In *Proceedings of the Joint 15th Linguistic Annotation Workshop and 3rd Designing Meaning Representations Workshop*, pages 96–105, Punta Cana, Dominican Republic. Association for Computational Linguistics.

Shira Wein. 2025. Ambiguity and Disagreement in Abstract Meaning Representation. In *Proceedings of*

Context and Meaning: Navigating Disagreements in NLP Annotation, pages 145–154, Abu Dhabi, UAE. International Committee on Computational Linguistics.

Ludwig Wittgenstein. 1953. *Philosophical investigations. Philosophische untersuchungen.* Macmillan, New York, USA.

Nianwen Xue, Ondřej Bojar, Jan Hajič, Martha Palmer, Zdeňka Urešová, and Xiuhong Zhang. 2014. Not an Interlingua, But Close: Comparison of English AMRs to Chinese and Czech. In *Proceedings of the Ninth International Conference on Language Resources and Evaluation*, pages 1765–1772, Reykjavik, Iceland. European Language Resources Association.

Xinliang Frederick Zhang and Marie-Catherine de Marneffe. 2021. Identifying Inherent Disagreement in Natural Language Inference. In *Proceedings of the 2021 Conference of the North American Chapter of the Association for Computational Linguistics: Human Language Technologies*, pages 4908–4915, Online. Association for Computational Linguistics.

A Appendix

Subfunc tor	Forms	Example
above	*nad* 'above/over'	*nad domem* 'above the house'
adjacency	*u, při* 'by'	*u domu* 'by the house'
alongside	*podle, podél* 'along'	*podél domu* 'along the house'
among	*mezi* 'among'	*chodit mezi domy* 'to walk among houses'
area	*po* 'on/around'	*chodit po domě* 'walk around the house'
around	*okolo, kolem* 'around'	*kolem domu* 'around the house'
behind	*za* 'behind/beyond'	*za domem* 'behind the house'
below	*pod* 'below/under'	*pod domem* 'under the house'
beside	*vedle* 'beside/next to'	*vedle domu* 'next to the house'
between	*mezi* 'between'	*cesta mezi domy* 'path between houses'
distr	*po* 'on'	*vysedávají po hospodách* 'hang out in pubs'
event	*na, při* 'on/at'	*na návštěvě* 'on a visit'
facing	*čelem k* 'facing'	*čelem k domu* 'facing the house'
foreground	*v čele* 'at the head of'	*v čele kolony* 'at the head of the column'
front	*před* 'in front of'	*před domem* 'in front of the house'
ingroup	*mezi* 'among'	*mezi auty vede Škoda* 'Skoda leads among cars'
inside	*v* 'in', *uvnitř* 'inside'	*v domě* 'in the house'
middle	*uprostřed* 'in middle of'	*uprostřed domu* 'in the middle of the house'
near	*blízko, poblíž* 'near'	*blízko domu* 'near the house'
opposite	*naproti* 'opposite'	*naproti domu* 'opposite the house'
outside	*stranou, mimo* 'outside'	*stranou domu* 'outside the house'
side	*po boku* 'alongside'	*po boku manželky* 'alongside the wife'
surface	*na* 'on'	*na domě* 'on the house'
within	*na, u* 'at/on/in'	*pracuje u divadla* 'work at the theater'
OTHER		

Table 4: Subfunctors (and selected forms) for LOC functor (meaning "where")

Func	Subfunctor	Example
ACMP	community	*pracovat s kolegou* 'to work with a colleague'
	association	*prodávat s byty i pozemky* 'to sell with apartments also land'
	excluded	*s výjimkou Jana pracují všichni* lit. 'with exception of Jan'
MANN	of-event	*pracovat s obtížemi* 'to work with difficulties'
	of-agent	*pracovat s nadšením* 'to work with enthusiasm'
	of-result	*pracovat s úspěchem* 'to work with success'
MEANS	tool	*pracovat s lopatou* 'to work with a shovel'
	tool-abstr	*obtěžovat se zprávami* 'to bother with news'
	transport	*jet s autem* 'to go with a car'
	material	*pracovat se dřevem* 'work with wood'
	mediator	*jet s cestovkou* 'to go with a tour guide'
EXT	ext	*pracovat s velkou intenzitou* 'to work with great intensity'
COND	because	*pracovat s přinucením* lit. 'to work with coercion'
	progress	*s jarem roste nálada* 'with spring comes a rise in mood'
	relation	*změnila se vznikem klubu* 'it changed with establishment of club'
	condition	*pracovat se sluncem nad hlavou* 'to work with sun overhead'
AIM	intent	*pracovat s cílem uspět* 'work with the aim of succeeding'
REG	regard	*s přírodou není všechno v pořádku* 'all is not well with nature.'
	topic	*s tou kytarou si vzpomínám, že...* 'with that guitar I remember...'
TWHEN	simult	*souběžně s konferencí* 'simultaneously with conference'
TSIN	validity	*s účinností od ledna* lit. 'with efficiency from January'
CPR	compared	*je se mnou stejně stará* 'she is the same age as (lit. with) me.'
MOD	mod	*s největší pravděpodobností odjel* lit. 'he left with highest probability'
CIRC	side-effect	*přijet s bábovkou* 'to arrive with a cake'
	idiom	*dělej se sebou něco* 'do something with yourself'
OTHER	other	

Table 5: Functors and subfunctors for circumstants expressed by Czech preposition *s* 'with'.

A_1	A_2	κ_1	p_{o1}	p_{e1}	κ_2	p_{o2}	p_{e2}
A	B	**0.787**	0.800	0.063	**0.548**	0.584	0.080
A	C	**0.803**	0.815	0.063	**0.603**	0.634	0.078
A	D	**0.813**	0.825	0.063	**0.636**	0.666	0.083
B	C	**0.877**	0.885	0.064	**0.629**	0.658	0.078
B	D	**0.872**	0.880	0.065	**0.641**	0.670	0.081
C	D	**0.893**	0.900	0.065	**0.668**	0.694	0.077

Table 6: Details of Cohen's κ calculation: the relative observed agreement p_o and hypothetical probability of agreement by chance p_e for each pair of annotators and both the tasks.

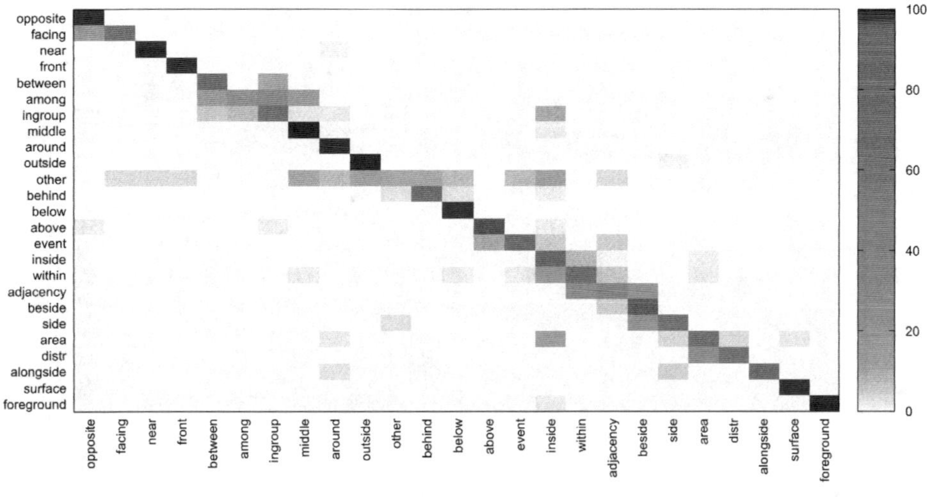

Figure 4: Confusion matrix for Task 1. A confusion matrix was calculated for each annotator against the created "golden data" and the values were summed for each pair of subfunctors. The matrix was normalized per rows, values were sorted to move the large values towards the diagonal as described in (Thoma, 2017) to group similarly behaving subfunctors together.

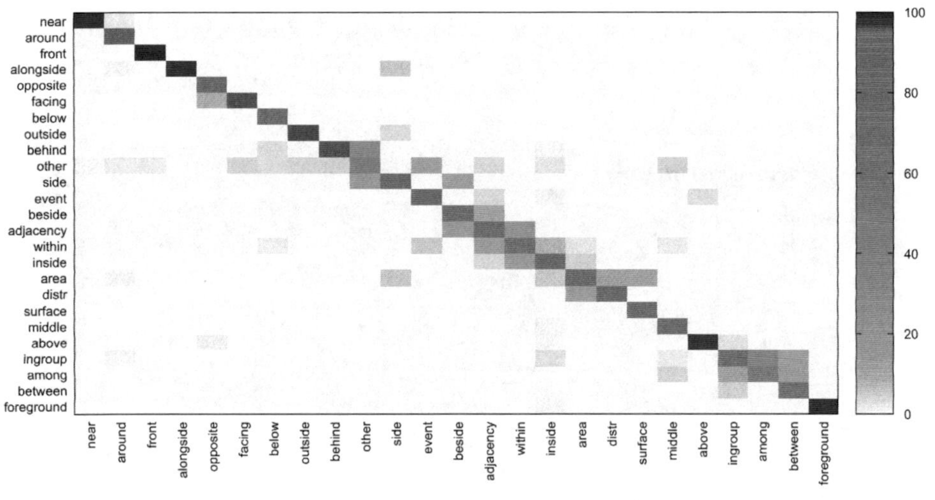

Figure 5: Confusion matrix for Task 1, normalized per columns. See Figure 4 for more details.

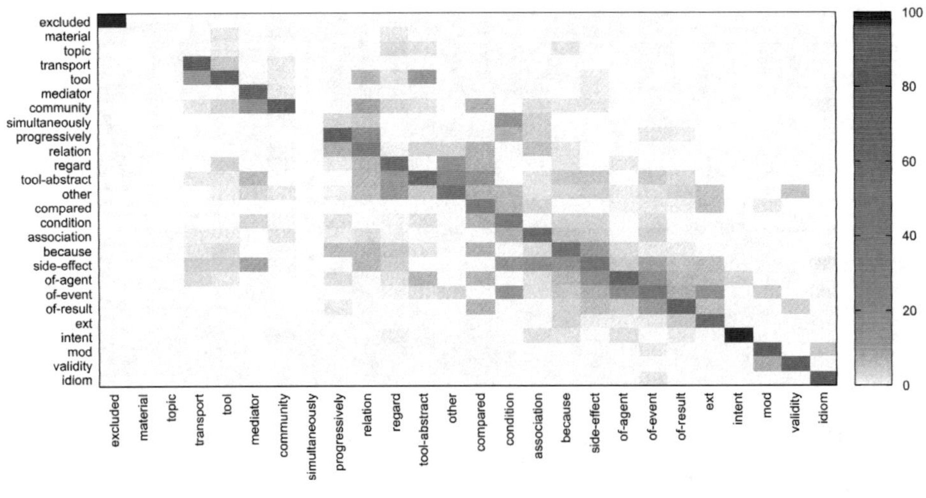

Figure 6: Confusion matrix for Task 2, normalized per columns. See Figure 4 for more details. See Figure 3 for the matrix normalized per rows.

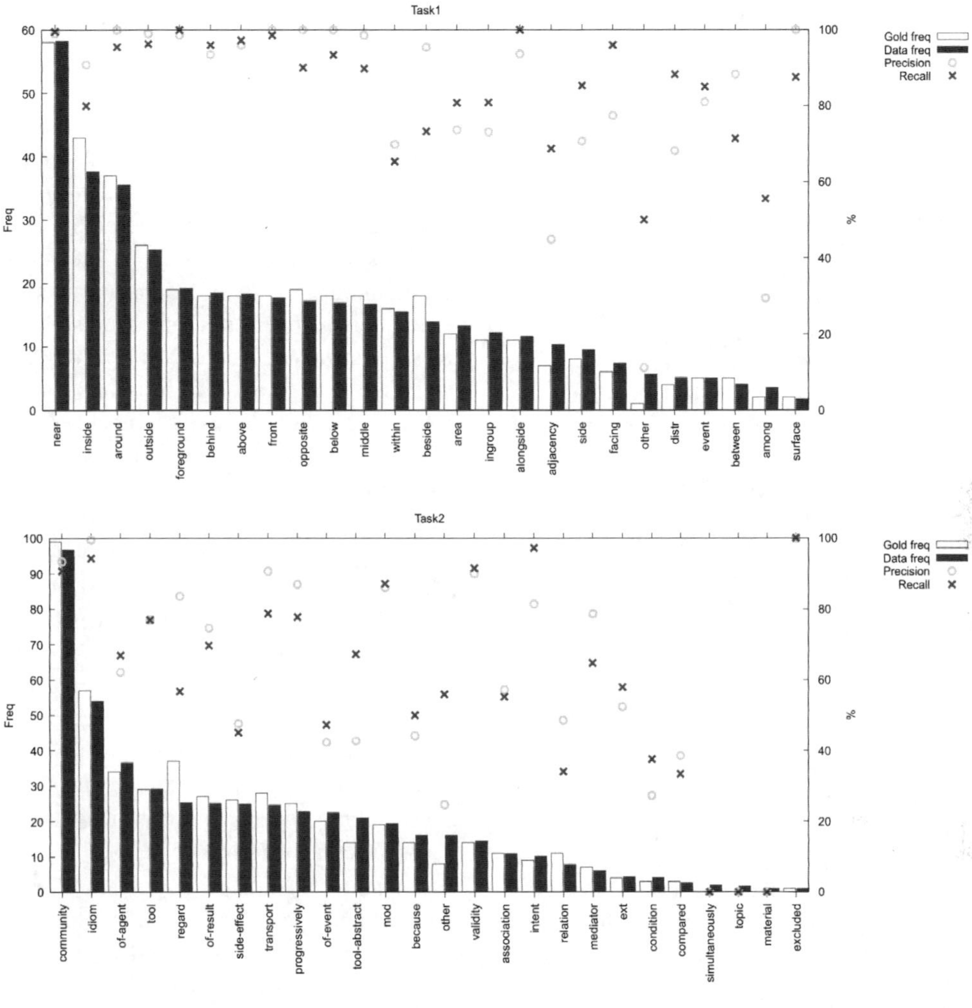

Figure 7: Comparison of subfunctor frequencies in the annotated data and in the golden data. To make frequencies comparable, the number of occurrences of each subfunctor in a sentence was divided by the number of all the values assigned by all the annotators to the sentence. Also shown are precision and recall for each subfunctor.

An Annotation Protocol for Diachronic Evaluation of Semantic Drift in Disability Sources

Nitisha Jain, Chiara Di Bonaventura, Albert Meroño-Peñuela, Barbara McGillivray
King's College London, 30 Aldwych, London, UK
{nitisha.jain,chiara.di_bonaventura,albert.merono,barbara.mcgillivray}@kcl.ac.uk

Abstract

Annotating terms referring to aspects of disability in historical texts is crucial for understanding how societies in different periods conceptualized and treated disability. Such annotations help modern readers grasp the evolving language, cultural attitudes, and social structures surrounding disability, shedding light on both marginalization and inclusion throughout history. This is important as evolving societal attitudes can influence the perpetuation of harmful language that reinforces stereotypes and discrimination. However, this task presents significant challenges. Terminology often reflects outdated, offensive, or ambiguous concepts that require sensitive interpretation. Meaning of terms may have shifted over time, making it difficult to align historical terms with contemporary understandings of disability. Additionally, contextual nuances and the lack of standardized language in historical records demand careful scholarly judgment to avoid anachronism or misrepresentation. In this paper we introduce an annotation protocol for analysing and describing semantic shifts in the discourse on disabilities in historical texts, reporting on how our protocol's design evolved to address these specific challenges and on issues around annotators' agreement.

1 Introduction

Language constantly evolves and adapts to speakers' communicative needs and socio-cultural changes; understanding these shifts is crucial for grasping the dynamic nature of language and its intricate relationship with social and cultural phenomena. The semantics of words of a language shift due to influences from social practices, events, and political circumstances (Keidar et al., 2022; Castano et al., 2022; Azarbonyad et al., 2017). The *functioning and disability of individuals*,[1] such as those affecting their cognitive, developmental, intellectual, mental, physical or sensory functions, is a key area of study pursuing equitable access in society, and in which language is in constant motion: inappropriate use of language can contribute to the perpetuation of stereotypes, discrimination, and stigmatization (Andrews et al., 2022). For example, the word "lame" was historically associated with physical disabilities affecting a person's ability to walk or move normally; but over time, it has semantically changed to mean "socially inept or out of touch" (Oxford University Press, 2024b), shifting meaning from a physical disability context to a more casual and potentially derogatory usage. Therefore, development of techniques to annotate such semantic change within the disability domain is essential for ensuring accurate interpretation and fostering a deeper understanding of historical texts. Without such methods, there is a risk of misrepresenting or overlooking the evolving meanings and social implications of disability-related terms across different historical contexts.

In Natural Language Processing (NLP), the task of Semantic Shift Detection (SSD) focuses on detecting, interpreting, and assessing potential changes in the meaning of words over time (Montanelli and Periti, 2023). The International Workshops on Semantic Evaluation (SemEval) (Schlechtweg et al., 2020) and Ever Evolving NLP (EvoNLP[2]) have proposed various tasks and models. In the Semantic Web, ontology evolution (Stojanovic, 2004) studies how and why ontologies and knowledge graphs change over time; various works have proposed models based on heuristics (Stavropoulos et al., 2019) and machine learning models for semantic change in biomedicine (Pesquita and Couto, 2012) and generalised domains (Meroño-Peñuela et al., 2021), with some studies looking into the impact of seman-

[1] WHO disability classification standards.

[2] https://sites.google.com/view/evonlp/home.

Proceedings of the 19th Linguistic Annotation Workshop (LAW-XIX-2025), pages 160–172
July 31, 2025 ©2025 Association for Computational Linguistics

tic change on reasoning and hierarchies (Pernisch et al., 2019, 2021). As explained in previous works (McGillivray et al., 2022; Hoeken et al., 2023), changes in language semantics over time can influence what is considered offensive. However, to the best of our knowledge no existing work facilitates resources for semantic change over large time spans (as these changes can be slow), considering both textual and semantic representations, and addressing discriminatory and harmful language in disability.

In this paper, we propose an annotation protocol for the analysis and evaluation of semantic change in the disability domain, which is built on two rounds of iteration. Our approach involves designing an annotation framework to capture both the descriptive and offensive nuances of historically relevant disability-related terms, accounting for their evolving connotations across different historical and social contexts. This includes structured guidelines for annotators to assess the perceived offensiveness, descriptive intent, and type of disability referenced in each instance. We present the quantitative and qualitative analyses on annotation disagreement that highlight the importance of capturing the nuanced and subjective nature of disability-related discourse, and discuss the four main challenges in annotating disability-related discourse over time. The annotation data and guidelines have been made available[3] to promote further research in this direction.

2 Background and Related Work

There are several previous studies directed towards the evolution of disability terminology across various mediums, including media representations, scholarly publications, and broader social discourse (Ferrigon and Tucker; Simon, 2017; Auslander and Gold, 1999). Importantly, these studies show the changing landscape of disability discourse, its impact on societal perceptions and attitudes, and the dynamic nature of language and its role in shaping perceptions of disability within diverse contexts (Andrews et al., 2022).

A number of research projects have addressed the issues of bias and representation in historical texts, developing several resources that focus on the language and portrayal of disability (Rahman, 2024; National Center on Disability and Journalism, 2021; DE-BIAS Project consortium, 2025). These initiatives aim to highlight and mitigate the marginalization of disabled individuals in historical records by providing analytical frameworks and lexical resources that bring attention to the social and cultural contexts in which disability-related terms were used in the past and how they should be used today.

Within the research area of Semantic Shift Detection, benchmark datasets and text corpora capable of supporting the analysis of word meaning change over time have been developed (cf. McGillivray et al. (2023) for an overview and Marongiu et al. (2024) for a discussion of this task in the context of semantic change research). The SemEval 2020 dataset (Schlechtweg et al., 2020) contains a multilingual set of annotated sentences from English, German, Latin, and Swedish historical texts; other gold standard datasets exist (Rodina and Kutuzov, 2020; Zamora-Reina et al., 2022). These datasets were all annotated by human experts, which ensures a high level of accuracy and contextual understanding, particularly important when dealing with nuanced and historically contingent language, but it is also a time-consuming and labor-intensive process. Ridge et al. (2024) present a dataset of historical British newspapers from the 19th century where the contexts of a number of terms related to vehicles were annotated with their meaning via voluntary crowdsourcing, leveraging the scalable, collective effort of non-expert contributors.

While existing annotated datasets from semantic change detection research constitute a promising avenue for studying semantic change and improving the understanding of historical language use, the existing resources solely utilize corpora amassed from general domains. As a result, they often overlook specialized areas such as disability discourse, where terminology carries distinct social and cultural significance that requires focused analysis. On the other hand, previous studies on the language of disabilities have not looked specifically at the challenges of corpus annotation in historical texts. Our study addresses both these gaps by focussing on an annotation protocol specifically tailored to the annotation of disability terms whose semantics has changed in historical texts.

In addition to the semantic change literature, our work also intersects with annotation challenges explored in socially sensitive domains. Similar challenges have been discussed in the hate speech detection literature, where offensiveness and inflammatory intent often vary by context, speaker

[3] https://doi.org/10.6084/m9.figshare.29198132

identity, and target community (Sap et al., 2019; Pavlopoulos et al., 2020). Recent work has introduced graded offensiveness scales, soft-labeling approaches, and community-informed annotation schemes to better reflect the subjective and socially contingent nature of such language (Vidgen et al., 2019; Mostafazadeh Davani et al., 2022). Our annotation protocol draws on these developments by adopting a five-point offensiveness scale and encouraging annotators to consider both historical context and social intent when evaluating terms.

3 Data Sources

For designing the annotation protocol for measuring the semantic change in the disability domain, we selected texts for annotation from Gale's *History of Disabilities: Disabilities in Society, Seventeenth to Twentieth Century*[4], a collection of monographs, manuscripts, and ephemera documenting disability history (17th-20th centuries) through personal memoirs, accounts of care and rehabilitation, advocacy efforts, and policies impacting individuals with disabilities, thus examining society's evolving perceptions of disability. Additionally, we collected an initial list of terms used to refer to disabilities from Wikipedia[5] and the Disability at Stanford project.[6]

4 Annotation Protocol

The purpose of the annotation is to trace the evolution of selected terms related to disabilities over time in historical texts. We conducted two annotation rounds to assess the quality of the sources and refine the annotation protocol. The pilot round was carried out by a team of five annotators working in Digital Humanities and Natural Language Processing and from career levels ranging from doctoral students to senior lecturers. The aim of this pilot was to assess the quality of the source texts for the annotation task at hand. The annotation protocol was built and refined based on the feedback given by participants in the pilot.

In the first version of the protocol, each annotation line displayed a focus sentence with the disability term (one of the selected terms) in bold, along with the sentence before and after it for context. Annotators were tasked to choose from a drop-down menu whether the term was 'Derogatory', 'Not derogatory', 'Not referring to a disability', or 'Unclear due to illegible OCR'—a necessary option given the limitations of historical documents. If the term did refer to a disability, annotators also indicated whether it referred to a 'mental' or 'physical' disability. This distinction was important for understanding how different types of impairments were perceived and treated historically, as societal attitudes and institutional responses often varied between mental and physical disabilities.

Feedback from the pilot annotation round revealed several important insights and challenges that guided the updates to the following round of the protocol. Annotators noted, for example, that *demented* often appeared in medical texts to classify individuals deemed "mentally insane" by historical standards. Though medically framed at the time, the term would now be seen as stigmatizing. Similarly, *Downie* was sometimes used as a personal name rather than a reference to Down syndrome, and in certain cases, it appeared in affectionate or familiar contexts—underscoring the importance of contextual interpretation.

The term *cripple* also prompted discussion among annotators. While it was sometimes used descriptively in medical contexts, it often appeared in passages reflecting harsh or dehumanizing attitudes. *These examples highlighted the limitations of a binary classification (Derogatory vs. Not derogatory), which could not capture the nuance of tone and intent.* Annotators also found the mental vs. physical distinction for disability types too narrow, noting that many instances involved cognitive or sensory disabilities (e.g., blindness, deafness) that fell outside these categories.

Based on this feedback from the pilot, we modified the protocol to better account for the historical and contextual subtleties encountered in the data. Again, each annotation line presents a focus sentence with the disability term highlighted, preceded by the sentence before it and the sentence after. The annotation consists now in choosing from the drop-down menu the best category to which the term can be assigned according to the following dimensions.

The first decision annotators make is to determine whether the term is used as part of a 'formal diagnosis' or within 'common language'. This distinction helps clarify whether the term is functioning within an institutionalized medical discourse or in more casual, everyday speech.

Next, annotators assess whether the term is used

[4]Gale's Disabilities in Society, Seventeenth to Twentieth Century Collection.

[5]Wikipedia list of disabilities with negative connotations.

[6]Disability at Stanford project.

with a 'descriptive' or 'offensive' intent. To capture varying degrees of offensiveness and contextual appropriateness, we implemented a *graded scale*, allowing annotators to position the term along a five-point scale:

1. *Neutral/Descriptive*: Factually descriptive and still acceptable in contemporary usage.
2. *Outdated but Neutral*: Historically accepted and descriptive, but now considered outdated or replaced by person-first language.
3. *Mildly Pejorative / Stigmatizing*: Sometimes used negatively but not inherently offensive; may reflect stereotypical or patronizing attitudes.
4. *Strongly Pejorative / Insulting*: Clearly used offensively or with dehumanizing intent.
5. *Highly Offensive / Dehumanizing*: Explicitly used as a slur or in oppressive, violent, or cruel contexts.

This graded scale was introduced to replace the earlier binary classification of 'Derogatory' vs. 'Not derogatory', which proved inadequate in capturing the nuances of language and intent found in historical texts. With a more granular approach we acknowledge that offensiveness exists on a spectrum and is deeply influenced by context, authorial intent, and audience perception—particularly in diachronic corpora.

Further, if the term in context refers to a disability, annotators are asked to mark the 'Type of Disability' it pertains to. Annotators can select from *cognitive*, *sensory*, and/or *physical* categories. This refinement allows us to better track how different forms of disability were represented and discussed over time, and how terminology may have shifted in relation to different kinds of impairments.

Finally, in an optional comment field, annotators can explain their decision or provide additional observations. These qualitative notes are crucial for later analysis of annotation disagreements and for understanding the reasoning processes behind individual annotations.

5 Annotation Process

In the pilot annotation round, we examined four terms (henceforth referred to as "keywords"): *abnormal*, *cripple*, *demented*, and *downie*. These were chosen for their historical relevance to disability and their shifting meanings and acceptability over time. The selection balanced terms referring to physical disabilities (*cripple*, *downie*) and cognitive or mental ones (*abnormal*, *demented*) to explore varied linguistic representations.

Abnormal, derived from Latin *abnormis* ("irregular"), was commonly used in 19th- and early 20th-century clinical texts to describe physical or mental deviations from a perceived norm. Though often descriptive, the term has accumulated negative connotations, reinforcing ideas of deviance and stigma.

Cripple once served as a general descriptor for individuals with physical disabilities, especially mobility impairments. While historically common in both medical and everyday language, it is now widely viewed as offensive due to its reductive and dehumanizing implications. Some activists have attempted to reclaim the term in recent years to subvert its derogatory implications (Wikipedia contributors, 2025).

Demented, from Latin *demens* ("out of one's mind"), was used in medical contexts to describe cognitive and psychiatric impairments. Though originally clinical, it has since acquired derogatory connotations and is often used pejoratively in modern speech.

Downie, a colloquial term sometimes aimed at individuals with Down syndrome, appeared in both derogatory and affectionate contexts. However, its frequent use as a personal surname made annotation difficult due to ambiguity and low inter-annotator agreement.

In the first round of annotation, for each keyword, we selected three textual excerpts from monographs and one from manuscripts through advanced search throughout the *Gale's History of Disabilities* collection (as described in §3). This approach aimed to capture both institutional and personal uses of the terms while accounting for sources' distributions.

In the subsequent annotation round, we excluded *downie* from the dataset due to its ambiguity. Most occurrences were personal surnames unrelated to disability, resulting in non-relevant instances and inconsistent annotator agreement. Additionally, the limited context in some documents made it difficult to determine whether the term was used derogatorily or descriptively. As a result, we selected the word *blind* for further analysis. The term *blind* has a long history, originating from Old English meaning "sightless" or "obscured" (Oxford University Press, 2024a). Historically, *blind* was commonly used to describe individuals with significant visual impairments. Although originally a neutral descriptor, modern disability discourse has raised concerns about its use, particularly in metaphorical contexts where it can perpetuate negative stereotypes (e.g., "blind to the truth"). In disability advocacy, there is increasing emphasis on person-first language (e.g., "person who is blind") or identity-first language (e.g., "blind person"), depending on individual and community preferences.

For this second round, we aimed to curate a larger annotation corpus for a more detailed analysis. For each of the four keywords, we first identified 15 monographs and 10 manuscripts from the collection through advanced keyword search. From these, a list of 40 sentences were randomly selected for each keyword (along with the previous and next sentences for context), resulting in a curated annotation corpus of 120 textual excerpts in total. The annotation workshop comprised 12 annotators from research teams within the authors' University. One annotator had a background in Linguistics and all others had background in Computer Science. The levels of experience ranged from early career researchers (doctoral students, postdocs) to senior lecturers. During the workshop, participants were first introduced to the annotation protocol and guidelines. Then, they worked in small groups of three to annotate the selected sentences along the dimensions discussed in §4 following a structured approach[7].

6 Analysis of annotations

In this section, we analyse the results of the annotation process described in §5. Specifically, we present a quantitative analysis regarding annotators' agreement in §6.1. In addition, we present a qualitative analysis discussing the challenges and some of the interesting cases that were observed during the annotation process in §6.2[8].

6.1 Quantitative Analysis

The total size of the annotation corpus in terms of the actual sentences to be annotated, measured as count of words is 6717 (*Abnormal* - 1581, *Blind* - 1359, *Cripple* - 1749, and *Demented* - 2028). Firstly, we show in Figure 1 the distribution of the curated annotation corpus over time[9] in terms

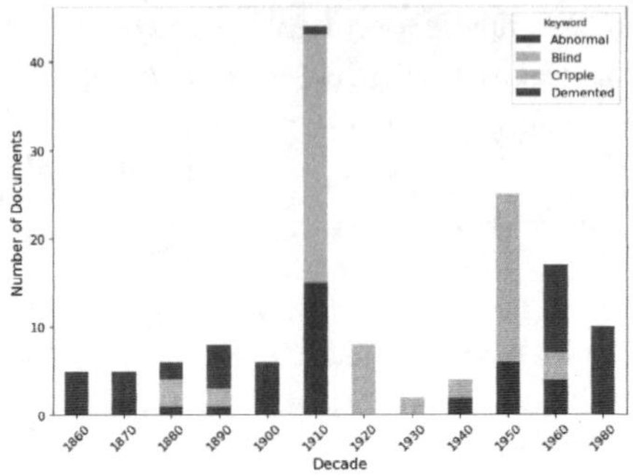

Figure 1: Publication dates of the documents in the annotation corpus (grouped by decades).

of number of texts from each decade with respect to the different keywords. The corpus contains texts from a varied range of time periods, starting from 1860s to 1980s. We notice that there is a peak in the 1910s, primarily driven by the word *cripple*, followed by *abnormal*. After this peak, there is a decline in document mentions during the 1920s and 1930s, with a slight resurgence in the 1950s and 1960s. The word *blind* sees a significant rise in the 1950s, while demented appears more frequently in the 1960s and 1980s. Early decades from the 1860s to 1900s show consistent but lower occurrences of these terms.

Figure 2 presents the distribution of labels obtained from the annotations (cumulative for all annotators) for three different annotation tasks across multiple keywords. The distribution of labels for the first task reveals how medical terms transfer into common discourse, and conversely, how colloquial expressions find their way into formal diagnostic contexts. In our dataset, *cripple* appears to lean more heavily into common language usage, while the other keywords maintain a more balanced representation between diagnostic and everyday speech. In the second task, at the neutral end (level 1), the terms begin with a relatively descriptive, clinical approach. As the labels progress through values 2 and 3, we see the gradual introduction of more pejorative and stigmatizing language. The transition is particularly striking for *cripple* and *demented*, which shows a significant shift towards more negative characterizations. Finally, in the third task we see a substantial agreement among annotators, with *blind* being recognised as predominantly sensory-focused, *demented* as heavily weighted towards cognitive characteristics, and *cripple* with strong physical connotation. *Abnormal* stands out as displaying a more polysemous

[7]the annotations will be made publicly available

[8]Note that these results correspond to the second round of annotations, the pilot was only leveraged to refine the annotation protocol and no agreement measurements were made

[9]wherever this information was explicitly available in the metadata from the collection

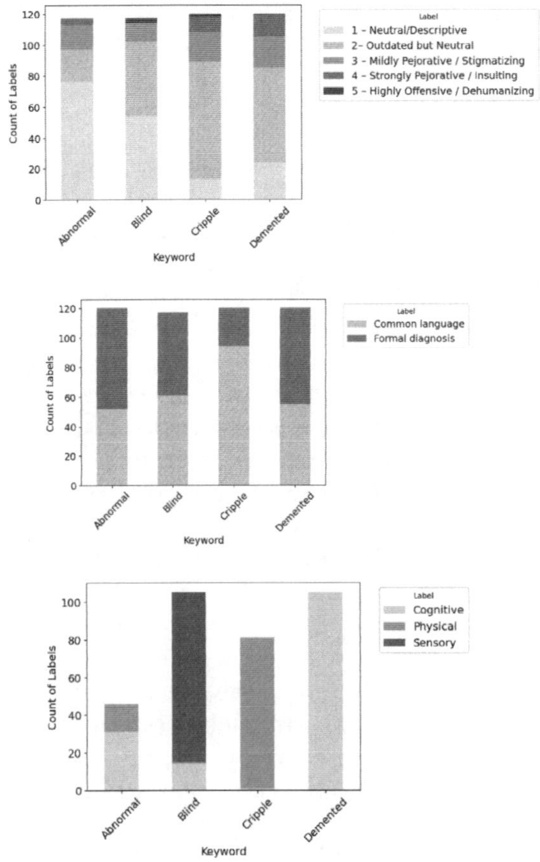

Figure 2: Distribution of annotation labels across different tasks and datasets. The subfigures show the label distributions for three annotation tasks: `Intent of Term`, `Use of Term` and `Type of Disability`.

profile, including both cognitive and physical interpretations[10].

6.1.1 Measuring annotator agreement

To assess the consistency of the annotations and the degree to which annotators agree on the interpretation of the terms, we calculated Cohen's Kappa (Cohen, 1960) and Fleiss' Kappa scores (Joseph and Fleiss, 2023) (Table 1). We also calculated Spearman's rank correlation (Spearman, 1961) to measure the agreement and variance among annotators who classified terms with varying degrees of offensiveness.

[10]This figure illustrates the overall distribution of labels across all annotators, but does not reflect inter-annotator agreement and should not be interpreted as indicative of consistency between annotators. Due to label imbalance and varied interpretation of terms, high label frequency does not necessarily imply high agreement, which is instead captured through chance-corrected metrics like Cohen's or Fleiss' Kappa.

Annotation Task	Keyword	$\overline{C\kappa}$	$F\kappa$	$\overline{S\rho}$
Intent of Term	Abnormal	0.18	0.17	0.22
	Blind	0.26	0.24	0.30
	Cripple	-0.12	-0.13	0.02
	Demented	0.06	0.02	0.52
Use of Term	Abnormal	0.26	0.25	-
	Blind	0.06	0.04	-
	Cripple	-0.05	-0.08	-
	Demented	0.36	0.36	-
Type of Disability	Abnormal	0.27	0.19	-
	Blind	-0.08	-0.15	-
	Cripple	0.33	-0.01	-
	Demented	1.00	1.00	-

Table 1: Average Cohen's Kappa ($\overline{C\kappa}$) and Fleiss' Kappa ($F\kappa$) for each annotation task and keyword. Averaged Spearman's Rank Correlation ($\overline{S\rho}$) for the `Intent of Term` annotations.

Cohen's Kappa ($C\kappa$). Cohen's Kappa (κ) was used to measure pairwise agreement between annotators, calculated as:

$$\kappa = \frac{P_o - P_e}{1 - P_e}$$

where P_o is the observed agreement and P_e is the agreement expected by chance. It is to be noted that in cases with highly skewed label distributions, P_e can be close to or equal to P_o, resulting in *low or even zero Kappa scores* despite frequent agreement between annotators. In extreme cases where both annotators used only a single class, $P_e = 1$, making the denominator zero and rendering Kappa *undefined* (NaN). For reporting purposes, we replaced such values with 1.00 to reflect perfect agreement in these cases. Keeping this in mind, the averaged Cohen's Kappa results in Table 1 reveal varying levels of agreement across annotation tasks and keywords. For the 'Intent of Term' task, the agreement is generally low, with *blind* showing the highest value (0.26), and *cripple* showing a negative Cohen's Kappa value (-0.12) indicating poor or no agreement between raters. In the 'Use of Term' task, the highest agreement is seen with the keyword *demented* (0.36), while the keyword *blind* has a low agreement (0.06). The keyword *cripple* shows a negative value (-0.05). In the 'Type of Disability' task, the agreement is stronger, particularly for *demented* (1.00 indicating complete agreement), suggesting a higher level of consistency in annotating this keyword. On the other hand, other keywords show much lower agreement, with *blind* showing the lowest score (-0.08) as the annotators chose differently among the *cognitive*, *sensory*, and *physical* categories. Overall, these results suggest that the annotators show varied levels of agreement when categorizing disability-related keywords[11]. Keywords like *demented* are more clearly interpreted by annotators, leading to higher agreement, whereas *cripple* and *blind* are perceived as more ambiguous or context-dependent, highlighting the challenges in achieving a consistent understanding of these terms, particularly in contexts that might be socially or culturally sensitive.

Fleiss' Kappa ($F\kappa$). Fleiss' Kappa (κ) was used to assess agreement across multiple annotators, using the same chance-corrected formulation:

$$\kappa = \frac{\bar{P} - \bar{P}_e}{1 - \bar{P}_e}$$

where $\bar{P}$ is the *mean observed agreement* and $\bar{P}_e$ the expected agreement by chance. As with Cohen's Kappa, *skewed label distributions* can lead to low or undefined (NaN) scores. We replaced undefined values with 1.00 in cases of unanimous single-class agreement. These scores generally indicates low-to-moderate agreement across the keywords. In the 'Use of Term' task, *demented* stands out with the highest Fleiss' Kappa, suggesting better consensus among annotators, while *cripple* and *blind* show much lower Fleiss' Kappa values, indicating significant disagreement. Notably, *cripple* has a negative Fleiss' Kappa in all tasks, reflecting widespread discord [12].

Spearman's rank correlation ($S\rho$). For the 'Intent of Term', since the annotators rate terms across categories from neutral/descriptive to highly offensive, Spearman's correlation provides insight into how consistently these annotators align in their evaluations. The average correlation scores highlight differences in annotator agreement across keywords. *Demented* has the highest overall agreement (0.52), suggesting that annotators had a more consistent understanding of how to classify this term. *Blind* (0.30) and *abnormal* (0.23) show moderate agreement. In contrast, *cripple* has the lowest agreement (0.02), indicating substantial variation in interpretation, possibly due to its historical connotations and evolving societal perceptions. This suggests that certain terms may be more prone to subjective interpretation, impacting annotation reliability[13].

6.2 Qualitative Analysis

This section presents a qualitative analysis of annotator disagreements during dataset annotation, with a selection of particularly insightful examples, which reflect the subjective nature of interpreting complex socio-linguistic constructs, especially in ethically and historically sensitive domains like disability-related language. Following the framework proposed by Röttger et al. (Röttger et al., 2022), who distinguish between descriptive and prescriptive annotation paradigms for subjective NLP tasks, we adopted the descriptive paradigm in our annotation process. This approach encourages annotator subjectivity, allowing us to capture a range of valid interpretations rather than enforcing a single normative viewpoint. Specifically, we discuss the unique challenges in time-sensitive annotations, that we group into four categories: (1) subjectivity in the interpretation, (2) contextual influence on the annotation, (3) Historical and linguistic evolution, (4) Categorisation challenges[14].

6.2.1 Subjectivity in the interpretation

Offensiveness vs. Stigmatization. The assessment of offensive language varied significantly across annotators. Although disability-related terms were not explicitly offensive in isolation, the surrounding context often conveyed stigmatizing messages. Annotators frequently highlighted portrayals of disability that reinforced harmful stereotypes—for example, associating blindness with poverty, abnormality with criminality, or framing disabled individuals as obstacles to social and economic progress. Such implicit negativity influenced how terms were judged, leading to disagreement about their offensiveness. For example, in the sentence *"The so-called 'cripples' were confined to a separate wing of the institution"*, one annotator viewed the term 'cripples' as mildly pejorative due to its stigmatizing undertones, while another interpreted it as neutral, reflecting historical norms. A third annotator took an intermediate position, recognizing the term's outdated but non-hostile nature. These differences underscore the subjective nature of assessing offensive language, particularly in historical texts where social norms have evolved.

[11] pairwise Kappa scores are presented in the Appendix (Table 2)

[12] A visual representation of the Fleiss' Kappa scores and their variation across different terms is presented in the Appendix (Figure 3)

[13] detailed analysis and visualization in the Appendix

[14] Further discussion and examples in Appendix B

Value of Qualitative Comments. The notes provided by annotators offered valuable insight into their reasoning and highlighted the complexity of the task. For instance, one annotator remarked that while 'abnormal' could be interpreted as informal, the historical context suggested it carried diagnostic weight. Another commented that the term 'cripple' felt stigmatizing but did not appear intended to insult. Such reflections underscore the importance of qualitative comments in resolving ambiguity and improving consistency in annotation.

6.2.2 Contextual influences on the annotation

Focus sentence vs. Whole context. In some cases, annotators reported that the ratings of intent of use would have been different based on whether they should have considered just the focus sentence or the whole context. Indeed, annotators found instances in which the use of a word was mildly offensive or not offensive at all, but their context was very offensive or contained other offensive words. For example, one original sentence concerning 'demented' said that *"dementia concerned mental retrogression"*, but the immediate context after discussed *"the intelligence of idiots* and that *idiocy in all its degrees means arrested or retarded development"*. Such discrepancies contributed to annotator disagreement, as some focused on the standalone sentence while others considered the full passage. This variability reveals the limitations of narrow-span annotation when assessing offensive language, especially in historical texts where offensive intent or stigma may accumulate across sentences. It also underscores the importance of supporting larger-span annotations to better capture temporally sensitive shifts in language use and meaning.

Unique Challenges in Semi-Structured Content. The annotators felt that the task of annotating uses of the potentially offensive words in titles, references, and citations was fundamentally different from working on free text, mostly due to the limited context.

6.2.3 Historical and linguistics evolution

Influence of Historical Context on Meaning. The historical context of language significantly influenced annotators' decisions. Terms like 'abnormal' and 'cripple' have undergone shifts in meaning over time, from clinical or neutral descriptors to terms with potential stigmatizing connotations. Annotators' varied responses reflect the difficulty of balancing the original historical context with modern understandings of disability language.

Semantic Change and the Origin of Slurs. Prompted by the cross-analysis of their annotations, the annotators openly discussed about the origin of slurs and how offensive language comes into existence in the first place. One annotator said that slurs have "only appeared recently" and that "it made no sense to have them back then, it is a newer phenomenon". The discussion focused on the fact that there are probably no "intentional" slurs in the dataset (because of the medical domain, and because of the time at which the text of the dataset was published), hypothesising that it is the post-hoc use of medical terms in discourse what prompts their semantic drift into offensive language.

6.2.4 Categorisation challenges

Formal Diagnosis vs. Common Language. Annotators faced challenges in classifying disability-related terms, particularly when distinguishing between formal medical diagnoses and common or colloquial usage. For instance, the sentence *"The child was described as abnormal in both behavior and appearance, requiring constant supervision"* was interpreted differently. While one annotator classified it as common language, reflecting everyday usage, others marked it as a formal diagnosis. This highlights the challenge of distinguishing between colloquial and medical language, especially when historical shifts in meaning blur the boundaries. For future time-sensitive annotations in disability sources we suggest practitioners to expand these two categories including, for instance, 'medical use but not formal diagnosis'.

Difficulties in Identifying Implied Disabilities. In some cases, annotators differed in marking implied disability types. For example, the sentence *"The blind man had remarkable memory and navigated the town with ease"* was identified as referring to sensory disability by two annotators, while another overlooked the implication. This suggests that implicit references to disability, especially when not explicitly stated, pose challenges for consistent annotation and require greater sensitivity to context.

Multiple Dimensions of Medical Conditions. The annotators notes highlighted the difficulty in assigning one single category to some medical conditions. For example, for contexts that mentioned the condition *epilepsy* the annotators were unclear on whether this is a "cognitive" or a "sensory" condition; they would have perhaps selected both. This might change across different conditions.

7 Observations and Conclusions

The annotation disagreements described in §6 reflect the inherent subjectivity in interpreting historical texts that contain socially charged language. Annotators brought divergent perspectives on the historical role of terminology, the socio-political context of the sentences, and the contemporary implications of stigmatizing language. These divergences align with observations in prior research that annotation of socio-psychological constructs often entails subjective and multidimensional judgments (Pavlick and Kwiatkowski, 2019).

The annotation guidelines provided to annotators did not fully account for these interpretive differences. Future annotation tasks involving socially sensitive language would benefit from clearer operational definitions, explicit guidance on balancing historical and modern interpretations, and perhaps more granular label schemes. Another key challenge, also noted in hate speech annotation literature, is the variation in perceived offensiveness based on the background of the annotators and their relationship to the communities referenced in the texts (Vidgen et al., 2019). This is especially relevant for disability discourse, where community preferences around person-first versus identity-first language and perceptions of terms as outdated or offensive can differ widely. While our annotators were trained to reflect on historical and social context, future annotation efforts would benefit from including individuals with lived experience of disability or from adopting participatory annotation approaches that foreground community perspectives. Additionally, methods that embrace annotation disagreement such as soft labeling (Wu et al., 2023) may better reflect the inherent subjectivity of such tasks than traditional majority vote approaches. Other annotation disagreement challenges, such as different readings of a sentence's tone, remain outside the capabilities of textual representations and we consider them much harder to address through annotation protocols alone.

The findings from this analysis suggest several implications for the development of annotation schemes in the context of socio-political constructs and sensitive domains such as disability discourse. First, annotation tasks involving socio-psychological or politically charged constructs should acknowledge that disagreements are not necessarily indicative of noise, but may instead reflect valid differences in perspective that offer richer interpretive possibilities (Mostafazadeh Davani et al., 2022). Second, annotation protocols might benefit from incorporating structured reflection or justification fields, prompting annotators to explicitly state the reasoning behind their choices. Finally, our study highlights the need for methodological innovations in annotation aggregation. Majority voting may obscure valuable minority perspectives that offer critical insights into the data. Alternative approaches such as adjudication by discussion or perspectivist approaches (Cabitza et al., 2023) may be better suited to capturing the complexities inherent in the annotation of multidimensional socio-linguistic phenomena. Our analysis shows the deeply subjective nature of such annotation tasks. Where social and ethical considerations intersect with linguistic analysis, disagreements may be inevitable and even desirable, provided they are systematically analysed and leveraged.

Acknowledgments

This work was partially supported by the HE project MuseIT, co-funded by the European Union under Grant Agreement No. 101061441. The views and opinions expressed in this work are those of the authors and do not necessarily reflect the views of the European Union or the European Research Executive Agency. We thank MuseIT partners including Nasrine and Sandor for their valuable feedback in the pilot round, and Lloyd May for initial discussions. Special thanks to Andrea for her detailed feedback on the first draft.

Authors' contributions

BMcG designed the study, acquired the data for the annotation, developed the annotation protocol and wrote sections 1, 2, 4, 5, and B. NJ helped with design of study, data collection and formatting for the annotation session, co-led the annotation session and collection of data, performed the quantitative analysis of the dataset and the annotations, wrote section 5 and contributed to 6.1, 6.2 and 7 and refined the paper overall. CDB helped with the data collection, co-leading the annotation session, and writing section 6.2. AMP helped with the data collection and writing section 6.2.

Limitations

We are aware of the following limitations. **(1)** We only focused on English using readily available resources. However, exploring the applicability of this annotation protocol to other languages would be an important direction for future work, which could show interesting patterns about disability over time across languages. **(2)** We investigated a limited number of disability keywords. Although we diversified our data selection to account for multiple sources, multiple centuries, multiple intent of term, use of term and types of disability, future work should expand this annotation protocol to more disability keywords. **(3)** We did not conduct a fine-grained annotation analysis based on annotators' background. This was out-of-scope for this paper but we acknowledge the importance of this analysis for future work centered around subjectivity, especially given that domain expertise (e.g., in historical or medical texts) could influence annotation quality and help address cases of low agreement.

References

Erin E Andrews, Robyn M Powell, and Kara Ayers. 2022. The evolution of disability language: Choosing terms to describe disability. *Disability and Health Journal*, 15(3):101328.

Gail K Auslander and Nora Gold. 1999. Disability terminology in the media: a comparison of newspaper reports in Canada and Israel. *Social Science & Medicine*, 48(10):1395–1405.

Hosein Azarbonyad, Mostafa Dehghani, Kaspar Beelen, Alexandra Arkut, Maarten Marx, and Jaap Kamps. 2017. Words are malleable: Computing semantic shifts in political and media discourse. In *Proceedings of the 2017 ACM on Conference on Information and Knowledge Management*, pages 1509–1518.

Federico Cabitza, Andrea Campagner, and Valerio Basile. 2023. Toward a perspectivist turn in ground truthing for predictive computing. In *Proceedings of the Thirty-Seventh AAAI Conference on Artificial Intelligence and Thirty-Fifth Conference on Innovative Applications of Artificial Intelligence and Thirteenth Symposium on Educational Advances in Artificial Intelligence*, AAAI'23/IAAI'23/EAAI'23. AAAI Press.

Silvana Castano, Alfio Ferrara, Stefano Montanelli, Francesco Periti, et al. 2022. Semantic shift detection in vatican publications: a case study from leo xiii to francis. In *CEUR WORKSHOP PROCEEDINGS*, volume 3194, pages 231–243. CEUR-WS.

Jacob Cohen. 1960. A coefficient of agreement for nominal scales. *Educational and psychological measurement*, 20(1):37–46.

DE-BIAS Project consortium. 2025. De-bias: Vocabulary – english.

Phillip Ferrigon and Kevin Tucker. Person-first language vs. identity-first language: An examination of the gains and drawbacks of disability language in society. *Journal of Teaching Disability Studies*, 1:1–12.

Sanne Hoeken, Sophie Spliethoff, Silke Schwandt, Sina Zarrieß, and Özge Alaçam. 2023. Towards detecting lexical change of hate speech in historical data. In *Proceedings of the 4th Workshop on Computational Approaches to Historical Language Change*, pages 100–111.

L Joseph and Levin Fleiss. 2023. *Statistical methods for rates and proportions*. Wiley-Blackwell.

Daphna Keidar, Andreas Opedal, Zhijing Jin, and Mrinmaya Sachan. 2022. Slangvolution: A causal analysis of semantic change and frequency dynamics in slang. *arXiv preprint arXiv:2203.04651*.

Paola Marongiu, Barbara McGillivray, and Anas Fahad Khan. 2024. Multilingual workflows for semantic change research. *Journal of Open Humanities Data*.

Barbara McGillivray, Malithi Alahapperuma, Jonathan Cook, Chiara Di Bonaventura, Albert Meroño-Peñuela, Gareth Tyson, and Steven Wilson. 2022. Leveraging time-dependent lexical features for offensive language detection. In *Proceedings of the The First Workshop on Ever Evolving NLP (EvoNLP)*, pages 39–54.

Barbara McGillivray, Anas Fahad Khan, and Paola Marongiu. 2023. A new clarin resource family for lexical semantic change – final report. Technical report, Zenodo.

Albert Meroño-Peñuela, Romana Pernisch, Christophe Guéret, and Stefan Schlobach. 2021. Multi-domain and explainable prediction of changes in web vocabularies. In *Proceedings of the 11th Knowledge Capture Conference*, pages 193–200.

Stefano Montanelli and Francesco Periti. 2023. A survey on contextualised semantic shift detection. *Preprint*, arXiv:2304.01666.

Aida Mostafazadeh Davani, Mark Díaz, and Vinodkumar Prabhakaran. 2022. Dealing with disagreements: Looking beyond the majority vote in subjective annotations. *Transactions of the Association for Computational Linguistics*, 10:92–110.

National Center on Disability and Journalism. 2021. National center on disability and journalism. National Center on Disability and Journalism.

Oxford University Press. 2024a. blind (adj., n.1, & adv.))). Oxford English Dictionary.

Oxford University Press. 2024b. lame, (adj. & n.). Oxford English Dictionary.

Ellie Pavlick and Tom Kwiatkowski. 2019. Inherent disagreements in human textual inferences. *Transactions of the Association for Computational Linguistics*, 7:677–694.

John Pavlopoulos, Jeffrey Sorensen, Lucas Dixon, Nithum Thain, and Ion Androutsopoulos. 2020. Toxicity detection: Does context really matter? In *Proceedings of the 58th Annual Meeting of the Association for Computational Linguistics*, pages 4296–4305, Online. Association for Computational Linguistics.

Romana Pernisch, Daniele Dell'Aglio, Matthiew Horridge, Matthias Baumgartner, and Abraham Bernstein. 2019. Toward predicting impact of changes in evolving knowledge graphs. ISWC.

Romana Pernisch, Daniele Dell'Aglio, and Abraham Bernstein. 2021. Beware of the hierarchy—an analysis of ontology evolution and the materialisation impact for biomedical ontologies. *Journal of Web Semantics*, 70:100658.

Catia Pesquita and Francisco M. Couto. 2012. Predicting the Extension of Biomedical Ontologies. *PLoS Computational Biology*, 8(9):e1002630.

Labib Rahman. 2024. Disability language guide. Stanford University.

Mia Ridge, Nilo Pedrazzini, Miguel Vieira, Arianna Ciula, and Barbara McGillivray. 2024. Language of mechanisation crowdsourcing datasets from the living with machines project. *Journal of Open Humanities Data*.

Julia Rodina and Andrey Kutuzov. 2020. Rusemshift: a dataset of historical lexical semantic change in russian. In *Proceedings of the 28th International Conference on Computational Linguistics*, pages 1037–1047.

Paul Röttger, Bertie Vidgen, Dirk Hovy, and Janet Pierrehumbert. 2022. Two contrasting data annotation paradigms for subjective NLP tasks. In *Proceedings of the 2022 Conference of the North American Chapter of the Association for Computational Linguistics: Human Language Technologies*, pages 175–190, Seattle, United States. Association for Computational Linguistics.

Maarten Sap, Dallas Card, Saadia Gabriel, Yejin Choi, and Noah A. Smith. 2019. The risk of racial bias in hate speech detection. In *Proceedings of the 57th Annual Meeting of the Association for Computational Linguistics*, pages 1668–1678, Florence, Italy. Association for Computational Linguistics.

Dominik Schlechtweg, Barbara McGillivray, Simon Hengchen, Haim Dubossarsky, and Nina Tahmasebi. 2020. Semeval-2020 task 1: Unsupervised lexical semantic change detection. *Preprint*, arXiv:2007.11464.

Cecilia Capuzzi Simon. 2017. Disability studies: A new normal. In *Beginning with Disability*, pages 301–304. Routledge.

Charles Spearman. 1961. The proof and measurement of association between two things.

T.G. Stavropoulos, S. Andreadis, E. Kontopoulos, and I. Kompatsiaris. 2019. Semadrift: A hybrid method and visual tools to measure semantic drift in ontologies. *Journal of Web Semantics*, 54:87–106. Managing the Evolution and Preservation of the Data Web.

Ljiljiana Stojanovic. 2004. *Methods and Tools for Ontology Evolution*. Ph.D. thesis, University of Karlsruhe.

Bertie Vidgen, Alex Harris, Dong Nguyen, Rebekah Tromble, Scott Hale, and Helen Margetts. 2019. Challenges and frontiers in abusive content detection. In *Proceedings of the Third Workshop on Abusive Language Online*, pages 80–93, Florence, Italy. Association for Computational Linguistics.

Wikipedia contributors. 2025. List of disability-related terms with negative connotations — Wikipedia, the free encyclopedia. [Online; accessed 18-March-2025].

Ben Wu, Yue Li, Yida Mu, Carolina Scarton, Kalina Bontcheva, and Xingyi Song. 2023. Don't waste a single annotation: improving single-label classifiers through soft labels. In *Findings of the Association for Computational Linguistics: EMNLP 2023*, pages 5347–5355, Singapore. Association for Computational Linguistics.

Frank D Zamora-Reina, Felipe Bravo-Marquez, and Dominik Schlechtweg. 2022. Lscdiscovery: A shared task on semantic change discovery and detection in spanish. *arXiv preprint arXiv:2205.06691*.

A Additional Results for Inter-annotator Agreement

Cohen's Kappa. The detailed pairwise results for Cohen's Kappa are shown in Table 2. With respect to Cohen's Kappa, we observe the following:

- Use of Terms: The "Use of Term" category shows mixed agreement among the annotators. For example, the term "Abnormal" has moderate agreement between A1 and A3 (0.50), but very low agreement between A1 and A2 (0.16). The terms "Blind" and "Cripple exhibit negative or low values in some comparisons, indicating weak or no agreement in those cases.
- Intent of Terms: The "Intent of Term" category shows a more consistent, although still low, agreement between annotators. The term

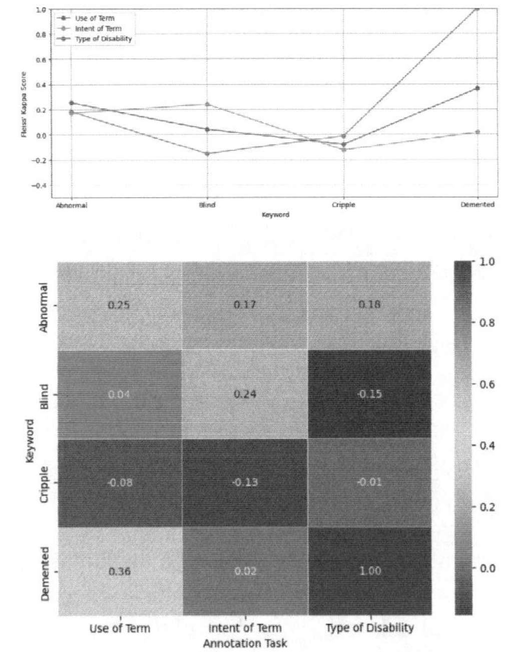

Figure 3: Comparative analysis of the Fleiss' Kappa scores across different keywords and annotation tasks.

"Blind" shows the strongest agreement between A1 and A3 (0.50), but the other terms exhibit lower kappa scores, suggesting more disagreement on the intent behind terms like "Abnormal" and "Cripple".

- Type of Disability: This category shows somewhat better agreement, especially for the terms "Demented" and "Cripple", which have full agreement or expected agreement scores between all pairs of annotators. In contrast, the term "Blind" shows negative or weak kappa scores across all pairs, suggesting minimal consensus on its classification as a type of disability.

Fleiss' Kappa. Figure 3 shows the Fleiss' Kappa scores and their variation across different terms.

Spearman's rank correlation. The results are visualized in Figure 4. Based on the results, we make the following observations for the annotations obtained for each keyword:

- Abnormal: The correlation between A1 and A2 (0.59) is moderate, indicating that their annotations show some alignment. However, A1 and A3 (0.19) and A2 and A3 (-0.10) show weak to negative correlations, suggesting discrepancies in the way these annotators interpreted the terms.

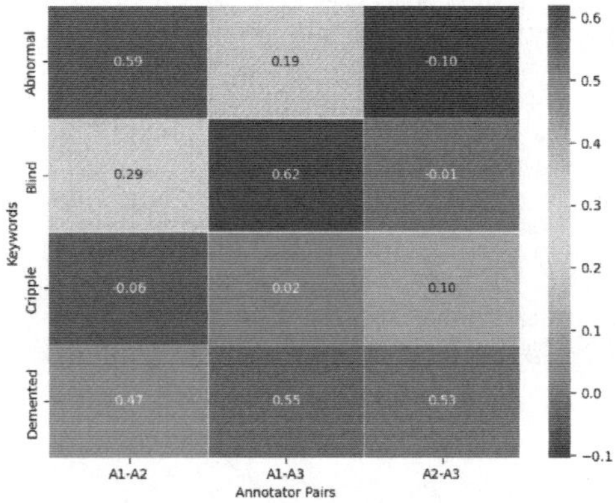

Figure 4: Comparative analysis of the Spearman's Rank Correlation scores across different keywords for the Intent annotations.

- Blind: The correlation between A1 and A3 (0.62) is relatively strong, indicating agreement between these two annotators. A1 and A2 (0.29) and A2 and A3 (-0.01) show weaker correlations, with A2 and A3 almost having no agreement at all.

- Cripple: All correlations are weak, with A1 and A2 (-0.06), A1 and A3 (0.02), and A2 and A3 (0.10), showing minimal or negative alignment. This suggests significant divergence in how these annotators approached the classification of terms.

- Demented: The correlations are generally higher, with A1 and A2 (0.47), A1 and A3 (0.55), and A2 and A3 (0.53) indicating a moderate to strong agreement across all annotators, suggesting more consistency in how these annotators rated the terms.

B Cases of Low Annotator Agreement

Here we present three examples of low annotator agreement.

Example 1: "Joe Hanlon, a cripple, had tits, and Cronin asked him for a match." This is an account from a journal, most likely documenting conditions in an institutional setting—perhaps a psychiatric hospital, asylum, or another care facility. The narrator describes instances of abuse by a person named Cronin, presumably a staff member or attendant, towards several patients. The journal writer's tone is matter-of-fact, possibly reflecting either the norms

Term/Disability Type	Cohen's Kappa (A1 vs A2)	Cohen's Kappa (A1 vs A3)	Cohen's Kappa (A2 vs A3)	Fleiss' Kappa
Abnormal (Use of Term)	0.16	0.50	0.11	0.25
Blind (Use of Term)	0.21	-0.42	0.40	0.04
Cripple (Use of Term)	0.15	-0.07	-0.22	-0.08
Demented (Use of Term)	0.34	0.20	0.55	0.36
Abnormal (Intent of Term)	0.37	0.15	0.02	0.17
Blind (Intent of Term)	0.15	0.50	0.14	0.24
Cripple (Intent of Term)	-0.13	-0.15	-0.09	-0.13
Demented (Intent of Term)	0.08	-0.11	0.22	0.02
Abnormal (Type of Disability)	0.05	0.74	0.03	0.19
Blind (Type of Disability)	-0.25	0.00	0.00	-0.15
Cripple (Type of Disability)	1.00	0.00	0.00	-0.01
Demented (Type of Disability)	1.00	1.00	1.00	1.00

Table 2: Kappa scores for different terms and types of disability.

of the time or an attempt to objectively record events. The language reflects the historical attitudes toward the term *cripple* are likely seen today as offensive, though they may have been considered clinical or neutral by the writer. In this sentence, the annotators unanimously categorized the use of term *cripple* as common language. However, their assessments of Intent diverged substantially. One annotator interpreted the intent as Outdated but Neutral, while another annotator labeled it Mildly Pejorative or Stigmatizing, and the third annotator classified it as Strongly Pejorative or Insulting. This variation may be attributed to different readings of the sentence's tone. For one annotator, the use of *cripple* in this context may have reflected outdated but descriptive language, whereas another annotator may have perceived the sentence structure and reference as dehumanizing, intensifying the perceived stigma. The third annotator's annotation fellsbetween these extremes, reflecting uncertainty about whether the term is merely descriptive or carries additional pejorative force.

Example 2: "In the heat of their technical testimony they forgot the cripple seated at the far end of the room." In this case, two annotators labeled Use of Term as Formal Diagnosis, while the third annotator categorized it as Common Language. The Intent annotations again showed marked variation: one annotator perceived the term as Outdated but Neutral, whereas another annotator assigned Mildly Pejorative or Stigmatizing, and the third annotator assigned Strongly Pejorative or Insulting. The second annotator's notes indicate that their decision was guided by the broader context of the sentence, which they felt framed the reference to the *cripple* in a neutral, factual manner. The third annotator, on the other hand, appeared to prioritize the contemporary offensiveness of the term. The disagreement over Use suggests differing interpretations of whether *cripple* was historically considered a formal medical designation or a colloquial term, showing the difficulty of aligning modern sensibilities with historical usage.

Example 3: "The poor, the lame, the blind, the crippled, the outcast." This sentence generated consistent annotations for Use of Term (all three annotators selected Common Language), but Intent annotations were highly variable. The second annotator labeled it Neutral/Descriptive, suggesting an understanding that the sentence was listing marginalized groups without pejorative intent. In contrast, the first annotator classified it as Mildly Pejorative or Stigmatizing, and the third annotator as Strongly Pejorative or Insulting. The inclusion of *outcast* alongside terms for disability may have contributed to the third annotator's interpretation of heightened stigma. Furthermore, this annotator's detailed notes, distinguishing between different types of disabilities referenced in the sentence (e.g., *lame* as physical, *blind* as sensory), suggest an analytic focus on the cumulative social exclusions implied by the sentence structure.

Pre-annotation Matters: A Comparative Study on POS and Dependency Annotation for an Alsatian Dialect

Delphine Bernhard, Nathanaël Beiner, Barbara Hoff
Université de Strasbourg, LiLPa UR 1339
F-67000 Strasbourg, France
{dbernhard,n.beiner,barbara.hoff}@unistra.fr

Abstract

The annotation of corpora for lower-resource languages can benefit from automatic pre-annotation to increase the throughput of the annotation process in a a context where human resources are scarce. However, this can be hindered by the lack of available pre-annotation tools. In this work, we compare three pre-annotation methods in zero-shot or near-zero-shot contexts for part-of-speech (POS) and dependency annotation of an Alsatian Alemannic dialect. Our study shows that good levels of annotation quality can be achieved, with human annotators adapting their correction effort to the perceived quality of the pre-annotation. The pre-annotation tools also vary in efficiency depending on the task, with better global results for a system trained on closely related languages and dialects.

1 Introduction

Automatic pre-annotation is often considered a cost-effective way of producing high-quality corpora, as it streamlines the process for human annotators. In the context of low-resource languages, pre-annotation can be a particularly beneficial practice, given that annotation tasks are often undertaken with limited human and financial resources. However, low-resource languages frequently lack training data or existing tools to obtain good quality pre-annotations.

In this article, we address the impact of pre-annotation on POS and dependency annotation in the Universal Dependencies (UD) framework (De Marneffe et al., 2021) for the Alsatian Alemannic dialects. Alsatian is a hypernym which refers to both Alemannic and Franconian dialectal varieties spoken in the Alsace region, in Northeastern France. The different Upper German dialects referred to by the term "Alemannic Alsatian dialects" are Northern Low Alemannic, spoken in the northern and central parts of Alsace, Southern Low Alemannic, spoken in the southern part of Alsace (south of Colmar), and High Alemannic, in the very south of the region. The Alemannic Alsatian dialects are closely related to other Alemannic German dialects, as for example Swiss German and Swabian, and to other dialectal varieties in the Oberdeutsch dialect family, as for example Bavarian.[1] Rhine Franconian is also spoken in the northwest of Alsace, but it is not included in our study, which focuses on Low Alemannic Alsatian. It is also worth mentioning that there is no consistent spelling standard for Alsatian dialects, which leads to high levels of variation in writing.

In this work, we compare three different pre-annotation methods, focusing on out-of-the-box tools that are easy to use without requiring extensive computational resources, advanced information technology skills or financial resources to pay for APIs. These methods rely either on tools trained for the closest standard language, German, or on a mix of German and related dialects, as well as an instruction-tuned generative large language model (LLM). Instruction-tuned LLMs have sparked the interest of researchers in recent years for annotation tasks with both positive and negative–or at least more cautious–conclusions. One of our goals was therefore to gain a better understanding of their advantages and pitfalls. We address the following research questions (RQ):

RQ1 Is it possible to obtain good annotation quality with zero-shot pre-annotation only, when no existing tools are available for the target language?

RQ2 Which pre-annotation method is the most useful?

RQ3 Can pre-annotation bias be mitigated by using a mix of pre-annotation tools or, on the contrary, does it have a detrimental effect on quality?

[1] Alemannic Alsatian dialects appear under the name "Elsässisch", on the lower left of the map of German dialects by Werner König, published in the *dtv-Atlas Deutsche Sprache*, 17. edition, Munich 2011, p. 230-231.

Proceedings of the 19th Linguistic Annotation Workshop (LAW-XIX-2025), pages 173–186
July 31, 2025 ©2025 Association for Computational Linguistics

RQ4 What are the advantages and pitfalls of instruction-tuned LLMs for our target tasks?

2 Previous Work

2.1 Impact of Pre-Annotation

The impact of pre-annotation for treebank construction has been investigated since as early as 1993 (Marcus et al., 1993), with mostly consensual findings about the advantages of pre-annotation leading to a reduced annotation time, without negative effects on annotation quality. Some of the following papers nevertheless describe potential issues with automatic pre-annotations, in particular the influence of the pre-annotation tool on human annotators.

Fort and Sagot (2010) show that automatic pre-annotation for POS in English reduces the annotation time, even when pre-annotations have moderate levels of accuracy, and does not impact inter-annotator agreement or accuracy. But at the same time pre-annotation can introduce some systematic errors and biases, especially if the pre-annotation is rather good.

Berzak et al. (2016) describe the problem of *anchoring*, which they define as "a well known cognitive bias in human decision making, where judgments are drawn towards pre-existing values", leading to a phenomenon that they call *"parser bias"*. They present a study to measure anchoring for POS tagging and dependency parsing in English and show that there is a bias towards the outputs of the specific pre-annotation tool being edited by the human annotators.

For languages other than English, Mikulová et al. (2022) investigate pre-annotation bias for Czech dependency syntax. They observe that annotations are more consistent when the data is pre-annotated, which might point at an influence of the automatic pre-annotation on the annotators. Overall, annotation is sped-up when the texts are pre-annotated and inter-annotator agreement improves.

The efficacy of automatic pre-annotation has also been studied in the context of languages characterised by a high level of variation in writing. Eckhoff and Berdičevskis (2016) train a parser for Old East Slavic and use it for pre-annotation in an experiment involving four annotators. Pre-annotation led to gains in speed, without apparently lowering annotation quality.

2.2 Zero-Shot Transfer of Taggers and Parsers across Languages and Varieties

Zero-shot[2] transfer has been proposed in recent years as a viable option for low-resource languages with neither existing taggers or parsers, nor big enough training corpora.

For POS tagging and dependency parsing, Lauscher et al. (2020) demonstrated that transfer performance is mainly influenced by the similarity in syntactic properties between the source and target languages. This finding was substantiated by de Vries et al. (2022), who explored zero-shot cross-lingual transfer learning using multilingual pre-trained models for POS tagging, with 65 source languages for training and 105 target languages for testing. They highlighted that including the target language, and to a lesser extent the source language, in the training dataset for the multilingual pre-trained model is particularly crucial. Vandenbulcke et al. (2024) confirmed previous observations that training on closely related languages is key. Transfer of parsers across different historical states of a language is investigated by Lücking et al. (2024), who show that parsers trained on contemporary English and German can be transferred to older language states with very modest drops in performance.

Methods have been proposed to improve tagger and parser efficiency in zero-shot transfer. To mitigate noise caused by spelling variations between source (training) and target (automatic annotation) languages, data transformation can be employed. Various automated methods have been suggested, typically utilizing data transformation techniques leading to an increased resemblance between source and target language data: phonemic and graphemic transformation rules (Hana et al., 2011), lexicon-based translation of words (Bernhard and Ligozat, 2013; Wang et al., 2022), random noise injection in training data (Aepli and Sennrich, 2022; Blaschke et al., 2023).

Finally, more recent work by Ezquerro et al. (2025) has investigated the use of generative large language models for zero-shot dependency parsing. They compared syntactic trees obtained via simple prompting of instructed-tuned LLMs against ran-

[2]Here we use the term zero-shot in the context of cross-lingual tasks, where a multilingual pre-trained model is fine-tuned on a language for a task and then directly applied on another language. Zero-shot is used in this sense by e.g. Aepli and Sennrich (2022), de Vries et al. (2022) and Vandenbulcke et al. (2024).

dom trees generated via different baselines. They reach negative conclusions, since most of the tested LLMs are not able to beat the strongest baselines.

3 Experimental Setup

3.1 Corpus

Our corpus consists of texts translated from French into Low Alemannic Alsatian and belonging to different genres and domains (see Table 1). Most of the sources were translated in the realm of our project, either by a professional translator or by a project participant. In addition, we included three sources with pre-existing translations into Low Alemannic Alsatian: the *Universal Declaration of Human Rights*,[3] which is already present in other Universal Dependencies treebanks, such as French ParTUT, the *Parable of the Prodigal Son* (Steiner and Matzen, 2016) and the *North Wind and the Sun* (Boula de Mareüil et al., 2018).

The corpus was tokenised using an adapted version of the tokenisation script developed by Blaschke et al. (2023) for Bavarian and split into 6 annotation batches. Each batch contains a number of sentences for each source that is proportional to the length of the corresponding source. The original sentence order is kept.

For the analysis presented here, we only retained sentences whose tokenisation was not corrected or modified during the manual annotation correction process, which would prevent the calculation of agreement scores with the pre-annotation. The tokenisation had to be corrected for e.g. contracted forms or epenthetic consonants. Table 2 details the number of sentences and words in each batch, for the analysed subset and in total.

3.2 Pre-annotation Methods

We compare three main pre-annotation methods, based on the analysis of zero-shot transfer methods in Section 2.2.

UDPipe (Straka, 2018) We used UDPipe 2 through the LINDAT UDPipe REST Service[4] and applied the two available German models: GSD (McDonald et al., 2013) and HDT (Borges Völker et al., 2019). Prior to annotating our corpus, we normalize accented vowels to their unaccented form and use a bilingual Alsatian-German lexicon of closed class words to translate Alsatian forms to their German equivalent (Bernhard, 2023). The aim of this pre-processing of Alsatian data is to make Alsatian look more like German and thus be able to use models trained on German directly, without retraining. We used the latest models available when performing the pre-annotation: for batches 1 to 4, the models trained on UD 2.12[5] were used, and for batches 5 and 6, the models trained on UD 2.15.[6] Only very slight changes in performance were reported between the two versions of the training data in the detailed model performance.

Mistral Large We used the free Mistral API with a prompt (see Appendix A) and two different temperature values: 0.1 and 0.7. The sentences were provided in the CoNLL-U format, with the requested annotations left empty. The Mistral Large model claims to excel in several languages, including German.[7] The prompt was refined during the course of the manual annotation period to correct minor details (typos, addition of relation subtypes based on evolutions of the guidelines). In addition to POS and dependency relations, the prompt also requested for a gloss in French. Since Mistral does not always output a correct CoNLL-U file, we semi-automatically corrected the following errors: extraneous POS and dependency annotations on multiword tokens, missing tokens and text metadata, spaces instead of tabulations, missing empty '_' columns. Moreover, the annotation sometimes fails unexpectedly for some sentences and the annotation was then retried. For one of the batches, we also experimented with "agents",[8] in order to decompose the annotation process in the following annotation steps: POS, French gloss and dependency relations, followed by a CoNLL-U format verification agent. The output of each agent was passed as input to the next agent.

ArboratorGrew trainable parsing service[9] on the ArboratorGrew annotation platform (Guibon et al., 2020). The parser (Guiller, 2020; Peng et al., 2022) is based on the architecture of Dozat and Manning (2017) and was trained using the test splits for the following UD corpora: 977 sentences from

[3] https://www.ohchr.org/en/human-rights/universal-declaration/translations/elsassisch?LangID=gsw

[4] https://lindat.mff.cuni.cz/services/udpipe/

[5] https://ufal.mff.cuni.cz/udpipe/2/models#universal_dependencies_212_models

[6] https://ufal.mff.cuni.cz/udpipe/2/models#universal_dependencies_215_models

[7] https://mistral.ai/fr/news/mistral-large-2407

[8] https://docs.mistral.ai/capabilities/agents/

[9] https://arborator.github.io/arborator-documentation/#/parser

Title	Author	Domain	Genre	Sentences	Words
Monday Tales	Alphonse Daudet	Literary	Short story	179	3,924
Universal Declaration of Human Rights	United Nations	Legal	Official charter	83	2,231
Decameron	Boccace	Literary	Short story	19	494
Peter and the Wolf	Sergueï Prokofiev	Literary	Symphonic tale	65	940
Parable of the Prodigal Son	Luke	Religion	Parable	29	631
The North Wind and the Sun	Esope	Literary	Fable	6	127
Chronicles on French Regional Languages	Michel Feltin-Palas	Journalism	Column	177	4,354
			TOTAL	558	12,701

Table 1: Corpus contents. "Words" refers to syntactic words.

Batch	Analysed part Sent.	Analysed part Words	Total Sent.	Total Words
1	74	1,670	88	1,978
2	88	1,771	93	1,967
3	84	1,672	92	1,972
4	85	1,769	93	1,957
5	89	2,248	94	2,380
6	91	2,220	98	2,447
Total	511	11,530	558	12,701

Table 2: Corpus batches.

Pre-annotation	Batch 1	2	3	4	5	6
UDPipe-GSD	✓	✓	✓	✓	✓	✓
UDPipe-HDT	✓	✓	✓	–	✓	✓
Mistral temp=0.7	✓	✓	✓	–	–	–
Mistral temp=0.1	–	✓	✓	–	✓	✓
Mistral agents	–	–	–	✓	–	–
ArboratorGrew	–	–	–	✓	✓	✓

Table 3: Distribution of pre-annotation settings across batches.

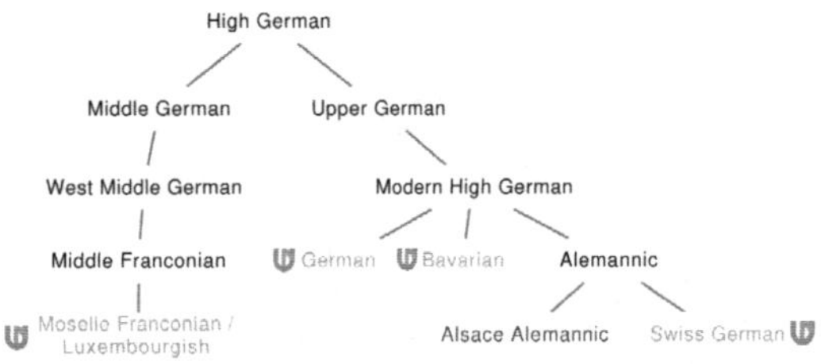

Figure 1: Simplified family tree of Alsace Alemannic based on Glottolog (Hammarström et al., 2024), with related languages available in UD.

German GSD (McDonald et al., 2013), 1,070 sentences from Bavarian MaiBaam (Blaschke et al., 2024), 100 sentences from Swiss German UZH (Aepli, 2018) and 20 sentences from Luxembourgish LuxBank (Plum et al., 2024). These languages were selected based on their proximity to Alsace Alemannic (see Figure 1). In addition, we added 25 Alsatian sentences which were annotated as examples for earlier versions of the annotation guide. In total, 2,192 sentences from 5 Germanic Languages were used to train ArboratorGrew. The Labelled Attachment Score (LAS) obtained during training was 0.83 (Epoch 55). Due to an unavailability of the parsing service during the first half of our annotation period, we started using ArboratorGrew only from batch 4 onwards.

Selection of the pre-annotation We randomly choose one of the available pre-annotations for each sentence and assign different pre-annotations to each annotator. This approach ensures that human annotators start from different pre-annotations, preventing any potential uniform and unique influence on their annotations. For each annotation batch, at least 3 different pre-annotation methods were used (see Table 3).

3.3 Manual Correction Process

The corpus was annotated by two annotators who are co-authors of this paper: A1 and A2. Both are native speakers of Alsace Low Alemannic, have obtained a master's degree in linguistics and written Master theses on the Alsatian dialects. The initial guidelines had been drafted by one of the two annotators based on a study of existing grammars in Alsatian and existing POS annotation guidelines (Bernhard et al., 2018). Both annotators were given an initial training batch, which was used to make them familiar with the annotation tool and the guidelines. After each batch, the annotators discussed their annotations in order to reach a consensual `validated` annotation (see Figure 2 for an example validated annotation). The decisions reached during their discussions were also inte-

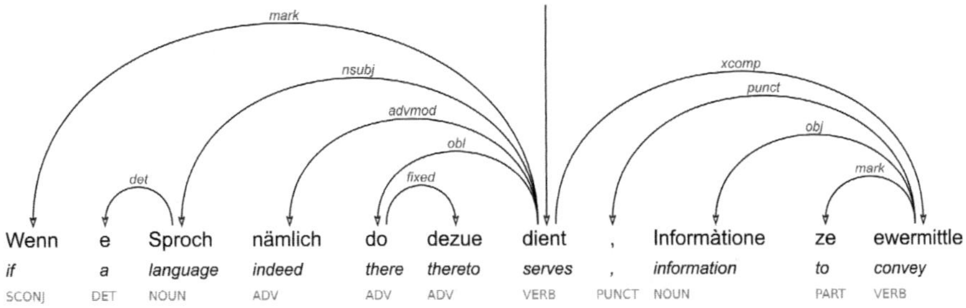

Figure 2: Example annotated sentence with English glosses.

grated in the annotation guide.[10]

The annotation tool was ArboratorGrew (Guibon et al., 2020): the pre-annotated CoNLL-U files were uploaded on the platform and then annotated in blind annotation mode. The whole annotation process reported in this paper took place over a period of four months.

3.4 Agreement Assessment

We used the following scores to measure agreement between pre-annotations, manual corrections and the final validated annotations:
POS: Cohen's κ (Cohen, 1960) for POS labels, as well as accuracy.
Dependencies: Adaptation of Krippendorff's α (Krippendorff, 1970) to dependency relations proposed by Skjærholt (2014), as well as UAS (Unlabelled Attachment Score), LAS (Labelled Attachment Score) and LAcc (dependency Label Accuracy) (Eisner, 1996; Nivre et al., 2004; Buchholz and Marsi, 2006).[11]

4 Results

4.1 Results per Annotation Batch

Figure 3 shows the evolution of inter-annotator agreement over time for both tasks. The agreements tend to increase, with a steeper rise and a higher variability in agreement for dependencies. Agreement levels for POS are more consistent, indicating that the task is less difficult. Overall, the increase in agreement suggests that annotators improve their consistency over time, possibly due to improved guidelines, better training, or increased familiarity with the annotation task.

[10]Details about the annotation guide and specific linguistic properties of the dataset will be described in another article.

[11]For all dependency measures, we reuse the scripts developed by Skjærholt (2014) and available at `https://github.com/arnsholt/syn-agreement/`. Similarly to (Dipper et al., 2024), we converted them to Python 3.

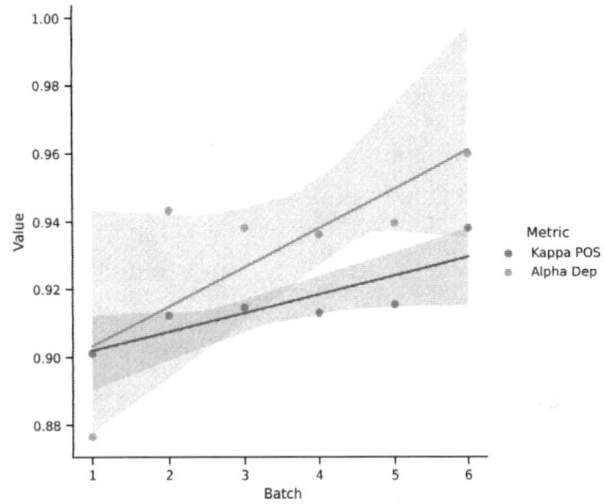

Figure 3: Evolution of inter-annotator agreement scores.

Figure 4 illustrates the evolution of the agreement between the annotators and the automatic pre-annotation over time. For A1, agreement with the pre-annotations remains relatively stable, with a slight downward trend. For A2, the declining trend is more marked for dependencies, with high variability, while for POS the agreement slightly improves. The decline in the agreement for dependencies is likely due to the quality of the automatic pre-annotations: over time, the annotators are more actively correcting errors. The difference in POS agreement trends between A1 and A2 could suggest varying levels of reliance on pre-annotations. Overall, both annotators align more with POS pre-annotations, while increasingly correcting errors in pre-annotations for dependencies.

Finally, Figure 5 illustrates the evolution of agreement between the two annotators and the validated annotation. Both annotators show an increasing agreement trend over batches, indicating an improvement in their annotation consistency over time. In contrast to Figure 4, agreement is consistently higher for dependencies than for POS: this might point at an over-reliance on POS pre-

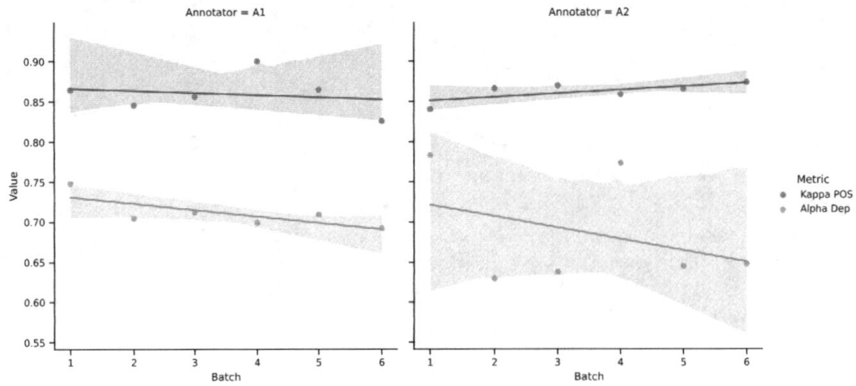

Figure 4: Evolution of agreement scores with respect to the pre-annotation.

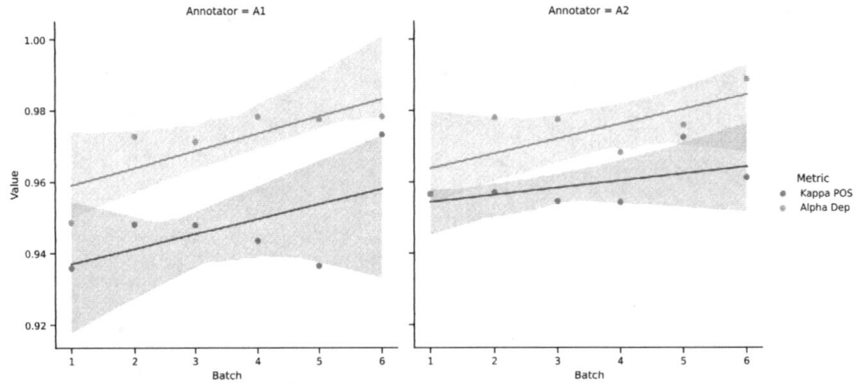

Figure 5: Evolution of agreement scores with respect to the validated annotation.

annotations, being perceived as good enough, and an under-reliance on dependency pre-annotations, being perceived as error-prone and deserving more corrections.

To conclude, lower agreements are observed with the pre-annotation and higher agreements with the validated version, with inter-annotator agreements in-between. This is a result of consensus building by the two annotators to reach the validated annotation (see Table 6 in Appendix D for the detailed agreement scores for each batch.). Overall, the inter-annotator agreements are high (POS $\kappa \geq 0.90$, dependency $\alpha \geq 0.88$), as well as agreements with the validated annotation (POS $\kappa \geq 0.94$, dependency $\alpha \geq 0.95$). Regarding **RQ1** (*Is it possible to obtain good annotation quality with zero-shot pre-annotation only, when no existing tools are available for the target language?*), our findings demonstrate that good levels of annotation quality can be attained even in the absence of pre-existing annotation tools for our target language. This suggests that relying on closely-related languages or multilingual LLMs can be a viable option in such cases. However, as we did not include a control setting in which the annotators started from scratch, we cannot compare the quality of the annotations with and without pre-annotation.

4.2 Analysis of the Pre-annotation Methods

Table 4 details the agreement scores broken down by pre-annotation method and Figure 6 displays the per-sentence POS accuracy and LAS with respect to the validated annotation for UDPipe-GSD, Mistral and ArboratorGrew. Mistral obtains the best results overall for POS, followed closely by ArboratorGrew. Both UDPipe models have lower levels of performance for this task. UDPipe-GSD obtains the best results for dependencies, both in terms of dependency attachments and dependency labels. ArboratorGrew also has good performance for this task, while Mistral obtains the lowest UAS and LAS. Interestingly, Mistral still gets good dependency label accuracy scores. Finally, the density plots in Figure 6 confirm that Mistral has a

Pre-annotation	Annot.	Sent.	Tok.	K POS	Acc POS	α Dep	UAS	LAS	LAcc
UDPipe-GSD	A1	148	3,293	0.84	0.86	0.82	0.76	0.63	0.74
	A2	125	2,815	0.82	0.84	0.83	0.79	0.63	0.71
	validated	273	6,108	0.80	0.82	0.79	0.76	0.60	0.70
UDPipe-HDT	A1	144	3,218	0.79	0.81	0.73	0.64	0.53	0.64
	A2	72	1,792	0.78	0.80	0.77	0.66	0.56	0.67
	validated	216	5,010	0.75	0.77	0.72	0.64	0.51	0.63
Mistral	A1	149	3,126	0.93	0.93	0.62	0.60	0.52	0.73
	A2	214	4,446	0.91	0.92	0.50	0.56	0.48	0.72
	validated	363	7,572	0.88	0.89	0.52	0.55	0.45	0.69
ArboratorGrew	A1	70	1,713	0.89	0.90	0.64	0.74	0.62	0.74
	A2	100	2,297	0.89	0.90	0.68	0.75	0.63	0.74
	validated	170	4,010	0.85	0.87	0.64	0.73	0.59	0.71

Table 4: Scores for each pre-annotation method.

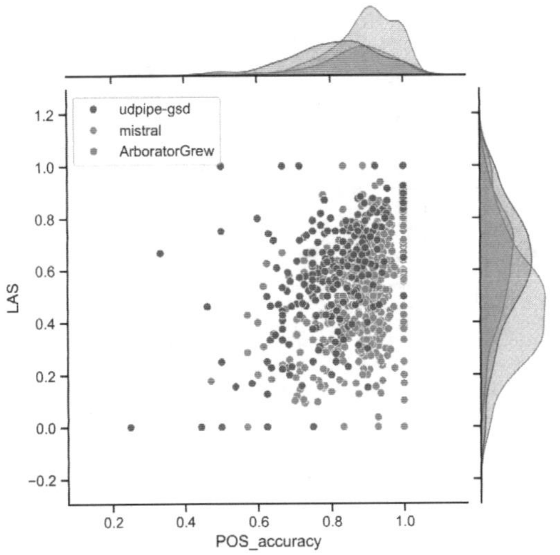

Figure 6: Per sentence POS accuracy and LAS for UDPipe-GSD, Mistral and ArboratorGrew with kernel density estimate (KDE) plots.

higher concentration of sentences with higher POS accuracy, but lower LAS. UDPipe-GSD and AboratorGrew have a higher concentration of points towards the top half LAS values.

If we compare mean dependency distances[12] across the same sentences, Mistral is characterized by shorter distances (avg=3.05, median=3.17), while UDPipe-GSD has larger distances (avg=3.40, median=3.47) closer to what is observed in the validated sentences (avg=3.41, median=3.59), showing that dependency analyses by Mistral tend to favour connections with less intervening words.

Figure 7 compares the pre-annotations of a sentence against the version validated by the annotators. The pre-annotations from UDPipe-GSD, Mistral and ArboratorGrew contain errors in both POS tags and dependencies. While all three pre-annotation tools correctly identified the root of the sentence, all three mistook the perfect tense as a copular structure. The noun phrase "De Mösiö Hamel" (*Mister Hamel*) was correctly identified as the subject of the sentence by all three tools, but both the internal structure and the POS of the elements was a source of error. It is also interesting to note that all three tools annotated the word "gànz" as an adverb (both in POS and for its dependency), whereas the annotators followed annotation guidelines and annotated this word with the POS 'ADJ', although it functions as an adverb. This example shows that there are different types of errors between different pre-annotations: UDPipe-GSD performed worst for POS tags, but best for dependencies, with only one error. On the contrary, Mistral performed best for POS tags, but lower for dependencies. ArboratorGrew lies in between.

For **RQ2** (*Which pre-annotation method is the most useful?*), we find that there are notable differences among the pre-annotation methods, according to the task: simpler POS or dependency labelling tasks can be performed in-context with an instruction-tuned LLM; however more complex dependency attachment resolution is better achieved by models specifically trained for dependency parsing. The best compromise between both tasks is achieved by ArboratorGrew: the model has been trained on comparatively less data than both UDPipe models (2,192 sentences vs. 13,814 sentences in GSD-train and 153,035 sentences in HDT-train), but on a mix of closely related languages and dialects, with variation in writing characteristic of dialects. This is in line with Philippy et al. (2023)

[12]Calculated by averaging the absolute distance between a word and its head, excluding the root (Liu et al., 2017).

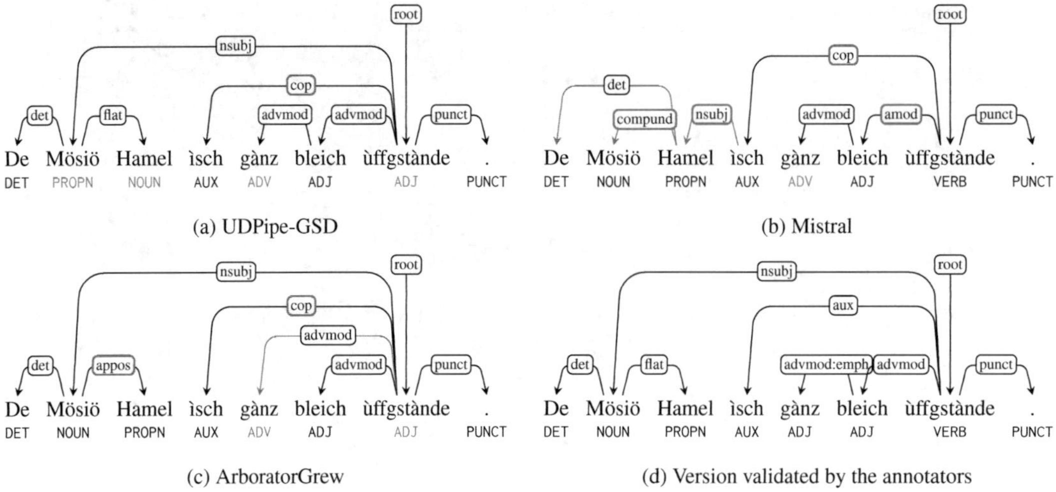

Figure 7: Comparison of the pre-annotations with the validated version for the sentence "De Mösiö Hamel ìsch gànz bleich ùffgstànde" – *'Mister Hamel stood up all pale'*. Errors are marked in red.

who show that cross-lingual transferability is linked to linguistic similarity. It also confirms observations by Blaschke et al. (2024) who obtained lower results for Bavarian with HDT than GSD, despite its larger training corpus: this could be due to an over-fitting of the HDT model for standard German, or to larger discrepancies in terms of genres and domains between the HDT corpus and the Bavarian and Alsatian corpora.

4.3 Pre-annotation Bias

Table 5 shows the correlations between the proportion of tokens pre-annotated by a tool and the global agreement of the annotators with the pre-annotation in a batch. The significant correlation scores show that there is a negative correlation for POS pre-annotation by UDPipe-HDT: the higher the proportion of tokens pre-annotated by UDPipe-HDT, the lower the agreement between the annotators and the POS pre-annotation. This means that the annotators tended to correct and modify the POS pre-annotations by UDPipe-HDT. On the other-hand, there is a positive correlation for dependency pre-annotation for UDPipe-GSD and, to a lesser degree UDPipe-HDT. The observations are in line with the performances of the systems shown in Table 4. Higher agreements with the pre-annotations for dependencies are observed when there is a higher proportion of the best performing tools among the pre-annotations and lower agreements with the POS pre-annotations occur when there is a higher proportion of the lowest performing system. This shows that the annotators were able to identify good and low-quality pre-annotations and tended to agree with correct pre-annotations.

Score	Pre-annotation	Spearman	Pearson
POS	UDPipe-GSD	-0.50	-0.30
	UDPipe-HDT	-0.82^{**}	-0.71^{*}
	Mistral	0.43	0.42
	ArboratorGrew	0.89^{*}	0.68
Dep	UDPipe-GSD	0.84^{***}	0.90^{***}
	UDPipe-HDT	0.79^{**}	0.89^{**}
	Mistral	-0.57	-0.66^{*}
	ArboratorGrew	-0.37	-0.38

Table 5: Spearman's and Pearson's correlations between the proportion of tokens pre-annotated by a tool and the agreement between the annotators and the pre-annotation in a batch. P-values: *** < 0.001, ** < 0.01 and * < 0.05.

Table 4 additionally shows that both A1 and A2 have similar patterns of agreement with the pre-annotation methods, and this agreement is dependent both on the pre-annotation and the task. For **RQ3** (*Can pre-annotation bias be mitigated by using a mix of pre-annotation tools or, on the contrary, does it have a detrimental effect on annotation quality?*), we observe that the annotators did not approach pre-annotations indiscriminately, but rather adapted their correction efforts to the pre-annotation, without uncritically accepting it. Diverse pre-annotation methods thus lead to different correction strategies.

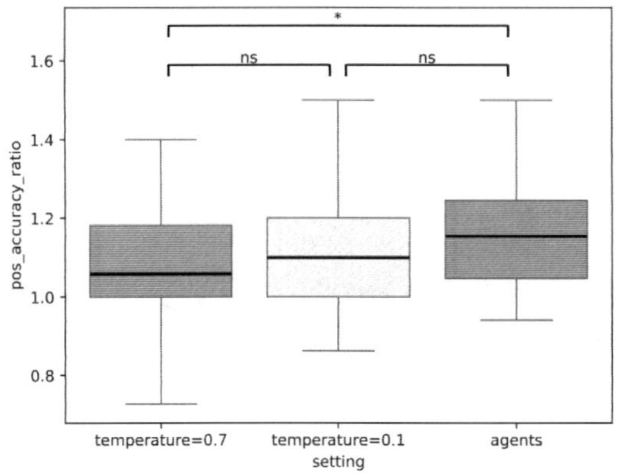

Figure 8: Sentence-level POS accuracy ratio of Mistral in different settings with respect to UDPipe-GSD. Outliers are not shown.

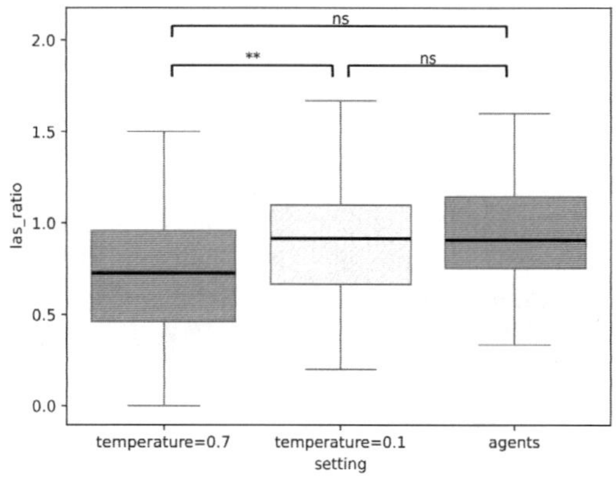

Figure 9: Sentence-level LAS ratio of Mistral in different settings with respect to UDPipe-GSD. Outliers are not shown.

4.4 Instruction-tuned LLMs for Pre-Annotation

Since the way we used Mistral evolved in the course of the annotation period, we perform a detailed analysis of Mistral settings (temperatures and agents) in comparison to UDPipe-GSD. For this, we compute sentence-wise ratios of Mistral over UDPipe-GSD for POS accuracy and LAS. By calculating these ratios sentence-wise, we control for the input sentences and their complexity.

Figure 8 shows the distribution of the POS accuracy ratios. These ratios have a median greater than 1, showing that Mistral performs better than UDPipe-GSD for POS tagging. The statistical significance of the difference between the different settings has been assessed using Mann-Whitney's U test (Mann and Whitney, 1947). Only the difference between the temperature of 0.7 and the use of agents is significant. This might indicate that breaking down a complex task into smaller, simpler tasks (here, using agents) can be beneficial.

Figure 9 shows the distribution of the LAS ratios. These ratios have a median inferior to 1, showing that Mistral performs worse than UDPipe-GSD for dependency parsing. Here, only the difference between both temperature settings is significant, with better performance for a temperature of 0.1. Overall, the settings with a higher temperature have the lowest performance: data annotation is not a creative task and it makes sense to set the temperature to its lowest possible value and keep only the most plausible annotation (Gilardi et al., 2023). For **RQ4** (*What are the advantages and pitfalls of instruction-tuned LLMs for our target tasks?*), we find that Mistral is most efficient for simpler labelling tasks at lower temperatures. Besides, as already mentioned, we had to post-process the output to obtain valid CoNLL-U files, which is a clear downside of this method.

5 Conclusion and Perspectives

In this work, we have compared three pre-annotation methods for POS and dependency annotation for Low Alemannic Alsatian. Since there is no pre-existing annotated corpus for the language, we used mostly zero-shot methods, relying on closely-related languages or an instruction-tuned LLM. We were able to obtain good annotation quality and showed that the human annotators adapted their correction effort to the perceived quality of the pre-annotation. Moreover, the best method for pre-annotation is task-dependent, with the ArboratorGrew model trained on a mixture of closely-related languages and dialects achieving the best overall performance for both tasks.

The corpus described in this paper is currently being reviewed for its release on the UD repository and will complement the resources already available for High German languages. We also used this corpus to train a parser specifically for Alsatian and pre-annotate a second corpus of texts natively written in Alsatian.

Limitations

Selection of pre-annotations for each sentence. The comparison of the pre-annotation systems does not rely on the exact same set of sentences for each system, since different pre-annotations were used for each sentence and human annotator. Therefore, we could not compare the methods on an identical sample of data. It is therefore possible that the random pre-annotation selection process was more advantageous for some systems (shorter and less complex sentences).

Pre-annotation methods. We only compared a restricted set of pre-annotation methods. For the instruction-tuned LLM, only Mistral Large was used, with a single type of prompt. The conclusions could therefore be different for another LLM or for other prompting schemes. Moreover, the pre-annotation tools were used out-of-the-box, without any attempt at tuning the hyperparameters.

Settings for the pre-annotation systems. The settings used for some of the pre-annotation systems (UDPipe training corpus version, Mistral prompt) evolved slightly in the course of the four month annotation period, which could impact the consistency of the observations.

Corpus and language. The corpus under study includes only one target language and it is unclear how our conclusions could be extended to other languages.

Acknowledgments

This work has been carried out within the framework of the ANR-21-CE27-0004 DIVITAL project supported by the French National Research Agency. We would like to thank Adrien Fernique and Carole Werner for translating the texts and Michel Feltin-Palas and Daniel Steiner for allowing us to use their content. We also thank Justine Binot for elaborating the initial Mistral Prompt and Carole Werner for training the ArboratorGrew model.

References

Noëmi Aepli. 2018. Parsing Approaches for Swiss German. Master's thesis, University of Zurich.

Noëmi Aepli and Rico Sennrich. 2022. Improving Zero-Shot Cross-lingual Transfer Between Closely Related Languages by Injecting Character-Level Noise. In *Findings of the Association for Computational Linguistics: ACL 2022*, pages 4074–4083, Dublin, Ireland. Association for Computational Linguistics.

Delphine Bernhard. 2023. Transfert zero-shot pour l'étiquetage morphosyntaxique : analyse de l'impact de la transformation des données à étiqueter pour les dialectes alsaciens. In *Actes des 5èmes journées du Groupement de Recherche CNRS " Linguistique Informatique, Formelle et de Terrain "*, pages 30–38, Nancy, France.

Delphine Bernhard, Pascale Erhart, Dominique Huck, and Lucie Steiblé. 2018. Part-of-speech annotation guidelines for the alsatian dialects. Zenodo: 10.5281/zenodo.1171925.

Delphine Bernhard and Anne-Laure Ligozat. 2013. Hassle-free POS-Tagging for the Alsatian Dialects. In Marcos Zampieri and Sascha Diwersy, editors, *Non-Standard Data Sources in Corpus Based-Research*, ZSM Studien, pages 85–92. Shaker.

Yevgeni Berzak, Yan Huang, Andrei Barbu, Anna Korhonen, and Boris Katz. 2016. Anchoring and Agreement in Syntactic Annotations. In *Proceedings of the 2016 Conference on Empirical Methods in Natural Language Processing*, pages 2215–2224, Austin, Texas. Association for Computational Linguistics.

Verena Blaschke, Barbara Kovačić, Siyao Peng, Hinrich Schütze, and Barbara Plank. 2024. MaiBaam: A Multi-Dialectal Bavarian Universal Dependency Treebank. In *Proceedings of the 2024 Joint International Conference on Computational Linguistics, Language Resources and Evaluation (LREC-COLING 2024)*.

Verena Blaschke, Hinrich Schütze, and Barbara Plank. 2023. Does Manipulating Tokenization Aid Cross-Lingual Transfer? A Study on POS Tagging for Non-Standardized Languages. In *Tenth Workshop on NLP for Similar Languages, Varieties and Dialects (VarDial 2023)*, pages 40–54, Dubrovnik, Croatia. Association for Computational Linguistics.

Emanuel Borges Völker, Maximilian Wendt, Felix Hennig, and Arne Köhn. 2019. HDT-UD: A very large Universal Dependencies Treebank for German. In *Proceedings of the Third Workshop on Universal Dependencies (UDW, SyntaxFest 2019)*, pages 46–57, Paris, France. Association for Computational Linguistics.

Philippe Boula de Mareüil, Frédéric Vernier, and Albert Rilliard. 2018. A Speaking Atlas of the Regional Languages of France. In *Proceedings of the Eleventh International Conference on Language Resources and Evaluation (LREC 2018)*, page 6, Miyazaki, Japan.

Sabine Buchholz and Erwin Marsi. 2006. CoNLL-X Shared Task on Multilingual Dependency Parsing. In *Proceedings of the Tenth Conference on Computational Natural Language Learning (CoNLL-X)*, pages 149–164, New York City. Association for Computational Linguistics.

Jacob Cohen. 1960. A coefficient of agreement for nominal scales. *Educational and psychological measurement*, 20(1):37–46.

Marie-Catherine De Marneffe, Christopher D. Manning, Joakim Nivre, and Daniel Zeman. 2021. Universal dependencies. *Computational linguistics*, 47(2):255–308.

Wietse de Vries, Martijn Wieling, and Malvina Nissim. 2022. Make the Best of Cross-lingual Transfer: Evidence from POS Tagging with over 100 Languages. In *Proceedings of the 60th Annual Meeting of the Association for Computational Linguistics (Volume 1: Long Papers)*, pages 7676–7685, Dublin, Ireland. Association for Computational Linguistics.

Stefanie Dipper, Cora Haiber, Anna Maria Schröter, Alexandra Wiemann, and Maike Brinkschulte. 2024. Universal Dependencies: Extensions for Modern and Historical German. In *Proceedings of the 2024 Joint International Conference on Computational Linguistics, Language Resources and Evaluation (LREC-COLING 2024)*, pages 17101–17111, Torino, Italia. ELRA and ICCL.

Timothy Dozat and Christopher D Manning. 2017. Deep Biaffine Attention for Neural Dependency Parsing. In *Proceedings of ICLR 2017*.

Hanne Martine Eckhoff and Aleksandrs Berdičevskis. 2016. Automatic parsing as an efficient pre-annotation tool for historical texts. In *Proceedings of the Workshop on Language Technology Resources and Tools for Digital Humanities (LT4DH)*, pages 62–70, Osaka, Japan. The COLING 2016 Organizing Committee.

Jason M. Eisner. 1996. Three New Probabilistic Models for Dependency Parsing: An Exploration. In *COLING 1996 Volume 1: The 16th International Conference on Computational Linguistics*.

Ana Ezquerro, Carlos Gómez-Rodríguez, and David Vilares. 2025. Better benchmarking LLMs for zero-shot dependency parsing. In *Proceedings of the Joint 25th Nordic Conference on Computational Linguistics and 11th Baltic Conference on Human Language Technologies (NoDaLiDa/Baltic-HLT 2025)*, pages 121–135, Tallinn, Estonia. University of Tartu Library.

Karën Fort and Benoît Sagot. 2010. Influence of pre-annotation on POS-tagged corpus development. In *Proceedings of the Fourth ACL Linguistic Annotation Workshop*, pages 56–63.

Fabrizio Gilardi, Meysam Alizadeh, and Maël Kubli. 2023. ChatGPT outperforms crowd workers for text-annotation tasks. *Proceedings of the National Academy of Sciences of the United States of America*, 120(30):1–3.

Gaël Guibon, Marine Courtin, Kim Gerdes, and Bruno Guillaume. 2020. When collaborative treebank curation meets graph grammars. In *Proceedings of The 12th Language Resources and Evaluation Conference*, pages 5293–5302, Marseille, France. European Language Resources Association.

Kirian Guiller. 2020. Analyse syntaxique automatique du pidgin-créole du Nigeria à l'aide d'un transformer (BERT) : Méthodes et Résultats. Master's thesis, Sorbonne Nouvelle - Paris 3.

Harald Hammarström, Robert Forkel, Martin Haspelmath, and Sebastian Bank. 2024. Glottolog 5.1.

Jirka Hana, Anna Feldman, and Katsiaryna Aharodnik. 2011. A Low-budget Tagger for Old Czech. In *Proceedings of the 5th ACL-HLT Workshop on Language Technology for Cultural Heritage, Social Sciences, and Humanities (LaTeCH '11)*, pages 10–18.

John D. Hunter. 2007. Matplotlib: A 2D graphics environment. *Computing in Science & Engineering*, 9(3):90–95.

Klaus Krippendorff. 1970. Estimating the reliability, systematic error and random error of interval data. *Educational and psychological measurement*, 30(1):61–70.

Anne Lauscher, Vinit Ravishankar, Ivan Vulić, and Goran Glavaš. 2020. From Zero to Hero: On the Limitations of Zero-Shot Language Transfer with Multilingual Transformers. In *Proceedings of the 2020 Conference on Empirical Methods in Natural Language Processing (EMNLP)*, pages 4483–4499, Online. Association for Computational Linguistics.

Haitao Liu, Chunshan Xu, and Junying Liang. 2017. Dependency distance: A new perspective on syntactic patterns in natural languages. *Physics of Life Reviews*, 21:171–193.

Andy Lücking, Giuseppe Abrami, Leon Hammerla, Marc Rahn, Daniel Baumartz, Steffen Eger, and Alexander Mehler. 2024. Dependencies over Times and Tools (DoTT). In *Proceedings of the 2024 Joint International Conference on Computational Linguistics, Language Resources and Evaluation (LREC-COLING 2024)*, pages 4641–4653, Torino, Italia. ELRA and ICCL.

Henry B Mann and Donald R Whitney. 1947. On a test of whether one of two random variables is stochastically larger than the other. *The annals of mathematical statistics*, pages 50–60.

Mitchell P Marcus, Mary Ann Marcinkiewicz, and Beatrice Santorini. 1993. Building a large annotated corpus of English: The Penn Treebank. *Computational linguistics*, 19(2):313–330.

Ryan McDonald, Joakim Nivre, Yvonne Quirmbach-Brundage, Yoav Goldberg, Dipanjan Das, Kuzman Ganchev, Keith Hall, Slav Petrov, Hao Zhang, Oscar Täckström, and 1 others. 2013. Universal dependency annotation for multilingual parsing. In *Proceedings of the 51st Annual Meeting of the Association for Computational Linguistics (Volume 2: Short Papers)*, pages 92–97.

Marie Mikulová, Milan Straka, Jan Štěpánek, Barbora Štěpánková, and Jan Hajic. 2022. Quality and Efficiency of Manual Annotation: Pre-annotation Bias. In *Proceedings of the Thirteenth Language Resources and Evaluation Conference*, pages 2909–2918, Marseille, France. European Language Resources Association.

Joakim Nivre, Johan Hall, and Jens Nilsson. 2004. Memory-Based Dependency Parsing. In *Proceedings of the Eighth Conference on Computational Natural Language Learning (CoNLL-2004) at HLT-NAACL 2004*, pages 49–56, Boston, Massachusetts, USA. Association for Computational Linguistics.

Fabian Pedregosa, Gaël Varoquaux, Alexandre Gramfort, Vincent Michel, Bertrand Thirion, Olivier Grisel, Mathieu Blondel, Peter Prettenhofer, Ron Weiss, Vincent Dubourg, Jake Vanderplas, Alexandre Passos, David Cournapeau, Matthieu Brucher, Matthieu Perrot, and Édouard Duchesnay. 2011. Scikit-learn: Machine learning in Python. *Journal of Machine Learning Research*, 12(null):2825–2830.

Ziqian Peng, Kim Gerdes, and Kirian Guiller. 2022. Pull your treebank up by its own bootstraps. In *Actes Des Journées Jointes Des Groupements de Recherche Linguistique Informatique, Formelle et de Terrain (LIFT) et Traitement Automatique Des Langues (TAL).*, pages 139–153, Marseille, France.

Fred Philippy, Siwen Guo, and Shohreh Haddadan. 2023. Towards a Common Understanding of Contributing Factors for Cross-Lingual Transfer in Multilingual Language Models: A Review. In *Proceedings of the 61st Annual Meeting of the Association for Computational Linguistics (Volume 1: Long Papers)*, pages 5877–5891, Toronto, Canada. Association for Computational Linguistics.

Alistair Plum, Caroline Döhmer, Emilia Milano, Anne-Marie Lutgen, and Christoph Purschke. 2024. LuxBank: The First Universal Dependency Treebank for Luxembourgish. In *Proceedings of the 22nd Workshop on Treebanks and Linguistic Theories (TLT 2024)*, pages 30–39, Hamburg,Germany. Association for Computational Linguistics.

Arne Skjærholt. 2014. A chance-corrected measure of inter-annotator agreement for syntax. In *Proceedings of the 52nd Annual Meeting of the Association for Computational Linguistics (Volume 1: Long Papers)*, pages 934–944, Baltimore, Maryland. Association for Computational Linguistics.

Daniel Steiner and Raymond Matzen. 2016. *D'Biwel uf Elsässisch*. Éditions du Signe, Strasbourg.

Milan Straka. 2018. UDPipe 2.0 prototype at CoNLL 2018 UD shared task. In *Proceedings of the CoNLL 2018 Shared Task: Multilingual Parsing from Raw Text to Universal Dependencies*, pages 197–207, Brussels, Belgium. Association for Computational Linguistics.

The pandas development team. 2024. pandas-dev/pandas: Pandas v2.2.3.

Zeno Vandenbulcke, Lukas Vermeire, and Miryam de Lhoneux. 2024. Recipe for Zero-shot POS Tagging: Is It Useful in Realistic Scenarios? In *Proceedings of the Fourth Workshop on Multilingual Representation Learning (MRL 2024)*, pages 137–147, Miami, Florida, USA. Association for Computational Linguistics.

Pauli Virtanen, Ralf Gommers, Travis E. Oliphant, Matt Haberland, Tyler Reddy, David Cournapeau, Evgeni Burovski, Pearu Peterson, Warren Weckesser, Jonathan Bright, Stéfan J. van der Walt, Matthew Brett, Joshua Wilson, K. Jarrod Millman, Nikolay Mayorov, Andrew R. J. Nelson, Eric Jones, Robert Kern, Eric Larson, and 16 others. 2020. SciPy 1.0: Fundamental algorithms for scientific computing in python. *Nature Methods*, 17:261–272.

Xinyi Wang, Sebastian Ruder, and Graham Neubig. 2022. Expanding Pretrained Models to Thousands More Languages via Lexicon-based Adaptation. In *Proceedings of the 60th Annual Meeting of the Association for Computational Linguistics (Volume 1: Long Papers)*, pages 863–877, Dublin, Ireland. Association for Computational Linguistics.

Michael L. Waskom. 2021. Seaborn: Statistical data visualization. *Journal of Open Source Software*, 6(60):3021.

A Outline of the Mistral Prompt

Please note that the details about UD POS tags and dependency relationships, as well as the description of the CoNLL-U format have been removed as these can be found on the Universal Depedencies website. The prompt was elaborated and optimised during earlier experiments with instruction-tuned LLMs, based on commonly acknowledged recommendations for prompting: defining the context and the role of the system, task description and constraints, addition of an example with the expected result, use of delimiters to identify subparts of the prompt.

```
You are an expert in Alsatian annotation. Your
task is to add the missing part-of-speech and
dependencies annotations to the Alsatian
sentences.

Here is the list of UPOS labels to use for
part-of-speech annotations:
<List of UPOS labels with names>

Here is the list of labels for Universal
Dependencies:
<List of relations with names>

Constraints: The output must respect the format
called CoNLL-U. Annotations are encoded in plain
text files (UTF-8, normalized to NFC, using only
the LF character as line break, including an LF
character at the end of file) with three types of
lines:
1.  Word lines containing the annotation of
a word/token/node in 10 fields separated by single
tab characters; see below.
2.  Blank lines marking sentence boundaries. The
last line of each sentence is a blank line.
3.  Sentence-level comments starting with hash (#).
Comment lines occur at the beginning of sentences,
before word lines.
Sentences consist of one or more word lines, and
word lines contain the following fields:
<List of fields in a CoNLL-U file>
The fields must additionally meet the following
```

```
constraints:
• Fields must not be empty.
• Fields other than FORM, LEMMA, and MISC must
not contain space characters.
• Underscore (_) is used to denote unspecified
values in all fields except ID.
Further, in UD treebanks the UPOS, HEAD, and
DEPREL columns are not allowed to be left
unspecified except in multiword tokens, where all
must be unspecified, and empty nodes, where UPOS
is optional and HEAD and DEPREL must be
unspecified.

####
Here is an example:

Sentence:
# sent_id = WKP_12043.19
# text = Isch dr Hans Baldung im Elsàss uf d Walt
    kumme?
1 Isch _ _ _ _ _ _ _ _
2 dr _ _ _ _ _ _ _ _
3 Hans _ _ _ _ _ _ _ _
4 Baldung _ _ _ _ _ _ _ _
5-6 im _ _ _ _ _ _ _ _
5 i _ _ _ _ _ _ _ SpaceAfter=No
6 m _ _ _ _ _ _ _ _
7 Elsàss _ _ _ _ _ _ _ _
8 uf _ _ _ _ _ _ _ _
9 d _ _ _ _ _ _ _ _
10 Walt _ _ _ _ _ _ _ _
11 kumme _ _ _ _ _ _ _ SpaceAfter=No
12 ? _ _ _ _ _ _ _ _

Annotation:
# sent_id = WKP_12043.19
# text = Isch dr Hans Baldung im Elsàss uf d Walt
    kumme?
1 Isch _ AUX _ _ 11 aux _ Gloss=est
2 dr _ DET _ _ 3 det _ Gloss=le
3 Hans _ PROPN _ _ 11 nsubj _ Gloss=Hans
4 Baldung _ PROPN _ _ 3 flat:name _ Gloss=Baldung
5-6 im _ _ _ _ _ _ _ _
5 i _ ADP _ _ 7 case _ SpaceAfter=No|Gloss=dans
6 m _ DET _ _ 7 det _ Gloss=le
7 Elsàss _ PROPN _ _ 11 obl:lmod _ Gloss=Alsace
8 uf _ ADP _ _ 10 case _ Gloss=en
9 d _ DET _ _ 10 det _ Gloss=le
10 Walt _ NOUN _ _ 11 obl _ Gloss=monde
11 kumme _ VERB _ _ 0 root _ SpaceAfter=No|Gloss=
    venir
12 ? _ PUNCT _ _ 11 punct _ Gloss=.
####

### Step 1: You must read and understand the
    Alsatian sentences.
### Step 2: Use your understanding from step 1 to
    add the POS, dependency and head labels
### Step 3: Provide the annotation of the given
    sentences.
The annotation should be in the CoNLL-U format.
Your output should consist exclusively of the
annotations. No other comments or text should be
included. Remove markdown formatting.
```

B Libraries Used

The following Python libraries were used for performing the analyses and drawing the plots:

- `conllu v. 6.0.0` (`https://github.com/EmilStenstrom/conllu/`)
- `matplotlib v. 3.9.4` (Hunter, 2007)
- `pandas v. 2.2.3` (The pandas development team, 2024)
- `scikit-learn v. 1.6.1` (Pedregosa et al., 2011)
- `scipy v. 1.13.1` (Virtanen et al., 2020)
- `seaborn v. 0.13.2` (Waskom, 2021)
- `starbars v. 3.1.1` (`https://github.com/elide-b/starbars`)

C Models Used

The following models were used:

- UDPipe:
  - GSD 2.12 and 2.15
  - HDT 2.12 and 2.15
- Mistral Large latest (the latest available Mistral model was always used):
  - unique prompt with temperatures 0.1 and 0.7
  - agents: 4 distinct agents all used in a row with temperature 0
    * UPOS: UPOS annotations
    * Gloss: French glosses
    * Dependencies: dependency annotations
    * CoNLL-U format checker

D Detailed Scores per Batch

Batch	Annot. 1	Annot. 2	Kappa POS	Acc POS	Alpha Dep	UAS	LAS	LAcc
1	A1	validated	0.94	0.94	0.95	0.92	0.85	0.90
		pre-annotation	0.86	0.88	0.75	0.67	0.58	0.72
	A2	validated	0.96	0.96	0.96	0.93	0.88	0.92
		pre-annotation	0.84	0.86	0.78	0.70	0.60	0.72
	A1	A2	0.90	0.91	0.88	0.87	0.77	0.84
2	A1	validated	0.95	0.95	0.97	0.94	0.89	0.93
		pre-annotation	0.85	0.86	0.70	0.65	0.55	0.71
	A2	validated	0.96	0.96	0.98	0.96	0.91	0.93
		pre-annotation	0.87	0.88	0.63	0.61	0.51	0.71
	A1	A2	0.91	0.92	0.94	0.92	0.82	0.87
3	A1	validated	0.95	0.95	0.97	0.93	0.88	0.92
		pre-annotation	0.86	0.87	0.71	0.65	0.53	0.69
	A2	validated	0.95	0.96	0.98	0.94	0.90	0.94
		pre-annotation	0.87	0.88	0.64	0.66	0.55	0.73
	A1	A2	0.91	0.92	0.94	0.89	0.81	0.88
4	A1	validated	0.94	0.95	0.98	0.94	0.88	0.92
		pre-annotation	0.90	0.91	0.70	0.73	0.63	0.76
	A2	validated	0.95	0.96	0.97	0.95	0.91	0.94
		pre-annotation	0.86	0.87	0.77	0.75	0.61	0.73
	A1	A2	0.91	0.92	0.94	0.90	0.81	0.87
5	A1	validated	0.94	0.94	0.98	0.94	0.91	0.95
		pre-annotation	0.86	0.88	0.71	0.70	0.57	0.70
	A2	validated	0.97	0.98	0.98	0.96	0.93	0.95
		pre-annotation	0.87	0.88	0.64	0.69	0.58	0.72
	A1	A2	0.92	0.92	0.94	0.92	0.86	0.91
6	A1	validated	0.97	0.98	0.98	0.95	0.91	0.95
		pre-annotation	0.83	0.84	0.69	0.67	0.55	0.69
	A2	validated	0.96	0.97	0.99	0.97	0.94	0.96
		pre-annotation	0.87	0.89	0.65	0.64	0.52	0.68
	A1	A2	0.94	0.94	0.96	0.93	0.87	0.91

Table 6: Detailed scores for each annotation batch.

Where it's at: Annotating Verb Placement Types in Learner Language

Josef Ruppenhofer[1], **Annette Portmann**[2], **Matthias Schwendemann**[2], **Christine Renker**[3], **Katrin Wisniewski**[2], **Torsten Zesch**[1],
[1]FernUniversität in Hagen, [2]Universität Leipzig, [3]Universität Bamberg,
Correspondence: torsten.zesch@fernuni-hagen.de

Abstract

The annotation of learner language is often an ambiguous and challenging task. It is therefore surprising that in Second Language Acquisition (SLA) research, information on annotation quality is hardly ever published. This is also true for verb placement, a linguistic feature that has received much attention within SLA. This paper presents annotations of verb placement in German learner texts at different proficiency levels. We argue that as part of the annotation process target hypotheses should be provided as ancillary annotations that make explicit each annotator's interpretation of a learner sentence. Our study demonstrates that verb placement can be annotated with high agreement between multiple annotators, for texts at all proficiency levels and across sentences of varying complexity. We release our corpus with annotations by four annotators on more than 600 finite clauses sampled across 5 CEFR levels.[1]

1 Introduction

Acquiring the different options for verb placement, and more generally constituent order, in finite clauses of German is a well-known challenge for learners and a frequent object of second language acquisition (SLA) studies on German (Jordens, 1990; Diehl et al., 2000; Gunnewiek, 2000; Tschirner and Meerholz-Härle, 2001; Jansen, 2008; Czinglar, 2013; Baten and Håkansson, 2015; Wisniewski, 2020; Schlauch, 2022; Schwendemann, 2023).

One key reason to study verb placement is its theoretical significance for theory building. While learners' *interlanguage* (IL) has been found to be highly variable, it is also known to be systematic (Selinker, 1972). Processability Theory (PT) (Pienemann, 1998, 2005) posits that German verb placement options are acquired in a fixed order by all learners regardless of other factors, such as learners' age or educational background. This systematicity is attributed to the fact that it depends on the *processability* of the grammatical structures producing the different orders. These grammatical mechanisms build on each other to the effect that there is no skipping or re-ordering possible among the five major placement options that PT focuses on. Unsurprisingly, such strong claims are contested within the field of SLA (De Bot et al., 2007; Hulstijn et al., 2015). A second important reason to verify claims about the acquisition of verb placement empirically is that some common instruments for proficiency testing that are used in educational settings rely on verb placement as a key diagnostic (e.g. MIKA-D in Austria (Glaboniat, 2020; Blaschitz, 2023)): a theory whose application affects educational trajectories in the real world had better be sound.

Recently, Ruppenhofer et al. (2024) published specifications for the computational implementation of a system detecting verb placement types as a prerequisite for an automated analysis of learner (L2) language development on a large scale. However, that paper did not show that a key prerequisite for automation holds, namely that verb placement analysis can be performed reliably by human annotators. Moreover, as far as we could ascertain, agreement on verb placement analysis also has never been evaluated within SLA, where most studies on the topic seem to be based on single coding by one of the authors.

While the above specifications suggest that this should be an eminently doable task on proficient native (L1) data, we think it needs to be tested empirically how well human coders agree on verb placement in **learner text**, which is orthographically, semantically, and/or morpho-syntactically non-canonical. As an illustration, consider example (1).

[1]https://github.com/dakoda-project/annotating_verb_placement_with_ths

Proceedings of the 19th Linguistic Annotation Workshop (LAW-XIX-2025), pages 187–200
July 31, 2025 ©2025 Association for Computational Linguistics

(1) Wann möchtst wir Treffen ?
when would-like we meeting ?
'When would you like (for) (us) to meet ?'

The last two tokens in (1) cannot combine if taken at face value: *wir* 'we' is a nominative case personal pronoun but *Treffen* 'meeting' is a noun. In this and other similar cases, any labeling of the learner data rests on adopting a particular interpretation of what the learner was trying to say.[2]

In the remainder of this paper, we argue for using an annotation protocol where verb placement annotations are performed in conjunction with the annotation of target hypotheses that can explicate the understanding of difficult learner productions such as (1). To that end, we present the design and results of an annotation study on essay data of L2 German learners at different levels of proficiency. We focus on the following research questions. How good is agreement between human annotators on verb placement overall? Can we observe differences related to the texts' proficiency levels (given in terms of CEFR ratings)? Is there an effect of sentence complexity on agreement?

2 Theoretical Background

To motivate our study design, we first present the SLA theory whose verb placement inventory we use for annotation and then discuss the use of target hypotheses in the analyses of learner data.

2.1 Processability Theory

The core of PT is the idea of a *processability hierarchy*. It encapsulates the idea that at least for some phenomena an acquisitional order from simpler to more complex structures results from the fact that the capabilities of the human language processor (Levelt, 1989) expand in a specific sequence as it develops new processing procedures for handling ever more advanced grammar rules. While the specific linguistic phenomena that exhibit fixed acquisition may differ across languages, the assumption is that all languages have phenomena of this kind because all languages must rely on grammatical processing procedures. In the case of German, verb placement is taken to be a core grammatical feature whose fixed acquisitional order is owed to the processability hierarchy. Table 1 illustrates the major patterns that Processability Theory (Pienemann, 1998) has focused on. These concern only finite clauses. In non-finite clauses, German verbs are always placed in final position so there is no variation to acquire. There also exist further minor finite sentence types with additional placement options. For instance, German allows so-called narrative verb-initial sentences. Since these minor sentence types are not the focus of the SLA literature, we set them aside here, too.

In **SVO** order, the verb is in second position, preceded by the S(ubject) and followed by an O(bject). **ADV**(erbial) is an order said to be used transitorily by learners (but ungrammatical in L1 German)[3], where an adverbial is placed before an SVO sequence for information structural reasons. **SEP**(aration) is a constellation that is used with complex verb clusters consisting of a finite modal or auxiliary in second position and a non-finite participle or infinitive in final position. Usually the finite and non-finite verbs are separated from each other by intervening arguments and/or modifiers. **INV**(ersion) is the L1-appropriate way of achieving the discursive ends intended by learners using ADV. But different from ADV, in INV the subject moves to the right of the verb so that only the adverbial remains to its left, which fulfills the constraint that in L1-German only one item should fill the preverbal slot. Once learners master INV, they no longer use ADV. The last placement type, **VEND** is used in subordinate clauses that are marked as such by subordinators or complementizers.

Note that some of the above placement types can co-occur. For instance, example (2) below shows both SEP(aration) of the finite and non-finite verbs *muss* and *suchen* and INV(ersion) of the subject pronoun *ich*. We refer the reader to Ruppenhofer et al. (2024) and their specifications for more discussion of such cases.

(2) Darum muss ich eine neue Wohnung
therefore must I a new apartment
suchen .
look-for .
'That's why I need to look for a new apartment.'

2.2 Annotating Target Hypotheses

Target hypotheses (THs) are a type of ancillary annotation that is often used in learner corpus linguistics. In that context, the TH makes explicit the aimed-for production the analyst assumes as

[2]We illustrate the multiple possible normalizations for example (1) below in Figure 1.

[3]Müller (2003) shows that there are some limited cases where ADV-like structures do occur in L1 German.

Short Name	Description	Example
SVO	canonical word order	*Ich* ***suche*** *eine neue Wohnung* . I look-for a new flat. 'I am looking for a new flat.'
ADV	adverb preposing	*Darum ich* ***suche*** *eine neue Wohnung* . therefore I look-for a new flat . 'Therefore, I am looking for a new flat.'
SEP	verb separation	*Ich* ***muss*** *darum eine neue Wohnung* <u>*suchen*</u> . I must therefore a new flat look-for . 'I have to look for a new flat.'
INV	inversion	*Darum* ***suche*** *ich eine neue Wohnung* . therefore look-for I a new flat . 'Therefore, I am looking for a new flat.'
V-END	verb-final	*Weil ich eine neue Wohnung* ***suche*** . because I a new flat look-for . 'Because I am looking for a new flat.'

Table 1: Verb placement types in German (Pienemann, 1998) (**bold** = finite verb; <u>underline</u> = non-finite verb)

a reference when performing error annotation on a learner production (Lüdeling, 2008). For German as an L2, MERLIN (Boyd et al., 2014) and the Falko corpora (Lüdeling et al., 2008) are well-known resources that feature THs. The guidelines of the Falko project (Reznicek et al., 2012) in fact distinguish several types of THs. So-called minimal target hypotheses (called TH1) are supposed to feature only the minimal edits to make a learner production morpho-syntactically grammatical (and automatically parsable), though not necessarily idiomatic and contextually appropriate. Extended target hypotheses (aka TH2), by contrast, are less constrained: they also aim to make the utterance semantically and pragmatically appropriate to the context. In addition to TH1s and TH2s, the Falko corpus also features TH0 hypotheses. These are like their TH1 counterparts except that word order changes necessary for TH1 are undone. This means that TH0 may contain ungrammatical word orders. Table 2 provides an illustration.

Inter-annotator agreement for TH-based annotation has not been reported or discussed very much, as most corpora with any type of TH are only singly annotated. A notable exception is the ComiGs corpus of picture story retellings (Köhn and Köhn, 2018). It includes a subset of learner texts for which two annotators produced both a TH1 and a TH2 following the Falko guidelines. The authors report a high level of agreement with a κ of 0.765 for which tokens on the learner text need to be changed. The reasons for the absence of multiple THs in most corpora likely are the time and cost required: the Falko guidelines for THs, for instance, span more than 20 pages.

The field of Grammatical Error Correction (GEC) distinguishes between reference normalizations that involve "minimal edits" (similar to Falko's minimal THs (TH1)) and reference normalizations that include "fluency edits" (similar to Falko's extended THs (TH2)). Of the datasets used in the recent Multilingual GEC shared task, most datasets only feature minimal edits and none seems to have multiple references at the same level of correction (Masciolini et al., 2025). To make up for the lack of multiple reference normalizations, the evaluation of GEC systems often uses reference-free metrics which enable the evaluation of model output without relying on a single (or, at best, a few) gold-standard references (Bryant et al., 2023).

3 Annotating Verb Placement with Ancillary Target Hypotheses

Broadly speaking, we can distinguish two types of difficult cases for verb placement analysis: (a) productions whose meaning is understandable but which are not obvious to normalize and (b) productions whose meaning is difficult to understand. Our introductory example (1) exemplifies the former situation: while we can understand the semantic import of the learner's utterance (especially in view of the task context of this production), the learner's production is syntactically incoherent and its normalization is not obvious.

Figure 1 shows several possible THs for the learner production in (1). The different THs themselves have different verb placement annotations and they lead to different conclusions about verb

L	Erstens gibt es viele Frage **muss** man im voraus zu überlegen. firstly gives it many questions must one in advance to consider 'First, there are many issues that one has to think about in advance.'	
TH0	Erstens gibt es viele Fragen, die **muss** man sich im Voraus überlegen.	raw word order
TH1	Erstens gibt es viele Fragen, die man sich im Voraus überlegen **muss** .	corrected order
TH2	Erstens gibt es viele Fragen, *über* die man im Voraus *nachdenken* **muss** .	fluency edit (italics)

Table 2: Example with three levels of target hypotheses from Falko L2 corpus (fu129_2006_10a)

placement on the learner layer. The first target hypothesis, TH-a, treats *wir* as an erroneous realization of the accusative form *uns* and interprets *Treffen* as an erroneously capitalized infinitive form rather than as a noun. In addition, the TH adds a subject pronoun *du* to make the sentence grammatical. Accordingly, the clause shows SEP(aration) between the finite verb 'möchtst' and the non-finite verb 'Treffen'. This also applies to the learner layer, which has counterparts for both verbal tokens as well as an intervening token. However, since the learner layer lacks a subject, it cannot be labeled as an instance of INV(ersion). By contrast, TH-b treats 'Treffen' as a noun and exhibits INV because the sole finite verb is followed by its subject and preceded by a non-subject. However, because the learner layer lacks a post-verbal subject, it cannot be labeled as INV. In fact, none of PT's labels applies.

An example of the second type of difficult case is found in (3). Here the verb *sagen* may or may not be taken to have a complement clause (cf. possible interpretations a-c). Depending on how the two finite verbs/clauses relate, we make different assumptions about the type of clause and verb placement we need to assign to the finite form *wurde*.

(3) und Sie sagen mir gut Konzert wurde 18
and she say me good concert became 18
märz.
March

(a) 'And she tells me there is a good concert on March 18th.'
(b) 'And she tells me okay. The concert was on March 18th.'
(c) 'And she tells me if the concert on March 18th turned out to be good.'

Given cases such as (1) and (3), it seems unavoidable to explicate coders' target hypotheses: simply comparing annotations on the learner layer without reference to THs risks making the annotations appear less valid and reliable than they might be. As a correlate, for instances where multiple THs are plausible, multiple gold standards for verb placement must be entertained.[4]

Beyond explicating the understanding attributed to the tokens on the learner layer, THs serve a second function that is important within the language acquisition context: they spell out the structure that was expected in context. For instance, in (4), the learner uses SVO (verb-second) in the complement clause. A possible TH for this clause would re-order it to final placement of the finite verb (*daß immer mehr Menschen lieber alleine als in einer Großfamilie leben*).

(4) ... so kann man Sagen, [dass immer mehr
... so can one say, [that always more
Menschen **leben** lieber alleine als in
people live preferably alone than in
einer Großfamilie].
a big-family].

' ..., then we can say that more and more people prefer living alone to living in an extended family.'

By the logic of Processability Theory, a data point such as (4) serves as a piece of negative evidence, suggesting that the learner has not mastered verb-final placement as they fail to use it in a context where it ought to be used. Without THs, no such evidence is available.

3.1 Source Data

The data on which we carried out our study comes from the MERLIN (Boyd et al., 2014) and DISKO (Wisniewski et al., 2022) corpora. Both of them include written texts, specifically essays, for which a manual CEFR rating is available. We used MERLIN data to represent the lower CEFR levels A1, A2, and B1, while we sample DISKO for more advanced B2 and C1 data.[5] We did not include texts rated as C2 since they are too few in number and of lesser interest as the acquisition of verb placement likely is completed prior to that level of proficiency.

[4]While we are concerned directly only with the analysis of verb placement, the idea of capturing multiple acceptable analyses of learner language should be relevant to learner language tree-banking in general.

[5]We consider the proficiency level TDN3 of the DISKO corpus to be equivalent to B2 for our purposes, whereas DISKO's level TDN5 serves as comparable to CEFR-level C1.

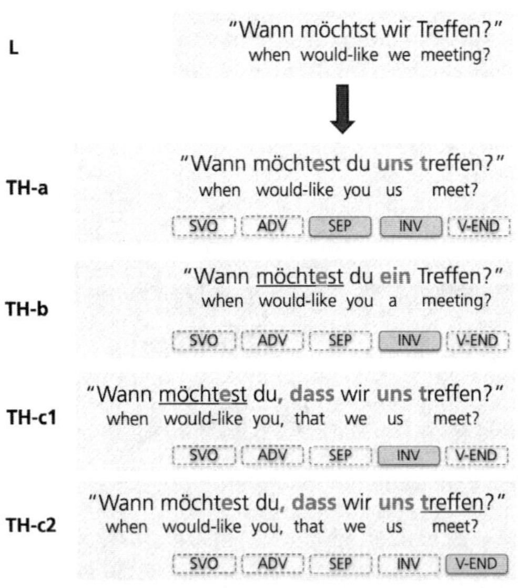

Figure 1: Different annotators might come up with different target hypotheses potentially leading to different analyses regarding verb placement. Note that TH-c produces two analyses because it assume two finite verbs/clauses.

The MERLIN corpus contains texts produced as part of standardized tests. The most common L1s in the German part of MERLIN[6] are Russian, Polish, Hungarian, French, and Spanish. The DISKO corpus contains language tests taken by L2 speakers studying at German universities. The most common L1s in DISKO are Russian, Arabic, and Spanish.

All annotations are performed on the learner data (abbreviated as **L**) as well as the annotated target hypothesis (**TH**). If the learner sentence was grammatical, the target hypothesis (and the resulting annotations) is usually a copy.

3.2 Type of target hypothesis to aim for

In the context of our annotation of verb placement types in the DAKODA project, annotators were instructed to produce target hypotheses that (i) reflect their interpretation of the learner text, (ii) are grammatical, and (iii) make minimal changes. They were, however, given no further criteria for which 'edit operations' they should consider more or less costly but instead use a holistic approach when weighing alternatives. Our instructions thus match neither the minimal (TH1s) nor the extended target hypotheses (TH2s) defined by Falko (Reznicek et al., 2012). While TH1s emphasize criteria (ii) and (iii), they may ultimately not reflect the contextually understood interpretation of a learner utterance in the interest of staying close to the lexico-syntactic material the learner provided. TH2s, by contrast, often don't observe desideratum (iii) and make more fluency edits than we would like to see from the annotators. For instance, for our purposes verbal constructions should not be replaced by nominal ones or vice versa. Nor should finite and non-finite constructions be switched, even at the cost of idiomaticity.

Our annotators were aware of the general 'downstream' analytic interest in verb placement, but they were not explicitly told to adhere to any additional desiderata such as the ones about preserving (finite) verbs. By refraining from imposing specific rules for which kinds of normalizations to prefer, we hoped to avoid suppressing alternative possible interpretations and alternative normalizations. Note that the TH guidance we used should not be seen as a poor man's approximation of TH1s: we purposely deviate from the Falko guidelines to enforce more faithfulness to interpretation than TH1s do, while allowing somewhat more formal variation than THs1 allow (but still less than TH2s do).[7]

The resulting data thus allows one to study how often annotators converge on the same or similar THs even without detailed guidance. This approach may be of interest for other research settings where the creation of highly controlled THs is not feasible.

3.3 Annotation Process

We split the annotation into 6 rounds. Per round, we asked for 100 finite clauses to be identified and annotated. For each round, we provided the annotators with a series of randomly sampled texts within which they were asked to perform a set of annotation steps (explained in the next paragraph) on the learner text until they had reached 10 finite clauses from the start in a given document. Limiting the annotation to at most 10 clauses from a given document/learner was done so as not to bias results to any particular learner. If a document contained fewer than 10 clauses, annotators were asked to annotate additional clauses in another document.

[6]The overall MERLIN corpus is trilingual with German, Italian, and Czech as targets of language acquisition.

[7]While we also hoped to see, as a welcome side effect, a speedup of TH construction relative to using the detailed Falko guidelines for TH1s, we did not perform an empirical comparison and thus do not know if any time savings materialized.

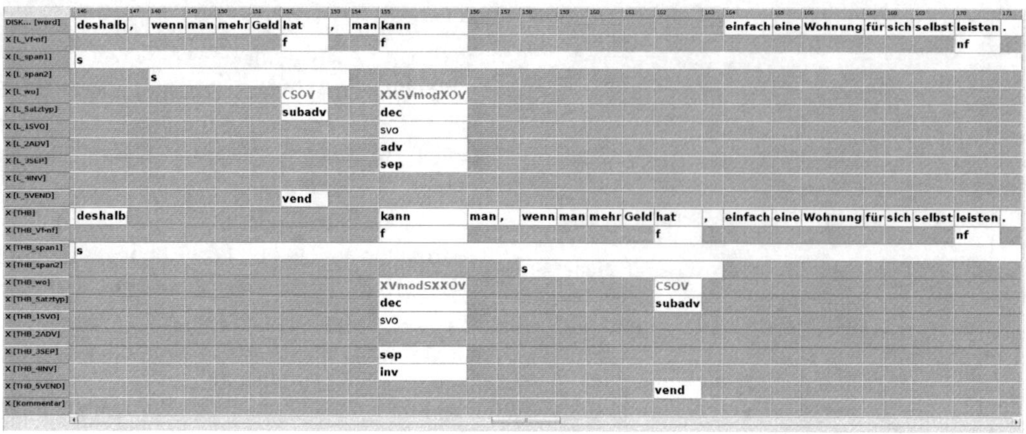

Figure 2: Annotation in Exmaralda
'If you have more money, you can readily afford a place of your own.'

Each round included documents from each of the five CEFR levels under consideration. Overall, data is drawn from 66 distinct documents.

Annotation Steps

- segment the text into sentences and clauses (as needed)
- identify any verbal forms and mark them as finite (f) or non-finite (nf)
- classify finite clauses into predefined sentence types (cf. Appendix A)
- record the ordering of the major constituents in each finite clause
- provide one or more labels characterizing the verb placement in a finite clause (cf. section 2.1)

Note that the annotators ran through the above annotation steps in one go. That is, we did *not* create an adjudicated set of finite verb instances before letting annotators proceed to the sentence type and verb placement analysis.[8] This choice was made with the expectation that agreement would be high for identifying finite verbs anyway.

Tool We used Exmaralda[9] (Schmidt and Wörner, 2014) because some of our annotators had prior familiarity with it and because our corpora are available in a format that Exmaralda can read. As we did not want to carry over any bias from automatic tools, the annotators worked on raw text, that is, they had no access to any manually or automatically assigned POS-tags or lemmas etc. For that reason, we explicitly asked for the annotations related to clause and verb identification in addition to verb placement labels.

Figure 2 shows a screenshot of annotations on a text from the DISKO corpus. In the example, the target hypothesis involves a reordering and the analysis of the matrix clause headed by the modal *kann* differs accordingly: for instance, while the learner clause exhibits ADV, the TH clause features INV.

Annotators We had 4 annotators ranging from master's students to post-docs with expertise in the area of German as a foreign or second language and familiarity with PT. They met to discuss questions after every round of annotation. A subgroup of two annotators finally produced an adjudicated gold standard. Importantly, this gold standard allows for multiple correct labels if they result from target hypotheses with different clausal orders.

4 Annotation Analysis

In the final dataset, we have 849 tokens annotated as verbs on the learner layer **L**. On the target hypothesis layer **TH**, we have 847 instances. Table 3 gives the breakdown per CEFR level. As we have complex sentences in our data even on the lower levels, we reached more than the 600 verb instances to be expected if we only had atomic finite clauses.

Figure 3 shows the combinations of sentence type and verb placement found on the learner layer. What we observe are mostly combinations that would be expected for German. For instance, INV(ersion) structures are commonly found in questions and declaratives, while verb-final (VEND) structures are found exclusively in

[8] In other words, unitizing was not completed before categorization in the sense of (Mathet et al., 2015).

[9] www.exmaralda.org

	L		TH	
Level	# verbs	% finite	# verbs	% finite
A1	159	.74	158	.73
A2	152	.73	151	.74
B1	161	.70	162	.70
B2	173	.68	173	.68
C1	204	.73	203	.73

Table 3: Total verb instances per CEFR level

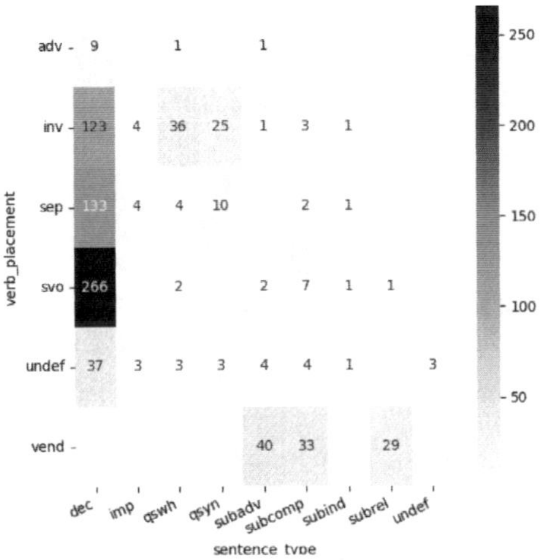

Figure 3: Combinations of sentence type (cf. Appendix A) and verb placement (cf. section 2) on the Learner layer

subordinate clause types. However, we can also observe some unexpected combinations involving SVO in various types of subordinate clauses.

4.1 Overall agreement

We first consider overall agreement per layer. Table 4 shows Fleiss κ values for 4 annotators calculated using the python re-implementation of the IRR_CAC package.[10] Importantly, as we had expected, agreement is very high for identifying finiteness. And in fact, agreement is also high for sentence type and verb placement, with surprisingly small differences between the two layers. The high agreement on annotations based on THs suggests that ancillary THs formulated without detailed Falko-style guidelines are adequate for our task.

4.2 By CEFR level

To address our second research question, we analyze the level of agreement obtained for texts with different **proficiency** levels to see if there is evidence for either of two seemingly conflicting intuitions. On the one hand, agreement might get better, the higher the proficiency level gets because more proficient texts are more grammatical and understandable. On the other hand, the constructions found in lower-proficiency texts may exhibit less variance and may be simpler, making clauses easier to analyze.

[10]https://github.com/afergadis/irrCAC

	L	**TH**
finiteness	.97	.98
sentence type	.84	.85
verb placement	.83	.83

Table 4: Overall agreement on learner text (**L**) and target hypothesis (**TH**) in terms of Fleiss' κ

Figure 4 provides plots for agreement by CEFR level. For the learner data, agreement on finiteness is high throughout, with a peak for documents at level B1. On the target hypothesis layer, the results are similar but the peak at B1 is absent.

For the annotation of sentence type on the TH layer, the texts at level A1 yield higher agreement than those at level B1, whereas on the learner layer the peak is at level B1. This may be due to non-target language-like characteristics of early learners' L2 German, whereas on L1 German the annotation of sentence type becomes more difficult, the more sophisticated the texts become. The finding for early L2 German learners might seem counter-intuitive at first sight. Since beginning learners make more errors, one might expect that it would be more difficult to agree on a common interpretation. However, early learner's language is also characterized by a smaller repertoire with a large proportion of ready-made chunks. This might constrain the range of interpretational options for annotators and thus make it an easier task to agree on annotations.

For verb placement, agreement improves slightly across levels for both learner and TH layers. On the learner layer, there is a dip for the highest level. However, overall the differences between CEFR levels do not seem very pronounced, which potentially means that both intuitions apply at the same time: we get fairly steady high agreement, though for different reasons at different levels.

4.3 By complexity

Addressing our third research question, we want to see if sentence **complexity**, operationalized here

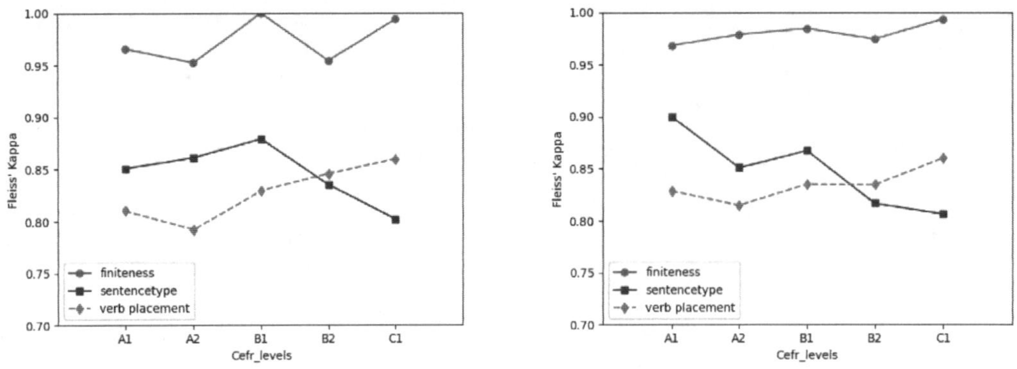

(a) Learner (**L**) (b) Target Hypothesis (**TH**)

Figure 4: Agreement by CEFR level

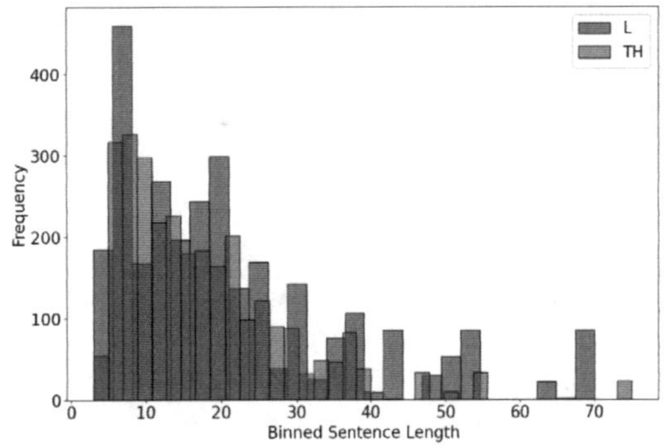

Figure 5: Distribution of sentence lengths

in rough terms as the number of tokens, influences agreement. Note that we use *complexity* here in the sense of (Bulté et al., 2024) as focused on formal features of linguistic items , in contrast to *difficulty*, which refers to items' cognitive load.

Figure 5 shows the right-skewed distribution of sentence lengths in both the learner and the TH layers. Most outliers at the end of the long tail are owed to the learner layer. Re-segmentation on the TH layer eliminates many of them.

We split the annotated instances into 10 bins of equal size. Figure 6 shows the agreement results for **L** and **TH**, respectively. Agreement on finiteness is a bit lower for the shorter sentences on the learner layer than on the TH layer. Agreement on sentence type trends downward as sentences get longer. For verb placement, agreement peaks for the 4th bin (median sent. length 12) on the leaner layer but for the 7th bin (median length 21) on the TH layer.

Notably, for both sentence type and verb placement, results are lower on the TH layer for the longest sentences than on the learner layer. This may be due to the fact that during the creation of target hypotheses the material could be re-segmented. This eliminated many long "sentences" that lack correct punctuation in the learner text. The long sentences that remain on the TH layer are complex ones that are harder to analyze.

4.4 Illustration of disagreements regarding verb placement

Some disagreements result from unclear grammatical relations.[11] In example (5), the token *alle* is mismatched with the verb *geht*. On one analysis, the author aimed for *allen geht es sehr gut*, where *allen* is an indirect object; on another, the author aimed for *alles geht sehr gut*, with *alles* as a subject.

(5) ich Hoffe alle **geht** sehr gut .
i hope all goes very well
'I hope everybody is doing very well. / I hope everything is going well'.

Other disagreements regarding verb placement are downstream of disagreements about whether a token is verbal or not. Example (6) is, even in its full context, very hard to make sense of. Some annotators treated *sein* as a non-finite form of the verb *sein* 'to be' that is in construction with the finite form *ist* 'is', while others didn't treat it as a verb but rather as the homophonous and homographic possessive determiner 'his'. On the first analysis, we observe an instance of a verbal bracket (SEP) , on the second analysis we do not.

[11]For discussion of disagreements about finiteness and sentence type, we refer the reader to appendix D.

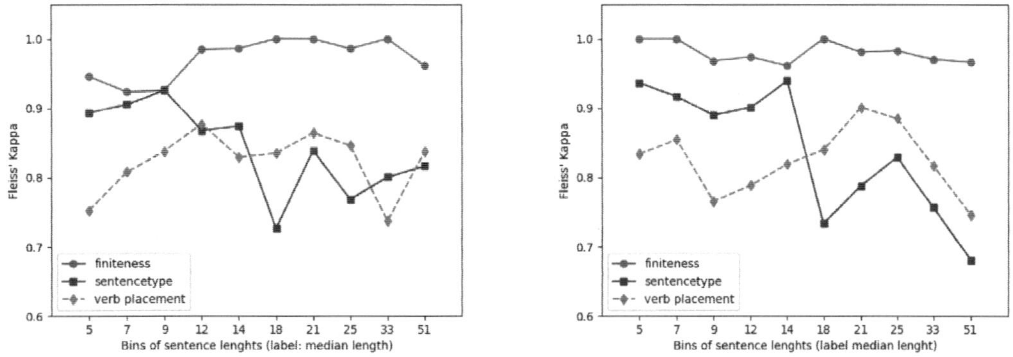

(a) Learner (**L**)

(b) Target Hypothesis (**TH**)

Figure 6: Agreement by sentence length

(6) wann ist deine Kinder **sein** .
when is your children {be/his}

Another group of disagreements includes cases such as (7) where one could either recognize a lexicalized separable prefix verb (e.g. *gutgehen*) that gives rise to a bracket when the parts are separated, or a compositional use where a simple verb (e.g. *gehen*) is modified or complemented by an adverb.

(7) Wie geht't's dir, mir geht **gut** und meine
how goes you, me goes good and my
famile auch .
family also .

'How are you doing? I'm well and my family is, too.'

Finally, we find cases of ambiguity between two verb placement types, for instance, between INV and ADV. In (8) the issue is whether the first token, *so*, is a modifier for the date phrase ('circa in 1975') or a clausal adverb ('Thus/therefore, in 1975 ...'). On the first analysis, there is only one preverbal constituent and the sentence exhibits INV. On the second analysis, there are two preverbal constituents and the sentence exhibits ADV.

(8) So im Jahr 1975 **bestanden** fast die Häfte
so in year 1975 consisted almost the half
von der Haushälte in Deutschland aus 3
of the households in Germany out-of 3
und mehr Personen .
and more persons .

'Thus/Circa in the year 1975 almost half the households consisted of three or more persons.'

5 Conclusion

Our corpus – the Multiply annotated verb placement corpus (MAVPC) – is the first dataset for SLA studies where verb placement is multiply coded and where target hypotheses are available as ancillary annotation rationales. We have shown that on essay data sampled from two corpora and stratified across CEFR levels, high levels of agreement could be achieved for the core annotation categories of finiteness, sentence type, and verb placement. This holds both on the raw learner text and on the THs. The corpus features not only the raw annotations of four annotators but also one or more gold standard labels that reflect contextually plausible interpretations of clausal structure and verb placement. The data can serve as a test set for automatic systems performing verb placement analysis.

While the high agreement on the Learner layer might suggest that THs are not needed at all, we would caution against that conclusion. The concomitant annotation of THs may improve agreement on the learner layer in a way that might be absent if no THs were constructed. Also, our data represents just one written text type and a limited set of L1s. Further studies on additional written text types and especially on spoken language are needed.

Acknowledgements

The authors were supported by BMBF (German Federal Ministry of Education and Research) as part of the project DAKODA (Datenkompetenzen in DaF/DaZ: Exploration sprachtechnologischer Ansätze zur Analyse von L2-Erwerbsstufen in Lernerkorpora des Deutschen [Data competencies in German as Foreign Language / German as a Second Language: Exploring language technology-based approaches to the analysis of L2 acquisition levels in learner corpora of German]), grant number 16DKWN035.

We would also like to thank Jamila Bläsing and Iulia Sucutardean for their support in annotating the data. Finally, we thank Nils Reiter for a fruitful exchange on the details of our agreement evaluation.

Limitations

The annotation carried out as part of this study covers only two corpora of learner essays. While we suspect that agreement would also be quite high in other written task settings, it is unclear just how well the findings would generalize. More significantly, this study does not include any transcripts of spoken learner language. Spoken language data, unlike our essay data, usually comes without punctuation and is transcribed not in terms of sentences or clauses but in terms of utterances or turns. Accordingly, manual annotation of verb placement on such data would be liable to exhibit disagreements resulting from differences in segmentation. In addition, spoken language transcripts contain disfluencies such as hesitations and repetitions which would have to be consistently factored into or out of the annotations. Further, since L1 spoken language admits certain structures that would be ungrammatical in the written modality, annotators should then not correct such structures on L2 data in their target hypotheses.

Our approach to TH creation relied on very little detailed guidance. While we think that that approach could be suitable for other research contexts, too, we acknowledge that it may limit the usefulness of the resulting annotations for re-use in research that requires high internal consistency across the breadth of grammatical phenomena.

References

Kristof Baten and Gisela Håkansson. 2015. The development of subordinate clauses in German and Swedish as L2s : a theoretical and methodological comparison. *Studies in Second Language Acquisition*, 37(3):517–547.

Verena Blaschitz. 2023. "Zeig mir bitte: Banane" – kritische (sprach-)wissenschaftliche Anmerkungen zum Deutschscreening "MIKA-D" [Please show me: banana – critical remarks from (language) science regarding the German language screening instrument MIKA-D]. *ÖDaF-Mitteilungen*, 39(12):174–197.

Adriane Boyd, Jirka Hana, Lionel Nicolas, Detmar Meurers, Katrin Wisniewski, Andrea Abel, Karin Schöne, Barbora Štindlová, and Chiara Vettori. 2014. The MERLIN corpus: Learner language and the CEFR. In *Proceedings of the Ninth International Conference on Language Resources and Evaluation (LREC'14)*, pages 1281–1288, Reykjavik, Iceland. European Language Resources Association (ELRA).

Christopher Bryant, Zheng Yuan, Muhammad Reza Qorib, Hannan Cao, Hwee Tou Ng, and Ted Briscoe. 2023. Grammatical error correction: A survey of the state of the art. *Computational Linguistics*, 49(3):643–701.

Bram Bulté, Alex Housen, and Gabriele Pallotti. 2024. Complexity and difficulty in second language acquisition: A theoretical and methodological overview. *Language Learning*, n/a(n/a).

Christine Czinglar. 2013. *Grammatikerwerb vor und nach der Pubertät: Eine Fallstudie zur Verbstellung im Deutschen als Zweitsprache [Grammar acquisition before and after puberty: A case study on verb placement in German as a second language]*. De Gruyter Mouton.

Kees De Bot, Wander Lowie, and Marjolijn Verspoor. 2007. A dynamic systems theory approach to second language acquisition. *Bilingualism: Language and Cognition*, 10(1):721.

Erika Diehl, Helen Christen, and Sandra Leuenberger. 2000. *Grammatikunterricht: Alles für der Katz? Untersuchungen zum Zweitsprachenerwerb Deutsch [Teaching Grammar: All For Naught? Investigations into the Second Language Acquisition of German]*, 1. edition. Niemeyer, Tübingen.

Manuela Glaboniat. 2020. MIKA-D. Eine Betrachtung aus testtheoretischer Perspektive [MIKA-D. An exmination from a test-theoretic perspective]. *ide - informationen zur deutschdidaktik*, 4:61 73.

Lisanne Klein Gunnewiek. 2000. *Sequenzen und Konsequenzen: zur Entwicklung niederländischer Lerner im Deutschen als Fremdsprache [Sequences and consequences: On the Development of Dutch Learners of German as a Foreign Language]*. Rodopi.

Jan H. Hulstijn, Rod Ellis, and Søren W. Eskildsen. 2015. Orders and sequences in the acquisition of l2 morphosyntax, 40 years on: An introduction to the special issue. *Language Learning*, 65(1):1–5.

Louise Jansen. 2008. Acquisition of German Word Order in Tutored Learners: A Cross-Sectional Study in a Wider Theoretical Context. *Language Learning*, 58(1):185–231.

Peter Jordens. 1990. The acquisition of verb placement in Dutch and German. *Linguistics*, 28(6):1407–1448.

Christine Köhn and Arne Köhn. 2018. An annotated corpus of picture stories retold by language learners. In *Proceedings of the Joint Workshop on Linguistic Annotation, Multiword Expressions and Constructions (LAW-MWE-CxG-2018)*, pages 121–132, Santa Fe, New Mexico, USA. Association for Computational Linguistics.

Willem J. M. Levelt. 1989. *Speaking: From Intention to Articulation*. The MIT Press.

Anke Lüdeling. 2008. Mehrdeutigkeiten und Kategorisierung: Probleme bei der Annotation von Lernerkorpora [Ambigutities and Categorization: Problems in the Annotation of Learner Corpora]. In Maik Walter and Patrick Grommes, editors, *Fortgeschrittene Lernervarietäten*, pages 119–140. Max Niemeyer Verlag.

Anke Lüdeling, Seanna Doolittle, Hagen Hirschmann, Karin Schmidt, and Maik Walter. 2008. Das lernerkorpus falko [the falko learner corpus]. *Deutsch als Fremdsprache*, 45(2):67–73.

Arianna Masciolini, Andrew Caines, Orphée De Clercq, Joni Kruijsbergen, Murathan Kurfalı, Ricardo Muñoz Sánchez, Elena Volodina, and Robert Östling. 2025. The MultiGEC-2025 shared task on multilingual grammatical error correction at NLP4CALL. In *Proceedings of the 14th Workshop on Natural Language Processing for Computer Assisted Language Learning*, pages 1–33, Tallinn, Estonia. University of Tartu Library.

Yann Mathet, Antoine Widlöcher, and Jean-Philippe Métivier. 2015. The unified and holistic method gamma (γ) for inter-annotator agreement measure and alignment. *Computational Linguistics*, 41(3):437–479.

Stefan Müller. 2003. Mehrfache Vorfeldbesetzung. *Deutsche Sprache*, 31(1):29–62. https://hpsg.hu-berlin.de/~stefan/Pub/mehr-vf-ds.html.

Manfred Pienemann. 1998. *Language processing and second language development. Processability theory*. Benjamins,.

Manfred Pienemann. 2005. An introduction to Processability Theory. In Manfred Pienemann, editor, *Cross-Linguistic Aspects of Processability Theory*, pages 1–60. John Benjamins.

Marc Reznicek, Anke Lüdeling, Cedric Krummes, Franziska Schwantuschke, Maik Walter, Karin Schmidt, Hagen Hirschmann, and Torsten Andreas. 2012. Das Falko-Handbuch. Korpusaufbau und Annotationen. Technischer Bericht, Humboldt-Universität zu Berlin. Version 2.01.

Josef Ruppenhofer, Matthias Schwendemann, Annette Portmann, Katrin Wisniewski, and Torsten Zesch. 2024. Every verb in its right place? a roadmap for operationalizing developmental stages in the acquisition of L2 German. In *Proceedings of the 2024 Joint International Conference on Computational Linguistics, Language Resources and Evaluation (LREC-COLING 2024)*, pages 6655–6670, Torino, Italia. ELRA and ICCL.

Julia Schlauch. 2022. Erwerb der Verbstellung bei neu zugewanderten Seiteneinsteiger:innen in der Sekundarstufe. Eine Fallstudie aus dem DaZ-Lerner:innenkorpus SeiKo [Aquisition of verb placement among newly arrived immigrants: Lateral entrants in secondary school. A case study based on the German-as-a-second-language learner corpus SeiKo]. *Korpora Deutsch als Fremdsprache*, 2(2):4362.

Thomas Schmidt and Kai Wörner. 2014. EXMARaLDA. In Jacques Durand, Ulrike Gut, and Gjert Kristoffersen, editors, *The Oxford Handbook of Corpus Phonology*. Oxford University Press.

Matthias Schwendemann. 2023. *Die Entwicklung syntaktischer Strukturen [The development of syntactic structures]*. Studien Deutsch als Fremd- und Zweitsprache. Erich Schmidt Verlag GmbH & Co. KG Berlin.

Larry Selinker. 1972. Interlanguage. *International Review of Applied Linguistics in Language Teaching*, 10(1-4):209–232.

E. Tschirner and B Meerholz-Härle. 2001. Processability Theory: Eine empirische Untersuchung [Processability Theory: An empirical investigation]. In K. Aguado and C. Riemer, editors, *Wege und Ziele: Zur Theorie, Empirie und Praxis des Deutschen als Fremdsprache (und anderer Fremdsprachen). Festschrift für Gert Henrici*, pages 155–175. Schneider, Hohengehren.

Katrin Wisniewski. 2020. SLA developmental stages in the CEFR-related learner corpus MERLIN: Inversion and verb-end structures in German A2 and B1 learner texts. *International Journal of Learner Corpus Research*, 6(1):1–37.

Katrin Wisniewski, Elisabeth Muntschick, and Annette Portmann. 2022. Schreiben in der Studiersprache Deutsch: Das Lernerkorpus DISKO [Writing in German as a Language of Instruction: The DISKO learner corpus]. In K. Wisniewski, W. Lenhard, J. Möhring, and L. Spiegel, editors, *Sprache und Studienerfolg bei Bildungsausländer/-innen*. Waxmann, Münster.

A Annotation of sentence types

The sentence type definitions in Table 5 are meant to apply only to *finite* clauses because PT's theorizing about verb placement does not include non-finite clauses. Thus, though German allows e.g. the use of infinitives and participles as imperatives, such constructions are not part of our annotation. Finally, note that while PT makes no explicit reference to sentence types in defining the verb placement types, previous findings point to a potential effect of sentence type on acquisition order (Diehl et al., 2000).

imp	imperative
dec	declarative main clause
qswh	matrix wh-questions
qsyn	matrix yes/no-question
subadv	adverbial clauses
subcomp	complement/object clauses
subind	embedded interrogative clauses
subrel	relative clauses
undef	other

Table 5: Sentence types

B Verb placement and developmental stages within Processability Theory

Within Processability Theory, categorizing the placement of verb tokens in learner text is done in service of determining the learners' so-called developmental stage. For instance, as noted in the body of the text, a learner who has mastered INV is more advanced than one who uses ADV. One important question is how mastery is assessed. Here, PT employs a so-called emergence criterion: a stage counts as acquired by an individual learner if some N instances are produced in contexts where the relevant verb constellation is expected by L1 standards, so-called obligatory contexts.

To exclude formulaic language and repetition from counting towards emergence, often a lexical diversity criterion for verbs is employed.

For instance, if INV placement is observed with only one verb that is less clear evidence that INV has been acquired than if instances were found for M verbs, where M usually is $\geq$3. The exact values of N and M vary somewhat in the PT literature.

Two considerations are important here. First, high overall accuracy is not required for emergence (cf. Wisniewski (2020)). Second, given how few learners figure in some corpora and how short their texts are, conclusions on individual learners or a cohort may be quite significantly influenced by a few verb tokens being categorized one way or another. For that reason we argue that at least the data should be public , if at all possible, and target hypotheses should be created to explicate the understanding of the learner layer.

C Additional agreement results

C.1 By round of annotation

We look at the development of agreement across rounds of annotation to see if we can observe a **training effect**. Our baseline assumption is that agreement will rise across successive rounds. Figure 7 shows the results for the learner layer and the target hypothesis. The level of agreement overall is high and the trends are broadly similar for both layers. The annotation of finiteness is always easiest. The annotation of sentence type tends to have higher agreement than that for verb placement. For verb placement on the learner layer, we find continual improvement through round 5 after an initial dip, and a slight drop-off for the last round. On the target hypothesis layer, the climb close to peak performance happens earlier.

C.2 Agreement by number of ratings

Some verbal instances in the dataset were not completely labeled on all layers by all annotators. We therefore wanted to see if the lacking annotations might reflect a greater difficulty of the relevant items. Figure 8 plots agreement depending on how many ratings the items minimally received. The figure suggests that agreement on the full dataset, where items were annotated by as few as 2 persons is, in fact, slightly better than on the subset where each item was annotated by everybody. We therefore think that the lacking annotations mostly result from the fact that we had no consistency enforcement in our annotation tool to make sure that items that were labeled as finite also received labeling on other layers. The setup thus allowed oversights to go unnoticed.

On the target hypothesis layer, we find the same trend as on the learner layer (cf. Fig 9).

D Further illustrations of annotator disagreements

Finiteness Disagreements with regard to **finiteness** are very rare overall. One subset of these cases represents instances where some annotators do not treat a token as verbal at all, while others do recognize a verb. For example (9), one subset

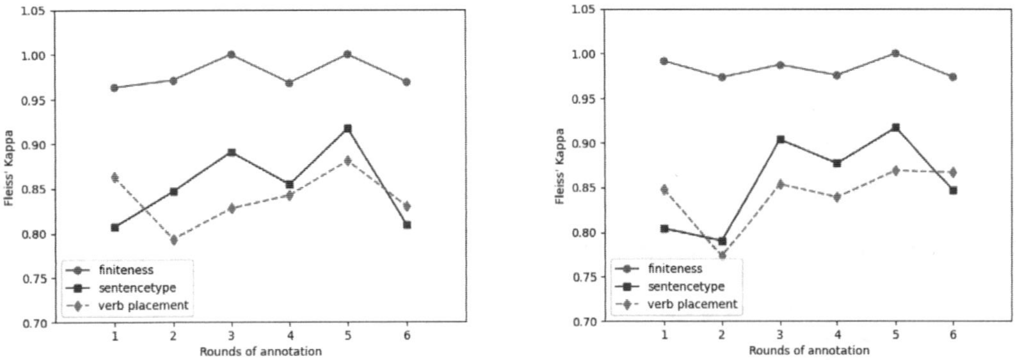

(a) Learner (**L**)

(b) Target Hypothesis (**TH**)

Figure 7: Agreement by round of annotation

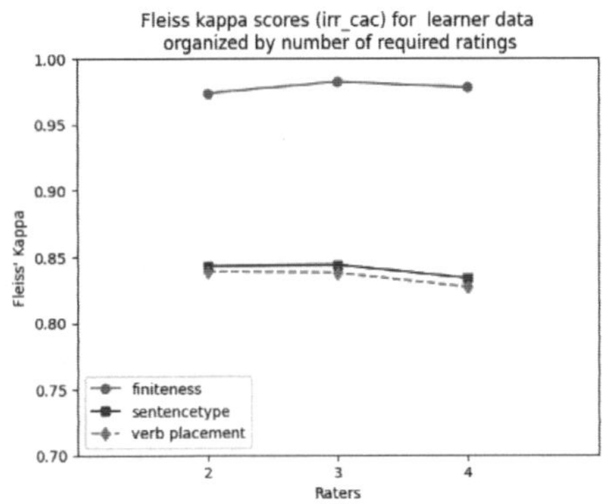

Figure 8: Agreement on learner layer for different numbers of required ratings

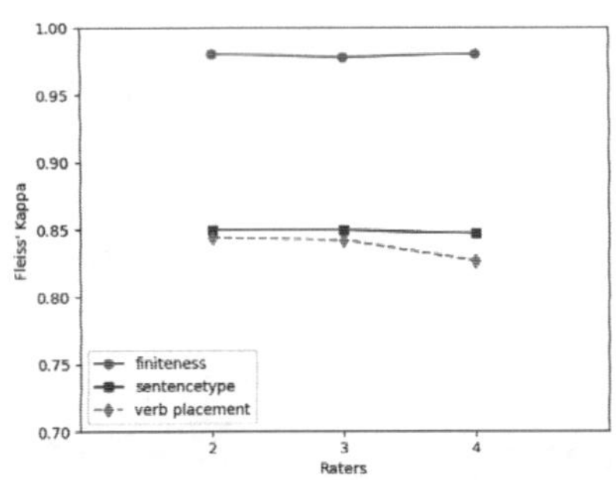

Figure 9: Agreement on target hypothesis layer for different numbers of required ratings

of annotators treated the token *besoche* 'visit' as a finite verbal form, whereas the second group of annotators treated it as a nominal form governed by the verb *nehme* 'take'.

(9) Ich nehme **besoche** meine Tochter .
I take visit my daughter .
'I visit my daughter .'

Example (10) is a case where all annotators perceive the token in question, *kommen* 'come', as verbal but differ as to finiteness. The disagreement is plausible since the *when*-clause lacks a subject, which normally suggests a non-finite construction. On the other hand, temporal adverbial clauses marked by *wann* 'when' ought to be finite according to the grammar of L1 German.

(10) Bringst du mir mit wann du hier in Deutschland **kommen** . .
bring you me with when you here in Germany come.
'You'll bringt it to me when you come here to Germany .'

Sentence type Disagreements with respect to sentence type may result from the tension between a sentence's form and its illocution. In (11), the sentence employs INV(ersion) as is appropriate for a yes/no question but the utterance is clearly a request.

(11) **Küsst** du für mich deine Kinder . .
kiss you for me your children.
'Kiss your children for me .'

The annotators were supposed to annotate based on form type (i.e. they should all have preferred the yes/no question analysis for 11) but they did not always manage to overrule conflicting signals from illocution.

A significant group of disagreements involve subordinate clauses with unexpected word order. In example (12), the token *leben* 'live' occurs in an object clause marked by the complementizer *dass* 'that' and governed by the verb *sagen* 'say'. The expected word order for that constellation is verb-final (VEND) but in fact *leben* seems to occupy the second position as would be appropriate for either a matrix clause or a complement clause without a complementizer. Matching the overall structure, one subgroup of annotators (correctly) recognized an object clause whereas another group annotated a matrix declarative, following the signal given by the word order.

(12) Betrachtet man die Entwicklung der letzten
considers one the development the last
Jahren so kann man Sagen, dass immer mehr
years so can one say, that always more
Menschen **leben** lieber alleine als in
people live preferably alone than in
einer Großfamilie .
a big-family.

'If we consider the developments of recent years, then we can say that more and more people prefer living alone to living in an extended family. .'

Another example is shown in (13), where a sentential relative clause exhibits main clause word order rather than verb-final order. Some annotators chose the relative clause analysis that fits the overall context while others chose an analysis as a declarative sentence that is consonant with the clause-internal word order.

(13) In mein Heimatland LandX , wohnen
In my home-country countryX , live
immer viele Menschen in einem Haushalt
always many people in one household
manchmal sogar eine ganze Familie was
sometimes even a whole family which
führ zu eine Hilfsbereite und relativ
lead to a helpful and relatively
Tolerante Gesellschaft .
tolerant society .

'In my home country countryX, many people live together in a single household, sometimes even a whole family, which makes for a helpful and tolerant society.
'

ICLE-RC: International Corpus of Learner English for Relative Clauses

Debopam Das
Åbo Akademi University
Tehtaankatu 2
20500 Turku, Finland
debopam.das@abo.fi

Izabela Czerniak
Åbo Akademi University
Tehtaankatu 2
20500 Turku, Finland
izabela.czerniak@abo.fi

Peter Bourgonje
University of Potsdam
Karl-Liebknecht-Str. 24-25
14476 Potsdam, Germany
bourgonje@uni-potsdam.de

Abstract

We present the ICLE-RC, a corpus of learner English texts annotated for relative clauses and related phenomena. The corpus contains a collection of 144 academic essays from the International Corpus of Learner English (ICLE; Granger et al., 2020), representing six L1 backgrounds – Finnish, Italian, Polish, Swedish, Turkish, and Urdu. These texts are annotated for over 900 relative clauses, with respect to a wide array of lexical, syntactic, semantic, and discourse features. The corpus also provides annotation of over 400 related phenomena (it-clefts, pseudo-clefts, existential-relatives, etc.). Here, we describe the corpus annotation framework, report on the IAA study, discuss the prospects of (semi-)automating annotation, and present the first results from our corpus analysis. We envisage the ICLE-RC to be used as a valuable resource for research on relative clauses in SLA, language typology, World Englishes, and discourse analysis.

1 Introduction

Relative clauses (henceforth RCs) are a type of subordinate clauses that typically modify nouns or noun phrases, and sometimes also adjectives[1], adverbs[2], PPs[3], VPs[4], and even entire clauses[5]. RCs in English (and beyond) have extensively been studied for a wide range of themes, such as syntactic and typological variation (Comrie, 1998; Grosu, 2012), semantic features (Cornish, 2018), discourse functions (Brandt et al., 2009), diachronic development (Fajri and Okwar, 2020), FLA/SLA (Doughty, 1991), parsing (Goad et al., 2021), and processing (Reali and Christiansen, 2007), to name but a few of more recent work.

In this paper, we present the ICLE-RC, a new corpus of English RCs and related phenomena. The latter includes constructions such as it-clefts, pseudo-clefts, and existential-relatives that employ words like *that*, *which*, or *who*, which are otherwise known as relative markers, frequently used to introduce relative clauses. The ICLE-RC uses a subset of the International Corpus of Learner English (ICLE; Granger et al., 2020). The first version of the ICLE-RC contains 144 ICLE texts, covering six L1 backgrounds – Finnish, Italian, Polish, Swedish, Turkish, and Urdu – with 24 texts from each. These texts are annotated for 924 RCs, with respect to a wide array of lexical, syntactic, semantic, and discourse features. These texts are also annotated for 407 related phenomena, which we call *other constructions* (henceforth OCs).

The paper is structured as follows: Section 2 outlines the motivation behind the creation of the ICLE-RC. The composition of the corpus is described in Section 3. We describe the annotation framework for RCs and OCs in Section 4 and Section 5, respectively. Section 6 reports on an IAA study, and highlights challenges in our RC annotation. The prospects of (semi-)automating the RC annotation is discussed in Section 7. We present the first results from our corpus analysis in Section 8. Related work is briefly described in Section 9. Section 10 concludes the paper with an outlook on the future work and applications of the corpus.

2 Motivation

The development of the ICLE-RC stems from a number of reasons. First, the corpus would provide real language data to assess English learners' use of RCs against the standard rules of English grammars (e.g., the use of *which* for a human referent, or the use of a comma for integrated RCs). Second, the six L1 backgrounds covered in the ICLE-RC represent six different language families (Pereltsvaig,

[1] *Pat is [beautiful], which, however, many consider her not.*
[2] *He moved [abroad] where he found a good job.*
[3] *He found a body [under the bridge] where nothing grows.*
[4] *She told me to [design it myself], which I simply can't.*
[5] *[Alex bought a mansion], which made him bankrupt.*

Proceedings of the 19th Linguistic Annotation Workshop (LAW-XIX-2025), pages 201–215

2023) – Finnish: Uralic; Italian: Romance; Polish: Slavic; Swedish: Germanic; Turkish: Turkic; and Urdu: Indo-Aryan[6]. This would allow identifying typological patterns for certain RC features potentially resulting from cross-linguistic influence (e.g., the use of extraposed RCs). This would also offer significant implications for research in World Englishes, in comparison to native varieties of English (e.g., by comparing the ICLE-RC with comparable corpora such as ICNALE (Ishikawa, 2023) as well as those of native academic English such as LOCNESS (Granger, 1998)). Third, the corpus would help us explore English learners' use of other constructions as alternative strategies of information structuring, in addition to RCs. Finally, although corpus-based studies exist for English RCs, they have mostly used small-size data sets designed to tackle very specific RC-oriented issues (see Section 9). To our knowledge, there is no large-scale corpus of English RCs with a feature-rich annotation framework. The ICLE-RC is designed to accommodate a wide variety of English texts, and support the annotation of RCs therein with a comprehensive coverage of linguistic features pertaining to lexical, syntactic, semantic, and discourse domains.

3 Data selection and setup of the corpus

The ICLE-RC derives from the ICLE (Granger et al., 2020), which is a corpus of academic essays written by undergraduate students from a given set of topics. These students are intermediate or advanced learners of English, coming from different L1 backgrounds such as Chinese, Dutch, Finnish, French, German, Greek, Hungarian, Italian, Japanese, Polish, Russian, Spanish, Swedish, Turkish, and Urdu. The data collection for the ICLE was initiated in the late 1990s, and has since been coordinated by Sylviane Granger at the Centre for English Corpus Linguistics at the University of Louvain. The corpus has grown over the years as a result of close collaboration with a large number of partner universities around the world. The most recent version of the corpus (ICLEv3) includes over 5.5 million words covering 25 L1 backgrounds[7].

The ICLE-RC includes 144 ICLE essays (100K+ words), which are equally distributed into 24 essays from six L1 backgrounds, namely Finnish, Italian, Polish, Swedish, Turkish, and Urdu. These 24 essays for each language are compiled from three institutions (with 8 essays from each), which are further balanced for the gender of the writer[8], whenever possible. The detailed distribution of the essays in the ICLE-RC is provided in Table 9 in the Appendix.

4 Annotation framework for RC

The relative clauses (RCs)[9] in the ICLE-RC are annotated for a wide range of lexical, syntactic, semantic, and discourse features. These features are grouped into seven primary categories, as listed in Table 1. The complete taxonomy of the annotation features is provided in Table 10 in the Appendix.

RELATIVE MARKER (RM): RMs are words that introduce an RC. RMs include the subordinator *that* and relative pronouns such as *which*, *who*, or *whose*. In the ICLE-RC, the RM feature includes three sub-features: `that`, `wh-word`, and `zero` (i.e., the absence of an overt RM for bare-relatives). These categories are exemplified below[10].

(1) Our duty should be to select programmes and to see only things ***that*** *open our mind.* [Italian; ITRS-1002]

(2) Those, ***who*** *cannot afford advertising campaigns led on a large scale*, have no chances of achieving success in any kind of business. [Polish; POLU-1006]

(3) **The status** ø *English has acquired today* is so dominant that it seems unlikely that the situation could ever change. [Finnish; FIJO-1003]

REFERENT FUNCTION: This feature identifies the grammatical function of the referent of the RM in the matrix clause. It includes seven categories: `subject`, `direct object`, `indirect object`, `predicative complement`, `adjunct`, and `clause`. Each category (except `clause`) further includes sub-categories; for example, `direct object`,

[6]The selection yields four Indo-European and two non-Indo-European languages.

[7]For specimen essays, check out the ICLE500 dataset.

[8]The classification follows from the ICLE.

[9]We only annotate full RCs, and exclude reduced RCs on grounds of parsing and processing difficulties (Acuña Fariña, 2000; McKoon and Ratcliff, 2003).

[10]**Conventions for examples:** The RC is in italics; the RM is in bold; the referent is underlined. In case of RM-zero, there is no overt RM, and the referent is marked in bold instead. The text inside the square brackets lists the L1 background and the file number of the source text. **Note:** Some examples contain grammatical/spelling errors (as written by L2 students).

#	feature	examples (of sub-features)	feature type
1	relative marker (RM)	*that*, *which*, *who*, zero	lexical/syntactic
2	grammatical function of referent	subject, object, predicative complement	syntactic
3	grammatical function of RM	subject, object, adjunct	
4	embedding of RC	embedded, non-embedded	
5	extraposition of RC	extraposed, non-extraposed	
6	type of referent	human, abstract entity	semantic/discourse
7	restrictiveness	integrated, supplementary	syntactic/discourse

Table 1: Primary categories of relative clause annotation

which refers to the direct object in the matrix clause, has three subtypes:

`direct-object-head-n`: The head noun of the direct object NP is the referent, as in (4). (If there is any complement and/or adjunct within that NP, the whole NP is considered as the referent.)

(4) ... they watch programms [sic] of cartoons ***which*** *are mostly in Hindi* ... [Urdu; PALW-1014]

`in-dir-obj-comp`: An NP which is part of a complement within the direct object NP is the referent, as in (5).

(5) The main objection is the fact that it creates the demand for things ***that*** *people do not need*. [Polish; POLU-1006]

`in-dir-obj-adjunct`: An (NP which is part of an) adjunct within the direct object NP is the referent, as in (6).

(6) According to that great king ... people ... should be punished by imposing on them the penalty equal in quality to **the criminal offences** ∅ *those people were charged with*. [Polish; POSI-1001]

MARKER FUNCTION: This feature identifies the grammatical function of the relativised item (represented by the RM) in the RC. It comprises nine categories, largely adapted from Huddleston and Pullum (2002): `subject`, `direct object`, `indirect object`, `predicative complement`, `genitive subject determiner`, `predicate`, `complement of auxiliary verb`, `head of a to-infinitival VP`, and `adjunct`. For illustration, we here define and exemplify only three of those categories (for information about all categories and sub-categories, see Table 10 in the Appendix).

`subject`: The relativised item functions as the subject in the RC, as in (7).

(7) These teachers ***who*** *want to prevent cheating* were once students. [Turkish; TRCU-1004]

`genitive subject determiner`: The relativised item (*whose*) is the genitive determiner in the subject NP of the RC, as in (8).

(8) ... his proposal is not only urgent but necessary as well for a democracy ***whose*** *purpose consists of controlling any political power*. [Italian, ITRS-1004]

`adjunct`: The relativised item functions as an adjunct or part of an adjunct in the RC. For adjuncts, the RC is usually introduced by *which*, *when*, or *where* (as in (9)).

(9) ... the newspapers have talked about child-porno and the right to have in one's possession videos or photos ***where*** *children are being exploited*. [Finnish; FIJY-1006]

EMBEDDING: This feature concerns whether the RC (and also its host clause) is embedded within a more superordinate matrix clause. The embedding clause is usually an attributive clause (e.g., *he said*) or a similar clause with a cognitive verb (e.g., *I think*), as in (10)[11]. Embedding rarely occurs in the ICLE-RC.

(10) The emphasis should be put on integration, since all cultures must be considered equal, and they should be able to co-exist in

[11] The embedder clause is marked by square brackets.

a highly civilized society, ***which*** *[we like to think] our own is.* [Swedish; SWUG-2007]

EXTRAPOSITION: Extraposition occurs when an RM does not immediately follow its referent. Instead, there are some intervening elements between the RM and its referent, as in (11). Unlike German which frequently allows extraposition of RCs (Gamon et al., 2002), the use of such constructions is found to be marginal in English (Levy et al., 2012), and also in the ICLE-RC.

(11) The once mighty state-churches have mostly diminished into mere baptizing-, wedding-, and funeral-organizers, ***whose*** *congregations rarely even believe in God.* [Finnish; FIHE-1015]

REFERENT TYPE: This represents a semantic/discourse category. The referent can be an entity, an abstract entity, or a proposition (a full clause). Furthermore, an entity can either be human or non-human. Examples of human, non-human, and abstract entity are given in (2), (9), and (10), respectively. (12) illustrates the proposition category.

(12) ... the product not advertised does not exist for customers, ***which*** *means it brings no profits.* [Polish; POLU-1006]

RESTRICTIVENESS: This feature identifies whether an RC is integrated or supplementary[12]. An integrated RC is an integral part of the referent NP that contains it. A supplementary RC, by contrast, is characterised by a weaker link to its referent or surrounding structures. In writing, the difference is often marked by putting a comma before the supplementary RCs. (13) and (14) exemplify integrated and supplementary RCs, respectively.

(13) The people ***who*** *happened to fall victim to this shameful disease* were persecuted. [Polish; POLU-1007]

(14) ... I haven't mentioned about inequality in the social life, ***which*** *is the extension of inequality in the family life.* [Turkish; TRCU-1003]

[12]The integrated-supplementary division of RCs corresponds to the distinction between restrictive and non-restrictive RCs (hence the feature name is 'restrictiveness'). For the differences between these two dichotomies, see Huddleston and Pullum (2002).

ADDITIONAL META-FEATURES: The essays are also marked for three additional features: `native language` (L1 background), `institution` (the source institution and also the country), and `gender` (of the writer; male or female). An example of the ICLE-RC annotation is provided in Table 11 in the Appendix.

5 Annotation framework for OC

In addition to RCs (and their linguistic features), the texts in the ICLE-RC are also annotated for a wide range of OCs (other constructions). OCs either resemble RCs (particularly because of the use of words such as *that* and *which*) but are not RCs proper, or they are a special type of RCs. OCs comprise six types, as defined and exemplified below.

IT-CLEFT: In a cleft construction, a single clause is split up into two clauses, each containing its own verb. An it-cleft construction begins with a dummy *it*, which is typically followed by a copula and an NP. The information in the *it*-clause is emphasised for the listener (foregrounded information). The clause that follows the *it*-clause is introduced by *that* (sometimes also *which* or *who*), and it contains information that is already understood (backgrounded information).

(15) It is the threat of a punishment that prevents us from committing felonies and offences. [Finnish; FIJO-1022]

PSEUDO-CLEFT: Pseudo-cleft constructions, like *it*-clefts, also configure themselves in terms of backgrounded and foregrounded information. Pseudo-clefts are typically introduced by *what*.

(16) What we learn in our schools today are not words of wisdom. [Swedish; SWUL-1003]

RELATIVE-THERE: This feature refers to existential clauses (introduced by the dummy pronoun *there*) that are followed by an RC.

(17) There are many reasons which leads to the failure of a marriage. [Urdu; PAGJ-1010]

FUSED RELATIVE: Fused relatives are a special type of RC in which the referent and the relativised element are fused together instead of being expressed separately as in regular RCs. Fused relatives are introduced by a wide range of RMs (otherwise used in regular RCs), such as *who(ever)*, *what(ever)*, *which(ever)*, or *where(ever)*.

(18) A student should think and try to draw conclusions on whichever lesson he is taking. [Turkish; TRME-3001]

SO: This feature identifies [*so* + ADJ + (*that*)] constructions, which usually present a reason-claim relation.

(19) Nowadays we are so used to television that we find difficult to think that it did not exist before... [Italian; ITRS-1001]

SUCH: This feature, like the previous SO feature, identifies [*such* + ADJ + (*that/which*)] constructions, which usually present a reason-claim relation.

(20) ... it can make people dependent on it to such an extent that they finally neglect their health, family and other vital things. [Polish; POSI-1002]

6 Reliability of annotation

The ICLE-RC is aimed to offer gold-standard data, and is entirely created from human annotation. The possibility of pre-annotating the source texts using heuristics based on (dependency or constituency) parsing output from parsers was excluded due to their limited success on learner English data[13]. The ICLE essays typically contain grammatical errors, missing words, truncated or incomplete sentences, and non-standard usages, and our preliminary experiments based on SpaCy dependency parses were not sufficiently satisfatory.

The RCs and OCs in the ICLE-RC were annotated by two annotators (two of the authors), who have many years of experience with various kinds of linguistic annotation. On average, the annotators took between 30 minutes and one hour to annotate a single essay (including revisions). The annotators used the UAM CorpusTool (version 2.8.16) (O'Donnell, 2008) to perform the annotation. A screenshot of an RC-annotation in UAM CorpusTool is provided in Figure 1 in the Appendix.

[13]For an overview of applying (UD) parsers to learner data, see Hashemi and Hwa (2016) and Huang et al. (2018).

In order to test the reliability of the corpus, we conducted an IAA study. The annotators independently annotated all 24 texts for the Polish part of the corpus. Given our multi-layered, feature-rich annotation scheme (Table 10), we calculated agreement only for the seven broad RC features: RM, REFERENT FUNCTION, MARKER FUNCTION, EMBEDDING, EXTRAPOSITION, REFERENT TYPE, and RESTRICTIVENESS.

It was found that the two annotators individually identified 163 RCs and 157 RCs, respectively, while both identified 151 common RCs[14]. According to Cohen's kappa (Landis and Koch, 1977), agreement was almost perfect for REFERENT FUNCTION and MARKER FUNCTION (0.86, 0.80), substantial for RM and REFERENT TYPE (0.77, 0.73), and moderate for RESTRICTIVENESS (0.58), as shown in Table 2. For the remaining two features, EMBEDDING and EXTRAPOSITION, prevalence prevented the calculation of meaningful κ-values. The agreement score was 89.35% for both features.

feature	type	κ-value
RM	lexical/syntactic	0.77
referent function	syntactic	0.86
marker function		0.80
referent type	semantic/discourse	0.73
restrictiveness	syntactic/discourse	0.58

Table 2: Inter-annotator agreement for five features

Importantly, the variation in agreement can be interpreted as indicative of the relative complexity of the annotation task for a target feature type. First, syntactic features (e.g., REFERENT FUNCTION, MARKER FUNCTION), in comparison to other feature types, are relatively more objective in nature. Hence, their identification is quite straightforward, which caused a very high degree of agreement. Second, the identification of RM (a lexical/syntactic feature) is quite uncomplicated when it is explicitly marked by *that* or a *wh*-word, but not necessarily the same when there is no overt RM (for bare-relatives). In our IAA study, the annotators also agreed overwhelmingly more on the presence of an RM than on their absences, which resulted in a higher degree of substantial agreement. Third, the identification of REFERENT TYPE operates on a semantic/discourse level, which brings subjectivity into analysis. This is evidenced by a lower degree

[14]The task of identifying RCs can sometimes pose considerable challenges due to the absence of an overt RM for bare-relatives, or the similarity between RCs and OCs.

of substantial agreement between the annotators. For instance, (21) presents such a case in which the referent 'a merciful God' was annotated as `entity` by the first annotator, but as `abstract-entity` by the second annotator.

(21) We treat it like a valuable gift from a merciful God ***who*** *enabled us to use our skills and abilities* ... [Polish; POSI-1002]

Finally, RESTRICTIVENESS presents an interesting case. RESTRICTIVENESS distinguishes integrated and supplementary RCs, and is determined based on syntactic cues; e.g., use of a comma for supplementary RCs, or the non-use of *that* for supplementary RCs (according to standard English grammars). RESTRICTIVENESS is also conveyed through discourse meaning, i.e., whether the RC presents an integral part of the meaning of the matrix clause, or as a separate, additional unit of information. In the ICLE(-RC), which is a corpus of L2 English student essays, the students did not seem to have strictly adhered to the standard grammatical rules for marking integrated and supplementary RCs. (22) presents such a case (an RC with *who),* where the annotators disagreed on identifying the RESTRICTIVENESS value.

(22) ... we can point out to the case of Oscar Wilde ***who*** *was tried for being a homosexual* ... [Polish; POLU-1007]

In those circumstances, the ICLE-RC annotators had to rely only on the available discourse meaning, which invited a greater amount of subjectivity in the interpretation. The challenge of determining restrictiveness has also been addressed in the RC literature (Bache and Jakobsen, 1980; Hundt et al., 2012). Ambiguities of this kind probably caused only a moderate degree of agreement between the annotators.

7 (Semi-)automating annotation

In order to assess the feasibility of automating our annotation procedure, we implemented a classifier based on `distilroberta-base` (Sanh et al., 2019). We annotated markers as spans in plain text, but for classification purposes, we tokenised[15] the entire corpus and mapped the span annotations onto words, resulting in IO (inside-outside) tags. We first trained a binary classifier, predicting whether or not a word is (part of) an RM. We use the first 76 files of the corpus as training data, and the remaining 20 files as test data. This results in 52,034 words in the training split and 11,663 words in the test split, of which only 144[16] are annotated as (being part of) an RM. We are thus dealing with a heavily unbalanced data set and therefore focus on the macro-averaged scores. The results for this binary classification set-up are included in Table 3.

	p	r	f1	support
none	0.99	1.00	1.00	11,519
relcl	0.83	0.36	0.50	144
accuracy			0.99	11,663
macro avg	0.91	0.68	0.75	11,663
weighted avg	0.99	0.99	0.99	11,663

Table 3: Binary classification results.

The same classification set-up is used to train and predict the values on the second level of the taxonomy in Table 10. We already face a severe class imbalance in the binary case (114 words labeled as (part of a) relative clause vs. 11,519 unlabeled words) and this only increases in multi-class classification set-ups where labels are further split up into different classes. This is reflected by the macro-averaged f1-scores: 0.46, 0.17, 0.38, 0.50, 0.50, 0,49, and 0.59 for RM, REFERENT FUNCTION, MARKER FUNCTION, EMBEDDING, EXTRAPOSITION, REFERENT TYPE, and RESTRICTIVENESS, respectively. The classification reports are included in Tables 12 to 18 in the Appendix.

Based on these results, we conclude that automatically suggesting RM spans with a binary classifier, which has a comparatively high precision, would be a feasible way to semi-automate the annotation procedure. In order to automatically provide candidate labels for the more fine-grained task of feature assignment, we consider the performance too low, and perhaps more training examples can further improve performance. Alternatively, using an LLM for this task might be a feasible strategy. Generative foundation models are not necessarily designed for text span annotation tasks, but recent studies have shown promising results (Kasner et al., 2025) and we consider this an important piece of future work.

[15]Using spaCy's `en_core_web_sm` model.

[16]The test split contains 119 RMs, resulting in on average 1.2 words per marker for the test split.

8 First results

The essays from different L1 backgrounds in the ICLE-RC vary with respect to the number of words and sentences, as shown in Table 4. For example, on average the students with Finnish L1 produced the lengthiest essays (867.04 words per essay) while the students with Swedish L1 produced the shortest essays (664.29 words per essay)[17], although both groups produced sentences of almost equal length (about 22 words per sentence).

language	# avg words	# avg sentences	# avg words per sentence
Finnish	867.04	39.38	22.02
Italian	718.33	27.21	26.40
Polish	705.92	33.17	21.28
Swedish	664.29	29.34	22.61
Turkish	786.75	39.25	20.04
Urdu	711.29	43.29	16.43
AVG	742.27	35.27	21.46

Table 4: General statistics for essays in the corpus

Table 5 shows the distribution of RCs for different L1 backgrounds, their rate and percentage of occurrence with respect to sentences. RCs are found to be a high-frequency feature for Italian: RCs occur in every 3.23 sentences, or 30.93% of the sentences contain an RC. By contrast, RCs occur least frequently for Urdu (only in every 11.81 sentences or in 8.47% of all sentences).

language	# RCs	# sentences	rate	%
Finnish	187	945	5.05	19.79
Italian	202	653	3.23	30.93
Polish	163	796	4.88	20.48
Swedish	147	705	4.80	20.85
Turkish	137	942	6.88	14.54
Urdu	88	1039	11.81	8.47
TOTAL	924	5080	5.50	18.19

Table 5: Distribution of RCs

Similarly, Table 6 shows the distribution of OCs for different L1 backgrounds, their rate and percentage of occurrence with respect to sentences. OCs are found to be used most frequently by the Polish and Finnish students, and least frequently by the Urdu students.

An important theme of investigation in our work is whether/how different RC features (and subfeatures) vary across languages. For the purpose of illustration, we only provide the distribution of two features: RM and RESTRICTIVENESS. First,

language	# OCs	# sentences	rate	%
Finnish	100	945	9.45	10.58
Italian	58	653	11.29	8.88
Polish	86	796	9.26	10.80
Swedish	56	705	12.58	7.94
Turkish	76	942	12.39	8.07
Urdu	31	1039	33.52	2.98
TOTAL	407	5080	12.48	8.01

Table 6: Distribution of OCs

Table 7 presents the distribution of RMs[18]. The Urdu students are found to structure RCs almost exclusively with an overt RM (*that* or a *wh*-word). By contrast, the occurrence of bare-relatives (with a `zero` marker) is found to be a highly frequent feature exploited by both the Finnish and Swedish students (about 20% of all RCs). Furthermore, the distribution of the overt RMs vary across these languages. For example, the subordinator *that* is used more frequently for Finnish, Swedish, and Turkish. By contrast, Italian, Polish, and Urdu show a more frequent use of a *wh*-word. Furthermore, the distribution of the *wh*-words shows a consistent pattern across these languages, with *which* being the most frequent *wh*-word, followed by *who* and then *where* (albeit with a larger margin). The remaining *wh*-words (*when*, *whose*, or *whom*) occur rarely in the corpus.

Next, the distribution of RCs for RESTRICTIVENESS (in Table 8) also shows variation across languages and RMs. For example, the frequency of supplementary RCs is found to be high for Italian and Polish (ca. 40%), intermediate for Finnish and Urdu (ca. 28-32%), and low for Swedish and Turkish (ca. 23%). One consistent pattern to emerge from the data, however, is that supplementary RCs are introduced by *that* by the students from all L1 backgrounds (albeit in small numbers). Such usage, strictly speaking, is not sanctioned by the (prescriptive) grammars. This might result from the insufficient learning outcomes of the L2 learners of English rather than an exposure to L1 varieties of English (both standard and non-standard), in which the co-occurrence of supplementary RCs and *that* is observed, albeit rarely (for an overview, see Hillberg, 2012).

It might be the case that (some of) these observed variations originate from the ways RCs are structured in the corresponding L1s. This can be validated by thoroughly examining the RC-related

[17]The official ICLE instructions stipulate ca. 600 words.

[18]The occurrence of 5 or fewer number of tokens for a category was excluded from the table.

RM-type	RM	Finnish	Italian	Polish	Swedish	Turkish	Urdu	Total/Avg
that	*that*	52 (27.81%)	38 (18.81%)	19 (11.66%)	46 (31.29%)	43 (31.39%)	14 (15.91%)	212 (22.94%)
wh-word	*which*	49 (26.20%)	65 (32.18%)	70 (42.94%)	35 (23.81%)	43 (31.39%)	38 (43.18%)	301 (32.58%)
	who	32 (17.11%)	49 (24.26%)	40 (24.54%)	24 (16.33%)	30 (21.90%)	23 (26.14%)	198 (21.43%)
	where	12 (6.42%)	13 (6.44%)	-	8 (5.44%)	6 (4.38%)	7 (7.95%)	49 (5.30%)
	when	-	-	-	-	-	-	13 (1.41%)
	whose	-	-	-	-	-	-	9 (0.97%)
	why	-	-	-	-	-	-	8 (0.87%)
	whom	-	-	-	-	-	-	-
	what	-	-	-	-	-	-	-
	how	-	-	-	-	-	-	-
zero	zero	37 (19.79%)	28 (13.86%)	21 (12.88%)	29 (19.73%)	9 (6.57%)	-	128 (13.85%)
TOTAL		187	202	163	147	137	88	924

Table 7: Distribution of RMs

restrictiveness	RM	Finnish	Italian	Polish	Swedish	Turkish	Urdu	Total/Avg
integrated	*that*	41 (21.93%)	25 (12.38%)	16 (9.82%)	41 (27.89%)	38 (27.74%)	9 (10.23%)	170 (18.40%)
	wh-word	56 (29.95%)	67 (33.17%)	60 (36.81%)	44 (29.93%)	59 (43.07%)	46 (52.27%)	332 (35.93%)
	zero	37 (19.79%)	28 (13.86%)	21 (12.88%)	28 (19.05%)	8 (5.84%)	4 (4.55%)	126 (13.61%)
supplementary	*that*	11 (5.89%)	13 (6.44%)	3 (1.84%)	5 (3.40%)	5 (3.65%)	5 (5.68%)	42 (4.55%)
	wh-word	42 (22.46%)	69 (34.16%)	63 (38.65%)	29 (19.73%)	27 (19.71%)	24 (27.27%)	254 (27.49%)
TOTAL		187	202	163	147	137	88	924

Table 8: Distribution of RCs for RESTRICTIVENESS

grammar of each L1, and comparing these results against those grammars to see whether any cross-linguistic factors influence the patterning of the RC features. We leave this task for the next stage in our work.

9 Related work

Although there are no large-scale corpora exclusively annotated for RCs, there exists a rich body of corpus-based studies on RCs in English. Weichmann (2015) provides a detailed, usage-based analysis of RCs (in 500 texts, with 80,000 parse trees) in the British component of the International Corpus of English (ICE)[19]. Biber et al.'s (1999) corpus-based account of English grammar, among many other grammatical phenomena, describes the use and distribution of RCs in a variety of registers. More commonly, specific aspects of RCs have been subject to corpus-based scrutiny, such as modified entity (Fox and Thompson, 1990), type of modification (Tse and Hyland, 2010), relativisers and their functions (Keenan and Comrie, 1977), referents of RCs (Kjellmer, 2008), (non-)humanness (Fox and Thompson, 1990), restrictiveness (Cornish, 2018), and bare-relatives (Lehmann, 2002). A significant line of research involves the analysis of RCs in historical corpora (Nevalainen and Raumolin-Brunberg, 2002; Johansson, 2006; Suárez-Gómez, 2006; Allen, 2022) and diachronic changes in the use of RCs (Leech et al., 2009; Xu and Xiao, 2015; Fajri and Okwar, 2020). Yet another important theme in RC research concerns the usage and variation of RCs in regional varieties of L1 English (Lehmann, 2002; Tagliamonte et al., 2005; Szmrecsanyi, 2013) as well as in World Englishes (Suárez-Gómez, 2015a,b). Finally, corpus-based research also explored phenomena related to RCs (OCs),

[19] https://www.ice-corpora.uzh.ch/en.html

such as pseudo-cleft (Breivik, 1999) and relative-*there* (Maschler et al., 2023).

10 Conclusions and outlook

The ICLE-RC is an extension of a subset of the ICLE, and it provides annotation for RCs and related phenomena, based on a comprehensive, multi-layered, feature-rich taxonomy. The first and present version of the ICLE-RC contains a collection of 924 RCs (and 407 OCs) from 144 academic essays, representing six L1 backgrounds and six corresponding language families. The annotations in stand-off XML format and the code for our classification experiments are available on GitHub[20]. The corpus is now in the post-production stage, and will soon be published as an open-access resource.

Our future work includes expanding the size and coverage of the corpus by adding more texts for the existing six languages as well as incorporating texts from other L1 backgrounds (from the ICLE), representing new (sub-)language families, such as Cantonese (Sino-Tibetan), Dutch (West Germanic), Greek (Hellenic), Japanese (Japonic), Farsi (Indo-Iranian), Russian (Slavic), and Tswana (Bantu). The extended corpus would enable us to employ statistical modeling on the data and draw reliable and comprehensive conclusions about the use of RCs by L2 English users.

We envisage that the ICLE-RC would be used as a valuable resource for research on RCs in various areas of linguistic analysis. In SLA and language typology, the corpus would help identifying varying patterns in the use of English RCs by L2 learners, and checking whether those patterns result from specific L1 backgrounds, or they, for example, conform to those stipulated by the NP accessibility hierarchy (Keenan and Comrie, 1977). The ICLE-RC can also be used to (re-)examine the properties of RCs in regional varieties of English, and validate or revise the resulting findings against the existing research in World Englishes. Furthermore, the corpus offers a rich repository of information-structuring devices (OCs, in addition to RCs), and this would aid research on discourse structure, supporting the analysis of fore-/back-grounding strategies, discourse referents, discourse segments, and discourse relations.

[20] `https://anonymous.4open.science/r/law2025-relative-clause-classification-663F`

Limitations and ethical considerations

The annotators that contributed to the annotations were employed by their affiliated universities at the time of working on this project.

The classification experiments using `distilroberta-base` were done on a CPU/laptop with 32GB of RAM and in total amounted to approx. 10 hours of training and evaluating.

Acknowledgments

We would like to thank the anonymous reviewers for their valuable feedback on the first submission version of the paper.

References

J.C. Acuña Fariña. 2000. Reduced relatives and apposition. *Australian Journal of Linguistics*, 20(1):5–22.

C.L. Allen. 2022. Pronominally headed relative clauses in early english. *English Language and Linguistics*, 26(1):105–132.

C. Bache and L.K. Jakobsen. 1980. On the distinction between restrictive and non-restrictive relative clauses in modern english. *Lingua*, 52(3):243–267.

D. Biber, S. Johansson, G. Leech, S. Conrad, and E. Finegan. 1999. *Longman Grammar of Spoken and Written English.* Pearson Education Limited.

S. Brandt, E. Kidd, E. Lieven, and M. Tomasello. 2009. The discourse bases of relativization: An investigation of young German and English-speaking children's comprehension of relative clauses. *Cognitive Linguistics*, 20(3):539–570.

L.E. Breivik. 1999. On the pragmatic function of relative clauses and locative expressions in existential sentences in the LOB Corpus. In *Out of corpora: Studies in honour of Stig Johansson (Language and Computers: Studies in Practical Linguistics, 26)*, pages 121–135. Rodopi.

B. Comrie. 1998. Rethinking the typology of relative clauses. *Language Design*, 1:59–86.

F. Cornish. 2018. Revisiting the system of English relative clauses: structure, semantics, discourse functionality. *English Language and Linguistics*, 22:431–456.

C. Doughty. 1991. Second Language Instruction Does Make a Difference: Evidence from an Empirical Study of SL Relativization. *Studies in Second Language Acquisition*, 13(4):431–469.

M.S.A. Fajri and V. Okwar. 2020. Exploring a Diachronic Change in the Use of English Relative Clauses: A Corpus-Based Study and Its Implication for Pedagogy. *SAGE Open*, 10(4).

B.A. Fox and S.A. Thompson. 1990. A Discourse Explanation of the Grammar of Relative Clauses in English Conversation. *Language*, 66(2):297–316.

M. Gamon, E. Ringger, Z. Zhang, R. Moore, and S. Corston-Oliver. 2002. Extraposition: a case study in German sentence realization. In *Proceedings of COLING 2002*.

H. Goad, N.B. Guzzo, and L. White. 2021. Parsing Ambiguous Relative Clauses in L2 English: Learner Sensitivity to Prosodic Cues. *Studies in Second Language Acquisition*, 43(1):83–108.

S. Granger. 1998. The computer learner corpus: A versatile new source of data for SLA research. In S. Granger, editor, *Learner English on Computer*, pages 3–18. Addison Wesley Longman, London & New York.

S. Granger, M. Dupont, F. Meunier, H. Naets, and M. Paquot. 2020. The International Corpus of Learner English. Version 3.

A. Grosu. 2012. Towards a More Articulated Typology of Internally Headed Relative Constructions: The Semantics Connection. *Language and Linguistics Compass*, 6(7):447–476.

H.B. Hashemi and R. Hwa. 2016. An Evaluation of Parser Robustness for Ungrammatical Sentences. In *Proceedings of the 2016 EMNLP*.

S. Hillberg. 2012. Relativiser that in Scottish English news writing. In *Outposts of Historical Corpus Linguistics: From the Helsinki Corpus to a Proliferation of Resources*.

Y. Huang, A. Murakami, T. Alexopoulou, and A. Korhonen. 2018. Dependency parsing of learner English. *International Journal of Corpus Linguistics*, 23(1):28–54.

R. Huddleston and G.K. Pullum. 2002. *The Cambridge grammar of the English language*. CUP, Cambridge, UK.

M. Hundt, D. Denison, and G. Schneider. 2012. Relative complexity in scientific discourse. *English language and linguistics*, 16(2):209–240.

S. Ishikawa. 2023. *The ICNALE Guide: An Introduction to a Learner Corpus Study on Asian Learners' L2 English*. Routledge.

C. Johansson. 2006. Relativizers in nineteenth-century English. In *Nineteenth-century English: Stability and change (Studies in English Language)*, page 136–182. Cambridge University Press.

Z. Kasner, V. Zouhar, P. Schmidtová, I. Kartáč, K. Onderková, O. Plátek, D. Gkatzia, S. Mahamood, O. Dušek, and S. Balloccu. 2025. Large language models as span annotators. *Preprint*, arXiv:2504.08697.

E. Keenan and B. Comrie. 1977. Noun Phrase Accessibility Hierarchy and Universal Grammar. *Linguistic Inquiry*, 8:63–99.

G. Kjellmer. 2008. "Troublesome Relatives": On *Whose Her* and Others. *English Studies*, 89(4):482–494.

R. Landis and G. Koch. 1977. The measurement of observer agreement for categorical data. *Biometrics*, 33:159–174.

G. Leech, M. Hundt, C. Mair, and N.I. Smith. 2009. *Change in contemporary English: A grammatical study*. Cambridge University Press.

H.M. Lehmann. 2002. Zero subject relative constructions in American and British English. In *New Frontiers of Corpus Research*, page 163–177. Rodopi.

R. Levy, E. Fedorenko, M. Breen, and E. Gibson. 2012. The processing of extraposed structures in English. *Cognition*, 122(1):12–36.

Y. Maschler, J. Lindström, and E. De Stefani. 2023. Pseudo-clefts: An interactional analysis across languages. *Lingua*, 291:103538.

G. McKoon and R. Ratcliff. 2003. Meaning Through Syntax: Language Comprehension and the Reduced Relative Clause Construction. *Psychological review*, 110(3):490–525.

T. Nevalainen and H. Raumolin-Brunberg. 2002. The rise of relative who in early Modern English. In *Relativisation on the North Sea Littoral*, page 109–121. Lincom Europa.

M. O'Donnell. 2008. The UAM CorpusTool: Software for corpus annotation and exploration. In Carmen M.. Bretones Callejas, editor, *Applied Linguistics Now: Understanding Language and Mind / La Lingüística Aplicada Hoy: Comprendiendo el Lenguaje y la Mente*, pages 1433–1447. Almería, Universidad de Almería.

A. Pereltsvaig. 2023. *Languages of the World: An Introduction*, 4th edition. Cambridge University Press.

F. Reali and M.H. Christiansen. 2007. Processing of relative clauses is made easier by frequency of occurrence. *Journal of Memory and Language*, 53:1–23.

V. Sanh, L. Debut, J. Chaumond, and T. Wolf. 2019. Distilbert, a distilled version of bert: smaller, faster, cheaper and lighter. *ArXiv*, abs/1910.01108.

C. Suárez-Gómez. 2006. *Relativization in Early English (950–1050): The Position of Relative Clauses*. Peter Lang.

C. Suárez-Gómez. 2015a. Relative clauses in Asian Englishes. *Journal of English Linguistics*, 42(2):245–268.

C. Suárez-Gómez. 2015b. The places where English is spoken: adverbial relative clauses in World Englishes. *World Englishes*, 34(4):620–635.

B. Szmrecsanyi. 2013. *Grammatical variation in British English dialects: A study in corpus-based dialectometry*. Cambridge University Press.

S. Tagliamonte, J. Smith, and H. Lawrence. 2005. No taming the vernacular! Insights from the relatives in northern Britain. *Language Variation and Change*, 17:75–112.

P. Tse and K. Hyland. 2010. Claiming a territory: Relative clauses in journal descriptions. *Journal of Pragmatics*, 42(7):1880–1889.

D. Weichmann. 2015. *Understanding relative clauses: A usage-based view on the processing of complex constructions*. De Gruyter Mouton.

X. Xu and R.Z. Xiao. 2015. Recent changes in relative clauses in spoken British English. *English Studies*, 96(7):1–21.

A Appendix

language	institution	gender	# essays
Finnish (Uralic)	University of Helsinki	F	4
		M	4
	University of Joensuu (now UEF)	F	4
		M	4
	University of Jyväskylä	F	4
		M	4
Italian (Romance)	University of Bergamo	F	6
		M	2
	Sapienza University of Rome	F	4
		M	4
	University of Turin	F	4
		M	4
Polish (Slavic)	Maria Curie-Skłodowska University	F	8
		M	0
	Adam Mickiewicz University	F	4
		M	4
	University of Silesia in Katowice	F	8
		M	0
Swedish (Germanic)	University of Gothenburg	F	4
		M	4
	Lund University	F	4
		M	4
	Växjö University	F	6
		M	2
Turkish (Turkic)	Mersin University	F	4
		M	8
	University of Mustafa Kemal	F	2
		M	2
	University of Çukurova	F	8
		M	0
Urdu (Indo-Aryan)	GC University Faisalabad	F	4
		M	8
	Govt College for Women Jhang	F	2
		M	2
	Lahore College for women university	F	8
		M	0
TOTAL			144

Table 9: Distribution of the essays in the ICLE-RC

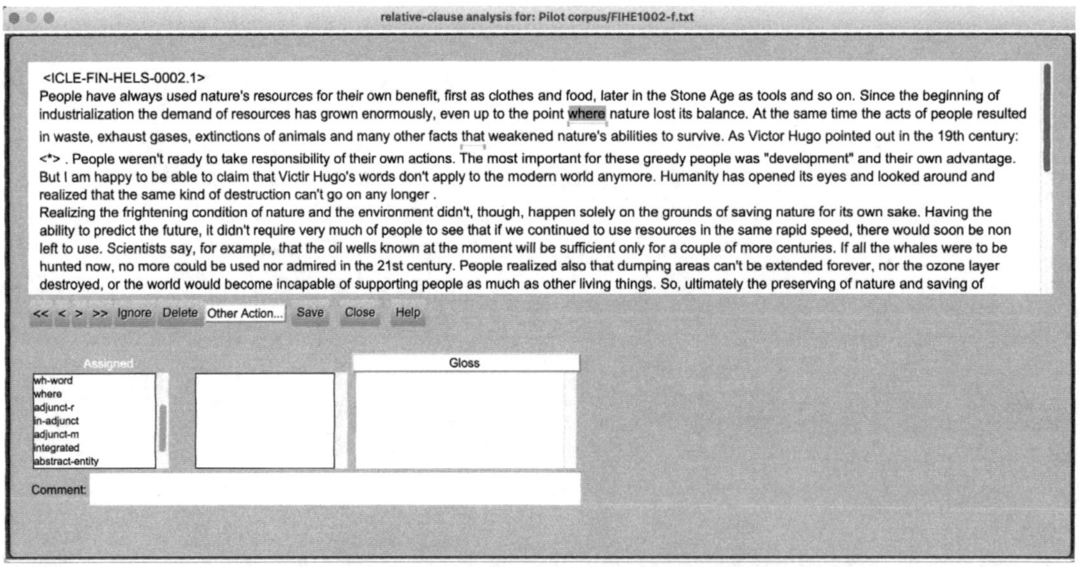

Figure 1: RC annotation in UAM CorpusTool

RC annotation feature			
level 1	**level 2**	**level 3**	**level 4**
RM	that		
	wh-word	*which*, *who*, *whose*, etc.	
	zero		
referent function	subject	subj-head-n	
		in-subj-comp	
		in-subj-adjunct	
	direct obj	dir-obj-head-n	
		in-dir-obj-comp	
		in-dir-obj-adjunct	
	indirect obj	indir-obj-head-n	
		in-indir-obj-comp	
		in-indir-obj-adjunct	
	predicative complement	pred-comp-np	pred-comp-head-n
			in-pred-comp-np-comp
			in-pred-comp-np-adjunct
		pred-comp-adjp	pred-comp-head-adj
			in-pred-comp-adjp-comp
			in-pred-comp-adjp-adjunct
		pred-comp-pp	pred-comp-head-p
			in-pred-comp-pp-comp
	adjunct	adjunct	
		in-adjunct	
	clause		
marker function	subject		
	direct obj		
	Indirect obj		
	predicative complement	pred-comp-full	
		in-pred-comp	
	gen-subj-det		
	predicate		
	aux-comp		
	head-to-inf-vp		
	adjunct		
embedding	yes		
	no		
extraposition	yes		
	no		
ref type	entity	human	
		non-human	
	abstract		
	proposition		
restrictiveness	integrated		
	supplementary		

Table 10: Taxonomy of features for RC annotation

The sentence in which the RC features are to be annotated: Unfortunately, life is not a situation comedy ***where*** *every problem is happily solved.* [Italian; ITTO-1002]		
meta-features	L1	Italian
	institution	University of Turin
	gender	female
RC features	RM	wh-word → *where*
	referent function	pred-comp → pred-comp-np → pred-comp-head-n
	marker function	adjunct
	embedding	no
	extraposition	no
	referent type	abstract entity
	restrictiveness	integrated

Table 11: Example of RC annotation

	p	r	f1	support
none	0.99	1.00	1.00	11,519
that	0.00	0.00	0.00	37
wh-word	0.83	0.90	0.86	58
zero	0.00	0.00	0.00	49
accuracy			0.99	11,663
macro avg	0.45	0.47	0.46	11,663
weighted avg	0.98	0.99	0.99	11,663

Table 12: Relative marker type classification results.

	p	r	f1	support
adjunct-r	0.00	0.00	0.00	46
clause-r	0.00	0.00	0.00	2
direct-obj-r	0.23	0.16	0.19	51
indirect-obj-r	0.00	0.00	0.00	5
none	0.99	1.00	0.99	11,519
pred-comp-r	0.00	0.00	0.00	11
subj-r	0.00	0.00	0.00	29
accuracy			0.99	11,663
macro avg	0.17	0.17	0.17	11,663
weighted avg	0.98	0.99	0.99	11,663

Table 13: Referent function classification results.

	p	r	f1	support
adjunct-m	0.50	0.18	0.27	22
direct-obj-m	0.00	0.00	0.00	47
none	0.99	1.00	0.99	11,519
pred-comp-m	0.00	0.00	0.00	3
subject-m	0.73	0.56	0.63	72
accuracy			0.99	11,663
macro avg	0.44	0.35	0.38	11,663
weighted avg	0.99	0.99	0.99	11,663

Table 14: Marker function classification results.

	p	r	f1	support
embed-no	0.81	0.38	0.52	137
embed-yes	0.00	0.00	0.00	7
none	0.99	1.00	0.99	11,519
accuracy			0.99	11,663
macro avg	0.60	0.46	0.50	11,663
weighted avg	0.99	0.99	0.99	11,663

Table 15: Embedding classification results.

	p	r	f1	support
extrapose-no	0.81	0.36	0.50	142
extrapose-yes	0.00	0.00	0.00	2
none	0.99	1.00	0.99	11,519
accuracy			0.99	11,663
macro avg	0.60	0.45	0.50	11,663
weighted avg	0.99	0.99	0.99	11,663

Table 16: Extraposition classification results.

	p	r	f1	support
abstract-entity	0.63	0.2	0.34	95
entity	0.82	0.49	0.61	47
none	0.99	1.00	0.99	11,519
proposition	0.00	0.00	0.00	2
accuracy			0.99	11,663
macro avg	0.61	0.43	0.49	11,663
weighted avg	0.99	0.99	0.99	11,663

Table 17: Referent type classification results.

	p	r	f1	support
integrated	0.62	0.18	0.28	118
none	0.99	1.00	1.00	11,519
supplementary	0.48	0.54	0.51	26
accuracy			0.99	11,663
macro avg	0.70	0.57	0.59	11,663
weighted avg	0.99	0.99	0.99	11,663

Table 18: Restrictiveness classification results.

ExpLay: A new Corpus Resource for the Research on Expertise as an Influential Factor on Language Production

Carmen Schacht
Ruhr-University Bochum, Germany
Faculty of Philology
Department of Linguistics
carmen.schacht@rub.de

Renate Delucchi Danhier
TU Dortmund University
Department of Cultural Studies
Institute for Diversity Studies
renate.delucchi@tu-dortmund.de

Abstract

This paper introduces the ExpLay-Pipeline, a novel semi-automated processing tool designed for the analysis of language production data from experts in comparison to the language production of a control group of laypeople. The pipeline combines manual annotation and curation with state-of-the-art machine learning and rule-based methods, following a silver standard approach. It integrates various analysis modules specifically for the syntactic and lexical evaluation of parsed linguistic data. While implemented initially for the creation of the ExpLay-Corpus, it is designed for the processing of linguistic data in general. The paper details the design and implementation of this pipeline. To demonstrate the pipeline's capabilities and explore linguistic markers of expertise, we present the initial release of the ExpLay-Corpus. This corpus comprises German oral descriptions of urban landscapes elicited from architectural students (characterized as a semi-expert population) and a group of matching laypersons. Using the ExpLay-Pipeline, preliminary analyses of syntactic and lexical complexity between these two groups were conducted. While the primary focus of this work lies on the architecture of the pipeline and its annotation methodology, these preliminary findings serve to showcase the pipeline's functionality and establish ExpLay as an accessible resource for future research on linguistic markers of expertise.

1 Introduction

This research is grounded in three core assumptions concerning the influence of expertise on cognition and language production.

First, it draws on the principle of *linguistic relativity* (Whorf, 1956; Slobin, 1996), which postulates that language plays a role in shaping thought, attention allocation, and cognition in general. Empirical support for linguistic relativity has been documented across various cognitive domains, including color perception (Winawer et al., 2007; Roberson et al., 2000), the conceptualization of motion events (Slobin, 1996; Papafragou et al., 2008) and the use of spatial frames of reference (Levinson, 2003; Majid et al., 2004).

Second, effects similar to *linguistic relativity* are observed beyond language: Expertise, whether professional or personal, can shape cognition in a manner analogous to language. For instance, a neuro-imaging study (Maguire et al., 2000) found structural alterations in the posterior hippocampus of taxi drivers compared to non-drivers, suggesting that its expansion results from extensive navigational experience. Other findings reveal a significant improvement in reaction time for e-sports players (Ersin et al., 2022) as well as decision making and dexterity (Jiang et al., 2020) for non-professional gamers (semi-experts), compared to laypeople. Effects of domain-specific expertise on attention and cognition have also been documented, for example in the field of architecture. In a previous eye-tracking study using stimuli similar to those in the present research, Mertins et al. (2020) found that architects and laypeople differ systematically in how they allocate visual attention. While laypeople focused more on human figures in indoor scenes; architects attending to outdoor scenes concentrated longer on architectural elements, particularly upper-level features like roofs, whereas laypeople remained focused on elements at eye level.

Third, rational communication aims to maintain linguistic code maximally efficient and to this end adapts dynamically to situational and communicative demands. Just as language influences cognition, expertise influences language production. This is reflected in domain-specific, conventionalized linguistic codes (Teich et al., 2021), which facilitate both perception and communication within specialized fields. Such patterns are evident in domain-related language use and mirror the cogni-

Proceedings of the 19th Linguistic Annotation Workshop (LAW-XIX-2025), pages 216–227
July 31, 2025 ©2025 Association for Computational Linguistics

tive effects of linguistic relativity discussed earlier. This phenomenon has been observed across various domains, including literary discourse (Degaetano-Ortlieb and Piper, 2019), the physical sciences (Halliday, 1988/2004), and diachronic shifts in scientific English (Degaetano-Ortlieb and Teich, 2022, 2018; Biber et al., 2011; Biber and Gray, 2016; Juzek et al., 2020) as well as scientific German (Jakobi et al., 2024). Domain-specific features also emerge in the use of linguistic structures such as compounding (Gamboa et al., 2025) and metaphor usage (Halliday, 1988/2004; Webster, 2018) in scientific and technical texts.

Despite growing interest in the cognitive effects of expertise, little is known about how architectural expertise influences spatial cognition and its linguistic encoding. This study addresses this gap by analyzing how architects describe urban and natural landscapes. To investigate the linguistic manifestations of expertise in architecture, a dedicated corpus resource was curated and subjected to a preliminary linguistic analysis.

As an initial exploratory step, the study focused on syntactic and lexical complexity as indicators of domain-specific language use, comparing the speech production of semi-expert participants (students of architecture) with that of non-expert controls (students of German language and literature). The metrics selected incorporate a range of syntactic and lexical measures, thereby capturing a broad variety of structural linguistic features that may exhibit domain-specific variation across the two groups. Given the central role of communicative efficiency, we decided to focus on linguistic complexity as a suitable entry point for exploration of experts' language use. A higher communicative efficiency is often associated with denser, more complex structures (compared to more linear constructions), suggesting the hypothesis that expert language production may exhibit greater structural complexity than that of non-experts.

This preliminary analysis primarily serves to demonstrate the capabilities of the parsing and evaluation pipeline presented in this paper. It is not intended as an exhaustive account of architectural expertise in language use.

2 Previous work

Most existing studies on complexity measures such as dependency length so far focus on dependency processing (Juzek et al., 2020; Futrell et al., 2015) rather than on dependency production. Moreover, they tend to treat expertise as a factor either in the processing of other expert's data (Jakobi et al., 2024) or in written expert language such as scientific discourse (Banks, 2003; Biber et al., 2011). Studies applying the Universal Dependencies (UD) framework (de Marneffe et al., 2021) to spoken data usually focus on the creation of spoken language treebanks (Dobrovoljc, 2022; Dobrovoljc and Nivre, 2016) rather than addressing differences between the groups of speakers who produced the linguistic data for those treebanks in the first place.

While Dobrovoljc and Nivre (2016) at least address some particularities of oral data during the annotation process of the resource, in general very little attention is given to the characteristics of the speakers who produced the linguistic material and possible differences among groups (such as experts vs. non-experts). To address the gap between these two areas, the present study curates experimentally elicited spoken data from both expert and non-expert participants. In doing so, it offers a novel corpus resource to facilitate further investigation into how expertise shapes linguistic structure in spoken language.

This approach is motivated in particular by the eye-tracking findings of Mertins et al. (2020), which revealed systematic domain-dependent differences in visual attention patterns between architects and non-architects. These findings suggest domain-specific cognitive processing, and, by extension, the possibility of domain-specific linguistic realizations of such cognitive behaviors, consistent with the study's core assumptions. So we aspire to use a corpus-based and computational linguistic approach to analyze verbalizations in a similar experimental set-up as the one used in the eye-tracking study.

To conduct an initial exploratory analysis of potential syntactical and lexical differences between expert and non-expert verbalizations in addition to the curation of the resource itself, this study draws on established (syntactic and lexical) complexity metrics. These include dependency distance (Gibson, 1998; Futrell et al., 2015), dependency and constituent-tree tree height (Yngve, 1960), dependency-based clause count (Biber, 1988; Lu, 2011), and constituency-based phrase count (Lu, 2011) as well as word class (Shi and Lei, 2021). Additionally, following the methodology of Park (2024) we apply Principal Component Analysis (PCA) to generate a combined syntactic complexity score, using the PC-loadings to determine the weightings of individual metrics contributing to the combined score.

3 ExpPlay release

The initial release of the ExpLay-Resource comprises the raw (unparsed) data, the parsing and evaluation pipeline, as well as the parsed corpus of experimentally elicited spoken language produced by experts and non-experts in the field of architecture. Following the *silver standard* approach described in (Rebholz-Schuhmann et al., 2010), the dataset was manually pre-processed, automatically parsed, and partially curated across multiple linguistic levels using the ExpLay-Pipeline introduced in this paper. This pipeline integrates several state-of-the-art tools for natural language processing, linguistic annotation, and the evaluation of linguistic structures. The full resource including the pipeline and corpus is made freely available on Gitlab.[1] The entire dataset can be accessed under a CC BY 4.0 license on OSF[2], to support open-access initiatives and facilitate accessible future research in linguistics.

3.1 Data collection

A controlled, online language production experiment was conducted via Zoom, in which participants were asked to orally describe a series of images depicting urban and natural environments (Figure 1). The images were presented one at a time in randomized order, and participants were given unlimited time to respond. The participants were instructed to describe each scene as if speaking to an artist who had never seen it and would need to recreate it through drawing. This task design intentionally avoided priming architecture students to adopt an expert-oriented communicative register, thereby ensuring that both groups (experts and non-experts) shared a common baseline assumption about their audience. As a result, any observed effects in the expert group's descriptions can be interpreted as reflecting general language processing and cognitive-linguistic tendencies influenced by the presence or absence of architectural expertise of the respective participant group, rather than from professional communication demands.

All descriptions were produced in German, which was the native language of all participants. Afterwards, a second group of laypeople with no architectural background completed the same task under identical conditions. for the present study, an initial sample of 13 participants per group was selected from a larger pool of participants. The control group was deliberately selected to closely match the architect group in gender, age, and multilingual status, thereby controlling for potential confounding variables while isolating the influence of domain-specific expertise. This study design allows to compare language use between participants with and without architectural training, while keeping other demographic and linguistic factors constant.

Because the expert sample in this study consists of architecture students rather than practicing architects with extensive professional experience, the level of domain-specific expertise must be interpreted with some caution and can thus be more appropriately characterized as a semi-expert group. Nevertheless, we still anticipate some measurable differences between students with architectural training and those without, reflecting varying degrees of architectural knowledge.

The resulting initial sample for the ExpLay-Resource comprises 13 participants per group: Among the experts, 5 were male and 8 female; among the laypeople, 4 were male and 9 female. All participants were between 19 and 32 years old. Each group included 12 monolingual and 1 bilingual speaker. All oral descriptions were recorded, transcribed, and subsequently analyzed.

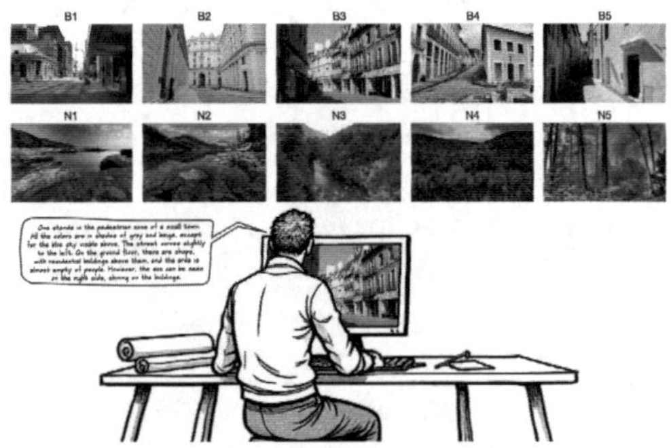

Figure 1: Experimental set-up in the verbalization experiment showing the used visual stimuli.

For this initial release of the ExpLay corpus, only the urban environment stimuli (images B1 to B5) were selected, as these are more likely to elicit domain-specific differences between expert and

[1] Gitlab: https://gitlab.ruhr-uni-bochum.de/schaccmr/explay-resource.git.

[2] The entire dataset is made freely available on OSF: https://osf.io/ky87h/?view_only=4a0c7ae6a07c4fe89bc8632787742616.

Dummy Token	Function	Category
%	Grammatical correction	1
&	Insertion of ellipsis (oral structure)	2
$	Insertion of ellipsis (stylistic structure)	2
§	Nominalization	3
@	Substantivized determiner/quantifier	3

Table 1: Overview of dummy tokens used to mark different types of insertions in the data.

non-expert participants due to their closer thematic alignment with architectural expertise. The natural environment stimuli will be included in a future release. Each participant contributed five text productions, resulting in a total of 130 descriptions in the current version of the resource.

3.2 Data curation

To prepare the transcripts for annotation, the oral productions were first extracted and cleaned according to a strict protocol aimed at ensuring comparability while preserving the integrity of the original data.

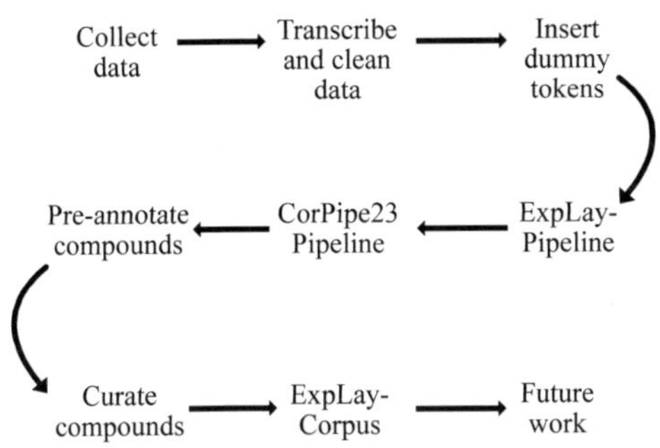

Figure 2: Workflow of ExpLay's curation process.

Cleaning involved the removal of filler particles and inaudible segments, which are excluded from the current release. Subsequently, the cleaned transcripts were manually annotated. Different dummy tokens (see Table 1 for details) were inserted to flag (1) ungrammatical structures that do not impede comprehension, (2) elliptical constructions typical of spontaneous speech or used for stylistic effect, and (3) elliptical references, such as nominalized adjectives. Category 3 tokens include the inferred original token in parentheses. Deleted structures are indicated with pipe symbols marking the start and end of the omitted span. Incomprehensible sentence parts (those severely ungrammatical to the point of impeding interpretation) were also marked. Although excluded from the parsed versions used for analysis, these segments are preserved in the unparsed data to support potential future research. Insertions are encoded using special characters that indicate the type of dummy-token (see Table 1). In the case of category 3 dummy-tokens, the original token is added in parenthesis after each insertion. Section 3.3 will show in more detail how those dummy-token insertions are handled in the pipeline, and Section 3.4 will show the different versions of the parse.

After annotating dummy tokens and incomprehensible structures, the transcripts are fed into the ExpLay-Pipeline described in Section 3.3. This pipeline performs automatic parsing and multi-level linguistic evaluation and is included as part of the ExpLay-Resource release. Subsequently, compound words were pre-annotated using a modified version of the Tuggener *compound-split* compound splitter (Tuggener, 2016) and then manually curated. In the final step, coreference annotation was conducted using the CorPipe23 system (Straka, 2023). An overview of the complete annotation and curation workflow of the ExpLay-Resource is illustrated in Figure 2, and Section 3.4 summarizes the resulting parsed data versions.

3.3 ExpLay-Pipeline

The ExpLay-Pipeline was implemented for the creation of the ExpLay-Corpus specifically and for the processing of expert-language data in general and is available in the repository. It is implemented in Python (Van Rossum and Drake, 2009), an untyped open-access programming language, and incorporates several state-of-the-art natural language processing systems (see Figure 4 for a depiction of the pipeline's architecture).

The ExpLay-Pipeline processes `.txt` files located in a designated directory, each containing curated transcripts that have undergone dummy-token annotation and the removal of ungrammatical structures (see 3.1). Meta-data of partici-

```
# sent_id = 0
# text = Zu sehen ist der Blick vom Bürgersteig aus auf eine Kreuzung .
# ['TOP', ['SINV', ['PP', ['IN', 'Zu'], ['NN', 'sehen']], ['VP', ['VBZ', 'ist']], ['NP', ['NP', ['DT', 'der'], ['NN', 'Blick']], ['PP', ['IN', 'von'], ['NP', ['NNP', 'dem'], ['NNP'
# ['TOP', ['SINV', ['PP', ['PART', 'Zu'], ['VERB', 'sehen']], ['VP', ['AUX', 'ist']], ['NP', ['NP', ['DET', 'der'], ['NOUN', 'Blick']], ['PP', ['ADP', 'von'], ['NP', ['DET', 'dem'].
1	Zu	zu	PART	PTKZU	_	2	mark	_	-|start_char=0|end_char=2
2	sehen	sehen	VERB	VVINF	VerbForm=Inf	0	root	_	-|start_char=3|end_char=8
3	ist	sein	AUX	VAFIN	Mood=Ind|Number=Sing|Person=3|Tense=Pres|VerbForm=Fin	2	aux:pass	_	-|start_char=9|end_char=12
4	der	der	DET	ART	Case=Nom|Definite=Def|Gender=Masc|Number=Sing|PronType=Art	5	det	_	-|start_char=13|end_char=16
5	Blick	Blick	NOUN	NN	Case=Nom|Gender=Masc|Number=Sing	2	nsubj:pass	_	-|start_char=17|end_char=22
6-7	vom	_	_	_	_	_	_	_	-|start_char=23|end_char=26
6	von	von	ADP	APPR	_	8	case	_	----
7	dem	der	DET	ART	Case=Dat|Definite=Def|Gender=Masc|Number=Sing|PronType=Art	8	det	_	----|Entity=(c1--2
8	Bürgersteig	Bürgersteig	NOUN	NN	Case=Dat|Gender=Masc|Number=Sing	2	obl	_	-|end_char=38|Entity=c1)|start_char=27
9	aus	aus	ADP	APZR	_	8	fixed	_	-|start_char=39|end_char=42
10	auf	auf	ADP	APPR	_	12	case	_	-|start_char=43|end_char=46
11	eine	ein	DET	ART	Case=Acc|Definite=Ind|Gender=Fem|NumType=Card|Number=Sing|PronType=Art	12	det	_	-|end_char=51|Entity=(c2--2|start_char=47
12	Kreuzung	Kreuzung	NOUN	NN	Case=Acc|Gender=Fem|Number=Sing	2	obl	_	-|end_char=60|Entity=c2)|start_char=52
13	.	.	PUNCT	$.	_	2	punct	_	-|start_char=60|end_char=61
```

Figure 3: Exemplary parse of a sentence from participant P002/ stimulus B1. Note that the linear representation of the constituent trees was truncated for the illustration.

pants must be encoded in the filename in a fixed order using the format: participant-ID, gender, expert-status, stimulus-ID and language status (e.g. `P001_F_L_B1_M_.txt`). Each `.txt`-file in the directory is parsed individually, returning both individual and aggregate output statistics. During pre-processing, three versions of each transcript are created from each original `.txt` file: (1) A *raw-version* with all ungrammatical structures and dummy-tokens removed, (2) a *cleaned-corrected version*, which mirrors the raw-version but retaining the correction dummy-tokens and (3) an *all-dummy-version*, containing all dummy-tokens but excluding ungrammatical structures. To ensure compatibility with parsing tools, the pipeline removes the special character markers from the text-string and stores them as a separate object. Therefore, the original text production transcript itself cannot contain any of the special characters used to mark the dummy-tokens, as the pipeline would interpret those as dummy-token markers.

All three versions are then parsed using the stanza pipeline (Qi et al., 2020) applying the following processors: `tokenize`, `POS`, `lemma` and `depparse`. Stanza is an NLP toolkit that provides models for several different languages and a range of NLP tasks. The `POS` processor returns part-of-speech (POS) annotations and the `depparse` processor generates dependency annotations – both following the Universal Dependencies (UD) framework, which aims to standardize the format of various annotations, such as dependencies and POS-tags. The stanza pipeline returns the parsed data in the standardized `.conllu` format(Universal Dependencies Consortium, n.d.a), which is broadly supported by NLP tools. After parsing with stanza, the ExpLay-Pipeline re-introduces the dummy-token markers into the `.conllu` formatted parse by inserting the marker into the `MISC` column of the respective tokens in the `.conllu` file. This ensures that inserted tokens remain traceable for subsequent analysis.

Next, the parsed data is fed into the `Berkeley Neural Parser` (Kitaev and Klein, 2018), an NLP library providing state-of-the-art self-attentive language models for parsing various linguistic structures such as constituencies, which it returns in the form of an NLTK-tree object from the NLTK library (Bird et al., 2009). The parser uses the revised Penntreebank (PTB) tag-set of the English News Text Treebank (Bies et al., 2015) for the constituency nodes and the POS-tags. The multilingual model `benepar_en3` is used, as it is more robust than the German model and can also handle German data. After parsing the constituency structure of each version of a single production, the ExpLay-Pipeline creates a duplicate of the constituency tree and exchanges the revised PTB POS-tags for the upos-tags from the stanza-parse. This way, two trees are parsed, containing both sets of POS-tags. The trees are then stored as commentary lines between the sentence-ID and the parse in the `.conllu` format. Those are exported as `.conllu` files as single parses and added to a collective `.json` file containing the entire dataset of each version organized by the meta-data encoded in the filenames for easy access. For an exemplary parse of a sentence see Figure 3.

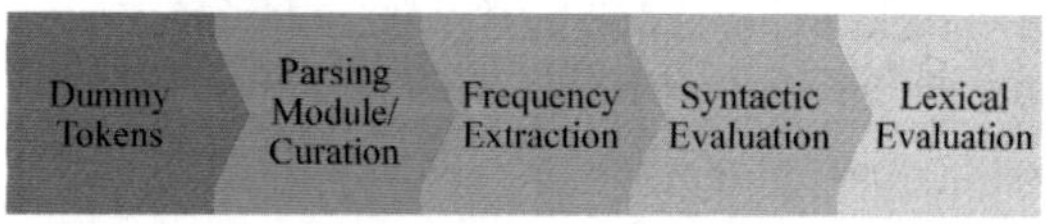

Figure 4: Architecture of the ExpLay-Pipeline.

Subsequently, the rawfile-version is passed to the frequency-extraction module of the pipeline, which collects various linguistic frequency measures both into single and collective `.csv` files. It collects simple surface measures such as word- and sentence-count and the usage of all POS-tags, but also more linguistically complex structural measures from the constituency and dependency frameworks based on previous findings regarding the influence of those metrics on syntactic complexity. These structural measures include dependency distance (Gibson, 1998; Futrell et al., 2015), dependency and constituent-tree tree height (Yngve, 1960), dependency-based clauses count (Biber, 1988; Lu, 2011), and constituency-based phrase count (Lu, 2011). It should be noted, that due to the spontaneous, oral nature of the linguistic data, sentence boundaries, although defined as precisely as possible during transcription, should ultimately be regarded as approximations.

The extracted frequency data is then exported as both individual and aggregated files for further analysis. The aggregated data from the raw-version is then processed through the syntactic and lexical analysis modules of the pipeline, which utilize the libraries Pandas (pandas development team, 2020), NumPy (Harris et al., 2020), SciPy (Virtanen et al., 2020) and Sklearn (Pedregosa et al., 2011). The syntactic module first assesses the normality of the data distribution using the Shapiro-Wilk test (Shapiro and Wilk, 1965) (see Equation 1). Depending on the outcome, statistical significance is evaluated using either a t-test for normally distributed data (Student, 1908) (see Equation 2 and 3) or the Mann-Whitney-U test (Mann and Whitney, 1947) (see Equation 4) for non-normally distributed data. It simultaneously tests for effect size using Cohen's delta (Cohen, 1988) (see Equation 5) if the data is distributed normally or a Rank-Biserial correlation (Cureton, 1956) (see Equation 7) for non-normal distributions.

$$W = \frac{\left(\sum_{i=1}^{n} a_i x_{(i)}\right)^2}{\sum_{i=1}^{n}(x_i - \bar{x})^2} \quad (1)$$

$$t = \frac{\bar{X}_1 - \bar{X}_2}{\sqrt{s_p^2\left(\frac{1}{n_1} + \frac{1}{n_2}\right)}} \quad (2)$$

$$s_p^2 = \frac{(n_1 - 1)s_1^2 + (n_2 - 1)s_2^2}{n_1 + n_2 - 2} \quad (3)$$

Following these calculations, all metrics showing significant group differences are collected and normalized using Z-score standardization (see Equation 8), centering the data around a mean of 0 and a standard deviation of 1 while preserving the general shape of the distribution. Principal Component Analysis (PCA) (Jolliffe, 2002) (see Equations 9 and 10) is then performed, following the approach outlined in Park (2024) to assess the contribution of each metric to overall group variance.

$$U = n_1 n_2 + \frac{n_1(n_1 + 1)}{2} - R_1 \quad (4)$$

$$d = \frac{\bar{X}_1 - \bar{X}_2}{s_p} \quad (5)$$

$$s_p = \sqrt{\frac{(n_1 - 1)s_1^2 + (n_2 - 1)s_2^2}{n_1 + n_2 - 2}} \quad (6)$$

$$r_{rb} = 1 - \frac{2U}{n_1 n_2} \quad (7)$$

Principal Component loadings from the PCA, that represent linear combinations of the original metrics, are used to derive weights for a combined syntactic complexity score, which is likewise realized as a linear combination of the significant metrics.

$$Z = \frac{X - \mu}{\sigma} \quad (8)$$

$$Z = XW \quad (9)$$

$$PC_k = \sum_{i=1}^{n} w_i^{(k)} X_i \quad (10)$$

Then the module calculates a combined syntactic complexity score as a weighted sum of all the significant metrics normalized with min-max-normalization (see Equations 11 and 12) into a final dataset for a last test of normality, significance and effect-size as well as Pearson's r (see Equation 13) for a correlation between the PCA results and the combined syntactic complexity score.

$$X' = \frac{X - X_{\text{min}}}{X_{\text{max}} - X_{\text{min}}} \quad (11)$$

$$C = \sum_{i=1}^{m} w_i \cdot X_i \quad (12)$$

$$r = \frac{\sum(X_i - \bar{X})(Y_i - \bar{Y})}{\sqrt{\sum(X_i - \bar{X})^2 \sum(Y_i - \bar{Y})^2}} \quad (13)$$

In the final step, the lexical module of the ExpLay-Pipeline estimates lexical complexity by computing the frequency of open and closed word classes, following the approach of Shi and Lei

(2021), who (among other factors) investigated lexical complexity on the basis of word class in the context of social class differences — a framework also applicable to the study of expertise as a factor influencing language. The classification is based on the upos-tags from the Stanza parse, following the Universal Dependencies (UD) project (Universal Dependencies Consortium, n.d.b):

- **Open class or lexical words:** ADJ, ADV, INTJ, NOUN, PROPN, VERB
- **Closed class or grammatical words:** ADP, AUX, CCONJ, DET, NUM, PART, PRON, SCONJ
- **Other:** PUNCT, SYM, X

Mirroring the process of the syntactic module, the lexical module applies the same statistical procedures as the syntactic module to assess distribution (test for normality), significance, and effect size. Both modules export the results as `.csv` files to a results folder in the directory. In addition, the modules also generate various plots visualizing the significance tests outcomes and the PCA results. The graphics are exported to a plot folder inside the results folder using the Python libraries Matplotlib (Hunter, 2007) and Seaborn (Waskom, 2021) for visualization.

3.4 ExpLay-Corpus

The resulting ExpLay-Corpus consists of three parsed versions per transcribed verbalization, corresponding to the three previously mentioned versions: The raw-version, the cleaned-corrected-version, and the all-dummy-version. These versions are stored in `.conllu` files, along with additional collective `.json` files containing the entire dataset. The results amount to three parses of the 130 texts and three files of the complete parse. Each individual parse consists of 11778 parsed tokens, derived from the raw-file version. Each of the three versions are enriched with two iterations of the constituency trees generated from the Benepar module, which are added before each sentence. The raw-file version was chosen for the evaluation modules as it best preserves the original text and includes minimal alternations, therefore providing a reliable basis for text-level comparison between the two groups. This choice can be manually adjusted should the application of the pipeline on future corpora require the evaluation of a different parse version.


```
{
    "id": [
        8
    ],
    "text": "Bürgersteig",
    "lemma": "Bürgersteig",
    "upos": "NOUN",
    "xpos": "NN",
    "feats": "Case=Dat|Gender=Masc|Number=Sing",
    "head": 2,
    "deprel": "obl",
    "start_char": 27,
    "end_char": 38,
    "misc": [
        "_",
        "[['Bürger', 'tail', '-'], ['Steig', 'head', 'Bürger']]"
    ]
},
```


Figure 5: Exemplary .json file entry from the production of P002/ stimulus B1 including the compound parse of the noun 'Bürgersteig' (Engl. sidewalk).

After parsing and evaluation with the ExpLay-Pipeline, the all-dummy-version was fed into the CorPipe23 (Straka, 2023) module for coreference parsing and pre-parsed using a derivation of the Tuggener (2016) *compound-split* compound splitter for compound words. The rationale behind this choice of parse iteration was that curation costs should be kept minimal, therefore only one of the parses should be annotated and curated for compound words. The all-dummy version was selected for compound word annotation to minimize curation efforts, as it can be easily mapped back to the raw-file version. The compound parse was then manually curated and stored in the `MISC` column of the respective token in the `.json` parse, using the format `'NoC'` for non-compound words or the pattern `'compound': [('first constituent', 'tail', '-'), ('second constituent', 'head', 'remaining part of compound', 'linking element')]` for compound words with two constituents (see Figure 5). This representation uses the maximum split approach and does not account for the branching direction in multi-constituent compounds.

4 Preliminary analysis of syntactic and lexical complexity

In a preliminary evaluation of the newly created corpus, the syntactic and lexical evaluation modules of the ExpLay-Pipeline were applied to the rawfile-parse of the corpus. This served two purposes: running a field test on the pipeline and the evaluation modules, as well as providing an initial exploration of the new resource.

4.1 Syntactic metrics

The previously described syntactical metrics evaluated in the pipeline include dependency distance, dependency and constituent tree height, dependency-based clause count, and constituency-based phrase count. Additionally, the pipeline also calculate surface measures such as sentence count and average tokens per sentence, but – as stated earlier – the annotated sentence boundaries should be considered with some reservations. For a complete display of the descriptive measures calculated for the ExpLay Corpus see Table 4 in Section A. The module then tests the data for normality, significance and effect size using the previously mentioned tests. Significant individual metrics are then combined into a combined syntactic complexity score. PCA is conducted on the chosen individual metrics and the resulting principal component loadings are used as weights for the combined score. Finally, a second round of normality, significance, and effect size tests is applied to the combined metric scores.

Metric	p-value	Cohen's d	RB
sent-count	0.75	0	0.03
tok-per-sent	0.25	0	-0.11
dep-dist	0.41	0.14	0
num-clauses	0.18	0	-0.14
dep-tree-height	0.31	0	-0.10
con-tree-height	**0.05**	0	**-0.02**
num-phrases	0.22	0	-0.13

Table 2: p-values, Cohen's d and Rank-Biserial correlation values of the single syntactic metrics before running the PCA.

4.2 Lexical metric

To calculate the lexical metric, the pipeline first calculates the count of open and closed word classes per text by adding up the counts of the single POS-tags per text according to the categorization of the UD-project. Then the same statistical tests as in the syntactic module are applied to those measures to test for normality, significance and effect size.

4.3 Results

Of the syntactic metrics analyzed for the 13 speakers per group reported in this paper, only constituent tree height showed a statistically significant group difference ($p < .05$), with a moderately small effect size. Experts exhibited slightly higher average tree heights than laypeople (see Table 4 in Section A), suggesting a tendency toward more deeply embedded, hierarchically complex sentence structures, in opposition to the laypeople's use of a slightly flatter syntax.

In contrast, surface-level syntactic features (e.g., sentence length, tokens per sentence) and lexical measures (e.g., distribution of word classes) did not differ significantly between groups, as can be seen in Table 2 for the significance values of the syntactic metrics, as well as in Table 3 for the evaluation of the lexical measures. Not only do the experts produce longer descriptions in general, they also display a slightly elevated use of open word classes compared to the laypeople, even though the differences did not turn out to be significant.

For a graphical visualization of the distribution of word classes among the two groups as well as for an exemplary output of the visualization module of the pipeline see also Figure 6. These features, however, are less sensitive to hierarchical syntactic depth as constituent tree height. The elevated tree height in expert speech points to denser phrasal layering, potentially reflecting more domain-specific and information-dense language use, in line with prior findings on expert discourse such as scientific writing. Laypeople on the other hand seem to use more shallow and linear constructions.

As no other syntactic measures reached significance, the combined syntactic complexity metric is identical to constituent tree height and is thus not reported separately.

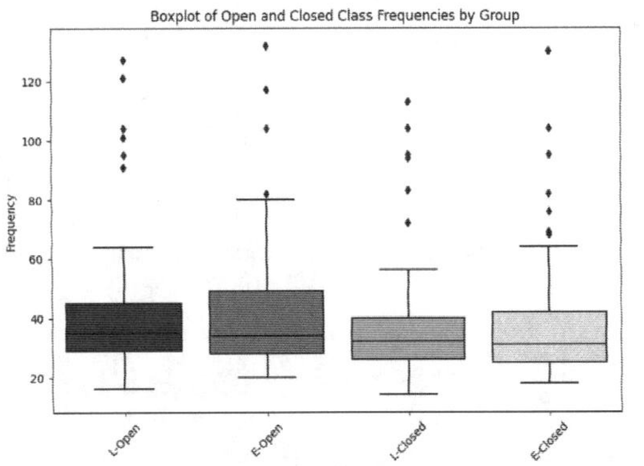

Figure 6: Boxplots of the descriptive values of the lexical metric.

4.4 Conclusion

The application of the ExpLay-Pipeline on datasets exports both individual and composite met-

Group	mean	sd	min	max	median	p-value	Cohen's d	RB
L-open	41.86	23.81	16.0	127.0	35.0	0.73	0	-0.04
L-closed	36.98	20.64	14.0	113.0	32.0	0.66	0.08	0
E-open	42.97	22.80	20.0,	132.0	34.0	**0.04**	0	**-0.02**
E-closed	38.62	21.99	18.0	130.0	31.0	0.12	0	-0.16

Table 3: Evaluation of the lexical metric.

rics, accompanied by normality assessments, significance tests, effect sizes, and Pearson correlations to assess group differences. The current paper's goal is primarily to showcase the range of syntactic and lexical measures the ExpLay-Pipeline can generate. We anticipate that increasing the participant number to at least 40 speakers per group in the future would enhance statistical power and reveal more differences between experts and laypeople.

These preliminary findings suggest that while both experts and non-experts use similar syntactic elements, they differ in the degree of syntactic complexity, with constituent tree height capturing features of structural depth possibly not reflected in other metrics. Given the exploratory nature of this initial analysis and the current limited number of speakers as well as the limitation to verbalizations of half of the described images, these results are not to be considered definitive. Future inclusion of the remaining parsed stimuli as well as more speakers will provide a more comprehensive basis for analysis.

However, this first evaluation offers initial evidence of domain-specific linguistic patterns in expert discourse in the domain of architecture in addition to the primary objective of this study: showcasing the functionality of the new pipeline. The observed increase in structural complexity (despite similar lexical and surface-level syntactic measures) raises the hypothesis of more complex linguistic structures in the expert population compared to the more linear constructions in the control group and consequently of a higher information density in expert language. This, in turn, opens up promising directions for future research, including semantic analyses and computational approaches of machine learning, to explore whether such structural differences persist across additional linguistic features.

Limitations

This study is limited in both its disciplinary scope and linguistic coverage: the data was collected for the specific domain of architectural expertise and in the German language, which may constrain the generalizability of the findings to other domains or languages. The current dataset includes speech from 26 participants (13 architects and 13 non-architects), each describing five stimuli. This relatively small sample size, along with the limited number of stimuli, restricts the statistical power and robustness of the analyses. Therefore, statistically significant results were not anticipated at this early stage. In addition to the limited sample size, the reduced level of expertise within the tested expert sample (that is more accurately characterized as a semi-expert group) must be taken into account. Future investigations may benefit from a follow-up study involving professional architects with greater practical experience. We expect that the effects observed in the preliminary present evaluation would be more pronounced with participants exhibiting a higher degree of domain-specific expertise.

While the manual pre-processing and annotation of the data were conducted with care, inter-annotator agreement was not assessed, which may introduce some degree of variability. Additionally, the annotation decisions, mirrored in the code and detailed documentation provided, rely on a specific theoretical framework, which may not align with all linguistic traditions. Future work will aim to expand the dataset substantially and to incorporate reliability measures to strengthen the generalizability and replicability of the findings.

Acknowledgments

We are grateful to the anonymous reviewers for their helpful comments. This research is partially funded by *Deutsche Forschungsgemeinschaft* (DFG, German Research Foundation) – Project-ID 232722074 – SFB 1102. Figure 1 includes elements generated using DALL·E 3, which were subsequently modified by the authors.

References

D. Banks. 2003. The evolution of grammatical metaphor in scientific writing. *Amsterdam Studies in the Theory and History of Linguistic Science Series*, 4:127–148.

D. Biber. 1988. *Variation across Speech and Writing*. Cambridge University Press.

D. Biber and B. Gray. 2016. *Grammatical Complexity in Academic English: Linguistic Change in Writing*. Studies in English Language. Cambridge University Press.

D. Biber, B. Gray, and K. Poonpon. 2011. Should we use characteristics of conversation to measure grammatical complexity in l2 writing development? *TESOL Quarterly*, 45(1):5–35.

A. Bies, J. Mott, and C. Warner. 2015. *English News Text Treebank: Penn Treebank Revised LDC2015T13. Web Download*. Linguistic Data Consortium, Philadelphia.

S. Bird, E. Klein, and E. Loper. 2009. *Natural language processing with Python: analyzing text with the natural language toolkit*. " O'Reilly Media, Inc.".

J. Cohen. 1988. *Statistical Power Analysis for the Behavioral Sciences. 2. Auflage*. Lawrence Erlbaum Associates, Hillsdale.

E. E. Cureton. 1956. Rank-biserial correlation. *Psychometrika*, 21(3):287–290.

M.-C. de Marneffe, C. D. Manning, J. Nivre, and D. Zeman. 2021. Universal Dependencies. *Computational Linguistics*, 47(2):255–308.

S. Degaetano-Ortlieb and A. Piper. 2019. The scientization of literary study. In *Proceedings of the 3rd Joint SIGHUM Workshop on Computational Linguistics for Cultural Heritage, Social Sciences, Humanities and Literature*, pages 18–28, Minneapolis, USA. Association for Computational Linguistics.

S. Degaetano-Ortlieb and E. Teich. 2018. Using relative entropy for detection and analysis of periods of diachronic linguistic change. In *Proceedings of the Second Joint SIGHUM Workshop on Computational Linguistics for Cultural Heritage, Social Sciences, Humanities and Literature*, pages 22–33, Santa Fe, New Mexico. Association for Computational Linguistics.

S. Degaetano-Ortlieb and E. Teich. 2022. Toward an optimal code for communication: The case of scientific english. *Corpus Ling.. Ling.. Theory*, 18(1):175–207.

K. Dobrovoljc. 2022. Spoken language treebanks in Universal Dependencies: an overview. In *Proceedings of the Thirteenth Language Resources and Evaluation Conference*, pages 1798–1806, Marseille, France. European Language Resources Association.

K. Dobrovoljc and J. Nivre. 2016. The Universal Dependencies treebank of spoken Slovenian. In *Proceedings of the Tenth International Conference on Language Resources and Evaluation (LREC'16)*, pages 1566–1573, Portorož, Slovenia. European Language Resources Association (ELRA).

A. Ersin, H. Ceren Tezeren, N. Ozunlu Pekyavas, B. Asal, A. Atabey, A. Diri, and İ Gonen. 2022. The relationship between reaction time and gaming time in e-sports players. *Kinesiology*, 54(1):36–42. Doi:10.26582/k.54.1.4.

R. Futrell, K. Mahowald, and E. Gibson. 2015. Large-scale evidence of dependency length minimization in 37 languages. *Proceedings of the National Academy of Sciences*, 112(33):10336–10341.

J. Gamboa, K. Braun, J. Järvikivi, and S. E. M. Allen. 2025. The distributional properties of long nominal compounds in scientific articles: an investigation based on the uniform information density hypothesis. *Corpus Linguistics and Linguistic Theory*, 21(1):137–171.

E. Gibson. 1998. Linguistic complexity: locality of syntactic dependencies. *Cognition*, 68(1):1–76.

M. A. K. Halliday. 1988/2004. On the language of physical science. In Jonathan J. Webster, editor, *The Collected Works of M. A. K. Halliday (Vol. 5)*, pages 140–158. Continuum, London and New York.

C. R. Harris, K. Jarrod Millman, S. J. van der Walt, R. Gommers, P. Virtanen, D. Cournapeau, E. Wieser, J. Taylor, S. Berg, N. J. Smith, R. Kern, M. Picus, S. Hoyer, M. H. van Kerkwijk, M. Brett, A. Haldane, J. Fernández del Río, M. Wiebe, P. Peterson, and 7 others. 2020. Array programming with NumPy. *Nature*, 585(7825):357–362.

J. D. Hunter. 2007. Matplotlib: A 2d graphics environment. *Computing in Science & Engineering*, 9(3):90–95.

D. N. Jakobi, T. Kern, D. R. Reich, P. Haller, and L. A. Jäger. 2024. Potec: A german naturalistic eye-tracking-while-reading corpus. *Preprint*, arXiv:2403.00506.

C. Jiang, A. Kundu, and M. Claypool. 2020. Game player response times versus task dexterity and decision complexity. In *Extended Abstracts of the 2020 Annual Symposium on Computer-Human Interaction in Play*, CHI PLAY '20, page 277–281, New York, NY, USA. Association for Computing Machinery.

I. T. Jolliffe. 2002. *Principal Component Analysis*. Springer Series in Statistics. Springer-Verlag, New York. Doi:10.1007/b98835.

T. S. Juzek, M.-P. Krielke, and E. Teich. 2020. Exploring diachronic syntactic shifts with dependency length: the case of scientific English. In *Proceedings of the Fourth Workshop on Universal Dependencies (UDW 2020)*, pages 109–119, Barcelona, Spain (Online). Association for Computational Linguistics.

N. Kitaev and D. Klein. 2018. Constituency parsing with a self-attentive encoder. In *Proceedings of the 56th Annual Meeting of the Association for Computational Linguistics (Volume 1: Long Papers)*, Melbourne, Australia. Association for Computational Linguistics.

S. C. Levinson. 2003. *Space in language and cognition: Explorations in cognitive diversity*. Cambridge University Press.

X. Lu. 2011. A corpus-based evaluation of syntactic complexity measures as indices of college-level esl writers' language development. *TESOL Quarterly*, 45(1):36–62.

E. A. Maguire, D. G. Gadian, I. S. Johnsrude, C. D. Good, J. Ashburner, R. S. J. Frackowiak, and C. D. Frith. 2000. Navigation-related structural change in the hippocampi of taxi drivers. *Proceedings of the National Academy of Sciences*, 97(8):4398–4403.

A. Majid, M. Bowerman, S. Kita, D. B. Haun, and S. C. Levinson. 2004. Can language restructure cognition? the case for space. *Trends in Cognitive Sciences*, 8(3):108–114.

H. B. Mann and D. R. Whitney. 1947. On a test of whether one of two random variables is stochastically larger than the other. *The Annals of Mathematical Statistics, Ann. Math. Statist.*, 18(1):50–60.

H. Mertins, R. Delucchi Danhier, B. Mertins, A. Schulz, and B. Schulz. 2020. The role of expertise in the perception of architectural space. In C. Leopold, C. Robeller, and U. (Hrsg. Weber, editors, *Research Culture in Architecture*, pages 279–288. Birkhäuser, Basel.

The pandas development team. 2020. pandas-dev/pandas: Pandas.

A. Papafragou, J. Hulbert, and J. Trueswell. 2008. Does language guide event perception? evidence from eye movements. *Cognition*, 108(1):155–184.

S. Park. 2024. Identifying key linguistic variables of second language speaking proficiency using principal component analysis. *Forum for Linguistic Studies*, 6(6):623–633.

F. Pedregosa, G. Varoquaux, A. Gramfort, V. Michel, B. Thirion, O. Grisel, M. Blondel, P. Prettenhofer, R. Weiss, V. Dubourg, J. Vanderplas, A. Passos, D. Cournapeau, M. Brucher, M. Perrot, and E. Duchesnay. 2011. Scikit-learn: Machine learning in Python. *Journal of Machine Learning Research*, 12:2825–2830.

P. Qi, Y. Zhang, Y. Zhang, J. Bolton, and C. D. Manning. 2020. Stanza: A Python natural language processing toolkit for many human languages. In *Proceedings of the 58th Annual Meeting of the Association for Computational Linguistics: System Demonstrations*.

D. Rebholz-Schuhmann, A. J. Jimeno-Yepes, E. M. van Mulligen, N. Kang, J. Kors, D. Milward, P. Corbett, E. Buyko, K. Tomanek, E. Beisswanger, and U. Hahn. 2010. The calbc silver standard corpus for biomedical named entities- a study in harmonizing the contributions from four independent named entity taggers. In *Nicoletta Calzolari (Conference Chair), et al*, Valletta, Malta. European Language Resources Association (ELRA. Proceedings of the Seventh International Conference on Language Resources and Evaluation (LREC'10).

D. Roberson, I. Davies, and J. Davidoff. 2000. Color categories are not universal: Replications and new evidence from a stone-age culture. *Journal of Experimental Psychology: General*, 129(3):369–398.

S. S. Shapiro and M. B. Wilk. 1965. An analysis of variance test for normality (complete samples)†. *Biometrika*, 52(3-4):591–611.

Y. Shi and L. Lei. 2021. Lexical use and social class: A study on lexical richness, word length, and word class in spoken english. *Lingua*, 262:103155.

D. I. Slobin. 1996. From "thought and language" to "thinking for speaking". In J. J. Gumperz and S. C. Levinson, editors, *Rethinking linguistic relativity*, pages 70–96. Cambridge University Press.

M. Straka. 2023. ÚFAL CorPipe at CRAC 2023: Larger context improves multilingual coreference resolution. In *Proceedings of the CRAC 2023 Shared Task on Multilingual Coreference Resolution*, pages 41–51, Singapore. Association for Computational Linguistics.

Student. 1908. The probable error of a mean. *Biometrika*, 6(1):1–25.

E. Teich, P. Fankhauser, S. Degaetano-Ortlieb, and Y. Bizzoni. 2021. Less is more/more diverse: On the communicative utility of linguistic conventionalization. *Frontiers in Communication*, 5.

D. Tuggener. 2016. *Incremental Coreference Resolution for German*. Phd thesis, University of Zürich, Zürich, Switzerland.

Universal Dependencies Consortium. n.d.a. Universal dependencies documentation: Format. `https://universaldependencies.org/format.html`. Accessed: 2025-04-06.

Universal Dependencies Consortium. n.d.b. Universal dependencies: Part-of-speech tags. `https://universaldependencies.org/u/pos/index.html`. Accessed: 2025-04-06.

G. Van Rossum and F. L. Drake. 2009. *Python 3 Reference Manual*. CreateSpace, Scotts Valley, CA.

P. Virtanen, R. Gommers, T. E. Oliphant, M. Haberland, T. Reddy, D. Cournapeau, E. Burovski, P. Peterson, W. Weckesser, J. Bright, S. J. van der Walt, M. Brett,

J. Wilson, K. J. Millman, N. Mayorov, A. R. J. Nelson, E. Jones, R. Kern, E. Larson, and 16 others. 2020. SciPy 1.0: Fundamental Algorithms for Scientific Computing in Python. *Nature Methods*, 17:261–272.

M. L. Waskom. 2021. seaborn: statistical data visualization. *Journal of Open Source Software*, 6(60):3021.

J. J. Webster. 2018. *18. The Language Of Science – A Systemicfunctional Perspective*, pages 345–363. De Gruyter Mouton, Berlin, Boston.

B. L. Whorf. 1956. *Language, Thought, and Reality*. Cambridge, Ma.

J. Winawer, N. Witthoft, M. C. Frank, L. Wu, A. R. Wade, and L. Boroditsky. 2007. Russian blues reveal effects of language on color discrimination. *Proceedings of the National Academy of Sciences*, 104(19):7780–7785.

V. H. Yngve. 1960. A model and an hypothesis for language structure. *Proceedings of the American Philosophical Society*, 104(5):444–466.

A Appendix

Metric	mean	sd	min	max	median
L-sent-count	7.58	3.96	3.0	29.0	7.0
L-tok-per-sent	11.82	2.49	7.17	18.33	11.57
L-dep-dist	2.74	0.36	1.89	3.62	2.77
L-num-clauses	0.26	0.21	0.0	1.0	0.25
L-dep-tree-height	2.62	0.46	2.0	4.67	2.6
L-con-tree-height	7.34	0.66	6.17	10.0	7.17
L-num-phrases	20.97	4.23	13.0	32.33	20.57
E-sent-count	7.48	3.71	3.0	24.0	7.0
E-tok-per-sent	12.53	2.92	7.88	20.0	12.2
E-dep-dist	2.79	0.36	2.1	3.73	2.72
E-num-clauses	0.33	0.26	0.0	1.0	0.27
E-dep-tree-height	2.66	0.35	2.13	4.0	2.6
E-con-tree-height	7.56	0.71	6.38	9.25	7.5
E-num-phrases	22.25	5.08	14.5	36.33	21.25

Table 4: Descriptive values of the syntactic metrics.

Towards Resource-Rich Mizo and Khasi in NLP: Resource Development, Synthetic Data Generation and Model Building

Soumyadip Ghosh
IIIT Hyderabad
soumya50052@gmail.com

Henry Lalsiam
North-Eastern Hill University
neihsialhenry25@gmail.com

Dorothy Marbaniang
Assam University, Silchar
dolly.marbz@gmail.com

Gracious Mary Temsen
University of Hyderabad
gmtemsen@uohyd.ac.in

Rahul Mishra
IIIT Hyderabad
rahul.mishra@iiit.ac.in

Parameswari Krishnamurthy
IIIT Hyderabad
param.krishna@iiit.ac.in

Abstract

In the rapidly evolving field of Natural Language Processing (NLP), Indian regional languages remain significantly underrepresented due to their limited digital presence and lack of annotated resources. This work presents the first comprehensive effort toward developing high quality linguistic datasets for two extremely low resource languages Mizo and Khasi. We introduce human annotated, gold standard datasets for three core NLP tasks: Part-of-Speech (POS) tagging, Named Entity Recognition (NER), and Keyword Identification. To overcome annotation bottlenecks in NER, we further explore a synthetic data generation pipeline involving translation from Hindi and cross-lingual word alignment. For POS tagging, we adopt and subsequently modify the Universal Dependencies (UD) framework to better suit the linguistic characteristics of Mizo and Khasi, while custom annotation guidelines are developed for NER and Keyword Identification. The constructed datasets are evaluated using multilingual language models, demonstrating that structured resource development, coupled with gradual fine-tuning, yields significant improvements in performance. This work represents a critical step toward advancing linguistic resources and computational tools for Mizo and Khasi.

1 Introduction

India is home to more than 1,963 languages (Census Commissioner, 2022), belonging to five major language families, yet the Indian Constitution officially recognizes only 22 (Indian-Constitution, 2022). While English and Hindi are spoken by approximately 10.2% and 43.63% of the population, respectively, the majority prefer using their regional languages. However, a vast number of these languages remain underrepresented in the field of Natural Language Processing (NLP), primarily due to the lack of curated resources and limited availability of digital text in native scripts. While high-resource languages benefit from abundant datasets, extremely low-resource languages like Mizo and Khasi (Sarkar et al., 2024) have very limited digital presence.

Example 1:

English: The sun is shining in the sky.

Khasi : Ka sngi ka shai thaba ha ka suin bneng.

Mizo: Ni chu vânah a ên mêk .

Example 2:

English: While thanking the Garo people on this day, the Registrar General High Court of Meghalaya, Mr E. Kharumnuid expressed his praise to the members of the Wangala Committee that he gets to witness this Festival.

Khasi: Haba ai ka jingkhublei sha ki jaitbynriew Garo ha kane ka sngi u Registrar General, High Court ka Meghalaya, u Bah E Kharumniud u la pynpaw ka jingïaroh ïa ki dkhot ka Committee jong ka Wangala kaba u la ïoh ban sakhi ïa kane ka tamasa.

Mizo: Hemi ni hian Garo mipuite chungah lawmthu a sawi rualin, Registrar General High Court of Meghalaya, Mr E. Kharumnuid chuan he Festival hi a hmuh theih avangin Wangala Committee member-te chu a fak thu a sawi.

Figure 1: Example sentences in Mizo and Khasi with their corresponding English translations.

Mizo, a Tibeto-Burman language (Thurgood and LaPolla, 2003), is spoken by approximately 831K people, while Khasi, an Austroasiatic language (Jenny and Sidwell, 2014), is spoken by around 1.4M (according to Census 2011) people in India. A more comprehensive linguistic description of Mizo can be found in Appendix A.1, and for Khasi in Appendix A.2. Figure 1 illustrates example sentences in Mizo and Khasi corresponding to the same English sentence.

In this work, we focus on the development of foundational linguistic resources to support NLP for Mizo and Khasi. Specifically, we created datasets for Part-of-Speech (POS) (Kumar et al., 2024) tagging, Named Entity Recognition (NER) (Murthy et al., 2018) and Keyword Identification (Bala et al., 2024).Given the lack of task-specific

Proceedings of the 19th Linguistic Annotation Workshop (LAW-XIX-2025), pages 228–239
July 31, 2025 ©2025 Association for Computational Linguistics

annotation guidelines for Mizo and Khasi, we adapted the Universal Dependencies (UD) (Universal Dependencies, 2025) framework for POS tagging and designed custom annotation schemes that reflect the unique syntactic and semantic characteristics of these two languages. Additionally, we created separate annotation guidelines for NER and Keyword Identification to ensure accurate dataset construction for each task.

To mitigate the challenge posed by the scarcity of gold-standard annotated data, especially for NER, we explored synthetic data generation using a Hindi NER dataset as a source. This involved translation into Mizo and Khasi, followed by word alignment using models such as Awesome-Align (Dou and Neubig, 2021) and VecMAP (Artetxe et al., 2017, 2018). The alignment process was carefully evaluated and refined to ensure the quality and usability of the resulting synthetic annotations. However, existing language models exhibit little to no understanding of Mizo and Khasi. To bridge this gap, we first constructed a monolingual corpus for both languages and performed multistage fine-tuning of multilingual models such as MuRIL (Khanuja et al., 2021), RemBERT (Conneau et al., 2019), and XLM-RoBERTa-Large (Chung et al., 2021).

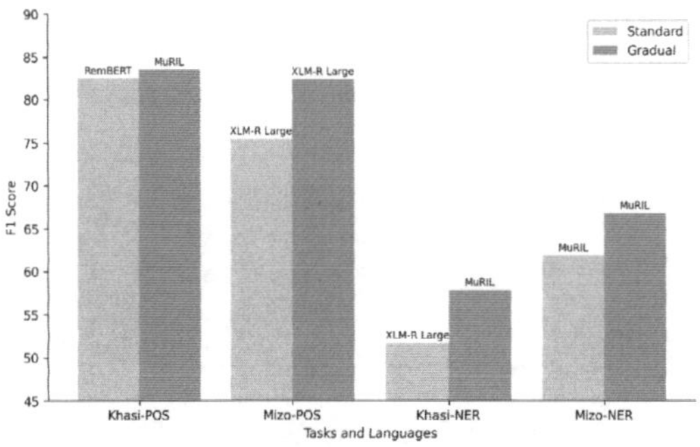

Figure 2: Comparison of best-performing models under standard and gradual fine-tuning approaches across different tasks in Khasi and Mizo. The best-performing models for each setting are indicated.

Building on this foundation, we further fine-tuned the models on task-specific datasets, employing both standard and gradual fine-tuning strategies. As illustrated in Figure 2, the gradual fine-tuning approach led to a significant boost in performance across POS tagging, NER and Keyword Identification tasks, demonstrating its effectiveness in low-resource settings.

By systematically developing and evaluating linguistically grounded resources, this work marks an important step toward enriching the NLP landscape for Mizo and Khasi languages currently transitioning from **Rising Stars** to **The Underdogs** (Joshi et al., 2020), supported by a growing suite of annotated datasets and tailored linguistic tools.

2 Related Work

2.1 POS Tagging

Cross-lingual transfer learning, as proposed by Kim et al. (2017), has been widely used for POS tagging in extremely low-resource languages by leveraging high-resource language data to improve model performance. Similarly, Chaudhary et al. (2021) introduced an active learning approach that reduces the dependency on manual annotations and mitigates conflicts in POS tag selection and optimization. More recently, Chaudhary et al. (2021) introduced the first UD-compliant POS tagging datasets for the low-resource Indic languages Angika, Magahi and Bhojpuri. Their work highlighted tokenization challenges and proposed a look-back tokenization fix that improved the F1 score, emphasizing the importance of script-aware adaptation in multilingual models. While weakly supervised POS taggers have shown promise for some low-resource languages, Kann et al. (2020) demonstrated their limitations for truly low-resource languages. The lack of good dictionaries and limited linguistic resources make traditional weak supervision methods less effective, especially for Mizo and Khasi. This highlights the need for new and better approaches.

2.2 NER & Keyword Identification

The primary challenge in NER tagging for low-resource languages is the lack of annotated data, which can be mitigated through multilingual approaches and mapping techniques. Murthy et al. (2018) demonstrated that for closely related languages, neural network layers can be divided for each language, leveraging cross-lingual features to enhance NER quality. Panchadara (2024) showed that merging datasets for Dravidian languages and utilizing mBERT and XLM-Roberta significantly improves accuracy. Dash et al. (2024) explored data augmentation techniques and community-driven resource creation to enhance NER performance for the Ho language. Similarly, Khemchandani et al. (2021) proposed RelateLM, a multilingual model that uses high-resource languages as pivots through translation and backtranslation. Tang et al. (2019) employed an attention-based deep learning technique for clinical text classification using keyword extraction, where a fine-tuned BERT model achieved 97.6% accuracy. Bala et al. (2024) introduced a keyword extraction and summarization dataset for Mizo, enriching news articles in the language. Nasar et al. (2019) explored Keyword Identification and summarization, highlighting the lack of datasets and discussing various challenges associated with the task. These studies highlight how leveraging linguistic similarities and cross-lingual transfer can improve NER and Keyword Identification task quality for low-resource languages.

2.3 Synthetic Data Generation & Alignment

Prior studies have explored synthetic data generation using LLMs to enhance model performance Tang et al. (2023); Gholami and Omar (2023). In parallel, word alignment has been widely studied for machine translation and cross-lingual NLP Dou and Neubig (2021). Recent work by Wu et al. (2024) demonstrated the effectiveness of optimizing LLM-based models through word alignment techniques. Our work builds upon these advances by integrating synthetic data generation with word alignment techniques to improve NER performance in extremely low-resource languages.

3 Data Development

3.1 Gold Standard Data

We crawled news articles from various permitted websites in Mizo and Khasi, covering diverse topics(Healthcare, Education, Politics, Culture, Environment, Local Governance, Entertainment, and Sports) written in their respective languages. After preprocessing, we used these data to create datasets for Part-of-Speech (POS) tagging, Named Entity Recognition (NER) and Keyword Identification. These gold-standard datasets were meticulously annotated by linguistic experts with proficiency in Mizo and Khasi, ensuring high-quality and reliable annotations for downstream NLP tasks.

Due to the absence of task-specific annotation guidelines for these languages, we initially adopted the Universal Dependencies (UD) (Universal Dependencies, 2025) framework for POS tagging and later refined it to better capture their linguistic characteristics. For NER, we developed a custom annotation framework from scratch to ensure consistency and accuracy. Figure 3 shows an example of the NER dataset, and Figure 4 shows the POS dataset for both languages. We have released all the annotated datasets publicly on the iHub-Data (iHub-Data, IIIT Hyderabad, 2025) India platform[1].

Khasi: Haba ai ka jingkhublei sha ki jaitbynriew Garo ha kane ka sngi u Registrar General, High Court ka Meghalaya, u Bah E Kharumniud u la pynpaw ka jingïaroh ïa ki dkhot ka Committee jong ka Wangala kaba u la ïoh ban sakhi ïa kane ka tamasa.

1	Haba	O
2	ai	O
3	ka	O
4	jingkhublei	O
5	sha	O
6	ki	O
7	jaitbynriew	b-NEMI
8	Garo	i-NEMI
9	ha	b-NETI
10	kane	i-NETI

...

Mizo: Chairperson thar C Zodinpuii hi Directorate of Social Welfare & Tribal Affairs-ah Joint Director-in ni 31.12.2023 ah pension in a chhuak.

1	Chairperson	b-NEMI
2	thar	O
3	C	b-NEP
4	Zodinpuii	i-NEP
5	hi	O
6	Directorate	b-NEO
7	of	i-NEO
8	Social	i-NEO
9	Welfare	i-NEO
10	&	i-NEO

...

Figure 3: Illustration of the NER dataset with entity tags applied to the first 10 tokens of example sentences in both languages.

Inter-Annotator Agreement (IAA) Scores

Task	Khasi	Mizo
POS	0.91	0.93
NER & Keyword Identification	0.88	0.90

Table 1: Inter-Annotator Agreement (IAA) scores (Cohen's Kappa) for POS, NER and Keyword Identification datasets in Khasi and Mizo.

To validate the annotated data, we conducted an analysis of Inter-Annotator Agreement (IAA) (Artstein, 2017) using Cohen's Kappa (Rau and Shih, 2021) score. Table 1 presents Cohen's Kappa scores, and Table 2 provides dataset statistics, with a detailed breakdown for each language.

[1]https://india-data.org/datasets-listing/natural-language-processing-(nlp)/

Khasi: Haba ai ka jingkhublei sha ki jaitbynriew Garo ha kane ka sngi u Registrar General, High Court ka Meghalaya, u Bah E Kharumniud u la pynpaw ka jingïaroh ïa ki dkhot ka Committee jong ka Wangala kaba u la ïoh ban sakhi ïa kane ka tamasa.

```
1    Haba          CONJ
2    ai            VERB
3    ka            DET
4    jingkhublei   NOUN
5    sha           PREP
6    ki            DET
7    jaitbynriew   NOUN
8    Garo          PROPN
9    ha            PREP
10   kane          DET
...
```

Mizo: Chairperson thar C Zodinpuii hi Directorate of Social Welfare & Tribal Affairs-ah Joint Director-in ni 31.12.2023 ah pension in a chhuak.

```
1    Chairperson   NOUN
2    thar          ADJ
3    C             PROPN
4    Zodinpuii     PROPN
5    hi            AUX
6    Directorate   NOUN
7    of            ADP
8    Social        NOUN
9    Welfare       NOUN
10   &             CCONJ
...
```

Figure 4: Illustration of the POS-tagged dataset showing the first 10 tokens annotated using the adapted UD framework.

Gold Dataset Statistics

Language	Sentences	Tokens	Types
POS Tagging			
Khasi	507	21.6K	7.5K
Mizo	502	17.3K	5.4K
NER & Keyword Identification			
Khasi	4.1K	203.1K	14.9K
Mizo	4.4K	116.2K	15.9K

Table 2: Statistics of gold-standard datasets for POS tagging, NER and Keyword Identification in Khasi and Mizo.

Monolingual Dataset Statistics

Language	Sentences	Tokens	Types
Khasi	253.3K	15.14M	269.9K
Mizo	318.4K	12.18M	294.8K

Table 3: Statistics of the Monolingual Corpora for Mizo and Khasi

3.2 Monolingual Corpus and Synthetic Data

Using the crawled data, we compiled a monolingual corpus for each language after extensive preprocessing and filtering. The preprocessing pipeline included removal of metadata, URLs, and non-native scripts (such as Devanagari, Bengali, etc). Additionally, we applied heuristic rules for noise reduction, including filtering out texts with high proportions of negative sentiment using a sentiment classifier, and removing sentences with excessive repetition or low information density. Table 3 summarizes the final statistics of the cleaned monolingual corpora.

Additionally, we created Hindi-Mizo and Hindi-Khasi parallel datasets, using WMT23 (Pal et al., 2023) English-Mizo and English-Khasi data in conjunction with Google Translate and BhashaVerse (Mujadia and Sharma, 2024). To address the scarcity of annotated data further, we generated synthetic NER datasets for both languages based on the Hindi NER dataset. Figure 6 illustrates the detailed procedure for the generation of synthetic data, and Table 5 presents the statistics of these datasets.

4 Methodology

4.1 Baseline models

We began our experiment with baseline models, using Google MuRIL, XLM-RoBERTa-Large, and Google RemBERT. MuRIL (Khanuja et al., 2021), developed by Google, is pre-trained on 16 Indian languages. RemBERT (Chung et al., 2021), also developed by Google, is trained on 110 languages. XLM-RoBERTa-Large (Conneau et al., 2019), developed by Facebook, is pre-trained on 100 languages.

For all three tasks and both languages, we first applied a zero-shot approach to the gold-standard data. For Mizo, XLM-RoBERTa-Large achieved the best performance in both POS tagging and NER. For Khasi, RemBERT performed best for POS tagging, while XLM-RoBERTa-Large was the top performer for NER and Keyword Identification. Table 4 presents the detailed results of our baseline models.

4.2 Model Finetune

As these models perform poorly in a zero-shot setting, a two-stage fine-tuning approach is adopted. In the first stage, the models are fine-tuned on a monolingual corpus to enhance their understanding of the target languages. Once language compre-

F1 Scores of Baseline Models

Language	MuRIL	RemBERT	XLM-R large
POS Tagging			
Khasi	9.47	14.19	11.62
Mizo	12.94	9.11	17.38
NER & Keyword Identification			
Khasi	8.59	9.31	16.28
Mizo	12.35	8.61	13.07

Table 4: Macro F1-scores for POS tagging, NER, and Keyword Identification in a zero-shot setting using baseline models.

hension is established, task-specific fine-tuning is performed. Two setups are explored: Standard and Gradual. Section 6 provides a detailed explanation of this process, while Table 7 presents the corresponding results.

5 Synthetic NER Data Generation

There is a severe lack of publicly available data for these languages on the internet, making it necessary to rely on synthetic data generation (Anonymous, 2025) to obtain large-scale resources without direct human involvement. However, direct translation from another language is not feasible, as it often results in variations in word count and word order (James and Krishnamurthy, 2025). This makes it difficult to map the NER tags, especially when using the BIO (Beginning, Inside, Outside) (Yohannes and Amagasa, 2022) format.

To address this, we used Hindi NER (Bahad et al., 2024) data (tagged in BIO format) as our source. We first translated the sentences without their tags into Mizo and Khasi (P M et al., 2024). After translation, we aligned the words using Awesome-Align and VecMAP.

- **Awesome-Align** (Dou and Neubig, 2021) is a cross-lingual word alignment tool that leverages multilingual BERT (mBERT) to generate high-quality word alignments between parallel texts.

- **VecMAP** (Artetxe et al., 2018, 2017) is a method for learning cross-lingual word embeddings by mapping word vectors from one language to another into a shared vector space, allowing better alignment and improving translation consistency.

Hindi: वे यहोशू के पास लौट आए।
(ve yahoshoo ke paas laut aae.)
Mizo: Josua hnênah an kîr leh a .

0-2 || वे → an
1-0 || यहोशू → Josua
2-1 || के → hnênah
3-1 || पास → hnênah
4-3 || लौट → kîr
5-5 || आए → a

Hindi: उसने अपनी आँखों से मुझे धन्यवाद दिया।
(usane apanee aankhon se mujhe dhanyavaad diya.)
Khasi: U khublei ianga da ki khmat.

0-0 || उसने → U
1-6 || अपनी → jongu
2-5 || आँखों → khmat
3-3 || से → da
4-2 || मुझे → ianga
5-1 || धन्यवाद → khublei
6-1 || दिया → khublei

Figure 5: Detailed alignment examples for Hindi–Khasi and Hindi–Mizo translations after refinement using Awesome-Align and VecMAP. Each example includes the original Hindi sentence, its transliteration, the corresponding target translation (Mizo & Khasi), and word-level alignments.

To train Awesome-Align, we utilized the WMT23 English-Mizo and English-Khasi parallel datasets (Pal et al., 2023). Since our source data was in Hindi, we first translated the English sentences into Hindi. Subsequently, we trained Awesome-Align using the Hindi-Mizo and Hindi-Khasi parallel datasets.

However, Awesome-Align internally relies on mBERT (Devlin et al., 2018), which has minimal to no representation of Mizo and Khasi. To mitigate this limitation, we first fine-tuned mBERT on our monolingual corpus. The initial results were suboptimal, prompting us to refine our approach. We partitioned the monolingual corpus into two subsets, each containing approximately 7.5 million tokens. The model was initially fine-tuned on the first subset, followed by an additional fine-tuning stage on the second subset. This two-stage fine-tuning process resulted in a perplexity score of 9.25, significantly enhancing the model's ability to process Mizo and Khasi text.

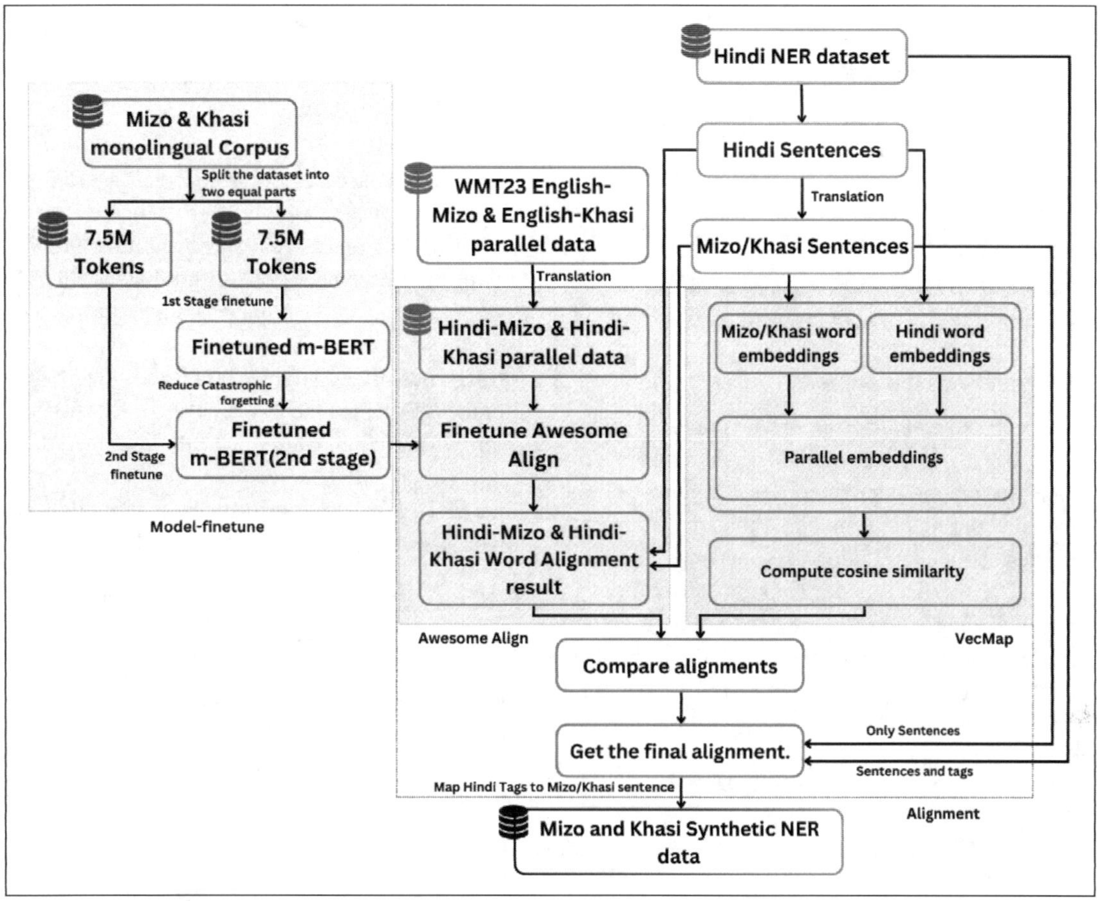

Figure 6: Pipeline for synthetic NER data generation.

Once Awesome-Align was trained, we used our Hindi source sentences and their Mizo/Khasi translations (Hindi ||| Mizo/Khasi) to generate word alignments. However, the model occasionally produced unaligned words or incorrectly mapped multiple words to a single word. To refine these alignments, we used VecMAP.

For VecMAP, we first generated Word2Vec (Mikolov et al., 2013) embeddings for Hindi, Mizo, and Khasi using our source Hindi sentences and their corresponding translations. We then mapped the Hindi embeddings to a common space with Mizo/Khasi embeddings and vice versa. Using cosine similarity, we corrected the unaligned words and improved alignments where Awesome-Align incorrectly assigned multiple words to a single word. This resulted in more accurate alignments. Figure 5 illustrates detailed examples of Hindi–Khasi and Hindi–Mizo alignments.

At this stage, we had Hindi NER data, along with translated Mizo/Khasi sentences and their word alignments. To map the NER tags, we first removed the BIO tags and then assigned the tags according to the alignments. Finally, we reapplied the BIO tags:

- **B (Beginning)** was assigned to the first token of an entity.
- **I (Inside)** was assigned to subsequent tokens within the entity.
- **O (Outside)** was assigned to tokens that did not belong to any entity.

This process allowed us to generate high-quality synthetic NER data for Mizo and Khasi, ensuring accurate tag mappings despite the complexities of translation and word alignment. Figure 6 illustrates the detailed procedure for synthetic data generation, and Table 5 presents the statistics of these datasets. All synthetic datasets have been publicly released on the iHub-Data India platform[2].

[2] https://india-data.org/datasets-listing

Synthetic NER data

Dataset	Sentences	Tokens	Types
Khasi	6.6K	220.3K	15.1K
Mizo	6.6K	175.2K	17.4K

Table 5: Statistics of the synthetic NER dataset for Mizo and Khasi.

6 Experiments and Results

6.1 1st Stage Finetune

While these models support several Indian languages and scripts, they do not accommodate Mizo and Khasi, as no datasets for these languages were included during pre-training. Although their vocabularies contain the Latin script, which is also used by Mizo and Khasi, the structural differences in these languages limit the models' ability to understand them effectively. Consequently, their zero-shot performance on Mizo and Khasi was significantly low.

Perplexity Scores from First-Stage Fine-Tuning

Language	MuRIL	RemBERT	XLM-R large
Khasi	5.19	8.13	8.57
Mizo	10.06	7.69	7.92

Table 6: Perplexity scores after the first stage of fine-tuning on the monolingual corpus.

To address this limitation, we fine-tuned these models on a monolingual corpus specifically curated for Mizo and Khasi. This fine-tuning process improved their language comprehension, making them more suitable for downstream NLP tasks. We evaluated the effectiveness of this adaptation using perplexity scores, with detailed results presented in Table 6.

6.2 2nd Stage Finetune (Task-Specific)

With these models now adapted to our target languages, they are ready for fine-tuning on specific NLP tasks. For each task, we employ two fine-tuning strategies: standard fine-tuning and gradual fine-tuning. In gradual training, we initially freeze all model layers and progressively unfreeze them over several epochs. Using these approaches, we achieved an F1 score improvement of approximately 62% for POS and 43% for NER and Keyword Identification in the standard fine-tuning setup, with an additional gain of 6% when applying gradual training.

6.2.1 POS Tagging

Part-of-Speech POS tagging involves labeling each word in a sentence with its corresponding grammatical categories such as noun, verb, adjective, or adverb. Building on our first-stage fine-tuned model, we further fine-tuned it on our gold-standard POS tagging dataset and evaluated its performance on the same dataset. In the standard fine-tuning setup, MuRIL performed slightly better for Mizo, while RemBERT yielded the best results for Khasi. However, with gradual training, MuRIL achieved the highest performance for Khasi, whereas XLM-RoBERTa-Large outperformed other models for Mizo. The detailed results are presented in Table 7.

6.2.2 NER Tagging & Keyword Identification

Named Entity Recognition (NER) involves extracting meaningful information from text by identifying and categorizing named entities such as person names, locations, and organizations. Additionally, tasks beyond NER, Keyword Identification, focus on extracting key terms that represent the main topics of a document. This is particularly useful for applications like search engine optimization, text summarization, and content classification.

To evaluate NER performance, we fine-tuned our first-stage fine-tuned models on synthetically generated NER data and used gold-standard data as a benchmark. In the standard fine-tuning setup, XLM-RoBERTa-Large achieved the best performance for Khasi, while MuRIL performed better for Mizo. However, in the gradual fine-tuning setup, MuRIL outperformed other models for Khasi, while it remained the best-performing model for Mizo. The detailed results are presented in Table 7.

7 Conclusion

The development of NLP resources for low-resource languages such as Mizo and Khasi is crucial for their digital preservation and broader linguistic accessibility. Through the creation of high-quality annotated datasets for POS tagging, NER, and Keyword Identification, this work establishes foundational linguistic resources to support future research and tool development for these underrepresented languages. In particular, our synthetic NER data generation pipeline leveraging translation and word alignment demonstrate the feasibility

F1 Score of Task-Specific Fine-Tuning Across Different Models

Language	Standard			Gradual		
	MuRIL	RemBERT	XLM-R-Large	MuRIL	RemBERT	XLM-R-Large
POS tagging						
Khasi	76.49	82.51	71.02	**83.52**	81.15	76.81
Mizo	79.53	73.26	75.41	81.35	79.60	**82.39**
NER and Keyword Identification						
Khasi	48.30	47.11	51.68	**57.84**	55.27	53.79
Mizo	61.88	58.69	59.27	**66.79**	64.08	64.92

Table 7: Macro F1 score comparison of fine-tuned MuRIL, RemBERT, and XLM-R Large on POS tagging and NER and Keyword Identification tasks for Mizo and Khasi under standard and gradual fine-tuning setups.

of bootstrapping annotated data in the absence of gold-standard resources.

Among the models evaluated, MuRIL and XLM-R Large emerged as the most effective choices, depending on the task. MuRIL performed best for Khasi POS tagging (f1: 83.52) and both Mizo NER (f1:66.79) and Khasi NER (f1:57.84), while XLM-R Large achieved the highest score (f1:82.39) for Mizo POS tagging, demonstrating how a well-structured fine-tuning strategy can significantly enhance model performance.

Future work can extend these efforts by expanding annotated datasets, refining task-specific guidelines, and increasing coverage across linguistic phenomena. Incorporating community-driven or semi-automated annotation strategies may further enhance the scalability and adaptability of resource creation, contributing to better representation and accessibility for Mizo, Khasi, and other low-resource languages.

Acknowledgment

This project is funded by I-Hub Data (iHub-Data, IIIT Hyderabad, 2025). We thank I-Hub Data as well for providing access to computational resources (GPU support), which enabled us to carry out the training and experiments effectively. We are grateful to Nagaraju Vuppala and Mayuri Dilip for their contributions to data management in the initial stages. Finally, we extend our sincere thanks to all anonymous reviewers for their valuable feedback and constructive suggestions, which helped improve the quality of this work.

Ethics Statement

This research promotes linguistic inclusivity by developing NLP resources for Mizo and Khasi, two extremely low-resource languages. Dataset creation involved collaboration with native speakers and language experts, ensuring ethical data collection and annotation while respecting linguistic and cultural contexts.

Textual data was collected from permitted news websites in full compliance with their terms of use. All human annotators participated voluntarily and were fairly remunerated for their work. The dataset contains no personally identifiable information, ensuring privacy and confidentiality.

While multilingual models were fine-tuned on these languages, potential biases remain due to the limited availability of digital resources. We encourage further community-driven efforts to enhance NLP for underrepresented languages.

We used LLM to refine sentence structure and check grammar in our paper, ensuring clarity while maintaining the originality of the content.

References

Anonymous. 2025. Does synthetic data help named entity recognition for low-resource languages? In *Submitted to ACL Rolling Review - December 2024*. Under review.

Mikel Artetxe, Gorka Labaka, and Eneko Agirre. 2017. Learning bilingual word embeddings with (almost) no bilingual data. In *Proceedings of the 55th Annual Meeting of the Association for Computational Linguistics (Volume 1: Long Papers)*, pages 451–462.

Mikel Artetxe, Gorka Labaka, and Eneko Agirre. 2018. A robust self-learning method for fully unsupervised cross-lingual mappings of word embeddings. *arXiv preprint arXiv:1805.06297*.

Ron Artstein. 2017. Inter-annotator agreement. *Handbook of linguistic annotation*, pages 297–313.

Sankalp Bahad, Pruthwik Mishra, Parameswari Krishnamurthy, and Dipti Sharma. 2024. Fine-tuning pre-trained named entity recognition models for Indian languages. In *Proceedings of the 2024 Conference of the North American Chapter of the Association for Computational Linguistics: Human Language Technologies (Volume 4: Student Research Workshop)*, pages 75–82, Mexico City, Mexico. Association for Computational Linguistics.

Abhinaba Bala, Ashok Urlana, Rahul Mishra, and Parameswari Krishnamurthy. 2024. Exploring news summarization and enrichment in a highly resource-scarce indian language: A case study of mizo. *arXiv preprint arXiv:2405.00717*.

Census Commissioner. 2022. Census of India 2011 - Language Atlas. [Accessed 05-06-2024].

Aditi Chaudhary, Antonios Anastasopoulos, Zaid Sheikh, and Graham Neubig. 2021. Reducing confusion in active learning for part-of-speech tagging. *Transactions of the Association for Computational Linguistics*, 9.

Hyung Won Chung, Thibault Févry, Henry Tsai, Melvin Johnson, and Sebastian Ruder. 2021. Rethinking embedding coupling in pre-trained language models. In *9th International Conference on Learning Representations, ICLR 2021, Virtual Event, Austria, May 3-7, 2021*. OpenReview.net.

Alexis Conneau, Kartikay Khandelwal, Naman Goyal, Vishrav Chaudhary, Guillaume Wenzek, Francisco Guzmán, Edouard Grave, Myle Ott, Luke Zettlemoyer, and Veselin Stoyanov. 2019. Unsupervised cross-lingual representation learning at scale. *CoRR*, abs/1911.02116.

Satya Ranjan Dash, Bikram Biruli, Yasobanta Das, Prosper Abel Mgimwa, Muhammed Abdur Rahmaan Kamaldeen, and Aloka Fernando. 2024. Named entity recognition (ner) in low resource languages of ho. In *Empowering Low-Resource Languages With NLP Solutions*, pages 157–182. IGI Global.

Jacob Devlin, Ming-Wei Chang, Kenton Lee, and Kristina Toutanova. 2018. BERT: pre-training of deep bidirectional transformers for language understanding. *CoRR*, abs/1810.04805.

Zi-Yi Dou and Graham Neubig. 2021. Word alignment by fine-tuning embeddings on parallel corpora. *arXiv preprint arXiv:2101.08231*.

Sia Gholami and Marwan Omar. 2023. Does synthetic data make large language models more efficient? *arXiv preprint arXiv:2310.07830*.

iHub-Data, IIIT Hyderabad. 2025. iHub-Data IIIT Hyderabad. Accessed: 9 Mar. 2025.

Indian-Constitution. 2022. Languages included in the eighth schedule of the indian constitution. [Accessed: 2 Mar. 2025].

Antony Alexander James and Parameswari Krishnamurthy. 2025. Pos-aware neural approaches for word alignment in dravidian languages. In *Proceedings of the First Workshop on Challenges in Processing South Asian Languages (CHiPSAL 2025)*, pages 154–159.

M. Jenny and P. Sidwell. 2014. *The Handbook of Austroasiatic Languages (2 vols)*. Grammars and Sketches of the World's Languages. Brill.

Pratik Joshi, Sebastin Santy, Amar Budhiraja, Kalika Bali, and Monojit Choudhury. 2020. The state and fate of linguistic diversity and inclusion in the nlp world. *arXiv preprint arXiv:2004.09095*.

Katharina Kann, Ophélie Lacroix, and Anders Søgaard. 2020. Weakly supervised pos taggers perform poorly on truly low-resource languages. In *Proceedings of the AAAI Conference on Artificial Intelligence*, volume 34, pages 8066–8073.

Simran Khanuja, Diksha Bansal, Sarvesh Mehtani, Savya Khosla, Atreyee Dey, Balaji Gopalan, Dilip Kumar Margam, Pooja Aggarwal, Rajiv Teja Nagipogu, Shachi Dave, et al. 2021. Muril: Multilingual representations for indian languages. *arXiv preprint arXiv:2103.10730*.

Yash Khemchandani, Sarvesh Mehtani, Vaidehi Patil, Abhijeet Awasthi, Partha Talukdar, and Sunita Sarawagi. 2021. Exploiting language relatedness for low web-resource language model adaptation: An indic languages study. *arXiv preprint arXiv:2106.03958*.

Joo-Kyung Kim, Young-Bum Kim, Ruhi Sarikaya, and Eric Fosler-Lussier. 2017. Cross-lingual transfer learning for pos tagging without cross-lingual resources. In *Proceedings of the 2017 conference on empirical methods in natural language processing*, pages 2832–2838.

Sanjeev Kumar, Preethi Jyothi, and Pushpak Bhattacharyya. 2024. Part-of-speech tagging for extremely low-resource Indian languages. In *Findings of the Association for Computational Linguistics: ACL 2024*, pages 14422–14431, Bangkok, Thailand. Association for Computational Linguistics.

Tomas Mikolov, Kai Chen, Greg Corrado, and Jeffrey Dean. 2013. Efficient estimation of word representations in vector space. *arXiv preprint arXiv:1301.3781*.

Vandan Mujadia and Dipti Misra Sharma. 2024. Bhashaverse: Translation ecosystem for indian subcontinent languages. *arXiv preprint arXiv:2412.04351*.

Rudra Murthy, Mitesh M Khapra, and Pushpak Bhattacharyya. 2018. Improving ner tagging performance in low-resource languages via multilingual learning. *ACM Transactions on Asian and Low-Resource Language Information Processing (TALLIP)*, 18(2):1–20.

Zara Nasar, Syed Waqar Jaffry, and Muhammad Kamran Malik. 2019. Textual keyword extraction and summarization: State-of-the-art. *Information Processing & Management*, 56(6):102088.

Abhinav P M, Ketaki Shetye, and Parameswari Krishnamurthy. 2024. MTNLP-IIITH: Machine translation for low-resource Indic languages. In *Proceedings of the Ninth Conference on Machine Translation*, pages 751–755, Miami, Florida, USA. Association for Computational Linguistics.

Santanu Pal, Partha Pakray, Sahinur Rahman Laskar, Lenin Laitonjam, Vanlalmuansangi Khenglawt, Sunita Warjri, Pankaj Kundan Dadure, and Sandeep Kumar Dash. 2023. Findings of the WMT 2023 shared task on low-resource Indic language translation. In *Proceedings of the Eighth Conference on Machine Translation*, pages 682–694, Singapore. Association for Computational Linguistics.

Kiranmaye Panchadara. 2024. Enhancing named entity recognition in low-resource dravidian languages: A comparative analysis of multilingual learning and transfer learning techniques. *Journal of Artificial intelligence and Machine Learning*, 2(1):1–7.

Gerald Rau and Yu-Shan Shih. 2021. Evaluation of cohen's kappa and other measures of inter-rater agreement for genre analysis and other nominal data. *Journal of english for academic purposes*, 53:101026.

Sunita Sarkar, Sneha Das, Basab Nath, and Somnath Mukhopadhyay. 2024. A multilingual neural machine translation model for low resource north eastern languages.

Matthew Tang, Priyanka Gandhi, Md Ahsanul Kabir, Christopher Zou, Jordyn Blakey, and Xiao Luo. 2019. Progress notes classification and keyword extraction using attention-based deep learning models with bert. *arXiv preprint arXiv:1910.05786*.

Ruixiang Tang, Xiaotian Han, Xiaoqian Jiang, and Xia Hu. 2023. Does synthetic data generation of llms help clinical text mining? *arXiv preprint arXiv:2303.04360*.

G. Thurgood and R.J. LaPolla. 2003. *The Sino-Tibetan Languages*. Routledge language family series. Routledge.

Universal Dependencies. 2025. Universal POS tags. Accessed: 7 March 2025.

Qiyu Wu, Masaaki Nagata, Zhongtao Miao, and Yoshimasa Tsuruoka. 2024. Word alignment as preference for machine translation. *arXiv preprint arXiv:2405.09223*.

Hailemariam Mehari Yohannes and Toshiyuki Amagasa. 2022. Named-entity recognition for a low-resource language using pre-trained language model. In *Proceedings of the 37th ACM/SIGAPP Symposium on Applied Computing*, SAC '22, page 837–844, New York, NY, USA. Association for Computing Machinery.

A Appendix

A.1 Linguistic Landscape of Mizo

Mizo, a Tibeto-Burman language (Thurgood and LaPolla, 2003), is written in the Roman script, which was introduced by Welsh Christian missionaries in the late 19th century. The early Mizo script was developed by Rev. J.H. Lorrain and Rev. F.W. Savidge in 1894. The Mizo alphabet consists of 25 letters, excluding F, Q, R, and X, as these letters do not exist in native Mizo words.

Beyond being a means of communication, Mizo serves as a symbol of identity, unity, and cultural heritage for the Zo people.It is **spoken by** approximately **831K** (according to Census 2011) people in India and is primarily used in Mizoram (Fig. 7). Additionally, Mizo (or closely related dialects) is spoken in parts of Manipur, Tripura, Assam, as well as in neighboring Myanmar and Bangladesh, where different Zo communities reside.

Figure 7: Map of India highlighting Mizoram[3], the primary region where Mizo is spoken.

Mizo evolved from various dialects spoken by different Zo tribes. Historically, the Lusei dialect (spoken by the Lusei/Lushai tribe) became dominant due to its early adoption in education, administration, and Christian missionary work. Over time, other dialects merged into what is now recognized as the standard Mizo language. However, distinct Zo dialects such as Hmar, Paite, Lai, Mara, and Vaiphei continue to be spoken by their respective communities.

Linguistically, Mizo is an agglutinative language, meaning words are formed by adding multiple affixes to a root word, allowing complex meanings to be expressed through morphological constructions rather than separate words..

A.2 Linguistic Landscape Khasi

Khasi belongs to the Austroasiatic language family (Jenny and Sidwell, 2014) and is predominantly spoken in Meghalaya, India, with approximately **1.4 million speakers** (according to Census 2011). It is written in the Roman script and has a rich oral tradition.

Khasi is the largest indigenous language in Meghalaya (Fig: 8) and is primarily spoken in the Khasi and Jaintia Hills, as well as the Ri Bhoi district. The Khasi people are linked to the Mon-Khmer sub-group of the Austroasiatic language family, with linguistic similarities to Mon-Khmer dialects spoken in Southeast Asia.

Figure 8: Map of India highlighting Meghalaya[4], the primary region where Khasi is spoken.

Historically, the Khasi people are known as Hynniewtrep (Children of Seven Huts), representing seven sub-groups: Khynriam, Pnar (Jaintia), Bhoi, War, Maram, Lyngngam, and Mnar. Among these, the Pnar (Jaintia), Bhoi, and War are significant regional variations. While Khasi has a standardized written form, dialectal variations exist across different regions.

[3]Source: https://tinyurl.com/5b6893an

[4]Source: https://tinyurl.com/5fyebpp3

Linguistically, Khasi is an agglutinative language, where words are formed by adding prefixes, suffixes, and infixes to a root word, allowing complex meanings to be built through morphological processes rather than separate words. .

A.3 Experimental Setup

Multilingual transformer-based models, including MuRIL, RemBERT, and XLM-RoBERTa-Large, were fine-tuned on Mizo and Khasi datasets. The models were initialized with pre-trained weights and further trained using our annotated datasets. Fine-tuning was conducted using the Hugging Face Transformers library on NVIDIA L40S GPU (96GB VRAM). The training process followed a two-stage fine-tuning approach:

- **Stage 1 (Monolingual Fine-Tuning)**
  - Batch size: **32**
  - Learning rate: **3e-5**
  - Epochs: **2**
- **Stage 2 (Task-Specific Fine-Tuning for NER/POS)**
  - Batch size: **16**
  - Learning rate: **2e-5**
  - Epochs: **3**

For optimization, the **AdamW** optimizer was used with a **linear decay learning rate schedule**.

Creating Hierarchical Relations in a Multilingual Event-type Ontology

Zdeňka Urešová, Eva Fučíková, Jan Hajič
Institute of Formal and Applied Linguistics
Faculty of Mathematics and Physics
Charles University
{uresova,fucikova,hajic}@ufal.mff.cuni.cz

Abstract

This paper describes the work on hierarchization of the SynSemClass event-type ontology. The original resource has been extended by a hierarchical structure to model specialization and generalization relations between classes that are formally and technically unrelated in the original ontology. The goal is to enable one to use the ontology enriched by the hierarchical concepts for annotation of running texts in symbolic meaning representations, such as UMR or PDT. similar

The hierarchy is in principle built bottom-up, based on existing SSC classes (concepts). This approach differs from other approaches to semantic classes, such as in WordNet or VerbNet. Although the hierarchical relations are similar, the underlying nodes in the hierarchy are not.

In this paper, we describe the challenges related to the principles chosen: single-tree constraint and finding features for the definitions of specificity/generality. Also, a pilot inter-annotator experiment is described that shows the difficulty of the hierarchization task.

1 Introduction

The SynSemClass (SSC) multilingual[1] event-type ontology (Uresova et al., 2020; Urešová et al., 2023b) is a lexical-semantic resource that links similar resources, such as FrameNet (Baker et al., 1998; Fillmore et al., 2003), WordNet (Miller, 1995; Fellbaum, 1998), VerbNet (Schuler, 2006) and others, and unifies them under a single scheme.

Each entry in SynSemClass (Urešová et al., 2023b), a *class*, corresponds to one eventive *concept* (state or process). Every concept is specified in multiple ways so that the human reader can understand what the concept is. The following are the main features describing a class, e.g., *kill* (Fig. 1):

- the prototypical **name**, e.g., *kill* stands for the event type *killing*),
- a brief **class definition** (in all languages), which characterizes the common meaning of all synonymous **class members** contained in it, e.g., *A Cause deprives a Victim of life*,
- a fixed set (a **Roleset**) of defined "situational participants" (**"semantic roles"**), e.g., *Cause, Victim, etc.*,
- each class member is further **linked** to one or more existing syntactic or semantic lexical resources for each language (as referenced above, e.g., to WordNet entries),
- each class member is **exemplified** by instances of real texts (and their translations to English) extracted from translated or parallel corpora,[2] e.g., *This is not only because it kills the unborn.*

The organization of this paper is as follows: Sect. 2 explains why we have decided to build the hierarchy, and in Sect. 3 we mention other works on this topic. In Sect. 4, our approach to hierarchical scheme is presented, Sect. 5 describes some challenging issues (Sect. 5.1) and tools used (Sect. 5.2). Sect. 6 discusses the current state of the hierarchy with some statistics. We conclude and draw future plans in Sect. 7. Sect. 8 in the extra space lists the limitations of the current state of the hierarchy.

2 Motivation

Although SynSemClass is a resource that is meant to be used in document annotation (perhaps in addition to or on top of another meaning representation scheme, such as Uniform Meaning Representation (UMR) (Bonn et al., 2024)), such annotation would

[1] English, Czech, German and Spanish.

[2] Such as the Prague Czech-English Dependency Corpus (https://ufal.mff.cuni.cz/pcedt2.0/en/index.html) the Paracrawl corpus (http://paracrawl.eu), and the XSRL dataset (https://catalog.ldc.upenn.edu/LDC2021T09), among others.

Proceedings of the 19th Linguistic Annotation Workshop (LAW-XIX-2025), pages 240–249
July 31, 2025 ©2025 Association for Computational Linguistics

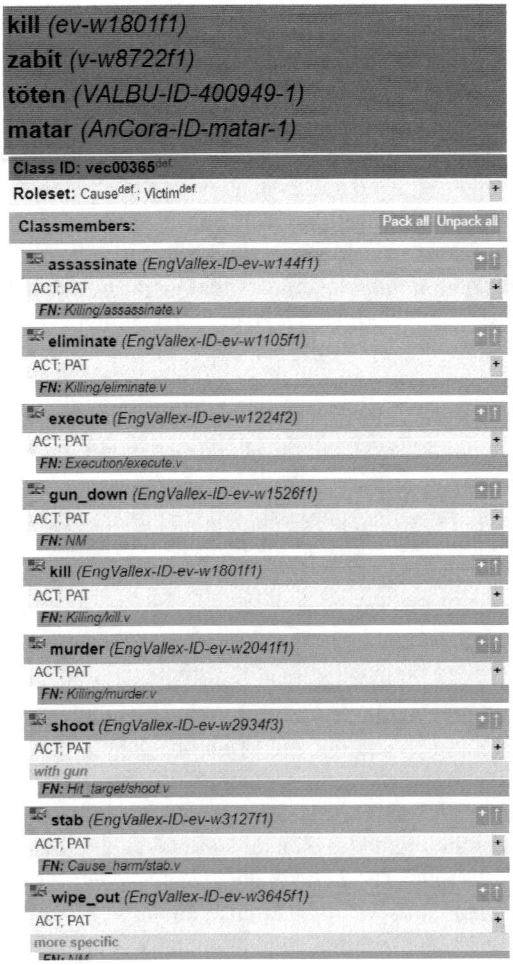

Figure 1: The abbreviated example of the SSC class *kill*.

be very difficult to perform accurately and efficiently given the properties of the SynSemClass ontology as described in the previous paragraph (Urešová et al., 2023a).

The problem is the unrelatedness of the different classes in the ontology: in the hypothetical (but certainly not uncommon) case that the annotator sees an expression (verb, noun, and MWE) that is not found among the class members of any class (or is found, but it is used in a new or different sense clearly not corresponding to the concept of the class in which it is found), *all* the classes would have to be considered, one by one, to find a suitable one (or determine that it does not exist in the resource).[3] There are now 1500+ classes in SynSemClass - so this is unfeasible to do efficiently.

Therefore, we have determined that a hierarchy over the concepts (as represented by the classes) in SynSemClass is necessary. The existence of such a hierarchy, connecting all the classes by a generalization/specialization relation, would reduce the effort required to find the appropriate class in the hierarchy by going top-down and selecting an appropriate hierarchical node (and the class represented by (linked from) it) in just a few steps.

However, given the existence of hierarchies integrated in other resources, one might ask why to build a new one. We have had two main reasons: first, the underlying SynSemClass resource is richer than the aforementioned ones in terms of being multilingual (or "interlingual") from the start, build bottom up, interlinked to other resources, has explicit mappings to syntactic resources in the languages it refers to, and has exemplification based on real corpora. Second, when inspecting the links to resources with similar hierarchies (WordNet, FrameNet, VerbNet) included in SynSemClass, there was often a multiple number of possible generalizations.[4] While the differences might be due to a different view on the synset/class concept, it is clear that there is no simple way to get a common hierarchy.

That is why we are exploiting the gap and trying to fill it; the main novelty is the complexity of the linked resources in the combined resource, that is, the hierarchy plus the data in the underlining ontology. We believe that both the actual creation and the use for textual annotation in the future can benefit from this complex information, which can guide annotators' understanding of the concepts in the hierarchy. In addition, this approach combines the "bottom-up view ", built within the SynSemClass ontology itself, with the top-down view when starting with the top-level ontology, as most current approaches do.

We are aware of the fact that such a hierarchy cannot be fully built in a simple tree-shaped form. However, we do believe that the core of such hierarchical set of relations can, despite the fact that the individual languages might sometimes have incompatible tendencies in expressing hyperonymy and

[3]One can imagine a better way of pre-annotation, namely the use of current state-of-the-art technology, such as LLMs. However, even that assumes at least some data to be fully annotated manually, if only for the development and evaluation of such tool(s).

[4]When going from SynSemClass to WordNet to hyperonym synset in WordNet and back to SynSemClass, there have been over 3 suggested possible generalization classes on average. For example, for the SynSemClass *propose*, there are five different top-level aligned WordNet semantic classes (communication, social, possession and cognition), with 7 different synsets suggested as direct hyperonyms.

hyponymy. The fact that the underlying ontology stress concepts rather than lexical (syn)sets should help, since all the context (links to entries in the other resources, including WordNet), syntactic and semantic properties present at each entry, can be taken into account when considering the often conflicting grounds for determining the hierarchical structure.

At the same time, if this hierarchy exists, SynSemClass could also serve other purposes, such as enabling a comparison to other lexical resources and their hierarchies thanks to the rich linking scheme within SynSemClass, linguistic and cognitive research on generalization and specialization, or language acquisition.

3 Related Work

The work described here relates closely to other lexical resources that include information about hierarchical relations among concepts, for example, WordNet (Fellbaum, 1998) or FrameNet (Baker et al., 1998).

The Princeton WordNet (PWN) is a large lexical database of English that groups words into interrelated sets of cognitive synonyms (synsets) and that is organized as a network where the synsets' relations are encoded through a super-ordinate relation (hyponymy/hyperonymy). PWN represents a concept as lists of the word senses that can be used to express the concept. Verb synsets also add the relation of troponymy in such a way that the nodes at the bottom of the tree denote specifications of a more general event (Fellbaum, 2005; Miller and Fellbaum, 2007). The multilingual EuroWordNet (Pianta et al., 2002; Ellman, 2003) introduced some major design changes, among them new semantic and lexical relations that may be specific to individual languages [5] (Vossen, 1998; Vossen et al., 1998; Tufis et al., 2004). In addition, a framework for a 'Global Grid' was established that defines a universal core lexical inventory and establishes guidelines for its cross-linguistic encoding (Fellbaum and Vossen, 2007).

FrameNet, a resource containing information about lexical and predicate argument semantics, is based on the principles of frame semantics, where frames (conceptual structures that describe different types of entities, situations and events) are organized into a network where more abstract frames (*super-frames*) are connected to less abstract frames (*sub-frames*). These relations include, but are not limited to: *Inheritance* - the relationship between a parent frame and its child frame; *Using* (or weak-inheritance) - the relation between a frame that is related in some way to a super-frame; *Subframe* - a relation between a complex frame that denotes a sequence of states and transitions and the individual frames that separately denote each state; and *Perspective* - the relation between frames denoting different perspectives over a neutral frame and the neutral frame itself. In addition to the hierarchy of frames arranged according to the frame-to-frame relations, FrameNet works with the second hierarchy, i.e., hierarchy of semantic types, which indicates the basic types of fillers of frame elements, marks non-lexical types of frames, and records important semantic differences between lexical units belonging to the same frame (Materna, 2014 [cit. 2024-11-14]).

Various proposals have been put forward to align the information contained in both resources aiming at the development of an ontology of events. BabelNet (Navigli and Ponzetto, 2010) is a prime example. For Slavic languages specifically, (Leseva and Stoyanova, 2022) set the foundations for the development of an ontology of stative predicates in Bulgarian and Russian by elaborating on FrameNet hierarchical classification through its mapping with WordNet.

Another example of an ontology that integrates information from lexical resources (with upper-level ontologies such as DOLCE (Borgo et al., 2022)) is The Rich Event Ontology (Brown et al., 2017), which provides a structure of event concepts connected at various levels of specificity and establishes relations between events and between events and the key objects and participants involved.

There are other ontologies, but as far as we know, there is no multilingual synonyms ontology with a hierarchical scheme built bottom-up. i.e., as in SynSemClass, with so much empirical material available for determining the hierarchical relations with much higher certainty (than WordNet(s)' only lexically-based synsets). We also have to stress here that the multilingual wordnets are developed top-down working with a shared set of so-called Base Concepts and an equivalence relation for each synset to the closest concept from an Inter-Lingual-Index. The general approach of EuroWordNet is to build wordnets mainly from existing resources (Vossen et al., 1998; Vossen, 2002). Compatibil-

[5]Currently, WNs exist for some 40 languages, see http://www.globalwordnet.org

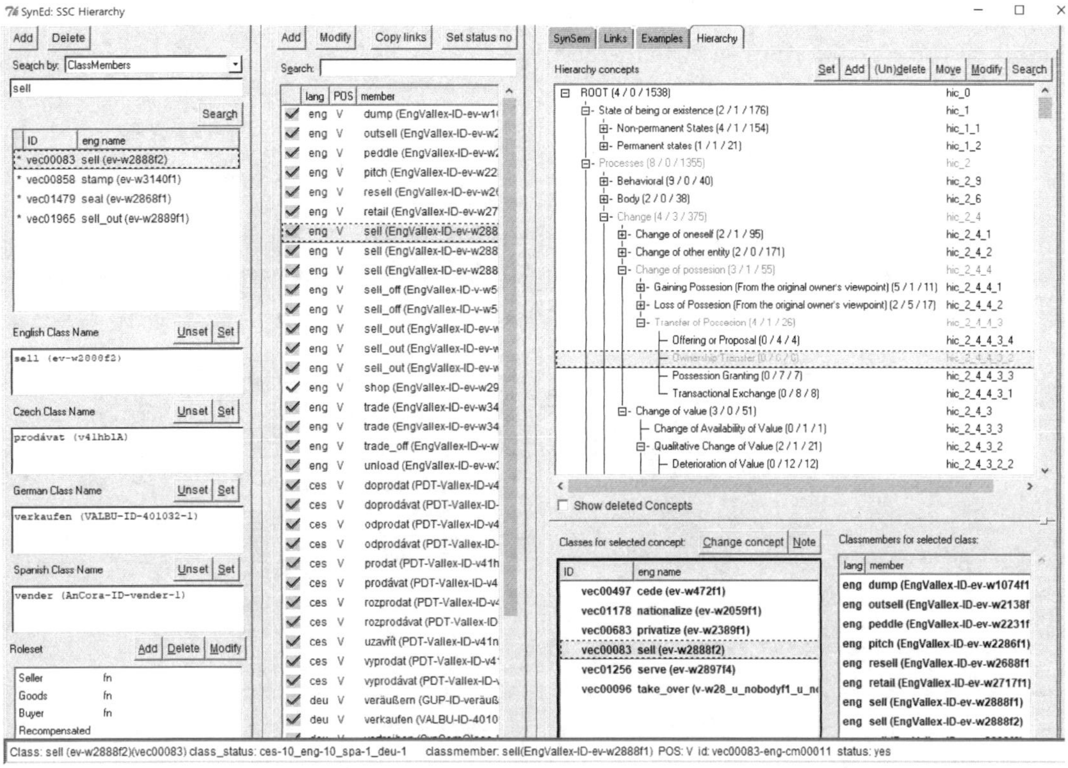

Figure 2: The hierarchical concept Ownership Transfer (abbreviated; shown in the editing tool)

ity between the EuroWordNet languages and the Inter-Lingual-Index with respect to lexical coverage and relations depends on which of the two basic methods for building the European wordnets was followed: either English synsets are translated into the target language and the relations are copied (Expand method), or synsets are created for the target language, interlinked with the PWN relations, and subsequently translated into English for mapping with ILI entries (Fellbaum and Vossen, 2007). For the discussion of near-synonymy, there are both theoretical lexicographic works such as (Lyons, 1968), and also the computationally-oriented view by (Edmonds and Hirst, 2002).

4 The Hierarchy

We have conceived the hierarchy as a single, rooted tree, in which ideally the SynSemClass classes are assigned 1:1 to its nodes and where the edges represent the *more general* or *more specialised* conceptual relation between the parent and the child nodes in the tree.

However, after testing a few examples, it was clear that this is not feasible to do directly, for the same reasons that the direct use of SynSemClass with its flat, set-like structure would be inefficient to use for annotation. Looking at any concept, the question that was not easy to answer was "which concept might be the next more general one among all the other SynSemClass concepts?" - without going through every other class. In Sect. 5 we explain how we proceeded, using some preprocessing to extract some candidates for these relations.

As a working solution, we have decided to scrap the 1:1 requirement of linking the hierarchy nodes to SynSemClass classes for now and temporarily allow both empty nodes in the hierarchy, as well as nodes with multiple SynSemClass classes assigned to them, to be split later. However, each SynSemClass class is (perhaps also temporarily) linked to *only one node* in the hierarchy to maintain at least some structure in it. We believe that this is not limiting at this time.

Having done so, we have to distinguish the original SynSemClass concepts as represented by the set of class members (verbs or nouns) in its flat structure (in this paper, we will call them **syc**s), and the nodes in the hierarchy tree (**hic**s, for hierarchical concepts).

Each **hic** (node in the hierarchy tree) is characterized by a series of features, or descriptors, as illustrated by the example in Fig. 2, for the **hic Ownership Transfer**:

- **definition**: *Refers to the complete shift of ownership or control from one party to another*,
- **mapping (linking) between the hic and syc(s)**: vec00497 (*cede*), vec01178 (*nationalize*), vec00683 (*privatize*), vec00083 (*sell* - highlited), vec01256 (*serve*), and vec00096 (*take_over*),
- **roleset(s)** coming from the **syc**(s) mapped: *Seller*, *Goods*, *Buyer* and *Recompensated*,[6]
- **class members from the classes mapped**, e.g., *dump, outsell, peddle, pitch, resell, retail, sell*,
- **example sentences** coming from **syc**(s) again (invisible on Fig. 2),
- its **parent** (more general concept) **hic** node: *Transfer of Possession*.

All of these parts constitute a complex description of **hic** (hierarchical concept). They serve (similarly to the SynSemClass class features and descriptors, as we see them) primarily for human understanding of the concepts.

We have created the base hierarchical structure (Sect. 5). To verify the approach fully, we have linked each class in the ontology (illustrated, e.g., in Fig. 1) to a node in the hierarchy.

The top level of the hierarchy is shown schematically in Fig. 3;[7] for the **hic** *Possession or Ownership*, we are showing the full expanded path (internal nodes in light blue) to this **hic** (which is a leaf in the hierarchy tree, shown in light green).

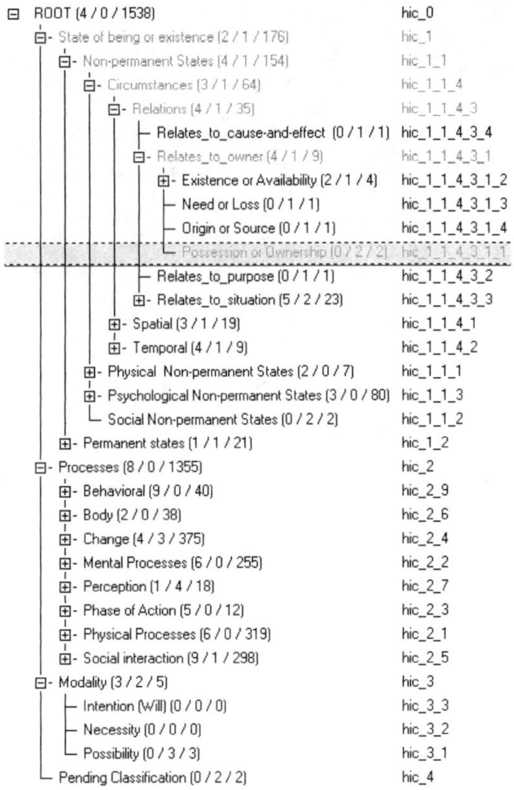

Figure 3: The tree w/path to Possession or Ownership

5 Building the Hierarchy

5.1 Issues of Full Hierarchization

The main identified problem is the very definition of the relation between **hic** s. At the beginning, we have intentionally abstained from using some predefined relation type(s), such as those from the Linguistic Linked Open Data (LLOD),[8] other Semantic Web ontologies, or even from the existing resources such as WordNet's hyponymy/hyperonymy (even though our idea was closest to this). Instead, we have been testing various node splits as we went along, refining the top-level hierarchy of essentially states vs. processes down the (sub)tree(s) being split from the root to the (current set of) leaves. We still see this relation as closest to "specialization" (of a higher-level concept in the hierarchy tree towards the lower-level one); the opposite direction would then be called "generalization."

Building such a hierarchical tree seems to be as difficult as categorization of things in the real world. The backbone of our scheme is the classification of real-world event types as states and processes. Since the resource used for our hierarchy, the SynSemClass ontology, represents the **sycs** concepts by a single class with a number of

[6]So far one **hic** may contain more rolesets, but ideally there should be only one, for the only class that should remain linked to (sec. 7).

[7]We are aware of the fact that *Modality* and *Phase of Action* (under *Processes*) are concepts that do not correspond to any **syc** "by definition" since SynSemClass does not cover non-content concepts. However, in our opinion, it is necessary to include them for full compositionality in the textual annotation, similarly to *abstract predicates* in UMR (Bonn et al., 2024).

[8]A sketch of possible conversion of SynSemClass into the relations and schemas available in LLOD is provided in (Uresova et al., 2020), but no hierarchical relations are included in that schema(s).

possible realizations (class members, i.e., words) with a unified roleset containing the situational participants (semantic roles), we found it convenient to use this feature as a starting point to build the initial classification.

Some **syc**s seemed to be classified and grouped under one **hic** quite easily due to the same set of roles. For example, under the **hic** *Communication* initially included all the **syc**s with *Speaker, Audience_Addressee, Information*. However, sorting then all the classes that fell within *Communication* was no longer easy. The appropriate criteria for further splitting and sorting have to be found. Questions arose not only regarding which meaning is more general and more specific but also regarding the subtle semantic distinctions that could be used to categorize (split) the given **hic** in a more subtle way, such as in *Transfer message*, *Discussion*, *Request*, *Communicated relation*, and *Mode of Speaking*.

Analyzing the relationships between individual **syc**s was difficult mainly because it posed a challenge:

- to specify what the (more general) parent **hic** is, especially when no suitable **syc** for the parent node has been found,
- to determine which sorting criteria are the most relevant,
- to determine which feature (criterion) of the concept is preferred when splitting a **hic** with a number of **syc**s assigned to it,
- to specify how to distinguish the specialized semantic relations within one **hic** due to the different views on the distinctive criteria of meaning,
- to be consistent in applying the criteria.

Because some **hic**s overlap in certain features, distinguishing and classifying their meanings is particularly complex. For example, some might argue that **hic** *Change* and **hic** *Transformative* are much alike; however, we believe that this splitting has its merits, and they thus belong to different second-level concepts.

For example, verbs of motion might be divided into different sets of **hic**s according to the criteria used. One might prefer to use the criterion of *way of the movement* and distinguish the concepts of going vs. the concept of driving, but it is also possible to prefer the criterion of *speed* and classify the concept of running vs. the concept of crawling, or the criterion of *who does the motion*: *Self-Motion* (movement driven by the entity itself) vs. *Transport* (movement driven by external factors). In all cases, eventually we will be able to arrive at a full tree and employ all the criteria mentioned above, but the trees will differ substantially. The general criterion of explicability, simplicity, and linguistic adequacy should then be applied to determine the order of application of the criteria (i.e., at which level, which criterion shall be used).

Another example is whether an additional role in the Roleset can be used as criterion for a split into more specialised **hic**s (such as in the case of a general class "change" (roleset: (thing, person) `Changing`) vs. the more specialised class "overcome" (roleset: `Protagonist`, `Hindrance`)), or the opposite, when a role from the Roleset becomes "built-in" into the more specialised class (such as in the case of the general class describing transport with roles `Transporter`, `Transported`, `Area_1`, `Area_2`, with a more specialised sub-**hic** *Setup Placement* (with class "plant" with its roleset `Transporter`, `Transported`, `Place`), which removes `Area_1` given that it is irrelevant to plant something. Another example of specialization is positivity vs. negativity: Loss vs. Gain, Improvement vs. Deterioration; granularity of cause (concepts of Contamination or Pollution vs. Water- and Liquid-induced damage), and several others.

These splitting criteria might differ between higher-level concepts. For example, while the difference in actor-caused (or actor-less) movement can prevail for the concepts of motion, for mental concepts, the "manner" criterion might prevail.

5.2 Tools Used

We have used an open source editor that was used in version 5.0 of SynSemClass[9] by adapting it - adding one additional tab to its editing canvas which shows the hierarchy as created so far and allows for assigning a **syc** to any **hic** in the hierarchy. It also allows for editing the **hic** tree by moving nodes around, adding new ones, and deleting them; definitions can also be added to its nodes.

To aid in creating the **hic** nodes of the hierarchy tree, we have also created a preprocessing tool that suggests **syc**s (i.e., the original SynSemClass

[9]https://github.com/fucikova/SynSemClass_multi/tree/main/Editor

classes) that appear to be semantically close enough to form either a subtree in the hierarchy, or the cluster could be used when considering a new general concept unifying them. The tool uses the sharing of semantic roles assigned to the classes and other hints to propose the clustering. Its results are collected in a table to aid in the effort to form the **hic** tree as a side resource.

6 Current State

All the classes (**syc**s) from SynSemClass have been assigned to the tree nodes of the conceptual hierarchy tree nodes (**hic**s). There are 1538 **syc**s in the version of SynSemClass that we have been working with. The current hierarchy has 663 nodes; this means that there are around 2.5 classes (**syc**s) per node in the hierarchy. This is still far from the goal of having (close to) 1:1 correspondence between **hic**s and **syc**s, but a larger number of nodes than many existing hierarchies currently have. In this section, we present some quantitative indicators.

6.1 Statistics and Description of the Hierarchy

The top level of the hierarchy (just under its root) has three branches[10] (Fig. 3):

1. States of Being or Existence: 139 nodes in total; they describe "static" concepts (existence, position, qualities, possession, mental states, etc.), linked from 176 **syc**s in total.

2. Processes: 518 nodes in total, describing processes (as opposed to states, as in the previous branch). There are 1355 **syc**s linked to these **hic**s, clearly indicating that there are still many split candidates in this branch, however typically with only 2-3 classes in them;

3. Modals: 4 nodes in total, describing modalities that are to be used as full concepts in textual annotation; given the SynSemClass principles, there are no classes that can be assigned to such "modality" concepts, except for five (e.g., *have a choice* in the "possibility" sense). This set of **hic**s will in fact need more work, since the **syc**s required to be linked to might not fit the philosophy of concepts in SynSemClass (which excludes auxiliaries, modals, copulas, etc.). Nevertheless, we believe that we need to have independent concepts for modals, phase-denoting and some "light" verbs, given the meaning they convey, which is then combined with the "content" eventives when annotating running texts.

A total of 35 conceptual nodes in the hierarchy tree have no class assigned to them yet, but they were introduced to keep the hierarchy tree fully connected (and might be populated later).

6.2 Structure of the Hierarchy Files

The current version of SynSemClass is 5.5;[11] For complete reproducibility, we also include the version used for the work that led to this paper.[12] After unpacking, there is

- File `hierarchy-tabular.xlsx`: tabular form of the hierarchy tree, one **hic** per row, sorted by the ID (column C). The hierarchy node name is in column A. In column B, the following statistics on **hic** are posted: number of sub-**hic**s, number of classes in **hic** and number of all classes in **hic** s within the subtree rooted in the current one.

- The XML files that represent both the SynSemClass version used and the proper hierarchy (`synsemclass_hierarchy.xml`).

7 Conclusions and Future Work

We have created a novel hierarchy of eventive concepts linked to an existing event-type ontology, SynSemClass. Each its class is linked to one node in the hierarchy. The hierarchy is a fully connected rooted tree, currently containing 663 **hic**s, with about 2.5 SynSemClass classes linked to each **hic**.

We have identified problems that arise while building such a hierarchy: defining each concept clearly, finding criteria for splitting nodes into its child nodes when multiple possibilities exist, and finding a set of SynSemClass classes representing each concept (node in the hierarchy) efficiently.

Perhaps not surprisingly, the existing resources do not consistently define its entries, as demonstrated by the multiplicity and fuzziness of relation mappings between these resources (using SynSemClass links). The hierarchies in these resources also differ substantially (FrameNet's vs. WordNet's hyponymy/hyperonymy relation vs. the shallow VerbNet hierarchy).

[10] Pending Classification is meant for undecided classes yet, so this branch is an artificial node only.

[11] `http://hdl.handle.net/11234/1-5915`

[12] `https://github.com/ufal/SynSemClassHierarchy/tree/main/Lexicons-LAW-XIX-2025`

No. of judgments	Both agree	1 annotator only (avg.)	IA agreement
50	20	26.5	28
100%	40%	53%	56%

Table 1: Gold data and inter-annotator agreement for assigning a class to the hierarchy tree

All of this poses a challenge for the refinement of the hierarchy over SynSemClass as we have developed it so far, in several respects:

- the hierarchy nodes which map to multiple SynSemClass classes must be split, after suitable criteria are identified for where to do the split, especially for nodes with a large number of classes;[13]
- the child nodes of **hic**s with no **syc** currently mapped to must be investigated in detail, to find out if there is a mistake in the composition of the **syc**(s), and if a split of the **syc** could be done to create such a (more general) concept that would be suitable to link from the currently empty **hic**s (which entails modifying SynSemClass);
- test the hierarchy in "real life", i.e., to use it for annotation of text in such a setup that will make clear in which way, and what proportion of running real text can be done with SynSemClass alone and what need the hierarchy;
- consider adding semantic features (such as animateness, abstractness) to the nodes of the hierarchy, or even to the SynSemClass entries themselves, to represent distinctions which did not make it into the hierarchy itself as a criteria for specialization.

We have performed a pilot annotation comparison (annotator agreement experiments) for the (re)assignment of 50 classes to the current hierarchy tree (Table 1). Two annotators independently assigned classes to the hierarchy, and the result was compared to the gold annotation and also between them.

The numbers indicate low accuracy against the data when annotators also agree, and only slightly above 50 percent accuracy for each of the two independently, and between themselves. This is to be expected since it is a very hard task, both mentally and from the statistical point of view (the random uniform baseline is 1/663). But it is an approximation of the text annotation task, since the SynSemClass classes (**syc**s) to be assigned to the hierarchy nodes (**hic**s) correspond, by and large, to the verb senses that text annotators will have to determine during such annotation, which will also serve as the relevant test and evaluation experiment.

The current full version of the hierarchy is published in a new version of SynSemClass (v5.5).[11] Nevertheless, there is still work to do, such as split some of the leaves of the hierarchy tree, populate some nodes with new links to the SynSemClass classes, and refine the concepts definitions.

8 Limitations

As is usual with any introspective approach in semantics in general and ontology work in particular, albeit supported by multiple lexical and corpus resources, the major limitation is our ability to understand the distinctions in the concepts we try to hierarchize and distinguish.

It might be the case that the fully connected tree constraint that we have chosen at the start is eventually untenable.[14] However, unless we specify the full hierarchy, no conclusions can be drawn.

Another limitation is that SynSemClass coverage needs to be improved (Fučíková et al., 2024).[15] In addition, the work on some abstract concepts, like modalities and concepts represented often by phase-denoting and some light verbs (i.e., concepts that take other eventives as arguments), has not been finished. Some SynSemClass classes would need to be rearranged to populate some internal **hic**s.

Finally, we acknowledge that this is work in progress and that additional work on splitting the remaining concepts in the hierarchy that are linked to more than one SynSemClass entry is needed. However, having the 663 current **hic**s assigned and structured in the hierarchy was, as we believe, the hardest part, both on the top levels and providing enough problems to solve at the more detailed levels down the hierarchy. The rest should go much more smoothly, despite the criteria selection problem discussed in Sect. 5.1.

[13]Ongoing work in progress: 217 additional hierarchy nodes are under evaluation and verification, and will appear in the final version.

[14]There are both cognitive and technical arguments in the literature; even WordNet does not follow this restriction, at least technically.

[15]It has not been used for annotation yet, except for small experiments (Urešová et al., 2019).

Acknowledgements

The work described here has been started while the authors have been supported by the Grant Agency of the Czech Republic under the EXPRO program as project “LUSyD” (grant No. GX20-16819X), and finished under the MŠMT international cooperation project "UMR" (grant No. LUAUS23283) and the LINDAT/CLARIAH-CZ Research Infrastructure (projects LM2018101 and LM2023062, supported by the Ministry of Education, Youth and Sports of the Czech Republic). The authors would like to thank all the annotators of the SynSemClass ontology and especially the ones who helped with the pilot hierarchy inter-annotator agreement experiment, Anna Staňková and Tomáš Razím. We would also like to thank the reviewers for their insightful comments.

References

Collin F. Baker, Charles J. Fillmore, and John B. Lowe. 1998. The Berkeley FrameNet Project. In *Proceedings of the 36th Annual Meeting of the Association for Computational Linguistics and 17th International Conference on Computational Linguistics - Volume 1*, ACL '98, pages 86–90, Stroudsburg, PA, USA. Association for Computational Linguistics.

Julia Bonn, Matthew J. Buchholz, Jayeol Chun, Andrew Cowell, William Croft, Lukas Denk, Sijia Ge, Jan Hajič, Kenneth Lai, James H. Martin, Skatje Myers, Alexis Palmer, Martha Palmer, Claire Benet Post, James Pustejovsky, Kristine Stenzel, Haibo Sun, Zdeňka Urešová, Rosa Vallejos, and 4 others. 2024. Building a broad infrastructure for uniform meaning representations. In *Proceedings of the 2024 Joint International Conference on Computational Linguistics, Language Resources and Evaluation (LREC-COLING 2024)*, pages 2537–2547, Torino, Italia. ELRA and ICCL.

Stefano Borgo, Roberta Ferrario, Aldo Gangemi, Nicola Guarino, Claudio Masolo, Daniele Porello, Emilio M. Sanfilippo, and Laure Vieu. 2022. DOLCE: A descriptive ontology for linguistic and cognitive engineering1. *Applied Ontology*, 17(1):45–69.

Susan Brown, Claire Bonial, Leo Obrst, and Martha Palmer. 2017. The Rich Event Ontology. In *Proceedings of the Events and Stories in the News Workshop*, pages 87–97, Vancouver, Canada. Association for Computational Linguistics.

Philip Edmonds and Graeme Hirst. 2002. Near-synonymy and lexical choice. *Computational Linguistics*, 28(2):105–144.

Jeremy Ellman. 2003. Eurowordnet: A multilingual database with lexical semantic networks: Edited by Piek Vossen. Kluwer Academic Publishers. 1998. isbn 0792352955, 179 pages. *Natural Language Engineering*, 9:427 – 430.

Christiane Fellbaum. 1998. *WordNet: An Electronic Lexical Database*. Language, Speech, and Communication. MIT Press, Cambridge, MA. 423 pp.

Christiane Fellbaum. 2005. Wordnet and wordnets. In Keith Brown, editor, *Encyclopedia of Language and Linguistics*, pages 2–665. Elsevier.

Christiane Fellbaum and Piek Vossen. 2007. Connecting the universal to the specific: Towards the global grid. In *Intercultural Collaboration*, pages 1–16, Berlin, Heidelberg. Springer Berlin Heidelberg.

Charles J. Fillmore, Ch. R. Johnson, and M. R. L.Petruck. 2003. Background to FrameNet: FrameNet and Frame Semantics. *International Journal of Lexicography*, 16(3):235–250.

Eva Fučíková, Cristina Fernández-Alcaina, Jan Hajič, and Zdeňka Urešová. 2024. Textual coverage of eventive entries in lexical semantic resources. In *Proceedings of the 2024 Joint International Conference on Computational Linguistics, Language Resources and Evaluation (LREC-COLING 2024)*, pages 15835–15841, Torino, Italy. European Language Resources Association.

Svetlozara Leseva and Ivelina Stoyanova. 2022. *Stative verbs: Conceptual structure, hierarchy, systematic relations*, pages 68–114. Prof. Marin Drinov Publishing House of BAS.

J. Lyons. 1968. *Introduction to Theoretical Linguistics*. Cambridge University Press.

Jiří Materna. 2014 [cit. 2024-11-14]. *Probabilistic Semantic Frames [online]*. Doctoral theses, dissertations, Masaryk University, Faculty of Informatics, Brno. SUPERVISOR : Karel Pala.

George Miller and Christiane Fellbaum. 2007. Wordnet then and now. *Language Resources and Evaluation*, 41:209–214.

George A. Miller. 1995. WordNet: A Lexical Database for English. *Commun. ACM*, 38(11):39–41.

Roberto Navigli and Simone Paolo Ponzetto. 2010. BabelNet: Building a very large multilingual semantic network. In *Proceedings of the 48th Annual Meeting of the Association for Computational Linguistics*, pages 216–225, Uppsala, Sweden. Association for Computational Linguistics.

Emanuele Pianta, Luisa Bentivogli, and Christian Girardi. 2002. Multiwordnet: developing an aligned multilingual database. In *Proceedings of the First International Conference on Global WordNet*.

Karin Kipper Schuler. 2006. *VerbNet: A Broad-Coverage, Comprehensive Verb Lexicon*. Ph.D. thesis, University of Pennsylvania.

Dan Tufis, Dan Cristea, and Sofia Stamou. 2004. Balka-Net: Aims, methods, results and perspectives – A general overview. *Romanian Journal of Information Science and Technology Special Issue*, 7:9–43.

Zdeňka Urešová, Cristina Fernández-Alcaina, Eva Fučíková, and Jan Hajič. 2023a. SynSemClass Czech and English Annotation Guidelines. Technical Report 73, UFAL MFF UK.

Zdeňka Urešová, Eva Fučíková, Cristina Fernández Alcaina, and Jan Hajič. 2023b. Synsemclass 5.0. available from the lindat/clariah-cz digital repository. http://hdl.handle.net/11234/1-5230.

Zdeňka Urešová, Eva Fučíková, Eva Hajičová, and Jan Hajič. 2019. Parallel Dependency Treebank Annotated with Interlinked Verbal Synonym Classes and Roles. In *Proceedings of the 18th International Workshop on Treebanks and Linguistic Theories (TLT, SyntaxFest 2019)*, pages 38–50, Paris, France. Université Paris Sorbonne Nouvelle, Association for Computational Linguistics.

Zdenka Uresova, Eva Fucikova, Eva Hajicova, and Jan Hajic. 2020. SynSemClass linked lexicon: Mapping synonymy between languages. In *Proceedings of the 2020 Globalex Workshop on Linked Lexicography*, pages 10–19, Marseille, France. European Language Resources Association.

Piek Vossen, editor. 1998. *EuroWordNet: a multilingual database with lexical semantic networks for European Languages.* Kluwer.

Piek Vossen. 2002. Wordnet, EuroWordNet and Global WordNet. *Revue Française de Linguistique Appliquée*, 7.

Piek Vossen, Laura Bloksma, and Horacio Rodriquez. 1998. The EuroWordNet Base Concepts and Top Ontology. Workingpaper, Vrije Universiteit.

Visual Representations of Temporal Relations between Events and Time Expressions in News Stories

Evelin Amorim[1,2], **António Leal**[4,3], **Nana Yu**[3], **Purificação Silvano**[3,1], **Alípio Jorge**[2,1]
[1]INESC TEC / Porto, Portugal
[2]University of Porto, FCUP / Porto, Portugal
[3]University of Porto, CLUP / Porto, Portugal
[4]University of Macau / Macau, China
evelin.f.amorim@inesctec.pt, antonioleal@um.edu.mo,
robertananayu@hotmail.com, msilvano@letras.up.pt, amjorge@fc.up.pt

Abstract

High-quality annotation is essential for the effective predictions of machine learning models. When annotations are dense, achieving accurate human labeling can be challenging since the most used annotation tools present an overloaded visualization of labels. Thus, we present Vitra (Visualizer of temporal relation annotations), a tool designed for viewing annotations made in corpora, specifically focusing on the temporal relations between events and temporal expressions. This tool aims to fill a gap in the available resources for this purpose. Our focus is on narrative text, which is a rich source for these types of elements. Vitra was developed to increase the human capacity for detecting annotation errors and uncover relations between narrative components or issues about the annotation scheme. To show how this can be done, we present an analysis of a subset of the Text2Story Lusa corpus, a dataset of Portuguese news stories. Such analysis focuses on the linguistic properties of the events and temporal expressions that occur in the annotated texts, in particular, of short news. We highlight that annotation is an iterative process that involves multiple rounds of revision, and our tool facilitates this process by helping users detect inconsistencies and improve the annotation scheme, thus offering added value to the community.

1 Introduction

Events and time expressions are essential elements in news stories. They both contribute to the narrative structure by linking actions, facts, and developments to specific points in time, helping readers grasp the sequence, causality, and context of events. Additionally, the relationship between events and time expressions plays a crucial role in establishing a timeline of occurrences.

Annotating events and time expressions and their relations is a well-known task in NLP (Doddington et al., 2004; Cassidy et al., 2014; Caselli and Vossen, 2017; Wang et al., 2022; Olsen et al., 2024). Therefore, several formats have been proposed to visually present this information to a lay target audience (Chen et al., 2023), like timelines (Nguyen et al., 2016; dos Santos Fernandes, 2023), infographics (Chen et al., 2019), and data comic (Zhao et al., 2021). However, these representations often lack the precision and focus needed for expert audiences, whose primary goal is to analyze data and inspect annotations in detail. Some visual representations, such as the Message Sequence Chart (MSC), have been used for this purpose (Hingmire et al., 2020; Amorim et al., 2021). However, these approaches do not specifically address the representation of events combined with time expressions in a visually intuitive manner, which would help in identifying annotation mistakes. This gap highlights the need for specialized visual tools that cater to the demands of expert users in tasks like annotation analysis and narrative inspection.

To address this gap, this work explores the following research questions:

RQ1 Which insights can be derived from visualizing the events and temporal expressions, and their temporal relationships?

RQ2 How effective is isolating time expressions and their related events, and arranging them on a timeline, for facilitating annotation inspection by expert audiences?

The first research question is whether the proposed visualization is suitable for representing temporal relations between events and time expressions in narratives. The usefulness of the visualization will be evaluated according to its capability to detect annotation errors and uncover relations between key narrative components or issues about the annotation scheme. Thus, we will characterize the Text2Story Lusa corpus, which is a narrative dataset manually annotated with Portuguese news

Proceedings of the 19th Linguistic Annotation Workshop (LAW-XIX-2025), pages 250–263

stories (Silvano et al., 2023b; Nunes et al., 2024) using Vitra (Visualizer of temporal relation annotations), our proposed visualization. The corpus was annotated using the Brat annotation tool (Stenetorp et al., 2012), and then, for this investigation, we converted the Brat standoff file format to the JSON format, which is a more general format. To this conversion, we employ the text2story package (Amorim et al., 2024), which also offers conversions from other types of annotation files. The second research question concerns its usability for the annotator. We elaborated on a questionnaire with six claims that intend to evaluate the overall design of the Vitra tool. Linguist experts with annotation experience were called to answer the proposed questionnaire.

By answering these research questions, the contributions of this work are the following:

1. Vitra, an open tool for visualization of events and time expressions to aid the iterative annotation process[1];

2. An analysis of how an effective visualization tool can aid in detecting annotation mistakes and improving multi-layer annotation schema quality;

3. A deep characterization of temporal relations between time expressions and events in a narrative dataset.

Our goal is to advance research on multi-layer dataset annotation by improving annotation quality through the integration of a visualization tool. Additionally, we aim to provide insights into the design and application of the proposed annotation scheme.

2 Related Work

The two fundamental concepts of our work are temporal relations between events and time expressions and their visualizations. Both have been extensively studied in recent years. Therefore, we divide this section into two parts to discuss research related to each topic. The first part discusses similar works about temporal relations. The second part is the visualization of temporal information.

[1]The code is available in `https://github.com/evelinamorim/sentencevisual`; a demo can be found in `https://nabu.dcc.fc.up.pt/annotationinspector/`

2.1 Temporal Relations

Several linguists, including Bell (1997) and Schokkenbroek (1999), argue that the narratives conveyed in news articles are inherently dependent on the temporal arrangement of events. The reconstruction of a narrative's timeline can be achieved through implicit temporal references, such as verb tense, or explicit temporal markers, namely time expressions (Filatova and Hovy, 2001). Time expressions are, in fact, essential for situating events within a temporal framework and determining the structural organization of a text. Moreover, they also play a crucial role in numerous downstream tasks in Natural Language Processing (NLP) and Information Retrieval (IR), such as timeline summarization, named entity recognition, temporal information retrieval, and question answering (Jatowt et al., 2022). Advancing these tasks, particularly the identification and extraction of time expressions (Lange et al., 2020; Sousa et al., 2023; Zhong and Cambria, 2023; Zhong et al., 2024), relies on the availability of annotated data and well-defined annotation schemes.

Various studies have proposed different annotation frameworks to represent not only the temporal information of events but also the characteristics of time expressions. One of the most significant contributions in this domain is the work of Pustejovsky et al. (2003), who introduced TimeML as an annotation specification designed to systematically encode time expressions, events, and their temporal relations in natural language texts (ISO-24617-1, 2012). In this framework, time expressions (labeled TIMEX3) are categorized into dates, times, durations, and sets, while the morphosyntactic and semantic properties of events (EVENT) are captured through attributes related to class, type, tense, part of speech, among others, and the temporal relations (TLINK) are represented by values like *before, after, during*, among others.

TimeML provides a robust methodology for encoding temporal information across various linguistic contexts, facilitating its application beyond English to languages such as Italian, Korean, Chinese, French, and Portuguese (Costa and Branco, 2012; Bittar, 2009; Silvano et al., 2024). Language-specific adaptations, including It-TimeML (Caselli et al., 2011) and KTimeML (Im et al., 2009), have been developed to address language-specific phenomena not adequately covered by ISO-TimeML. Based on these annotation frameworks, several annotated datasets have been created, encompassing a wide range of textual genres. Some examples include TimeBankPT—an adaptation of the English TimeBank — a Portuguese Annotated Dataset of news stories (Silvano et al., 2023b), and i2b2 (Sun et al., 2013), a dataset annotated with events and time expressions extracted from clinical narratives. Additionally, the NewsReader MEANTIME (Multilingual Event ANd TIME) corpus is a semantically annotated resource consisting of 480 news articles in English, Italian, Spanish, and Dutch (Minard et al., 2016). The dissemination of these annotated datasets has been facilitated through shared tasks, such as the TempEval series (Pustejovsky and Verhagen, 2009) and Clinical TempEval (Bethard et al., 2016), which target the extraction of three key tags: TIMEX3, EVENT, and TLINK.

Despite the availability of datasets containing annotated time expressions and their corresponding temporal relations with events, visualizing this information can often be challenging. In this regard, visualization tools play a critical role in facilitating linguistic analysis and validating annotation quality, thereby enhancing the interpretability and usability of annotated temporal data. Regarding the temporal analysis of news stories using visualization, Silvano et al. (2023a) and Silvano et al. (2024) analyzed temporal relations between events using a visualization called Bubble visualization. Our work aims to study the temporal relations of temporal expressions and their connected events, which means an analysis of a different annotation layer.

2.2 Visualizations of Temporal Information

Arranging temporal information in a visual timeline is a natural form of organizing events, time expression, and participants. For example, Gonçalves et al. (2023) presents a platform that provides a user's query search for related news stories in a database. The information is presented in a timeline of news stories, in temporal groups, among other representations for non-temporal information. Ye et al. (2024) uses the GPT model to annotate text, and then the main events are presented in a timeline. The authors tested the proposed approach using two use cases, one with a fictional book and another with a movie script. Most users who experimented with it found the tool easy to use and helpful in understanding the narratives.

Tang et al. (2018) proposed iStoryline, a tool that was built to generate hand-drawn narrative storylines. The input is a structured file with the entities and their relations in a time order. Then, a timeline of the story is built in a hand-drawn style. The authors also based the tool on extensive research of the relevant visual elements that design experts commonly employ when creating timelines of stories. Tang et al. (2020) also proposed a timeline tool, PlotThread, which generates timelines of stories and enhances them through reinforcement learning. In this platform, the user defines a storyline, and then an AI agent proposes alternatives to the user's storyline. Consequently, the user can improve the visualization. In the proposed visualization, the timelines of the participants can be inspected along with some remarkable events in which they participated. Wang et al. (2024) proposed another timeline visualization called E^2Storyline that presents entities and their relations using a novel matrix color system designed to convey relationships between entities in narratives. The authors tested the visualization with human users who reported easily identifying information from stories and understanding the relations between entities. None of these tools, however, focuses on the analysis of annotation and linguistic patterns. Usually, their goal is to improve the experience of narrative understanding for a lay user or, at most, provide a high-level analysis of narrative patterns for an expert.

Lai (2023), differently, focused on a deep analysis of annotations. The author proposed an R package to process annotated data from Rezonator, an annotation tool for discourse and grammar, and conversation analysis, among others. The package builds cliques of causal structures, Gants charts, co-reference chains, and many more visual devices to allow comparisons between participants in a dialog. Our visualization, nonetheless, is designed to portray the relations of temporal information and their connected events. This type of annotation can occur in different domains of texts, and as far as we know, this type of tool has not yet been proposed. Thus, our tool intends to fill this gap.

3 Methodology

Our methodology comprises two main steps that we detail below: data analysis of a subset from a Portuguese news stories dataset and the visual tool.

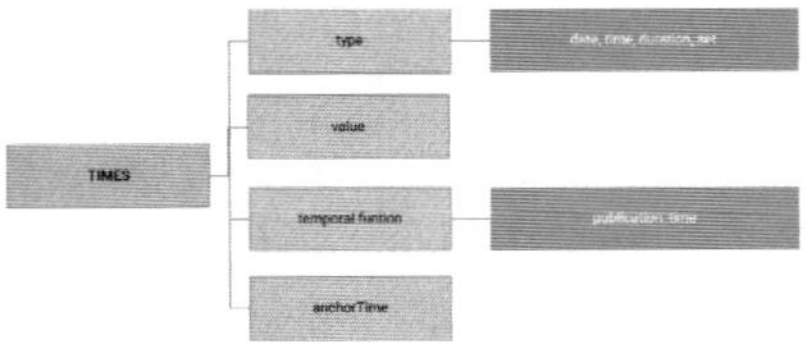

Figure 1: Attributes of the tag Time

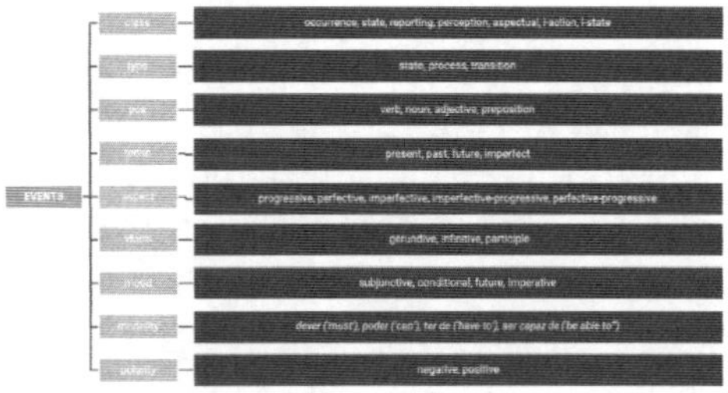

Figure 2: Attributes of the tag Events

3.1 Dataset and annotation

The corpus analyzed in this study has 67 news articles in European Portuguese, predominantly published between October and December 2020, sourced from a Portuguese news stories dataset (Silvano et al., 2023b). The articles were selected based on their narrative nature and a word count ranging from 100 to 200 words. The dataset covers diverse topics, including accidents, homicides, and robberies. Annotation was performed using the Brat Rapid Annotation Tool (Brat) (Stenetorp et al., 2012), adhering to the annotation scheme developed by Silvano et al. (2021) and Leal et al. (2022).

The annotation scheme used in the employed dataset integrates four levels of the ISO-24617 standard: the temporal level (ISO-24617-1, 2012), the referential level (ISO-24617-9, 2019), the spatial level (ISO-24617-7, 2020), and the semantic roles level (ISO-24617-4, 2014). The scheme is structured into two primary components: (1) the entity structure, encompassing labels for events, temporal expressions, participants, and spatial elements, and (2) the link structure, representing relationships such as temporal, objectal, spatial, and semantic role links. The annotation scheme has demonstrated coherence and interoperability through testing on the same dataset, yielding favorable results (Silvano et al., 2023a, 2024).

This study specifically focuses on temporal annotation, emphasizing the labels and attributes associated with the entity structures *Time* (Figure 1) and *Event* (Figure 2). These labels are utilized to identify and characterize temporal expressions and events. Additionally, the analysis incorporates the *Temporal Link* structure, which captures relationships among events, between events and temporal expressions, and among temporal expressions. Temporal links include attributes such as *Before*, *After*, *Includes*, *Is_included*, *During*, *Simultaneous*, *Identity*, *Begins*, *Ends*, *Begun_by*, and *Ended_by*.

The dataset was annotated by a PhD student in linguistics who was trained in the Brat annotation tool and the annotation scheme guidelines under the supervision of a senior linguist researchers. The annotation process followed a structured sequence of steps: (1) Temporal expressions, along with their corresponding attributes and values, were annotated across all news items; (2) Events associated with these temporal expressions were identified and annotated, including their attributes and values; (3) Temporal relationships between each event and its corresponding temporal expression were established, with directionality specified from the event to the temporal expression; (4) Temporal relationships between all temporal expressions were annotated, with directionality defined from the last temporal expression in the linear discourse order to the preceding one. The PhD student and the senior Linguistics researcher conducted multiple consensus meetings following the training phase to ensure the reliability of the annotations. These meetings aimed to ensure that the annotation complied with the manual as the student progressed through the news items. In cases where there were doubts, solutions were found that were based on linguistic theory. After this annotation phase, a second senior Linguistics researcher knowledgeable about the annotation procedures checked and validated the results.

3.2 Visualization

The visualization methodology was designed with two main objectives: (1) ensuring that narrative components — events, temporal expressions, and their relations — are easily identifiable by experts, and (2) structuring the information to facilitate the recognition of annotation mistakes and specific patterns.

To develop the Vitra tool, the team collaborated with linguists to understand the requirements for temporal structure annotation. Initially, we adopted a design similar to Brat (Stenetorp et al., 2012), where labeled elements appear within the raw text, highlighted by a color-coding system with relational links. However, this approach did not meet the linguists' needs, as it replicated the existing Brat interface, which does not isolate the relevant information and does not offer additional benefits. Consequently, we explored an alternative approach: isolating key information (time expressions, events, and relations) from the raw text using manual annotation. This separation improved visualization, aiding pattern identification. Given the central role of time expressions in this research, presenting them along a timeline was a natural choice. Events associated with time expressions were positioned to the left of the timeline, as they typically involve one or two instances at most.

The Figure 3 shows the final format after two more rounds of refinement with three linguist experts. Vitra was developed using programming languages such as Python, D3.js (Javascript), and the markup language HTML. The instructions are on the left side of the browser since it is the usual place for menus or referential information on a website. The sentences are separated in white blocks, thus, it is possible to highlight the current sentence under analysis by a human annotator. This functionality is activated after the human inspector clicks on the time expression he/she wants to analyze, and the corresponding sentence is highlighted. Different types of events and time expressions are assigned different borders and colors, as the instruction panel explains.

4 Results and Discussion

Our results are divided into data characterization regarding temporal information and the assessment of the visual tool proposed in this work.

4.1 Data characterization

The corpus contains an average of 175.97 tokens and 5.35 sentences per news article (cf. Table 1[2]).

	Tokens	Sentence
Avg.	175.97 ± 37.82	5.35 ± 1.29
Max.	239	9
Min.	82	3
Total	11,966	364

Table 1: Tokens and Sentences per News story

[2]We use the model pt_core_news_lg from the spacy library to tokenize the texts.

Regarding temporal expressions, the analysis of the attribute *Type* reveals that the most frequent temporal expressions correspond to *Date* (226), *Time* (43), and *Duration* (16), as shown in Table 2. The predominance of temporal expressions such as *Date* and *Time* is closely linked to the nature of the text analyzed. This type of text generally revolves around answering the central questions: 'Who?', 'What?', 'Where?', and, most importantly for our analysis, 'When?'. These results align with expectations given the analyzed text, which consists of brief news reports covering one or a few related events. Consequently, the temporal information is relatively straightforward, as temporal expressions typically indicate the relevant time interval related to the described situations. This is primarily achieved using *Date* expressions, which specify the day of the events, while *Time* expressions are used to a lesser extent to denote parts of the day. Example 4.1 illustrates this type of occurrence.

Example 4.1 *Um homem [...] morreu* ***hoje*** *na sequência do despiste do ciclomotor que conduzia [...] Os bombeiros receberam às* ***19:08*** *o alerta para o acidente (Lusa 40)*

A man died today after the moped he was driving skidded off the road. Firefighters received the alert for the accident at 7:08 pm.

The first temporal expression, categorized as *Date*, locates the event of "morrer"(to die) within a specific time interval that corresponds to a calendar day. The second temporal expression ("19:08"), classified as *Time*, provides additional information about the timing of the "receber" (to receive) event. This event is located within a narrower time interval, which is a subset of the timeframe indicated by the initial *Date* expression. These two temporal expressions are linked by a TLink described as *isIncluded*.

Example 4.2 illustrates the cases of *Duration*, which occur less frequently. The reason for the low occurrence of this type is that these expressions do not denote chronologically identifiable time intervals; that is, they do not answer the question 'When?'. As a result, they are not essential for understanding the primary information in this type of news.

Example 4.2 *Ali Bongo Ondimba esteve* ***vários meses*** *em convalescença (Lusa 346)*

Ali Bongo Ondimba spent several months convalescing

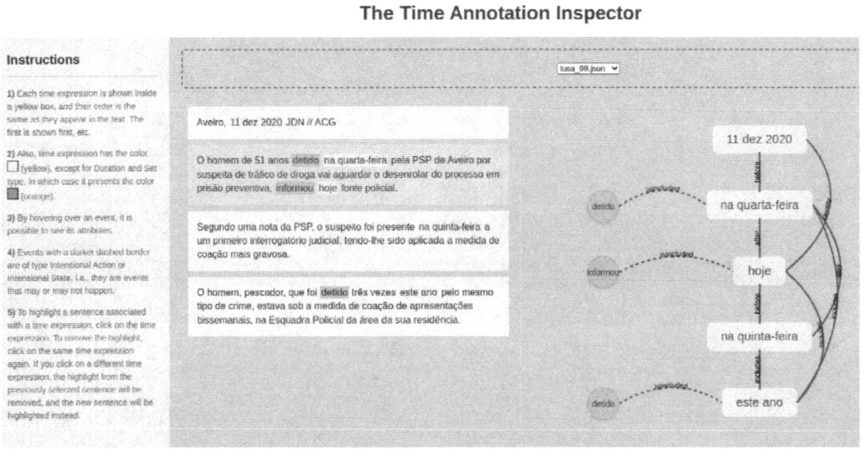

Figure 3: The Time Inspector Visualization

Concerning the temporal relations between events and temporal expressions, Figure 4a illustrates that, in most cases, the time interval denoted by the temporal expressions typically includes the time interval in which the situations are located (75%). The second most common relation observed is one where these two time intervals are simultaneous (13,2%). These findings support the earlier conclusion that, in these news stories, temporal expressions are usually dates (or expressions that function as dates) that locate the narrated situations within well-defined time intervals. Example 4.1 demonstrates a situation where the *isIncluded* relation is established between the expressions "morrer" (died) and "hoje" (today), while the *Simultaneous* relation occurs between "receber"(receive) and "19:08".

Other temporal relations between events and temporal expressions occur infrequently. Some expressions contribute to the temporal location of situations through the definition of the initial or final boundary of the relevant time interval (links *begunBy* (5.9%) and *endedBy* (1.5%)). Additionally, temporal expressions that have an aspectual role in measuring situations are also rare (only 4.4% of *During*) (cf. Figure 4a).

The analysis of temporal relations between temporal expressions reveals a significant variation in the results, as shown in Figure 4b. The most frequent relation between them is when the second temporal expression in the linear order of the discourse denotes a time interval that temporally precedes the time interval denoted by the first expression in the linear order of the discourse, accounting for 31.5%. This is followed by cases where both expressions refer to the same time interval (Identity), which makes up 28.1% of the results. In fourth place, we find the posteriority relation, where the temporal order matches the sequence of the expressions in the discourse, representing 13.4% of cases. Lastly, there are inclusion relations: 13% of cases involve the interval indicated by the second expression being included within the interval indicated by the first expression, while 14% of cases see the second expression's interval encompassing the first expression's interval.

The dominance of the *Before* relation likely stems from the structured format commonly used in news articles to convey information. Typically, a news article refers to events, which generally fall under the class of *Occurrence* (133 cases). These events are often described in sentences that identify the source of the information and include a *Reporting* event (43 cases) (Silvano et al., 2023a). In these instances, the *Occurrence* event is located before the *Reporting* event. Example 4.3 illustrates such cases.

Example 4.3 *Um homem [. . .] foi detido no concelho de Góis, [. . .] anunciou* ***hoje*** *a GNR. Segundo um comunicado [. . .], a detenção [..] ocorreu n****a terça-feira*** *(Lusa 43)*

A man was arrested in the municipality of Góis, the GNR announced today. According to a statement, the arrest took place on Tuesday

In this context, the first temporal expression, "hoje" (today), indicates the timing of the reporting event "anunciar" (to announce). The second temporal expression, "a terça-feira" (on Tuesday), specifies when the main event described in the news (the arrest) took place. As a result, the second temporal expression occurs chronologically before the first expression.

Another reason for the recurrence of the *Before* relation is related to the structure of the news articles. Typically, a news text begins with a lead, which presents the central information necessary for understanding the story, followed by additional details that are less critical. This structure often includes references to previous events, which have earlier temporal contexts, helping to explain the causes of the main event. This is the case of Example 4.4, where the temporal expression "hoje" (today) locates the main event of the news - the arrest of the murder suspect-, indicating that it occurs after the murder event itself, which is situated in time by the expression "o domingo" (on Sunday).

Example 4.4 *A PJ deteve* ***hoje*** *o suspeito de matar um homem [...] no* ***domingo***, *[...] em Cête. (Lusa, 5)*

The PJ arrested today the suspect of killing a man on Sunday in Cête.

The *Identity* relation is the second most frequent, as mentioned previously. This is because news articles often report on events that develop from the main event introduced in the lead, placing them within the same time interval. The fourth most frequent type of relation identified is temporal succession. This indicates that, in this genre of text, the chronological order of events does not always align with the linear narrative structure. Relations involving inclusion rank third and fifth. These are linked with expressions of type *Date*, which usually refer to time intervals represented by calendar terms, and expressions of type *Time*, which denote smaller segments of these intervals. For instance, in Example 4.1, the expression "19:00", categorized as *Time*, establishes an *isIncluded* relation with the expression "hoje" (today), which is classified as *Date*. These temporal relations are associated with a detailed breakdown of the information previously mentioned in the news lead.

Tables 2 and 3 in Appendix A detail all the attributes' statistics of time expressions and events, respectively.

4.2 Visualization

Verifying the annotation using Vitra has led to several improvements both in the annotation process itself and in the overall framework. The proposed tool generates a much "cleaner" image, allowing the selection of only some elements that are part of the annotation's temporal level. This possibility of selection and simplification makes it much easier to identify (1) whether all the necessary relations have been made, i.e., whether important information is missing, and (2) whether the connections made are correct. This can be challenging in Brat, as the elements needing connection are often apart, and the sheer volume of annotations can create a "dense" visualization. Furthermore, the use of a color code enables us to quickly determine if temporal expressions have been annotated correctly with the appropriate attributes. In Vitra, the connecting lines provide an easy way to verify whether the relationships are correct and whether all temporal expressions and events are linked, allowing for the reconstruction of the event chronology. Examples of these advantages can be found in the scenarios presented in Appendix C.

All in all, Vitra facilitates the comparison of a large number of annotated news articles, focusing on just one simplified annotation level. The visualization allows us to easily identify errors and inconsistencies in annotation across many news articles, thus contributing to improving the overall annotation quality of the entire corpus and the annotation manual itself.

To have a more independent assessment of the effectiveness of the visualization, we decided to develop a questionnaire with six claims related to the goals of this research, which are identifying annotation mistakes and recognizing patterns in the temporal structure of annotations. For each claim, we adopted a discrete Likert scale whose lowest number (1) in the score was associated with "Strongly Disagree", while the highest number (5) was associated with "Strongly Agree". Although this method has limitations, as pointed out by South et al. (2022), it is a standard quality evaluation method for visualizations. The list of all the claims is detailed in Appendix B. In addition to that, we left a text box for additional comments from the evaluators.

We invited three linguistics experts to complete a questionnaire designed to evaluate the proposed visualization. One of the experts had previously participated in the development of Vitra, therefore, we included two additional experts to eliminate any potential bias from the individual involved in the tool's development discussions. All three experts had similar profiles, were graduate students of lin-

(a) Temporal Relations between Events and Time Expressions

(b) Temporal Relations between Time Expressions

Figure 4: Comparison of temporal relations: (a) between events and time expressions, and (b) between time expressions.

guistics, already had experience with annotation tools like Brat, and knew the annotation schema used in the dataset that we employed in our experiments visualization. To compare with Brat visualization, four linguistics experts completed the same questionnaire designed to evaluate the Brat visual annotation tool. The only exception was the last question, which aimed to draw a comparison with Brat. The profiles of these four experts were similar to those of the linguists who answered the questionnaire for the evaluation of Vitra's visualization.

The first three claims of the questionnaire concern the interface, i.e., if the users were able to identify the events, times, and relations. Regarding this aspect, the users found Vitra's visualization mostly intuitive since the scores for the first three questions were between 4 and 5. The results were similar for Brat, where the scores also range from 4 to 5. The claims (4) and (5) of the survey were concerned with whether Vitra aids the process of identifying annotation mistakes and temporal patterns. Two of them scored 4 for the claim related to annotation errors (4), and one scored 5. Maybe this is related to the fact that Vitra's visualization does not present all the information of the annotation, for instance, the attributes of the events. For the Brat evaluation, claim 4, which is concerned with the identification of the errors, presented a great variation between the respondents. The scores for Brat in this issue were 2, 3, 4, and 5, showing that at least half of the linguistics experts think that Brat presents flaws in the inspection of annotations. In the assessment of Vitra in the discovery of temporal patterns (claim 5), two of them scored 5, while the other evaluator scored 4. Possibly, this is due to the arrangement of the temporal information, separated and combined with their relations, which aids in seeing all the temporal information as a whole. Regarding the Brat evaluation, three respondents scored 4 for the claim 5, while one scored 2. This suggests that the proposed visualization is competitive with respect to uncovering the temporal patterns with Brat.

We acknowledge that the number of respondents in our surveys evaluating Brat and Vitra, four and three participants, respectively, is not statistically significant. In most research, at least a sample size of 15 respondents is recommended; otherwise, the sample size is too small to draw a reliable conclusion (Sauro and Lewis, 2016). Consequently, the agreement scores derived from this sample size are also not statistically significant. However, our qualitative analysis, detailed with some examples in Appendix C, demonstrates the usefulness of this new visualization for analyzing the annotation schema and identifying errors.

5 Conclusion and Future Work

In this study, we investigate the application of visualization representation in the inspection of temporal relations involving events and time expressions. Narratives present dense information concerning events and time expressions. Hence, human annotators are presented with visually overloaded information in annotation tools when labeling narratives. In this investigation, we used a Portuguese dataset of news stories to answer the following research question.

RQ1) What insights can be derived from visualizing the events and temporal expressions and their temporal relationships

In our results, we showed that some unusual patterns in the temporal relations can be easily detected in the visualization of temporal expressions, events, and their relations. This is probably due to the nature of the proposed visualization, which sets aside temporal expressions, their related events, and their relations. In the Brat annotation tool, and usually in text annotation tools for documents, the raw text is presented along with all the relations and all entities. However, when facing a multilayer scheme, annotators can be challenged using a visualization like Brat since this is a more complex task.

Thus, answering the first research question, we conclude that unusual patterns in a multilayer annotation scheme are more salient in a visual representation that is devoted to the specific layers on which the focus of the investigation is. Some specific and relevant insights for our studied annotation scheme were observed, leading to adjustments in the annotation guidelines. A few use cases of insights are detailed in Appendix C.

RQ2) How effective is isolating time expressions and their related events, and arranging them on a timeline, for facilitating annotation inspection by expert audiences?

Isolating was beneficial for human annotators. In our questionnaire, the annotator experts positively assessed the identification of events, time expression, and their relations. Hence, all of them agreed that the proposed visualization facilitates the process of identifying errors or patterns.

We aim to advance the study of visual representations for human annotators as well as the quality of multilayer scheme annotations, which present complexities and challenges in development and assessment. In future work, we intend to add other annotation formats to Vitra, which can allow different types of arrangements, like the events in a timeline or even participants. Additionally, we plan to integrate Vitra into the Inception annotation tool (Klie et al., 2018), which is a more modern tool than BRAT. By doing this, we seek to stimulate human annotators to use our tool to aid the labeling process.

6 Limitations

The first limitation of our work is the small number of linguists who evaluate our tool, which could lead to a biased evaluation. The second limitation is that the tool still lacks interactive constraints. Currently, the annotator cannot correct annotation errors or move elements in the visual representation. These features could enhance the experience of the human annotator and broaden the functionalities of the representation. The third and last limitation that we can observe in this work is that the visualization is tied to the annotation scheme presented by Silvano et al. (2023a). However, we plan, as future work, to include other types of annotation schemes that include events and temporal expression as well.

Acknowledgements

This work is financed by National Funds through the Portuguese funding agency, FCT - Fundação para a Ciência e a Tecnologia, within project LA/P/0063/2020. DOI 10.54499/LA/P/0063/2020 | https://doi.org/10.54499/LA/P/0063/2020. The authors would also like to acknowledge the project StorySense, with reference 2022.09312.PTDC (DOI10.54499/2022.09312.PTDC).

References

Evelin Amorim, Ricardo Campos, Alípio Jorge, Pedro Mota, and Rúben Almeida. 2024. text2story: A python toolkit to extract and visualize story components of narrative text. In *Proceedings of the 2024 Joint International Conference on Computational Linguistics, Language Resources and Evaluation (LREC-COLING 2024)*, pages 15761–15772.

Evelin Amorim, Alexandre Ribeiro, Inês Cantante, Alípio Jorge, Brenda Santana, Sérgio Nunes, Purificação Silvano, António Leal, and Ricardo Campos. 2021. Brat2viz: a tool and pipeline for visualizing narratives from annotated texts. In *Proceedings of Text2Story-Fourth Workshop on Narrative Extraction From Texts held in conjunction with the 43rd European Conference on Information Retrieval (ECIR 2021)*.

Allan Bell. 1997. *The Language of News Media*. Blackwell.

Steven Bethard, Guergana Savova, Wei-Te Chen, Leon Derczynski, James Pustejovsky, and Marc Verhagen. 2016. SemEval-2016 task 12: Clinical TempEval. In *Proceedings of the 10th International Workshop on Semantic Evaluation (SemEval-2016)*, pages 1052–1062, San Diego, California. Association for Computational Linguistics.

André Bittar. 2009. Annotation of events and temporal expressions in French texts. In *Proceedings of the Third Linguistic Annotation Workshop (LAW III)*, pages 48–51, Suntec, Singapore. Association for Computational Linguistics.

Tommaso Caselli, Valentina Bartalesi Lenzi, Rachele Sprugnoli, Emanuele Pianta, and Irina Prodanof. 2011. Annotating events, temporal expressions and relations in Italian: the it-timeml experience for the ita-TimeBank. In *Proceedings of the 5th Linguistic Annotation Workshop*, pages 143–151, Portland, Oregon, USA. Association for Computational Linguistics.

Tommaso Caselli and Piek Vossen. 2017. The event storyline corpus: A new benchmark for causal and temporal relation extraction. In *Proceedings of the Events and Stories in the News Workshop*, pages 77–86.

Taylor Cassidy, Bill McDowell, Nathanael Chambers, and Steven Bethard. 2014. An annotation framework for dense event ordering. In *Proceedings of the 52nd Annual Meeting of the Association for Computational Linguistics (Volume 2: Short Papers)*, pages 501–506.

Qing Chen, Shixiong Cao, Jiazhe Wang, and Nan Cao. 2023. How does automation shape the process of narrative visualization: A survey of tools. *IEEE Transactions on Visualization and Computer Graphics*.

Zhutian Chen, Yun Wang, Qianwen Wang, Yong Wang, and Huamin Qu. 2019. Towards automated infographic design: Deep learning-based auto-extraction of extensible timeline. *IEEE transactions on visualization and computer graphics*, 26(1):917–926.

Francisco Costa and António Branco. 2012. TimeBankPT: A TimeML annotated corpus of Portuguese. In *Proceedings of the Eighth International Conference on Language Resources and Evaluation (LREC'12)*, pages 3727–3734, Istanbul, Turkey. European Language Resources Association (ELRA).

George R Doddington, Alexis Mitchell, Mark A Przybocki, Lance A Ramshaw, Stephanie M Strassel, and Ralph M Weischedel. 2004. The automatic content extraction (ace) program-tasks, data, and evaluation. In *Lrec*, volume 2, pages 837–840. Lisbon.

Catarina Justo dos Santos Fernandes. 2023. Visualizing news stories from annotated text. Master's thesis, Faculdade de Enegenharia da Universidade do Porto.

Elena Filatova and Eduard Hovy. 2001. Assigning time-stamps to event-clauses. In *Proceedings of the Workshop on Temporal and Spatial Information Processing - Volume 13*, TASIP '01, USA. Association for Computational Linguistics.

Francisco Gonçalves, Ricardo Campos, and Alípio Jorge. 2023. Text2storyline: generating enriched storylines from text. In *European Conference on Information Retrieval*, pages 248–254. Springer.

Swapnil Hingmire, Nitin Ramrakhiyani, Avinash Kumar Singh, Sangameshwar Patil, Girish Palshikar, Pushpak Bhattacharyya, and Vasudeva Varma. 2020. Extracting message sequence charts from hindi narrative text. In *Proceedings of the First Joint Workshop on Narrative Understanding, Storylines, and Events*, pages 87–96.

Seohyun Im, Hyunjo You, Hayun Jang, Seungho Nam, and Hyopil Shin. 2009. KTimeML: Specification of temporal and event expressions in Korean text. In *Proceedings of the 7th Workshop on Asian Language Resources (ALR7)*, pages 115–122, Suntec, Singapore. Association for Computational Linguistics.

ISO-24617-1. 2012. Language resource management - semantic annotation framework (semaf) - part 1: Time and events (semaf-time, iso-timeml). Standard, Geneva, CH.

ISO-24617-4. 2014. Language resource management-semantic annotation framework (semaf) - part 4: Semantic roles (semaf-sr). Standard, Geneva, CH.

ISO-24617-7. 2020. Language resource management-semantic annotation framework (semaf) - part 7: Spatial information. Standard, Geneva, CH.

ISO-24617-9. 2019. Language resource management-semantic annotation framework (semaf) - - part 9: Reference annotation framework (raf). Standard, Geneva, CH.

Adam Jatowt, Antoine Doucet, and Ricardo Campos. 2022. Diachronic analysis of time references in news articles. pages 918–923.

Jan-Christoph Klie, Michael Bugert, Beto Boullosa, Richard Eckart de Castilho, and Iryna Gurevych. 2018. The INCEpTION platform: Machine-assisted and knowledge-oriented interactive annotation. In *Proceedings of the 27th International Conference on Computational Linguistics: System Demonstrations*, pages 5–9, Santa Fe, New Mexico. Association for Computational Linguistics.

Ryan Ka Yau Lai. 2023. From annotation to analysis: Exploring conversational dynamics with rezonater. In *Proceedings of the 37th Pacific Asia Conference on Language, Information and Computation*, pages 303–313.

L. Lange, A. Iurshina, H. Adel, and J. Strötgen. 2020. Adversarial alignment of multilingual models for extracting temporal expressions from text. In *Proceedings of the 5th Workshop on Representation Learning for NLP*, pages 103–109.

António Leal, Purificação Silvano, Evelin Amorim, Inês Cantante, Fátima Silva, Alípio Mario Jorge, and Ricardo Campos. 2022. The place of ISO-space in Text2Story multilayer annotation scheme. In *Proceedings of the 18th Joint ACL - ISO Workshop on Interoperable Semantic Annotation within LREC2022*, pages 61–70, Marseille, France. European Language Resources Association.

Anne-Lyse Minard, Manuela Speranza, Ruben Urizar, Begoña Altuna, Marieke van Erp, Anneleen Schoen, and Chantal van Son. 2016. MEANTIME, the NewsReader multilingual event and time corpus. In *Proceedings of the Tenth International Conference on Language Resources and Evaluation (LREC'16)*, pages 4417–4422, Portorož, Slovenia. European Language Resources Association (ELRA).

Phong H Nguyen, Kai Xu, Rick Walker, and BL William Wong. 2016. Timesets: Timeline visualization with set relations. *Information Visualization*, 15(3):253–269.

Sérgio Nunes, Alípio Mario Jorge, Evelin Amorim, Hugo Sousa, António Leal, Purificação Silvano, Inês Cantante, and Ricardo Campos. 2024. Text2Story lusa: A dataset for narrative analysis in European Portuguese news articles. In *Proceedings of the 2024 Joint International Conference on Computational Linguistics, Language Resources and Evaluation (LREC-COLING 2024)*, pages 15773–15782, Torino, Italia. ELRA and ICCL.

Helene Olsen, Étienne Simon, Erik Velldal, and Lilja Øvrelid. 2024. Socio-political events of conflict and unrest: A survey of available datasets. In *Proceedings of the 7th Workshop on Challenges and Applications of Automated Extraction of Socio-political Events from Text (CASE 2024)*, pages 40–53.

James Pustejovsky, José Castaño, Robert Ingria, Roser Saurí, Rob Gaizauskas, Andrea Setzer, Graham Katz, and Dragomir Radev. 2003. Timeml: Robust specification of event and temporal expressions in text. pages 28–34.

James Pustejovsky and Marc Verhagen. 2009. SemEval-2010 task 13: Evaluating events, time expressions, and temporal relations (TempEval-2). In *Proceedings of the Workshop on Semantic Evaluations: Recent Achievements and Future Directions (SEW-2009)*, pages 112–116, Boulder, Colorado. Association for Computational Linguistics.

Jeff Sauro and James R Lewis. 2016. *Quantifying the user experience: Practical statistics for user research*. Morgan Kaufmann.

Christina Schokkenbroek. 1999. News stories: Structure, time and evaluation. *Time & Society*, 8(1):59–98.

Purificação Silvano, Evelin Amorim, António Leal, Inês Cantante, Maria de Fátima Henriques da Silva, Alípio Jorge, Ricardo Campos, and Sérgio Sobral Nunes. 2023a. Annotation and visualisation of reporting events in textual narratives. In *Proceedings of Text2Story 2023: Sixth Workshop on Narrative Extraction From Texts*.

Purificação Silvano, António Leal, Fátima Silva, Inês Cantante, Fatima Oliveira, and Alípio Mario Jorge. 2021. Developing a multilayer semantic annotation scheme based on ISO standards for the visualization of a newswire corpus. In *Proceedings of the 17th Joint ACL - ISO Workshop on Interoperable Semantic Annotation*, pages 1–13, Groningen, The Netherlands (online). Association for Computational Linguistics.

Purificação Silvano, Evelin Amorim, António Leal, Inês Cantante, Alípio Jorge, Ricardo Campos, and Nana Yu. 2024. Untangling a web of temporal relations in news articles. In *Proceedings of Text2Story 2024 - Seventh Workshop on Narrative Extraction From Texts*, volume 3671 of *CEUR Workshop Proceedings*, pages 77–92.

Purificação Silvano, Alípio Jorge, António Leal, Evelin Amorim, Hugo Sousa, Inês Cantante, Ricardo Campos, and Sérgio Nunes. 2023b. Text2story lusa annotated corpus. Data set.

Hugo Sousa, Ricardo Campos, and Alípio Jorge. 2023. Tei2go: A multilingual approach for fast temporal expression identification. In *Proceedings of the 32nd ACM International Conference on Information and Knowledge Management*, CIKM '23, page 5401–5406, New York, NY, USA. Association for Computing Machinery.

Laura South, David Saffo, Olga Vitek, Cody Dunne, and Michelle A Borkin. 2022. Effective use of likert scales in visualization evaluations: A systematic review. In *Computer Graphics Forum*, volume 41, pages 43–55. Wiley Online Library.

Pontus Stenetorp, Sampo Pyysalo, Goran Topić, Tomoko Ohta, Sophia Ananiadou, and Jun'ichi Tsujii. 2012. Brat: a web-based tool for nlp-assisted text annotation. In *Proceedings of the Demonstrations at the 13th Conference of the European Chapter of the Association for Computational Linguistics*, pages 102–107.

Weiyi Sun, Anna Rumshisky, and Ozlem Uzuner. 2013. Evaluating temporal relations in clinical text: 2012 i2b2 challenge. *Journal of the American Medical Informatics Association : JAMIA*, 20.

Tan Tang, Renzhong Li, Xinke Wu, Shuhan Liu, Johannes Knittel, Steffen Koch, Thomas Ertl, Lingyun Yu, Peiran Ren, and Yingcai Wu. 2020. Plotthread: Creating expressive storyline visualizations using reinforcement learning. *IEEE Transactions on Visualization and Computer Graphics*, 27(2):294–303.

Tan Tang, Sadia Rubab, Jiewen Lai, Weiwei Cui, Lingyun Yu, and Yingcai Wu. 2018. istoryline: Effective convergence to hand-drawn storylines. *IEEE transactions on visualization and computer graphics*, 25(1):769–778.

Xiaozhi Wang, Yulin Chen, Ning Ding, Hao Peng, Zimu Wang, Yankai Lin, Xu Han, Lei Hou, Juanzi Li, Zhiyuan Liu, et al. 2022. Maven-ere: A unified large-scale dataset for event coreference, temporal, causal, and subevent relation extraction. *arXiv preprint arXiv:2211.07342*.

Yunchao Wang, Guodao Sun, Zihao Zhu, Tong Li, Ling Chen, and Ronghua Liang. 2024. E2 storyline: visualizing the relationship with triplet entities and event discovery. *ACM Transactions on Intelligent Systems and Technology*, 15(1):1–26.

Li Ye, Lei Wang, Shaolun Ruan, Yuwei Meng, Yigang Wang, Wei Chen, and Zhiguang Zhou. 2024. Storyexplorer: A visualization framework for storyline generation of textual narratives. *arXiv preprint arXiv:2411.05435*.

Jian Zhao, Shenyu Xu, Senthil Chandrasegaran, Chris Bryan, Fan Du, Aditi Mishra, Xin Qian, Yiran Li, and Kwan-Liu Ma. 2021. Chartstory: Automated partitioning, layout, and captioning of charts into comic-style narratives. *IEEE Transactions on Visualization and Computer Graphics*, 29(2):1384–1399.

Xiaoshi Zhong and Erik Cambria. 2023. Time expression recognition and normalization: a survey. *Artificial Intelligence Review*, 56(9):9115–9140.

Xiaoshi Zhong, Chenyu Jin, Mengyu An, and Erik Cambria. 2024. Xtime: A general rule-based method for time expression recognition and normalization. *Knowledge-Based Systems*, 297:111921.

A Time Expressions and Events Attributes Statistics

Time Expressions		
Attribute Name	Attribute Value	N.
Type	Date	226
	Duration	16
	Time	43
Temporal Function	Publication Time	67
Total		294

Table 2: Time Expressions Statistics

Events		
Attribute Name	Attribute Value	N.
Class	Occurrence	133
	Reporting	43
	State	16
	I_State	8
	I_Action	1
	Aspectual	1
	Perception	1
Type	Transition	173
	State	24
	Process	7
Pos	Verb	177
	Noun	13
	Adjective	5
	Preposition	6
Tense	Past	133
	Imperfect	5
	Future	7
	Present	10
Aspect	Perfective	161
	Imperfective	5
	Progressive	1
Polarity	Positive	201
VForm	Participle	18
	Infinitive	9
	Gerundive	2
Movement	Motion Literal	4
Modality	*Poder* (may)	7
	Dever (should)	1
Mood	Future	5
	Conditional	2
	Subjunctive	1
Total	204	

Table 3: Events Expressions Statistics

B Questionnaire About the Visualization

1. The visualization is easy to navigate.

2. The narrative components - time expressions and events - are visually distinct.

3. The relationships between narrative components are clearly represented.

4. The visualization effectively supports the identification of annotation errors in time expressions, events, and their relations.

5. The visualization enables the identification of temporal patterns.

6. Compared to the BRAT annotation tool, the proposed visualization provided a better depiction of the relations between all the time expressions and their connected events

C Examples of Identified Error Annotation and Insights

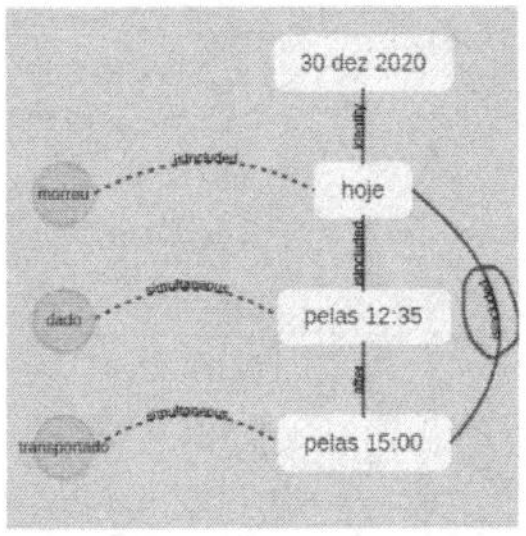

Figure 5: In the visualization of lusa_49, the connections were correct. However, these temporal connections did not capture the critical information about the temporal relation between the time interval denoted by "pelas 15 horas" (around 3 p.m.) and the time interval denoted by "hoje" (today). Thus, we added to the annotation manual that temporal expressions can connect to two or more temporal expressions, ensuring that the correct chronology is captured. This figure already represents that missing link.

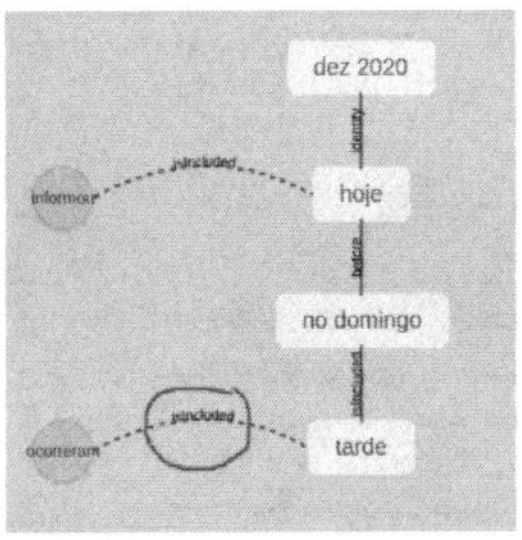

Figure 6: In the scenario of the lusa_82 news story, the event "ocorreram" (occurred) was initially linked to "no domingo" (on Sunday), which did not allow us to infer that the event took place during the time frame denoted by "tarde" (afternoon). We needed to modify the guidelines to connect "ocorreram" to "tarde." This adjustment enables us to infer a relationship between "ocorreram" and "no domingo," establishing a transitive relation. The figure already illustrates the correct temporal representation.

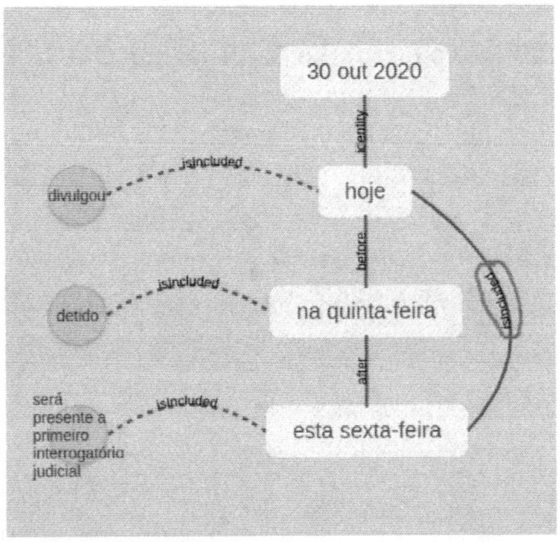

(a) The relation between "esta sexta" (this Friday) and "hoje" (today) is incorrect in the Lusa_35 news story. The IsIncluded link was annotated instead of the Identity link. This figure shows the representation that highlights this annotation error.

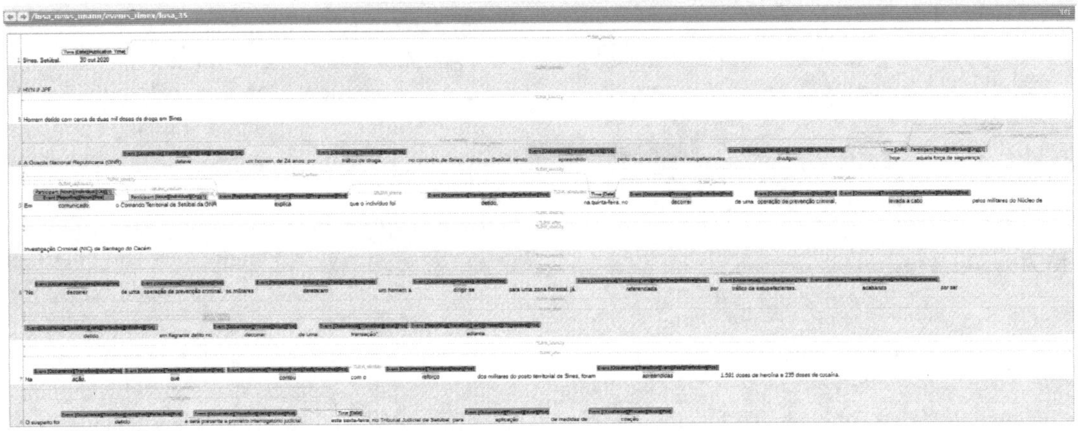

(b) BRAT visualization of anotations of news story lusa_35

Figure 7: Comparing the lusa_35 news story using the proposed visualization and BRAT.

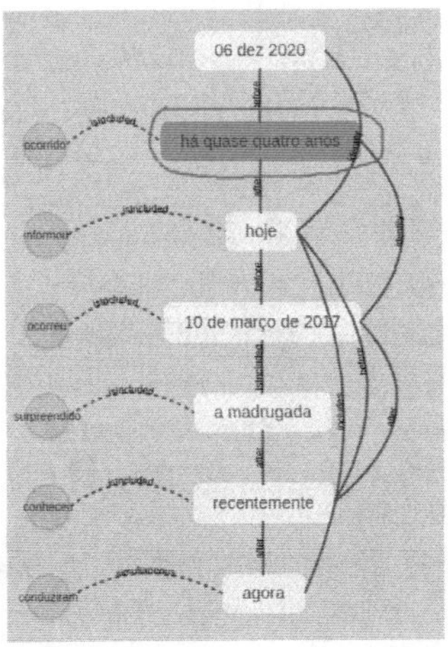

Figure 8: In the visualization of lusa_76, "há quase 4 anos" (almost 4 years ago) is not a temporal expression of type Duration, so it should be in yellow (not orange).

Annotating *candy speech* in German YouTube comments

Yulia Clausen and **Tatjana Scheffler**
CRC 1567 Virtual Lifeworlds
Ruhr-University Bochum, Germany
{yulia.clausen|tatjana.scheffler}@rub.de

Abstract

We describe the phenomenon of *candy speech* – positive emotional speech in online communication – and introduce a categorization of its various types based on the theoretical framework of social interaction by Goffman (1967). We provide a dataset of 46,286 German YouTube comments manually annotated with candy speech types; 14,580 comments in this data contain a total of 21,785 candy speech expressions. We discuss issues in the annotation and evaluation of such higher-level semantic properties of text.

1 Introduction

The theoretical framework of social interaction introduced by Goffman (1967) is centered around *face-work*, where *face* represents a 'positive social value a person effectively claims for [themselves] [...] an image of self delineated in terms of approved social attributes' (p. 5). In this approach, social interactions involve emotionally charged linguistic utterances which directly influence a person's image or face. Goffman (1967) assumes various states and processes related to face: An individual is said to be 'in face' when they feel confident and assured, hence one strives to 'maintain one's face', i.e., to sustain a positive image of oneself. At the same time, one fears to 'lose face', which could result in a damage to one's image. In cooperative discourse, mutual face support is desired and even expected, and, if heeded, ensures that faces are maintained. Furthermore, 'face-saving' and 'face-giving' strategies can be applied when face is lost. The former allows an individual to sustain an impression that they have not lost their face, while the latter refers to the process by which others help an individual to 'gain face'.

In linguistics, face-work plays a central role, as it provides insight into how language functions not only as a medium for conveying information, but also as a means to manage social relationships, shape interpersonal dynamics, and construct identities in interactions. Nonetheless, very few studies have addressed positive interactions in social media from a corpus-based perspective via annotation of significant amounts of realistic data or using computational approaches. Annotation efforts have so far centered on *negative* online interactions, and linguistic expressions that negatively influence another person's or group's public image have been extensively studied. The area of negative communication practices has been delineated in great detail, with distinctions between hate speech, offensive language, toxicity, and many other subtypes (see Poletto et al., 2021, for a survey, and references therein). In contrast, little empirical work has been done on the positive side, despite the fact that (as we believe) positive face-work is similarly complex, and despite the fact that positive social engagement leads many users to strongly associate with certain virtual communities and spend large amounts of time interacting online. The lack of empirical research on positive face-work means that we know very little on how it looks and how to identify it in online data. Studying the types of phenomena that make up positive interactions in digital media may enable us to automatically find and possibly enhance positive face-work, and may help us understand how virtual communities and identities are constructed through language.

In this study, we focus on *candy speech* – a term we use for positive face-work in online discourse that provides face support for others. We develop a classification of candy speech types that allows for a differentiated view of face-supporting strategies. Some previous work has already documented the prevalence of (certain types of) positive speech in social media (e.g., Chakravarthi and Muralidaran 2021; Jiménez-Zafra et al. 2023 on 'hope speech' or Njoo et al. 2023 on 'empowerment language'). Face work, in particular positive face work, has

Proceedings of the 19th Linguistic Annotation Workshop (LAW-XIX-2025), pages 264–269
July 31, 2025 ©2025 Association for Computational Linguistics

however rarely been directly addressed in corpus or computational linguistic studies (but see Dutt et al., 2020; Klüwer, 2011; Klüwer, 2015; Virtanen, 2022). Specifically, Klüwer's (2011; 2015) work on small talk in task-oriented dialogs, which she frames in face-work terms, is relevant for our study. Klüwer (2011; 2015) develops a taxonomy of dialog acts for non-task-oriented passages in virtual reality dialogs based on the notion that these interactions typically serve social purposes: to either request support for one's own face, or to provide face support for the interlocutor. In our classification of candy speech, we build on and extend Klüwer's face supporting dialog acts based on social media interactions between real humans.

Our main contributions are the following:

- We develop a definition and subcategorization of candy speech in social media comments.
- We annotate a subset of a German YouTube corpus and discuss first observations regarding the distribution of candy speech expressions.
- We present an evaluation method for comparing span-based candy speech annotations and apply it to our corpus data.

2 Dataset

We work with the data from the NottDeuYTSch corpus (Cotgrove, 2018), which contains over 33 million words taken from approximately 3 million YouTube comments published between 2008 and 2018 by a young German-speaking audience. Comments posted on social media platforms often represent emotional discourse. In addition, it is known that YouTube comments in particular contain many positive social interactions, for example within fan groups and other communities (Cotgrove, 2025), thus being suitable for our purposes.

We selected 16 videos authored by seven creators, together with all their comments. To reflect the topic distribution in the original corpus, the creators/videos were selected randomly; however, we made sure that the creators represent different sectors (e.g., music, tutorials) so that the commenting communities can be expected to differ in the frequency and types of candy speech expressions. The annotated dataset consists of a total of 46,286 comments, grouped into 16 'documents' according to the video they relate to.[1]

[1]The dataset and annotation guidelines are available via the OSF platform: `https://osf.io/r9uek/`.

3 Candy speech

3.1 Definition

Following Goffman's (1967) theory, we define candy speech as face-support that aims to help others maintain and restore their positive (self-)image. Candy speech thus is constituted by expressions of positive attitudes and feelings on social media towards individuals (e.g., content creators or commenters) and their posts (videos, comments, etc.). The purpose of candy speech is to encourage, cheer up, support or empower others. Candy speech can be viewed as the counterpart to hate speech, as it likewise aims to influence the self-image of the target person or group, but in a positive way. In the following section, we describe our classification of candy speech expressions against the backdrop of face-work strategies.

3.2 Classification

Our classification includes 10 annotation categories: eight distinct types of candy speech and two additional categories. An overview of all candy speech types is given in Table 1. The additional categories are *implicit* and *ambiguous*. The annotation *implicit* is used for indirect expressions of one of the eight explicit types. The label *ambiguous* applies to cases in which the lack of context prevents an expression from being clearly classified as candy speech or not.

The candy speech types realize face-supporting strategies directed at others, which we broadly divide into two classes: those conveying positive disposition toward individuals and those claiming shared common ground (Stalnaker, 2002) with an individual or a group. Positive disposition is realized by the types *affection declaration*, *compliment*, *encouragement*, *gratitude*, *positive feedback* and *sympathy*. It can also be expressed implicitly. Claiming of common ground is done via using markers of *group membership* or signaling *agreement*.

Additionally, we label each comment containing candy speech as *initiative* or *reactive*, which allows us to differentiate between spontaneous acts of face support (initiative) and replies to other comments (reactive). Reactive comments can represent face-supporting or face-saving acts, depending on whether they refer to candy speech expressions (e.g., agreement) or aim at counteracting face threats initiated by others (e.g., compliments on positive achievements of the target person).

Type	Short definition	Example
affection declaration	admiration, love and affection towards others	*I like you XD*
compliment	acknowledgment of skills, personal characteristics or achievements of others	*You create really great videos !*
encouragement	comments that aim to encourage others	*Keep at it !*
gratitude	sincere gratitude expressed unprompted	*Thanks for motivating me !*
group membership	markers of group membership, e.g., belonging to a fan community	*I am a #lochinator*
positive feedback	positive attitude toward a post, video, comment etc.	*The song is mega mega cool .*
sympathy	words of compassion and understanding	*the new ones are worth a chance, too !*
agreement	agreement with an opinion or statement that represents candy speech	*Yeaaah so amazing*
implicit	indirect expression of candy speech	*Why don't you go to Supertalent ?*
ambiguous	unclear whether candy speech or not	*OMG*

Table 1: Types of candy speech expressions (examples are translated from German).

4 Annotation

4.1 Procedure

The annotations were performed with the annotation tool Inception (Klie et al., 2018). Each comment was checked for the presence of candy speech, and the identified candy speech expressions were annotated on the exact span level with one of the predefined types. Note that one comment can contain several candy speech expressions, and such expressions can also overlap. For each expression, we aimed at labeling the shortest possible span, e.g., instead of annotating several consecutive expressions of the same type as one span, each clause was annotated separately. Furthermore, our annotation scheme allows for overlapping spans in order to preserve the grammaticality of each annotated expression. E.g., *Ihr seit soooooo süss und eure Parodien der Hammer* ('You are soooooo sweet and your parodies are awesome') was labeled both as *affection declaration* and *positive feedback*.

The annotations were conducted by two annotators – an author of this paper (annotator 1) and a graduate student with linguistic background (annotator 2). At the beginning of the annotation process, the annotation guidelines with the definition of candy speech and a number of predefined candy speech types were compiled and shared with annotator 2. In the annotation training period, both annotators annotated the same portion of the data and discussed the results. Annotator 2 proceeded with the annotation, while regularly discussing the results with annotator 1. When new cases/types emerged, the annotation guidelines were updated and previous annotations were adapted accordingly.

Annotator 1 annotated one document; annotator 2 annotated 13 documents. Annotations performed by annotator 2 were reviewed by annotator 1 and any disagreements were discussed until a consensus was reached and corrected if necessary. Two additional documents were annotated separately by each annotator; these results were not discussed and used to calculate the inter-annotator agreement.

4.2 Inter-annotator agreement

The basic inter-annotator agreement (IAA) was measured on the comment level in binary form, i.e., whether a given comment contains candy speech or not. The results based on percentage agreement and Cohen's κ (Cohen, 1960) are given in Table 2. The annotators show good agreement of $\kappa \geq 0.7$ on the detection of whether comments contain candy speech. Note that most comments are quite short, with an average of 16.5 tokens per comment.

Evaluating agreement for span annotations such as candy speech expressions is not a trivial task.

Document	# comments	%	κ
Doc1	204	85.2	.70
Doc2	242	89.6	.76

Table 2: Binary IAA on the comment level.

There are generally two options: First, classical chance-corrected inter-annotator agreement (Artstein and Poesio, 2008) could be applied if the task is seen as a classification task, assigning items to classes. However, in this case we should choose a suitable method which allows for multiple classes to be assigned to the same token. In addition, the most likely item choice (for practical reasons) for evaluation would be word tokens – and this does not take into account that several words often belong together to make up one candy speech expression (see Table 1). Thus, missing one candy speech expression should not count for different numbers of mismatches depending on the length of the phrase. Similar issues arise for other span-based annotations, such as named entity recognition (NER). A second option for evaluating span-based annotations comes from the NER literature and is based on matching markables (labeled spans) between a candidate and a reference annotation. Since all standardly available NER scorers however share the assumption that spans cannot overlap (Nakayama, 2018; Batista and Upson, 2020; Palen-Michel et al., 2021; Lignos et al., 2023), we implemented our own span-based F-score to compare two candy speech annotations. We calculate precision (P), recall (R) and F1 scores by counting whether the type and character span of each annotated candy speech expression matches between the two annotators (strict agreement) as well as whether both annotators identified the same type(s) of candy speech in a given comment (type agreement only; disregarding spans). The results show good agreement at the type level, and moderate agreement in the (very strict) fine-grained evaluation (see Table 3).

		Strict			Type		
Doc	#	P	R	F1	P	R	F1
Doc1	204	.66	.51	.58	.79	.61	.69
Doc2	242	.55	.48	.51	.84	.73	.78

Table 3: IAA on the fine-grained annotation.

4.3 Statistics on the annotated data

14,580 (31.5%) of the comments contain at least one candy speech expression.[2] In total, 21,785 expressions of candy speech were found. Table 4 shows the distribution per type.

Type	Count	%
affection declaration	3,933	18.1
compliment	3,504	16.1
encouragement	1,009	4.6
gratitude	474	2.2
group membership	558	2.6
positive feedback	11,403	52.3
sympathy	101	0.5
agreement	269	1.2
implicit	255	1.2
ambiguous	279	1.3
Total	21,785	100

Table 4: Distribution of candy speech types.

Positive feedback is the most frequent type and covers over 50% of all annotated expressions. It represents a more 'general' type of candy speech that occurs with all kinds of videos. *Affection declaration* and *compliment* are also frequent, with a proportion of 18% and 16%, respectively. The other types were found in less than 5% of all candy speech expressions, which can be explained by the fact that they are more specific and often closely linked to the video theme. For example, *sympathy* occurred mainly in the comments to a video about a natural disaster, while *gratitude* was most frequently found in the comments to a fitness tutorial.

Emojis/emoticons occurring without accompanying text, but with a clear positive meaning, were counted as *positive feedback* (275 instances; 2.4%). Beißwenger and Pappert (2019) have previously noted the significance of emojis for face-work of this kind. Other single emojis were counted as *group membership* (if they were clearly interpretable as the creator's symbol; see Scheffler 2024) or as *ambiguous* (if both negative and positive interpretations could in principle be possible; Scheffler and Nenchev 2024). These were less frequent, however (3 and 29 instances, respectively).

Initiative comments prevail over the reactive ones (92% vs. 8%, respectively). All types of

[2]For the documents annotated by both annotators, we consider the version of annotator 1.

candy speech occurred in both modes, except for *agreement*, which is only possible in responses.

5 Conclusion and discussion

This study contributes to the identification and promotion of positive online discourse. We have defined the phenomenon of candy speech as positive face-work in online communication and provided a detailed annotation scheme for its different types. Further, we discussed challenges related to the annotation and evaluation of this type of span-based semantic properties.

Our work facilitates a deeper understanding of positive face-work in online settings by showing that candy speech varies across several dimensions: its 'target' (e.g., an individual or their output), the domain/topic of the creator/video (e.g., expressions of *gratitude* are most common with videos offering practical advice), and the level of intensity (e.g., *affection declaration* may reflect stronger emotions than *compliments* or *positive feedback*). Empirical research into candy speech and its linguistic realizations can yield insights into how virtual communities constitute themselves and support each other. The dataset we provide can be used to train computational models to detect (and potentially generate) various types of candy speech, and positive language more broadly, e.g., for mitigating face threats.

As the next step, we plan to look into a finer-grained differentiation of our majority class *positive feedback* as well as of the reactive comments with respect to face-supporting and face-saving acts.

Acknowledgments

We are grateful to Dennis Reisloh for providing a large part of the annotations. We would like to thank the anonymous reviewers for their helpful comments. This research was funded by the Deutsche Forschungsgemeinschaft (DFG, German Research Foundation), CRC 1567, Project ID 470106373.

References

Ron Artstein and Massimo Poesio. 2008. Survey article: Inter-coder agreement for computational linguistics. *Computational Linguistics*, 34(4):555–596.

David Batista and Matthew Antony Upson. 2020. nervaluate.

Michael Beißwenger and Steffen Pappert. 2019. How to be polite with emojis: a pragmatic analysis of face work strategies in an online learning environment. *European Journal for Applied Linguistics*, 7(2):225–253.

Bharathi Raja Chakravarthi and Vigneshwaran Muralidaran. 2021. Findings of the shared task on hope speech detection for equality, diversity, and inclusion. In *Proceedings of the First Workshop on Language Technology for Equality, Diversity and Inclusion*, pages 61–72, Kyiv. Association for Computational Linguistics.

Jacob Cohen. 1960. A coefficient of agreement for nominal scales. *Educational and Psychological Measurement*, 20(1):37–46.

Louis A. Cotgrove. 2018. Nottinghamer Korpus Deutscher YouTube-Sprache (The NottDeuYTSch Corpus). LINDAT/CLARIAH-CZ digital library at the Institute of Formal and Applied Linguistics (ÚFAL), Faculty of Mathematics and Physics, Charles University.

Louis A. Cotgrove. 2025. *Abogeil! The language of German teens on YouTube*. Number 63 in amades - Arbeiten und Materialien zur deutschen Sprache. IDS-Verlag, Mannheim.

Ritam Dutt, Rishabh Joshi, and Carolyn Rose. 2020. Keeping up appearances: Computational modeling of face acts in persuasion oriented discussions. In *Proceedings of the 2020 Conference on Empirical Methods in Natural Language Processing (EMNLP)*, pages 7473–7485, Online. Association for Computational Linguistics.

Erving Goffman. 1967. *Interaction Ritual: Essays on Face-to-Face Behavior*. Pantheon Books, New York.

Salud María Jiménez-Zafra, Miguel Ángel Garcia-Cumbreras, Daniel García-Baena, José Antonio Garcia-Díaz, Bharathi Raja Chakravarthi, Rafael Valencia-García, and Luis Alfonso Ureña-López. 2023. Overview of HOPE at IberLEF 2023: Multilingual hope speech detection. In *Procesamiento del Lenguaje Natural, Revista*, 71, pages 371–381.

Jan-Christoph Klie, Michael Bugert, Beto Boullosa, Richard Eckart de Castilho, and Iryna Gurevych. 2018. The INCEpTION Platform: Machine-Assisted and Knowledge-Oriented Interactive Annotation. In *Proceedings of the 27th International Conference on Computational Linguistics: System Demonstrations*, pages 5–9. Association for Computational Linguistics.

Tina Klüwer. 2011. "I like your shirt" - dialogue acts for enabling social talk in conversational agents. In *Intelligent Virtual Agents*, pages 14–27, Berlin, Heidelberg. Springer Berlin Heidelberg.

Tina Klüwer. 2015. *Social talk capabilities for dialogue systems*. Ph.D. thesis, Saarland University, Saarbrücken.

Constantine Lignos, Maya Kruse, and Andrew Rueda. 2023. Improving NER research workflows with SeqScore. In *Proceedings of the 3rd Workshop for Natural Language Processing Open Source Software (NLP-OSS 2023)*, pages 147–152, Singapore. Association for Computational Linguistics.

Hiroki Nakayama. 2018. seqeval: A python framework for sequence labeling evaluation. Software available from https://github.com/chakki-works/seqeval.

Lucille Njoo, Chan Park, Octavia Stappart, Marvin Thielk, Yi Chu, and Yulia Tsvetkov. 2023. TalkUp: Paving the way for understanding empowering language. In *Findings of the Association for Computational Linguistics: EMNLP 2023*, pages 9334–9354, Singapore. Association for Computational Linguistics.

Chester Palen-Michel, Nolan Holley, and Constantine Lignos. 2021. SeqScore: Addressing barriers to reproducible named entity recognition evaluation. In *Proceedings of the 2nd Workshop on Evaluation and Comparison of NLP Systems*, pages 40–50, Punta Cana, Dominican Republic. Association for Computational Linguistics.

Fabio Poletto, Valerio Basile, Manuela Sanguinetti, Cristina Bosco, and Viviana Patti. 2021. Resources and benchmark corpora for hate speech detection. *Language Resources and Evaluation*, 55(2):477–523.

Tatjana Scheffler. 2024. Emojis und Gruppenidentität auf Twitter. In Simon Meier-Vieracker, editor, *Reingegrätscht: Eine kleine Linguistik des Fußballs*, pages 73–81. Narr, Tübingen.

Tatjana Scheffler and Ivan Nenchev. 2024. Affective, semantic, frequency, and descriptive norms for 107 face emojis. *Behavior Research Methods*, 56(8):8159–8180.

Robert Stalnaker. 2002. Common Ground. *Linguistics and Philosophy*, 25(5):701–721.

Tuija Virtanen. 2022. Virtual performatives as facework practices on Twitter: Relying on self-reference and humour. *Journal of Pragmatics*, 189:134–146.

Variety delights (sometimes) – Annotation differences in morphologically annotated corpora

Andrea Dömötör[1], Balázs Indig[1,2], Dávid Márk Nemeskey[1],
[1]National Laboratory for Digital Heritage
[2]ELTE Faculty of Informatics
{domotor.andrea,nemeskey.david}@btk.elte.hu
indig.balazs@inf.elte.hu

Abstract

The goal of annotation standards is to ensure consistency across different corpora and languages. But do they succeed? In our paper, we experiment with morphologically annotated Hungarian corpora of different sizes (ELTE DH gold standard corpus, NYTK-NerKor, and Szeged Treebank) to assess their compatibility as a combined training corpus for morphological analysis and disambiguation. Our results show that combining any two corpora not only failed to improve the results of the trained tagger, but even degraded them due to the inconsistent annotations. Further analysis of the annotation differences among the corpora revealed inconsistencies of several sources: a different theoretical approach, lack of consensus, and tagset conversion issues.

Keywords: morphology, corpus annotation, corpus evaluation, POS tagging

1 Introduction

Annotation standards such as Universal Dependencies (UD) (Nivre et al., 2017) are intended to facilitate consistent annotation across corpora and languages. Linguistic annotation is time-consuming; therefore, combining different corpora that share the same annotation scheme could be an effective strategy to increase corpus size. In our research, we explored this possibility with morphologically annotated corpora in Hungarian. Training a text processing tool with several different Hungarian corpora has previously been proven to be an effective method for the recognition of named entities (Simon et al., 2022). Our assumption was that a larger training corpus would increase the performance of a lemmatizer and morphological analyzer tool as well.

However, linguistic annotation is a complex task and different theoretical approaches may allow subjectivity even within a well-defined annotation scheme. Therefore, it is highly questionable whether the corpora that are expected to be compatible are indeed so; and if not, whether it is possible to ensure a higher level of compatibility without manually re-annotating one of them.

In this paper we examine the compatibility of three morphologically annotated Hungarian corpora by using them as training data for POS-tagging tools. In Section 3 we present the corpora, their tagsets, and the tagger tools in detail. The section also describes our experiment setup: each corpora was split into train, dev, and test subsets which we used in different combinations for training and testing. Our results presented in Section 4 showed that pairing different corpora lowered the performance in each case. To analyze the differences in the tagsets and annotation schemes of the corpora, we performed further training and testing experiments where we used one corpus for training and another for testing (Section 5). The error analysis of these revealed inconsistencies of several sources: a different theoretical approach, lack of consensus, and tagset conversion issues.

Our findings contribute to the standardization of annotation schemes for Hungarian, including the revision of the UD guidelines. We also detected some issues in the corpora and the UD-conversion tool that we used that need to be addressed in the future.

2 Related Work

The issue of combining different corpora was previously addressed by Straka and Straková (2017) in the evaluation of UDPipe version 1.1. They trained the pipeline on a wide range of languages where multiple UD corpora were available. The tagger and parser models were trained both on the individual corpora and on combinations of different corpora. Generally, they found that the models achieved better results when only one corpus was used for training, combining different corpora de

Proceedings of the 19th Linguistic Annotation Workshop (LAW-XIX-2025), pages 270–278
July 31, 2025

graded performance. They also conducted more detailed experiments for smaller corpora with the goal of examining the possibility to enrich limited training data from other corpora. The paper shows the results in those cases only where the enrichment of the training corpus resulted in better performance in dependency annotation. This means a total of 12 corpora in ancient Greek, Czech, English, French, Italian, Latin, Slovenian, and Swedish languages. Extending the original datasets from other corpora improved the performance of POS tagging in 6 cases, morphological feature identification in 4, and lemmatization in 7 cases. Thus, increasing corpus size from other sources did not work in every case, not even for small corpora. The authors explain this with the inconsistencies in the annotations of the different corpora (*"the Universal Dependencies are yet not so universal as everyone would like"*).

Wisniewski and Yvon (2019) examine the discrepancies in annotations of UD corpora, focusing primarily on English and French treebanks, as these are among the most extensively represented languages. To detect differences between the corpora, they used the method of Boyd et al. (2008), which states that if two identical sequences are annotated differently, then one of the sequences is likely to be inconsistent. According to Wisniewski and Yvon (2019), inconsistencies may naturally occur within a corpus as well, but in all the cases examined, the ratio of conflicting annotations was higher between different corpora than within one. The authors conducted another experiment to characterize differences between corpora. In this, they trained a binary classifier to decide which of the two corpora a sentence belongs to. The intuitive assumption is that the higher the error rate of this classifier is, the more similar the two corpora are. The classifier was trained on words, POS tags, and word + POS tag pairs. The most successful classification was achieved with the last combination, which suggests that varying annotations of identical words (or sequences of words) characterize the corpora well, indicating that the differences between the annotations of different corpora are systematic.

It can thus be said that the discrepancies in annotation schemes among different corpora of the same language are a known issue that affects multiple languages.

3 Corpora and Tools Used

For our experiments, we used three manually annotated Hungarian corpora of different sizes. The largest among them is the Szeged Treebank (Vincze et al., 2010), which is currently used as the training corpus for HuSpacy (Orosz et al., 2023). Its total size is 1 362 505 tokens. The bulk of the original annotations (Csendes et al., 2004) was automatically converted to the Universal Dependencies standard[1]. On a small part of the corpus[2] (42 032 tokens), the converted UD annotations were manually checked and corrected; this is the only subset openly available in the UD treebank repository (Nivre et al., 2020).

The second largest corpus we used is NYTK-NerKor[3] (Simon and Vadász, 2021), which contains a total of 1 017 340 tokens, while the smallest ELTE DH gold standard corpus (K. Molnár and Dömötör, 2023)[4] consists of 496 060 tokens. Both corpora were annotated with the same methodology. They used the emtsv (Indig et al., 2019) text processing pipeline for pre-processing, and its output was manually corrected by human annotators. The rule-based morphological analyzer module (Novák et al., 2016) of the pipeline assigns all possible morphological and morphosyntactic analyses to each word of the input text. The annotations are linked to each morpheme of the word (Example 1). The POS tagger module, PurePos (Orosz and Novák, 2013) disambiguates the analyses suggested by the analyzer module and provides the lemma and the morphological tag of the word (Example 2). The emtsv tag is a simplified combination of the emMorph tags of each morpheme of the word.

(1) *tető[/N]-n[Supe]*
roof-SUPESSS

'on (the) roof'

(2) Word: *tetőn – 'on (the) roof'*
Lemma: *tető – 'roof'*
Tag: `[/N][Supe]`

[1] https://github.com/huspacy/huspacy-resources/tree/master/data/processed/szeged-corpus

[2] https://github.com/UniversalDependencies/UD_Hungarian-Szeged/

[3] https://github.com/nytud/NYTK-NerKor/

[4] https://github.com/ELTE-DH/gold-standard

This means that the emtsv tags are not merely POS-tags. They also contain all the morphosyntactic information that is represented in the morphological features in Universal Dependencies. The emtsv tagset can be converted automatically to UD; both NerKor and the ELTE DH corpus used the emmorph2ud2 (Vadász and Simon, 2019) converting tool to add the UD annotation layer. The UD tags were not manually checked in either of the corpora, but NerKor did apply some dictionary- and rule-based corrections in cases where their scheme differed from the UD guidelines[5]. The ELTE DH corpus did not change the output of the UD conversion tool (as it is supposed to be unambigous).

In summary, all three corpora have UD morphological annotations and two of them also contain emtsv tags, meaning the three corpora could potentially be merged to form a substantially larger and more comprehensive training dataset for morphological analyzers and POS-tagging tools. All three corpora are genre heterogeneous, containing overlapping and unique text types. Combining the corpora thus achieves not only a larger size but also greater genre diversity. The genres found in the corpora are summarized in Table 1.

For testing the compatibility of the corpora, we trained the lemmatizer and morphological analyzer modules of HuSpaCy and PurePos on each. HuSpaCy is a project that provides Hungarian models for spaCy, the latter of which does not officially support the language. Similarly to spaCy, it uses UD POS tags and morphological features. PurePos is an HMM-based automatic morphological annotation tool optimized for the emtsv tagset with the option of pre-analysis using the rule-based emMorph (Novák et al., 2016) module.

For the train-dev-test split of the corpora, we used the division of HuSpaCy's original training data (derived from the Szeged Treebank). The cutting ensured that each subcorpus is represented in the train, dev, and test sets with the same proportion, and that each set contained complete sentences only. First, the corpora were used separately for training and testing, then we attempted to combine them in pairs.

All models were trained for at most 50 epochs. For HuSpaCy, we disabled all components aside from the senter, tagger, morphologizer and lemmatizer modules. Due to inconsistencies in the HuSpaCy dependencies, we were unable to retrain the transformer-based models and only report results for the `hu_core_news_lg`[6] model. For context, these results can be compared with the numbers achieved by the public spaCy (Honnibal et al., 2020) models for other languages. The results of a total of 82 models in 24 languages are available on the official website.[7] The average performance of the models in POS tagging, morphological features identification, and lemmatization is shown in Table 2.

4 Results

4.1 HuSpaCy

Table 3 shows the results of HuSpaCy trained on different corpora and their combinations. In part-of-speech tagging (POS), NerKor achieved the best result. The performances in lemmatization seem to correspond to the sizes of the individual corpora. In identifying morphological features (Feats), the Szeged Treebank significantly underperformed compared to the other two corpora. However, it can generally be said that all three corpora meet or exceed the average performance of spaCy models in other languages, presented in Table 2.

In the bottom part of the table, we see that combining different corpora degraded the results in almost every case. The results of the smallest corpus (ELTE DH) slightly improved when combined with NerKor. In another instance, we see an improvement is the lemmatization accuracy of the ELTE–Szeged pairing, which surpasses that of the ELTE DH corpus but still stays below the accuracy achieved by the Szeged corpus alone. The worst result was obtained by pairing the two larger corpora, NerKor and the Szeged Treebank. According to these results, ELTE DH and NerKor seem more compatible than any other corpus pair. This might be due to the fact that both used the same converter tool to create their UD layers.

4.2 PurePos

We conducted similar experiments with PurePos on the two corpora containing emtsv annotations (ELTE DH and NerKor). First the analyzer was trained without using the emMorph module, meaning it had to learn the tagset solely from the data without pre-analysis available. Similarly to the

[5] https://github.com/nytud/NYTK-NerKor/blob/main/ud_pos_feats.md

[6] https://huggingface.co/huspacy/hu_core_news_lg

[7] https://spacy.io/models

	ELTE DH	NYTK-NerKor	Szeged Treebank
Literary	✓	✓	✓
Scientific-popular	(articles) ✓	(wikipedia) ✓	
Blog	✓		
Legal	✓	✓	✓
News		✓	✓
Web		✓	
Student essays			✓
IT-related			✓

Table 1: Genres of the corpora

POS	Morph	Lemma
0,966	0,944	0,940

Table 2: Average accuracy values of spaCy models in different languages

Corpus	train	dev	test	POS	Lemma	Feats
ELTE DH	485 525	5250	5285	0,982	0,975	0,977
NerKor	997 002	10 167	10 148	0,986	0,982	0,979
Szeged	1 340 639	11 418	10 448	0,983	0,987	0,969
ELTE DH + NerKor	1 482 527	15 417	15 433	0,984	0,977	0,978
ELTE DH + Szeged	1 826 164	16 668	15 733	0,976	0,979	0,954
NerKor + Szeged	2 337 641	21 585	20 596	0,914	0,918	0,897

Table 3: HuSpaCy results trained on different corpora

experiments with HuSpaCy, we trained PurePos separately on each corpus as well as on their combination. The results are shown in Table 4. The UD and emMorph lemmas are presented in separate columns because NerKor assigns two types of lemma to the words: the original (emMorph) lemmas were adjusted to the UD scheme during the UD conversion. Thus, we included both lemma variants in our training experiments.

We can see that the two corpora performed equally in the tagging task despite their different sizes. In lemmatization, the UD lemmas of NerKor proved to be easier to learn than the emMorph lemmas, whereas the two types attained the same accuracy in the ELTE DH corpus (which further was incidentally the same as the results for the emMorph lemmas in NerKor). We find again that combining the two corpora not only failed to improve the results but downright degraded them.

Table 5 presents results from the same training setup but this time we used the built-in emMorph pre-analyzer module so the task of the model trained from the corpora was disambiguation only. For reference, it is worth examining how much of the words are already unambiguous. This was most easily measurable in the xml version of the ELTE DH corpus, as it contains all alternative emtsv analyses. Accordingly, for nearly half (45.7%) of the words both the lemma and the tag are unambiguous. This sets a baseline for (and a lower limit on) the performance of PurePos on this corpus.

Compared to Table 4, the results are mixed. The emMorph pre-analyzer improved both the tagging and lemmatization performance on the ELTE DH corpus significantly; in the latter task, PurePos + emMorph even outperforms HuSpaCy. The comperatively lower results on NerKor suggest that the annotations of NerKor tend to differ from the emtsv pre-analyses.

5 Corpus and tagset differences

The results shown in the previous section suggest significant annotation inconsistencies between the

Corpus	train	test	Tag	Lemma (UD)	Lemma (emMorph)
ELTE DH	485 525	10 535	0,948	0,925	0,925
NYTK-NerKor	997 002	20 315	0,948	0,940	0,925
ELTE DH + NerKor	1 482 527	30 850	0,942	0,923	0,919

Table 4: PurePos results trained on various corpora without emMorph pre-analysis

Corpus	train	test	Tag	Lemma (UD)	Lemma (emMorph)
ELTE DH	485 525	10 535	0,963	0,982	0,982
NYTK-NerKor	997 002	20 315	0,936	0,948	0,954
ELTE + NerKor	1 482 527	30 850	0,942	0,958	0,958

Table 5: PurePos results trained on various corpora with emMorph pre-analysis

examined corpora that might be caused by differences in the tagset or in the use of certain tags. In this section we discuss in detail the inconsistencies we found.

5.1 UD POS tags

The UD POS tagsets are quite consistent in the three corpora, we only found two differences. The first one is marginal: Szeged Treebank uses a special `SYM` tag for emoticons while the other two corpora tag them as `X`. The other difference, the usage of the `AUX` (auxiliary verb) tag is more common and problematic. The ELTE DH corpus does not have `AUX` tag at all and the Szeged Treebank and NerKor tags different words with it.

In the UD guidelines[8] an auxiliary is described as "a function word that accompanies the lexical verb of a verb phrase and expresses grammatical distinctions not carried by the lexical verb". The guidelines differentiate tense, passive, modal, agreement auxiliaries, and verbal copulas within this category. The Hungarian UD guidelines are quite narrow on the issue, it states that "we consider the verbs “volna”, “fog”, “talál” and “szokott” as AUX in Hungarian". *Volna* and *fog* are tense auxiliaries for the past conditional and future tenses respectively, while *talál* and *szokott* express modality (*'happen to'*) and aspect (*'used to'*). This list seems rather arbitrary and none of the corpora adhere to it.

Szeged Treebank uses the `AUX` tag for the two tense auxiliaries *volna* and *fog*, as well as for copulas. *Volna* has only one form and is attached to a finite verb (Example 3a). *Fog* has the paradigm for person and number and accompanies an infinitive (Example 3b). Finally, the copula is also conjugated for person and number, but it has present and past tenses as well (Example 3c).

The UD tags in the other two corpora are conversions from the emtsv tagset, which does not have an auxiliary tag itself. As the UD conversion in the ELTE DH corpus was fully automatic, the `AUX` tag is missing from the corpus altogether. In Nerkor, the auxiliary *volna* is tagged as `[/V]` (verb with no inflections) which allows their automatic conversion to `AUX`. However, this was not an option for *fog* and the copula as those have inflections and coincide with other verbs (e.g. *fog* also means "to grasp/hold").

(3) a. *Elmondhattad* *volna*
tell-PST-MOD-SG2 COND

'You could have told (me)'

b. *El* *fogja* *mondani*
PVB FUT-SG3 tell-INF

'He/She will tell'

c. *Ez* *gyors* *volt*
this-PRON fast-ADJ was-COP-SG3-PAST

'It was fast'

The UD guidelines mention modal auxiliaries as well, which is controversial in the Hungarian linguistic tradition (Kalivoda and Prószéky, 2024). They are commonly described as finite verb + infinitive constructions, but they do not form a well-defined category. Therefore, annotating them as

[8]https://universaldependencies.org/guidelines.html

AUX would inevitably require arbitrary decisions about which words to include as modal auxiliary.

In order to detect other systematic differences in the annotation schemes of the three corpora, we conducted further experiments where we used one corpus for training and another one for testing. Table 6 shows the POS-tagging results with HuSpaCy.

	ELTE DH	NerKor	Szeged
ELTE DH	0,982	0,950	0,930
NerKor	0,944	0,986	0,944
Szeged	0,922	0,937	0,983

Table 6: POS-tagging results across corpora. Each row shows the results of the model trained on the corpus indicated in the first column.

Not surprisingly, using the same corpus for training and testing provides the best result. For more insight on annotation differences, we examined the F-scores by tag. We found that most common tags (NOUN, ADJ, VERB, NUM, DET, PART, SCONJ, PUNCT) show stable results with any training and testing setup. Some tags' scores however, drop significantly when the training and testing data are from different corpora.

This is the case with proper nouns (PROPN) that can be explained with annotation differences and anomalies in the UD conversion. Emtsv does not have a specific tag for proper nouns, so the converter tool converts every uppercased noun to PROPN. This can be problematic with multiword proper names that contain adjectives and other words as well, such as certain institution names. The ELTE DH corpus annotates the elements of these based on their morphology; therefore, the adjectival parts of multiword names are converted to ADJ instead of PROPN. NerKor solves this issue by using 'part of proper name' (caseless noun, i.e. [/N]) tags for each inner token in a named entity. With this approach named entities are handled as a whole, and the morphological features of the inner elements are not displayed. Another approach could be to keep the original emtsv tags of the elements and modify the UD converter accordingly (by including uppercased adjectives).

Another common issue is the distinction of coordinate conjuncts (CCONJ), subordinate conjuncts (SCONJ) and adverbs (ADV). The confusion between CCONJ and SCONJ (which happened when Szeged Treebank was paired with another corpus) is likely due to the UD conversion. Emtsv has only one [/Cnj] tag for both coordinate and subordinate conjuncts. The converter differentiates based on a lexicon that lists 10 elements as subordinate conjuncts. Other conjuncts are converted to CCONJ, often wrongly. The list of subordinate conjuncts needs to be extended with elements such as *mintha* 'like/as if', *hogyha* 'if', *minthogy* 'since/whereas', etc.

The confusion between conjuncts and adverbs (and also pronouns) is quite common, as several lexical items are in fact ambigous. A closer look at these tags in the corpora revealed that Szeged Treebank overuses the ADV tag. There are 10 lemmas that Szeged Treebank exclusively tags as ADV while in NerKor and ELTE DH they are (and should be) tagged as conjuncts, such as *emellett* 'besides', *mialatt* 'while' and *ugyanakkor* 'at the same time'. The dropping F-score of the ADV tag in the Szeged – other corpus pairings is likely due to these erroneous annotations.

5.2 UD features

The feature sets of the corpora also show some differences. Szeged Treebank has some unique features that are not present in the other two corpora. Poss is a boolean feature for possessive pronouns, determiners, or adjectives. Szeged Treebank uses it for possessive pronouns, while ELTE DH and NerKor mark the possessiveness of pronouns with the Number[psed] (possessed object's number) feature. Other feature exclusively used in Szeged Treebank is NumType[sem] that is not mentioned in the UD guidelines but according to Szeged Treebank's data it specifies some semantic categories of numeric lexical items such as time (*7.20*), result (e. g. of a futball match: *2:0*) or quotient (*50:50*). The functions of Type and Cas features in Szeged Treebank are not exactly clear. Type is used for website names and gets values of *w* or *o*. Cas is probably an obsolete version of Case where the case values are coded with numbers. Lastly, Szeged Treebank is not consistent with the name of the reflexive pronoun feature. It appears both in form of Reflex (which is the correct form according to the UD guidelines and is used in the other two corpora) and Reflexive.

There are slight differences in the feature value sets as well. Some values are not represented in all three corpora because they are rare. This is the case with the absolute superlative Degree=Abs and the "general locative" Case=Loc used for the archaic locative of some Hungarian cities. Other value differences are caused by the UD conversion of emtsv. The dative and genitive cases have the same suffix in Hungarian (*-nak/-nek*, see Example 4) and emtsv always annotates them as dative, there is no tag for the genitive case. Therefore, the UD converter converts all nominals with the dative/genitive suffix to dative, which means that the ELTE DH corpus has no `Case=Gen` feature value. NerKor, however, seems to have changed some of the `Case=Dat` values to genitive, probably with the intention of matching Szeged Treebank. The method of identifying the genitive case is not documented thus it is unsure whether the `Case=Gen` features are correct.

(4) a. *a* *cég* *elemző-i-nek*
the company analyst-PL-GEN
közlés-e
announcement-POSS.SG3

'the announcement of the company's analysts'

b. *átad-t-a* *a* *cég*
hand-PST-SG3 the company
elemző-i-nek
analyst-PL-DAT

'He/She handed it/them to the company's analysts'

Other difference between ELTE DH and NerKor is that NerKor distinguishes between adjectival participles and adjectives, using `[/V][_ImpfPtcp/Adj]`, `[/V][_PerfPtcp/Adj]`, and `[/V][_ModPtcp/Adj]` tags for the former, while in the ELTE DH corpus, this distinction only appears in detailed emMorph analysis; the simple emtsv tag is `[/Adj]` in every case. While the UD converter converts both adjectives and participles to `ADJ`, the difference still affects the UD features, as in NerKor an extra `VerbForm` feature is added for participles, which does not appear in either the ELTE DH or the Szeged Treebank, where the annotation for adjectival participles matches that of simple adjectives.

Another issue with the UD conversion is that it loses some cases that are present in emtsv. For example, the comitative case is not handled at all by the converter script; therefore, it converts to the default nominative. Nouns in the distributive case are converted to `ADV` which results in dropping all the features. As the derivational suffix for the distributive case is productive, the noun POS tag and the `Case=Dis` feature should be kept.

Lastly, Szeged Treebank has some erroneous `PronType` values, like `PrsPron` instead of `Prs` or pronoun types coded with single letters (probably a remainder from an older version of the corpus).

The overall results of the features with train and test sets of different corpora are shown in Table 7. It seems that ELTE DH and Szeged Treebank make the least compatible pairing. This is probably mostly due to the previously mentioned conversion issues, some of which have been corrected in NerKor.

	ELTE DH	**NerKor**	**Szeged**
ELTE DH	0,977	0,931	0,896
NerKor	0,926	0,979	0,925
Szeged	0,889	0,906	0,969

Table 7: Feature results across corpora. Each row shows the results of the model trained on the corpus indicated in the first column.

Examining the F-scores by feature revealed that pairing different corpora makes the results of `NumType` and `PronType` features drop the most (in addition to those already mentioned). The most confused values of the `NumType` feature are `Card` (cardinal numbers) and `Frac` (fractions). A notable difference we found in the use of these values is that Szeged Treebank uses the `Frac` value for numbers with decimals while these numbers have `NumType=Card` values in ELTE DH and NerKor. The main issue with `PronType` is the distinction of personal (`Prs`) and demonstrative (`Dem`) pronouns, especially between ELTE DH and Nerkor. Emtsv has different tags for these pronoun types (`[/N|Pro]` and `[/Det|Pro]`, respectively) that were often confused by the PurePos models with every corpus setup. After the UD conversion, both pronouns get the `PRON` POS tag; they only differ in the `PronType` feature. Although personal and demonstrative pronouns are often homonymous in Hungarian, the generally low scores of these pronoun types suggest that it might be worth checking their annotations for possible errors.

5.3 emtsv

The emtsv tags of NerKor and ELTE DH are inherently very diverse, as they include several features. According to Vadász and Simon (2019), there are

2088 possible combinations[9]. The two corpora together contain 2024 different tags, only 1025 of which are common between them. This emphasizes the relevance of rule-based analyzer modules (like the emMorph module in PurePos) because a tag variation this great is almost impossible to cover with a training corpus. As emtsv was designed specifically for Hungarian it has several features that are not present in Universal Dependencies. For comparison, the three discussed corpora have altogether 1790 UD POS + feature combinations, 593 of which are common among them. We mapped these UD POS + feature combinations with their respective emtsv tags and found that nominals (nouns, adjectives, and proper nouns) show the greatest diversity. Special features include derivations, semantic categories (like nations or colors), and syntactic (like attributive a predicative adjectives) and word form (like abbreviations and acronyms) features. This much granularity in the tagset is not ideal for machine learning but it can be very valuable for corpus linguists.

The results of PurePos when trained and tested on different corpora are shown in Table 8. As expected, the performance of the models is 4-5% lower in the cross-evaluation setup.

	ELTE DH	**NerKor**
ELTE DH	0,948	0,891
NerKor	0,902	0,942

Table 8: PurePos tagging results across corpora. Each row shows the results of the model trained on the corpus indicated in the first column.

The main differences beetwen the annotation schemes of ELTE DH and NerKor were already discussed in the previous sections. With the UD conversion these differences split between the POS tags and the features.

6 Summary

In summary, the consistency of annotations proved to be more crucial than corpus size in training morphological analyzers. The results obtained from the combination of different corpora demonstrated that even small discrepancies in the annotation schemes can pose significant challenges to the tagging tools.

The annotation differences of the corpora are from several sources. In some cases they are deliberate like the different handling of multiword proper names in ELTE DH and NerKor. Annotations may also differ due to the lack of consensus regarding a phenomenon or category, which is the case with auxiliaries in Hungarian. In other cases the cause of difference was the fact that one of the corpora over-simplified (or complicated) a tag or simply made mistakes. An example for the former is the different annotations of participles in ELTE DH and NerKor, and for the latter we can mention the overuse of `ADV` in Szeged Treebank, mostly at the expense of conjuncts.

Our research also revealed some issues with the emtsv–UD converter tool. For future work we plan to extend the list of subordinate conjuncts and add the missing cases.

As we got good results with training with the corpora separately, the question arises whether compatibility of different corpora is really that essential. In our opinion, having detailed guidelines is crucial for an international standard like Universal Dependencies. The fact that this is still missing for Hungarian presents an ongoing challenge for the Hungarian NLP community. Fixing the issues revealed in our research, such as the obsolete features in Szeged Treebank and the annotation of participles in ELTE DH, is also an important future work.

However, emtsv is an inherently language-specific annotation scheme for Hungarian, which makes the emMorph analysis and the emtsv tag layer a suitable way for the corpora to retain their unique character.

[9] `https://github.com/nytud/panmorph/blob/master/emmorph.tsv`

References

Adriane Boyd, Markus Dickinson, and Detmar Meurers. 2008. On detecting errors in dependency treebanks. *Research on Language and Computation*, 6:113–137.

Dóra Csendes, János Csirik, and Tibor Gyimóthy. 2004. The szeged corpus: A pos tagged and syntactically annotated hungarian natural language corpus. In *Proceedings of the 5th International Workshop on Linguistically Interpreted Corpora LINC 2004 at The 20th International Conference on Computational Linguistics COLING 2004*, pages 19–23.

Matthew Honnibal, Ines Montani, Sofie Van Landeghem, and Adriane Boyd. 2020. spaCy: Industrial-strength Natural Language Processing in Python.

Balázs Indig, Bálint Sass, Eszter Simon, Iván Mittelholcz, Noémi Vadász, and Márton Makrai. 2019. One format to rule them all – the emtsv pipeline for hungarian. In *Proceedings of the 13th Linguistic Annotation Workshop. Association for Computational Linguistics*, pages 155–165.

Emese K. Molnár and Andrea Dömötör. 2023. Gondolatok a gondola-tokról. Morfológiai annotációt javító módszerek tesztelése gold standard korpuszon. In *XIX. Magyar Számítógépes Nyelvészeti Konferencia*, pages 341–356, Szeged.

Ágnes Kalivoda and Gábor Prószéky. 2024. Hungarian auxiliaries revisited. *Acta Linguistica Academica*, 71:202–218.

Joakim Nivre, Marie-Catherine de Marneffe, Filip Ginter, Jan Hajič, Christopher D. Manning, Sampo Pyysalo, Sebastian Schuster, Francis Tyers, and Daniel Zeman. 2020. Universal Dependencies v2: An evergrowing multilingual treebank collection. In *Proceedings of the 12th Language Resources and Evaluation Conference*, pages 4034–4043, Marseille, France. European Language Resources Association.

Joakim Nivre, Daniel Zeman, Filip Ginter, and Francis Tyers. 2017. Universal Dependencies. In *Proceedings of the 15th Conference of the European Chapter of the Association for Computational Linguistics: Tutorial Abstracts*, Valencia, Spain. Association for Computational Linguistics.

Attila Novák, Borbála Siklósi, and Csaba Oravecz. 2016. A New Integrated Open-source Morphological Analyzer for Hungarian. In *Proceedings of the Tenth International Conference on Language Resources and Evaluation (LREC 2016)*, pages 1315—-1322, Portorož.

György Orosz, Gergő Szabó, Péter Berkecz, Zsolt Szántó, and Richárd Farkas. 2023. Advancing Hungarian Text Processing with HuSpaCy: Efficient and Accurate NLP Pipelines. In *Text, Speech, and Dialogue*, pages 58–69, Cham. Springer Nature Switzerland.

György Orosz and Attila Novák. 2013. PurePos 2.0: a hybrid tool for morphological disambiguation. In *Proceedings of the International Conference on Recent Advances in Natural Language Processing (RANLP 2013)*, pages 539–545, Hissar, Bulgaria. INCOMA Ltd. Shoumen.

Eszter Simon and Noémi Vadász. 2021. Introducing NYTK-NerKor, A Gold Standard Hungarian Named Entity Annotated Corpus. In *Text, Speech, and Dialogue - 24th International Conference, TSD 2021, Olomouc, Czech Republic, September 6-9, 2021, Proceedings*, volume 12848 of *Lecture Notes in Computer Science*, pages 222–234. Springer.

Eszter Simon, Noémi Vadász, Dániel Lévai, Dávid Márk Nemeskey, György Orosz, and Zsolt Szántó. 2022. Az NYTK-NerKor több szempontú kiértékelése. In *XXVIII. Magyar Számítógépes Nyelvészeti Konferencia*, pages 403–416, Szeged. Szegedi Tudományegyetem TTIK, Informatikai Intézet.

Milan Straka and Jana Straková. 2017. Tokenizing, POS tagging, lemmatizing and parsing UD 2.0 with UDPipe. In *Proceedings of the CoNLL 2017 Shared Task: Multilingual Parsing from Raw Text to Universal Dependencies*, pages 88–99, Vancouver, Canada. Association for Computational Linguistics.

Noémi Vadász and Eszter Simon. 2019. Konverterek magyar morfológiai címkekészletek között. In *XV. Magyar Számítógépes Nyelvészeti Konferencia*, pages 99–111, Szeged. Szegedi Tudományegyetem, Informatikai Intézet.

Veronika Vincze, Dóra Szauter, Attila Almási, György Móra, Zoltán Alexin, and János Csirik. 2010. Hungarian Dependency Treebank. In *Proceedings of LREC 2010*, Valletta, Malta. ELRA.

Guillaume Wisniewski and François Yvon. 2019. How Bad are PoS Tagger in Cross-Corpora Settings? Evaluating Annotation Divergence in the UD Project. In *Proceedings of the 2019 Conference of the North American Chapter of the Association for Computational Linguistics: Human Language Technologies, Volume 1 (Long and Short Papers)*, pages 218–227, Minneapolis, Minnesota. Association for Computational Linguistics.

Addressing Variability in Interlinear Glossed Texts with Linguistic Linked Data

Maxim Ionov
University of Zaragoza, Spain
max.ionov@gmail.com

Natalia Patiño Mazzotti
Goethe University Frankfurt, Germany
nataliapatinomazzotti@gmail.com

Abstract

In this paper, we identify types of uncertainty in interlinear glossed text (IGT) annotation, a common notation for language data in linguistic research. Using the Linked Data paradigm, we provide guidelines for encoding IGT to address these uncertainties, enhancing interpretability and interoperability without compromising expressivity. Finally, we present *ligt-search*, a command-line tool with Python bindings provided as part of *ligttools* suite, that uses these guidelines to offer searching and filtering capabilities across multiple datasets in an interoperable way.

1 Introduction

1.1 Background

Interlinear glossed text (IGT) is a notation commonly used to represent language examples in descriptive and typological linguistics. It is designed to provide an intuitive way of showing language material so that it could be understood without needing to know the language. IGT data may consist of any number of layers added under the original text (hence *interlinear*): word-by-word translation, grammatical meaning of morphemes, transliteration, free translation, etc. Some layers have morpheme-by-morpheme alignment between each other, e.g. morpheme segmentation and grammatical meaning of morphemes. Consider the following example from Tundra Yukaghir:

(1) Ieruuče lalime-le me=köjle-s-um.
hunter sledge-ACC PF=break-CAUS-TR.3SG
'The hunter broke the sledge.'
(Schmalz, 2013, p. 66)

This example consists of three layers: morphological segmentation, glosses aligned with the transcription layer, and free translation. The second word is divided into two elements: a root glossed as 'sledge' and a morph *-le*, glossed as the accusative case. The next word[1] consists of the clitic *me=* attached to the verb *kölje* 'break' followed by the causative suffix *-s* and *-um* glossed as TR.3SG, that is, transitive and third person singular.

Generally, datasets and published works that contain IGT follow the Leipzig Glossing Rules, LGR (Comrie et al., 2008), a set of guidelines and recommended glosses for common grammatical categories, such as PL to annotate plural grammatical meaning or ACC for accusative case.

Additionally to these guidelines, a list of abbreviations (markers) for less common grammatical categories is usually included with the data, especially in cases in which a grammatical category is relevant in a given language but not necessarily cross-linguistically.

1.2 Variability in IGT

Since the Leipzig Glossing Rules are guidelines, great variability is allowed to annotate data. The flexibility that these guidelines provide allows them to adapt according to the language, distinguishing several subcategories of a particular grammatical category, when needed. Example (2) introduces a very specific gloss BEFORE.UU, which in the context of the Ese Ejja language is used for subordinated clauses coding coreferentiality between the two (unique)[2] arguments of the main and dependent clauses:

(2) poki-ximawa, eya kya-eno pwaje
go-**BEFORE.UU** 1ABS APF-sad be.FUT
'Before (I) leave, I will be sad.'
(Vuillermet, 2014, p. 358)

[1]The term 'word' is used here as a simplification to refer to a visually separated unit of annotation. The strict definition does not impact the annotations since only morphs and complete examples have corresponding translations. For more on the concept of word, see Schiering et al. (2010); Haspelmath (2023).

[2]According to Vuillermet, Unique arguments are the only arguments of intransitive verbs.

Proceedings of the 19th Linguistic Annotation Workshop (LAW-XIX-2025), pages 279–284
July 31, 2025

Generally, coreference of subjects or lack thereof (a grammatical category known as switch-reference) is marked via the glosses SS (same subject) and DS (different subject). In Ese Ejja, marking the specific syntactic function of the coreferent argument is crucial, since it triggers different marking. In this example, both arguments involved in the coreference are subjects of intransitive clauses, which the author specifies as unique arguments.

In cases like (2), using a non-standard gloss is important since it provides additional information about the grammatical category (i.e. the type of clause and the co-reference of specific arguments).

However, this might hinder its interpretability and interoperability given that different sources might contain different glossing to encode the same grammatical category. The following examples show this variability for the category of evidentiality in Shipibo-Konibo (Panoan):

(3) a. Jawen jema-ronki ani iki.
POS3 village:ABS-**HSY** large COP
'Her village is very large.'
(Valenzuela, 2003, p. 534)

b. Jawen jema-ronki ani iki.
POSS3 village:ABS-**REP** large COP
'Her village is very large.'
(Valenzuela, 2008, p. 34)

In (3), the morpheme *-ronki* which encodes reportative evidential, has been glossed differently in two different instances. Note, that it is not immediately clear from the examples alone if the analyses of this morph in these two cases are identical or this is the case of different granularity for these two markers. The same example shows a more trivial but common case of variability in glossing, which shows the glosses POSS and POS referring to the same grammatical category. In this case, it is immediately clear that this is, in fact, the same category, but this can still cause problems for search or automatic methods.

In some cases, a morph can be analyzed in several ways, once again leading to inconsistent glossing. In the following example, the clausal clitic *=ti* in Yurakaré, that initially was thought to be a different-subject marker (DS), has been alternatively analysed as a nominalizer (NMZR) in more recent literature:

(4) a. më lëtëmë=chi mala-m=**ti**
2SG.PRN jungle–DIR go.SG-2SG.S–**DS**
sëë mi-n-nënë-ni
1SG.PRN 2SG-IO-cook-INTL:1SG.S
'While you go to the jungle, I'll cook.'
(Van Gijn, 2006, p. 312)

b. ta-ka-n-toro=**ti**
1PL.OBJ-3SG.OBJ-BEN-finish=**NMZR**
baytu tishi ta-sibbë=chi
go.1PL.EXH now 1PL.POSS-house=DIR
'When we finish it, let's go to our house immediately.'
(Gipper and Yap, 2019, p. 366)

These three examples demonstrate different cases of annotation inconsistency and variability:

- Multiple labels for the same category (3);
- Difference in granularity of labels (or overlap) (2);
- Alternative analyses (4).

Note, that this does not stem from an "incorrect" use of LGR, but is, in fact, an expected property described in the rules. However, it poses challenges for understanding the data and aggregating over it, both for people and algorithms. In simplest cases, like with glosses POS and POSS, this can be solved by cleaning the data, selecting a single label and normalising the annotation, but for the most part, modifying the glosses would lead to information loss, e.g. in case of (4), where the choice of a marker depends on the function of a morpheme that the author (annotator) wants to highlight. IGT annotations provide an interpretation of the data by a linguist that depends on many factors, and replacing one marker with with a seemingly similar one might change this interpretation. A better solution would be to preserve the original annotations but *explain* them, i.e. add semantics: establish relationships between annotations, group alternative labels, link to external databases of grammatical categories. In the next sections we show how to combine all that by employing the Linked Data paradigm.

The rest of the paper is organized as follows: Section 2 introduces the Linked Data paradigm and describes Ligt, a Linked Data vocabulary for representing IGT. In Section 3 we use Ligt to address each of the aforementioned issues with IGT annotation. Section 4 presents *ligt-search*, a tool that allow to search across Ligt datasets with different annotations.

Finally, Section 5 concludes the paper and outlines directions for future research.

2 Linguistic Linked Data and Ligt

2.1 Linked Data Paradigm

Linked Data is a set of best practices for publishing and connecting structured data on the Web using open standards (Berners-Lee, 2008). It is built around four key principles: using Universal Resource Identifiers (URIs) to uniquely identify entities, making them accessible via HTTP, providing structured descriptions using open standards such as RDF and SPARQL, and providing links to related resources via URIs. This approach allows for the creation of a machine-readable, semantically interconnected web of data, enabling data interoperability and reuse across domains in line with FAIR principles.

Linguistic Linked Data, LLD (Chiarcos et al., 2012; Cimiano et al., 2020) applies these principles specifically to linguistic resources such as lexicons and corpora. By representing linguistic entities with URIs, describing them in RDF, and linking them to external datasets, LLD facilitates semantic interoperability and integration across linguistic and NLP applications. The result is a distributed, reusable, and extensible ecosystem of linguistic data that supports advanced querying, cross-lingual research, and long-term data sustainability.

2.2 Ligt

Ligt is an RDF vocabulary designed for modelling IGT as Linked Data (Chiarcos and Ionov, 2019). It was developed as a generalisation over shallow RDF representations of traditional formats of storing IGT annotations, namely, Toolbox, FLEx and Xigt (Chiarcos et al. (2017) has a detailed description of the formats, their limitations, and these shallow representations). Since its inception, the vocabulary has been applied to multiple datasets, covering language data from hundreds of languages (Nordhoff, 2020b,a; Nordhoff and Krämer, 2022; Ionov, 2021) showing significantly increasing interoperability of collections of IGT coming from different sources stored in different formats.

The most commonly used components of the model are presented on Fig. 1: A dataset consists of texts or collections of IGT, both of which contain a number of `ligt:Utterances`. Utterances, in turn, consist of tiers of annotation which contain the smallest units of annotation — `ligt:Items`. The tiers can be either word-level or morph-level, with the property `ligt:correspondsTo` creating alignment between tiers.[3]

An important but underused feature of Ligt is that it allows having multiple tiers of the same type and multiple annotations for the same unit. Surprisingly, this is lacking in many common formats,[4] but as we show in Section 3.3, it is incredibly important for encoding parallel annotations.

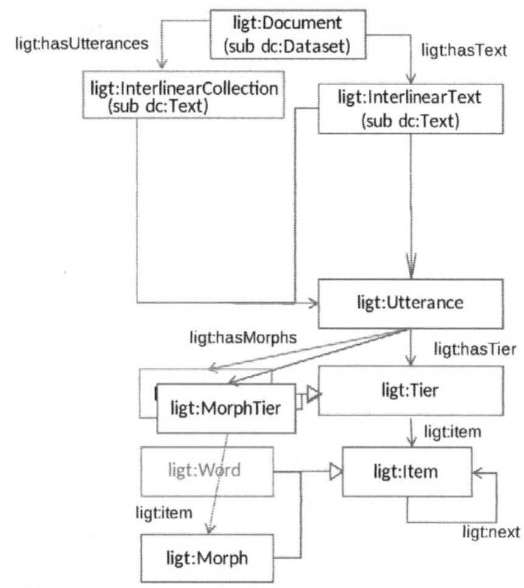

Figure 1: A simplified Ligt data model

3 Addressing Types of Annotation Variability in IGT

3.1 Multiple Labels

Probably the most straightforward issue leading to variation in annotation of IGT across datasets is having multiple labels referring to the same category. This can happen due to personal preferences of the annotator, convenience, or linguistic tradition. An example of this can be found in (3) with the markers REP and HSY both coding the hearsay type of evidentiality.

To address both cases, a user could provide a mapping from the label to a definition of the grammatical category in an external knowledge base. In practice, it is not strictly necessary to use a knowledge base for that, and the annotations can be mapped to an RDF entity defined ad-hoc in the dataset, however this solution lacks interoperability and will require a mapping from properties in each dataset that the user wants to query. With the mappings to a knowledge base, as long as all the datasets map to the same one, the data is interoperable.

[3]Full model description can be found at https://ligt-dev.github.io/ligt/.

[4]As far as we know, only Xigt representation allows this.

For example, the following triples map both evidentiality markers from (3) to hearsay evidentiality in the Ontology of Linguistic Annotation (OLiA) (Chiarcos and Sukhareva, 2015), specifically, to its module based on the UniMorph initiative (Batsuren et al., 2022):[5]

```
<http://purl.org/olia/unimorph.owl#HRSY>
                                    skos:notation "HSY"@en .
<http://purl.org/olia/unimorph.owl#HRSY>
                                    skos:notation "REP"@en .
```

Written like this, the mappings can be added to the triple store alongside with the data or used by SPARQL engines to add the new relations during runtime. The following SPARQL fragment selects morphs annotated as both HSY and REP:

```
...
?morph ligt:gloss ?label .
?meaning skos:notation ?label .
FILTER(?meaning = unimorph:HRSY)
...
```

This example is quite simple, and the same could have been achieved with a simple correspondence table between tagset-specific and universal tags. However, using RDF technologies provides several advantages: First, extending the mappings to several different knowledge bases is trivial. Second, while Ligt is designed to model the *syntax* of IGT, external mappings provide *semantics*: tags are not mere strings, but RDF entities which contain (depending on a knowledge base) additional information, including paradigmatic relationships with other tags.

3.2 Difference in Granularity

A more challenging issue in compatibility of glosses is partial overlap or difference in granularity between the two labels. For example, the aforementioned tag BEFORE.UU in (2) indicates a special case of switch reference, and could be mapped to the same category as the marker SS (same subject). However, with that we lose additional information, encoded in the gloss: a temporal relation between the dependent and the main clauses (BEFORE) and the type of coreference with regards to the semantic roles (unique-to-unique).

In order to create a mapping, we need to provide all the values that it expresses and map them to the string label with the property `skos:notation`, like in the previous section. However, this gloss corresponds to heterogeneous set of values: it combines grammatical categories with syntactic and semantic roles. While it is possible to find a suitable vocabulary to represent syntactic roles and clausal relationship — with OLiA discourse extension (Chiarcos, 2014), we have to create a property for the coreference type ourselves.[6]

```
:uu a owl:Class ;
     rdfs:label "Unique-to-Unique Coreference"@en ;
     rdfs:comment "A coreferent configuration where both
     referring expressions are the only arguments of an
     intransitive verb."@en .
:before_uu a owl:Class ;
    owl:intersectionOf (olia:PrecedenceRelation :uu) ;
    skos:notation "BEFORE.UU"@en .
```

With this, we can introduce the mapping between the gloss and the class as in the previous section:

```
:before_uu skos:notation "BEFORE.UU"@en .
```

Since the gloss is dataset-specific, we create the corresponding class ad-hoc. Despite that, we still have access to additional information about its components according to the relationships established for the ad-hoc class. For example, the following SPARQL fragment extracts labels of all the components of the class that corresponds to the label BEFORE.UU:

```
SELECT ?component ?label WHERE {
  ?compositeClass skos:notation "BEFORE.UU"@en ;
                  owl:intersectionOf ?list .

  ?list rdf:rest*/rdf:first ?component .
  OPTIONAL { ?component rdfs:label ?label }
}
```

3.3 Parallel Analyses

The final issue concerns alternative analyses. In (4), we see an example of that: clitic =*ti* is glossed differently in the same context in two different publications. Unlike the first issue, not only the label is different, but the underlying value as well: DS, a marker indicating switch-reference, was changed to NMZR, a nominalizer, which is a marker indicating a *process* of nominalisation.[7]

The previous solutions were applied to the marker itself, not to its instance, since those issues concerned every usage of a marker. In this case, we cannot apply the same method, since the change is in a specific annotation. However, Ligt provides native support for multiple analyses for both individual words and whole tiers. In this case, we only need to add an additional `ligt:Item` (a subclass

[5]This is just one of possible data sources that the annotations can be mapped to, and the same principle would work with any other repository of grammatical categories. More information on this can be found in (Ionov, 2021).

[6]While this is not necessary, this might be beneficial, especially if the new property would be created as a subclass of an existing context.

[7]As a side note, this is yet another demonstration of heterogeneity of IGT annotations: while switch-reference is a grammatical category, nominalisation is a process. So it is not only a change in the value, but in a type of the annotation.

of `ligt:Analysis`) in the appropriate part of the tier with morphs:[8]

```
:morphs a ligt:MorphTier ;
        ligt:item :m3_1, :m3_2, m3_3, m3_3_alt .
:w3 a ligt:Word ; rdfs:label "mala-m=ti" .
:m3_1 a ligt:Morph ; ligt:correspondsTo :w3 ;
      rdfs:label "mala" ; ligt:gloss "go.SG" ;
      ligt:next :m3_2 .
:m3_2 a ligt:Morph ; ligt:correspondsTo :w3 ;
      rdfs:label "-m" ; ligt:gloss "2SG.S" ;
      ligt:next :m3_2 .
:m3_3 a ligt:Morph ; ligt:correspondsTo :w3 ;
      rdfs:label "=ti" ; ligt:gloss "DS" .
:m3_3_alt a ligt:Morph ; ligt:correspondsTo :w3 ;
          rdfs:label "=ti" ; ligt:gloss "NMZR" .
```

4 Searching and filtering IGT with *ligt-search*

Following this analysis, we developed *ligt-search*, a tool which allows users to search across local and remote Ligt datasets. Integrated into a package *ligttools*,[9] it can be used either as a standalone command-line utility or called from Python code. In order to allow users combine datasets with different annotations, the tool accepts mappings and additional annotations for each dataset. This way, it addresses the issues discussed in this paper. As a result, not only it allows using datasets from different sources, it provides an opportunity to use opinionated annotations stored locally for the data that is being accessed remotely.

Combined with the other tool in the package, *ligt-convert*, which supports conversion from FLEx, ToolBox and CLDF formats at the time of writing, this allows searching across heterogeneous datasets in common IGT formats.

5 Summary and Outlook

In this paper, we identified three types of variability in IGT annotation and, using RDF vocabulary Ligt, proposed ways to address them to make the annotations more comparable and compatible across datasets. We also introduced *ligt-search*, a tool that uses these techniques to allow users search across IGT datasets in a flexible way, allowing them to provide their own mappings and additional annotations. In the future, this should become a basis for a user-friendly tool that could combine local and remote data, regardless of annotation inconsistencies and personal preferences.

[8] A good practice would be to add a metadata object to both analyses to provide provenance, which we skip here since it is not directly related to the issue.

[9] https://github.com/ligt-dev/ligttools

References

Khuyagbaatar Batsuren, Omer Goldman, Salam Khalifa, Nizar Habash, Witold Kieraś, Gábor Bella, Brian Leonard, Garrett Nicolai, Kyle Gorman, Yustinus Ghanggo Ate, and 1 others. 2022. Unimorph 4.0: Universal morphology. In *Proceedings of the Thirteenth Language Resources and Evaluation Conference*, pages 840–855.

Tim Berners-Lee. 2008. Linked Data. https://www.w3.org/DesignIssues/LinkedData.html. [Online; accessed 10-April-2025].

C. Chiarcos and Maria Sukhareva. 2015. OLiA - Ontologies of Linguistic Annotation. *Semantic Web*, 6:379–386.

Christian Chiarcos. 2014. Towards interoperable discourse annotation. discourse features in the ontologies of linguistic annotation. In *Proceedings of the Ninth International Conference on Language Resources and Evaluation (LREC'14)*, pages 4569–4577, Reykjavik, Iceland. European Language Resources Association (ELRA).

Christian Chiarcos and Maxim Ionov. 2019. Ligt: An LLOD-Native Vocabulary for Representing Interlinear Glossed Text as RDF. In *2nd Conference on Language, Data and Knowledge (LDK 2019)*, volume 70 of *Open Access Series in Informatics (OASIcs)*, pages 3:1–3:15, Dagstuhl, Germany. Schloss Dagstuhl – Leibniz-Zentrum für Informatik.

Christian Chiarcos, Maxim Ionov, Monika Rind-Pawlowski, Christian Fäth, Jesse Wichers Schreur, and Irina Nevskaya. 2017. Llodifying linguistic glosses. In *Language, Data, and Knowledge: First International Conference, LDK 2017, Galway, Ireland, June 19-20, 2017, Proceedings 1*, pages 89–103. Springer.

Christian Chiarcos, Sebastian Nordhoff, and Sebastian Hellmann. 2012. *Linked Data in Linguistics: Representing and Connecting Language Data and Language Metadata*. Springer Science & Business Media.

Philipp Cimiano, Christian Chiarcos, John P McCrae, and Jorge Gracia. 2020. *Linguistic Linked Data: Representation, Generation and Applications*. Springer Nature.

Bernard Comrie, Martin Haspelmath, and Balthasar Bickel. 2008. The Leipzig Glossing Rules: Conventions for interlinear morpheme-by-morpheme glosses. https://www.eva.mpg.de/lingua/pdf/Glossing-Rules.pdf.

Sonja Gipper and Foong Ha Yap. 2019. Life of= ti: Use and grammaticalization of a clausal nominalizer in yurakaré. In *Nominalization in Languages of the Americas*, pages 363–390. John Benjamins Publishing Company.

Martin Haspelmath. 2023. Defining the word. *WORD*, 69(3):283–297.

Maxim Ionov. 2021. APiCS-Ligt: Towards Semantic Enrichment of Interlinear Glossed Text. In *3rd Conference on Language, Data and Knowledge (LDK 2021)*, volume 93 of *Open Access Series in Informatics (OASIcs)*, pages 27:1–27:8, Dagstuhl, Germany. Schloss Dagstuhl – Leibniz-Zentrum für Informatik.

Sebastian Nordhoff. 2020a. From the attic to the cloud: mobilization of endangered language resources with linked data. In *Proceedings of the Workshop about Language Resources for the SSH Cloud*, pages 10–18, Marseille, France. European Language Resources Association.

Sebastian Nordhoff. 2020b. Modelling and annotating interlinear glossed text from 280 different endangered languages as linked data with LIGT. In *Proceedings of the 14th Linguistic Annotation Workshop*, pages 93–104, Barcelona, Spain. Association for Computational Linguistics.

Sebastian Nordhoff and Thomas Krämer. 2022. IMT-Vault: Extracting and enriching low-resource language interlinear glossed text from grammatical descriptions and typological survey articles. In *Proceedings of the 8th Workshop on Linked Data in Linguistics within the 13th Language Resources and Evaluation Conference*, pages 17–25, Marseille, France. European Language Resources Association.

René Schiering, Balthasar Bickel, and Kristine A. Hildebrandt. 2010. The prosodic word is not universal, but emergent. *Journal of Linguistics*, 46(3):657–709.

Mark Schmalz. 2013. *Aspects of the grammar of Tundra Yukaghir*. Ph.D. thesis, Universiteit van Amsterdam.

Pilar M. Valenzuela. 2003. *Transitivity in Shipibo-Konibo grammar*. Ph.D. thesis, University of Oregon.

Pilar M Valenzuela. 2008. Evidentiality in shipibo-konibo, with a comparative overview of the category in panoan. *Studies in evidentiality*, pages 33–61.

Rik Van Gijn. 2006. *A grammar of Yurakaré*. Ph.D. thesis, Radboud University Nijmegen.

Marine Vuillermet. 2014. The multiple coreference systems in the ese ejja subordinate clauses. In *Information Structure and Reference Tracking in Complex Sentences*, pages 341–371. John Benjamins Publishing Company.

Illuminating Logical Fallacies with the CAMPFIRE Corpus

Austin Blodgett[1], Claire Bonial[1], Taylor Pellegrin[2], Melissa Torgbi[3], Harish Tayyar Madabushi[3]
[1] U.S. Army Research Laboratory, [2] Oak Ridge Associated Universities, [3] University of Bath
austin.blodgett.civ@army.mil, claire.n.bonial.civ@army.mil, thudson@terpmail.umd.edu, mat66@bath.ac.uk, htm43@bath.ac.uk

Abstract

Misinformation detection remains today a challenging task for both annotators and computer systems. While there are many known markers of misinformation—e.g., logical fallacies, propaganda techniques, and improper use of sources—labeling these markers in practice has been shown to produce low agreement as it requires annotators to make several subjective judgments and rely on their own knowledge, external to the text, which may vary between annotators. In this work, we address these challenges with a collection of linguistically-inspired litmus tests. We annotate a schema of 25 logical fallacies, each of which is defined with rigorous tests applied during annotation. Our annotation methodology results in a comparatively high IAA on this task: Cohen's κ in the range .69-.86. We release a corpus of 12 documents from various domains annotated with fallacy labels. Additionally, we experiment with a large language model baseline showing that the largest, most advanced models struggle on this challenging task, achieving an F1-score with our gold standard of .08 when excluding non-fallacious examples, compared to human performance of .59-.73. However, we find that prompting methodologies requiring the model to work through our litmus tests improves performance. Our work contributes a robust fallacy annotation schema and annotated corpus, which advance capabilities in this critical research area.

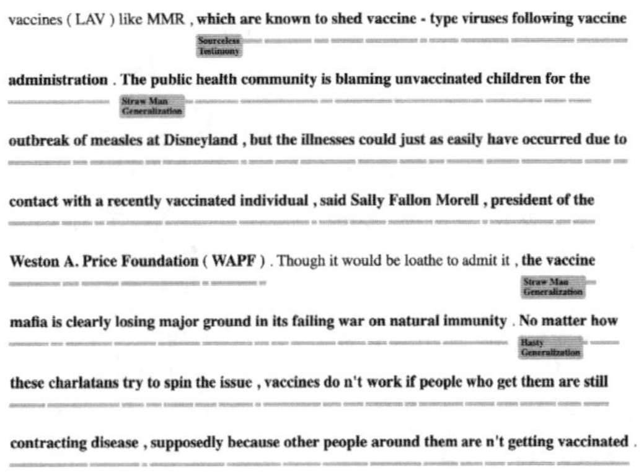

Figure 1: We show a visualization of fallacies identified in text. Although these are manual annotations shown, our corpus supports automatic markup of documents producing such a visualization for readers requiring automatic assessment of the credibility of a document, particularly in topic areas where fact-checking is not readily available.

1 Introduction

Identifying and addressing misinformation remains a challenging, labor-intensive task today. Particularly in situations that are fast-changing—such as natural or infrastructural disasters, disease outbreaks, military conflicts, and political crises—the spread of misinformation can easily outpace the available resources and human capital needed to address it. Automatic and human-in-the-loop strategies show some potential to reduce the cost of labor for identifying misinformation, but there remain challenges to algorithmically and robustly identifying misinformation in arbitrary text. We envision reliable tools that can facilitate the automatic markup of text with likely misinformation markers (see Figure 1).

To address these challenges, we developed the CAMPFIRE (Combined Annotations of Misinformation, Propaganda, and Fallacies Identified Robustly and Explainably) corpus—a corpus of texts on various topics (COVID-19, the Russian invasion of Ukraine, and the 2023 Ohio train derailment) annotated with markers useful for identifying misinformation. Although we divide these markers into testable and untestable beliefs, fallacies, and propaganda types, in this paper we narrow our focus to logical fallacy annotation. One advantage of focusing on logical fallacies as opposed to fact verification is that they allow us to scrutinize the soundness of a text's arguments in a content-neutral

Proceedings of the 19th Linguistic Annotation Workshop (LAW-XIX-2025), pages 285–296
July 31, 2025

way, even if many of the facts involved are not yet known. We address weaknesses of previous annotation schemas for fallacies by developing rigorous linguistic tests—inspired by the notion of frames and frame elements (Fillmore and Baker, 2001)—for each annotation label so that they can be applied consistently and objectively across domains. We find that our annotation methodology reduces the subjectivity of fallacy annotation, resulting in relatively high inter-annotator agreement (IAA): our agreement on a triple-annotated dataset, as measured by Cohen's κ, is in the range .69-.86 based on pairwise comparison of three annotators.

Technologies for identifying and addressing misinformation are particularly relevant today, given the popularity of generative, large language models (LLMs), the reliance of LLMs on online text, and the tendency of these systems to hallucinate. To establish baseline system performance on fallacy identification and recognition, we experiment with two of the largest, most advanced models (GPT-4o, GPT-o1) to predict CAMPFIRE fallacy labels. Performance leaves much to be desired: GPT-o1 achieves the best F1-score of .08 when excluding non-fallacious examples. Although this demonstrates the continued challenge of this task, we find that providing the litmus tests used by our annotators improves model performance.

After describing related work (Section 2), we present our theoretical framework, based upon first identifying the relevant, valid reasoning types (Section 3), followed by our annotation schema, including litmus tests ensuring diagnostic criteria for certain fallacy labels (Section 4). We then describe our corpus and annotation procedures, concluding with resulting IAA measures demonstrating the clarity and robustness of our schema (Section 5). We conduct experiments to establish baseline LLM performance in recognizing fallacies across three evaluation documents (Section 6).[1] Our discussion compares the challenges of human and system performance on this task, and we propose that our litmus tests reduce subjectivity in this task (Section 7). We conclude with suggestions for further system improvement on the critical task of fallacy and misinformation detection (Section 8).

2 Related Work

There has been an surge of research in NLP on detecting misinformation and related tasks, including fake news detection and automatic fact-checking, stance and sentiment analysis, and rumor detection, resulting in various workshops and shared tasks. Thus, there are a variety of annotation schemas and datasets focused broadly on the detection and analysis of misinformation, which may have some overlapping categories with our research. These datasets include the SemEval 2020 annotated dataset (Da San Martino et al., 2020a), and the credibility indicators outlined by Zhang et al. (2018). Here, we survey related work supporting the areas of fact-checking, propaganda techniques, and fallacy detection.

Both fact-checking generally and fake news detection more specifically require comparing claims against some ground truth, widely accepted facts. Hu et al. (2021) focus on fake news detection that compares claims against knowledge graphs. Instead of focusing on a document-level classification of fake news, Fung et al. (2021) cross-check individual elements of the document that better captures fake news where only a small portion of the document has been manipulated. One distinction between CAMPFIRE and fake news detection research is our focus on misinformation markers that do not require outside knowledge or ground truth facts to compare against. Our focus facilitates misinformation detection in subject-matter domains that are fast-changing, where the facts of a situation are not yet known or understood, such as the early weeks of the COVID-19 pandemic.

Propaganda techniques facilitate the acceptance and spread of certain claims, often in lieu of credible evidence and argumentation. Da San Martino et al. (2020b) offer a survey of relevant work on propaganda detection. Da San Martino et al. (2019) developed a corpus annotated with 18 labels describing propaganda techniques in which the annotators chose both the label and the span of the annotation, obtaining a γ inter-annotator agreement of .53. Recently, LLMs have been leveraged for propaganda detection. Sprenkamp et al. (2023) leverage GPT-3 and GPT-4 for classifying the propaganda techniques in the SemEval 2020 Task 11 dataset.[2] The best GPT-4 performance achieves an

[1]Our corpus and full experimental results and prompts can be found here: `https://github.com/melissatorgbi/CAMPFIRE`

[2]Many of the categories in this dataset overlap with CAMPFIRE propaganda techniques (e.g., APPEAL TO FEAR, FLAG-WAVING, REPETITION, SLOGAN), but several are classed as

F1-score of 58%, while the state-of-the-art system, which uses a fine-tuned RoBERTa model, achieves an F1-score of 63% (Abdullah et al., 2022). This demonstrates that the mere increase in scale of an LLM does not guarantee superior performance on this challenging task. Furthermore, the performance across the detection of particular techniques and fallacies varies wildly— LOADED LANGUAGE (F1-score of 72%) and NAME CALLING (F1-score of 65%) set the upper bound, while REPETITION (22% F1-score), BANDWAGON, and REDUCTIO AD HITLERUM (24% F1-score) sit on the lower bound. From this, we hypothesize that techniques with a clearer linguistic signature (as we would expect from LOADED LANGUAGE and NAME CALLING) are much easier to detect.

Like propaganda techniques, logical fallacies make a claim that may appear persuasive but is not supported by credible evidence or a logically sound argument. The *Argotario* corpus (Habernal et al., 2017, 2018) is one of the few corpora focused exclusively on logical fallacies, but their research crowd-sources annotations of just five logical fallacies. Bonial et al. (2022) attempt to replicate the *Argotario* annotation with expert annotators annotating logical fallacies in various publications, and show that the categories do not facilitate good IAA, nor can the distinctions be replicated by a system in a few-shot learning setting.

In Sahai et al. (2021), potential fallacies are collected automatically from Reddit by searching for mentions of fallacies in comments, and then these are filtered through crowdsourced judgments. Here again, IAA is somewhat low, particularly for HASTY GENERALIZATION, where agreement was measured via Cohen's κ at .38. This underscores the challenge of this annotation task. The authors explore several models for automatic prediction of fallacies, including BERT and MGN, with resulting F1-scores between 13 and 42% on the task most comparable to ours of labeling a comment with a particular fallacy. Unsurprisingly, given the correspondingly low IAA, the lowest F1-score is for HASTY GENERALIZATION.

We apply several lessons learned from related work. First, our schema supplies rigorous and detailed litmus tests facilitating objective determination of each annotation category. Second, the CAMPFIRE schema is refined until achieving satisfactory IAA, as the systems trained on data marked up with categories with relatively low IAA demonstrate correspondingly poor performance on those categories. Third, CAMPFIRE annotations focus on misinformation markers that can be identified from linguistic or structural features of a text, rather than external knowledge, as this reduces ambiguity in the annotation process and makes our schema more applicable in fast-changing domains where the facts are not yet known.

CAMPFIRE fallacies (e.g., BAND WAGON and REDUCTIO AD HITLERUM).

3 Theoretical Framework

A fallacy is an error in reasoning, argument, or methodology that leads to an unsound inference. A fallacy may be intentional or unintentional. Because fallacies are erroneous forms of inference, it is useful to categorize fallacies based on the type of inference they attempt to make. CAMPFIRE's fallacy taxonomy groups fallacies based on five inference types:

- **Deductive** inference draws a conclusion as a logical consequence of a premise. This includes inference using logical connectives *and*, *not*, *if... then*, etc., propositions that are true by definition (e.g., *cats are mammals*), as well as mathematical proof. A deductive fallacy can involve use of contradictions, skipping steps in an inference, or presenting an intuition, association, or bias as a universal principle. Deductive fallacies in CAMPFIRE include: FALSE DILEMMA, APPEAL TO NATURE, APPEAL TO NOVELTY, APPEAL TO TRADITION, THOUGHT-TERMINATING CLICHE.

- **Inductive** inference draws a conclusion that *likely* follows from a premise. For example, inductive inference might use observations about a population to infer a general claim that is supported by the observations. An inductive fallacy can involve relying on insufficient observations or relying on a biased sample of observations that are not representative of the population the general principle is meant to describe. Inductive fallacies in CAMPFIRE include: HASTY GENERALIZATION, CORRELATION-CAUSATION FALLACY, SLIPPERY SLOPE.

- **Abductive** inference draws a hypothesis that is meant to explain a set of observations, but is not observed directly. Note that in abductive reasoning, unlike inductive reasoning, the hypothesis is only *consistent with* the observations and functions as a guess of how to explain them. Thus abductive inferences still need to be tested inductively before being considered credible. An abductive fallacy involves concluding that a hypothesis is true because it is consistent with observations without providing evidence for it. Abductive fallacies in CAMPFIRE include: APPEAL TO IGNORANCE, CONSPIRACY THEORY, SCAPEGOAT.

- **Testimony** is the process of obtaining information from a source. As an inference type, testimony can be thought of having the premises *source A says X* and *source A is credible and qualified* and the conclusion *X is true*. A testimony fallacy can involve relying on an uncredible or unqualified source, relying on testimony without identifying the source, or using the commonality of a belief as evidence that it is true. Testimonial fallacies in CAMPFIRE include: BANDWAGON, IRRELEVANT AUTHORITY, SOURCELESS TESTIMONY, AMBIGUOUS SOURCE, APPEAL TO CONFIDENCE/DISBELIEF, PLAIN FOLKS.

- **Rebuttal** is the process of critique of an argument in order to invalidate it. Rebuttal might involve identifying contradictions or inconsistencies in an argument (rebuttal of *deduction*), presenting counter-evidence or scrutinizing the reliability of evidence (rebuttal of *induction*), posing a more plausible hypothesis (rebuttal of *abduction*), or scrutinizing the credentials and credibility of sources of testimony (rebuttal of *testimony*). Rebuttal fallacies often involve rejecting evidence, arguments, or testimony for irrelevant or frivolous reasons. Rebuttal fallacies in CAMPFIRE include: APPEAL TO ACCIDENT, APPEAL TO FABRICATION, APPEAL TO COVER-UP, REJECTION BY AD HOMINEM, GUILT BY ASSOCIATION, GUILT BY ANALOGY, STRAW MAN GENERALIZATION, TWO WRONGS MAKE A RIGHT.

Fallacies are grouped into the five categories above based on inference type—deductive, inductive, abductive, testimony, or rebuttal. Each fallacy is assumed to be an unsound attempt to draw some inference, and different types of fallacies are organized by the type of inference they attempt to draw. Organizing the taxonomy this way also allows us to explain why techniques in each category are fallacious, because we can compare them to credible forms of inference and identify the differences.

4 Annotation Schema

We recognize three major challenging sources of ambiguity in the annotation of fallacies:

- In what circumstances should a given fallacy apply—how similar must the text be to the fallacy schema?
- What span of text should a fallacy be 'anchored' to—what span should receive the fallacy label?
- How much external knowledge should annotators rely on when annotating?

These challenges inform the design of our annotation schema. We address them using a collection of strategies meant to reduce the annotators' burden to make subjective judgments.

Annotating clauses. The annotation anchor of each CAMPFIRE fallacy label is always a *clause*. Each clause is a span of tokens within a sentence. We use a preprocessing script to first identify clauses in a text before annoatating. This script parses text into universal dependency trees (de Marneffe et al., 2021). Dependencies that correspond to a clause (*root, csubj, csubj:pass, ccomp, advcl, advcl:relcl, acl, acl:relcl, xcomp, parataxis*) are used to select the token span under that subtree. We also include coordinated clauses (under *conj*) and—for the sake of identifying testimonial fallacies—prepositional phrases evoking a reporting events (e.g., 'according to ... ') are also treated as "clauses" for purposes of annotation. This procedure produces a (possibly nested) list of text spans each with the potential to be an annotation anchor. This allows for more fine-grained annotation than annotation by sentence, but involves less subjectivity than asking annotators to choose an arbitrary span by hand.[3] Because some fallacies can conceivably span over many clauses or sentences, each fallacy guideline also includes rules for identifying its conventional annotation anchor in order to further reduce this source of ambiguity.

Fallacy Guidelines. In practice, identifying fallacies can be a very challenging task because ar-

[3]See Furman et al. (2023) for discussion of span disagreement that motivated our decision to simplify the annotation span by using the clause as an anchor, and thereby reduce this source of disagreement.

guments in the real world that invoke a fallacy do not all take the same structural form or rely on the same lexical items or linguistic markers. Additionally, a real-world argument might have degrees of similarity to a known fallacy, in which case annotators might disagree about how similar it must be in order to deserve a fallacy label. To address this challenge, we develop rigorous annotation guidelines for each fallacy in our schema to drastically reduce this source of ambiguity. We start by observing that each fallacy has a logical form with premises and a conclusion. Each fallacy also has 'frame elements,' concepts evoked by the fallacy that must be in a particular relationship with each other for the fallacy label to apply.

Figure 2, for example, shows the guidelines for the SLIPPERY SLOPE fallacy. Text that is labeled as SLIPPERY SLOPE must evoke frame elements: Person/group **A** who initiates the events and Events **E** and **E'** which are the starting and resulting events of the slippery slope. The advantage of relying on frame elements and other litmus tests is that annotators are asked whether they can identify concepts in the text corresponding to the correct frame elements and whether these elements meet particular criteria, greatly reducing the subjectivity of the task.

During annotation, annotators consider a fallacy's logical form, frame elements, and tests to decide if that fallacy label can be applied. During adjudication, annotators again consult the guidelines to resolve disputes. Although frame elements are not annotated explicitly, they provide a rigorous litmus test to identify fallacies as objectively as possible.

Limiting External Knowledge. Another major challenge in the design of this schema was the issue of reliance on external knowledge. Early group annotations of fallacies revealed that often correctly identifying a fallacy in some text depended greatly on annotators' knowledge about the particular subject being discussed. Annotators with different levels of expertise or different preconceptions tended to make different judgments, resulting in lower agreement. We decided early on to reduce this source of ambiguity by focusing on fallacies that could be identified without relying on external knowledge or relying on it as little as possible. For example, an early version of our schema included the label STRAW MAN which is a fallacy of relevance where an opponent's position is mischaracterized in order to make it seem weaker than

logical form

A allows/causes event **E** therefore A will allow/cause event **E**$'$.

[If we allow pet cats]$_{premise}$, *[it's just a matter of time until someone has a pet alligator.]*$_{conclusion}$

frame elements

- Person/Group **A**: Initiator of the events **E** and **E**$'$
- Event **E** : Starting event
- Event **E**$'$: Resulting event
  - Test 1: **E** and **E**$'$ are intentional or presented as intentional.
  - Test 2: **E**$'$ is presented as a more extreme version of **E**.
  - Test 3: **E** is presented as an indirect cause of **E**$'$, i.e. if **E** does not occur, **E**$'$ is assumed not to occur.

Anchor: **E**$'$

Figure 2: For each fallacy, our guidelines present the logical form and an example illustrating it. Additionally, required frame elements and litmus tests for determining if those frame elements are present in a sentence are provided.

it is and therefore easier to critique. But identifying STRAW MAN fallacies places a burden on the annotator to know what the opponent's true position is. Since that level of external knowledge is not practical and may vary between annotators, we narrowed this fallacy to STRAW MAN GENERALIZATION which can be identified with little external knowledge. See the Table 4 in the Appendix for the full list of fallacies, definitions, and examples.

5 Corpus

In this section, we present the corpus of our research into the detection of misinformation across a diverse range of documents. The corpus in total comprises fourteen documents sourced from a variety of publications, including scholarly works, tabloids, and major news organizations. Our corpus distribution across topics is summarized in Table 1. These documents were selected to represent the multiple avenues for the dissemination of misinformation across the population as well as to cover opposing positions on a number of topics. The corpus we present here is a subset of what is planned for the CAMPFIRE corpus which we continue to develop. Additionally, we note again that while

Annotation Task	Topic
Triple Annotations	Covid (1) Ukrainian Conflict (1) Ohio Train Derailment (1)
Double Annotations	Covid (4) Ukrainian Conflict (2) Ohio Train Derailment (0)
Single Annotations	Covid (4) Ukrainian Conflict (1) Ohio Train Derailment (0)

Table 1: A summary of our corpus of fourteen documents focusing on three topics. Double and triple annotations are annotated by multiple annotators independently and then adjudicated together.

	Annotator Pair		
Cohen's κ	**A1-A2**	**A2-A3**	**A1-A3**
Overall	.78	.86	.69
- Fallacy Y/N	.77	.89	.72
- Fallacy Label	.61	.72	.47

Table 2: We break our IAA evaluation into three metrics: 1) The overall Cohen's κ which accounts for the judgment of whether a fallacy is present or not and the correct fallacy label. 2) Fallacy Y/N measures Cohen's κ IAA on whether a fallacy is present. 3) Fallacy Label evaluates Cohen's κ IAA for only examples where either the gold or predicted label is a fallacy. We show IAA scores for each pair of annotators.

our full corpus annotation includes the annotation layers of beliefs types and propaganda techniques, in the present paper we focus only on the Fallacy annotations.

The process of document selection began with the selection of a range of medical documents on the topic COVID-19 at the start of the pandemic. The topics of these papers spanned the safety in wearing masks, the effectiveness of herd immunity, vaccination safety, and long-term illnesses. As we've developed our misinformation guidelines, we've broadened our annotation work to include the international conflict of the Russo-Ukrainian War, and an ecological disaster, known as the Ohio train derailment.

5.1 Annotation Procedure

The annotation process itself was a multi-stage endeavor that involved a team of three native English-speaking annotators with undergraduate or graduate-level training in linguistics. The annotators were trained over the course of two weeks to identify and annotate misinformation markers. Each annotator worked independently to annotate the documents according to the provided guidelines. This initial round of solo annotation allowed them to individually develop their expertise in recognizing and marking instances of misinformation across the four layers. After the initial annotations were completed, the annotators convened to discuss their findings and collaboratively establish a Gold standard for a subset of documents that were double and triple annotated. IAA scores were also collected to establish which fallacy labels were fairly clear, and which required updates either to the guidelines or to the categorization itself.

5.2 Agreement Metrics

All three annotators independently annotated three documents (containing a total of 194 annotation targets) and then convened to develop agreed-upon, gold standard annotations. We leverage these to establish IAA and to use as our evaluation set in Section 6. Table 2 shows our agreement results. We measured agreement in several ways. First, we measured the overall Cohen's κ IAA for each pair of our three annotators with results ranging from .69-.86. Because most clauses do not contain a fallacy and annotators usually agree on whether a fallacy is present, this overall IAA score is skewed by the vast number of NONE labels. To account for this in our evaluation, we also measure IAA on the judgement of whether a fallacy is present or not (Fallacy Y/N in Table 2) with results ranging from .72-.89. Lastly, we evaluate IAA on fallacy labels excluding cases where both annotators agree that a fallacy is not present (Fallacy Label in Table 2) with results ranging from .47-.72. This was the most challenging of the three metrics.

Overall, our level of agreement exceeds reported scores for other comparable annotations schemas and demonstrates the clarity and reliability of our schema, despite having 25 annotation category labels in a challenging task.

Additionally, Figure 3 shows confusion matrices for human and GPT-o1 performance respectively against our gold labels. What can readily be seen from this figure is that, for humans, the largest source of confusion of labels is the decision of whether the text should be labeled with a fallacy or should be labeled NONE, whereas for our experiments with GPT-o1, both the decision of whether a fallacy is present and the decision of which fallacy to apply are large sources of confusion.

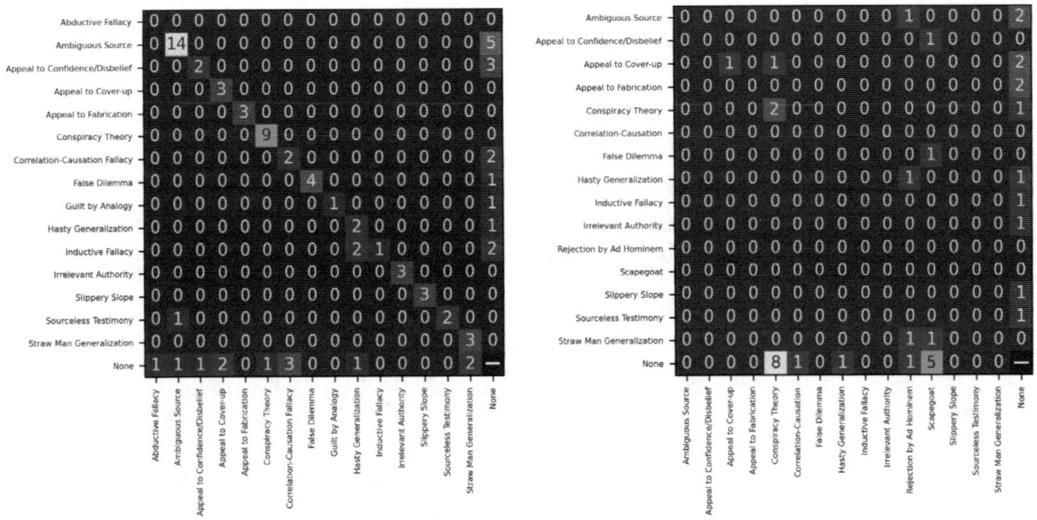

Figure 3: Confusion matrices for human performance (Left) and GPT-o1 performance (Right) respectively. The left matrix shows human annotations (columns) compared to gold adjudicated labels (rows) based on triple-annotated and double annotated documents. For comparison, the right matrix shows GPT-o1 predicted labels (columns) compared to gold (rows) based on triple-annotated documents. The dash in the lower right corner of each matrix stands in for the vast majority of NONE examples (1,104 examples for humans, 222 for GPT-o1) where both the gold and predicted labels agree that a fallacy is not present to prevent skewing the results.

6 Experiments: LLM Baseline

To establish baseline system performance on the task of recognizing and labeling fallacies, we use OpenAI's gpt-4o-2024-08-06 (GPT-4o) and o1-2024-12-17 (GPT-o1). These models were selected as representative of current LLM capabilities due to their large size. GPT-o1 was chosen alongside GPT-4o for its reported ability to handle complex reasoning which may be beneficial for this task. The temperature for GPT-4o and GPT-o1 were 0 and 1 respectively, which were the lowest options for each model to make the outputs more deterministic. Three documents that had been triple annotated and adjudicated were selected for evaluation, thereby giving us a clear picture of how LLM performance compares to manual annotation. A total of 22 tests were run, including experiments to investigate what information from the guidelines to include in the prompt.

6.1 Prompt Variations

Initial experiments were conducted to determine the amount and type of information to include in the prompt. These experiments were primarily tested on a single pilot document that contained the most fallacies of the three evaluation documents, and later extended to include the other two documents for final evaluation.[4] The prompt experiments involved varying combinations of the following elements, all drawn from the annotation guidelines:

- Fallacy Names
- 1-2 Sentence Fallacy Definitions
- Frame Element Listing
- Fallacy Examples

In one variation, we also instructed the model to output frame elements as instantiated by the annotation target sentence.

In the prompt, the model was given the whole document in text, and then a list of the clauses to label. We experimented with giving the model the full list of clauses in a single prompt, as well as iterating over each clause with a full list of fallacies and iterating over each clause and each fallacy, then asked the model to produce a label for a single clause and a single fallacy each time. The model was instructed to label each clause with a fallacy name or NONE which was then compared to a

[4]We acknowledge that leveraging items from our test set in our prompt experimentation could have led to over-optimization and better performance on those specific items. Ideally, we would conduct prompt experimentation on a separate set; however, our corpus size limited this possibility. Additionally, we note that the relatively poor performance overall indicates that optimizing on the test items did not dramatically skew performance.

gold label. The prompt variation that produced the highest F1-score on the pilot document was selected for further experiments.

Overall, our prompt experiments demonstrated that, in comparison to just providing the fallacy names, providing the fallacy definition improved performance, as does adding the frame element description and asking the model to output the frame elements in its response. Somewhat surprisingly, we found that adding examples of the fallacies did not improve performance. We tested two variants of this: first leveraging the simple, invented examples from the guidelines (see Table 4 in the Appendix for examples), and then adding corpus examples of the fallacies. Neither variation improved performance, and in fact the additional corpus examples decreased performance further. We posit that adding examples hurts performance because it cues the model into lexical similarities with examples, whereas the fallacies are based to a greater extent on semantic properties of the reasoning chain across clauses.

We found that providing a list of fallacies produced better results than iterating over individual fallacies. We also found that providing a listing of all clauses and asking the model to label all of them individually in one output response greatly improved performance over presenting the entire document and then asking the model to annotate a single clause at a time, iterating over clauses. We attribute this to the importance of the overall document context in understanding fallacies.

Thus, the best-performing prompt variation selected provided a task description, followed by a listing of all fallacies, each supplemented with its definition and a description of the required frame elements. The entire document was given in text, followed by the same text split into a listing of clauses. The model was then asked to output the fallacy label or "none" for each clause, and provide the instantiated frame elements for each detected fallacy.[5]

6.2 Results: Baseline Performance

Table 3 reports evaluation metrics for the two models tested using the best prompt variation. Similar to our IAA evaluation in section 5.2, we measure F1-scores in several ways. First, we measured the overall F1-score comparing annotators and models against our gold data. Because most clauses do not contain a fallacy and annotators usually agree on whether a fallacy is present, this overall F1-score is skewed by the vast number of NONE labels. To account for this in our evaluation, we also measure F1 on the judgement of whether a fallacy is present or not (Fallacy Y/N in Table 3). Lastly, we measure F1 on predicting fallacy labels excluding cases where both gold and predicted labels agree that a fallacy is not present (Fallacy Label in Table 2). This last metric presents the most challenging problem for both humans and LLMs.

We measure F1-scores among three annotators of .96-.98, but this score is greatly skewed by the presence of NONE labels. When drilling deeper, we find scores of .98-.99 on the judgement of whether a fallacy is present and .59-.73 on the more challenging task of predicting the correct label, excluding cases where both the annotated and gold labels agree that a fallacy is not present.

In comparison, when we calculate F1-scores for GPT-4o and -o1 against the gold standard, the models achieve .90 and .89 overall F1 respectively. Again, this is greatly skewed by the vast majority of NONE labels from non-fallacious sentences. When we inspect further, we find that models each achieve .95 scores when judging whether a fallacy is present. But on the more challenging metric of choosing the correct label excluding cases where both the predicted and gold labels agree that a fallacy is not present, GPT-4o and GPT-o1 score only .05 and .08 respectively, demonstrating that this task is far from solved.

When we drill down to examine how often the model can correctly predict that a fallacy is present and what the fallacy label is, we find that GPT-4o only correctly labels 1 of 14 gold fallacy labels from our evaluation set, while GPT-o1 correctly labels just 3. Qualitative analysis is provided in the Discussion.

7 Discussion

Our results show that our annotation schema and methodology— moving from a decision tree supporting recognition of a fallacy, to inference type, and finally to litmus tests involving frame elements to decide upon the specific fallacy—support relatively high overall annotator IAA on this challenging and generally subjective task. Additionally, our prompt variation experiments support the notion that having litmus tests for particular fallacies, in the form of required frame elements, also supports

[5]Full prompts can be viewed on our github: https://github.com/mcliooatorgbi/CAMPFIRE.

F1-score	GPT-4o	GPT-o1	Human
Overall	.90	.89	.96-.98
- Fallacy Y/N	.95	.95	.98-.99
- Fallacy Label	.05	.08	.59-.73

Table 3: Evaluation of two models against 3 linguist annotators. We break our evaluation into three metrics: 1) The overall F1-score which accounts for the judgment of whether a fallacy is present or not and the correct fallacy label. 2) Fallacy Y/N measures F1-score on whether a fallacy is present. 3) Fallacy Label evaluates F1-score for only examples where either the gold or predicted label was a fallacy.

model performance. When our annotation team disagreed upon the appropriate fallacy label, adjudication involved presenting the frame elements found in that sentence in support of a particular fallacy. Similarly, requiring the model to output the frame elements boosts performance. Thus, we posit that breaking the annotation task down in multiple steps and criteria for decision making decreases subjectivity in fallacy classification.

We readily acknowledge, however, that our analysis regarding model performance must be tempered by the fact that GPT-o1, the best-performing model, is only able to accurately label 3 of 14 gold-standard fallacies. Of the three fallacies that -o1 correctly identified, two are CONSPIRACY THEORY, an Abductive fallacy, and one is APPEAL TO COVER-UP, a Rebuttal fallacy. The three correctly identified cases are given below:

1. *The media...doesn't want you talking about East Palestine and Nordstream* - APPEAL TO COVER-UP
2. *A pandemic is their last attempt for total control* - CONSPIRACY THEORY
3. *A coordinated censorship attack is being waged against the entire independent media by Google, YouTube and Facebook* - CONSPIRACY THEORY

Example (3) above was the only fallacy correctly labeled by GPT-4o as well. We note that all three annotators agreed on these labels for each of these three cases.

When we explore several cases where the model posited that a fallacy existed where there was none, we find that GPT-o1 most often labeled clauses as CONSPIRACY THEORY fallacies: 8 of 17 predicted fallacies were assigned this label. Indeed, the model seems to have the best handle on the notion of a CONSPIRACY THEORY, as there was no clear set of lexical triggers associated with this set, and conceptually the false positives did involve the powerful, conspiratorial entity frame element, but no clear conspiratorial event required for annotation. Next most frequently, GPT-o1 assigned SCAPEGOAT fallacies where the word "blame" was mentioned in 7 of 17 predicted fallacies. Finally, AD HOMINEM was assigned in 4 cases where there were insulting names such as "charlatan." Thus, in many of these cases, while one frame element was found in the clause (often cued by a key lexical item), all required elements were not present.

8 Conclusion & Future Work

When we consider our manual and model annotation results overall, we posit that model performance could be brought closer to human performance with prompting strategies as well as structured output that required frame elements and litmus tests to be passed. Only if the model can provide all frame elements can the annotation of a particular fallacy be assigned. This process of requiring the model to "show its work" when it comes to the fallacy assigned is quite similar to how annotators argued for and settled disputes over fallacy labels.

In addition to exploring more sophisticated prompting strategies, we are currently working to further expand our corpus to levels adequate to experiment with finetuning a model. We are eager to see if a fine-tuned model can excel at this task, or if larger models with more advanced "reasoning" capabilities can outpace even fine-tuned models given the right prompting strategies.

With improved model performance over a larger corpus, we will also begin to explore if there is any difference in performance in detecting fallacies that are missteps in different reasoning types. It has been posited that LLMs are inductive, bottom-up reasoners moving from specific observations to generalizations (Olsson et al., 2022); thus, we may expect performance on inductive fallacies to be superior to deductive and abductive fallacies. However, we also note an opportunity to leverage fallacy recognition evaluation in order to further explore whether or not these models are "reasoning" at all (cf. Lu et al. (2024)).

Limitations

Although we annotated a schema of 25 fallacy types and demonstrated improvement of inter-annotator agreement over previous work, there is still much room for improvement in the types of fallacies to identify, the agreement and objectivity of annotators, and the reliability of automated systems in performing this task. So far, our annotations have focused on single-author texts. We hope to add annotations of multi-author debate and discourse in future work.

Ethical Considerations

All annotators who participated in this research were paid adequately for their work and were included as authors. Annotators met regularly to discuss ways to improve the annotation process and make it easier, and their expert input was relied on throughout the development of our schema. Misinformation detection is a complex issue with important societal implications, and we recognize the possibility for bias to influence our data creation. We take steps to reduce the possibility for bias wherever possible. We believe our approach of focusing on logical structures of arguments has allowed us to annotate in a content-neutral way and thus reduce potential sources of bias.

References

Malak Abdullah, Ola Altiti, and Rasha Obiedat. 2022. Detecting propaganda techniques in english news articles using pre-trained transformers. In *2022 13th International Conference on Information and Communication Systems (ICICS)*, pages 301–308. IEEE.

Claire Bonial, Austin Blodgett, Taylor Hudson, Stephanie Lukin, Jeffrey Micher, Douglas Summers-Stay, Peter Sutor, and Clare Voss. 2022. The search for agreement on logical fallacy annotation of an infodemic. In *Proceedings of the Thirteenth Language Resources and Evaluation Conference*, pages 4430–4438.

Giovanni Da San Martino, Alberto Barrón-Cedeño, Henning Wachsmuth, Rostislav Petrov, and Preslav Nakov. 2020a. SemEval-2020 task 11: Detection of propaganda techniques in news articles. In *Proceedings of the Fourteenth Workshop on Semantic Evaluation*, pages 1377–1414, Barcelona (online). International Committee for Computational Linguistics.

Giovanni Da San Martino, Stefano Cresci, Alberto Barrón-Cedeño, Seunghak Yu, Roberto Di Pietro, and Preslav Nakov. 2020b. A survey on computational propaganda detection. In *Proceedings of the Twenty-Ninth International Joint Conference on Artificial Intelligence, IJCAI-20*, pages 4826–4832. International Joint Conferences on Artificial Intelligence Organization. Survey track.

Giovanni Da San Martino, Seunghak Yu, Alberto Barrón-Cedeño, Rostislav Petrov, and Preslav Nakov. 2019. Fine-grained analysis of propaganda in news article. In *Proceedings of the 2019 Conference on Empirical Methods in Natural Language Processing and the 9th International Joint Conference on Natural Language Processing (EMNLP-IJCNLP)*, pages 5636–5646, Hong Kong, China. Association for Computational Linguistics.

Marie-Catherine de Marneffe, Christopher D. Manning, Joakim Nivre, and Daniel Zeman. 2021. Universal dependencies. *Computational Linguistics*, 47(2):255–308.

Charles J. Fillmore and Collin F. Baker. 2001. Frame semantics for text understanding. In *Proceedings of WordNet and Other Lexical Resources Workshop*, Pittsburgh. NAACL, NAACL.

Yi Fung, Christopher Thomas, Revanth Gangi Reddy, Sandeep Polisetty, Heng Ji, Shih-Fu Chang, Kathleen McKeown, Mohit Bansal, and Avi Sil. 2021. InfoSurgeon: Cross-media fine-grained information consistency checking for fake news detection. In *Proceedings of the 59th Annual Meeting of the Association for Computational Linguistics and the 11th International Joint Conference on Natural Language Processing (Volume 1: Long Papers)*, pages 1683–1698, Online. Association for Computational Linguistics.

Damián Ariel Furman, Pablo Torres, José A. Rodríguez, Laura Alonso Alemany, Diego Letzen, and Vanina Martínez. 2023. Which argumentative aspects of hate speech in social media can be reliably identified? In *Proceedings of the Fourth International Workshop on Designing Meaning Representations*, pages 136–153, Nancy, France. Association for Computational Linguistics.

Ivan Habernal, Raffael Hannemann, Christian Pollak, Christopher Klamm, Patrick Pauli, and Iryna Gurevych. 2017. Argotario: Computational argumentation meets serious games. In *EMNLP (System Demonstrations)*.

Ivan Habernal, Patrick Pauli, and Iryna Gurevych. 2018. Adapting serious game for fallacious argumentation to german: pitfalls, insights, and best practices. In *Proceedings of the Eleventh International Conference on Language Resources and Evaluation (LREC 2018)*.

Linmei Hu, Tianchi Yang, Luhao Zhang, Wanjun Zhong, Duyu Tang, Chuan Shi, Nan Duan, and Ming Zhou. 2021. Compare to the knowledge: Graph neural fake news detection with external knowledge. In *Proceedings of the 59th Annual Meeting of the Association for Computational Linguistics and the 11th International Joint Conference on Natural Language Processing*

(*Volume 1: Long Papers*), pages 754–763, Online. Association for Computational Linguistics.

Sheng Lu, Irina Bigoulaeva, Rachneet Sachdeva, Harish Tayyar Madabushi, and Iryna Gurevych. 2024. Are emergent abilities in large language models just in-context learning? In *Proceedings of the 62nd Annual Meeting of the Association for Computational Linguistics (Volume 1: Long Papers)*, pages 5098–5139.

Catherine Olsson, Nelson Elhage, Neel Nanda, Nicholas Joseph, Nova DasSarma, Tom Henighan, Ben Mann, Amanda Askell, Yuntao Bai, Anna Chen, and 1 others. 2022. In-context learning and induction heads. *arXiv preprint arXiv:2209.11895*.

Saumya Sahai, Oana Balalau, and Roxana Horincar. 2021. Breaking down the invisible wall of informal fallacies in online discussions. In *Proceedings of the 59th Annual Meeting of the Association for Computational Linguistics and the 11th International Joint Conference on Natural Language Processing (Volume 1: Long Papers)*, pages 644–657, Online. Association for Computational Linguistics.

Kilian Sprenkamp, Daniel Gordon Jones, and Liudmila Zavolokina. 2023. Large language models for propaganda detection. *arXiv preprint arXiv:2310.06422*.

Amy X Zhang, Aditya Ranganathan, Sarah Emlen Metz, Scott Appling, Connie Moon Sehat, Norman Gilmore, Nick B Adams, Emmanuel Vincent, Jennifer Lee, Martin Robbins, and 1 others. 2018. A structured response to misinformation: Defining and annotating credibility indicators in news articles. In *Companion Proceedings of the The Web Conference 2018*, pages 603–612.

A Fallacy Definitions and Examples

We provide a listing of all our fallacy labels, organized by fallacy type, as well as guidelines examples of each fallacy in Table 4.

Inference Type	Fallacy Label	Guidelines Example
Deductive	FALSE DILEMMA	If we don't get a cat then we have to get a dog.
	APPEAL TO NATURE / NOVELTY / TRADITION	Raw meat is more natural for cats / We have to get that new cat food / Old-fashioned cat food is the best.
	THOUGHT-TERMINATING CLICHE	It just is the way it is.
Inductive	HASTY GENERALIZATION	My cat is black, so all cats are black.
	CORRELATION-CAUSATION	Many cat owners have asthma.
	SLIPPERY SLOPE	If we allow pet cats, it's just a matter of time until someone has a pet alligator.
Abductive	APPEAL TO IGNORANCE	No one has proven that cats can't understand humans.
	CONSPIRACY THEORY	There is an evil, secret organization of people who want to kidnap our pet cats.
	SCAPEGOAT	The shortage of cat food is all because of immigrants.
Testimony	BANDWAGON	90% of people prefer cats.
	IRRELEVANT AUTHORITY	I heard from a friend that cats can sense radio waves.
	SOURCELESS TESTIMONY	It is known that cats can sense radio waves.
	AMBIGUOUS SOURCE	Scientists say that cats can sense radio waves.
	APPEAL TO CONFIDENCE-DISBELIEF	Cats couldn't possibly be a good pet.
	PLAIN FOLKS	You can trust me, I'm just an ordinary pet owner like you.
Rebuttal	APPEAL TO ACCIDENT / FABRICATION / COVER-UP	Some people say cats are mean, but those are just the bad cats / People who like cats are brainwashed by the pro-cat shadow government / The news never tells you about all the people who were murdered by their cats.
	REJECTION BY AD-HOMINEM	I don't trust the opinion of a cat person.
	GUILT BY ASSOCIATION / ANALOGY	John's brother stole a dog, so John can't be trusted! / Cat owners are like fascists, always creating rules for their pets.
	STRAW MAN GENERALIZATION	Dog lovers think that cats are evil!
	TWO WRONGS MAKE A RIGHT	People say cats can be mean, but what about dogs?!

Table 4: Listing of the fallacy labels used in our schema; these are categorized by the inference type involved, where each fallacy represents a fallacious step in that type of reasoning. We also provide a simple, invented example of the fallacy listed in our guidelines.

Cheap Annotation of Complex Information: A Study on the Annotation of Information Status in German TEDx Talks

Carmen Schacht Tobias Nischk Oleksandra Yazdanfar Stefanie Dipper
Sprachwissenschaftliches Institut / CRC Information Density and Linguistic Encoding
Fakultät für Philologie, Ruhr-Universität Bochum
firstname.lastname@rub.de

Abstract

We present an annotation experiment for the annotation of information status in German TEDx Talks with the main goal to reduce annotation costs in terms of time and personnel. We aim for maximizing efficiency while keeping annotation quality constant by testing various different annotation scenarios for an optimal ratio of annotation expenses to resulting quality of the annotations. We choose the RefLex scheme of Riester and Baumann (2017) as a basis for our annotations, refine their annotation guidelines for a more generalizable tagset and conduct the experiment on German Tedx talks, applying different constellations of annotators, curators and correctors to test for an optimal annotation scenario. Our results show that we can achieve equally good and possibly even better results with significantly less effort, by using correctors instead of additional annotators.

1 Introduction

Information status concerns the way in which referents are referenced in a text: e.g. as a newly introduced entity (*a nice picture*), as a generally known entity (*the sun*), as a previously mentioned entity (*she*), etc. In language, information status is mainly reflected in the form of referring expressions, e.g. personal pronouns for a pre-mentioned entity or indefinite article for a newly introduced entity.

Investigating information status is a complex endeavor, as there exist various competing terminologies and classifications. In our work, we follow Riester and Baumann (2017) in their approach to the annotation of information status, applying the *RefLex* scheme, an annotation scheme encoding detailed information on contextual and extra-textual givenness of referents. The scheme covers both the referential and lexical dimensions of information status. Only the referential level is relevant to the work described in this study.

This work is part of a larger project on word order in German, investigating the influence of information status and information-theoretical factors such as surprisal and information density (Shannon, 1948). In particular, we are interested in the relationship between information status and information density. We therefore annotate data according to the RefLex scheme. Since the annotation of such a complex phenomenon requires expert annotators, it is rather costly in terms of time and personnel. Hence, we aim to find a more economical solution to the commonly expensive annotation and curation of information status.

In this paper we present the results of an annotation experiment that we conducted by testing various annotation scenarios for time and personnel efficiency as well as accuracy of the annotations. Specifically, we compare the traditional approach – multiple annotation and subsequent curation, which is usually considered a guarantee of high annotation quality – with a simpler approach in which a single annotation is subsequently corrected. Our results show that we can achieve equally good and possibly even better results with significantly less effort, by using correctors instead of additional annotators.

2 Related Work

Linguistic annotation is a corpus-linguistic method with a long tradition, where quality control plays an important role. Traditionally, the quality of annotations is measured using chance-corrected measures of inter-annotator agreement (IAA), also called inter-rater reliability (IRR), such as Fleiss' kappa or Cohen's kappa (Fleiss, 1971; Cohen, 1960; Carletta, 1996). These measures assume that two or more annotators annotate the same text independently of each other.

Another type of quality control is when only one annotator annotates the text and subsequently

Proceedings of the 19th Linguistic Annotation Workshop (LAW-XIX-2025), pages 297–307
July 31, 2025 ©2025 Association for Computational Linguistics

an expert annotator goes over these annotations and corrects them if necessary. In this case, the two versions – before and after correction – can be compared with each other applying measures such as F-score, measuring the accuracy of one version with regard to the other.

It can be assumed that fewer errors will be detected with this method than with multiple annotations. For example, the two large German-language treebanks were annotated according to these two paradigms: The first method – double annotation – was applied to the annotation of the TIGER treebank, the second method – annotation plus subsequent correction – to the annotation of TüBa-D/Z (Dipper and Kübler, 2017).

Grouin et al. (2014) evaluate the effect of differently-annotated types of training data (with double annotations, with a curated gold version, with an automatic pre-annotation that has been manually corrected) on the performance of a CRF classifier. In contrast to our approach, the annotation quality as such is not compared and evaluated directly, but indirectly, based on the performance of the trained system. Furthermore, in contrast to our experiment, they deal with a simple annotation task (identification of personal information in clinical documents).

A number of papers compare the quality of annotation with vs. without automatic pre-annotation; for an overview see, e.g., Mikulová et al. (2022). In contrast, we do not use automatic pre-annotation in our study.

3 The Data

The fragments that we annotated are extracts from the transcriptions of a total of five TEDx Talks which were given in German on a range of different topics. The texts are subject to licenses that permit free redistribution.[1]

From each talk, we annotated 100 referential expressions from two different sections of the talk, resulting in 10 fragments with 1,000 annotated units in total.[2]

We chose TEDx Talks for the annotation experiment as we considered them an adequate cross-section of content, while keeping the genre of the data – semi-scripted oral talks – constant. We excluded talks that involved particularities as for example rap, for this would distort the homogeneity of the dataset too much.

All annotations, curations, and corrections were created and handled in the annotation tool INCEpTION (Klie et al., 2018). Details of the procedure are provided in the following sections.

4 Annotation Guidelines

We base our experiments on the annotation of information status according to the RefLex scheme proposed by Riester and Baumann (2017). RefLex is a comprehensive annotation scheme that provides a total of 12 different labels, which can be divided into 7 classes, see Table 1. In addition, the features '+generic' and '+predicative' can be added to each expression. Markables are nominal phrases (NPs, incl. pronouns) and specific adverbs (e.g. *here*). If the NP is directly embedded in a prepositional phrase (PP), the entire PP is annotated. Possessive pronouns are also annotated.

In the following we describe the modifications we have made to RefLex. Table 2 provides an overview of the tags used in our study.

Label names Among other things, we have shortened the label names for the annotation. First, we omit the prefix 'r-' from all labels.[3] Second, we replace some of the longer names by short ones, see Table 3, e.g. `displaced` instead of 'r-given-displaced' or `known` instead of 'r-unused-known'.

Markables We define admissible markables as follows: A markable is either an NP (or PP, as specified in RefLex), a possessive pronoun or a deictic adverbial (*hier* 'here', *jetzt* 'now').

For complex phrases with embedded phrases, relative clauses or appositions, we annotate (i) the entire phrase (i.e. its head) and (ii) each of the embedded phrase(s).

Idioms are annotated as an entire span. Foreign language material is not considered, except for when it is referred back to. Incomprehensible passages, e.g. due to spelling mistakes or transcription errors, are ignored.

[1]The TEDx Talks are part of this playlist: `https://www.youtube.com/playlist?list=PLzPiBVgAHXijVDasy92X6lZkl0DvFgSEg`, accessed 2024-02-26. Our annotations are based on the subtitles extracted from these videos.

[2]The annotation guidelines as well as the annotated data are made freely available: `https://gitlab.ruhr-uni-bochum.de/comphist/law25_infstat`.

[3]The prefix 'r-' marks tags from the referential dimension rather than the lexical dimension of the RefLex tagset. As mentioned above, we only annotate the referential dimension, so the prefix is redundant information.

Table 1: Annotation tags of the r-level	
Tag	Contextual class
r-given-sit	Referents contained in text-external context (communicative situation)
r-environment	
r-given	Referents mentioned in previous discourse context
r-given-displaced	
r-cataphor	Discourse-new entities that depend on other expressions in the discourse context
r-bridging	
r-bridging-contained	Globally unique entities that are discourse-new and independent of the discourse context
r-unused-unknown	
r-unused-known	
r-new	Non-unique, discourse-new entities
r-expletive	Non-referring expressions
r-idiom	
+generic	Optional features
+predicative	

Table 1: Overview of the RefLex tagset (from Riester and Baumann, 2017, p. 9).

Label	Form	Description	Examples
new	indef, also complex	referent newly introduced; but may embed **given, known** etc.	***eine ganz andere Art der Freiheit***
given	def NP or pers/dem pron or pron adv or adv	referent mentioned before, possibly as text span	***sie***; ***da; dort; damals***; text span referent only in case of dem pron or pron adv: ***das*** *stimmt*; ***daran*** *denke ich oft*
bridging	not complex	referent mentioned before is a silent/implicit argument	
	1. def NP (no pron/adv)		***die Wohnung*** [(silent:) *in diesem Haus*]; ***diese Aussage*** [*nämlich dass ...*]; ***das glücklichste Land*** [*von allen*]
	2. quantifying pron or NP		***alle/manche/niemand*** [*von denen*]; ***3l*** [*Milch*]
situation	1st or 2nd person, deictic	referent extratextual	***ich; dein; hier; jetzt***
cataphor	*es*; pron adv (only pron)	referent introduced subsequently	*denken* ***daran****, dass ...*
known	def, not complex	1. encyclopedic knowledge	***der Papst***; locations; known persons
	def + indef	2. classes, always generic (**+G**)	***(die) Menschen*** *sind neugierig*; ***am Abend***; ***Löwen in Afrika***
unknown	def, complex	reference by description, everything **new** or **known**	***die Bilder von Vögeln***; unknown persons
contained	def, complex	containing embedded **given / bridging / situation / contained**	***seine Frau***; ***die Wohnung in diesem Haus***
displaced	def	referent mentioned more than 5 clauses ago	
expletive	*es; sich*	semantically empty expression	***es*** *gibt keinen Grund*; *ich erinnere* ***mich*** *an ...*
idiom		does not introduce a referent, intransparent semantics	
noref		does not introduce a referent, transparent semantics	
	def + indef	1. formulaic incl. secondary prepositions	***zu Hause; vielen Dank; in jedem Fall an Hand; an Stelle; auf Grund; in Folge; mit Ausnahme***
	quantified	2. quantified adverbial expressions	***viel Zeit***
+generic (+G)		only in case of **new, given** and **known**	***ein Löwe*** *ist ...*
+discontinuous (+D)		discontinuous constituent, incl. floating quantifier	***Dinge*** *machen,* ***die ...*** ; ***das*** *ist auch* ***alles*** *sinnvoll*

Table 2: Overview and descriptions of the tags used in the annotation study.

RefLex Label	Our Label
r-given-sit, r-environment	situation
r-unused-known	known
r-ununsed-unknown	unknown
r-bridging-contained	contained
r-given-displaced	displaced
–	noref
+generic	+generic (+G)
–	+discontinuous (+D)

Table 3: Mapping between the original RefLex and our label names.

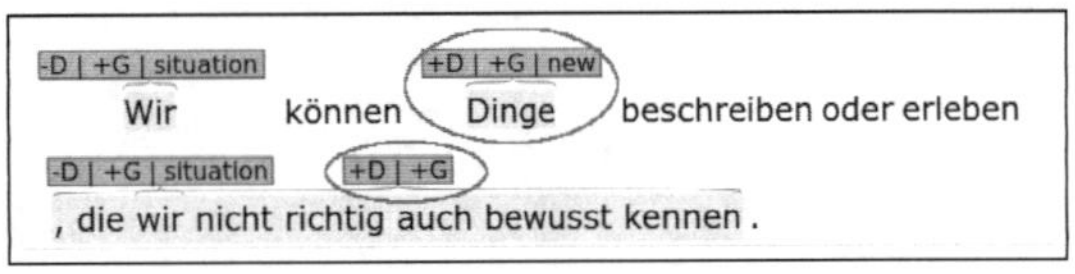

Figure 1: Annotation of example (1), featuring a discontinuous constituent (screenshot of INCEpTION).

Discontinuous constituents We added a special feature to mark constituents as discontinuous, as in (1). In the German original version, the relative clause is separated from its antecedent *Dinge* 'things'. In the annotation, the label `new`, which applies to the entire construction, is only annotated on the head noun *things*. In addition, the feature `+D` (for "discontinuous") is annotated at the head and at the relative clause, to mark them as one constituent.

(1) *Wir können Dinge beschreiben oder erleben, die wir nicht richtig auch bewusst kennen.*
'We can describe or experience things that we are not really aware of.'

Figure 1 shows the annotation for this example. The relevant annotations are highlighted in red (the second highlighted annotation `+D|+G` refers to the entire relative clause, whose words are marked in light green). The default value `-D` is automatically added by INCEpTION.

Generic In addition to the label `+/-D`, there is another special feature in Figure 1: `+/-G`, which stands for "+/-generic". Its default value is `-G`, but has been changed by the annotator for all the markables shown in the example, as *wir* 'we' refers to human beings in general in this example.

Note that we do not evaluate the annotations of these extra features `+/-D` and `+/-G` in our experiments.

Merging two labels RefLex distinguishes the two labels 'r-given-sit' and 'r-environment': Both refer to expressions for referents that are present in the immediate text-external context. 'r-environment' expressions additionally involve a deictic gesture (e.g. *this chair*), whereas 'r-given-sit' expressions do not (e.g. *I, we*). This distinction cannot always be made clearly without knowledge of the extra-textual context.

In (2), for example, it is conceivable that a picture or film of the supermarket and in particular of the fruit in the supermarket was shown during the TEDx Talk and the speaker pointed to the picture while uttering the phrase *this fruit* (highlighted in the English translation of the example). On the other hand, the phrase could also be understood as referring to the subsequent description.

(2) *Als erstes bin ich in einen Supermarkt gegangen und habe mir Obst angeschaut und dieses Obst gefunden: Obst, einzeln verpackt, weil Birnen und Äpfel sind ja tatsächlich schwer zu trennen.*
'The first thing I did was go to a supermarket to look at fruit and found *this fruit*: Fruit, individually wrapped, because pears and apples are actually difficult to separate.'

Hence, we abandon the distinction and keep one label `situation` for both RefLex labels.

New label We define a new label called `noref`, which is part of the class of non-referring expressions. Like idioms and expletives, such expressions do not introduce a referent. However, whereas the label `idiom` marks semantically intransparent spans, the new `noref`-label captures semantically transparent instances, such as *vielen Dank* 'thanks a lot', *zu Hause* 'at home', or so-called secondary prepositions like *auf Grund* 'due to; by reason of' or *mit Ausnahme* 'with the exception'.

Even though adding new labels always adds to the complexity of the tagset and thereby increases the risk of annotation errors, the addition of the `noref` label was judged to cover a relevant portion of information previously unaddressed and is therefore warranted.

Form-based characteristics We have enriched the definitions by consistently referring to possible

Form	Def	Examples
Articles		
Indefinite	indef	*ein Rad*
None	indef	*Räder*
Definite	def	*das Rad*
Demonstrative	def	*dieses Rad*
Possessor	def	*mein/Ottos Rad*
Quantifiers	def	*alle Räder; jedes Rad*
Quantifiers	indef	*keine/viele Räder*
Pronouns		
Demonstrative	def	*das; dieses*
Pronominal adv	def	*daran*
Indefinite	indef	*jemand*

Table 4: Forms of articles and pronouns and corresponding type of definiteness (column 'Def').

forms of the referring phrases, to facilitate annotation decisions and render them more robust against errors. In particular, the definitions have a strong focus on the form of the article, if any, or the type of pronoun or adverb, see Table 2, column 'Form'. Moreover, we added detailed definition of definiteness, see Table 4.

We also specified additional criteria for the labels `bridging`, `contained`, `unknown` and `known`, to allow for an easier distinction between those labels, see Table 2, column 'Description'.

Decision hierarchy There are often several options for annotating a phrase. For example, the second occurrence of *wir* 'we' in example (1) can be annotated either as `situation` or as `given` (because it has been mentioned previously). Similar cases often occur with referents labeled as `known` which are referenced multiple times.

Our guidelines specify that the label `given` (and `displaced`) should generally be annotated in preference, resulting, e.g., in coreference chains such as `unknown-given-given` or `known-displaced`. There are two exceptions to this rule: First, regarding the label `situation` as in (1), all coreferent occurrences are annotated as `situation`, cf. Figure 1. Secondly, generic *man* 'one/you/they' is always annotated as `known`.

Linguistic tests We define linguistic tests to aid the annotation decision process. These tests concern mainly the decision whether an expression is considered to refer to a class or to individuals. This is realized by testing whether the expression refers to every single member of the assumed class or to a subset of individuals.

For example, if we want to annotate the phrase *modernster Methoden* 'state-of-the-art methods' in example (3), we can ask the following test question: Does this apply to every single state-of-the-art method? In the example, however, we are dealing with a contextually restricted subset of methods (which are relevant for virtual worlds), so `known` (for a known class) is not used, but `new` for a newly introduced subset.

(3) *virtuelle Welten helfen uns, unsere Wahrnehmung, unsere menschliche Wahrnehmung, zu stärken mit Hilfe modernster Methoden und Techniken.*
'virtual worlds help us to strengthen our perception, our human perception, with the help of *state-of-the-art methods* and techniques.'

5 Experiments

Annotation and curation of linguistic resources is time consuming and costly, especially in the case of a complex phenomenon like information status and a detailed tagset such as the RefLex scheme. To keep annotation costs minimal, we conducted an annotation experiment to test for an optimized annotation mode, which allows for minimal costs in resources and maximal accuracy. We assumed that the expenses of the usual annotation and curation process, involving multiple annotators and curators, could be reduced significantly by installing different settings of annotation while maintaining a reasonable accuracy and therefore quality of the annotated data.

To test this, we set up various annotation scenarios in different personnel settings and tested for time and staff 'costs' in relation to the resulting annotation quality. There were four expert annotators (the authors) involved in the experiment. Before running the experiment, the annotators annotated and curated several passages in two training datasets for annotation training. All annotators were also involved in the fine-tuning of the annotation guidelines. After the training phase, the guidelines were finalized. Then the experiment was conducted. All annotations, curations, and corrections where created and handled in the annotation tool INCEpTION (Klie et al., 2018).

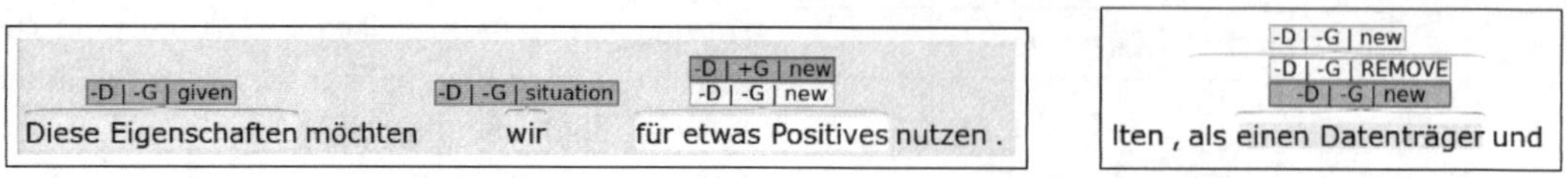

Figure 2: Original annotations and and corrections of example (4) (left), and a REMOVE correction, marking the erroneous span in example (5) (right).

Correcting annotations Figure 2 uses example (4) to show how we have implemented the correction steps in INCEpTION. The annotations shown in green are those of the annotator. The labels in yellow and purple come from two correctors.

For the correction steps, new layers (with new colors) were created in INCEpTION, with the same labels as the original annotation layer plus an additional label REMOVE (see below). The correctors could only see the original annotations of one annotator and not the corrections of the other corrector.

(4) *Diese Eigenschaften möchten wir für etwas Positives nutzen.*
'We want to use these qualities *for something positive*.'

Figure 2, left part, shows that the two existing annotations of example (4) were found to be correct by both correctors, so they didn't change anything. However, the phrase *for something positive* 'for something positive' was not considered by the annotator. Both correctors (shown in yellow and purple) have re-annotated this phrase.[4]

Removing an erroneous annotation of correcting the extent of an annotation span is a special case in the correction process. For this case, a new label REMOVE is employed, which is used to mark the incorrect span. A new correct span including a label is added, if needed. Figure 2, right part, shows the annotation of example (5). The original annotator did not include the preposition *als* 'as' in the span, which has been corrected accordingly by the corrector (shown in yellow).

(5) *als einen Datenträger*
'as a data storage medium'

Experimental settings The experiment included three different annotation settings (also see Table 10 in Appendix A for an overview of these settings):

Set 1 First, all four annotators annotated and collectively curated a gold version of 5 × 100 annotations.

Set 2 Secondly, only three of the annotators annotated and curated 2 × 100 annotations, and a single corrector corrected the annotations of one of the three annotators per batch.

Set 3 The last setting involved two annotators annotating and curating the gold version and the other two both correcting the same single annotation per batch, but independently from each other. In total, 3 × 100 annotations were annotated, curated and corrected in this setting.

The gold versions were created by the annotators themselves in a joint discussion round. This means that the gold versions are certainly influenced by the existing annotations, but this is trivially true for every gold version that is created on the basis of existing annotations.

The correctors did not participate in the curation. They only saw one of the annotations and corrected this annotation. They had no access to the other annotations or to the gold version.

So the relevant question is: Can the correctors arrive at a similarly high-quality "gold" result as the curators? Since a correction is significantly cheaper than a curation (requires less time and personnel), this would save a lot.

In order to make the two basic scenarios – multiple annotation followed by curation on the one hand vs. single annotation followed by correction on the other – as comparable as possible, the correction is based on one of the annotations that is also used to create the gold version (as one of several annotations).

6 Results

To evaluate the quality of the various annotation scenarios, we use two different measures: Fleiss' kappa as a measure of inter-annotator agreement and F_1-score as a measure of the annotators' and

[4]As already noted, we ignore differences regarding the labels +/-D and +/-G.

Set	Labels (κ)	Spans (%)
1	0.63	73.58
2	0.73	67.67
3	0.76	88.19

Table 5: Inter-annotator agreement: Fleiss' kappa for exact matching spans and proportion of matching spans across the different settings.

Annotator	Labels (F_1)	Spans (F_1)
Person1	0.75	0.93
Person2	0.70	0.93
Person3	0.64	0.88
Person4	0.63	0.88

Table 6: Annotator vs. gold: F_1-scores for labels and spans between each annotator and the curated gold version.

Corrector	Labels (F_1)	Spans (F_1)
Person1	0.75	0.92
Person2	0.81	0.95
Person3	0.79	0.93
Person4	0.86	0.96

Table 7: Corrector vs. gold: F_1-scores for labels and spans between each corrector and the curated gold version.

correctors' accuracy with regard to the gold standard and as a measure for the correctors' agreement among them.[5]

Agreement among the annotators We first analyzed agreement between the annotators, see Table 5. Only spans that were exact matches were included in the evaluation using Fleiss' kappa. The second column shows the proportion of these spans in all spans. The table already shows solid scores for the labels in the first phase, which increase continuously, indicating a robust baseline of inter-annotator scores for the further evaluation of the experiment.

Distance between annotations and gold Next, we examined how far the individual annotators were from the curated gold version. We calculated this distance in the form of aggregated F-scores across all annotated text fragments per annotator, see Table 6. Only exact matches were counted as correct. We distinguish between F-scores for spans and for labels, to differentiate between correctly identifying spans and subsequently labeling them correctly. The span scores were calculated as the harmonic mean of span precision and recall. The label scores are the micro-averaged harmonic mean of label precision and recall per person. As Table 6 shows, label F-scores range from 0.63 to 0.75 while span F-scores are considerably higher at 0.88 to 0.93, indicating a relatively robust span identification across annotators, while label identification seems to pose some challenges.

For us, a highly relevant question is how far away the results from the different tasks are from the optimal gold version. In other words, we want to compare two distances: (i) How far are the individual annotators from the curated gold version? (ii) How far are the corrected versions from the gold version? If the corrected versions are further away from the gold version, this would mean that the corrections have introduced additional errors and worsened the annotation overall. The expectation would therefore be that the corrected version is as close as possible to the gold version, so that a correction can serve as a substitute for an elaborate double annotation with subsequent curation.

Question (i) has been answered above (see Table 6). Question (ii) is addressed next.

Distance between corrections and gold For the evaluation of the corrected labels, we also used an absolute match heuristic, where only exact matches were counted as correct. However, to account for the fact that spans could be added or removed by the correctors, we introduce an additional label called `NONE`, which covers two possible scenarios: (i) A span was added by the corrector but does not exist in the gold standard (gold = `NONE`, correction = `foo`). (ii) A span in the gold standard was omitted by the corrector (gold = `foo`, correction = `NONE`).[6]

[5]In our view, chance-corrected measures such as Fleiss' kappa are not applicable to the other scenarios because it is to be expected that the gold version as well as the corrector's version are biased by the given annotations and therefore the assumptions concerning chance agreement are no longer correct.

[6]This approach also allows us to also account for cases in which the extent of a span has been corrected (as shown in Figure 2, right part), in that `REMOVE` annotations are treated as

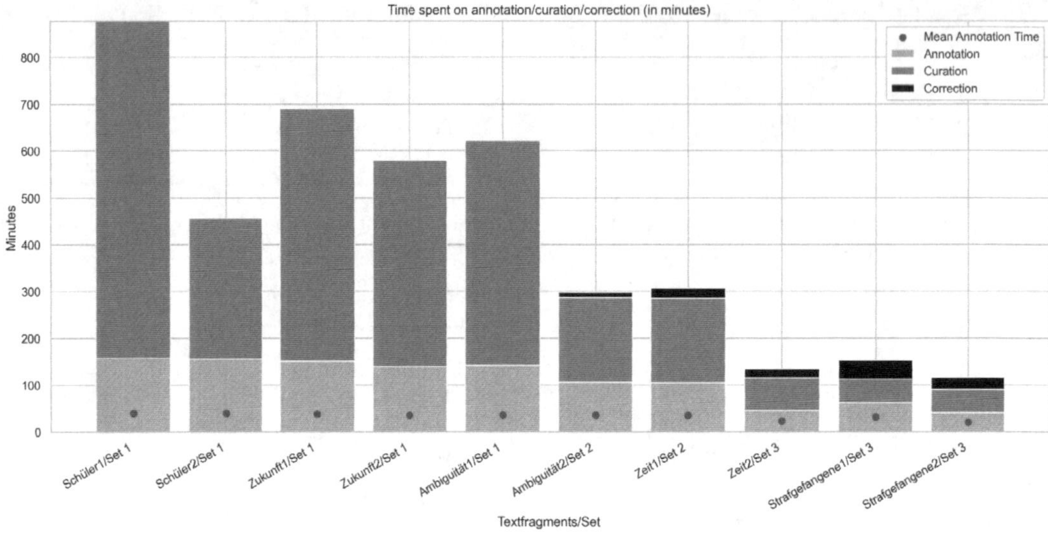

Figure 3: Accumulated annotation, curation and correction times per text fragment. Note that total annotation time represented in the bars decreases substantially due to employing fewer annotators per scenario, but average annotation time stays relatively constant.

Task	Labels (F_1)	Spans (F_1)
Annotation	0.68	0.91
Correction	0.80	0.94

Table 8: Annotation vs. correction: macro-average of the annotation and correction F_1-scores for labels and spans.

	Labels (F_1)	Spans (F_1)
Correctors	0.95	0.97

Table 9: Corrector vs. corrector: F_1-scores for labels and spans between the correctors.

For comparing corrections with the gold version, we calculated span and label F-scores for each individual corrector across all corrections, see Table 7. The table shows that practically all F-scores are substantially higher than the F-scores of the original annotators in both span and label identification.

Table 8 shows the macro-averaged F-scores of both tasks. The F-scores of the correction task clearly outperform the overall annotation scores, indicating an increase in data quality for the correction scenario as compared to the usual annotation setting of multiple annotations and subsequent curation.

Agreement among the correctors Finally, we also compared the correctors with each other using the F_1-score, by considering one of the correctors as the "gold" version to which the other corrector is compared. As above, the span scores were calculated as the harmonic mean of span precision and recall and the label scores as the micro-averaged harmonic mean of label precision and recall, see Table 9 for the results. Both label and exact span agreement are exceptionally high, indicating highly consistent identification of relevant text spans and similar interpretive strategies.

Comparing time and personnel across the scenarios To evaluate the influence of the various annotation settings on time and personnel spent on the annotation process, all annotation, curation and correction times were tracked, see Figure 3 for the respective settings and measured times.

The bars encode the accumulated time required per text. The different settings include either annotation plus curation (Set 1), or annotation, curation plus correction in different weightings (Sets 2 and 3). Average annotation time is marked by a blue dot within the columns.

NONE annotations.

The first five bars represent the accumulated time requirements for annotating (light blue) and curating (azure) the text fragments in Set 1, by four annotators and curators. That is, the lower part of these bars shows the sum of the four individual annotation times and the upper part of the bars shows the curation time multiplied by four (because four curators were involved). The time requirements shown therefore correspond to the personnel costs that would have to be invested.

The next two bars show the total time of Set 2, comprising three annotators and curators plus one corrector (midnight blue). The final three bars represent Set 3, with only two annotators/curators and two correctors. Note that this is the minimal amount of annotators/curators necessary to realize traditional annotation and curation.

As expected, the overall time is trivially reduced significantly from setting to setting (as fewer people are involved in the annotation and curation per setting). In addition, a training effect can be observed during curation: every second text fragment from the same text is curated faster than the first (e.g., compare the curation time of the first and second bar or of the third and fourth bar). The curation time also appears to be decreasing in general, although this may also be an effect of the respective texts.

However, Figure 3 also shows that the average annotation time (the blue dots) stays relatively constant. This shows that, in contrast to curation, there is practically no training effect with annotation, or only a marginal one.

Set 3 is the setting in which the time required for the conventional annotation setting – involving 2 annotators + joint curation – can best be compared directly with the correction setting, involving 1 annotator + 1 corrector. Figure 4 relates the two alternatives directly to each other. The left column of each pair shows the accumulated time for two annotators (light blue) and the curation time multiplied by two (azure). The right column of each pair shows the sum of the average annotation time (blue) and the average curation time (midnight blue). The comparison clearly shows the drastic time gain due to the correction setting.

Considering that the F-scores for span and label identification in the correction setting not only stay constant between the conditions of annotation/curation and annotation/correction, but even increase, the annotation costs saved in terms of time and personnel are considerable.

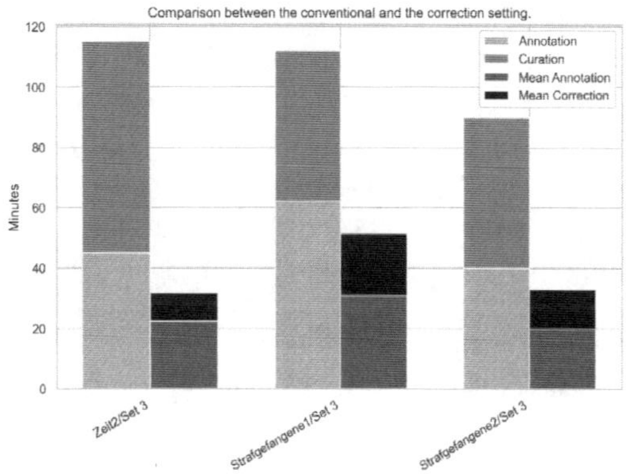

Figure 4: Comparison of accumulated time required by the conventional setting (left bars) and the correction setting (right bars).

7 Conclusion

We set out to investigate various annotation scenarios and their respective efficiency in terms of time and personnel employed and conducted an annotation mode experiment where we compared the scenarios of (i) four annotators and four curators, (ii) three annotators and three curators tested against a single corrector and finally (iii) two annotators and two curators tested against two correctors.

As has been shown in Section 6, the F-scores for span and label identification of the correctors not only stayed constant compared to the annotator F-scores, but even exceeded those annotators' values while reducing the total time of the entire annotation process approximately by half, even when considering the control curation condition in this calculation. We therefore argue that the third scenario of annotating and correcting is preferable to the conventional annotation and curation setting not only in terms of time and personnel, but also in terms of annotation quality, as the corrections closely match the gold version as can be inferred from the respective F-scores. We could thus show that time-efficient annotation – even in the case of highly complex tagsets such as the RefLex tagset – does not necessarily need to come at the traditionally high annotation cost.

Limitations

The study is based on data from only one type of text, TEDx Talks, and on only one type of annotation, information status. Overall, a rather small amount of data (1000 annotations from 5 different texts) was annotated. Whether the same or similar results can be obtained for other text and annotation types is an open question.

All annotators were involved in all parts of the study from the beginning and contributed to the development of the guidelines as well as annotating, curating and correcting data themselves. The significance of the study would have been stronger if these tasks had been carried out by different experts, for example if the developers of the guidelines had not annotated the data.

Since all annotators were directly involved in the development of the annotation guidelines as well as in the annotation, curation and correction processes, a marginal training effect may have positively influenced the overall annotation quality. Compared to a setup involving separate teams for annotation, curation, and correction, the resulting quality metrics may be slightly elevated. Nevertheless, the relatively stable mean annotation time across tasks highlights the substantial efficiency gains achieved through the integrated correction settings. These gains represent a notable improvement over conventional annotation workflows that rely on multiple independent annotations followed by subsequent curation – both in terms of time investment and the resulting data quality.

Acknowledgments

We are grateful to the anonymous reviewers for their helpful comments. Funded by/gefördert durch die Deutsche Forschungsgemeinschaft (DFG) – Projektnummer 232722074 – SFB 1102 (Project C6).

References

Jean Carletta. 1996. Assessing agreement on classification tasks: the kappa statistic. *Computational Linguistics*, 22(2):249–254.

Jacob Cohen. 1960. A coefficient of agreement for nominal scales. *Educational and Psychological Measurement*, 20(1):37–46.

Stefanie Dipper and Sandra Kübler. 2017. German treebanks: TIGER and TüBa-D/Z. In Nancy Ide and James Pustejovsky, editors, *Handbook of Linguistic Annotation*, pages 595–639. Springer, Berlin.

Joseph L. Fleiss. 1971. Measuring nominal scale agreement among many raters. *Psychological Bulletin*, 76(5):387–382.

Cyril Grouin, Thomas Lavergne, and Aurélie Névéol. 2014. Optimizing annotation efforts to build reliable annotated corpora for training statistical models. In *Proceedings of LAW VIII - The 8th Linguistic Annotation Workshop*, pages 54–58, Dublin, Ireland. Association for Computational Linguistics and Dublin City University.

Jan-Christoph Klie, Michael Bugert, Beto Boullosa, Richard Eckart de Castilho, and Iryna Gurevych. 2018. The INCEpTION platform: Machine-assisted and knowledge-oriented interactive annotation. In *Proceedings of the 27th International Conference on Computational Linguistics: System Demonstrations*, pages 5–9. Association for Computational Linguistics.

Marie Mikulová, Milan Straka, Jan Štěpánek, Barbora Štěpánková, and Jan Hajic. 2022. Quality and efficiency of manual annotation: Pre-annotation bias. In *Proceedings of the Thirteenth Language Resources and Evaluation Conference*, pages 2909–2918, Marseille, France. European Language Resources Association.

Arndt Riester and Stefan Baumann. 2017. *The RefLex Scheme — Annotation Guidelines*, volume 14 of *SinSpeC — Working Papers of the SFB 732 "Incremental Specification in Context"*. OPUS, Stuttgart.

Claude E. Shannon. 1948. A mathematical theory of communication. *The Bell System Technical Journal*, 27(3):379–423.

A Appendix

Setting / Text	Person1	Person2	Person3	Person4	Distribution of Tasks
Set 1					
Schüler-1	100 ann+cur	100 ann+cur	100 ann+cur	100 ann+cur	4 anno / 4 cur
Schüler-2	100 ann+cur	100 ann+cur	100 ann+cur	100 ann+cur	4 anno / 4 cur
Gesellschaft-1	100 ann+cur	100 ann+cur	100 ann+cur	100 ann+cur	4 anno / 4 cur
Gesellschaft-2	100 ann+cur	100 ann+cur	100 ann+cur	100 ann+cur	4 anno / 4 cur
Ambiguität-1	100 ann+cur	100 ann+cur	100 ann+cur	100 ann+cur	4 anno / 4 cur
Set 2					
Ambiguität-2	100 ann+cur	100 ann+cur	100 ann+cur	**100 corr**	3 anno / 3 cur / 1 corr
Zeit-1	100 ann+cur	100 ann+cur	100 ann+cur	**100 corr**	3 anno / 3 cur / 1 corr
Set 3					
Zeit-2	**100 corr**	100 ann+cur	100 ann+cur	**100 corr**	2 anno / 2 cur / 2 corr
Strafgefangene-1	100 ann+cur	**100 corr**	100 ann+cur	**100 corr**	2 anno / 2 cur / 2 corr
Strafgefangene-2	100 ann+cur	100 ann+cur	**100 corr**	**100 corr**	2 anno / 2 cur / 2 corr

Table 10: Detailed overview over annoation, curation and correction scenarios. 'Person1' to 'Person4' shows the tasks of the four expert annotators in the respective settings. '100 ann+cur' means that this person created 100 annotations (independently of the others) and then curated the gold version together with the other annotators. This means that four people were involved in annotating and curating ('4 anno / 4 cur', column 'Distribution of Tasks'). From Set 2 onwards, Person4 no longer annotated and curated, but instead corrected the 100 annotations of one of the annotators ('100 corr'). From Set 3 onwards, two people corrected the same 100 annotations of one annotator, independently from each other.

Annotating Spatial Descriptions in Literary and Non-Literary Text

Emilie Sitter, **Omar Momen,** **Florian Steig,**
Berenike Herrmann, and **Sina Zarrieß**
CRC 1646 – Linguistic Creativity in Communication
Faculty of Linguistics and Literary Studies
Bielefeld University, Germany
{emilie.sitter,omar.hassan,f.steig,berenike.herrmann,sina.zarriess}@uni-bielefeld.de

Abstract

Descriptions are a central component of literary texts, yet their systematic identification remains a challenge. This work suggests an approach to identifying sentences describing spatial conditions in literary text. It was developed iteratively on German literary text and extended to non-literary text to evaluate its applicability across textual domains. To assess the robustness of the method, we involved both humans and a selection of state-of-the-art Large Language Models (LLMs) in annotating a collection of sentences regarding their descriptiveness and spatiality. We compare the annotations across human annotators and between humans and LLMs. The main contributions of this paper are: (1) a set of annotation guidelines for identifying spatial descriptions in literary texts, (2) a curated dataset of almost 4,700 annotated sentences of which around 500 are spatial descriptions, produced through in-depth discussion and consensus among annotators, and (3) a pilot study of automating the task of spatial description annotation of German texts. We publish the codes and all human and LLM annotations for the public to be used for research purposes only.[1]

1 Introduction

Literary and non-literary texts are full of descriptions that help readers see, hear, feel, smell, and even taste what is happening in a story or text, making the places and entities experiencable. While the analysis of literary text has become an important area of annotation studies, existing work typically targets narrative elements, such as characters or plot structure (Bethard et al., 2012; Reiter, 2015; Bamman et al., 2020; Zehe et al., 2021; Jahan et al., 2021; Reiter et al., 2022; Soni et al., 2023). In the domain of non-literary text, a lot of recent NLP work deals with multimodal image descriptions scraped from alt-texts on the web or collected via human annotations, cf. (Young et al., 2014; Sharma et al., 2018; Pont-Tuset et al., 2020; Garg et al., 2024; Alaçam et al., 2024). However, to our knowledge, no tool or dataset distinguishes between descriptive and non-descriptive language and identifies descriptions in naturally occurring text. In this work, we present an approach to annotating and detecting descriptions in unimodal, literary, and non-literary text. To give our study a concrete target and domain, we focus on descriptions of space.

Since the 1990s, the concept of space has gained increasing attention in the cultural and social studies (Döring and Thielmann, 2008). In linguistics and NLP, the analysis of spatial language in text has received moderate but continuous attention. To date, existing work on annotations of spatial language mainly aimed at detecting mentions of spatial entities (named entity recognition) or other spatial concepts, like paths or trajectories (Pustejovsky et al., 2015; Pustejovsky, 2017).

This work focuses on identifying sentences describing static space. The following sentence is an example of a spatial description in a story that works without naming any named spatial entities:

(1) Auf dem zertretenen Rasen zwischen Haus und Zaun, roh gezimmert, stand ein länglicher Tisch mit Bank und Sesseln.[2]
On the trampled lawn between the house and the fence, rough-hewn, was an oblong table with a bench and chairs.

In literary texts in particular, such descriptions are a fundamental unit for creating a space of action and opening up a world to the reader by routing the narrative in a physical environment. Despite the increasing interest in space and spatial descriptions,

[1] https://github.com/emilie-si/LAW2025-Descriptions

[2] Arthur Schnitzler: Doktor Gräsler, Badearzt (1917)

Proceedings of the 19th Linguistic Annotation Workshop (LAW-XIX-2025), pages 308–325
July 31, 2025

identifying them in a natural context—in our study, novels or travel reports—remains a challenge. The paper contributes to the broader goal of understanding spatial and descriptive language in various textual domains and improving its automatic detection. We propose a set of annotation guidelines to extract spatially descriptive sentences from literary and non-literary texts beyond self-evident cases. As examples we use the two German corpora KOLIMO (Herrmann and Lauer, 2018; Horstmann, 2019) and Wikivoyage (Nolda, 2024; Wikimedia Foundation Inc., 2025).

Based on samples extracted from these two corpora, we created a set of annotated sentences. To ensure that all annotators' perspectives are considered, we systematically discussed the cases of disagreement. A final label was assigned based on the mutual agreement of all annotators on a plausible classification. Since human annotations are expensive and time-consuming, we also explore how to automate this annotation task. Based on the manually annotated dataset, we test the ability of LLMs to identify spatial descriptions. In doing so, we aim to contribute to a more comprehensive understanding of spatial language processing.

2 Background: Descriptions and Space

2.1 Descriptions

We draw on background from different disciplines to develop our approach to annotating descriptions. Since our main focus is on literary text, we rely on work from literary studies (Ronen, 1997; Hahn et al., 2025), digital humanities (Herrmann et al., 2022; Schumacher, 2023), and psychology (Draschkow and Võ, 2017; Henderson and Hollingworth, 1999).

It can be assumed that humans generally have an intuitive understanding of what is descriptive (Wolf, 2007; Nünning, 2007). Depending on the domain and genre of a text, spatial conditions can be presented in different contexts and for different reasons. The primary function of spatial descriptions is to convey spatial information (Ryan, 2012). They enable readers to build a mental figuration of spatial information (Denis, 2008, 2018) and serve as a building block for constructing narrative space (Dennerlein, 2009; Wolf, 2007).

The boundary between narrative and descriptive is more than often fluid. We are thus taking up the long-standing question of how to reliably distinguish between narrative and descriptive (Mosher, 1991; Ronen, 1997; Wolf, 2007). According to Wolf, a distinction can be made by "the presence or absence of the core elements of typical narratives: motivated actions that involve anthropomorphic agents, are interrelated not only by chronology but also by causality and teleology and lead to, or are consequences of, conscious acts or decisions, frequently as results of conflicts" (Wolf, 2007). Similarly, for Dennerlein "uneventfulness and the communication of stable properties of a spatial situation" are the central criteria of spatial descriptions (Dennerlein, 2009, own translation).

However, there are countless cases in which these two criteria are either not exclusively or not fully met (Ronen, 1997). This work shows how we deal with such cases.

2.2 Spatial Frames

The sentences relevant in our annotation task should describe visually cohesive spaces with scenic quality. In the literary studies, Ruth Ronen's concept of "spatial frames" refers to this relatively restricted sub-area of space: spatial frames are "the actual or potential surroundings of fictional characters, objects and places" (Ronen, 1986). Spatial frames encompass only the (potential) environment of a narrator or the characters in a story: everything that could be perceived as being "here" during narration and where an action can (potentially) take place (Zoran, 1984; Ryan et al., 2016). The notion of spatial frames as "shifting scenes of action" Ryan et al. (2016) highlights the scenic nature of spatial frames.

The entire space in which a story takes place can be understood as a series of many individual spatial frames (Zoran, 1984). Spatial frames are different to specific locations. They represent particular, immovable points in space that can be localized either on a real map or on the map of a story world (Schumacher, 2023; Ryan et al., 2016). Places become spatial frames as soon as they convey more meaning than a mere geographical location on a map.

Grounding our description identification approach on Ronen's (1986) concept of Spatial Frames has certain advantages. It excludes instances of spatial language that do not exactly describe spatial conditions, such as route descriptions or mere geographical and factual information (as in "*Berlin is the capital of Germany*"). But, compared to more restrictive concepts, it includes any kind of space as long as action could take place there within a story ("*Berlin is big and noisy.*"). Spatial Frames in a story do not only encompass a character's actual spatial surroundings but everything that, within the story, can *potentially* be their environment (Ronen, 1986). Since we annotated isolated sentences without context, it cannot always be judged what would be an actual surrounding in a story and what is, for instance, only imagined, dreamed, or described from afar. Spatial frames comprise exactly the section of spatial language that we want to capture in our annotation task.

2.3 Scenes

Objects share some qualities with spatial frames, such as their three-dimensionality and perceptibility (they can be experienced on various levels, such as visually, acoustically, haptically). However, in contrast to scenes in which we can be embedded and events can take place, we can look at discrete objects only from an outside point of view (Henderson and Ferreira, 2004).

Drawing an analogy between textually described scenes and visually depicted scenes (in real life or in photographs), we rely on the concept of Scene Grammar (Draschkow and Võ, 2017; Võ and Wolfe, 2013; Võ et al., 2019; Wolfe et al., 2011) to distinguish objects from scenes. Assuming that scene perception functions in a similar way to language perception, it serves as an approach for understanding the generation of mental models of described scenes. Scene Grammar comprises the environmental rules that help us to recognize real-world visual scenes at first glance by only coarse spatial information (Draschkow and Võ, 2017; Võ et al., 2019; Oliva, 2005).

According to Scene Grammar, a combination of individual, static anchor objects (e.g., shower, washbasin, toilet) and smaller-scale local objects attached to anchors (e.g., towel, soap bar, toilet paper) forms a complete scene (e.g., bathroom) (Võ et al., 2019; Draschkow and Võ, 2017; Oliva, 2005). In our annotation task, we rely on Scene Grammar to exclude descriptions of anchor objects on their own (such as "*The towel is red.*"). However, a combination of explicitly ("*Next to the clean shower, there is a red towel.*") or implicitly ("*The bathroom is clean.*") described individual objects indicates that the subject of the description is a scene. We can then consider it a spatial frame.

3 Annotation Procedure

This section introduces the set-up of our annotation task, the procedures for guideline development and data curation, as the final annotation guidelines.

3.1 Approach

We asked our annotators to identify spatial descriptions on the level of complete, isolated sentences (we do not consider passages describing space that are shorter or longer than exactly one complete sentence). The annotators' task was to make a binary distinction, i.e., whether an instance is a spatial description or not. Moreover, annotators could annotate instances as "unclear" and could add a comment explaining their uncertainty. All sentences were annotated independently by one of the paper's authors and two out of a group of four in-lab trained annotators.

3.2 Iterative Guideline Development

We followed Reiter's (2020) proposed methodology for developing annotation guidelines. This approach aims to develop generic but precise guidelines for the practical annotation of a phenomenon that has already been described theoretically.

We started the guideline development for the literary data, assuming that it is more difficult to identify static spatial descriptions in literary and narrative than in non-narrative texts. The initial round of annotations was conducted in a relatively open manner, aiming to better understand the phenomenon and to identify ambiguities and challenges. The guidelines were then iteratively developed and refined based on existing research on the subjects of space, description, and scenes. They are formulated in bullet points and contain examples for all cases described (Reiter, 2020; Reiter et al., 2019).

After annotating a subset of sentences, we discussed the individual diverging samples and further sharpened the guidelines as reported in Section 3.4. If annotators chose different categories or the label "unclear" due to a lack of clarity in the guidelines, these were adjusted accordingly. All annotators were informed of the update.

3.3 Data Curation

To obtain a curated ground-truth dataset, we took into account all annotators' subjective decisions and re-evaluated divergent annotations through discussion. A final label was assigned based on mutual agreement. The aim was to finally select categories as comprehensible and acceptable to as many annotators as possible. Guideline adjustments of later annotation iterations were incorporated retroactively into previously annotated subsets. This procedure ensured the creation of a curated dataset with the most appropriate categories.

Please refer to Section 5 for further analysis of annotator agreement and Section 7 for further discussion.

3.4 Annotation Guidelines

This section summarizes the guidelines that were iteratively developed for identifying spatial descriptions in literary text.

1. Spatial descriptions describe "spatial frames": any space that can potentially be a character's immediate environment in a story (Ronen, 1986). They describe an actually perceptible scene (2-a) instead of, for instance, only background knowledge about a location (2-b).

(2) a. There was a scent of flowers in the pretty looking garden. (✓)
  b. The garden was redesigned last year. (✗)

2. Spatial descriptions must contain information about the spatial and perceptible environment at a certain place. Spatial frames can be captured by describing what can be perceived at a certain point in space. Rather than just mentioning a spatial frame (3-b), there has to be some descriptive element (3-a).

(3) a. This forest is dark. (✓)
  b. This is a forest. (✗)

3. Spatial descriptions can also convey acoustic, tactile, olfactory, or other sensory signals that contribute to the perception of space (4-a) (Wolf, 2007). Describing the spatial frame not necessarily requires visual sensations, as we can infer the spatial conditions through these other sensory modalities (Dennerlein, 2009).

(4) a. In the basement it was cold and a mildewy scent hung in the air. (✓)

4. Spatial descriptions describe a scene (5-a) instead of a single object (5-b). We can define a scene as an arrangement of two or more implicitly or explicitly mentioned independent elements in a semantic relationship.

(5) a. There is a green bottle on the table. (✓)
  b. My bottle is green. (✗)

5. An isolated sentence must not contain any unresolved references to previous text (e.g. pronouns) (6-b). Any spatial description can be understood without any further textual context (6-a).

(6) a. The living room was furnished tastefully. (✓)
  b. It was furnished tastefully. (✗)

6. Descriptions do not report any action. The described space is static, its properties are stable over time. There is no unique, temporary action (which would often be expressed by a verb for a spontaneous, individual action or movement, such as "walk") at the time of description of the space (7-c). Descriptive parts of sentences that are embedded in narrative sentences Schumacher (2023) are not relevant for our annotation task. The following exceptions can be made: a) typical and recurring actions of generic actors who are not individual characters in the passage (Dennerlein, 2009) (7-a) and b) the act of perception reported while describing space (by verbs of perception, such as "see" or "hear") (7-b).

(7) a. Shibuya Crossing is constantly filled with pedestrians. (✓)
  b. We saw the small bridge that crosses the river. (✓)
  c. We crossed the river over a small bridge. (✗)

7. For the description of generic, natural phenomena and light, we apply a WIDLII (*When In Doubt, Leave it In*) approach (Steen et al., 2010). With natural phenomena (weather and wind, tides and waves, daylight phases, sunrises and sunsets, clouds, light from lamps or candles) there is usually some kind of movement: waves roll over the water, clouds drift across the sky, the sun rises or sets. The described natural phenomena must not contain a narrative and have to be generic and repetitive instead of one-off movements (8-a).

(8) a. The sun sank, painting the horizon a breathtaking red. (✓)

8. Only concrete space is of interest to us. Described space can be real or fictional, imaginary, remembered, phantastic, or dreamed, as long as it is not purely metaphorical or an abstraction of a character's mental processes (9-a).

(9) a. There was a maze of thoughts tangled up in my mind. (✗)

9. The spatial descriptions must be complete German sentences, but a verb is not necessarily required (10-a).

(10) a. Colorful flowers, ripe fruit, large trees in the garden. (✓)

4 Spatial Descriptions Dataset

Our annotation work resulted in a dataset of spatial descriptions extracted from two fundamentally different German corpora of literary and non-literary texts: KOLIMO and Wikivoyage. KOLIMO, the "Corpus of Literary Modernism", has its focus on 19th century fiction (Herrmann and Lauer, 2018; Horstmann, 2019). The copyright on these texts has expired, and they are public domain. KOLIMO is a convenient literary corpus because of its size and its availability in digital form with extensive metadata. As a non-literary counterpart, we chose Wikivoyage, an online travel guide, as we expected to find many spatial descriptions there (Nolda, 2024; Wikimedia Foundation Inc., 2025). The German version of Wikivoyage is distributed under the CC BY-SA 4.0 license.

We developed our guidelines for spatial descriptions primarily based on KOLIMO. As a non-literary counterpart that is highly different not only in genre but also in its time of origin, Wikivoyage enables us to explore the extent to which the annotation scheme can be transferred to another domain.

For annotating on the sentence level, the full texts required some preprocessing. We excluded texts shorter than 10 sentences, assuming that it is unlikely that authors will dedicate complete sentences to exclusively describe spatial surroundings in very short texts. We eliminated incomplete sentences and only included sentences that begin with a capital letter and end with a punctuation mark.

	KOLIMO	Wikivoyage
Time Span	1850–1939	2012–2024
# Texts	43,012	20,195
# Filtered Texts	14,901	17,781
# Filtered Sentences	7,783,056	876,775
# Annotated Sentences	3854	800
Spatial Descriptions Ratio	8.4%	20%

Table 1: Statistics of the two corpora used in our study.

Bullet points, as they can be found in Wikivoyage, inherently indicate the beginning of a sentence and, therefore, cannot appear within a sentence. Moreover, only sentences with a minimum length of five words are considered for annotation. Table 1 reports the size of the complete dataset.

For better comparability between the two subsets, we pre-filtered the data. For each corpus, we determined the 10 most frequent non-named spatial entities (by lemma) (Kababgi et al., 2024) based on a list of spatial entities generated by Herrmann et al. (2022). Inflected forms or spatial entities as part of compound words (as they are frequent in German) were taken into account as far as possible (see Appendix A). We condensed the datasets to only sentences that contain one or more of the 10 most frequent spatial entities.

Pre-filtering definitely contributed to the proportion of spatial description among all annotated sentences, as reported in Table 1. We ensure that all sentences contain at least one spatial entity and, therefore, are spatial to some degree. Otherwise, at least in the literary data, a lower proportion of descriptions would be expected (Ronen, 1997).

5 Analysis: Agreement and Challenges

5.1 Quantitative Evaluation

For a quantitative evaluation of annotator agreement, three annotators independently annotated subsets of 300 sentences in random order. Disagreement cases were discussed individually and used to further refine the annotation guidelines and to train the annotators (see Section 3.4). Starting with literary sentences, we measured their Inter-Annotator Agreement (IAA) by Krippendorff's alpha (Krippendorff, 2013) and the F1 score in every iteration, as shown in Table 2. Instances annotated as "unclear" were counted as "not a spatial description" since our focus is on clear cases of descriptions. The highest achieved Krippendorff's Alpha in the best annotation iteration (iteration 2) is .66. Table 2 also shows that the continuous adaptation of

	It. 1 (Lit.)	It. 2 (Lit.)	It. 3 (Lit.)	It. 4 (Non-lit.)
# Sent.	294	295	300	300
A1-A2-A3 (K–α)	.63	.66	.60	.44
A1-A2 (F1)	.70	.65	.65	.58
A1-A3 (F1)	.67	.69	.74	.58
A2-A3 (F1)	.61	.72	.56	.40
A1-LLM (F1)	.64	.62	.71	.13
A2-LLM (F1)	.62	.73	.53	.12
A3-LLM (F1)	.51	.64	.67	.09
Curated-LLM (F1)	.70	.65	.70	.08

Table 2: Agreement between annotators and best LLM (Qwen2.5:32B with long English prompt (EN-long)). The table reports the agreement between the annotators and the annotators and the model in four iterations (It. 1 to It. 4) of annotating 300 sentences across both Literary and Non-literary datasets. (Some sentences of these sets were used to develop the prompt and are therefore not considered in this evaluation.)

the guidelines and excessive training of the annotators resulted in the agreement decreasing again in iteration 3.

The guidelines for literary text were slightly adapted to account for the non-literary corpus. These sentences exhibit a different structural composition. Surprisingly, they were not as easy to identify with the existing set of rules, which is again reflected in the decreasing IAA of iteration 4. For the pilot study, we tested the applicability of the existing rules to the non-literary texts, but these need to be further adapted in order to consistently identify spatial descriptions in this corpus.

5.2 Qualitative Evaluation: Literary Text

Literary text often allows for more than one correct interpretation (Gius et al., 2019; Gius and Jacke, 2017; Amidei et al., 2018). A particular challenge in our corpus is to distinguish the narrative or partially narrative sentences from those that are exclusively descriptive. Often, some degree of subjectivity underlies the annotation, as in the following examples:

In Example 1 in Appendix B, the annotators disagreed concerning the concreteness of the described space. One annotator was arguing that in this case the city is a concrete space that is actually described, while others assumed that the sentence reflects the mental state of the narrator.

As for Example 2 in Appendix B, the annotators could not agree whether the sentence can be considered as an action, or if sleepers lying on the earth should correctly be interpreted as a stable property of the described space.

Annotators also interpreted Example 3 in Appendix B differently. It was not clear whether describing what the room *not* is would be sufficient or too little information for a spatial description.

5.3 Qualitative Evaluation: Non-literary Text

In Wikivoyage, sentences with specific and temporary actions are rare, but the corpus contains many geographical descriptions, route descriptions, and street courses. These are spatial in a certain way but do not exactly represent spatial frames. Descriptions of mere geographical locations only provide information on where a specific place (a named entity) can be located on a map, as in Example 4 in Appendix B. If only slightly more spatial information is provided (as in Example 5) it becomes unclear whether the passage should still be classified as a geographical description or already constitutes a spatial frame.

Route descriptions describe the way from one to another location and possible landmarks along the way (Denis, 2018). These kinds of descriptions do not correspond to the immediate, perceptible surroundings at a specific location and can therefore be excluded from our annotation scheme (see Example 6 in Appendix B). However, when they also describe spatial properties, as in Example 7, they could be interpreted as spatial frames.

In the literary corpus, the vast majority of sentences is complete. Ellipses can be considered complete sentences. In literary text, they can serve as rhetorical devices (see Example 8 in Appendix B). In Wikivoyage, on the other hand, we found sentences without any verbs, serving as enumerations, abbreviations, or points on a bullet list (as in Example 9 in Appendix B). By definition, these are complete sentences as they begin with a capital letter and end with a punctuation mark. As long as there is a semantic relationship between the listed elements, the absence of a verb does not necessarily make a sentence an uninterpretable array of random objects (Henderson and Ferreira, 2004). To prevent doubts as to whether it is even possible to describe without a verb, the guidelines had to be adapted to state explicitly that the occurrence of a verb is not a decisive criterion for annotation.

6 Pilot Study: Automatic Annotation

Our aim is to eventually have a larger dataset of spatial descriptions across different textual domains. To this end, we carried out a prompting experiment with LLMs to classify the literary and non-literary sentences in our dataset (§ 4) in a zero-shot setting.

6.1 Experimental Setup

To track the effect of the variables in this experiment (input prompt, model family, and model size), we used four different prompts and seven different models to classify the 3854 literary and 800 non-literary sentences, resulting in 28 automatic annotations for each sentence. We measured the performance of these annotations using the human annotations as the ground truth.

We developed four different prompts in English and German, with varying levels of detail based on the annotation guidelines. We chose to use the German prompt only in the *long* version, as there were no significant differences between languages in the other levels of detail. Then we explored the prompts' performance on 70 randomly selected sentences from the set of annotated literary sentences. These 70 sentences were not considered in the further evaluation. The prompts were modified slightly for the non-literary sentences (see Appendix C).

LLMs have been evolving rapidly, and no single model offers the best performance across the board. Different model families and sizes each have their advantages and disadvantages. To account for this, we tested several different models: GPT-4o, one of OpenAI's current proprietary LLMs; Gemma2 and Qwen2.5, two open-source LLMs. For each of these two open-source models, we tested 3 different model sizes, ranging from 2B to 32B parameters. We report the experiment's settings in Appendix D.

We could successfully get a clear answer as (YES/NO) for almost all the responses in our prompting experiments; only in very few cases we had to manually look at the response to figure out the answer. Eventually, we transformed all the responses into binary labels. This enabled us to evaluate the performance of the 28 model-prompt variants against the human annotations. We measured accuracy, precision, recall, and F1 score of each variant. Additionally, we report the ratio of sentences predicted as spatial descriptions to the total number of sentences in the dataset for each variant, considering that the ratio in human annotations (prior probability) is .08 for literary texts and .20 for non-literary texts.

6.2 Results

We report the results of the top five models (according to F1 score on literary sentences) in Table 3. The results of all model-prompt variants for the literary and non-literary dataset are reported in Appendix E. Results of the literary dataset in Table 3 show that all models achieve high accuracies (.82-.95), but face a severe precision-recall tradeoff, resulting in lower F1 scores (.45-.67). Most models show a low ratio of predicting descriptions, roughly aligning with the low ratio of descriptions in the human annotations. We notice that the best-performing models on the literary dataset show very different results on the non-literary dataset. The accuracies deteriorate by 10-15 points, and the models are either extremely restrictive in classifying sentences as descriptions or make a lot of mistakes when being less restrictive (row 3).

The variants with the highest F1 for literary sentences (.67, .64, .57) are (Qwen2.5:32B, EN-long), (GPT-4o, EN-long), and (Qwen2.5:7B, EN-medium) respectively. (Qwen2.5:32B, EN-long) is better at precision, while precision and recall of (GPT-4o, EN-long) are more balanced. As for model families, Qwen is performing generally better than Gemma, and it also outperforms the closed-source representative GPT-4o. Larger size does not always guarantee (significantly) better performance across each model family, as highlighted by Qwen2.5:7B results, which are relatively better than those of the 32B variant at the (EN-medium) prompt variant. However, we notice that the 3B versions of Qwen2.5 chose NO for all sentences, resulting in zero true positives, and hence zero precision, recall, and F1. For prompt variants, generally, the longer detailed prompts perform better than the shorter ones, and the German prompt does not improve over the English version. Exceptions show that the 7B version of Qwen performs better with briefer prompts than detailed ones, and that Gemma models perform better with the German prompt than the English one.

In Table 2, we compare the F1 scores between annotator pairs and between each annotator and our best-performing model-prompt variant on the literary dataset (Qwen2.5:32B, EN-long). The results show that the F1 score of the automatic annotations falls in the same range as the F1 scores of the annotator pairs. In the literary dataset, the val-

		Literary Dataset					Non-Literary Dataset				
Model	**Prompt**	**Acc.**	**P**	**R**	**F1**	**Rat.**	**Acc.**	**P**	**R**	**F1**	**Rat.**
Qwen2.5:32B	EN-long	**.95**	**.83**	.56	**.67**	.06	.81	1.0	.06	.12	.01
GPT-4o	EN-long	.94	.64	.63	.64	.08	.84	.97	.19	.32	.04
Qwen2.5:7B	EN-med.	.93	.56	.57	.57	.09	.76	.40	.42	.41	.21
Gemma2:27B	DE-long	.86	.37	.86	.52	.20	.84	.81	.26	.40	.06
Gemma2:9B	DE-long	.82	.31	**.88**	.45	.24	.84	.87	.21	.34	.05

Table 3: Evaluation results of the top five models according to F1 on the literary dataset. We selected only the best-performing prompt variant for each of these models. We report **Acc**uracy, **P**recision, **R**ecall, **F1**, and **Rat**io of predicted sentences as spatial descriptions to the total number of sentences in each dataset (literary dataset: 3784 sentences; non-literary dataset: 800 sentences).

ues range between .56 and .74 for annotator pairs, and between .51 and .73 for LLM-Human pairs. For non-literary texts, the values are lower for both annotator pairs and LLM–human pairs, with extremely low F1 scores for the latter. These low scores on the non-literary dataset suggest a significant change in task difficulty for LLMs across different genres. They highlight the need for genre-specific prompts, reflecting the varying annotation guidelines between genres.

In summary, the pilot study illustrates the usability of LLMs at the task of classifying sentences as spatial descriptions. For the literary sentences, they produce annotations with an acceptable degree of accuracy and a precision-recall trade-off, considering the inherently uncertain nature of the task. We found that the (Qwen2.5:32B, EN-long) model-prompt variant yields predictions that agree the most with human annotations for literary texts. Moreover, we found that no single model-prompt variant could perform consistently well across both literary and non-literary datasets. The guidelines and then the prompts were developed for the literary sentence. The transfer to Wikivoyage—an experiment as part of the pilot study—demonstrated that the guidelines and prompts have to be adapted to obtain reliable annotations, taking into account the different textual domains and times of origin.

It is also important to note that the pilot study was conducted on the subset of data restricted to sentences describing specific spatial entities reported in § 4. Therefore, the extent to which our prompts generalize to the full corpora remains uncertain at this stage.

7 Discussion

Natural language and especially literary text is inherently complex and often ambiguous. In our aim to identify spatial descriptions, we encountered several sources of disagreement. Apart from uncertainties in the texts themselves, disagreement also resulted from unclear cases within the annotation guidelines and practical factors such as annotator error. In this section, we discuss the major reasons for annotator disagreement. Unresolvable ambiguities within the data itself are the most prominent factor for disagreement. Isolated sentences do not always provide clear evidence as to whether they constitute a spatial description according to our definition. (See, for instance, Example 10 in Appendix B: without context, our annotators could interpret it as a description of an actual, spatial scene as well as a pure abstraction and therefore not spatial. Examples 11 and 12 were ambiguous for our annotators due to the polysemy of certain words.) Pavlick and Kwiatkowski's (2019) results, on the other hand, suggest that an increased amount of context would not necessarily contribute to an increased IAA. We therefore assume that there will always be at least a certain level of disagreement between annotators simply due to the polyvalence of literary text (Gius and Jacke, 2017).

When the guidelines lack precision, however, it can result in fuzziness and different interpretations not of the text itself, but of the annotation scheme. Gius and Jacke (2017) claim that any fuzziness in the categorization must be minimized as much as possible. The inherent polyvalence of the texts does not justify ambiguity in the category definitions. On the other hand, it is generally not possible to formulate guidelines that unambiguously account for 100% of all cases (Reiter et al., 2019). Our attempts to make the guidelines as precise as possible resulted in a detailed seven-page document. Amidei et al. (2018) warn of guidelines becoming too narrow and restrictive. They would be at risk of failing to capture the variability and polyvalence inherent to human language. In iteration 3 of our annotation, we had the most extensive list of guidelines in use. As Table 2 reports, the agreement between the annotators decreased. The guidelines would have covered most of the cases, but the cognitive load for the annotators was too high and they were too narrow to generalize well across our data.

A third and minor, but still a noticeable reason for an imperfect IAA was human errors (Pavlick and Kwiatkowski, 2019). When processing a large number of individual sentences in succession, the cognitive effort of the annotators was considerable and could occasionally lead to the selection of incorrect categories.

We argue that certain levels of disagreement are not only unavoidable but even indicative of the nuanced nature of descriptive and spatial language. We did not expect perfect agreement between the human annotators and even less between humans and LLMs. Instead, the objective was to produce a curated dataset of spatial descriptions in which any ambiguity arises solely from legitimate differences in the interpretation of language, accounting for the subjectivity of the individual annotators (Reiter et al., 2019; Amidei et al., 2018). The annotation process provided valuable insights into how humans interpret descriptive and spatial language and how annotation guidelines mediate this interpretation.

In general, we observe that the task of description annotation features a certain amount of subjectivity, resulting in label variation in our data. While traditional NLP paradigms aimed at eliminating human label variation as much as possible, recent work argues for embracing rather than excluding or ignoring it (Plank, 2022; van der Meer et al., 2024). By making the different iterations of our annotations and guidelines available, we also hope to contribute to this emerging line of research.

Conclusion

This work presents an approach to identifying spatial descriptions in literary text. A group of human annotators and of LLMs annotated individual sentences to determine whether they are spatial descriptions. While space and spatiality are topics that have received considerable attention in the (digital) humanities, literary studies, and, to some extent, in computational linguistics, this work is among the first to explicitly focus on the systematic identification of descriptions. We propose a set of annotation guidelines for spatial descriptions and report the performance of multiple LLMs in this annotation task. Our analyses revealed several systematic challenges for the manual and automatic annotation of descriptions, such as annotator subjectivity in assessing semantic aspects like concreteness and ambiguities as well as issues with substantial differences between datasets and class imbalance. A valuable next step could now be to investigate the impact of additional in-context examples or task-specific fine-tuning. Moreover, the relatively low agreement score of .44 for non-literary texts indicates that the annotation guidelines require further adjustment for this domain.

Limitations

One major limitation of this work is extending the existing annotation scheme to non-literary text. There are substantial differences between the two corpora we worked with not only in their textual structure but also in the time period they cover. The guidelines developed for literary text were less applicable to non-literary texts than expected. It turned out that for a reliable annotation of non-literary sentences, new guidelines and completely new prompts, along with a re-training of the annotators, would have been required.

Moreover, KOLIMO covers the literary domain (German-language texts from the late 19th century and early 20th century) much more extensively than Wikivoyage represents the non-literary domain. We are aware that travel reports cannot be equated with a general "non-literary" language, which includes many more text types and genres.

A possible extension of the dataset for a follow-up study could therefore include other corpora, especially from the non-literary side, in order to investigate annotators' and LLM's abilities to identify spatial descriptions in this data. However, also corpora of other languages than German could be of interest.

Our approach to counting the most frequent spatial entities is inherently flawed, as Herrmann et al.'s (2022) spatial entity list is by far not comprehensive. It was generated to cover literary fiction from the 19th and 20th century and therefore works better for KOLIMO than the contemporary texts in Wikivoyage. For instance, "Flughafen" ('airport') is not part of the list, however, due to our matching of compounds, this entity will be considered as an instance of "Hafen" ('harbor', 'port'). Moreover, it comprises only single words, while spatial entities could also be expressed as nominal phrases (see e.g., Barth (2021)).

A better approach instead of the list and regular expressions would be to use a neural model for a proper counting of the most frequent entities and then selecting the relevant sentences. However, at the time of creating the data set, we were not aware of any model for German that could automatically extract all relevant spatial entities from our large datasets. Moreover, for the time being we only aimed to control the dataset for our annotators in order to avoid annotating sentences entirely at random. The purpose of the pre-filtering is not to identify spatial sentences but to create a set of filtered candidate sentences that is more meaningful than a set composed of completely random corpus sentences.

Acknowledgments

This research has been funded by the Deutsche Forschungsgemeinschaft (DFG, German Research Foundation) – CRC-1646, project number 512393437, project A05.

References

Özge Alaçam, Ronja Utescher, Hannes Grönner, Judith Sieker, and Sina Zarrieß. 2024. WikiScenes with descriptions: Aligning paragraphs and sentences with images in Wikipedia articles. In *Proceedings of the 13th Joint Conference on Lexical and Computational Semantics (*SEM 2024)*, pages 93–105, Mexico City, Mexico. Association for Computational Linguistics.

Jacopo Amidei, Paul Piwek, and Alistair Willis. 2018. Rethinking the agreement in human evaluation tasks. In *Proceedings of the 27th International Conference on Computational Linguistics*, pages 3318–3329, Santa Fe, New Mexico, USA. Association for Computational Linguistics.

David Bamman, Olivia Lewke, and Anya Mansoor. 2020. An annotated dataset of coreference in English literature. In *Proceedings of the Twelfth Language Resources and Evaluation Conference*, pages 44–54, Marseille, France. European Language Resources Association.

Florian Barth. 2021. Konzept und klassifikation literarischer raumentitäten. pages 1281–1293. ISBN: 9783885797012 Publisher: Gesellschaft für Informatik, Bonn.

Steven Bethard, Oleksandr Kolomiyets, and Marie-Francine Moens. 2012. Annotating story timelines as temporal dependency structures. In *Proceedings of the Eighth International Conference on Language Resources and Evaluation (LREC'12)*, pages 2721–2726, Istanbul, Turkey. European Language Resources Association (ELRA).

Michel Denis. 2008. Assessing the symbolic distance effect in mental images constructed from verbal descriptions: A study of individual differences in the mental comparison of distances. 127(1):197–210.

Michel Denis. 2018. *Space and spatial cognition: a multidisciplinary perspective*. Routledge.

Katrin Dennerlein. 2009. *Narratologie des Raumes*. De Gruyter. Publication Title: Narratologie des Raumes.

Dejan Draschkow and Melissa Le-Hoa Võ. 2017. Scene grammar shapes the way we interact with objects, strengthens memories, and speeds search. 7(1):16471.

Jörg Döring and Tristan Thielmann. 2008. *Einleitung: Was lesen wir im Raume? Der Spatial Turn und das geheime Wissen der Geographen*, pages 7–46. transcript Verlag, Bielefeld.

Roopal Garg, Andrea Burns, Burcu Karagol Ayan, Yonatan Bitton, Ceslee Montgomery, Yasumasa Onoe, Andrew Bunner, Ranjay Krishna, Jason Michael Baldridge, and Radu Soricut. 2024. ImageInWords: Unlocking hyper-detailed image descriptions. In *Proceedings of the 2024 Conference on Empirical Methods in Natural Language Processing*, pages 93–127, Miami, Florida, USA. Association for Computational Linguistics.

Evelyn Gius and Janina Jacke. 2017. The hermeneutic profit of annotation: On preventing and fostering disagreement in literary analysis. 11(2):233–254. Publisher: Edinburgh University Press.

Evelyn Gius, Nils Reiter, and Marcus Willand. 2019. A shared task for the digital humanities chapter 2: Evaluating annotation guidelines. 4(3).

Kurt Hahn, Anne-Kathrin Reulecke, Steffen Schneider, and Julia Zimmermann, editors. 2025. *Descriptio*, 1 edition, volume 263 of *Litterae*. Rombach Wissenschaft, Baden-Baden.

John M. Henderson and Fernanda Ferreira. 2004. Scene perception for psycholinguists. In *The Interface of Language, Vision, and Action*. Psychology Press. Num Pages: 58.

John M. Henderson and Andrew Hollingworth. 1999. High-level scene perception. 50:243–71.

J. Berenike Herrmann, Joanna Byszuk, and Giulia Grisot. 2022. Using word embeddings for validation and enhancement of spatial entity lists.

J. Berenike Herrmann and Gerhard Lauer. 2018. Korpusliteraturwissenschaft. zur konzeption und praxis am beispiel eines korpus zur literarischen moderne. 92:127–156.

Jan Horstmann. 2019. KOLIMO: Korpus der literarischen moderne.

Labiba Jahan, Rahul Mittal, and Mark Finlayson. 2021. Inducing stereotypical character roles from plot structure. In *Proceedings of the 2021 Conference on Empirical Methods in Natural Language Processing*, pages 492–497, Online and Punta Cana, Dominican Republic. Association for Computational Linguistics.

Daniel Kababgi, Giulia Grisot, Federico Pennino, and J. Berenike Herrmann. 2024. Recognising nonnamed spatial entities in literary texts: a novel spatial entities classifier. In *CHR 2024: Computational Humanities Research Conference*, pages 472–481.

Klaus Krippendorff. 2013. Computing krippendorff's alpha-reliability.

Harold F. Mosher. 1991. Toward a poetics of "descriptized" narration. 12(3):425–445. Publisher: Duke University Press, Porter Institute for Poetics and Semiotics.

Andreas Nolda. 2024. Wikivoyage-korpus: Korpusquellen der deutschen sprachversion von wikivoyage im TEI-format.

Ansgar Nünning. 2007. Towards a typology, poetics and history of description in fiction. In Walter Bernhart and Werner Wolf, editors, *Description in Literature and Other Media*, volume 2 of *Studies in Intermediality (SIM)*, pages 91–128. Brill.

Aude Oliva. 2005. CHAPTER 41 - gist of the scene. In Laurent Itti, Geraint Rees, and John K. Tsotsos, editors, *Neurobiology of Attention*, pages 251–256. Academic Press.

Ellie Pavlick and Tom Kwiatkowski. 2019. Inherent disagreements in human textual inferences. *Transactions of the Association for Computational Linguistics*, 7:677–694.

Barbara Plank. 2022. The "problem" of human label variation: On ground truth in data, modeling and evaluation. In *Proceedings of the 2022 Conference on Empirical Methods in Natural Language Processing*, pages 10671–10682, Abu Dhabi, United Arab Emirates. Association for Computational Linguistics.

Jordi Pont-Tuset, Jasper Uijlings, Soravit Changpinyo, Radu Soricut, and Vittorio Ferrari. 2020. Connecting vision and language with localized narratives. In *Computer Vision–ECCV 2020: 16th European Conference, Glasgow, UK, August 23–28, 2020, Proceedings, Part V 16*, pages 647–664. Springer.

James Pustejovsky. 2017. *ISO-Space: Annotating Static and Dynamic Spatial Information*, pages 989–1024. Springer Netherlands, Dordrecht.

James Pustejovsky, Parisa Kordjamshidi, Marie-Francine Moens, Aaron Levine, Seth Dworman, and Zachary Yocum. 2015. SemEval-2015 task 8: SpaceEval. In *Proceedings of the 9th International Workshop on Semantic Evaluation (SemEval 2015)*, pages 884–894, Denver, Colorado. Association for Computational Linguistics.

Nils Reiter. 2015. Towards annotating narrative segments. In *Proceedings of the 9th SIGHUM Workshop on Language Technology for Cultural Heritage, Social Sciences, and Humanities (LaTeCH)*, pages 34–38, Beijing, China. Association for Computational Linguistics.

Nils Reiter. 2020. Anleitung zur erstellung von annotationsrichtlinien. In *Anleitung zur Erstellung von Annotationsrichtlinien*, pages 193–202. De Gruyter.

Nils Reiter, Judith Sieker, Svenja Guhr, Evelyn Gius, and Sina Zarrieß. 2022. Exploring text recombination for automatic narrative level detection. In *Proceedings of the Thirteenth Language Resources and Evaluation Conference*, pages 3346–3353, Marseille, France. European Language Resources Association.

Nils Reiter, Marcus Willand, and Evelyn Gius. 2019. A shared task for the digital humanities chapter 1: Introduction to annotation, narrative levels and shared tasks. 4(3).

Ruth Ronen. 1986. Space in fiction. 7(3):421–438. Publisher: Duke University Press, Porter Institute for Poetics and Semiotics.

Ruth Ronen. 1997. Description, narrative and representation. 5(3):274–286. Publisher: Ohio State University Press.

Marie-Laure Ryan. 2012. Space.

Marie-Laure Ryan, Kenneth Foote, and Maoz Azaryahu. 2016. *Narrating Space / Spatializing Narrative: Where Narrative Theory and Geography Meet*. Ohio State University Press.

Mareike Schumacher. 2023. *Orte und Räume im Roman: Ein Beitrag zur digitalen Literaturwissenschaft*. Digitale Literaturwissenschaft. Springer.

Piyush Sharma, Nan Ding, Sebastian Goodman, and Radu Soricut. 2018. Conceptual captions: A cleaned, hypernymed, image alt-text dataset for automatic image captioning. In *Proceedings of the 56th Annual Meeting of the Association for Computational Linguistics (Volume 1: Long Papers)*, pages 2556–2565, Melbourne, Australia. Association for Computational Linguistics.

Sandeep Soni, Amanpreet Sihra, Elizabeth Evans, Matthew Wilkens, and David Bamman. 2023. Grounding characters and places in narrative text. In *Proceedings of the 61st Annual Meeting of the Association for Computational Linguistics (Volume 1: Long Papers)*, pages 11723–11736, Toronto, Canada. Association for Computational Linguistics.

Gerard Steen, Aletta G. Dorst, J. Berenike Herrmann, Anna A. Kaal, Tina Krennmayr, and Trijntje Pasma. 2010. *A Method for Linguistic Metaphor Identiication. From MIP to MIPVU*, volume 14 of *Converging Evidence in Language and Communication Research (CELCR)*. John Benjamins Publishing Company.

Michiel van der Meer, Neele Falk, Pradeep K. Murukannaiah, and Enrico Liscio. 2024. Annotator-centric active learning for subjective NLP tasks. In *Proceedings of the 2024 Conference on Empirical Methods in Natural Language Processing*, pages 18537–18555, Miami, Florida, USA. Association for Computational Linguistics.

Melissa Le-Hoa Võ, Sage EP Boettcher, and Dejan Draschkow. 2019. Reading scenes: how scene grammar guides attention and aids perception in real-world environments. 29:205–210.

Melissa Le-Hoa Võ and Jeremy M. Wolfe. 2013. Differential electrophysiological signatures of semantic and syntactic scene processing. 24(9):1816–1823. Publisher: SAGE Publications Inc.

Wikimedia Foundation Inc. 2025. Wikivoyage – freie reiseinformationen rund um die welt.

Werner Wolf. 2007. Description as a transmedial mode of representation. general features and possibilities of realization in painting, fiction and music. In Werner Wolf and Walter Bernhart, editors, *Description in Literature and Other Media*, volume 2 of *Studies in Intermediality (SIM)*, pages 1–87. Brill.

Jeremy M. Wolfe, Melissa Le-Hoa Võ, Karla K. Evans, and Michelle R. Greene. 2011. Visual search in scenes involves selective and nonselective pathways. 15(2):77–84.

Peter Young, Alice Lai, Micah Hodosh, and Julia Hockenmaier. 2014. From image descriptions to visual denotations: New similarity metrics for semantic inference over event descriptions. *Transactions of the Association for Computational Linguistics*, 2:67–78.

Albin Zehe, Leonard Konle, Lea Katharina Dümpelmann, Evelyn Gius, Andreas Hotho, Fotis Jannidis, Lucas Kaufmann, Markus Krug, Frank Puppe, Nils Reiter, Annekea Schreiber, and Nathalie Wiedmer. 2021. Detecting scenes in fiction: A new segmentation task. In *Proceedings of the 16th Conference of the European Chapter of the Association for Computational Linguistics: Main Volume*, pages 3167–3177, Online. Association for Computational Linguistics.

Gabriel Zoran. 1984. Towards a theory of space in narrative. 5(2):309–335. Publisher: Duke University Press, Porter Institute for Poetics and Semiotics.

A Spatial Entities in the Corpora

In Table 4, we report the most frequent spatial entities in the two corpora.

B Example Sentences

In Table 5, we list a selection of sentences from the two corpora that do not unambiguously describe spatial frames.

C Prompts

In this section, we report the prompt variants in our experiment (§ 6). Based on the annotation guidelines, we formulate four different prompts as reported below.

C.1 EN-short

```
Your goal is to decide whether a sentence is a SPATIAL DESCRIPTION or not.

You will be provided with a sentence. You will answer with YES if that sentence is a SPATIAL DESCRIPTION. Otherwise, you will answer with NO.

In a SPATIAL DESCRIPTION, sensory features of spatial entities are described. These spatial entities form a static scene.
```

C.2 EN-medium

```
Your goal is to decide whether a sentence is a SPATIAL DESCRIPTION or not.

You will be provided with a sentence. You will answer with YES if that sentence is a SPATIAL DESCRIPTION. Otherwise, you will answer with NO.

A SPATIAL DESCRIPTION must meet all of the following criteria:

1. There is a description of a scene that consists of multiple entities.

2. The scene is static, it does not change.

3. There are descriptions of features that can be seen, felt, heard or smelled.
```

KOLIMO			Wikivoyage		
Entity	**Translation**	**Count**	**Entity**	**Translation**	**Count**
Stadt	City/Town	48003	Zimmer	Room	51408
Hafen	Port	16829	Stadt	City	45505
Museum	Museum	12975	Tür	Door	45287
Bahnhof	Station	11966	Fenster	Window	36323
Insel	Island	11777	Straße	Street/Road	35709
Park	Park	15051	Berg	Mountain	33416
Straße	Street/Road	20943	Tisch	Table/Desk	32672
See	Lake	12603	Platz	Place	31033
Platz	Place	13340	Erde	Earth	26549
Berg	Mountain	21811	Bett	Bed	21246

Table 4: The most frequent spatial entities in the two corpora according to the spatial entities collection by Herrmann et al. (2022). We also considered compounds and inflected forms of the reported lemmas.

```
4. The focus is on descriptions, not
actions.
```

C.3 EN-long (KOLIMO)

```
Your goal is to decide whether a
sentence is a SPATIAL DESCRIPTION or
not.

You will be provided with a sentence.
You will answer with YES if that
sentence is a SPATIAL DESCRIPTION.
Otherwise, you will answer with NO.

A SPATIAL DESCRIPTION must meet all
of the following criteria:

- Space which can be described
is the immediate environment where
events could take place (at least
theoretically), will take place in
the future or have taken place in the
past

- There are descriptive elements, not
just the mere mention of space

- Scenes (arrangements of objects,
background and foreground which are
at least implicit) are described, not
just a single object

- No unresolved references—what is
described is always unambiguous

- There is no action, except for
action that is expressed by verbs of
perception and is related to space
(see, hear ...)

- Generic, repeated actions can be
part of a spatial description (e.g.
sunset)

- Weather (rainfall, wind, clouds),
daylight (solar altitude, dusk and
dawn), ocean movements (waves, tide)
and light (natural or artificial) are
part of spatial descriptions, unless
they explicitly take place suddenly
or are part of individual actions

- The described space is static,
stable and does not change during the
description

- The described space is tangible
(real, fictional, imagined,
remembered, fantastic or dreamed),
but not exclusively metaphorical or
an abstraction

- The described qualities include all
senses and are not limited to the
visual

- Only complete descriptions are
relevant, even if many sentences
contain descriptive elements among
```

	Sentence	Translation	Source
1	Die Stadt erscheint mir kalt und fremd und widert mich.	The city seems cold and foreign to me and disgusts me.	Felix Hollaender: Die Briefe des Fräulein Brandt (1918)
2	Rings auf der bloßen Erde lagen lauter Schläfer.	All around on the bare earth were lying many sleepers.	Jakob Wassermann: Alexander in Babylon (1905)
3	Auch ist drinnen kein Platz mehr.	There is no room left inside either.	Fritz Mauthner: Der neue Ahasver (1882)
4	Die Kleinstadt Adorf liegt im Vogtlandkreis am Nordrand des Elstergebirges.	The small town of Adorf is located in Vogtlandkreis on the northern edge of the Elster mountains.	Wikivoyage: Adorf
5	Katharinenkapelle: Die Kapelle steht auf dem 493 m hohen Katharinenberg, es ist der zweithöchste Berg des Kaiserstuhls.	Katharinenkapelle: The chapel stands on the 493 meters high Katharinenberg, it is the second highest mountain in the Kaiserstuhl.	Wikivoyage: Endingen am Kaiserstuhl
6	Vorbei am Balcon du Ranc pointu fällt die Straße nun ab um die ersten Häuser und Campingplätze von Saint-Martin-d'Ardèche zu erreichen [sic].	Passing the Balcon du Ranc pointu, the road now descends to reach the first houses and campsites of Saint-Martin-d'Ardèche.	Wikivoyage: Gorges de l'Ardèche
7	Neben den Badestränden kann man auf den Cerro La Cruz laufen, einem etwa 1000 m hohen Berg, auf dem sich ein großes Kreuz befindet (ca. 30-45 min Fußmarsch je nach Kondition).	In addition to the beaches, you can walk up the Cerro La Cruz, a mountain about 1000 meters high, on which there is a large cross (approx. 30-45 min walk depending on fitness level).	Wikivoyage: Via Carlos Paz
8	Girlanden mit Lampions quer über den Hof von Flurfenster zu Flurfenster.	Garlands with lanterns across the courtyard from corridor window to corridor window.	Hans Ostwald: Das Zillebuch (1929)
9	Delaware Park: Größter Park in Buffalo mit gepflegten Grünflächen und einem See.	Delaware Park: Largest Park in Buffalo with well-tended green spaces and a lake.	Wikivoyage: Buffalo/Norden
10	Vor mir wachsen die geheimnisvollen, glutroten Korallen aus der Tiefe des Wassers, sie breiten ihr mystisches Geäst aus über den Himmel, sie flechten ein Netz durch Luft und Wolken, ein Netz von blutfarbenen Zweigen, an dem weiße Perlen schimmern.	In front of me, the mysterious, glowing red corals grow from the depths of the water, spreading their mystical branches across the sky, weaving a net through the air and clouds, a net of blood-colored branches on which white pearls shimmer.	Nataly von Eschstruth: Die Bären von Hohen-Esp (1922)

	Sentence	Translation	Source
11	Auch hatte sie hier den Apparat dicht neben sich, während das andere Telephon sich im Bibliothekzimmer befindet.	She also had the device [or *phone*] right next to her, while the other phone was in the library room.	Hugo Bettauer: Die freudlose Gasse (1924)
12	Ein Wachtmantel von gelbem Tuch mit grünem Kragen – grün und gelb waren die Farben der Stadt – hing am Nagel, ein Bauer mit einem bunten, klugen Zeisig von der Decke.	A watchman's coat of yellow cloth with a green collar—green and yellow were the colors of the city—hung from the nail, a cage [or *peasant*] with a colorful, clever siskin from the ceiling.	Wilhelm Raabe: Das letzte Recht (1910)

Table 5: Examples for annotated sentences.

others

- The sentences are complete and in German

C.4 EN-long (Wikivoyage)

Your goal is to decide whether a sentence is a SPATIAL DESCRIPTION or not.

You will be provided with a sentence. You will answer with YES if that sentence is a SPATIAL DESCRIPTION. Otherwise, you will answer with NO.

A SPATIAL DESCRIPTION must meet all of the following criteria:

- Space which can be described is the immediate environment where events could take place (at least theoretically), will take place in the future or have taken place in the past

- There are descriptive elements, not just the mere mention of space

- Scenes (arrangements of objects, background and foreground which are at least implicit) are described, not just a single object

- No unresolved references: what is described is always unambiguous

- There is no action, except for action that is expressed by verbs of perception and is related to space (see, hear ...)

- Generic, repeated actions can be part of a spatial description (e.g. sunset)

- Weather (rainfall, wind, clouds), daylight (solar altitude, dusk and dawn), ocean movements (waves, tide) and light (natural or artificial) are part of spatial descriptions, unless they explicitly take place suddenly or are part of individual actions

- The described space is static, stable and does not change during the description

- The described space is tangible (real, fictional, imagined, remembered, fantastic or dreamed), but not exclusively metaphorical or an abstraction

- The described qualities include all senses and are not limited to the visual

- No route descriptions from A to B

- The geographical location of a named entity is not a spatial description

- Only complete descriptions are

relevant, even if many sentences contain descriptive elements among others

- The sentences are complete and in German

C.5 DE-long (KOLIMO)

Du sollst entscheiden, ob ein Satz eine RAUMBESCHREIBUNG ist oder nicht.

Du bekommst einen Satz, und du wirst mit JA antworten, falls dieser Satz eine RAUMBESCHREIBUNG ist. Ansonsten wirst du mit NEIN antworten.

Eine RAUMBESCHREIBUNG muss alle folgenden Kriterien erfüllen:

- Raum, der beschrieben werden kann, ist die unmittelbare Umgebung, in der das Geschehen (zumindest theoretisch) stattfinden könnte, in der Zukunft stattfinden wird oder in der Vergangenheit stattgefunden hat

- Es gibt beschreibende Elemente, nicht die bloße Nennung von Raum

- Es werden Szenen (zumindest implizite Arrangements von Objekten, Hintergrund und Vordergrund) beschrieben, nicht nur ein einzelnes Objekt

- Keine unaufgelösten Referenzen - es ist immer eindeutig, was beschrieben wird

- Es gibt keine Handlung, außer solche, die durch Verben der Wahrnehmung ausgedrückt wird und sich auf den Raum bezieht (sehen, hören . . .)

- Generische, wiederholte Handlungen können Teil einer Raumbeschreibung sein (z.B. das Untergehen der Sonne)

- Wetter (Niederschlag, Wind, Wolken), Tageslichtphasen (Sonnenstand, Dämmerung), Meeresbewegungen (Wellen, Gezeiten) und Licht (von Lampen oder der Sonne) sind Teil von Raumbeschreibungen, solang sie nicht explizit plötzlich und in individuellen Handlungen vorkommen

- Der beschriebene Raum ist statisch, stabil und verändert sich nicht während der Beschreibung

- Der beschriebene Raum ist konkret (real, fiktional, imaginiert, erinnert, phantastisch, geträumt), aber nicht ausschließlich metaphorisch oder eine Abstraktion

- Die beschriebenen Qualitäten umfassen alle Sinne und sind nicht auf das Visuelle beschränkt

- Nur vollständige Beschreibungen sind relevant, auch wenn viele Sätze unter anderem raumbeschreibende Elemente enthalten

- Die Sätze sind vollständig und auf Deutsch

C.6 DE-long (Wikivoyage)

Du sollst entscheiden, ob ein Satz eine RAUMBESCHREIBUNG ist oder nicht.

Du bekommst einen Satz, und du wirst mit JA antworten, falls dieser Satz eine RAUMBESCHREIBUNG ist. Ansonsten wirst du mit NEIN antworten.

Eine RAUMBESCHREIBUNG muss alle folgenden Kriterien erfüllen:

- Raum, der beschrieben werden kann, ist die unmittelbare Umgebung, in der das Geschehen (zumindest theoretisch) stattfinden könnte, in der Zukunft stattfinden wird oder in der Vergangenheit stattgefunden hat

- Es gibt beschreibende Elemente, nicht die bloße Nennung von Raum

- Es werden Szenen (zumindest implizite Arrangements von Objekten, Hintergrund und Vordergrund) beschrieben, nicht nur ein einzelnes Objekt

- Keine unaufgelösten Referenzen – es ist immer eindeutig, was beschrieben wird

- Es gibt keine Handlung, außer solche, die durch Verben der Wahrnehmung ausgedrückt wird und sich auf den Raum bezieht (sehen, hören . . .)

- Generische, wiederholte Handlungen können Teil einer Raumbeschreibung sein (z.B. das Untergehen der Sonne)

- Wetter (Niederschlag, Wind, Wolken), Tageslichtphasen (Sonnenstand, Dämmerung), Meeresbewegungen (Wellen, Gezeiten) und Licht (von Lampen oder der Sonne) sind Teil von Raumbeschreibungen, solang sie nicht explizit plötzlich und in individuellen Handlungen vorkommen

- Der beschriebene Raum ist statisch, stabil und verändert sich nicht während der Beschreibung

- Der beschriebene Raum ist konkret (real, fiktional, imaginiert, erinnert, phantastisch, geträumt), aber nicht ausschließlich metaphorisch oder eine Abstraktion

- Die beschriebenen Qualitäten umfassen alle Sinne und sind nicht auf das Visuelle beschränkt

- Keine Streckenbeschreibungen von A nach B

- Die geographische Lage einer benannten Entität ist keine Raumbeschreibung

- Nur vollständige Beschreibungen sind relevant, auch wenn viele Sätze unter anderem raumbeschreibende Elemente enthalten

- Die Sätze sind vollständig und auf Deutsch

D LLMs Prompting Experiment Settings

We run all the open-source model experiments using their 8-bit quantization versions via the HuggingFace transformers library. We use a single NVIDIA RTX A6000 GPU to run all our open-source experiments, while we call OpenAI's API for the GPT-4o experiments. We set the LLMs' generation temperature to zero at all our prompting calls, and we set the seed to 42 whenever possible, to allow for reproducibility.

E Evaluation of LLMs Annotations

We report the results for our 28 model-prompt variants in this section. Table 6 shows the results of GPT-4o prompt variants, while the results of the open-source model-prompt variants are reported in Table 7.

Model	Prompt	Literary Dataset					Non-Literary Dataset				
		Acc.	P	R	F1	Rat.	Acc.	P	R	F1	Rat.
GPT-4o	EN-short	.87	.38	**.81**	.51	.18	.72	.38	**.70**	.50	.37
	EN-med	.93	.57	.55	.56	**.08**	.85	.67	.43	**.53**	.13
	EN-long	.94	**.64**	.63	**.64**	**.08**	.84	**.97**	.19	.32	.04
	DE-long	.93	.58	.69	.63	.10	.82	.76	.16	.27	.04

Table 6: GPT-4o Results.

Family	Size	Prompt	Literary Dataset					Non-Literary Dataset				
			Acc.	P	R	F1	Rat.	Acc.	P	R	F1	Rat.
Gemma2	2B	EN-short	.64	.17	.88	.29	.43	.46	.26	.96	.41	.72
		EN-med	.82	.29	.82	.43	.24	.61	.32	.83	.46	.52
		EN-long	.60	.17	**.96**	.29	.47	.56	.30	**.97**	.46	.63
		DE-long	.76	.24	.84	.37	.30	.78	.47	.58	.52	.25
	9B	EN-short	.53	.14	.90	.24	.54	.57	.29	.77	.42	.54
		EN-med	.81	.30	.89	.44	.26	.72	.39	.75	.51	.38
		EN-long	.78	.26	.89	.41	.29	.83	.60	.43	.50	.14
		DE-long	.82	.31	.88	.45	.24	.84	.87	.21	.34	.05
	27B	EN-short	.60	.16	.91	.28	.47	.60	.30	.75	.43	.50
		EN-med	.80	.28	.88	.43	.27	.73	.40	.72	.52	.36
		EN-long	.68	.20	.95	.33	.40	.83	.56	.62	**.59**	.22
		DE-long	.86	.37	.86	.52	.20	.84	.81	.26	.40	.06
Qwen2.5	3B	EN-short	.92	.00	.00	.00	.00	.80	.00	.00	.00	.00
		EN-med	.92	.00	.00	.00	.00	.80	.00	.00	.00	.00
		EN-long	.92	.00	.00	.00	.00	.80	.00	.00	.00	.00
		DE-long	.92	.00	.00	.00	.00	.80	.00	.00	.00	.00
	7B	EN-short	.85	.31	.60	.41	.17	.66	.31	.57	.40	.37
		EN-med	.93	.56	.57	.57	**.09**	.76	.40	.42	.41	**.21**
		EN-long	.83	.30	.77	.43	.22	.82	.58	.35	.44	.12
		DE-long	.87	.36	.70	.47	.17	.82	.80	.10	.18	.02
	32B	EN-short	.92	.50	.73	.59	.12	.71	.36	.61	.46	.33
		EN-med	.94	.63	.65	.64	**.09**	.81	.54	.38	.45	.14
		EN-long	**.95**	**.83**	.56	**.67**	.06	.81	**1.0**	.06	.12	.01
		DE-long	.94	.62	.71	.66	.10	.81	**1.0**	.06	.12	.01

Table 7: Open-source models Results.

A GitHub-based Workflow for Annotated Resource Development

Brandon Waldon **Nathan Schneider**
Georgetown University
{bw686, nathan.schneider}@georgetown.edu

Abstract

Computational linguists have long recognized the value of version control systems such as Git (and related platforms, e.g., GitHub) when it comes to managing and distributing computer code. However, the benefits of version control remain under-explored for a central activity within computational linguistics: the development of annotated natural language resources. We argue that researchers can employ version control practices to make development workflows more transparent, efficient, consistent, and participatory. We report a proof-of-concept, GitHub-based solution which facilitated the creation of a legal English treebank.

1 Introduction

Linguistic annotation is an important pillar of the empirical enterprise that supports modern computational linguistics. A recent review notes that "corpus resources... remain highly relevant for testing and studying [NLP] systems" (Opitz et al., 2025: 4), even as these resources take a less central role in system training. By augmenting corpus data with high-quality annotations, "people skilled at language analysis can ensure meaningful evaluation of NLP systems" (ibid).

However, creating a valuable annotated dataset is time-consuming and labor-intensive, and some common practices can undermine the usefulness and quality of the end result. For example, behind each "gold" annotation may be several non-trivial analytical decisions reached through careful adjudication. Unfortunately, researchers tend not to make, or publicly share, detailed records of these processes. As a result of low project **transparency**, dataset users may have no way of determining the original justification for a given annotation.

Moreover, linguistic annotation practices tend to vary widely in terms of the assistive tools made available to annotators. Providing annotators with access to tools that automatically visualize and/or validate annotations can facilitate more **efficient** and more **consistent** (i.e., less error-prone) resource development (Bontcheva et al., 2010; Stenetorp et al., 2012). However, there are high overhead costs for creating such tools from scratch, meaning that less mature annotation projects are often pursued with more primitive annotation technologies.

Finally, not all workflows permit the kinds of robust community **participation** that help to sustain linguistic annotation projects over time. Though most projects are sustained primarily by the efforts of a core development team, outside researchers can make valuable contributions by identifying annotation errors or adding new annotations. To make full use of these non-core contributors, it is desirable to develop resources on platforms that facilitate open communication between a project's core developers and the broader research community.

We argue that researchers can address these issues with resource development workflows that employ version control systems (such as Git) and online services for interacting with such systems (such as GitHub). Though computational linguists have long recognized the value of version control for managing and distributing computer code, we demonstrate that version control systems and services also serve to make linguistic annotation procedures more **transparent**, **efficient**, **consistent**, and **participatory**.

In what follows, we recap the core principles behind version control generally and Git/GitHub in particular. We then present our GitHub-based annotation workflow in general form. Next, we report a proof-of-concept implementation, which facilitated the creation of a treebank of legal English.

2 Version control and Git/GitHub

In this section, we briefly review the concept of a version control system (VCS) and the core principles underlying Git/GitHub, with a focus on prop-

Proceedings of the 19th Linguistic Annotation Workshop (LAW-XIX-2025), pages 326–331

erties that facilitate our proposed workflow.

A VCS records changes to a file repository over time, allowing teams to track modifications, compare versions, and revert to previous states when needed. VCS adoption enables developers to create and modify files while maintaining a complete project history within the repository.

Git is a widely employed VCS. A Git **branch** is a parallel instance of the repository with a change history that may diverge from that of the central version of the project (as reflected by the 'main' branch). Branches allow project contributors to develop new features or fixes without affecting the main codebase before the changes are ready to be integrated. A Git **commit** records the changes made to repository files at a specific point in time. Each commit contains a unique hash identifier and includes a message describing the changes made. Commits create a traceable history of modifications, allowing viewers to understand when and why particular changes were implemented.

GitHub is a web-based hosting service for managing and sharing Git projects. While Git provides the foundational version control capabilities, GitHub extends these with a social platform that enables web-based collaboration. On GitHub, **pull requests** enable developers to propose changes from their working branch to the main branch. Pull requests serve as a collaborative space where team members can review file changes, provide feedback, and discuss modifications before changes are merged from a working branch to the main branch. GitHub **actions** specify automated procedures triggered by repository events (such as commits or pull requests). Actions serve to automate repetitive tasks such as testing code or writing files.

3 Application to linguistic annotation

Notably, GitHub has already proven to be valuable for large-scale linguistic annotation projects such as Universal Dependencies (de Marneffe et al., 2021), which employs GitHub as a forum for discussing annotation guidelines and as a tool for maintaining existing datasets.[1] Our proposed workflow goes a step further by integrating GitHub directly at the resource development stage. This level of integration results in a comprehensive record of annotation decisions (and annotator discussions) for each individual annotation in the dataset.

This workflow (Figure 1) starts with two conceptual roles performed by project participants: the *annotator* role and the *manager* role.[2] The manager organizes the annotation project by populating a subdirectory of the repository with "stub" entries. These entries include pre-annotated text, possibly with some pre-processing (e.g., tokenization). These entries, and/or their associated filenames, may also include project-relevant metadata.

From the main GitHub branch where stub entries reside, the annotator creates a working branch.[3] Within this working branch, the annotator completes stub entries, adding annotations according to the project guidelines. Each time an annotator commits changes to their working branch, two GitHub actions are automatically triggered: a visualization action and a validation action. The visualization action creates a graphical representation of the annotated data and commits it to the annotator's branch. The validation action triggers a script that heuristically verifies that the annotation conforms to conventions of the annotation schema.

When an annotator completes their annotations, they initiate a pull request to merge their changes back into the main branch. The manager reviews the pull request. This review is facilitated by the action-generated graphical representation, which enables the manager to inspect the proposed contribution without having to manually read through the raw text of the annotation file. The manager and annotator can also review the output of the validation action to ensure the annotation is well-formed.

The manager and annotator can discuss the proposed contributions by leaving comments on the pull request. Ultimately, the manager has two options: approve the changes and merge them into the main branch, or request additional edits from the annotator. In the latter case, the annotator makes edits on the annotator branch and then requests a subsequent review from the manager.

Upon successful merging of annotated entries into the main branch, a statistics action is auto-

[1] `https://github.com/universaldependencies`

[2] A single individual may perform multiple roles, and the tasks of a single role may be delegated to multiple individuals.

[3] Because the manager adds stub files directly to the main branch, that branch will consist of both incomplete and complete files until all annotations are merged. This creates minor inconveniences for data browsing and statistics collection. On an alternative implementation, the manager is tasked with creating each stub file on a dedicated branch, immediately opening a draft pull request assigned to the annotator. This modified approach would maintain a cleaner main branch containing only completed annotations; it would also eliminate the need for external assignment tracking.

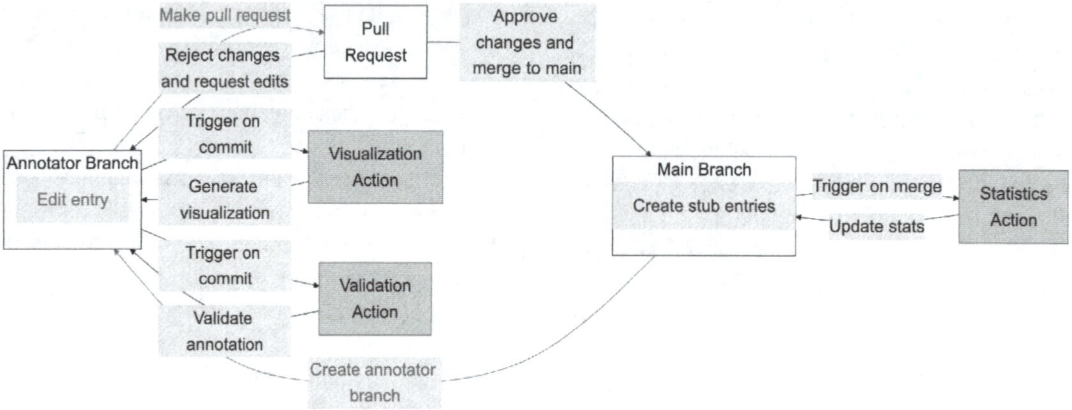

Figure 1: Workflow schema. Blue text indicates *manager* tasks; green text indicates *annotator* tasks.

matically triggered. This process updates project statistics, which may include information about overall project progress or summary statistics of the annotations themselves.

In what follows, we show that this workflow can be implemented in a way that promotes the four values presented in Section 1: **transparency**, **consistency**, **efficiency** and community **participation**.

4 Demonstration: treebanking

We applied this workflow while developing a treebank of legal US English in CGELBank (Reynolds et al., 2023), a treebanking formalism that extends the descriptive theory of English syntax presented in the Cambridge Grammar of the English Language (CGEL, Huddleston and Pullum, 2002).

The core team consisted of five researchers. Each team member performed the tasks of the annotator role, while the tasks of the manager role were performed primarily by the two senior members of the team. One member working in the manager role populated the main branch with stub files in the project-native `.cgel` data format (Figure 2; see Reynolds et al. 2023, Sec. 5 for more discussion), with each file corresponding to one sentence of the treebank. In addition to the raw sentence text and other relevant metadata, each stub file contained an automated tokenization of the sentence.

The annotated sentences were sourced from US federal statutes as compiled in the US Code by the Office of the Law Revision Counsel (OLRC) of the US House of Representatives.[4] The OLRC publishes the US Code in XML format according to a standardized schema known as United States Legislative Markup (USLM). Each sentence of the

```
# sent_id = ...
# text = the Attorney General
# sent = the Attorney General
(NP
    :Det (DP
        :Head (D :t "the"))
    :Head (Nom
        :Head (N :t "Attorney")
        :Mod (AdjP
            :Head (Adj :t "General"))))
```

Figure 2: Example of the `.cgel` data format, illustrating analysis of the noun phrase *the attorney general.*

treebank is associated with an ID derived from unique USLM metadata associated with the parent element of the sentence. For ease of browsing and cross-referencing the treebank data, we found it helpful to designate a short unique prefix to each sentence ID, e.g. `usc-039` for sentence 39.

For each sentence, the assigned annotator created a new working branch from the main branch of the project's GitHub-hosted repository. The annotator then manually corrected the automated tokenization and added lemma and part-of-speech tags according to CGELBank conventions (Reynolds et al., 2024). Tree editing was facilitated by ActiveDOP (van Cranenburgh, 2018), a browser-based graphical treebanking tool which utilizes an active learning parser (disco-dop, van Cranenburgh et al. 2016). To enable editing of `.cgel`-format trees, we extended a CGELBank-customized version of ActiveDOP reported by Reynolds et al. (2023). Once the annotator was finished using the tool, they exported the `.cgel`-format tree from ActiveDOP and appended it to the corresponding stub file. The an-

[4] https://uscode.house.gov/

notator then saved and committed their file changes to their working branch.

Some annotators opted to interface with Git from the command line (and subsequently 'push' their commits to the project's GitHub repository), while others utilized GitHub's built-in text editor user interface to edit and commit changes directly from their web browser. Once the annotator's changes had been committed to their working branch on GitHub, a visualization action automatically generated a LaTeX rendering of the `.cgel`-format tree as a `.pdf` file and committed that file to the working branch. A second validation action verified that the tree did not have any obvious errors.

The annotator then opened a pull request on the main branch. Another team member, assuming the manager role, reviewed the pull request by inspecting the changed files. The LaTeX rendering provided the reviewer with a convenient, easy-to-read graphical representation of the user's annotation. The reviewer and annotator could discuss the annotation through comments left on the pull request. In the event that the reviewer requested changes, the annotator could modify the relevant `.cgel` file, which automatically re-triggered the visualization action to update the LaTeX `.pdf` of the tree. This procedure is partly illustrated in Figure 3.

Once the reviewer approved the annotation and merged it to the main branch, an automatically-triggered action generated summary statistics of the treebank, including counts of lexical nodes and category/function labels, average tree depth, and a list of high-frequency lemmas.

5 Discussion

Our project repository[5] is not simply a static collection of gold annotations; the repository's commit history and pull request comments also form a dynamic public record of the decision-making processes that led to that gold data. This feature of our development workflow enhances project **transparency**, providing future dataset users with a means of determining how we adjudicated hard cases of linguistic analysis.

As a new treebanking formalism with a relatively small research community, CGELBank lacks the breadth of specialized annotation tools enjoyed by more established projects, e.g., Universal Dependencies (de Marneffe et al., 2021).[6] We used

[5]`https://github.com/nert-nlp/legal-cgel/`

[6]`https://universaldependencies.org/tools.html`

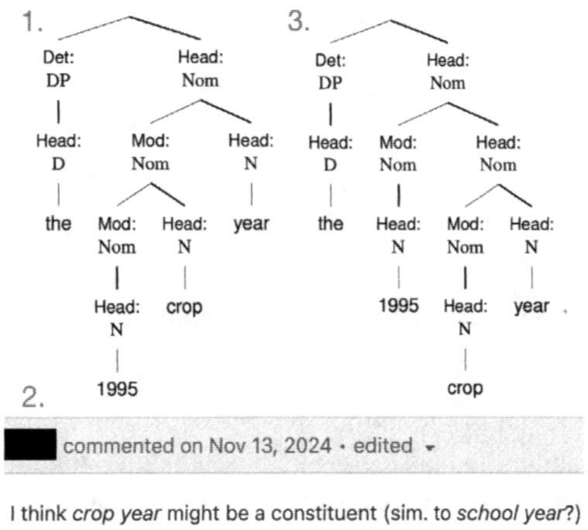

Figure 3: (1): excerpt of a GitHub action-generated LaTeX visualization for an annotator's CGELBank tree annotation; (2): excerpt of a reviewer comment on the pull request containing the annotation; (3): the visualization action is re-triggered after the annotator commits their edits, yielding a modified LaTeX rendition.

GitHub actions – relatively simple scripts which execute in a GitHub repository – to deliver some of the functionality of standalone annotation tools (i.e., automated visualization and validation), in addition to using and extending a bespoke CGELBank annotation tool. We used these actions in a way that allowed the annotator and reviewer to **efficiently** discuss and adjudicate a proposed annotation. These actions – especially the automated valiation – also promote **consistency** by enabling annotators and reviewers to quickly spot errors.

Lastly, the public nature of GitHub strongly encourages community **participation**. Anyone with a GitHub account can comment on the project by posting a GitHub *issue* (a discussion thread used to track project-related matters). The broader community can also create pull requests to suggest corrections to the dataset (or to add new data).

6 Related work

To a limited extent, previous work has discussed the utility of version control for developing annotated linguistic resources. Palmer and Xue (2010) recommend that annotators employ a VCS protocol to promote data security and integrity as a resource is developed. San (2016) implements a Git-based procedure to develop a dataset of phonetic transcriptions for three indigenous Australian languages. On this procedure, annotators' contributions are tracked through Git commits, and Git "hooks" (automated scripts) automatically recompute corpus statistics upon merge. Our proposed workflow builds on this approach by leveraging the social functionality of GitHub to facilitate adjudication, foster community participation, and create a persistent open record of the design and analysis choices that shape the final corpus product.

Previous work has also explored the value of VCS technologies for maintaining previously-developed resources. Rosenberg (2012) and Steiner (2017) discuss how version control could help research communities record (and disseminate) changes and corrections to speech corpus annotations. Dumitru et al. (2024) design and implement a VCS for managing *dynamic* speech corpora of the kind envisioned by Rosenberg.

Previous work has focused largely on applying VCS protocols in the context of annotated speech corpora. To our knowledge, we report the first application of a VCS-based workflow to syntactic treebanking. However, as discussed in Section 3, GitHub already plays a significant role in the ongoing maintenance of the Universal Dependencies project, including as a forum for discussing errors and updates to annotation conventions.

7 Limitations

Though our workflow offers several advantages for linguistic annotation, we have not presented a quantitative comparison of annotation speed or accuracy against alternative workflows. Additionally, while GitHub actions provide useful automation, developing and maintaining custom validation and visualization scripts requires a non-trivial number of technical prerequisites, including familiarity with the YAML-based workflow syntax associated with GitHub actions. Finally, annotators unfamiliar with version control in general (or Git in particular) may face a learning curve associated with the core concepts of Git repository management.

8 Conclusion

We presented a GitHub-based workflow for linguistic annotation. We provided a proof-of-concept implementation of this workflow for syntactic treebanking, demonstrating that this workflow promotes four values that enhance the usefulness and quality of annotated linguistic resources. Future work could extend this approach to other types of linguistic annotation tasks beyond treebanking, such as semantic role labeling or discourse analysis. Moreover, the workflow could be adapted to support multiple independent annotations followed by adjudication, leveraging Git's branching model to manage parallel annotation efforts.

Finally, there are opportunities to integrate GitHub with external annotation tools through the GitHub Apps framework,[7] which enables third-party software to directly perform common GitHub operations such as writing commits, opening/commenting on pull requests, and triggering automated workflows. In ongoing work, we are extending such functionality to ActiveDOP (van Cranenburgh, 2018), the tree editor employed in our CGELBank treebanking demonstration, so that annotators can participate in a GitHub-based workflow without leaving the annotation environment.

Computational linguistics continues to depend on high-quality linguistic annotation to support empirically-informed natural language analysis and data-driven system development. By embracing version control practices and technologies, we can foster more rigorous, collaborative, and sustainable approaches to this essential practice.

9 Acknowledgments

We thank Micaela Wells, Devika Tiwari, and Meru Gopalan, who participated as annotators for the CGELBank project described in the paper. We additionally thank Meru Gopalan for his assistance in developing the visualization action script described in Section 4. We also thank Brett Reynolds for providing helpful feedback on many annotations. Finally, we gratefully acknowledge the insightful comments of three anonymous LAW reviewers. This research was supported in part by NSF award IIS-2144881 (to NS).

References

Kalina Bontcheva, Hamish Cunningham, Ian Roberts, and Valentin Tablan. 2010. Web-based collaborative corpus annotation: Requirements and a framework implementation. In *New Challenges for NLP Frameworks (NLPFrameworks 2010)*, pages 20–27, Valletta, Malta. ELRA Language Resources Association.

Marie-Catherine de Marneffe, Christopher D. Manning, Joakim Nivre, and Daniel Zeman. 2021. Universal Dependencies. *Computational Linguistics*, 47(2):255–308.

Vlad Dumitru, Matthias Boehm, Martin Hagmüller, and Barbara Schuppler. 2024. Version control for

[7] https://docs.github.com/en/apps/overview

speech corpora. In *Proceedings of the 20th Conference on Natural Language Processing (KONVENS 2024)*, pages 303–308, Vienna, Austria. Association for Computational Linguistics.

Rodney Huddleston and Geoffrey K. Pullum, editors. 2002. *The Cambridge Grammar of the English Language*. Cambridge University Press, Cambridge, UK.

Juri Opitz, Shira Wein, and Nathan Schneider. 2025. Natural language processing RELIES on linguistics. *Computational Linguistics*. To appear.

Martha Palmer and Nianwen Xue. 2010. *Linguistic Annotation*, chapter 10. John Wiley & Sons, Ltd.

Brett Reynolds, Aryaman Arora, and Nathan Schneider. 2023. Unified syntactic annotation of English in the CGEL framework. In *Proc. of LAW*, pages 220–234, Toronto, Canada.

Brett Reynolds, Nathan Schneider, and Aryaman Arora. 2024. CGELBank annotation manual v1.1. *Preprint*, arXiv:2305.17347.

Andrew Rosenberg. 2012. Rethinking the corpus: moving towards dynamic linguistic resources. In *Proceedings of Interspeech 2012*, pages 1392–1395, Portland, USA. International Speech Communication Association.

Nay San. 2016. Using version control to facilitate a reproducible and collaborative workflow in acoustic phonetics. In *Proceedings of the Sixteenth Australasian International Conference on Speech Science and Technology (SST2016)*, pages 341–344, Parramatta, Australia. Australasian Speech Science and Technology Association.

Ingmar Steiner. 2017. A devops manifesto for speech corpus management. In *Proceedings of the 28th Conference on Electronic Speech Signal Processing (ESSV)*, pages 160–166, Saarbrücken, Germany. Deutsches Forschungszentrum für Künstliche Intelligenz.

Pontus Stenetorp, Sampo Pyysalo, Goran Topić, Tomoko Ohta, Sophia Ananiadou, and Jun'ichi Tsujii. 2012. brat: a web-based tool for NLP-assisted text annotation. In *Proceedings of the Demonstrations at the 13th Conference of the European Chapter of the Association for Computational Linguistics*, pages 102–107, Avignon, France. Association for Computational Linguistics.

Andreas van Cranenburgh. 2018. Active DOP: A constituency treebank annotation tool with online learning. In *Proceedings of the 27th International Conference on Computational Linguistics: System Demonstrations*, pages 38–42, Santa Fe, New Mexico. Association for Computational Linguistics.

Andreas van Cranenburgh, Remko Scha, and Rens Bod. 2016. Data-oriented parsing with discontinuous constituents and function tags. *Journal of Language Modelling*, 4(1):57–111.

The incremental process of building an annotation scheme for clinical narratives in Portuguese: the contribution of human variation analysis

Ana Luísa Fernandes[1,2,5], Purificação Silvano[1,2,5], António Leal[2,5,6], Nuno Guimarães[1,2], Rita Rb-Silva[2,3,4], Luís Filipe Cunha[1,2], Alípio Jorge[1,2]

[1]INESC TEC, [2]University of Porto, [3]CI-IPOP, [4]RISE-Health, MEDCIDS, [5]CLUP
Porto, Portugal
[6]University of Macau, China
Correspondence: ana.l.fernandes@inesctec.pt

Abstract

The development of a robust annotation scheme and corresponding guidelines is crucial for producing annotated datasets that advance both linguistic and computational research. This paper presents a case study that outlines a methodology for designing an annotation scheme and its guidelines, specifically aimed at representing morphosyntactic and semantic information regarding temporal features, as well as medical information in medical reports written in Portuguese. We detail a multi-step process that includes reviewing existing frameworks, conducting an annotation experiment to determine the optimal approach, and designing a model based on these findings. We validated the approach through a pilot experiment where we assessed the reliability and applicability of the annotation scheme and guidelines. In this experiment, two annotators independently annotated a patient's medical report consisting of six documents using the proposed model, while a curator established the ground truth. The analysis of inter-annotator agreement and the annotation results enabled the identification of sources of human variation and provided insights for further refinement of the annotation scheme and guidelines.

1 Introduction

Manual annotation is a cornerstone of both linguistic research and natural language processing (NLP) (cf. e.g., Snow et al., 2008; Bhardwaj et al., 2010; Flickinger et al., 2017), enabling the research of linguistic phenomena and providing "gold labels" for training and assessing models in multiple NLP tasks (Pustejovsky and Stubbs, 2012; Pustejovsky et al., 2017; Levi and Shenhav, 2022). In addition to supporting data-driven approaches, manual annotation contributes to formalizing linguistic theories by offering a structured framework for empirical validation (Hovy and Lavid, 2010). Developing a comprehensive annotation scheme is critical to ensure that the annotation is systematic, consistent, interoperable, and comprehensive. A well-designed scheme enables the accurate representation of complex linguistic phenomena grounded in theory while maintaining practical applicability for annotators (Beck et al., 2020). When the data pertains to highly specialized subject matter, such as medical discourse, or involves the intersection of distinct domains, such as linguistics and medicine, the demands on scheme design increase substantially. In such cases, the annotation scheme and corresponding guidelines must be particularly precise and detailed to ensure accurate interpretation. This complexity challenges scheme designers and places additional cognitive and interpretive burdens on annotators (Graham and van der Meer, 2015). Among the additional challenges in annotating clinical narratives is the significant heterogeneity of the content and writing styles of medical reports, which vary not only across healthcare institutions (Zhu et al., 2023), but also between different departments or services within the same hospital. These texts are often written in a free and spontaneous manner, reflecting an inherent diversity of topics and concepts specific to the medical domain. Moreover, clinical texts differ substantially from non-clinical texts due to the highly technical and specialized nature of the field, as well as the frequent use of abbreviations, which significantly increases the complexity of their processing (Moharasan and Ho, 2019). Additionally, biomedical terminology is inherently complex, and it is common for certain terms to have different meanings depending on the context in which they are used. This further underscores the need for clear and context-sensitive annotation guidelines (Irrera et al., 2024).

A critical aspect of the annotation process is the assessment of both the effectiveness of the annotation scheme and the annotators' understanding of the guidelines. Successful annotation depends on the clarity, coherence, and comprehensiveness of

Proceedings of the 19th Linguistic Annotation Workshop (LAW-XIX-2025), pages 332–343
July 31, 2025

the documentation, as well as the annotators' training and familiarity with the scheme (Artstein and Poesio, 2008). Well-developed guidelines — featuring explicit definitions and illustrative examples — are essential for achieving reliable and accurate annotations (Pustejovsky and Stubbs, 2012). The validation of annotation schemes typically involves a combination of pilot studies, iterative guideline refinement, and qualitative analyses of problematic cases. The annotation process generally entails collecting judgments from multiple annotators for each data instance, a practice widely recognized for enhancing annotation quality (Snow et al., 2008). A commonly used metric to assess the quality of the annotation is inter-annotator agreement (IAA), which provides a quantitative assessment of annotation consistency (Artstein and Poesio, 2008). High IAA scores suggest clear and effective guidelines, whereas low agreement may stem from a variety of causes (Artstein, 2017; Basile et al., 2021; Bayerl and Paul, 2024), often revealing ambiguities or conceptual difficulties that require further attention.

Analyzing sources of annotation disagreement is determinant in improving annotation frameworks, providing valuable information on areas where guidelines may need clarification or extension (Artstein and Poesio, 2008; Hovy and Lavid, 2010). Although human variation in clinical annotation is natural, it is generally undesirable because, for example, the annotation can be used to develop information extraction algorithms for clinical research, where data must be unambiguous. Therefore, ambiguity must be eliminated, and disagreement in the annotation should be minimal or ideally nonexistent. Nevertheless, analyzing such variation in earlier stages of the annotation process can serve as a valuable diagnostic tool, revealing limitations or ambiguities in the current annotation design and accompanying guidelines. Observing patterns of annotator disagreement helps refine the guidelines and ultimately contributes to reducing annotation errors (Finlayson and Erjavec, 2017; Beck et al., 2020).

The primary objective of this paper is to describe a methodology to develop and validate an annotation scheme. We focus specifically on strategies aimed at minimizing human variation throughout the annotation process. To this end, we present a case study involving the design of an annotation scheme for medical reports written in European Portuguese. Our main contributions are as follows: (1) a methodological proposal for the design and validation of annotation schemes; (2) a case study illustrating the role of human variation analysis in refining annotation schemes and guidelines; (3) an annotation scheme for representing both linguistic and medical information in European Portuguese medical reports.

The paper is structured as follows. Section 2 reviews related work. Section 3 presents the case study, beginning with a description of the annotation scheme (3.1), followed by the results of the evaluation and a discussion (3.2) of how the findings informed improvements to the scheme and guidelines (3.2.2). The paper concludes with final remarks and directions for future work (4).

2 Related work

The development and validation of annotation schemes is a labor-intensive and demanding task. Yet, it is essential for both linguistic research and NLP applications. Over the past four decades, annotation strategies have evolved significantly. Since the early 1990s, when annotation became central to training machine learning models and practices were mostly improvised (Ide, 2017), there has been substantial progress toward systematizing and formalizing annotation methodologies.

A considerable body of work has focused on establishing principled standards for creating and validating annotation schemes. For example, Graham and van der Meer (2015) propose a seven-step annotation process. This process begins with selecting and preparing data, followed by formulating labels and attributes grounded in linguistic theory, and drafting the annotation scheme and accompanying guidelines. Subsequent steps include piloting the scheme on a sample dataset, evaluating the outcomes through IAA, and revising the scheme and guidelines if needed. The process concludes with large-scale annotation, periodic evaluations, and, finally, model training. A comparable approach is presented by Pustejovsky et al. (2017) through the MATTER annotation cycle (Model, Annotate, Train, Test, Evaluate, Revise), which emphasizes the iterative nature of annotation development. A key component of this cycle is the MAMA loop (Model-Annotate-Model-Annotate), whereby annotation schemes are continually tested and refined.

Designing a robust annotation scheme is inherently complex and critical for producing high-quality annotated datasets. As emphasized by Finlayson and Erjavec (2017), this process should be multi-phased, collaborative, and supported by appropriate tools. Additionally, the complexity of annotation tends to increase with the level of linguistic detail involved (Flickinger et al., 2017).

Once the scheme is designed, it is necessary to rigorously evaluate the annotation scheme and its guidelines. Among various evaluation approaches, IAA agreement remains one of the most widely adopted and recognized. Artstein (2017) points out that IAA is not just a measure of reliability; it is also a tool for refining annotation schemes and understanding how annotators interpret them. Artstein and Poesio (2008) conceptualize IAA as an indicator of annotation "trustworthiness". Commonly used metrics for measuring IAA include Cohen's kappa (Cohen, 1960), Krippendorff's alpha (Krippendorff, 2004), and simple percentage agreement. Bhardwaj et al. (2010) introduce Anveshan (Annotation Variance Estimation), a framework designed to evaluate patterns of annotator agreement and disagreement. This framework includes IAA agreement analysis and outlier detection based on annotation values.

However, reporting IAA results alone is often insufficient. Additional contextual information is necessary for meaningful interpretation. Bayerl and Paul (2024) advocate for including essential metadata to ensure transparent assessment of agreement, such as annotator expertise (e.g., novices, domain experts, scheme developers). Furthermore, Bayerl and Paul (2024) identify factors that can influence IAA agreement such as the annotation domain, the number of categories in the annotation scheme, the number and expertise of annotators, the training provided to annotators, the purpose of the annotation task, and the specific agreement metrics used. From a different perspective, Basile et al. (2021) challenge the idea of a singular "correct" annotation. They identify three primary sources of disagreement — annotator-related, data-driven, and context-dependent — and argue for embracing disagreement within evaluation frameworks, promoting the use of multiple annotations and adaptive metrics.

Analyzing the sources of annotator disagreement can be a productive strategy for improving annotation schemes and guidelines. Teruel et al. (2018) and Hovy and Lavid (2010) demonstrate that such analysis can lead to greater clarity in annotation instructions and scheme structure. Likewise, Levi and Shenhav (2022) advocate for breaking down annotation tasks into distinct layers to effectively isolate and address sources of disagreement. Dickinson and Tufis (2017) highlight the value of "iterative enhancement" — a process that involves identifying errors to accelerate annotation and improve its quality. This iterative process often results in enhanced guidelines and refined annotation schemes. Beck et al. (2020) discuss five different sources of problems in annotations: ambiguities and variations in the data, uncertainty among the annotators, errors, and biases. According to the authors, failing to address these issues can have undesirable consequences for different phases of the annotation process, while resolving them can yield more robust scientific results.

While the majority of the reviewed studies emphasize important aspects to consider in the development and validation of annotation schemes, they rarely provide a detailed, step-by-step account of the entire annotation process. In contrast, our work aims to fill this gap by offering a comprehensive framework for structuring the annotation workflow. Specifically, we highlight the critical role of analyzing human variation as a means to iteratively refine both the annotation scheme and the accompanying guidelines.

3 A case study

In this section, we present the methodology developed to design and validate our annotation scheme, as outlined in Figure 1.

The proposed approach is structured into four distinct phases, each comprising multiple steps that guide the annotation process from conception to evaluation. To illustrate the practical application of our methodology, we conduct a case study in which we implement and assess an annotation scheme tailored to extract both grammatical and medical information embedded within clinical narratives. The source material includes admission reports, discharge summaries, and general clinical notes. This annotation scheme serves as the foundation for constructing an annotated corpus of medical records written in European Portuguese, specifically from patients diagnosed with Acute Myeloid Leukemia (AML), a relatively understudied condition, being the extraction of structured data from clinical narratives essential to support and facilitate research efforts. Additionally, the proposed annotation scheme and the resulting annotated dataset will enable a detailed investigation of the semantic characteristics of medical records, particularly for

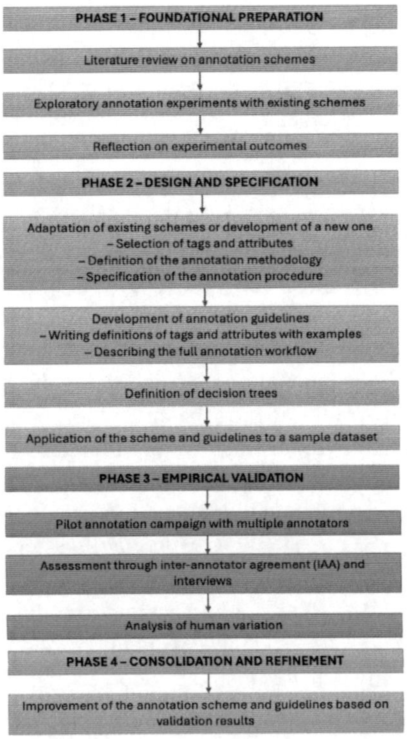

Figure 1: The proposed methodology for the development and validation of the annotation scheme.

temporal features.

Subsection 3.1 details the methodology employed in the development of the annotation scheme, while Subsection 3.2 discusses the procedures used to validate the scheme.

3.1 The development of the annotation scheme and guidelines

The initial step of Phase 1 involved a comprehensive review of the literature to identify existing frameworks for annotating clinical reports with morphosyntactic, semantic, and medical information[1]. Over the years, several proposals have focused on the annotation of grammatical information — particularly entities and temporal relations — as well as the integration of clinical information via medical ontologies (e.g., Roberts et al., 2009; Styler IV et al., 2014; Oliveira et al., 2022; Nunes et al., 2024).

Given our objective to represent both the temporal properties and key medical aspects of clinical reports in European Portuguese, we prioritized annotation schemes that provided robust frameworks for these two dimensions. For grammatical information, the Text2Story annotation scheme offered a comprehensive and multilayered proposal for capturing various temporal features in textual data. This scheme (Silvano et al., 2021; Leal et al., 2022) was developed in alignment with the ISO 24617 standard (International Organization for Standardization, 2012), and was originally applied to annotate morphosyntactic and semantic elements in European Portuguese news articles. Its temporal layer builds upon ISO TimeML (ISO-24617-1, 2012), a widely adopted standard with demonstrated applicability across diverse contexts, and includes adaptations tailored to the specificities of Portuguese. The Text2Story annotation scheme has several key advantages over alternative frameworks such as PropBank, Abstract Meaning Representation, and Penn Treebank since these are characterized as closed systems, with predefined structures and fixed category sets that constrain their flexibility and limit their applicability across diverse domains or layers of annotation. In contrast, ISO 24617, from which ISO TimeML is one part, offers a more open and modular architecture, supporting the integration of multiple layers of annotation. Additionally, ISO 24617 was conceived as an interoperable standard, designed to accommodate a range of theoretical models and natural languages, allowing for its adaptation, with minimal modifications, to different linguistic and contextual settings.

Concerning medical information, our review highlighted two annotation schemes — i2b2 (Sun et al., 2013) and MERLOT (Campillos et al., 2018) — as particularly relevant. Both were specifically designed for the medical domain and have demonstrated promising results in producing large-scale, complex clinical annotations, along with achieving high IAA scores. The selection of these schemes was based on a preliminary analysis that considered not only the coverage of relevant clinical categories but also the robustness of the models. Subsequently, practical annotation experiments were conducted using these frameworks to evaluate their performance in annotating our specific corpus. For this preliminary comparative analysis, six pseudonymized admission reports from patients treated at IPO-Porto, Portugal, were manually annotated using three different annotation schemes. The results demonstrated that the Text2Story annotation scheme was more effective in capturing morphosyntactic and semantic information. However,

[1]For a more detailed review of the annotation schemes designed for clinical narratives, the reader is referred to (Fernandes et al., 2025)

it was inadequate for representing domain-specific medical content. Conversely, while the i2b2 and MERLOT schemes facilitated the annotation of relevant clinical concepts, the labels employed were overly broad and lacked the specificity required for fine-grained semantic representation in the medical domain. The summary of the results of this comparison can be found in Table 5 in the Appendix A[2].

Following this initial evaluation, it became clear that none of the existing annotation schemes could be adopted without substantial modification. To further investigate the identified limitations and inform the development of a more suitable scheme, we analyzed a broader corpus of 100 pseudonymized clinical narratives from IPO-Porto, comprising admission reports, discharge summaries, and general clinical notes. This extended analysis was conducted in collaboration with a medical specialist from IPO-Porto to identify the essential clinical information that should be captured in the annotation process.

Grounded on the results of our analysis, we commenced Phase 2 - Design and Specification of the annotation scheme and guidelines. For grammatical information, we concluded that the Text2Story scheme provided a comprehensive set of labels for encoding the morphosyntactic and semantic properties of events and temporal expressions. In addition to entity structures (events and temporal expressions), the Text2Story scheme — consistent with the ISO TimeML standard — also includes link structures such as Temporal Links (TLinks), which support the representation of temporal relations among events. The selection of domain-specific medical labels was guided by the UMLS Metathesaurus ontology (Bodenreider, 2004), providing a systematic and internationally recognized framework. The definitions of the medical labels presented in this work were also informed by the contributions of Leite (2024), whose research on the same corpus proposed a preliminary set of clinically relevant categories validated by a specialized physician. Several of these categories were retained, while others were adapted or refined to better suit the present annotation goals.

Building on this foundation, a set of domain-specific tags was introduced to support the structured representation of medically relevant information. These include Sign or Symptom, Personal History (Past Medical History, Comorbidity or Undefined), Intercurrence, Examination, Examination Result, Principal Diagnosis, Characterization of the Disease, Medical Procedure, Treatment, Drug Administration Route, and Treatment Response. Adding these tags solved the problem of overly broad categories present in other schemes. Additionally, a decision tree was developed for selecting domain-specific medical labels to ensure consistency and accuracy in the annotation process, minimizing ambiguities and enhancing the replicability of results. Since the annotation of clinical narratives involves interpreting medical terms in different contexts, the hierarchical structure of the decision tree helps guide annotators in selecting the most appropriate labels, reducing inter-annotator variability. This enhancement appears to be particularly advantageous for both annotators with a medical background and those without. For the former, familiarity with this method, widely used in clinical settings to support decision-making (Bae, 2014), facilitates a more intuitive and effective adoption of the annotation scheme. For the latter, the decision tree serves as a structured guide that aids in understanding the annotation criteria, reducing the need for extensive prior knowledge of medical terminology and promoting greater standardization in the annotation process. Once the initial version of the annotation model was defined, it was iteratively tested and refined using the annotated data until it was capable of representing all relevant information present in the clinical records. Throughout this iterative process, comprehensive annotation guidelines were developed. These guidelines include detailed descriptions of each annotation phase, definitions and attributes for all labels, illustrative examples drawn from the dataset, and clarifications for complex or ambiguous cases encountered during annotation. This version of the scheme and guidelines can be found in the GitHub repository.

3.2 Assessment of the annotation scheme and guidelines

Phase 3 of our proposal involves the validation of the annotation scheme and its guidelines, with a focus on evaluating its consistency, reliability, and interpretability. As discussed in Section 2, IAA is a widely accepted strategy for assessing the quality of annotation guidelines and the clarity of the annotation model itself.

To carry out this evaluation, we conducted a

[2]A detailed analysis of the results from these experiments, and a thorough justification of the selection of the most suitable scheme will be the subject of future publication.

small-scale experiment involving two linguistics students with prior experience in annotation tasks. The INCEpTION tool (Klie et al., 2018) was configured with our proposed annotation scheme, and the annotators were provided with both the scheme and its accompanying guidelines. They were instructed to annotate a set of synthetic clinical reports, which included one group consultation note, three discharge reports, and one general report concerning a patient diagnosed with AML. These reports were generated by a specialist physician from IPO-Porto to ensure clinical relevance and realism. The reports can be found in the GitHub repository.

In addition to the IAA analysis, we implemented a curation-based evaluation strategy to further assess the validity and practical applicability of the annotation scheme and guidelines. The curator, who held a background in both linguistics and pharmaceutical sciences, reviewed the annotated documents to identify common annotation errors and challenges faced by the annotators. This process facilitated the detection of inconsistencies, such as the assignment of divergent labels to semantically similar events, which were often traced back to ambiguities or insufficient clarity in the annotation guidelines. Such findings were instrumental in refining both the scheme and its documentation, thereby improving the overall robustness and reliability of the annotation process.

Subsequently, we computed IAA metrics, which are reported in the following section. The agreement was quantified using Cohen's Kappa and Krippendorff's Alpha, two well-established statistical measures for evaluating reliability (Artstein, 2017). Values closer to 1 indicate stronger agreement and, by extension, a more reliable annotation scheme. Furthermore, treating the curator's annotations as the reference (or "gold standard"), we also measured the annotation distance between each annotator and the curator to assess alignment with expert judgment.

Finally, we conducted a detailed qualitative analysis of the sources of disagreement, to understand the underlying factors contributing to human variation in annotation. These findings provided insights that informed subsequent refinements to both the annotation scheme and the supporting guidelines.

3.2.1 The analysis of IAA and curation

The analysis of IAA and curation outcomes provides valuable insights into the effectiveness and clarity of the annotation scheme and its accompanying guidelines. As shown in Table 1, the identification of text spans corresponding to events and time expressions and temporal links (TLinks) between events, events and time expressions, and between time expressions achieved substantial agreement, as indicated by Cohen's kappa values (Landis and Koch, 1977). Notably, agreement between individual annotators and the curator is higher than that observed between annotators, for both text spans and TLinks. In particular, the agreement between Annotator 1 (ANN1) and the curator for text span identification reached the threshold for almost perfect agreement, suggesting strong alignment with the curation standard.

Table 1: IAA (initial pilot) on span and relation annotations (exact match criteria) between ANN1, ANN2, and the curator, based on the curated reference.

type	annotators	krippendorff_alpha	cohen_kappa
relation	ANN2, Curator	0.761	0.760
	ANN1, Curator	0.754	0.754
	ANN1, ANN2	0.614	0.614
span	ANN2, Curator	0.741	0.742
	ANN1, Curator	0.910	0.910
	ANN1, ANN2	0.682	0.684

A closer examination of the divergences between annotators and the curator regarding text span annotation reveals two primary sources of disagreement: (i) cases in which both annotators recognize the same event or temporal expression but differ in the extent of the annotated span; and (ii) cases in which only one annotator identifies the event or temporal expression.

In the first category, although both annotators consistently identify the same underlying event — typically marked by the same nuclear noun — discrepancies arise due to variations in the delimitation of the annotated span. These differences are attributable to factors such as: (a) the inclusion or omission of leading or trailing whitespace; (b) divergent judgments on whether to annotate the full nominal phrase, including modifiers or complements, versus only its nucleus (e.g., [antecedentes relevantes] 'relevant antecedents' vs. [antecedentes] 'antecedents'); (c) inclusion of quantifiers (e.g., [duas consolidações] 'two consolidations' vs. [consolidações] 'consolidations'); (d) the presence or absence of prepositions introducing the expression (e.g., [em remissão completa] '(in) complete remission' vs. [remissão completa] 'complete remission'); and (e) the presence of multiple semantic units within a single span, such as "cariótipo normal" ('normal karyotype'), which one annotator treats as a single markable, while the other annotates "cariótipo" ('karyotype') and "normal" ('normal') as separate events.

The second category comprises 22 instances in which one annotator identified a markable that the other did not. These omissions often stem from challenges in interpreting domain-specific language and document structure. For instance, in one recurring case, the term "resumo" ('summary') — used to introduce a retrospective overview of the patient's clinical history — is annotated as a General Event Class by one annotator, while the other omits it, possibly not recognizing its functional role. Similar inconsistencies are observed with specialized medical terminology unfamiliar to one or both annotators. Terms such as "blastos" ('blasts') and "piperacilina-tazobactam" are annotated as events by one annotator, while the other does not annotate them. The same applies to acronyms and abbreviations from the medical domain (e.g., "7+3", "NPM1+", "FLT3+", "EV"), which are variably interpreted either as temporal expressions or domain-specific events.

Finally, several cases of disagreement can be attributed to differences in grammatical interpretation. For example, in the phrase "fez indução" ('did induction'), one annotator treats "fez" ('did') as a main verb and accordingly annotates it as an event, while the other classifies it as a light verb, and instead identifies "indução" ('induction') as the semantic nucleus, thereby excluding "fez" from annotation. Such differences highlight the challenges posed by complex syntactic constructions and further underscore the importance of clear, unambiguous annotation guidelines.

Turning to the analysis of inter-annotator agreement (IAA) on event attributes, as presented in Table 2, the results reveal considerable variability in agreement levels across different attributes. Agreement values between Annotators 1 (ANN1) and 2 (ANN2) range from fair ($\kappa = 0.22$ for Aspect) to almost perfect ($\kappa = 0.95$ for Part of Speech).

The low agreement for the Aspect attribute suggests potential issues in the clarity or interpretation of the guideline's definition. The current description — "The grammatical category that expresses the way an event is structured internally and unfolds over time (over an interval or in a moment), taking into account whether its duration is indeterminate or whether it has boundaries" — may have inadvertently introduced confusion. Although the Aspect attribute is intended to reflect grammatical aspect, its definition appears to overlap conceptually with lexical aspect, which is covered under the Class and Event Type attributes. This ambiguity likely contributed to the lower agreement for Aspect, especially when compared to the higher levels observed for Class ($\kappa = 0.56$) and Event Type ($\kappa = 0.68$), suggesting that annotators found it easier to identify lexical rather than grammatical aspectual properties.

The agreement for Verb Form is also relatively low ($\kappa = 0.37$), which is somewhat unexpected. This attribute involves the recognition of non-finite verb forms — typically a straightforward task for annotators with linguistic expertise. Interestingly, this agreement value is lower than that observed for Tense ($\kappa = 0.78$), despite the latter also involving morphological identification, albeit of finite verb forms. This discrepancy may indicate that the annotation of non-finite forms introduces ambiguities not present in the identification of tense.

As anticipated, the Part-of-Speech attribute yielded the highest agreement ($\kappa = 0.95$), reflecting the annotators' strong background in linguistics and the relative simplicity of identifying major word classes. In contrast, Polarity achieved only substantial agreement ($\kappa = 0.60$), which is somewhat surprising given that polarity identification is similarly considered a relatively simple classification task. This suggests that further clarification or refinement of the annotation criteria for Polarity may be beneficial.

With respect to the Specialized Event Class attribute, the agreement between annotators was substantial ($\kappa = 0.73$). Considering that the annotators have domain expertise in linguistics rather than medicine, this level of agreement suggests that the annotation manual's definitions and examples drawn from the clinical domain are generally accessible and comprehensible. Nevertheless, these results also point to opportunities for refinement, particularly in enhancing the clarity of domain-specific guidelines to further support non-expert annotators.

As for Time spans, the results are very diverse: the agreement values between annotators are less than chance agreement regarding "Temporal Function" (because one of the annotators did not perform this annotation), but are perfect and almost perfect regarding Time Type as revealed by Table 3.

Table 4 presents the results of IAA for temporal relation annotations across varying threshold lev-

Table 2: IAA scores (initial pilot) on event attributes between ANN1, ANN2, and the curator, based on the curated reference.

type	annotators	krippendorff_alpha	cohen_kappa
aspect	ANN1, ANN2	0.227	0.252
	ANN2, Curator	0.460	0.440
	ANN1, Curator	0.126	0.145
class	ANN1, ANN2	0.568	0.566
	ANN2, Curator	0.789	0.786
	ANN1, Curator	0.769	0.767
event	ANN1, ANN2	0.683	0.680
	ANN1, Curator	0.816	0.814
	ANN2, Curator	0.851	0.848
polarity	ANN1, ANN2	0.606	0.606
	ANN1, Curator	0.920	0.920
	ANN2, Curator	0.608	0.607
pos	ANN1, ANN2	0.959	0.959
	ANN2, Curator	0.889	0.889
	ANN1, Curator	1.000	1.000
specialized	ANN1, ANN2	0.731	0.730
	ANN2, Curator	0.792	0.792
	ANN1, Curator	0.820	0.819
tense	ANN1, ANN2	0.787	0.783
	ANN1, Curator	1.000	1.000
	ANN2, Curator	0.705	0.703
vform	ANN1, ANN2	0.379	0.375
	ANN1, Curator	0.462	0.429
	ANN2, Curator	0.690	0.667

Table 3: IAA results (initial pilot) for time expression attributes between ANN1, ANN2, and the curator, based on the curated reference.

type	annotators	krippendorff_alpha	cohen_kappa
temporal function	ANN1, ANN2	-0.326	0.063
	ANN2, Curator	-0.389	0.049
	ANN1, Curator	0.523	0.520
time type	ANN1, ANN2	1.000	1.000
	ANN2, Curator	1.000	1.000
	ANN1, Curator	0.904	0.902

els. As the threshold increases from 0 to 3, both the number of matched temporal links (TLinks) and the proportion of those matches that include agreement on the relation type (e.g., Before, After, Overlap) also increase. This suggests that applying more relaxed matching criteria — specifically regarding the span boundaries — improves alignment between annotators. Consequently, the percentage of agreement on TLink attributes rises from 26.7% at threshold 0 to 31.9% at thresholds 2 and 3. At threshold 0, among a total of 212 TLinks established between events, events and time expressions, and between time expressions, annotators agreed on the TLink in 41% of the cases, and only in 26% of the cases (56 out of 87) did they agree on the TLink attribute. However, when filtered to exclude the cases where annotators disagreed on the TLink attribute and considering only the 56 cases of agreement, the proportion of agreement significantly increases to 64.4%. Although further detailed analysis is required to identify the underlying causes of disagreement, these results point to the complexity of annotating temporal relations and suggest that clearer annotation guidelines may be necessary to ensure more consistent labeling. Additionally, these findings underscore the importance of further training for annotators to enhance reliability in this domain.

Table 6 in the Appendix A presents the distribution of label annotations in the initial pilot study after curation, while Table 7 shows the distribution of attributes for the specialized events in the same pilot study.

Table 4: Results of IAA between annotators in TLINKs and TLINKs attributes (initial pilot).

threshold	#TLink matches	#matches in TLink type	% agreement TLink matches	% agreement matches in TLink type	% agreement matches in TLink type (filtered)
0	87	56	0.414	0.267	0.644
1	103	64	0.490	0.305	0.621
2	109	67	0.519	0.319	0.615
3	110	67	0.524	0.319	0.609

3.2.2 Improvement of the annotation scheme and guidelines

The analysis of the curation results and IAA presented in Section 3.2 highlighted several issues that required clarification in the annotation scheme and its associated guidelines, particularly concerning the definition of markables. Although a detailed definition for markables was already provided in the guidelines, we decided to refine the instructions by specifying that markables should not include whitespace before or after the span, nor punctuation marks such as commas. Additionally, the statistical analysis revealed the need for further clarification regarding the annotation of noun complements and modifiers, as well as quantifiers. Specifically, when an event is accompanied by a temporal complement or modifier, such as "quadro recente" ('recent case'), the modifier should be annotated with the Time label and receive the attributes defined by TIDES 2005 (Ferro et al., 2005). To facilitate this, an open field labeled Value was introduced. Furthermore, in cases where events are preceded by quantifiers, such as "duas consolidações" ('two consolidations'), the quantifier should not be annotated as part of the event but should instead be captured in the quantification field.

Concerning lexicalized and semi-lexicalized expressions, although the guidelines already specified that the entire expression should be marked — including prepositions — we decided to include the example "em remissão completa" ('in complete remission'), as it is a recurrent expression in medical reports.

Another issue pertained to the annotation of abbreviations. For instances such as "O FLT3 foi +" ('the FLT3 was +'), where the symbol "+" represents the event 'positive', a mechanism was needed to ensure proper annotation. To address this, an open field called Observations was introduced, enabling the abbreviation to be annotated as an event with its full form recorded in that field.

With polarity, we clarified that events preceded by negative quantifiers, such as "nada" ('nothing'), or by negative verbs, such as "deixar de + infinitive" ('to stop + infinitive'), should also be annotated with a negative polarity attribute.

Some annotation errors arose due to the annotators' lack of medical knowledge. Although the decision tree assists in the selection of domain-specific labels, we believe that the annotation process would be further facilitated if annotators received brief training on the specific disease reported in the medical records — in this case, Acute Myeloid Leukemia. Familiarity with domain-specific concepts would enable annotators to better identify and apply the relevant labels. To this end, we incorporated a short video presentation, accessible via QR code, created by a specialist physician at IPO-Porto.

In addition to analyzing the curation results and IAA, we conducted interviews with annotators to identify the main difficulties encountered during the annotation process. The aim was to refine the annotation scheme and improve its applicability. One issue that was raised was related to the label General Event Class, which included an attribute called Class. This terminology caused ambiguity, complicating the annotation process. To resolve this, the scheme was reorganized, renaming General Event Class to General Event, while retaining the name of the Class attribute. To maintain terminological consistency, the label Specialized Event Class was also renamed to Specialized Event. Another issue highlighted by the annotators was the redundancy in annotating events within the Specialized Event Class, which required dual labeling with both Specialized Event Class and General Event Class. This redundancy arose because certain attributes, such as Polarity and Part of Speech, were only defined for the General Event Class. To address this, these attributes were integrated directly into the Specialized Event Class, eliminating the need for dual labeling. However, attributes exclusive to the General Event Class were not incorporated, as events in the Specialized Event Class typically correspond to nouns and adjectives, which only receive Polarity and Part-of-speech attributes. Another challenge reported by annotators was related to inter-document annotation. Annotators experienced difficulty identifying which relationships should be established between different medical reports for the same patient. To address this, the guidelines were clarified to specify how events and expressions should be linked across multiple reports. It was established that the Doctime (date of report creation) should always be connected to both the previous and subsequent report dates. Events in the reports should only link to the previous report via TLINK Identity when pertinent to the understanding of the patient's story. Additionally, two new attributes, Admission Date and Discharge Date, were introduced for dates. When a report is written during a hospitalization period, the Doctime of that report should be linked to both the Admission Date and Discharge Date of the corresponding report. When the Doctime corresponds to the Discharge Date, only the latter should be assigned.

Figure 2 in the Appendix A shows the annotation of a corpus excerpt using the latest version of the annotation scheme. The final version of the scheme and the corresponding guidelines can be accessed in the GitHub repository.

4 Final remarks

In this work, our main goal was to describe the incremental process of developing and validating an annotation scheme, along with its corresponding guidelines, capable of integrating both linguistic and medical domain information in an inter-document annotation. The results of the annotation and curation phases enabled improvements to both the scheme and the guidelines through an iterative refinement process. Developing an annotation scheme requires ongoing efforts toward improvement. With that in mind, we intend to further explore issues related to the identification of grammatical features and to develop a question–answer system that facilitates the selection of domain-specific labels, even for annotators without prior knowledge of the field.

Acknowledgments

This work is financed by National Funds through the Portuguese funding agency, FCT - Fundação para a Ciência e a Tecnologia, within project LA/P/0063/2020. DOI 10.54499/LA/P/0063/2020 | https://doi.org/10.54499/LA/P/0063/2020. The authors also acknowledge the support of the StorySense project (DOI 10.54499/2022.09312.PTDC).

References

R. Artstein. 2017. Inter-annotator agreement. In N. Ide and J. Pustejovsky, editors, *Handbook of Linguistic Annotation*, pages 297–313. Springer Netherlands.

Ron Artstein and Massimo Poesio. 2008. Inter-coder agreement for computational linguistics. *Computational Linguistics*, 34(4):555–596.

Jong-Myon Bae. 2014. The clinical decision analysis using decision tree. *Epidemiology and Health*, 36:e2014025.

Valerio Basile, Michael Fell, Tommaso Fornaciari, Dirk Hovy, Silviu Paun, Barbara Plank, Massimo Poesio, and Alexandra Uma. 2021. We need to consider disagreement in evaluation. In *Proceedings of the 1st Workshop on Benchmarking: Past, Present and Future*, pages 15–21, Online. Association for Computational Linguistics.

Petra Saskia Bayerl and Karin I. Paul. 2024. What determines inter-coder agreement in manual annotations? a meta-analytic investigation. *Computational Linguistics*.

Christin Beck, Hannah Booth, Mennatallah El-Assady, and Miriam Butt. 2020. Representation problems in linguistic annotations: Ambiguity, variation, uncertainty, error and bias. In *Proceedings of the 14th Linguistic Annotation Workshop*, pages 60–73, Barcelona, Spain. Association for Computational Linguistics.

Vikas Bhardwaj, Rebecca Passonneau, Ansaf Salleb-Aouissi, and Nancy Ide. 2010. Anveshan: A framework for analysis of multiple annotators' labeling behavior. In *Proceedings of the Fourth Linguistic Annotation Workshop*, pages 47–55, Uppsala, Sweden. Association for Computational Linguistics.

O. Bodenreider. 2004. The unified medical language system (umls): Integrating biomedical terminology. *Nucleic Acids Research*, 32:D267–D270.

L. Campillos, L. Deléger, C. Grouin, T. Hamon, A.-L. Ligozat, and A. Névéol. 2018. A french clinical corpus with comprehensive semantic annotations: Development of the medical entity and relation limsi annotated text corpus (merlot). *Language Resources and Evaluation*, 52:571–601.

Jacob Cohen. 1960. A coefficient of agreement for nominal scales. *Educational and Psychological Measurement*, 20:37 – 46.

Markus Dickinson and Dan Tufis. 2017. Iterative enhancement. In Nancy Ide and James Pustejovsky, editors, *Handbook of Linguistic Annotation*, pages 257–276. Springer.

Ana Luísa Fernandes, Purificação Silvano, Nuno Guimarães, Rita Rb-Silva, Tahsir Ahmed Munna, Luís Filipe Cunha, António Leal, Ricardo Campos, and Alípio Jorge. 2025. Human experts vs. large language models: Evaluating annotation scheme and guidelines development for clinical narratives. In *Proceedings of the Text2Story 2025 – Eighth International Workshop on Narrative Extraction from Texts*, pages 149–160, Lucca, Italy. CEUR-WS.org.

Lisa Ferro, Laurie Gerber, Inderjeet Mani, Beth Sundheim, and George Wilson. 2005. Tides 2005 standard for the annotation of temporal expressions. Available online at: `http://www.timeml.org/timex2/`.

Mark A. Finlayson and Tomaž Erjavec. 2017. Overview of annotation creation: Processes & tools. In Nancy Ide and James Pustejovsky, editors, *Handbook of Linguistic Annotation*, pages 167–192. Springer.

Dan Flickinger, Stephan Oepen, and Emily Bender. 2017. Sustainable development and refinement of complex linguistic annotations at scale. In Nancy Ide and James Pustejovsky, editors, *Handbook of Linguistic Annotation*, pages 353–377. Springer.

Yvonne Graham and Jacques van der Meer. 2015. Interannotator agreement for qualitative data analysis in research: Methods and strategies. *Qualitative Research Journal*, 15(3):1–18.

Eduard Hovy and Julia Lavid. 2010. Towards a 'science' of corpus annotation: A new methodological challenge for corpus linguistics. *International Journal of Translation Studies*, 22:13–36.

Nancy Ide. 2017. Introduction: The handbook of linguistic annotation. In Nancy Ide and James Pustejovsky, editors, *Handbook of Linguistic Annotation*, pages 1–10. Springer, Dordrecht.

International Organization for Standardization. 2012. *ISO 24617:2012 - Language Resource Management – Semantic Annotation Framework*. ISO.

Orazio Irrera, Simone Marchesin, and Gianmaria Silvello. 2024. Metatron: Advancing biomedical annotation empowering relation annotation and collaboration. *BMC Bioinformatics*, 25(1):1–41.

ISO-24617-1. 2012. Language resource management - semantic annotation framework (semaf) - part 1: Time and events (semaf-time, iso-timeml). Standard, Geneva, CH.

J.-C. Klie, M. Bugert, B. Boullosa, R. Eckart de Castilho, and I. Gurevych. 2018. The inception platform: Machine-assisted and knowledge-oriented interactive annotation. In *Proceedings of the 27th International Conference on Computational Linguistics: System Demonstrations*, pages 5–9. Association for Computational Linguistics.

Klaus Krippendorff. 2004. *Content Analysis: An Introduction to Its Methodology*, 2nd edition. Sage Publications, Thousand Oaks, CA.

J. Richard Landis and Gary G. Koch. 1977. The measurement of observer agreement for categorical data. *Biometrics*, 33(1):159–174.

A. Leal, P. Silvano, E. Amorim, I. Cantante, F. Silva, A. Jorge, and R. Campos. 2022. The place of iso-space in text2story multilayer annotation scheme. In *Proceedings of the 18th Joint ACL - ISO Workshop on Interoperable Semantic Annotation within LREC2022*, pages 61–70. European Language Resources Association.

M. A. Leite. 2024. Ontology-based extraction and structuring of narrative elements from clinical texts. Mater´s thesis, Universidade do Porto.

Eitan Levi and Shaul R. Shenhav. 2022. A decomposition-based approach for evaluating inter-annotator disagreement in narrative analysis. *arXiv preprint*.

G. Moharasan and Tu-Bao Ho. 2019. Extraction of temporal information from clinical narratives. *Journal of Healthcare Informatics Research*, 3(2):220–244.

M. Nunes, J. Boné, J. C. Ferreira, P. Chaves, and L. B. Elvas. 2024. Medialbertina: An european portuguese medical language model. *Computers in Biology and Medicine*, 182:109233.

L. E. S. e Oliveira, A. C. Peters, A. M. P. da Silva, C. P. Gebeluca, Y. B. Gumiel, L. M. M. Cintho, D. R. Carvalho, S. Al Hasan, and C. M. C. Moro. 2022. Semclinbr—a multi-institutional and multi-specialty semantically annotated corpus for portuguese clinical nlp tasks. *Journal of Biomedical Semantics*, 13(1):13.

James Pustejovsky, Harry Bunt, and Annie Zaenen. 2017. Designing annotation schemes: From theory to model. In Nancy Ide and James Pustejovsky, editors, *Handbook of Linguistic Annotation*, pages 31–63. Springer, Dordrecht.

James Pustejovsky and Amber Stubbs. 2012. *Natural Language Annotation for Machine Learning*. O'Reilly Media, Inc.

Angus Roberts, Robert J. Gaizauskas, Mark Hepple, George Demetriou, Yikun Guo, Ian Roberts, and Andrea Setzer. 2009. Building a semantically annotated corpus of clinical texts. *Journal of biomedical informatics*, 42 5:950–66.

P. Silvano, A. Leal, F. Silva, I. Cantante, F. Oliveira, and A. Jorge. 2021. Developing a multilayer semantic annotation scheme based on iso standards for the visualization of a newswire corpus. In *Proceedings of the 17th Joint ACL - ISO Workshop on Interoperable Semantic Annotation*, pages 1–13, Groningen, The Netherlands (online). Association for Computational Linguistics.

Rion Snow, Brendan O'Connor, Daniel Jurafsky, and Andrew Ng. 2008. Cheap and fast – but is it good? evaluating non-expert annotations for natural language tasks. In *Proceedings of the 2008 Conference on Empirical Methods in Natural Language Processing*, pages 254–263, Honolulu, Hawaii. Association for Computational Linguistics.

William F. Styler IV, Steven Bethard, Sean Finan, Martha Palmer, Sameer Pradhan, Piet C de Groen, Brad Erickson, Timothy Miller, Chen Lin, Guergana Savova, and James Pustejovsky. 2014. Temporal annotation in the clinical domain. *Transactions of the Association for Computational Linguistics*, 2:143–154.

W. Sun, A. Rumshisky, and O. Uzuner. 2013. Annotating temporal information in clinical narratives. *Journal of Biomedical Informatics*, 46:S5–S12.

Marta Teruel, Cristian Cardellino, Federico Cardellino, Laura Alonso Alemany, and Serena Villata. 2018. Increasing argument annotation reproducibility by using inter-annotator agreement to improve guidelines. In *Proceedings of the Eleventh International Conference on Language Resources and Evaluation (LREC 2018)*, Miyazaki, Japan. European Language Resources Association (ELRA).

E. Zhu, Q. Sheng, H. Yang, Y. Liu, T. Cai, and J. Li. 2023. A unified framework of medical information annotation and extraction for chinese clinical text. *Artificial Intelligence in Medicine*, 142:1–12.

A Appendix

Table 5: Comparison of the analyzed annotation frameworks

Feature	Text2Story	i2b2	Merlot
Medical domain coverage	-	+	++
Morphosyntactic and grammatical domain coverage	+++	+	+
Existence of the TLINK before_overlap (captures temporal info "recently")	-	+	-
Existence of the TLINK identity (captures coreference of same event)	+	-	-

Table 6: Distribution of annotation labels in the corpus of the initial pilot.

Label	Count
Specialized Events	100
General Events	64
Times	22
TLinks	228

Table 7: Distribution of Specialized Event tags

Category	Count
Personal History	3
Sign or Symptom	17
Examination	12
Examination Result	11
Principal Diagnosis	5
Treatment	19
Intercurrence	10
Characterization of the Disease	11
Treatment Response	10
Drug Administration Route	2

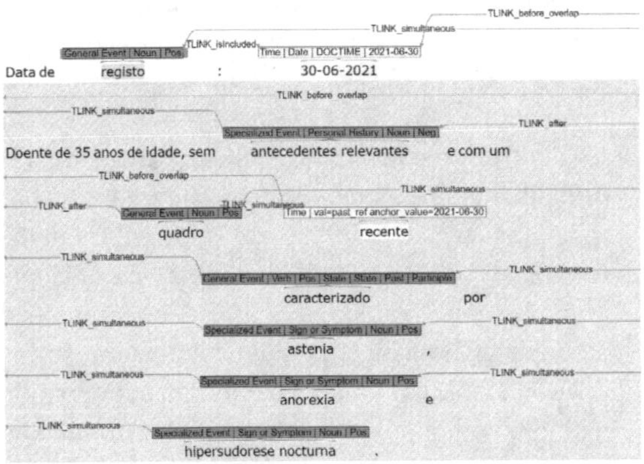

Figure 2: Annotation of an excerpt from a medical report using the latest version of the annotation scheme. Events are marked in blue and temporal expressions in yellow. The annotated excerpt illustrates the identification of various attributes associated with both events and temporal expressions, as well as the temporal relations between events and between events and temporal expressions. "Registration date: 06/30/2021. The patient is a 35-year-old with no relevant medical history, presenting with recent symptoms of asthenia, anorexia, and night sweats".

Expanding the UNSC Conflicts Corpus by Incorporating Domain Expert Annotations and LLM Experiments

Karolina Zaczynska
University of Potsdam
Applied Computational Linguistics Discourse Research Lab
Potsdam, Germany
zaczynska@uni-potsdam.de

Abstract

In this work we expand the UN Security Council Conflicts corpus (UNSCon) (Zaczynska et al., 2024) on verbal disputes in diplomatic speeches in English. By including annotations of a UNSC expert, we target the problem of annotating verbal conflicts in a domain with its own culture and rules. On the one hand, we aim to catch all conflicts detected by political domain experts which as a result will be interpretable only by people with advanced political science backgrounds. On the other hand, we target linguistically marked verbalisations that are domain-independent and potentially easier to detect for language models. This balancing act resulted in a refined annotation scheme, and we re-annotate and expand the corpus size by 40% by including new debates. We perform a pilot study using a Large Language Model to include lexical markers of negative evaluation within the conflict spans, which until now were not annotated separately. Classification experiments on the conflict labels in the corpus using Transformer models demonstrate that models trained on the political domain improve the results.

1 Introduction

The UNSC Conflicts corpus (UNSCon) presented in our previous work (Zaczynska et al., 2024) aims to serve as a resource for understanding verbal conflicts in United Nations Security Council (UNSC) speeches. It is novel in its attempt to operationalise conflicts defined as verbal disputes and critique in a diplomatic setting, and works on disagreement detection for speeches that are mostly pre-written. We developed an annotation scheme of Conflicts including content and linguistic markers, allowing for the detection of different types of Conflicts without requiring expert knowledge of the topic. The annotations were performed by computational linguists, and had not yet been compared to those from political scientists. To address this, in this work we conduct experiments with a UN Security Council expert, identify key disagreements and suggest modifications to the annotation guidelines to improve the corpus.

Limited to debates on two topics and speeches from 2014 and 2016, UNSCon covers a restricted range of targets and periods. We expand the corpus by adding 40 new speeches on the subject *Iraq* from the years 2002, 2003, 2019, and 2020, in order to increase the diversity in topics and targets. With the expanded corpus, we perform classification experiments on Conflict types and compare them to results from the original UNSCon paper. We see that although the increasingly imbalanced label distribution between Conflicts and No Conflicts in the new dataset poses a challenge for the models, we improve scores by using RoBERTa models trained on argumentation and the political domain.

Detecting lexical markers of negative evaluation within Conflict spans is a crucial part of annotating these spans and is required for certain Conflict labels. Currently, annotations are applied to Elementary Discourse Units (EDUs), which are typically sentences or clauses. These annotations define Conflict types within the EDUs but do not specify the lexical markers themselves. To enhance the corpus' granularity, we conduct a pilot study using Large Language Models (LLMs) to identify the lexical markers inside the Conflict spans (EDUs) and categorise different types of lexical markers that indicate negative evaluation.

To summarise our contributions, we expand the corpus on two levels, qualitatively and quantitatively:

- We aim to improve the quality of annotations and the annotation scheme by incorporating suggestions made by an UNSC domain expert (§3).
- We expand the corpus: (1) by incorporating speeches from an additional topic (§4), and

Proceedings of the 19th Linguistic Annotation Workshop (LAW-XIX-2025), pages 344–358
July 31, 2025

(2) by incorporating automatically detected lexical markers of negative evaluation within the Conflict text spans using an LLM (§5.1 and 6.1).

- We provide new classification experiments for Conflict type detection on the refined and expanded UNSCon, compare the results with those obtained from the original corpus, and demonstrate improvements testing on RoBERTa models trained on similar tasks and domains (§5.2 and 6.2).

The updated dataset and the code for experiments are available in our GitHub repository.[1]

The remainder of the paper is structured as follows: First, we present related work and detail the annotation scheme for Conflict types as defined in Zaczynska et al. (2024) (§2). Next, we describe the annotation experiments conducted with a political scientist (§3) and the updated Conflicts annotation scheme based on identified disagreements. Then, we introduce our expanded dataset with new annotation guidelines and the additional speeches included (§4). We outline the experiments and classification setups (§5), discuss the results (§6), and, finally, draw conclusions (§7).

2 Background

In our former work presenting the UNSCon (Zaczynska et al., 2024), we define Conflicts as verbal disagreements or critique directed at someone present at the UNSC debate, without necessarily referring to a military or physical conflict. There are different types of Conflict:

(1) Negative Evaluations (NegE) describe Conflicts where the speaker directly criticises another country (DIRECT NEGE). Speakers can also criticise an intermediate entity serving as a proxy instead of directly targeting another country (INDIRECT NEGE). Below is an example from a speech given on Ukraine after a resolution criticising a referendum planned in Crimea was vetoed by the Russian Federation. It starts with a direct critique on Russia's voting behaviour (labelled with the Conflict type DIRECT NEGE) and continues with a critique of the referendum that Russia supports (labelled as INDIRECT NEGE):

(1) Russia's decision to veto the resolution is therefore profoundly unsettling. – DIRECT NEGE
The referendum to be held tomorrow in Crimea is dangerous and destabilizing. – INDIRECT NEGE
It is unauthorized and invalid. – INDIRECT NEGE
(S/PV.7138, Australia)[2]

(2) Challenge and Corrections (CC) describe Conflicts where a speaker accuses another one of lying (CHALLENGE) and where a speaker provides a correction to that allegedly false statement (CORRECTIONS). The next example is taken from a speech in which the speaker from the Russian Federation is addressing accusations made by the United States:

(2) The Permanent Representative of the United States blamed Russia for illegally pursuing its ambitions. – CHALLENGE
That does not apply to us; – CORRECTION
it is a phrase taken from the foreign policy arsenal of the United States.
(S/PV.7138, Russian Federation)

For an EDU to be a Conflict, it must be possible to identify a target (addressee) of the critique by examining the speech. The annotation scheme specifies a set of target types for the Conflict, along with the specific countries being targeted. The UNSCon includes 87 speeches from debates discussing two topics: the *Ukraine* conflict, and the *Women, Peace and Security agenda* (WPS) focusing on gender (in)equality and crimes committed during peace keeping missions. The annotation spans are Elementary Discourse Units (EDUs) based on Rhetorical Structure Theory (Mann and Thompson, 1988). EDUs are usually sentences or clauses.

The work on the UNSCon is based on transcriptions of meetings in the UNSC (Schoenfeld et al., 2019), which serve as a foundation for various analyses in linguistics, computational linguistics, and political science. For example, Anisimova and Zikánová (2024) examine how diplomats convey evaluative speech using appraisal theory (Martin and White, 2005) for their analysis. Other studies focus on extracting country mentions in UNSC discussions using Wikidata for Named Entity Linking

[1] https://github.com/linatal/Expanding_UNSCon

[2] All examples are taken from the UNSCon and labelled with the original debate-id and country name the speaker represents.

(Glaser et al., 2022) and Named Entity Recognition (Ghawi and Pfeffer, 2022). Network analyses have also been conducted on UNSC topics from Afghanistan debates (Eckhard et al., 2021). Scartozzi (2022) look at discourse related to climate change in the UNSC.

Reinig et al. (2024) created a new resource of German parliamentary debates, annotated with fine-grained speech act types distinguishing between cooperation and conflict communication. Focusing on discourse in political debates around the US election 2016, Visser et al. (2020) annotated argument relations using the relation classes Inference, Conflict, and Rephrase. Focussing on dialogues they use the term Conflict differently than in the UNSCon, indicating incompatible propositions.

3 Evolution of the Annotation Scheme based on Domain Expert Annotations

In this section, we compare parallel Conflict annotations of the UNSCon speeches made by a UN Security Council expert with the original ones made by computational linguists. The analysis is the basis for the refined annotation scheme we present in the following sections. We first present the Inter-Annotator Agreement (IAA), along with some general observations, followed by a detailed analysis of the most common disagreements in the annotations.

3.1 General Observations and IAA

For the annotation experiments, we provided the political domain expert with annotation guidelines and used the pre-segmented raw texts from the original dataset.[3] Annotations were performed on all 87 speeches. Since we are working with potentially overlapping span annotations, we calculated IAA between the UNSCon annotations in the original corpus and the domain expert's annotations using unitising Krippendorff's alpha (Krippendorff, 2004). For INDIRECT versus DIRECT NEGE Conflict types versus NO CONFLICT, the IAA is 0.3, and for Targets, it ranges from 0.32 to 0.37. For CHALLENGE versus CORRECTION versus NO CONFLICT, the IAA is 0.37. The agreement is lower than what Zaczynska et al. (2024) reported for their experiments but still moderate, considering that their annotators received training during weekly meetings to resolve borderline cases. In contrast, our annotator conducted annotations mainly based on the provided guidelines without additional training.

In the original dataset, Conflicts usually span entire sentences, with a few exceptions. We observe that the political scientist annotator often chose to annotate individual propositions rather than full sentences as Conflict spans. When both NEGE and CC were applicable, the original UNSCon annotations preferred CC (which is according to the annotation guidelines), while the political domain expert frequently chose NEGE instead of CORRECTION. Generally, the political domain expert often labelled CORRECTION differently: Of the 148 EDUs labelled as CORRECTION in the original dataset, 17% (35 EDUs) were classified as NegEval by the political domain expert, and 21% (31 EDUs) were even marked as NO CONFLICT. Beyond that, there are similar disagreements to those identified by Zaczynska et al. (2024), such as interchanging INDIRECT with DIRECT NEGE. Of the 424 EDUs labelled as INDIRECT NEGE in the original dataset, 13% (56 EDUs) were classified as DIRECT NEGE by the political scientist. The following subsections address the disagreements we found between the annotations.

3.2 Diplomatic Phrasing

The choice of words is important in diplomacy; a restrained vocabulary allows nuanced control when agreeing or disagreeing with others to prevent unintended enthusiasm or offence (Stanko, 2001).[4] Thus, it is not surprising the political domain expert annotated Conflicts based on diplomatic rules, which the UNSCon did not include. For example, the sentence in bold below was marked by the domain expert as DIRECT NEGE due to its suggestion of a complaint about the Council's delayed discussion.[5] In contrast, productive meetings would be indicated by phrases like "it is a good opportunity [...]".

(3) The United States deeply appreciates the support from our colleagues around the table and from the many States that have called for a peaceful end to the crisis in Ukraine. This is, however, a sad and remarkable moment. **It is the seventh time that the Security Council**

[3] Both available online: https://github.com/linatal/UNSCon

[4] Some studies suggest this ambiguity is used strategically to achieve objectives (Bach et al., 2025; Scott, 2001).

[5] **Emphases** here and in the following examples are by paper's author.

has convened to discuss the urgent crisis in Ukraine. The Council is meeting on Ukraine because it is the job of this body to stand up for peace and to defend those in danger. (S/PV.7138, United States)

To maintain a clear linguistic operationalisation of Conflicts in the corpus, we chose not to include these implicit Conflicts. Consequently, this example shows, that the UNSCon may not contain all sentences marked with this type of critique, also in the updated version.

3.3 Instructions

A similar subtle critique as in (3) is present in the next example as an instructive formulation. Here, the representative of China communicates that more time should have been given before voting on the solution. This was not annotated in the original UNSCon, but it was marked by the political domain expert as DIRECT NEGE:

(4) We believe that the Security Council **should have had ample time** for further consultation to maximize our efforts to seek agreement and forge consensus to the largest extent possible. (S/PV.7643_spch008, China)

This example highlights the challenge of distinguishing between critical directives and, conversely, motivating or positively suggesting something in political speech.

Examining the domain expert annotations, we found differing assessments of whether instructive words carried conflict-related meaning. The next example includes "must", which caused the domain expert to annotate the sentence as Conflict, given its formulation as a strong demand implying criticism of Russia. The repetition reinforces this effect.

(5) Russia **must** pull back its forces to their bases and decrease their numbers to agreed levels. It **must** allow international observers access to Crimea. It **must** demonstrate its respect for the sovereignty and territorial integrity of Ukraine, [...]. It **must** engage in direct dialogue with Ukraine, as Ukraine has repeatedly requested, [...]. (S/PV.7138_spch012, Australia)

In a study by Gruenberg (2009) on the language used in UNSC resolutions, a small taxonomy of instructive words is presented, ranking them from

Emotive Words From Weakest to Strongest
Concerned
Grieved
Deplored
Condemned
Alarmed
Shocked
Indignant
Censured

Instructive Words From Weakest to Strongest
Decide
Call upon
Recommend
Request
Urge
Warn
Demand

Figure 1: Range of emotive and instructive words from weakest to strongest taken from Gruenberg (2009).

weakest to strongest (see Figure 1). For instructive sentences, we use the hierarchy provided by Gruenberg (2009) to update the Conflict annotations accordingly, since it resembles the assessments of our domain expert. Annotators are now advised to consider marking instructive words stronger than "recommend" as NEGE, noting that this should be assessed case-by-case. In the range of instructive words shown in Fig. 1 we can rank "must" between "request" and "urge".

3.4 Emotive Words

The Security Council employs a diverse vocabulary to express its institutional stance on different entities. While in the UNSCon the next two sentences were not annotated as Conflict, the domain expert chose DIRECT NEGE and explained this with the UK representative's decision to use "condemn". At the same time, we saw that sentences including "call upon" or 'urge" were not annotated. Gruenberg (2009) categorised emotive words by intensity (see Figure 1), where "condemned" falls in the middle range.

(6) The United Kingdom **condemns** the abduction at gunpoint and public parading of an OSCE Vienna Document inspection team and its Ukrainian escorts. (S/PV.7138, United States)

Similar to instructive words, for the improved UNSCon annotations, we include the hierarchy of emotive words by Gruenberg (2009) into the annotation guidelines and recommend considering the annotation of Conflicts based on emotive words that are similar or stronger than "condemned".

3.5 Sarcasm and Rhetorical Questions

From what we observed in the corpus, rhetorical questions and sarcasm often indicate a confrontational tone of statements in the UNSC speeches (and were accordingly annotated as Conflict by the UNSC expert), but were not annotated in the original corpus because they did not fit into existing Conflict type annotation rules. Another reason for including these types of utterances in the Conflict annotation scheme is informed by literature from political science, which discusses how sarcasm and humour are used in diplomacy to provoke, undermine discourse, or argue (Brassett et al., 2021; Chernobrov, 2023). The next example shows no lexical marker of negative evaluation, but the Russian representative uses a sarcastic tone to criticise other Council speakers. The political domain expert annotator labelled both annotations as DIRECT NEGE.

(7) **Some colleagues** today have achieved **high levels of rhetoric**. I must mention that the Ukrainian colleague nevertheless went far beyond anything permissible. [...]. (S/PV.7138_spch020, Russia)

In the example, the use of "some colleagues" can be interpreted as a defamatory reference to someone in the room; using "high levels of rhetoric" is a confrontational way of criticising others' speeches. It is sarcastic since the literal meaning is positive, but pragmatically it is intended to express a critique. In the next example, the representative of Lithuania uses a rhetorical question to criticise the statements given by the Russian representative, framing separatist groups as "peaceful protesters". Again, this sentence was marked by the domain expert, but not in the original dataset.

(8) A few days ago, a Ukrainian helicopter was downed by a rocket-propelled grenade, hardly a weapon so-called peaceful protesters - as labelled by the Russian side - can buy at the local corner market. **That certainly does not sound like the implementation of Geneva agreement by the separatists and their state sponsors?** (S/PV.7165_spch016, Lithuania)

Since we encountered several such instances, we added a new label FIGURATIVE LANGUAGE (FIGL) to the Conflict guidelines, covering sarcasm (saying something opposite of what is meant) and rhetorical questions (asking a question not to receive an answer, but to make a point or convey irony). The Appendix in section A provides more detailed guidelines for detecting sarcasm and rhetorical questions.

3.6 Cultural Differences in expressing Conflict

Conflicts from certain countries are more subtle compared to others, often avoiding direct naming of the addressee of the critique. Requiring lexical markers and identifying a target may result in missing Conflicts in less confrontational speeches. Some statements were marked as NEGE by the UNSC expert when the targeted country in the Council was inferred through background knowledge of the discourse. However, when they cannot be determined by the speech alone, they are not in the original corpus.

In the next example, the last sentence is a candidate for Conflict and was marked by the political scientist, but the speech is so implicit in not naming a target that it is unclear whether it refers to a country or a non-governmental group, making it difficult to determine the conflict type. Therefore we decided not to include this and similar Conflicts in the dataset, even if it means losing some conflict statements.

(9) We are troubled in particular by the continuing violence and aggressive provocations by illegal armed groups, including the seizure of key public buildings and the recent assassination attempt against the Mayor of the eastern city of Kharkiv. **All provocative actions and hostile rhetoric aimed at destabilizing Ukraine must cease immediately.** (S/PV.7165_spch010, Korea)

We also observed that some countries use more sarcasm and rhetorical questions than others. These cultural differences in communication were not included in the previous annotation scheme, which we now have addressed by including these as Conflict types.

4 Corpus Extension by Size

In this section we describe the extension of the UNSCon not only through applying the refined annotation guidelines to existing speeches but also by including new speeches from new debates.

To broaden the scope of the UNSCon, which concentrates on Ukraine and the WPS agenda, we included debates on Iraq. These debates focus on an (imminent) military conflict in Iraq, highlighting a crisis in international relations and the formation of opposing factions within UNSC countries — one supporting the military operation (including the US and Great Britain), and another opposing it

	#EDUs	
Conflict Type	**UNSCon**	**extended**
Direct NegE	771	1621
Indirect NegE	501	516
Challenge	101	138
Correction	128	214
Sarcasm	-	52
Rhetorical Question	-	120
Conflict	1501	2642
No Conflict	4497	7162
Sum	**5998**	**9804**

Table 1: UNSCon statistics original and updated version.

(Russian Federation, France, and others). We also included 2019 and 2020 debates on Iraq covering topics like the formation of a new Iraqi government, the violent response of the previous Iraqi government to demonstrations, and the threat posed by Islamic State (IS) terrorist groups in Iraq. Having a broader range of topics not directly related to military conflicts is more representative of other UNSC discussions, though they have a smaller total amount of Conflicts.

4.1 Corpus Statistics Expanded UNSCon

The corpus extension was carried out by the paper's author. For the EDU segmentation of the newly added speeches, we used Kamaladdini Ezzabady et al. (2021)'s MELODI system, which is available as part of the GitLab project page for their DisCut22 Discourse Annotator Tool.[6] We chose this system due to its accessibility and because it reported an f1-score of over 0.9 on the EDU segmentation task within the DISRPT2021 shared task. We expanded the corpus by segmenting and annotating it further, increasing the number of Elementary Discourse Units (EDUs) by 39%, and the number of Conflict annotations by 43%, resulting in a total of 9,806 EDUs (before: 5,998), and 131 speeches from 14 different debates (previously 87 speeches from 6 debates). The updated corpus now includes Conflicts originating from speeches delivered by 23 different countries (before: 21) and these speeches are targeted at 13 different countries (before: 5). Table 1 shows a more detailed comparison of the label distribution between the two versions of UNSCon.

[6]https://gitlab.irit.fr/melodi/andiamo/discoursesegmentation/discut22

We observe a greater imbalance between Conflicts and No Conflicts, with a tendency towards more No Conflict EDUs compared to the original version. With the inclusion of debates on additional topics, such as the spread of IS, we see that most countries criticise IS rather than each other, which is why they were not annotated as Conflicts. This may pose a challenge for classifiers; however, we view this as a more accurate representation of the general nature of speeches given at the UNSC, as the previous dataset predominantly consisted of highly controversial debates, mostly centred on the Ukraine crisis.

4.2 Inter-Annotator Agreement Expanded UNSCon

To evaluate the extension of the corpus done by the paper's author and the refined annotation guidelines, we had a second annotator (a computational linguistics student) annotate over 10% of the extended corpus. We selected speeches mainly from the new topic Iraq, as well as those containing instructive and figurative language. For NEGE, Cohen's Kappa is 0.71, which is slightly less than Zaczynska et al. (2024) report. For Krippendorff's Alpha (unitising) we report 0.6 for NEGE (two labels), 0.57 for Target Council (six labels), 0.59 Target Intermediate (six labels), and 0.65 for Country Name (nine labels). For Challenge Type (two labels), we report an Krippendorff's Alpha of 0.68, Target Challenge (five labels) 0.64, Country Name (eight labels) 0.64. For NEGE and CC, it appears that when there is agreement on the position and conflict type, agreement regarding the targets is similar to the previous labels. However, for FIGL, we observe a different pattern. For FIGL Type, we see a reasonable agreement with 0.61, but a lower agreement for the Targets (0.27 for Target Type and 0.25 for Country Type). This indicates a challenge in including this new Conflict type, as neither Sarcasm nor Rhetorical Questions necessarily clearly verbalise a target of the critique. However, with only a few instances of annotation for FIGL (166 EDUs), these observations should be taken cautiously.

5 Experiments

The next section outlines our setups for two sets of experiments: first, a pilot study on half of the dataset to incorporate lexical marker annotations for UNSCon, and second, an experiment utilising

Transformer models for fine-tuning on the Conflict type classification task.

5.1 Expansion of Conflicts with Lexical Markers

We perform a pilot study on using LLMs to extract the spans that include lexical markers of negative evaluation. Additionally, we let the LLM categorise the extracted lexical marker according to categories that are expanded and are more structured compared to the original guidelines.

- "Adjectival_Attribution": Adjectival attributions like *bad, dreadful, worrying*)
- "Noun": Nouns with a negative connotation (e.g., *traitor, annexation*)
- "Adverb": Adverbs that intensify criticism (e.g., *poorly, even, only*)
- "Verb": Verbs with a negative connotation (e.g., *infiltrating, invading*)
- "Negation_Phrase_or_Quantifier": Negation phrases and quantifiers (e.g., *not at all, not a single*)
- "Evaluative_Pattern": Recognisable evaluative patterns (e.g., *It is unfortunate that..., There is something worrying about...*)
- "Instructive_Words": Strong instructive words (e.g., *urge, must, warn, demand*)
- "Emotive_Words": Strong emotive words (e.g., *condemned, armed, shocked*)

For our pilot study, we use GPT4o (OpenAI, 2024) to annotate about half of the dataset (5,049 EDUs). Other open source models (llama-3.3-70b-versatile[7], gemma2-9b-it[8]) we tested did not produce satisfactory output. This might be due to the relatively complex task which consists of three steps: first, detecting if there are one or more lexical markers, second, categorising them, and third, extracting the substring(s) from an EDU. The final prompt we used for the experiment is provided in the Appendix B.

5.2 Classification Setup

We classify conflicts from diplomatic sources according to four distinct subtasks:

- 2-class setup, no FIGL: For comparability with the former classification setup, which did not include figurative language. We exclude the FIGL label for this setup.
- 3-class setup, no FIGL: For comparability with former classification setup, models should label each EDU choosing from one of the three categories: No Conflict, NEGE, CC.
- 4-class setup: models should label each EDU choosing from one of the four categories: No Conflict, NEGE, CC, FIGL.

We did not include more fine-grained classification on Conflict labels because of the performance drop we see for the 3 and 4-class setup (see section 6).

We test the following models on the UNSCon-extended for the classification tasks: We evaluated the best performing system reported in Zaczynska et al. (2024), namely RoBERTa-argument[9], which was trained on a variety of text types for binary classification tasks of arguments versus non-arguments. Given that none of the formerly tested models were trained on the political text domain, we additionally evaluated the following two models: PolicyBERTa-7d[10] (henceforth: RoBERTa-policy) is trained for topic detection based on the Manifesto Project, a project that collected election manifestos to study parties' policy preferences. Additionally, we also tested ArgumentMining-EN-ARI-AIF-RoBERTa_L (Ruiz-Dolz et al., 2021)[11] (henceforth: RoBERTa-relations) a model trained on a dataset tailored to a more fine-grained task than binary argumentation detection, specifically focusing on Argument Relation Mining, which involves classifying text into Inference, Conflict, and Rephrase relations. This model was trained on the datasets US2016 (Visser et al., 2020), containing annotated television debates and social media reactions to the US campaign in 2016, and on QT30 (Hautli-Janisz et al., 2022), a corpus focused on arguments and conflicts in Broadcast Debate. We follow the previous configurations as detailed in Zaczynska et al. (2024)(learning rate 1e-5, batch size of 32, with 2 training epochs and a weight decay of 0.01). We train the classifier to assign labels

[7] https://github.com/meta-llama/llama-models/blob/main/models/llama3_3/MODEL_CARD.md

[8] https://huggingface.co/google/gemma-2-9b-it

[9] https://huggingface.co/chkla/roberta-argument

[10] https://huggingface.co/niksmer/PolicyBERTa-7d

[11] https://huggingface.co/raruidol/ArgumentMining-EN-ARI-AIF-RoBERTa_L

for EDUs. All scores reported for the models are the result of 10-fold cross-validation.

6 Results and Discussion

6.1 Linguistics Markers

We perform a comparative analysis of the categories and lexical markers identified in a test set of 134 EDUs, using output from GPT4o and comparing it with another LLM, Gemini 2.0 Flash (Gemini). For calculating Cohen's Kappa, we ignore the text span length and focus solely on comparing the lists of categories assigned to each EDU by the two systems. For categories, we observe an average Cohen's Kappa of 0.45. In our multi-label setting, where multiple lexical marker annotations can exist per EDU, Cohen's Kappa is only partially appropriate because it allows the comparison of only one single point with another. We therefore also provide set comparison using the Jaccard index, where for each EDU, we compare all lexical markers and categories found for one EDU from Gemini against GPT4o as sets of strings and extract an overlap measure. For lexical marker categories, we observe an average Jaccard index of 0.63, and for extracted strings 0.59. Comparing the two outputs qualitatively, we see similar results regarding what is identified as a lexical marker of negative evaluation in the text; however, the chosen span of annotation differs. While GPT4o extracts phrases (for example, *camp of war in opposition to the United Nations and its Charter*), Gemini extracts individual words (*war, aggression, opposition*), and therefore, this also affects the categorisation: Because GPT4o focuses on phrases, it more frequently selects "Recognisable evaluative pattern" (*do its bidding -> Recognisable evaluative pattern, Negative verb*), whereas Gemini selects more specific word types (*make, do, bidding -> Verbs with a negative connotation, Strong instructive words*). Thus, while there is significant overlap of the chosen regions within the EDUs as being identified as lexical markers between both model outputs, the different spans negatively impact the IAA.

Looking at the distribution of lexical marker categories found in the annotated dataset we see that for all Conflict types the most prominent lexical markers are nouns with a negative attribution, followed by verbs (see Figure 2). A list of most frequent words (lemmatised using SpaCy library (Honnibal et al., 2020)) is in the Appendix C.

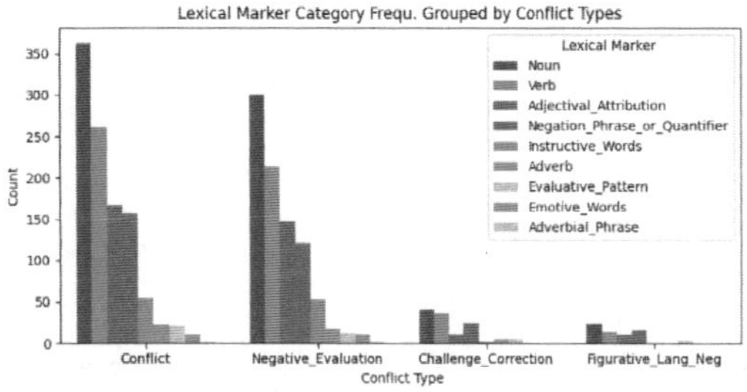

Figure 2: Frequency of found Lexical Marker Categories per Conflict Types.

6.2 Model Performance Classification

In Table 2, we present the classification results for the 3-class and 4-class setups. In our classification experiments on Conflict types using various RoBERTa-based models, we observe that for the binary setup (excluding FIGL, as it is absent from the old dataset), the results reported in Zaczynska et al. (2024) outperform our models fine-tuned on the new dataset. They report an f1-macro score of 0.74, whereas we achieve a best result of 0.70 for RoBERTa-relations. Comparing the performance of RoBERTa-argument on the old dataset with the new one, we note slightly better results for the binary and 3-class setups in the former (f1-macro 0.48 versus 0.45). We hypothesise that, although it offers more training instances, this is due to the increased label imbalance in the new corpus.

Comparing the results on our new dataset, RoBERTa-policy performs slightly better than RoBERTa-argument, although still lower than RoBERTa-relations. RoBERTa-policy was trained on topic detection using party manifestos, which are more similar to diplomatic texts than the diverse texts RoBERTa-argument was trained on.

Examining the 3-class setup (labels NegE, CC, or No Conflict), RoBERTa-relations again yields the best scores, outperforming RoBERTa-argument fine-tuned on the old dataset. We think that the good performance of RoBERTa-relations is due to the fact that it was trained on fine-grained Argument Relations classification and on political debates. The classification results thus suggest that domain-specific training — even when not on diplomatic texts but more broadly on political domains — enhance performance on Conflict classification tasks.

	UNSCon extended			orig. UNSCon
	RoBERTa^{argument}	RoBERTa$^{policy}_{topics}$	RoBERTa$^{argument}_{relations}$	RoBERTa^{argument}
	2-class setup (Conflict / No Conflict, without FigL)			
precision	0.72	0.72	0.73	**0.78**
recall	0.68	0.68	0.69	**0.78**
f1-macro	0.70	0.69	0.70	**0.74**
accuracy	0.78	0.79	**0.79**	0.78
	3-class setup (NegE / CC / No Conflict)			
precision (macro avg)	0.45	0.45	0.64	**0.72**
recall (macro avg)	0.45	0.45	0.48	**0.76**
f1-macro	0.45	0.45	**0.51**	0.48
accuracy	0.77	0.78	**0.78**	0.76
	4-class setup (FigL / NegE / CC / No Conflict)			
precision (macro avg)	0.34	0.58	**0.62**	N/A
recall (macro avg)	0.34	0.33	**0.42**	N/A
f1-macro	0.33	0.34	**0.47**	N/A
accuracy	0.77	0.76	**0.77**	N/A

Table 2: Classification results of the (1) 2-class setup: comparing the reported performance of the best model from Zaczynska et al. (2024) on the original UNSCon, and different RoBERTa-based models fine-tuned on the extended corpus, excluding FigL for comparability; (2) 3-class setup: comparing results reported on the original UNSCon fine-tuned on RoBERTa-argument with fine-tuned models on the new corpus, again excluding FIGL label; and (3) 4-class setup: comparing fine-tuned models on the new corpus including FIGL label.

7 Conclusion

This paper presents an extended version of the UNSC Conflicts Corpus as introduced by Zaczynska et al. (2024), by expanding both the annotation guidelines and corpus size, and incorporating more detailed annotations of lexical markers of Conflicts using an LLM. Working with diplomatic texts, and being annotated by computational linguists, we provide a detailed evaluation of political scientist annotations on the corpus and discuss identified disagreements. Annotating communicative phenomena in language within NLP, especially in a domain with its own culture and rules such as the diplomatic setting, presents a balancing act regarding annotation guidelines. One must choose between creating guidelines that target diplomatic language usage only interpretable by people with advanced political science backgrounds, and linguistically marked verbalisations that are relatively domain-independent and possible to pick up on by NLP classifiers. We refined the annotation scheme and kept both the original notion of a mandatory lexical verbalisation of Conflict, and also included Conflict labels that might need cultural knowledge to detect, like figurative language.

Our classification experiments on Conflict types using Transformer models show that integrating a model trained on a similar task and domain improves the performance. Despite this, the results indicate that smaller Conflict types like CHALLENGE CORRECTION (CC) (which involves detecting when someone claims another speaker is lying, and the correction of this alleged lie), and FIGURATIVE LANGUAGE (FIGL) (which includes sarcasm and rhetorical questions) require more data to achieve satisfactory outcomes. Looking at the classification results for each Conflict label, we observe that all models struggled to accurately classify less frequent classes. In addition to the small number of training samples, this also may be attributed to the inherent difficulty of the task. Detecting FIGURATIVE LANGUAGE, for instance, remains a challenge in NLP (Liu et al., 2022). However, training on dedicated task-specific datasets might enhance performance (Sanchez-Bayona and Agerri, 2024). For future work we will conduct a further qualitative analysis of the lexical markers and types extracted by the LLM and will expand the experiments to the full dataset. Additionally, we plan to broaden the current limited list of emotive and instructive words by Gruenberg (2009) into a larger taxonomy, using the list of lexical markers found in the experiments by the LLM, including terms expressing negative assessments found in the speeches.

Limitations

The study relies on annotations from a single political scientist, and gold annotations for the new UNSCon dataset was also done by one annotator, which may introduce bias into the analysis of annotation disagreements. Regarding our observations on cultural differences in expressing Conflicts, we must note that some speeches are originally given in other languages and then translated into English by UN personnel. Although the UNSC employs institutional mechanisms to ensure high-quality translations (such as monitoring programs, terminology, and proofreading),[12] these translations might introduce some bias or alter meanings or tone, potentially affecting the annotation of Conflicts. This issue may be particularly relevant for fine-grained annotations of sarcasm. Replicating the study in a language other than English might yield different Conflict annotations.

Acknowledgments

The paper was supported by the Deutsche Forschungsgemeinschaft (DFG), project "Trajectories of Conflict: The Dynamics of Argumentation in the UN Security Council" (448421482) and the German Academic Exchange Service (Deutscher Akademischer Austauschdienst) by a research grant for doctoral students. We thank our annotators Dr. Antonio Pires and Dietmar Benndorf for their work and their valuable feedback on the annotation guidelines. We thank Costanza Rasi for helping with the automatic EDU segmentation. We thank Prof. Manfred Stede and Dr. Peter Bourgonje on their helpful feedback on the paper.

References

Mariia Anisimova and Šárka Zikánová. 2024. Attitudes in diplomatic speeches: Introducing the CoDipA UNSC 1.0. In *Proceedings of the 20th Joint ACL - ISO Workshop on Interoperable Semantic Annotation @ LREC-COLING 2024*, pages 17–26, Torino, Italia. ELRA and ICCL.

Parker Bach, Carolyn E Schmitt, and Shannon C McGregor. 2025. Let me be perfectly unclear: strategic ambiguity in political communication. *Communication Theory*, page qtaf001.

James Brassett, Browning , Christopher, , and Muireann O'Dwyer. 2021. EU've got to be kidding: Anxiety, humour and ontological security. 35(1):8–26.

[12]https://www.rferl.org/a/UN_Interpreters_Make_Sure_Nothing_Is_Lost_In_Translation/1995801.html

Dmitry Chernobrov. 2023. Strategic humor and post-truth public diplomacy. Discussion paper, ARRAY(0x56430ed8ae38). © 2023.

Bernard Comrie and Jerrold Sadock. 1974. Toward a linguistic theory of speech acts. *Philosophical Quarterly*, 26(104):285.

Martina Ducret, Lauren Kruse, Carlos Martinez, Anna Feldman, and Jing Peng. 2020. You don't say... linguistic features in sarcasm detection. In Felice Dell'Orletta, Johanna Monti, and Fabio Tamburini, editors, *Proceedings of the Seventh Italian Conference on Computational Linguistics CLiC-it 2020 : Bologna, Italy, March 1-3, 2021*, Collana dell'Associazione Italiana di Linguistica Computazionale, pages 171–177. Accademia University Press. Code: Proceedings of the Seventh Italian Conference on Computational Linguistics CLiC-it 2020 : Bologna, Italy, March 1-3, 2021.

Steffen Eckhard, Ronny Patz, Mirco Schönfeld, and Hilde van Meegdenburg. 2021. International bureaucrats in the un security council debates: A speaker-topic network analysis. *Journal of European Public Policy*, 30(2):214–233.

Raji Ghawi and Jürgen Pfeffer. 2022. Analysis of country mentions in the debates of the UN Security Council. In *Information Integration and Web Intelligence*, pages 110–115, Cham. Springer Nature Switzerland.

Luis Glaser, Ronny Patz, and Manfred Stede. 2022. UNSC-NE: A named entity extension to the UN Security Council debates corpus. *Journal for Language Technology and Computational Linguistics*, 35(2):51–67.

Justin Gruenberg. 2009. An analysis of united nations security council resolutions: Are all countries treated equally? *Case Western Reserve Journal of International Law*, 41(2):513.

Annette Hautli-Janisz, Zlata Kikteva, Wassiliki Siskou, Kamila Gorska, Ray Becker, and Chris Reed. 2022. QT30: A corpus of argument and conflict in broadcast debate. In *Proceedings of the Thirteenth Language Resources and Evaluation Conference*, pages 3291–3300, Marseille, France. European Language Resources Association.

Matthew Honnibal, Ines Montani, Sofie Van Landeghem, and Adriane Boyd. 2020. spaCy: Industrial-strength Natural Language Processing in Python.

Aditya Joshi, Pushpak Bhattacharyya, and Mark J. Carman. 2017. Automatic sarcasm detection: A survey. *ACM Comput. Surv.*, 50(5).

Morteza Kamaladdini Ezzabady, Philippe Muller, and Chloé Braud. 2021. Multi-lingual discourse segmentation and connective identification: MELODI at disrpt2021. In *Proceedings of the 2nd Shared Task on Discourse Relation Parsing and Treebanking (DISRPT 2021)*, pages 22–32, Punta Cana, Dominican Republic. Association for Computational Linguistics.

Klaus Krippendorff. 2004. Measuring the reliability of qualitative text analysis data. 38(6):787–800.

Emmy Liu, Chenxuan Cui, Kenneth Zheng, and Graham Neubig. 2022. Testing the ability of language models to interpret figurative language. In *Proceedings of the 2022 Conference of the North American Chapter of the Association for Computational Linguistics: Human Language Technologies*, pages 4437–4452, Seattle, United States. Association for Computational Linguistics.

William C. Mann and Sandra A. Thompson. 1988. Rhetorical structure theory: Toward a functional theory of text organization. *Text - Interdisciplinary Journal for the Study of Discourse*, 8(3):243–281.

J. R. Martin and P. R. R. White. 2005. *The Language of Evaluation*. Palgrave Macmillan UK.

Antonio Jesús Moreno-Ortiz and María García-Gámez. 2022. Corpus annotation and analysis of sarcasm in twitter: #CatsMovie vs. #TheRiseOfSkywalker. *Atlantis. Journal of the Spanish Association for Anglo-American Studies*, pages 186–207.

OpenAI. 2024. Gpt-4 technical report. *Preprint*, arXiv:2303.08774.

Ines Reinig, Ines Rehbein, and Simone Paolo Ponzetto. 2024. How to do politics with words: Investigating speech acts in parliamentary debates. In *Proceedings of the 2024 Joint International Conference on Computational Linguistics, Language Resources and Evaluation (LREC-COLING 2024)*, pages 8287–8300, Torino, Italia. ELRA and ICCL.

Hannah Rohde. 2006. Rhetorical questions as redundant interrogatives. *UC San Diego: San Diego Linguistic Papers*.

Ramon Ruiz-Dolz, Jose Alemany, Stella M. Heras Barbera, and Ana Garcia-Fornes. 2021. Transformer-based models for automatic identification of argument relations: A cross-domain evaluation. *IEEE Intelligent Systems*, 36(6):62–70.

Elisa Sanchez-Bayona and Rodrigo Agerri. 2024. Meta4xnli: A crosslingual parallel corpus for metaphor detection and interpretation. *ArXiv*, abs/2404.07053.

Cesare M Scartozzi. 2022. Climate change in the UN Security Council: An analysis of discourses and organizational trends. *International Studies Perspectives*, 23(3):290–312.

Mirco Schoenfeld, Steffen Eckhard, Ronny Patz, Hilde van Meegdenburg, and Antonio Pires. 2019. The un security council debates 1992-2023. *Preprint*, arXiv:1906.10969.

Norman Scott. 2001. Ambiguity versus precision: The changing role of terminology in conference diplomacy - diplo resource. In *Langauge and Diplomacy*.

Stephen Skalicky and Scott Crossley. 2018. Linguistic features of sarcasm and metaphor production quality. In *Proceedings of the Workshop on Figurative Language Processing*, pages 7–16, New Orleans, Louisiana. Association for Computational Linguistics.

Nick Stanko. 2001. Use of language in diplomacy - diplo resource. In *Langauge and Diplomacy*.

Jacky Visser, Barbara Konat, Rory Duthie, Marcin Koszowy, Katarzyna Budzynska, and Chris Reed. 2020. Argumentation in the 2016 US presidential elections: annotated corpora of television debates and social media reaction. 54(1):123–154.

Karolina Zaczynska, Peter Bourgonje, and Manfred Stede. 2024. How diplomats dispute: The UN security council conflict corpus. In *Proceedings of the Joint International Conference on Computational Linguistics, Language Resources and Evaluation (LREC-COLING 2024)*.

Džemal Špago. 2020. Rhetorical questions as aggressive, friendly or sarcastic/ironical questions with imposed answers. *ExELL*, 8(1):68–82.

A Appendix Annotation Guidelines Extension

The following text is taken from the annotation guidelines and explains the annotations for Figurative Language. Figure 3 shows the annotation steps for Conflict types with the refined annotation guidelines.

Based on the results of our UNSC expert annotation experiments, we have expand the annotations guidelines by (Zaczynska et al., 2024) by including a new Conflict type, FIGURATIVE LANGUAGE (FIGL), which includes sarcastic statements (label: SARCASM) or rhetorical questions (label: RHETORICAL QUESTION) that serve to express a negative evaluation of another country. Sarcasm and rhetorical questions are figurative language, meaning they convey a message that is different from what is literally said (Skalicky and Crossley, 2018; Ducret et al., 2020).

Sarcasm. Sarcasm is defined as specific instances of verbal irony which serve to provide ironic criticism or praise that is somehow contrary to reality (Skalicky and Crossley, 2018). Sarcastic sentences are likely to be semantically or emotionally incongruent with their preceding sentences but also incongruent with the situation in which sarcasm is used. Detecting sarcasm might not be straightforward when only looking at the text. Thus, the annotators must also rely on understanding of the context beyond the statement to discern between sarcasm and sincerity. Following Moreno-Ortiz and García-Gámez (2022); Joshi et al. (2017) we annotate sarcasm as negative in nature, and the message must contain some form of criticism and an implied negative sentiment for it to be classified as Conflict type SARCASM.

Rhetorical Questions. A rhetorical question is an utterance that has the structure of a question does not expect an answer (Rohde, 2006). It can be seen as a mechanism to express sarcasm (Moreno-Ortiz and García-Gámez, 2022). Rhetorical questions are often lexically and syntactically not easily distinguishable from other types of questions. However, there are some linguistic cues that make a question more obviously rhetorical: Does it include strong negative polarity items (*at all*, *any*, *ever*)? Can it be preceded by the expression after all and followed by a *yet*-clause (Špago, 2020; Comrie and Sadock, 1974)?

In summary, the annotators mark EDUs as FIGURATIVE LANGUAGE if the following applies: Does the EDU/sentence use irony that indicates a negative evaluation or critique toward a country? This can be signified by: 1) SARCASM, meaning that the text expresses an evaluation whose literal polarity is the opposite of the intended polarity, or 2) RHETORICAL QUESTION, which is asked not primarily to elicit information, but to make a (negative) statement.

B Prompt Used for Lexical Marker Extraction

The following shows the prompt we used to extract the lexical markers and the categories per EDU from or corpus.

System / Instruction to the Model
You are an expert language processing system. Please analyse the text below for verbal conflicts or critique.

—

Task

Given the following text:
{{TEXT_EDU}}
Perform **three** steps:

1. **Check for Presence of Lexical Markers**
Determine whether the text contains any words/phrases that indicate negative evaluations, which we define as critique or distancing from another entity (person, country, group, etc.). Specifically, look for any of the following:

   - "Adjectival_Attribution": Adjectival attributions (e.g., *bad*, *dreadful*, *worrying*)
   - "Noun": Nouns with a negative connotation (e.g., *traitor*, *annexation*)
   - "Adverb": Adverbs that intensify criticism (e.g., *poorly*, *even*, *only*)
   - "Verb": Verbs with a negative connotation (e.g., *infiltrating*, *invading*)
   - "Negation_Phrase_or_Quantifier": Negation phrases and quantifiers (e.g., *not at all*, *not a single*)
   - "Evaluative_Pattern": Recognisable evaluative patterns (e.g., *It is unfortunate that...*, *There is something worrying about...*)
   - "Instructive_Words": Strong instructive words (e.g., *urge*, *must*, *warn*, *demand*)
   - "Emotive_Words": Strong emotive words (e.g., *condemned*, *armed*, *shocked*)

   Response: Indicate **Yes** or **No** (e.g., 'Present?: Yes' / 'Present?: No').

2. **Extract Lexical Marker Categories**
If you found negative markers, list which categories these markers belong to (e.g., "Adjectival_Attribution"," "Negative_Noun", "Negation_Phrase_or_Quantifier", etc.).
*Response**: Provide the categories as a comma-separated list, choosing from the following categories: 'Adjectival_Attribution', 'Noun', 'Adverb', 'Verb', 'Negation_Phrase_or_Quantifier', 'Evaluative_Pattern', 'Instructive_Words', 'Emotive_Words' or write 'None' if no markers are found.

3. **List the Lexical Markers**
List the actual words or phrases that caused you to identify negative evaluations. **Response**: Provide a comma-separated list of markers (e.g., 'bad, dreadful, invaded'), or write 'None' if no markers are found.

—

Output Format

- Present?: [Yes or No] - Lexical Marker Categories: [comma-separated categories or 'None'] - Lexical Markers: [comma-separated words/phrases or 'None']

C Most Frequent Lexical Marker of Negative Evaluation

LM Category	10 most frequent words
Noun	crisis (45), violence (33), terrorists (31), war (30), threat (26), conflict (21), terrorism (20), weapon (18), armed (18), crime (17)
Instructive Words	must (100), urge (17), call (10), should (8), demand (6), reject (3), halt (2), strongly (2), condemn (2), immediate (2)
Adjectival Attribution	illegal (19), serious (17), difficult (10), unacceptable (10), illegally (7), arm (6), dangerous (6), critical (6), criminal (6), deeply (5)
Negation Phrase or Quantifier	not (99), no (59), can (23), without (22), do (19), nothing (14), never (8), despite (6), non (3), nor (3)
Verb	destabilize (19), condemn (17), attack (15), undermine (14), threaten (13), kill (13), seize (12), shoot (12), destroy (10), fail (9)

Table 3: Most frequent Lexical Markers (LM) found per category, lemmatised using SpaCy library (model *en_web_core_sm*).

D Flowchart Conflict Annotations

E Visualisation Streams of Conflicts between Source and Target Comparing both Corpus Versions

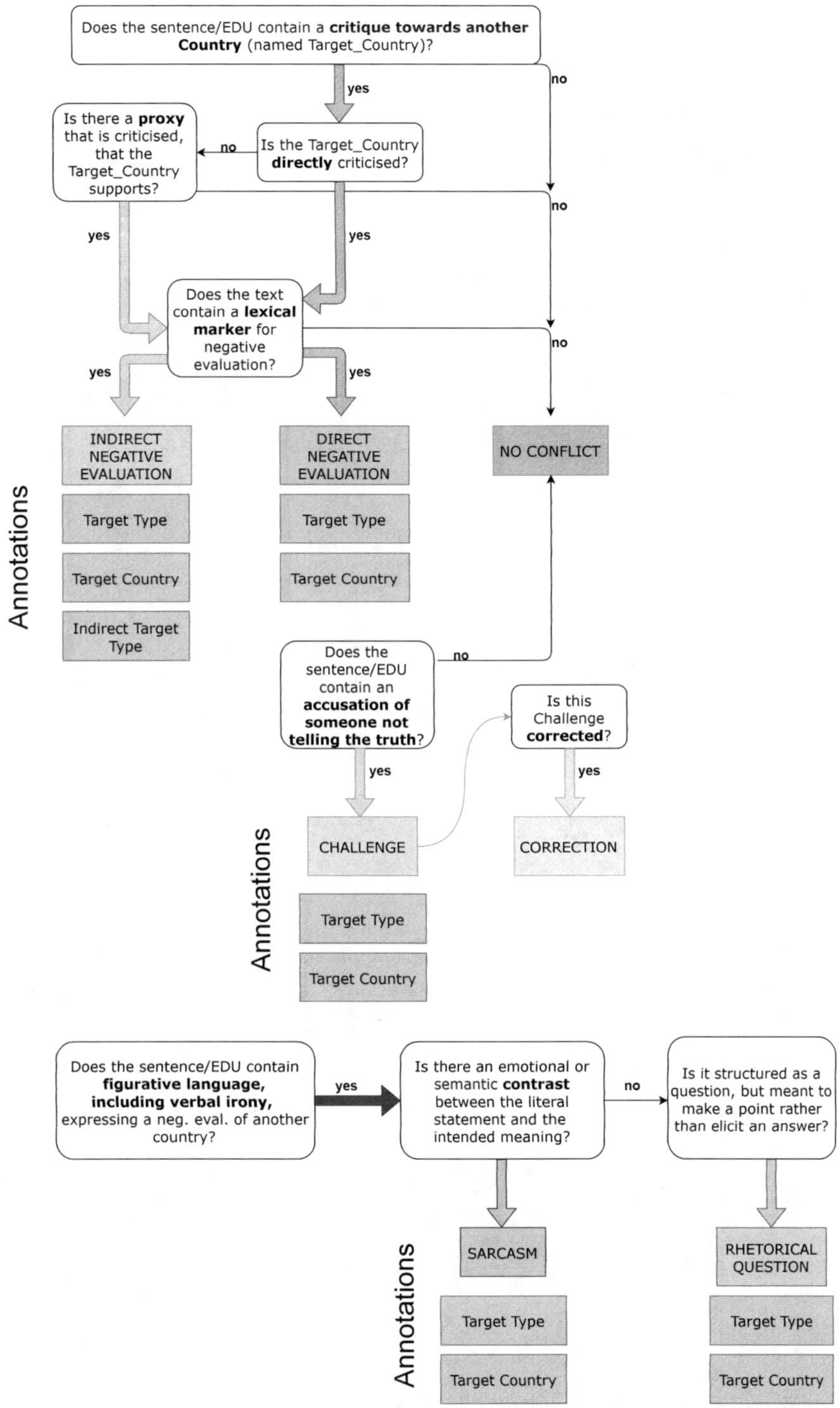

Figure 3: Annotation Steps of Conflict Type and Target Annotations Visualised in a Flowchart.

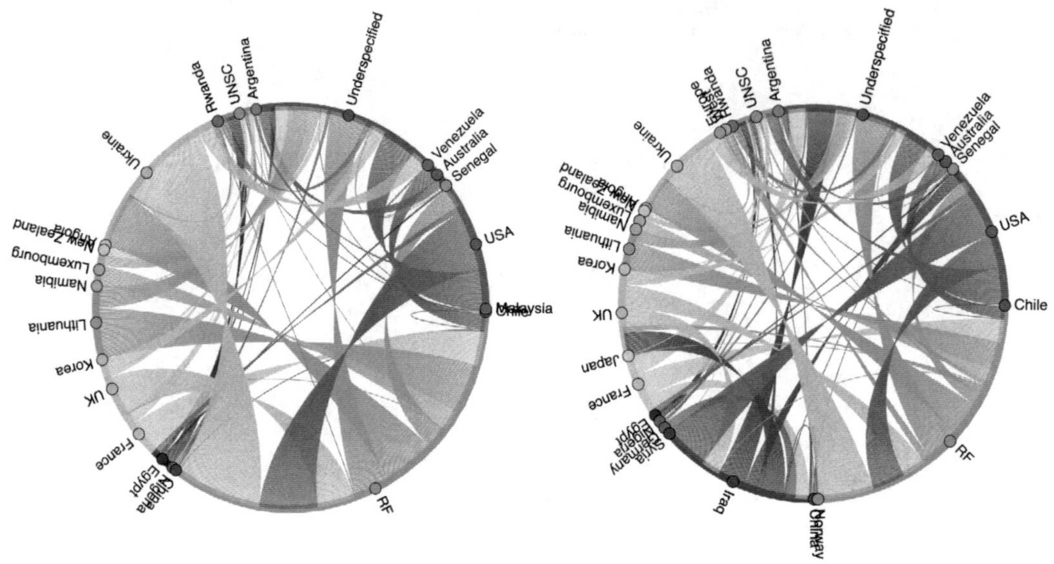

Figure 4: Visualisations of the source and target of Conflicts from the original UNSCon (left) and the extended UNSCon (right circle). An HTML version of the figure is available in our GitHub repository. RF stands for the Russian Federation, UK for the United Kingdom of Great Britain and Northern Ireland, and USA for the United States of America.

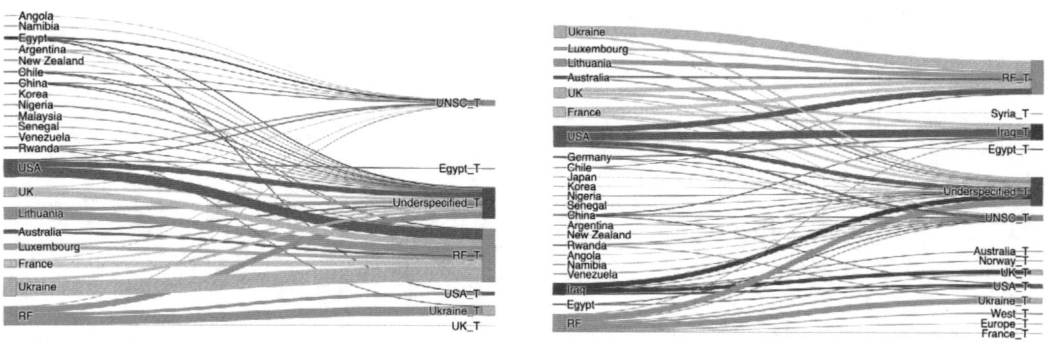

Figure 5: Sankey graphs of the source and target of Conflicts from the original UNSCon (left) and the extended UNSCon (right sankey). The source is on the left side, the target (marked by _T) is on the right side.

Guidelines for Fine-grained Sentence-level Arabic Readability Annotation

Nizar Habash,[†] Hanada Taha-Thomure,[‡] Khalid N. Elmadani,[†]
Zeina Zeino,[‡] Abdallah Abushmaes[††]

[†]Computational Approaches to Modeling Language Lab, New York University Abu Dhabi
[‡]Zai Arabic Language Research Centre, Zayed University
[††]Abu Dhabi Arabic Language Centre
`nizar.habash@nyu.edu, Hanada.Thomure@zu.ac.ae`

Abstract

This paper presents the annotation guidelines of the Balanced Arabic Readability Evaluation Corpus (**BAREC**), a large-scale resource for fine-grained sentence-level readability assessment in Arabic. **BAREC** includes 69,441 sentences (1M+ words) labeled across 19 levels, from kindergarten to postgraduate. Based on the Taha/Arabi21 framework, the guidelines were refined through iterative training with native Arabic-speaking educators. We highlight key linguistic, pedagogical, and cognitive factors in determining readability and report high inter-annotator agreement: Quadratic Weighted Kappa 81.8% (substantial/excellent agreement) in the last annotation phase. We also benchmark automatic readability models across multiple classification granularities (19-, 7-, 5-, and 3-level). The corpus and guidelines are publicly available.[1]

1 Introduction

Text readability plays a crucial role in comprehension, retention, reading speed, and engagement (DuBay, 2004). When texts exceed a reader's ability, they can lead to frustration and disengagement (Klare, 1963). Readability is shaped by both the content and presentation (Nassiri et al., 2023). In educational settings, readability leveling is widely used to align texts with students' reading abilities, promoting independent and more effective learning (Allington et al., 2015; Barber and Klauda, 2020).

Fine-grained readability systems, like Fountas and Pinnell's 27-level scale in English (Fountas and Pinnell, 2006), and Taha's 19-level Arabic system (Taha-Thomure, 2017), guide progression from early readers to adult fluency. These levels support instructional goals and can be mapped to broader categories for practical use in NLP.

We present the Balanced Arabic Readability Evaluation Corpus (**BAREC**), a large-scale dataset of 69K+ sentences[2] (1M+ words) across a broad space of genres and 19 readability levels. Based on the Taha/Arabi21 framework (Taha-Thomure, 2017), which has been instrumental in tagging over 9,000 children's books, **BAREC** guidelines enable standardized, sentence-level readability evaluation across diverse genres and educational levels, ranging from kindergarten to postgraduate comprehension (see Table 1). Our contributions are as follows:

RL	Grade	Example
1	KG	Ball كُرَة
3	1st	The bedroom غُرْفَةُ النَومِ
6	2nd	سُلوكي مَسْؤولِيَتْي My behavior is my responsibility
10	4th	كانت الحديقة واسعة، تطل على شاطئ النيل، The garden was spacious, overlooking the Nile.
14	8th	تعريف أصول الفقه Definition of Islamic Jurisprudence Principles
17	Uni	بين طعن القَنا وخَفْق البُنودِ Between lance thrusts and ensign flutters

Table 1: Examples by Reading Level (RL) and grade.

- We **define detailed annotation guidelines** for Arabic sentence-level readability across a fine-grained 19-level scale.
- We **apply and refine these guidelines** through annotation of a diverse, large-scale corpus, analyzing annotator agreement and sources of difficulty in this nuanced task.
- We **build and evaluate readability models** across multiple granularities (19, 7, 5, and 3 levels) to provide baseline results for various research and application needs.

Next, §2 reviews related work, §3 outlines the annotation framework, §4 covers data selection, and §5 discusses evaluation results.

[1]`http://barec.camel-lab.com`

[2]We use *sentence* to refer to syntactic sentences as well as shorter standalone text segments (e.g., phrases or titles).

Proceedings of the 19th Linguistic Annotation Workshop (LAW-XIX-2025), pages 359–376
July 31, 2025

Authors	Project	Metric	Levels	Unit	Size	Content
Al-Khalifa and Al-Ajlan (2010)	Arability	Readability	3	Document	150	School Textbooks
Forsyth (2014)	DLI Corpus	ILR	5 (3)	Document	179	L2 Learner
Kilgarriff et al. (2014)	KELLY	CEFR	6	Word	9,000	Most Frequent
Taha-Thomure (2017)	Taha/Arabi21	Readability	19	Document	9,000	Children's Books
Al Khalil et al. (2020)	SAMER Lexicon	Readability	5	Word	40,000	General Vocab
Habash and Palfreyman (2022)	ZAEBUC	CEFR	6	Document	214	Prompted Essays
Naous et al. (2024)	ReadMe++	CEFR	6	Sentence	1,945	Multi-domain
Soliman and Familiar (2024)	Arabic Vocab Profile	CEFR	2	Word	1,200	L2 Learner (A1, A2)
El-Haj et al. (2024)	DARES	Grade Level	12	Sentence	13,335	School Textbooks
Alhafni et al. (2024)	SAMER Corpus	Readability	3	Word	159,265	Literature
Bashendy et al. (2024)	QAES	AES	7×5	Document	195	Argumentative Essays
Our Work	BAREC	Readability	19 (7–5–3)	Sentence	69,441	Multi-domain

Table 2: Overview of Arabic readability and proficiency-related corpora.

2 Related Work

Automatic Readability Assessment Automatic readability assessment has been widely studied, resulting in numerous datasets and resources (Collins-Thompson and Callan, 2004; Pitler and Nenkova, 2008; Feng et al., 2010; Vajjala and Meurers, 2012; Xu et al., 2015; Xia et al., 2016; Nadeem and Ostendorf, 2018; Vajjala and Lučić, 2018; Deutsch et al., 2020; Lee et al., 2021). Early English datasets were often derived from textbooks, as their graded content naturally aligns with readability assessment (Vajjala, 2022). However, copyright restrictions and limited digitization have driven researchers to crowdsource readability annotations from online sources (Vajjala and Meurers, 2012; Vajjala and Lučić, 2018) or leverage CEFR-based L2 assessment exams (Xia et al., 2016).

Arabic Readability Efforts Arabic readability research has explored text leveling and assessment in multiple frameworks (Nassiri et al., 2023).

Taha-Thomure (2017) proposed a 19-level Arabic text leveling framework for educators, inspired by Fountas and Pinnell (2006) and focused on children's literature. Targeting full texts (books), particularly for early education, with 11 of the 19 levels covering up to 4th grade, the system supports teachers in matching books to students' reading abilities. Taha-Thomure (2017)'s procedural framework outlines ten qualitative and quantitative criteria: text genre, abstractness of ideas, vocabulary and its proximity to dialects, text authenticity, book production quality, content suitability, sentence structure, illustrations, use of diacritics, and word count. The Arab Thought Foundation adopted this framework under its Arabi21 initiative, which funded the leveling of over 9,000 children's books.

Other efforts applied CEFR leveling to Arabic, including the KELLY project's frequency-based word lists, manually annotated corpora such as ZAEBUC (Habash and Palfreyman, 2022) and ReadMe++ (Naous et al., 2024), and vocabulary profiling (Soliman and Familiar, 2024). El-Haj et al. (2024) introduced DARES, a readability assessment dataset collected from Saudi school materials. The SAMER project (Al Khalil et al., 2020) developed a lexicon with a five-level readability scale, leading to the first manually annotated Arabic parallel corpus for text simplification (Alhafni et al., 2024). Bashendy et al. (2024) presented a corpus of Arabic essays annotated across organization and style traits.

Automated readability assessment in Arabic has evolved from rule-based models using surface features (Al-Dawsari, 2004; Al-Khalifa and Al-Ajlan, 2010) to machine learning approaches with POS, morphology (Forsyth, 2014; Saddiki et al., 2018), and script features like OSMAN (El-Haj and Rayson, 2016). Recent work (Liberato et al., 2024) shows strong results with pretrained models on the SAMER corpus.

Our Approach Building on prior work, we curated the BAREC corpus across diverse genres and readability levels, manually annotating it at the sentence level using adapted Taha/Arabi21 guidelines (Taha-Thomure, 2017). Sentence-level annotation balances the coarse granularity of document-level labels and the limited context of word-level labels. This allows finer control and more objective assessment of textual variation. Table 2 compares BAREC with earlier efforts. To our knowledge, BAREC is the largest and most fine-grained manually annotated Arabic readability resource.

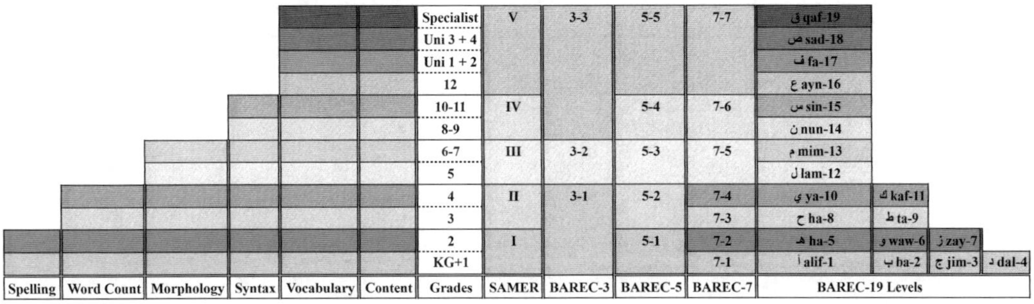

Figure 1: The **BAREC** *Pyramid* illustrates the relationship across **BAREC** levels and linguistic dimensions, three collapsed variants (3 levels, 5 levels and 7 levels), and educational grades.

3 BAREC Annotation Guidelines

3.1 Annotation Desiderata

Our guidelines and annotation decisions follow several key principles. **Comprehensive Coverage** ensures representation across all 19 levels, from kindergarten to postgraduate, with finer distinctions at early stages. **Objective Standardization** defines levels using consistent linguistic and content-based criteria, avoiding overreliance on surface features like word or sentence length. **Bias Mitigation** promotes inclusivity across Arab world regions and cultural content. **Balanced Coverage** supports diversity in levels, genres, and topics, especially addressing material scarcity in areas like children's literature. **Quality Control** is maintained through trained annotators and regular checks for inter-annotator agreement and consistency. Finally, **Ethical Considerations** include respecting copyrights and fairly compensating annotators.

3.2 Readability Levels

BAREC readability annotation assigns one of 19 levels to each sentence in the corpus. We retain Taha-Thomure (2017)'s 19-level naming system based on the Abjad order: **1-alif**, **2-ba**, **3-jim**, ... **19-qaf**, but extend and adjust the original guidelines, which were designed for book-level annotation to this task. The **BAREC** pyramid (Figure 1) illustrates the scaffolding of these levels and their mapping to guidelines components, school grades, and three collapsed versions of level size 7, 5, and 3. All four level types (19-7-5-3) are fully aligned to allow easy mapping from fine-grained to coarse-grained levels, but manual annotation only happened on 19 levels. For example, level **11-kaf** maps to level **4** (of 7), level **2** (of 5) and level **1** (of 3). See Table 3 for representative examples.

3.3 Readability Annotation Principles

Reading and Comprehension Readability reflects how easily independent readers can both read and comprehend a text without teacher or parent support. We focus on basic pronunciation (recovering lexical diacritics) and literal understanding, not on grammatical analysis or deep interpretation.

Sentence-level Focus We assess readability at the sentence level, independent of broader context, source, or author intent. This deliberate choice avoids genre-based assumptions and enables fair, objective comparison across diverse texts. Mapping sentence-level judgments to larger units is left for future work.

Target Audience While religious content is part of basic public education in the Arab world, we make no assumptions about readers' religious backgrounds or prior knowledge. Readability is judged purely on linguistic and cognitive grounds. Our guidelines reflect Modern Standard Arabic (MSA) as used in Egypt, the Gulf, and the Levant, leaving variations in other regions for future work.

Readability Level Keys Annotators start from the lowest (easiest) level and raise it based on key features: lexical, morphological, syntactic, or semantic. See Sections 3.4 and 3.5 below for details.

A Note on Arabic Diacritics While diacritics can aid comprehension, we assess readability without relying on them. This departs from Taha-Thomure (2017), who consider diacritics a key design feature in children's books. In ambiguous cases, we choose the simpler meaning, e.g., هذه سلطة بدون خيار *hðh slTˉhbdwn xyAr*[3] is read as 'a salad without cucumbers' not 'an authority without choices'.

[3]HSB transliteration (Habash et al., 2007).

RL	Arabic Sentence/Phrase	Translation	Reasoning
1-alif	أَرْنَب	**Rabbit**	*One bisyllabic familiar noun*
2-ba	ملعبٌ واسعٌ	**A large playground**	*Noun-adjective*
3-jim	أنا أحب الـ لون الأحمر.	I love **the** color red.	*Definite article*
4-dal	الشمس تشرق في الصباح الباكر.	The sun rises early **in the morning**.	*Prepositional phrase*
5-ha-	القطة تستريح على السرير وتستمتع بأشعة الشمس الدافئة.	The cat rests on the bed **and enjoys the warm sunshine**.	*A conjoined sentence*
6-waw	سُلوكي مَسْؤوليَّتي	My behavior is **my responsibility**	*Five syllable word*
7-zay	الأصدقاء يحتفلون بعيد ميلاد صديقهم بكعكة وهدايا رائعة.	**Friends** celebrate their friend's birthday with cake and amazing gifts.	*Broken plural*
8-ha	أَسْتَمِعُ إلى كُلّ فِقْرةٍ مِنَ الفِقْرَتَيْنِ الآتِيَتَيْنِ، ثُمَّ أُجيبُ:	I listen to each of the following two paragraphs, **then** I answer:	*ثُمَّ (then) is in level 8-ha ح*
9-ta	وقال بكلام فصيح مزعج: يا سمك يا سمك هل أنت على العهد القديم مقيم	He said in annoying, eloquent words: **Oh fish, oh fish**, do you abide by the old promise	*Vocative construction*
10-ya	وَسَأَلْتُكَ هَلْ كُنْتُمْ تَتَّهِمُونَهُ بِالْكَذِبِ قَبْلَ أَنْ يَقُولَ مَا قَالَ فَذَكَرْتَ أَنْ لاَ،	I asked you whether **you were** accusing him of lying before he said what he said, and you said no.	*Auxiliary Kaana*
11-kaf	حسام سعيدٌ قلبُه بسبب فوز فريقه.	Hossam, his **heart is happy** because of his team's victory.	*Acting derivative (happy is predicative)*
12-lam	لا أحد يجمع هذه الزهور معًا في باقة، فهي منتشرة جدًا — حتى إنه كان من المعروف عنها أنها تنمو بين أحجار الرصف، وتنبثق في كل مكان مثل الحشائش الضارة — وتحمل اسمًا قبيحًا جدًا وهو «زهور الكلاب» أو «الهندباء البرية».	No one puts these flowers together in a bouquet, they are so common—**they have even been known to grow between paving stones, and spring up everywhere like weeds**—and they have the very unsightly name of "dog-flowers" ɒ"dandelions."	*Parenthetical phrase*
13-mim	ومن يفعل المعروف مع غير أهله يجازَ كما جوزي مجير أم عامر	**And whoever offers good deeds to someone undeserving will be rewarded like he who gave shelter to a hyena**	*Conditional phrase*
14-nun	حيث إن هذه الزيادة في الجسيمات المشحونة تشير إلى خروج المركبة من نطاق تأثير الرياح الشمسية الذي يسمى الغلاف الشمسي (والذي يعتبر حسب بعض التعاريف حدود المجموعة الشمسية).	This increase in **charged particles** indicates the spacecraft's departure from the influence of the **solar wind**, which is called **the heliosphere** (which, according to some definitions, is the border of the **solar system**).	*General geography vocabulary*
15-sin	وكان من عادتها أن تقارن بينها وبين بطلة الرواية إذا أحسَّت منه إعجابًا بها أو ثناءً عليها، وتسأله في ذلك أسئلةً ذكيةً خبيثةًلا تسهل المغالطة في جوابها، إلا على سبيل المزاح والمداعبة.	It was her habit to compare herself with the heroine of the novel when she felt his admiration or praise for her, asking him smart and tricky questions **that did not allow answering deceptively**, except by joking and teasing.	*Specialized vocabulary that requires understanding the concept to comprehend its use*
16-ayn	ويذهب المؤرخون إلى أن النابغة الذبياني كان من المُحَكّمين، تقام له في هذه الأسواق قبة يذهب إليها الشعراء ليعرضوا شعرهم، فمن أشاد به ذاع صيته، وتناقلت شعره الركبان.	Historians assert that **Al-Nabigha Al-Dhubyani** was one of the **arbiters**. In these markets, a dome is erected for him where poets go to present their poetry. Whomever he praised, **his fame spread**, and his poetry circulated among the **caravans**.	*Specialized and uncommon vocabulary*
17-fa	بين طعن القَنا وخَفْق البُنود	Between the thrusts of **lances** and the fluttering of **ensigns**	*Heritage vocabulary familiar to a novice specialist*
18-sad	إلاّ الأواريَّ لأيًا ما أُبَيّنُهَا والنُّؤيُ كالحَوْضِ بالمَظلومَةِ الجَلَدِ	**I wasn't able to see except with extreme effort and difficulty like a water basin in solid undrillable land**	*Specialist vocabulary, symbolic poetic ideas requiring prior knowledge*
19-qaf	كأن حدوج المالكية غدوةً خلايا سفينٍ بالنواصف من دد	As if **the camel saddles of the Malikiyya caravan leaving the Dadi valley were great ships**	*Advanced specialist vocabulary, symbolic poetic ideas requiring prior knowledge*

Table 3: Representative subset of examples of the 19 **BAREC** readability levels, with English translations, and readability level reasoning. Underlining is used to highlight the main keys that determined the level.

3.4 Dimensions of Textual Features

To determine the **BAREC** level, we define six textual dimensions that identify *key* features necessary to unlock each level:

1. Number of Words Counts unique printed words (ignoring punctuation and diacritics). Used only up to level **11-kaf** (max 20 words).

2. Orthography & Phonology Focuses on word length (syllables) and letters like Hamzas. Final diacritics are ignored (words read in *waqf*), e.g., أَرْنَبٌ *Âar.nabũ* 'rabbit' has 2 syllables: *ar-nab*.

3. Morphology Covers derivation and inflection (tense, voice, number, etc.). Simpler forms appear at lower levels (e.g., present tense before past, singular before plural). Used up to level **13-mim**.

4. Syntactic Structures Tracks sentence complexity, from single words (**1-alif**) to complex constructions. Used up to level **15-sin**.

5. Vocabulary Central at all levels. Overlapping dialect and MSA vocabulary appear at easier levels; technical terms are introduced at harder levels. Arabized foreign words are treated as part of the language, while non-Arabic script is excluded.

6. Ideas & Content Evaluates needed prior knowledge, symbolic unpacking, and conceptual linking. Levels progress from familiar to specialized knowledge and from literal to abstract ideas. We recognize that such evaluations are complex and may vary subjectively among readers within the same age or education group.

Problems and Difficulties Annotators are instructed to report issues such as spelling errors, colloquial language, or sensitive topics. Difficulty is noted when annotations cannot be made due to conflicting guidelines.

The BAREC pyramid (Figure 1) illustrates which aspects are used (broadly) for which levels. For example, spelling criteria are only used up to level **7-zay**, while syntax is used until level **15-sin**, and word count is not used beyond level **11-kaf**. A full set of examples with explanations of leveling choices is in Table 3. The ***Annotation Cheat Sheet*** used by the annotators in Arabic and its translation in English are included in Appendix A. The full guidelines are publicly available.[1] For more on Arabic linguistic features, see Habash (2010).

3.5 Annotation Process

Sentence Segmentation Since our starting point is a text excerpt, typically a paragraph or two (∼500±200 words) from each source, we begin with sentence-level segmentation and initial text flagging. We followed the Arabic sentence segmentation guidelines by Habash et al. (2022).

Sentence Readability Annotation Each annotator is presented with a batch of 100 randomly selected sentences to annotate. The annotation was done through a simple Google Sheet interface (see Appendix A.3), which provides details such as sentence word count, and the guidelines constraints for the selected level to provide feedback confirmation to the annotator. The annotators are instructed to follow this procedure: **First** they read the sentence and make sure it has no flaws that can lead to excluding it. **Second**, they think about the meaning of the sentence noting any ambiguities due to diacritic absence or limited context, and consciously decide on the simpler reading in case of multiple readings. **Third**, they make an initial assessment of the lowest possible level based on word count. **Fourth**, they look for specific phenomena that allow increasing the level to the highest possible. For example, the sixth sentence in Table 3, سلوكي مسؤوليتي *slwky msŵwlyty* 'my behavior is my responsibility' has two words, which automatically sets it as level **2-ba** or higher. The presence of the first person pronominal clitic ي+ *+y* elevates the level to **3-jim**; however, the fact that the second word has five syllables raises the level further to **6-waw**. No other keys can take it higher.

Annotation averaged 2.5 hours per 100-sentence batch (1.5 minutes per sentence), reflecting the careful and rigorous approach taken by annotators to ensure high-quality, consistent labeling across a diverse and challenging dataset.

3.6 Annotation Team

The BAREC annotation team included six native Arabic-speaking educators (A0-A5), most with advanced degrees in Arabic Literature or Linguistics. A0 had prior experience in computational linguistics annotation, while A1-A5 brought extensive expertise in readability assessment from the Taha/Arabi21 project. A0 handled sentence segmentation and initial text selection; and A5 led the annotation team in assigning readability labels. Annotator profiles, covering demographic, educational, linguistic, and teaching backgrounds, are listed in Appendix A.4.

3.7 Training and Quality Control

Annotators A1-A5 received thorough training, including three shared pilot rounds that enabled in-depth discussion and refinement of the guidelines.

To ensure consistency, the initial 10,658 sentences (Phase 1) were double-reviewed before annotating the full 69K (1M+ words). Inter-annotator agreement (IAA) was assessed on 19 blind batches (excluding pilots 1 and 2), followed by group unification to support quality control and prevent drift. Only unified labels appear in the official release. The multiple IAA annotations will be released separately to support research on readability annotations.[1] Details on IAA are in Section 5.3).

In total, the annotators labeled 92.6K sentences; 25% were excluded from the final corpus: 3.3% were problematic (typos and offensive topics), 11.5% from early double annotations, and 10.3% from IAA rounds (excluding unification).

Category	Domain	Foundational	Advanced	Specialized	All
Documents	Arts & Humanities	562 (29%)	478 (25%)	327 (17%)	**1,367 (71%)**
	Social Sciences	44 (2%)	168 (9%)	163 (8%)	**375 (20%)**
	STEM	27 (1%)	85 (4%)	68 (4%)	**180 (9%)**
	All	**633 (33%)**	**731 (38%)**	**558 (29%)**	**1,922 (100%)**
Sentences	Arts & Humanities	24,978 (36%)	15,285 (22%)	10,179 (15%)	**50,442 (73%)**
	Social Sciences	2,270 (3%)	5,463 (8%)	6,586 (9%)	**14,319 (21%)**
	STEM	533 (1%)	1,948 (3%)	2,199 (3%)	**4,680 (7%)**
	All	**27,781 (40%)**	**22,696 (33%)**	**18,964 (27%)**	**69,441 (100%)**
Words	Arts & Humanities	274,497 (26%)	222,933 (21%)	155,565 (15%)	**652,995 (63%)**
	Social Sciences	26,692 (3%)	110,226 (11%)	138,813 (13%)	**275,731 (27%)**
	STEM	12,879 (1%)	48,501 (5%)	49,265 (5%)	**110,645 (11%)**
	All	**314,068 (30%)**	**381,660 (37%)**	**343,643 (33%)**	**1,039,371 (100%)**

Table 4: **BAREC** corpus statistics in documents, sentences, and words, across domain and readership levels.

4 BAREC Corpus

4.1 Corpus Selection

In the process of corpus selection, we aimed to cover a wide educational span as well as different domains and topics. We collected the corpus from $1,922$ documents, which we manually categorized into three domains: **Arts & Humanities**, **Social Sciences**, and **STEM**,[4] and three readership groups: **Foundational**, **Advanced**, and **Specialized**.[5] Table 4 shows the distribution of the documents, sentences and words across domains and groups. The corpus emphasizes educational coverage, with a higher-than-usual proportion of foundational-level texts. Domain variation reflects text availability and reader interest (more Arts & Humanities, less STEM). Texts were sourced from 30 resources, all either public domain, within fair use, or used with permission. Some were selected due to existing annotations. Notably, 25% of sentences came from new sources that were manually digitized. See Appendix C for resource details.

4.2 Readability Statistics

Figure 2 shows sentence distribution across **BAREC**-19 levels and their mappings to coarser levels (7, 5, and 3). The distribution is uneven, with 63% of sentences in the middle levels (**10-ya**∼fourth grade to **14-nun**∼ninth grade) reflecting natural text complexity and real-world usage.

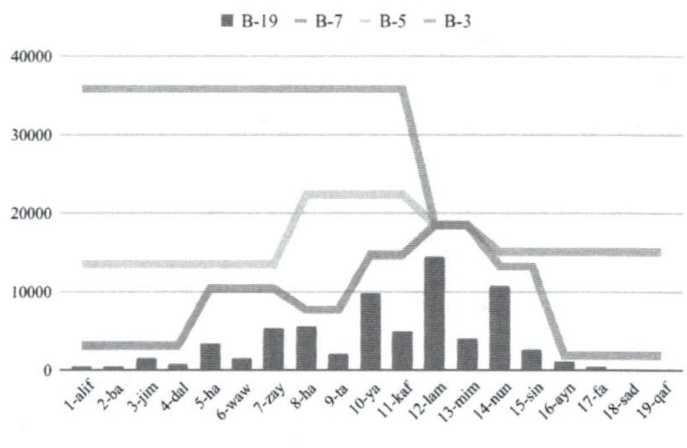

Figure 2: The distribution of sentences across **BAREC**-19 levels (blue), and their mapping to coarser levels.

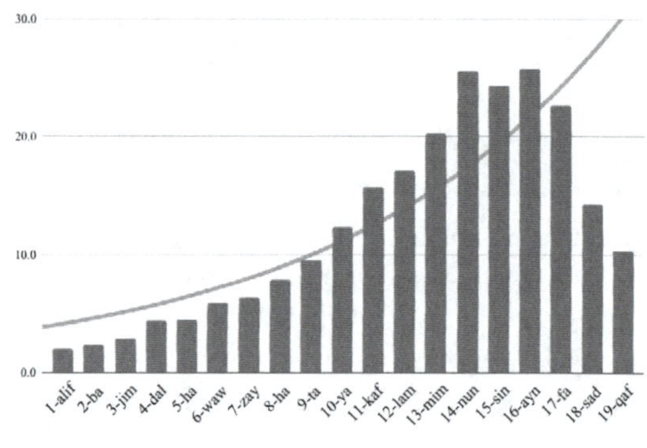

Figure 3: The average sentence word count across **BAREC**-19 levels, with trend line.

Figure 3 shows average sentence length by level, which correlates strongly with readability (Pearson r=81%). The drop at higher levels may result from shorter classical poetry lines.

Figure 4 shows *relative* distribution of readership groups and domains across readability levels. Foundational texts dominate lower levels and specialized texts higher ones. STEM and Social Science texts have a higher relative appearance in the upper mid levels.

[4]**Arts & Humanities:** literature, philosophy, religion, education, and related news. **Social Sciences:** business, law, social studies, education, and related news. **STEM:** science, technology, engineering, math, education, and related news.

[5]**Foundational:** Learners up to 4th grade (age 10), focused on basic literacy skills. **Advanced:** Adult readers with average abilities, handling moderate complexity texts. **Specialized:** Advanced readers (typically 9th grade+), engaging with domain specific texts.

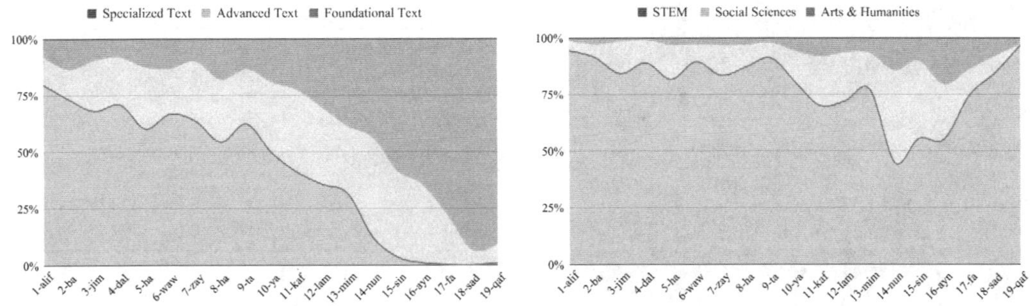

Figure 4: The relative distribution of readership groups and domains across **BAREC** levels.

5 Evaluation and Analysis

5.1 Metrics

We evaluate readability models and IAA using Accuracy, Adjacent Accuracy, Average Distance, and Quadratic Weighted Kappa (QWK), with QWK as our primary metric.

Accuracy (Acc) The percentage of cases where the predicted class matches the reference class in the 19-level scheme ($\mathbf{Acc}^{19}$), as well as three variants, $\mathbf{Acc}^{7}$, $\mathbf{Acc}^{5}$, and $\mathbf{Acc}^{3}$, which collapse the 19-level scheme into 7, 5, and 3 levels, respectively (Section 3.2).

Adjacent Accuracy (±1 $\mathbf{Acc}^{19}$) The proportion of predictions that are either exactly correct or off by at most one level.

Average Distance (Dist) The average absolute difference between two sets of labels. For example, the distance between **2-ba** and **4-dal** is 2.

Quadratic Weighted Kappa (QWK) An extension of Cohen's Kappa (Cohen, 1968; Doewes et al., 2023), measuring agreement between predicted and true labels, with a quadratic penalty for larger misclassifications.

5.2 Corpus Splits

We split the corpus at the document level into **Train (∼80%)**, **Dev (∼10%)**, and **Test (∼10%)**. Sentences from IAA studies are distributed across splits. For resources with existing splits, such as CamelTB (Habash et al., 2022) and ReadMe++ (Naous et al., 2024), we adopted their original splits. Table 5 reports the splits by documents, sentences, and words. Due to IAA and external corpus constraints, final proportions slightly deviate from exact 80-10-10. See Appendix B for full and split readability level distributions.

Split	#Documents	#Sentences	#Words
Train	1,518 (79%)	54,845 (79%)	832,743 (80%)
Dev	194 (10%)	7,310 (11%)	101,364 (10%)
Test	210 (11%)	7,286 (10%)	105,264 (10%)
All	1,922 (100%)	69,441 (100%)	1,039,371 (100%)

Table 5: **BAREC** corpus splits.

Stage	#Sets	Distance	$\mathbf{Acc}^{19}$	±1$\mathbf{Acc}^{19}$	QWK
Pilot 3	1	1.69	37.5%	58.5%	79.3%
Phase 1	2	1.38	48.4%	64.4%	80.2%
Phase 2A	6	1.21	49.4%	67.4%	72.4%
Phase 2B	10	0.80	67.6%	78.3%	78.8%
Overall / Macro	19	1.04	58.2%	72.3%	76.9%
Phase 2 / Macro	16	0.96	60.8%	74.2%	76.4%
Phase 2 / Micro	16	0.95	61.1%	74.4%	81.8%

Table 6: Average pairwise inter-annotator agreement (IAA) across different annotation stages. Macro/Micro indicate the form of averaging, over sets or sentences, respectively. Phase 2 = Phase 2A and 2B.

5.3 Inter-Annotator Agreement (IAA)

Pairwise Agreement Table 6 summarizes results for 19 IAA sets (excluding Pilots 1 and 2). We observe steady improvement from Pilot 3 to Phase 2B, with reduced distance and higher accuracy. The overall macro-average QWK is 76.9%, indicating substantial agreement and suggesting that most disagreements are minor (Cohen, 1968; Doewes et al., 2023). In Phase 2, the final and largest phase, the micro-average QWK rises to 81.8%.

Figure 5 presents a confusion matrix of sentence-level pairwise agreements for Phase 2 IAA sentences, using F-scores to account for the unbalanced level distribution. The strong diagonal (exact matches) reflects a high degree of agreement, consistent with the overall IAA results. However, accuracy varies across levels, with more disagree-

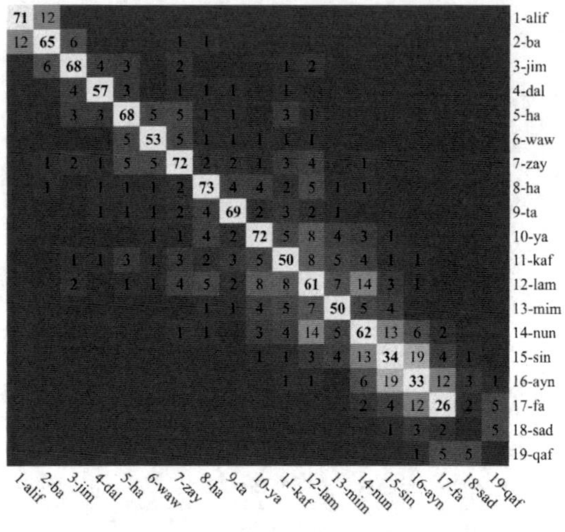

Figure 5: Confusion matrix for annotator pairwise agreement on Phase 2 IAA sentences normalized as F-scores.

ment at the harder higher levels. This may stem from the guidelines emphasizing vocabulary and content at the higher levels, features that are inherently more subjective than the textual feature cues used at lower levels.

Unification Agreement After each IAA study, annotators determined a unified readability level (UL) for each sentence. The UL falls within the Max-Min range of annotator labels 99.2% of the time and matches one of the annotators 86.8% of the time. Table 7 compares the micro-average performance of annotators in Phase 2, using both pairwise comparisons and the comparison between the UL and the rounded average level (AL) of annotators' choices. Table 7 also presents the results mapped to lower granularity levels (7, 5 and 3). We observe that overall, the AL-UL distance is smaller than the average pairwise distance among the annotators, and that its ±1 Acc is much higher, which suggests the average (AL) is more often than not closer to UL than any pair of annotators are to each other. The comparison across granularity levels shows that although the absolute Distance decreases, its relative magnitude (compared to the label range) increases. As expected, both Acc and ±1 Acc are higher with coarser level groupings. Appendix A.5 presents the results for each annotator against UL.

Error analysis To better understand annotator disagreement, we manually analyzed 100 randomly selected sentences with divergent readability labels. Table 8 presents representative examples

	19 Level	7 Level	5 Level	3 Level
Pairwise Distance	0.95	0.39	0.30	0.23
Relative to Range	5.0%	5.5%	6.0%	7.5%
Acc	61.1%	73.1%	75.2%	80.0%
±1 Acc	74.4%	92.0%	95.0%	97.3%
AL-UL Distance	0.52	0.26	0.22	0.18
Relative to Range	2.7%	3.7%	4.4%	5.9%
AL-UL Acc	61.2%	75.5%	78.9%	82.9%
AL-UL ±1 Acc	90.1%	98.5%	99.4%	99.5%

Table 7: Comparison of pairwise agreement micro averages across level granularities for all Phase 2 IAA sentences. UL = Unified Label; AL = Average Label.

with explanations. We found that 25% of disagreements were due to basic linguistic features (e.g., morphology, syntax, spelling), 12% involved emotional or symbolic content, 18% related to general advanced vocabulary, and 45% stemmed from domain-specific terminology in STEM, Humanities, or Social Sciences. This suggests that specialized vocabulary is the leading source of inconsistency, often due to differing expectations about what counts as general versus domain-specific language, and how specialization is defined. Some variation also stems from subjective views on what an *educated* Standard Arabic reader should know. In the future, we plan to develop readability lexicons to anchor our guidelines, building on efforts like the SAMER Lexicon (Al Khalil et al., 2020) and the Arabic Vocabulary Profile (Soliman and Familiar, 2024), but targeting 19 levels.

5.4 Automatic Readability Assessment

To establish a baseline for sentence-level readability classification, we fine-tune AraBERTv02 (Antoun et al., 2020) using the Transformers library (Wolf et al., 2019). Training is conducted on an NVIDIA V100 GPU for three epochs with a learning rate of 5×10^{-5}, a batch size of 64, and a cross-entropy loss function for multi-class classification across 19 levels. Table 9 presents the model's learning curve. We evaluate performance using varying proportions of the training data: $\frac{1}{8}$, $\frac{1}{4}$, $\frac{1}{2}$, and the full dataset. As shown in the table, model performance improves consistently with larger training data. Compared to the Phase 2 IAA micro averages (Table 6), the model's best Distance is 15.3% higher, and its best Accuracy is 5.3% absolute (8.7% relative) lower. However, the QWK is only marginally lower by just 0.8% absolute.

For a more extensive discussion of the automatic annotation results, see Elmadani et al. (2025).

Sentence (Arabic)	A1	A2	A3	A4	A5	UL	MM	Comments
أبي.. أبي.. *Dad .. Dad .. [lit. my father .. my father ..]*	2	2	2	3	3	**3**	*1*	First person singular pronoun is level 3.
احْتِضانُ الأُمِّ لَهُم. *The mother's embrace for them.*	9	12	5	5	5	**5**	*7*	Disagreement over احتضان 'embrace': standard or dialect aligned.
أشعر بالتعب والجوع.. *I feel tired and hungry..*	9	9	9	9	4	**9**	*5*	Vocabulary describing emotions (level 9).
يتم ضمان حيادية الإدارة بموجب القانون. *Administrative neutrality is guaranteed by law.*	12	12	12	14	12	**12**	*2*	Disagreement over حيادية 'neutrality': general advanced or specialized.

Table 8: Examples of Annotator Disagreements with Unified Levels (UL) and Max-Min Differences (MM)

Train	Distance	Acc^{19}	±1 Acc^{19}	QWK	Acc^{7}	Acc^{5}	Acc^{3}
12.5%	1.35	45.0%	61.3%	77.2%	56.8%	63.0%	71.3%
25.0%	1.33	46.9%	63.0%	77.6%	58.8%	64.3%	72.3%
50.0%	1.16	52.4%	68.1%	80.7%	62.9%	67.6%	74.0%
100.0%	1.09	55.8%	69.4%	81.0%	64.9%	69.1%	74.7%

Table 9: Performance at different training data sizes across multiple evaluation metrics.

6 Conclusions and Future Work

This paper presented the annotation guidelines of the Balanced Arabic Readability Evaluation Corpus (**BAREC**), a large-scale, finely annotated dataset for assessing Arabic text readability across 19 levels. With over 69K sentences and 1 million words, it is, to our knowledge, the largest Arabic readability corpus, covering diverse genres, topics, and audiences. We report high inter-annotator agreement (QWK 81.8% in Phase 2) that ensures reliable annotations. Benchmark results across multiple classification granularities (19, 7, 5, and 3 levels) demonstrate both the difficulty and feasibility of automated Arabic readability prediction.

Looking ahead, we plan to expand the corpus by increasing its size and diversity to include more genres and topics. We also aim to add annotations for vocabulary leveling and syntactic treebanks to study the effect of vocabulary and syntax on readability. Future work will analyze readability variations across genres and topics. Additionally, we intend to integrate our tools into a system that assists children's story writers in targeting specific reading levels.

The **BAREC** dataset, its annotation guidelines, and benchmark results, are publicly available to support future research and educational applications in Arabic readability assessment.[1]

Acknowledgments

The **BAREC** project is supported by the Abu Dhabi Arabic Language Centre (ALC) / Department of Culture and Tourism, UAE.

We acknowledge the support of the High Performance Computing Center at New York University Abu Dhabi.

We are deeply grateful to our outstanding annotation team: Mirvat Dawi, Reem Faraj, Rita Raad, Sawsan Tannir, and Adel Wizani, Samar Zeino, and Zeina Zeino.

Special thanks go to Karin Aghadjanian, and Omar Al Ayyoubi of the ALC for their continued support.

We would also like to thank the Zayed University ZAI Arabic Language Research Center team, in particular Hamda Al-Hadhrami, Maha Fatha, and Metha Talhak, for their valuable contributions to typing materials for the project. We also acknowledge Ali Gomaa and his team for their additional support in this area.

Finally, we thank our colleagues at the New York University Abu Dhabi Computational Approaches to Modeling Language (CAMeL) Lab, Muhammed Abu Odeh, Bashar Alhafni, Ossama Obeid, and Mostafa Saeed, as well as Nour Rabih (Mohamed bin Zayed University of Artificial Intelligence) for their helpful conversations and feedback.

Limitations

One notable limitation is the inherent subjectivity associated with readability assessment, which may introduce variability in annotation decisions despite our best efforts to maintain consistency. Additionally, the current version of the corpus may not fully capture the diverse linguistic landscape of the Arab world. Finally, while our methodology strives for inclusivity, there may be biases or gaps in the corpus due to factors such as selection bias in the source materials or limitations in the annotation process. We acknowledge that readability measures can be used with malicious intent to profile people; this is not our intention, and we discourage it.

Ethics Statement

All data used in the corpus curation process are sourced responsibly and legally. The annotation process is conducted with transparency and fairness, with multiple annotators involved to mitigate biases and ensure reliability. All annotators are paid fair wages for their contribution. The corpus and associated guidelines are made openly accessible to promote transparency, reproducibility, and collaboration in Arabic language research.

References

Ahmed Abdelali, Kareem Darwish, Nadir Durrani, and Hamdy Mubarak. 2016. Farasa: A fast and furious segmenter for Arabic. In *Proceedings of the Conference of the North American Chapter of the Association for Computational Linguistics (NAACL)*, pages 11–16, San Diego, California.

Abbas Mahmoud Al-Akkad. 1938. *Sarah*. Hindawi.

Imam Muhammad al Bukhari. 846. *Sahih al-Bukhari*. Dar Ibn Khathir.

M Al-Dawsari. 2004. The assessment of readability books content (boys-girls) of the first grade of intermediate school according to readability standards. *Sultan Qaboos University, Muscat*.

Hend S Al-Khalifa and Amani A Al-Ajlan. 2010. Automatic readability measurements of the Arabic text: An exploratory study. *Arabian Journal for Science and Engineering*, 35(2 C):103–124.

Muhamed Al Khalil, Nizar Habash, and Zhengyang Jiang. 2020. A large-scale leveled readability lexicon for Standard Arabic. In *Proceedings of the Twelfth Language Resources and Evaluation Conference*, pages 3053–3062, Marseille, France. European Language Resources Association.

Bayan Al-Safadi. 2005. *Al-Kashkoul: selection of poetry and prose for children* (الكشكول: مختارات من الشعر والنثر للأطفال). Al-Sa'ih Library (مكتبة السائح).

A. Alfaifi. 2015. *Building the Arabic Learner Corpus and a System for Arabic Error Annotation*. Ph.D. thesis, University of Leeds.

Bashar Alhafni, Reem Hazim, Juan David Pineros Liberato, Muhamed Al Khalil, and Nizar Habash. 2024. The SAMER Arabic text simplification corpus. In *Proceedings of the 2024 Joint International Conference on Computational Linguistics, Language Resources and Evaluation (LREC-COLING 2024)*, pages 16079–16093, Torino, Italia. ELRA and ICCL.

Richard L Allington, Kimberly McCuiston, and Monica Billen. 2015. What research says about text complexity and learning to read. *The Reading Teacher*, 68(7):491–501.

Shatha Altammami, Eric Atwell, and Ammar Alsalka. 2019. The arabic–english parallel corpus of authentic hadith. *International Journal on Islamic Applications in Computer Science And Technology-IJASAT*.

Wissam Antoun, Fady Baly, and Hazem Hajj. 2020. AraBERT: Transformer-based model for Arabic language understanding. In *Proceedings of the 4th Workshop on Open-Source Arabic Corpora and Processing Tools, with a Shared Task on Offensive Language Detection*, pages 9–15, Marseille, France. European Language Resource Association.

Amelia T. Barber and Susan L. Klauda. 2020. How reading motivation and engagement enable reading achievement: Policy implications. *Policy Insights from the Behavioral and Brain Sciences*, 7(1):27–34.

May Bashendy, Salam Albatarni, Sohaila Eltanbouly, Eman Zahran, Hamdo Elhuseyin, Tamer Elsayed, Walid Massoud, and Houda Bouamor. 2024. Qaes: First publicly-available trait-specific annotations for automated scoring of arabic essays. In *Proceedings of The Second Arabic Natural Language Processing Conference*, pages 337–351.

Houda Bouamor, Nizar Habash, Mohammad Salameh, Wajdi Zaghouani, Owen Rambow, Dana Abdulrahim, Ossama Obeid, Salam Khalifa, Fadhl Eryani, Alexander Erdmann, and Kemal Oflazer. 2018. The MADAR Arabic dialect corpus and lexicon. In *Proceedings of the Eleventh International Conference on Language Resources and Evaluation (LREC 2018)*, Miyazaki, Japan. European Language Resources Association (ELRA).

Jacob Cohen. 1968. Weighted kappa: Nominal scale agreement provision for scaled disagreement or partial credit. *Psychological bulletin*, 70(4):213.

Kevyn Collins-Thompson and James P. Callan. 2004. A language modeling approach to predicting reading difficulty. In *Proceedings of the Human Language Technology Conference of the North American Chapter of the Association for Computational Linguistics: HLT-NAACL 2004*, pages 193–200, Boston, Massachusetts, USA. Association for Computational Linguistics.

Tovly Deutsch, Masoud Jasbi, and Stuart Shieber. 2020. Linguistic features for readability assessment. In *Proceedings of the Fifteenth Workshop on Innovative Use of NLP for Building Educational Applications*, pages 1–17, Seattle, WA, USA → Online. Association for Computational Linguistics.

Afrizal Doewes, Nughthoh Arfawi Kurdhi, and Akrati Saxena. 2023. Evaluating quadratic weighted kappa as the standard performance metric for automated essay scoring. In *Proceedings of the 16th International Conference on Educational Data Mining*, pages 103–113, Bengaluru, India. International Educational Data Mining Society.

William H DuBay. 2004. The principles of readability. *Online Submission*.

Kais Dukes, Eric Atwell, and Nizar Habash. 2013. Supervised collaboration for syntactic annotation of quranic arabic. *Language resources and evaluation*, 47(1):33–62.

Matthias Eck and Chiori Hori. 2005. Overview of the IWSLT 2005 evaluation campaign. In *Proceedings of the Second International Workshop on Spoken Language Translation*, Pittsburgh, Pennsylvania, USA.

Mahmoud El-Haj and Paul Rayson. 2016. OSMAN — a novel Arabic readability metric. In *Proceedings of the Tenth International Conference on Language Resources and Evaluation (LREC'16)*, pages 250–255, Portorož, Slovenia. European Language Resources Association (ELRA).

Mo El-Haj, Sultan Almujaiwel, Damith Premasiri, Tharindu Ranasinghe, and Ruslan Mitkov. 2024. DARES: Dataset for Arabic readability estimation of school materials. In *Proceedings of the Workshop on DeTermIt! Evaluating Text Difficulty in a Multilingual Context @ LREC-COLING 2024*, pages 103–113, Torino, Italia. ELRA and ICCL.

Mo El-Haj and Saad Ezzini. 2024. The multilingual corpus of world's constitutions (MCWC). In *Proceedings of the 6th Workshop on Open-Source Arabic Corpora and Processing Tools (OSACT) with Shared Tasks on Arabic LLMs Hallucination and Dialect to MSA Machine Translation @ LREC-COLING 2024*, pages 57–66, Torino, Italia. ELRA and ICCL.

Khalid N. Elmadani, Nizar Habash, and Hanada Taha-Thomure. 2025. A large and balanced corpus for fine-grained Arabic readability assessment. In *Proceedings of the 63rd Annual Meeting of the Association for Computational Linguistics (ACL 2025)*, Vienna, Austria. Association for Computational Linguistics.

Lijun Feng, Martin Jansche, Matt Huenerfauth, and Noémie Elhadad. 2010. A comparison of features for automatic readability assessment. In *Coling 2010: Posters*, pages 276–284, Beijing, China. Coling 2010 Organizing Committee.

Jonathan Forsyth. 2014. Automatic readability prediction for modern standard Arabic. In *Proceedings of the Workshop on Open-Source Arabic Corpora and Processing Tools (OSACT)*.

Irene C Fountas and Gay Su Pinnell. 2006. *Leveled books (k-8): Matching texts to readers for effective teaching*. Heinemann Educational Books.

Nizar Habash, Muhammed AbuOdeh, Dima Taji, Reem Faraj, Jamila El Gizuli, and Omar Kallas. 2022. Camel treebank: An open multi-genre Arabic dependency treebank. In *Proceedings of the Thirteenth Language Resources and Evaluation Conference*, pages 2672–2681, Marseille, France. European Language Resources Association.

Nizar Habash and David Palfreyman. 2022. ZAEBUC: An annotated Arabic-English bilingual writer corpus. In *Proceedings of the Thirteenth Language Resources and Evaluation Conference*, pages 79–88, Marseille, France. European Language Resources Association.

Nizar Habash, Abdelhadi Soudi, and Tim Buckwalter. 2007. On Arabic Transliteration. In A. van den Bosch and A. Soudi, editors, *Arabic Computational Morphology: Knowledge-based and Empirical Methods*, pages 15–22. Springer, Netherlands.

Nizar Y Habash. 2010. *Introduction to Arabic natural language processing*, volume 3. Morgan & Claypool Publishers.

Muhamed Al Khalil, Hind Saddiki, Nizar Habash, and Latifa Alfalasi. 2018. A Leveled Reading Corpus of Modern Standard Arabic. In *Proceedings of the Language Resources and Evaluation Conference (LREC)*, Miyazaki, Japan.

Adam Kilgarriff, Frieda Charalabopoulou, Maria Gavrilidou, Janne Bondi Johannessen, Saussan Khalil, Sofie Johansson Kokkinakis, Robert Lew, Serge Sharoff, Ravikiran Vadlapudi, and Elena Volodina. 2014. Corpus-based vocabulary lists for language learners for nine languages. *Language Resources and Evaluation*, 48(1):121–163.

G.R. Klare. 1963. *The Measurement of Readability*. Iowa State University Press.

Fajri Koto, Haonan Li, Sara Shatnawi, Jad Doughman, Abdelrahman Sadallah, Aisha Alraeesi, Khalid Almubarak, Zaid Alyafeai, Neha Sengupta, Shady Shehata, Nizar Habash, Preslav Nakov, and Timothy Baldwin. 2024. ArabicMMLU: Assessing massive multitask language understanding in Arabic. In *Findings of the Association for Computational Linguistics: ACL 2024*, pages 5622–5640, Bangkok, Thailand. Association for Computational Linguistics.

Bruce W. Lee, Yoo Sung Jang, and Jason Lee. 2021. Pushing on text readability assessment: A transformer meets handcrafted linguistic features. In *Proceedings of the 2021 Conference on Empirical Methods in Natural Language Processing*, pages 10669–10686, Online and Punta Cana, Dominican Republic. Association for Computational Linguistics.

Juan Liberato, Bashar Alhafni, Muhamed Khalil, and Nizar Habash. 2024. Strategies for Arabic readability modeling. In *Proceedings of The Second Arabic Natural Language Processing Conference*, pages 55–66, Bangkok, Thailand. Association for Computational Linguistics.

Pierre Lison and Jörg Tiedemann. 2016. OpenSubtitles2016: Extracting Large Parallel Corpora from Movie and TV Subtitles. In *Proceedings of the Language Resources and Evaluation Conference (LREC)*, Portorož, Slovenia.

Farah Nadeem and Mari Ostendorf. 2018. Estimating linguistic complexity for science texts. In *Proceedings of the Thirteenth Workshop on Innovative Use of NLP for Building Educational Applications*, pages 45–55, New Orleans, Louisiana. Association for Computational Linguistics.

Tarek Naous, Michael J Ryan, Anton Lavrouk, Mohit Chandra, and Wei Xu. 2024. ReadMe++: Benchmarking multilingual language models for multi-domain readability assessment. In *Proceedings of the 2024 Conference on Empirical Methods in Natural Language Processing*, pages 12230–12266, Miami, Florida, USA. Association for Computational Linguistics.

Naoual Nassiri, Violetta Cavalli-Sforza, and Abdelhak Lakhouaja. 2023. Approaches, methods, and resources for assessing the readability of arabic texts. *ACM Trans. Asian Low-Resour. Lang. Inf. Process.*, 22(4).

Emily Pitler and Ani Nenkova. 2008. Revisiting readability: A unified framework for predicting text quality. In *Proceedings of the 2008 Conference on Empirical Methods in Natural Language Processing*, pages 186–195, Honolulu, Hawaii. Association for Computational Linguistics.

Hind Saddiki, Nizar Habash, Violetta Cavalli-Sforza, and Muhamed Al Khalil. 2018. Feature optimization for predicting readability of Arabic l1 and l2. In *Proceedings of the 5th Workshop on Natural Language Processing Techniques for Educational Applications*, pages 20–29.

Eli Smith and Cornelius Van Dyck. 1860. *New Testament (Arabic Translation)*.

Eli Smith and Cornelius Van Dyck. 1865. *Old Testament (Arabic Translation)*.

Rasha Soliman and Laila Familiar. 2024. Creating a CEFR Arabic vocabulary profile: A frequency-based multi-dialectal approach. *Critical Multilingualism Studies*, 11(1):266–286.

Hanada Taha-Thomure. 2007. *Poems and News (أشعار وأخبار)*. Educational Book House (دار الكتاب التربوي للنشر والتوزيع).

Hanada Taha-Thomure. 2017. *Arabic Language Text Leveling (معايير هنادا طه لتصنيف مستويات النصوص العربية)*. Educational Book House (دار الكتاب التربوي للنشر والتوزيع).

Toshiyuki Takezawa, Genichiro Kikui, Masahide Mizushima, and Eiichiro Sumita. 2007. Multilingual spoken language corpus development for communication research. In *International Journal of Computational Linguistics & Chinese Language Processing, Volume 12, Number 3, September 2007: Special Issue on Invited Papers from ISCSLP 2006*, pages 303–324.

Ibn Tufail. 1150. *Hayy ibn Yaqdhan*. Hindawi.

Unknown. 12th century. *One Thousand and One Nights*.

Sowmya Vajjala. 2022. Trends, limitations and open challenges in automatic readability assessment research. In *Proceedings of the Thirteenth Language Resources and Evaluation Conference*, pages 5366–5377, Marseille, France. European Language Resources Association.

Sowmya Vajjala and Ivana Lučić. 2018. OneStopEnglish corpus: A new corpus for automatic readability assessment and text simplification. In *Proceedings of the Thirteenth Workshop on Innovative Use of NLP for Building Educational Applications*, pages 297–304, New Orleans, Louisiana. Association for Computational Linguistics.

Sowmya Vajjala and Detmar Meurers. 2012. On improving the accuracy of readability classification using insights from second language acquisition. In *Proceedings of the Seventh Workshop on Building Educational Applications Using NLP*, pages 163–173, Montréal, Canada. Association for Computational Linguistics.

Thomas Wolf, Lysandre Debut, Victor Sanh, Julien Chaumond, Clement Delangue, Anthony Moi, Pierric Cistac, Tim Rault, R'emi Louf, Morgan Funtowicz, and Jamie Brew. 2019. Huggingface's transformers: State-of-the-art natural language processing. *ArXiv*, abs/1910.03771.

Menglin Xia, Ekaterina Kochmar, and Ted Briscoe. 2016. Text readability assessment for second language learners. In *Proceedings of the 11th Workshop on Innovative Use of NLP for Building Educational Applications*, pages 12–22, San Diego, CA. Association for Computational Linguistics.

Wei Xu, Chris Callison-Burch, and Courtney Napoles. 2015. Problems in current text simplification research: New data can help. *Transactions of the Association for Computational Linguistics*, 3:283–297.

A BAREC Annotation Guidelines Cheat Sheet and Annotation Interface

A.1 Arabic Original

مستوى بارق	صف	ACTFL	عدد كلمات	تهجئة وإملاء	تصريف واشتقاق	تراكيب نحوية	مفردات	فكرة ومحتوى
أ	روضة-1	مبتدئ أدنى	1	• كلمات من مقطع واحد أو مقطعين	• الفعل المضارع المفرد	• كلمة واحدة	• اسم جنس • اسم علم (متداول بسيط تركيبيا) • ضمير منفصل • مفردات متطابقة مع العامية - سامر I • الأرقام (العربية أو الهندية) 1-10	• فكرة مباشرة وصريحة وحسية. • لا رمزية في النص.
ب	1	مبتدئ أدنى	≤2	• كلمات من 3 مقاطع		• جملة اسمية (هو يلعب) • إضافة حقيقية (باب البيت) • صفة وموصوف (باب كبير)	• فعل • صفة • مفردات متشابهة مع العامية - سامر I • العدد الأصلي بالأحرف • الأسماء الخمسة: أبو، أخو	
ج		مبتدئ متوسط	≤4	• كلمات من 3 مقاطع	• سوابق: ال التعريف • سوابق: واو العطف • لواحق: ضمير المتكلم المفرد المتصل	• بدل كل: (صديقي أحمد) • بدل إشارة: (هذا البيت)	• مفردات فصيحة شائعة - سامر I • اسم الإشارة المفرد • الأرقام (العربية أو الهندية) 11-100	
د		مبتدئ متوسط	≤6	• كلمات تستخدم مد الألف (آ)	• الفعل المضارع الجمع • سوابق: حروف جر متصلة • ظرف منون	• جملة فعلية بدون مفعول به • جار ومجرور	• حروف الجر	
ه	2	مبتدئ أعلى	≤8	• كلمات من 4 مقاطع	• لواحق: ضمير متصل مفرد أو جمع • المثنى (في الأسماء والصفات) • جمع المؤنث السالم	• جملة فعلية مع مفعول به واحد اسم • جمل معطوفة • أدوات استفهام أساسية: ماذا، متى، من، أين، ما، كيف • صيغة التعجب "ما أفعل"	• العدد الترتيبي • الأرقام (العربية أو الهندية) 101-1,000 • اسم اشارة مثنى، جمع	• المحتوى من حياة القارئ. • لا رمزية في النص.
و		مبتدئ أعلى	≤9	• كلمات من 5 مقاطع	• الفعل الماضي المفرد والجمع • جمع مذكر سالم	• جملة فيها فعلين (مثلا جملة فعلية مفعولها أن المصدرية)	• مفردات فصيحة - سامر I	
ز		متوسط أدنى	≤10	• كلمات من +6 مقاطع • أفعال/أسماء معتلة الأخر	• الفعل الماضي المثنى •الفعل المضارع المثنى • فعل الأمر المفرد • لواحق: ضمير المثنى المتصل • جمع التكسير • واو القسم (والله)	• مفعول فيه (ظروف زمان ومكان) • حال • أداة الاستفهام هل	• مفردات فصيحة شائعة - سامر II	• بعض الرمزية أو عدم التصريح المباشر بكل المقصود في الجملة
ح	3	متوسط أدنى	≤11		• فعل الأمر الجمع • نون النسوة في الأسماء والأفعال • سوابق أخرى: سين الاستقبال، واو الاستئناف، فاء العطف • أدوات ربط (ثم، حتى، أو، أم، لكن، أمّا)	• المفعول المطلق • المفعول لأجله • المفعول معه • جملة فعلية تتعدى إلى مفعولين	• مفردات فصيحة - سامر I و سامر II • أحرف النفي • الأرقام (العربية أو الهندية) 1,001-1,000,000	• بعض الرمزية يحتاج معها القارئ إلى مساعدة من يشرح له المقصود من الفكرة
ط		متوسط أوسط	≤12		• فعل الأمر للمثنى • أداة الاستفهام: أ (أسمعتَ؟) • باء القسم • القسم: أداة القسم والمقسم به وجواب القسم.	• المنادى	• مفردات تصف حالات مزاجية وشعورية إيجابية وسلبية مثل الفرح، السعادة، الغضب، الأسف، الحسرة	• هناك شيء من الرمزية على مستوى الحدث في الجملة يدركها القارئ بنفسه أو من خلال معارفه السابقة
ي	4	متوسط أوسط	≤15		• المبني للمجهول	• إن وأخواتها • كان وأخواتها • خبر مقدم / مبتدأ مؤخر • العنعنة/السند • رُبّ (حرف جر شبيه بالزائد) • جملة الصلة وجملة الصفة • جملة الحال وجملة المفعول به	• أسماء الوصل المفردة • (قد – لقد) • (ممّا – عمّا – عمَّ – علامَ – فيمَ – إلامَ - بِمَ...)	
ك		متوسط أعلى	≤20		• المشتقات العاملة (مثلا اسم الفاعل)	• جملة أسمية خبرها جملة أسمية • إضافة لفظية (طويل القامة)	• أسماء الوصل المثنى والجمع	• هناك درجة من الرمزية وحاجة للمعرفة السابقة كي يُفهم المقصود من الجملة
ل	5	متقدم أدنى			• التصغير	• جمل اعتراضية (تفسير، دعاء) • استثناء • حصر • بدل (مثلا بدل بعض أو اشتمال) • تمييز	• مفردات فصيحة - سامر III • اسم الفعل (مثلا آمين) • الأرقام (العربية أو الهندية > 1,000,000 • ذو • (بل - بلى - أجل - قط)	
م	6-7	متقدم أوسط			• نون التوكيد • تاء القسم	• الجمل شرطية (مركبة - عادية) • حرف الجزم لما	• كلمات تصف حالات نفسية عميقة مثل الاكتئاب، الضياع، الاستنفار النفسي • استخدام كلمات منحوتة غير متداولة (مثلا هجرع للخفيف الأحمق مشتقة من هرع و هجع) • الرموز (ش.م.)	• أفكار رمزية ومعنى باطن خاصة على صعيد البعد النفسي للشخصيات أو الأحداث.
ن	8-9	متقدم أعلى				• التوكيد المعنوي • المدح والذم • جملة أن المصدرية في محل رفع مبتدأ • صيغة التعجب "أفعل به من"	• مفردات فصيحة - سامر IV • مفردات قانونية، علمية، دينية، سياسية،... غير متخصصة/عامة • فو - حمو	• تعابير ثقافية محلية قد لا يفهمها من لا يشترك في نفس الثقافة.
س	10-11	متقن أدنى				• تراكيب غير متداولة فيها التباس يحتاج إلى التشكيل الإعرابي لفكه	• المفردات المتخصصة التي لا تكفي معرفة الكلمة وحدها لفهمها، وإنما يحتاج إلى معرفة الفكرة/المفهوم لفهمها • الترخيم في أسماء العلم (مثلا أفاطم؟)	• أفكار رمزية، مجردة، علمية، أو شعرية وتحتاج إلى معارف لغوية ومعرفية سابقة للبناء عليها لأجل فهمها
ع	12	متقن أوسط					• مفردات فصيحة - سامر V • مفردات متخصصة ومفردات عربية عالية غير شائعة كثيرا في الفضاء العام. • مفردات في الغالب بعيدة عن اللهجات العامية.	
ف	جامعة 1-2	متقن أعلى					• مفردات عِلمية وتراثية غير متداولة اليوم وغير مألوفة لغير المتخصص المبتدئ	
ص	جامعة 3-4	متفوق					• مفردات عِلمية وتراثية غير متداولة اليوم وغير مألوفة لغير المتخصص	
ق	متخصص	متميز					• مفردات عِلمية وتراثية غير متداولة اليوم وغير مألوفة لغير المتخصص الباحث	
هناك صعوبة	هذا الوسم يستخدم في حالة وجود صعوبة في تقييم المستوى، المفضل استخدام هذا الوسم حتى نتمكن كفريق عمل أن نجد حلا (مثلا بتعديل المعايير أو إضافة تفاصيل شرحية لها)							
هناك مشكلة	بصورة عامة، نستخدم هذا الوسم للجمل الحاوية على:				• أخطاء إملائية (مثلا همزات، تاء مربوطة، ألف مقصورة/ياء) • أخطاء في التشكيل • ركاكة لغوية (أمية، عامية، ترجمة سيئة من لغة أجنبية) • مواضيع غير لائقة (عنصرية، حيازية، تنمرية، إباحية، إلخ) • جمل وعبارات معظمها مكتوب بلغات غير العربية أو بغير الخط العربي	ولكن في الحالات التالية نوسم الجمل ونضيف أحد الحروف التالية في عامود الملاحظات: • خطأ في همزة الوصل/همزة القطع >> (أ) • كلمات خادشة >> (ع) • الخطأ في التشكيل في بداية الجملة >> (ت) • الياء غير المنقوطة في آخر الكلمة >> (ي)		

A.2 English Translation

BAREC Level	Grade	ACTFL	Word Count	Spelling/Pronunciation	Morphology	Syntax	Vocabulary	Idea/Content
1-alif	Pre1-1	Novice Low	1	• One-syllable and two-syllable words	• Singular imperfective verb	• One word	• Common noun • Proper noun (frequent and simple) • Personal pronouns (non-clitics) • Vocabulary identical to dialectal form - SAMER I • Numbers (Arabic or Indo-Arabic) 1-10	• Direct, explicit, and concrete idea. • No symbolism in the text.
2-ba	1	Novice Low	≤2	• Three-syllable words			• Verb • Adjective • Vocabulary similar to dialectal form - SAMER I • Spelled cardinal numbers • The five nouns: *Abw (father)*, *Axw (brother)*	
3-jim		Novice Mid	≤4		• Prtoclitic: Definite article *Al+* • Proclitic: Conjunction *wa+* • Enclitic: First Person Singular pronoun	• Apposition (full) • Demonstratives	• Common MSA vocabulary - SAMER I • Singular demonstrative pronoun • Numbers: 11-100	
4-dal		Novice Mid	≤6	• Words with an elongated Alif (e.g. /ʔāsif/)	• Plural imperfective verb • Prepositional proclitics • Nunated adverbials	• Verbal sentence w/o direct object • Preposition and object	• Prepositions	
5-ha	2	Novice High	≤8	• Four-syllable words	• Enclitic: Singular and Plural pronouns • Dual (in nouns and adjectives) • Sound feminine plural	• Verbal sentence with one nominal direct object • Conjoined sentences • Basic interrogative particles: what, when, who, where, how • Exclamatory form: how <comparative adjective>	• Ordinal numbers • Numbers: 101-1,000 • Dual and plural demonstrative pronoun	• Content is from the reader's life. • No symbolism in the text.
6-waw		Novice High	≤9	• Five-syllable words	• Singular and plural perfective verb • Sound masculine plural	• Sentence with two verbs (e.g., a verbal sentence a clausal direct object introduced with *Masdar 'an [~to/that]*)	• MSA vocabulary - SAMER I	
7-zay		Intermediate Low	≤10	• Six-syllable or more words • Verbs/nouns with weak final letters	• Dual perfective verb • Dual imperfective verb • Singular imperative verb • Enclitics: dual pronoun • Broken plurals • Waw of oath	• Adverbial accusative (time and place adverbs) • Circumstantial accusative • Interrogative particle *hal*	• High frequency MSA vocabulary - SAMER II	• Some symbolism, or not everything is stated directly in the sentence.
8-ha	3	Intermediate Low	≤11		• Plural imperative verb • Feminine plural suffix (*nun*) in nouns and verbs • Other proclitics: future *sa+*, continuation *wa+*, conjunction *fa+* • Conjunctions (e.g., then, until, or, whether, but, as for)	• Absolute object (emphasizing the verb) • Object of purpose • Object of accompaniment • Verbal sentence with two direct objects	• MSA vocabulary - SAMER I and II • Negation particles • Numbers: 1,001-1,000,000	• Some symbolism that requires the reader to seek help to understand the idea.
9-ta		Intermediate Mid	≤12		• Dual imperative verb • Interrogative Hamza • Ba of oath • Oath: The particle of oath, the object of the oath, and the answer to the oat	• Vocative	• Vocabulary describing positive and negative emotional and mood states like joy, happiness, anger, regret, sorrow	• Some symbolism at the event level in the sentence that the reader understands through prior knowledge.
10-ya	4	Intermediate Mid	≤15		• Passive voice	• *Inna* and its sisters (particles introducing a subject) • *Kana* and its sisters (past tense verbs) • Preposed predicate, postponed subject • Chain of narration • *rubba* preposition construction • Relative clauses • Circumstantial and object clauses	• Singular relative pronouns • Verbal particles *qad* and *laqad* • Preposition-Conjunctions: *mimma*, *fima*...	
11-kaf		Intermediate High	≤20		• Acting derivatives (e.g., the active participle)	• Nominal sentence with a nominal predicate • False idafa (tall in stature)	• Dual and plural relative pronouns	• A degree of symbolism and a need for prior knowledge to understand the meaning of the sentence.
12-lam	5	Advanced Low			• Diminutive form	• Parentheticals (explanation, blessing) • Exception • Exclusivity • Apposition (e.g., partitive or containing) • Specification (*tamyiyz* construction)	• MSA vocabulary - Samer III • Frozen Verbs (e.g., *Āmiyn* Amen) • Numbers: > 1,000,000 • Five Nouns: Dhu (possession nominal) • Interjections: *bala*, *Ajal*, etc.	
13-mim	6-7	Advanced Mid			• Energetic mood (emphatic *nun*) • Ta of oath	• Conditional sentences • Jussive particle *lamma* (not yet)	• Words describing deep psychological states like depression, loss, psychological alertness • Use of coined, uncommon words • Abbreviations (e.g., LLC)	• Symbolic ideas and deeper meanings, especially in terms of the psychological dimension of characters/events. • Local cultural expressions that may not be understood by those outside the
14-nun	8-9	Advanced High				• Semantic emphasis • Praise and dispraise • *Masdar 'an* clause as a subject • Exclamatory form: <comparative adjective> *bih min*	• MSA vocabulary - SAMER IV • General legal, scientific, religious, political vocabulary, etc. • Five Nouns: *fw*, *Hmw*	
15-sin	10-11	Superior Low				• Uncommon constructions that are ambiguous and need diacritization for clarification	• Specialized vocabulary that requires understanding the concept/idea to comprehend it • Shortening in proper names (e.g., *fatim* for *fatima*)	• Symbolic, abstract, scientific, or poetic ideas that require prior linguistic and cognitive knowledge to understand.
16-ayn	12	Superior Mid					• MSA vocabulary - SAMER V • Specialized and highly elevated Arabic vocabulary. • Vocabulary mostly distant from dialects.	
17-fa	University Year 1-2	Superior High					• Scientific and heritage vocabulary not in use today, but familiar to a novice specialist	
18-sad	University Year 3-4	Distinguished					• Scientific and heritage vocabulary not in use today, but familiar to a specialist	
19-qaf	Specialist	Distinguished+					• Scientific and heritage vocabulary not in use today, but familiar to the advanced researcher specialist	
Difficulty	This tag is used when there is difficulty in assessing the level. It is preferred to use this tag so that the team can find a solution (for example, by adjusting the criteria or adding explanatory details).							
Problem	Generally, we use this tag for sentences containing:		• Spelling mistakes (e.g., Hamzas, Ta Marbuta, Alif maqsura/Ya) • Errors in diacritics • Linguistic awkwardness (illiteracy, colloquialism, poor translation from a foreign language) • Inappropriate topics (racism, bias, bullying, pornography, etc.) • Sentences and phrases mostly written in languages other than Arabic or in non-Arabic script			However, in the following cases, we provide the level and add a note in the comments column: • Error in Hamzat al-Wasl/Hamzat al-Qat' >> (أ) • Offensive words >> (ع) • Error in diacritics at the beginning of the sentence >> (ث) • Dotted Yaa missing at the end of the word >> (ي)		

A.3 Annotation Interface

Sentence/Phrase	Length	Level		Word Count	Spelling/Pronunciation	Morphology	Syntax	Vocabulary	Idea/Content	Notes
الجملة \ العبارة	عدد الكلمات	المستوى		عدد الكلمات	تهجئة/إملاء	تصريف واشتقاق	تراكيب نحوية	مفردات	فكرة / محتوى	ملاحظات
خَبَّرَ	1	و (صف 2)	6-waw	٩ هو أعلى عدد كلمات مطبعية غير متكررة بدون علامات الترقيم	• كلمات من ٥ مقاطع (بدون حساب حركات الإعراب)	• الفعل الماضي المفرد والجمع • جمع مذكر سالم	• جملة فيها فعلين (مثلا جملة فعلية مفعولها أن المصدرية)	• مفردات فصيحة - سامر ١	• المحتوى من حياة القارئ. • لا رمزية في النص.	
جودي بقربي	2	ز (صف 2)	7-zay	١٠ هو أعلى عدد كلمات مطبعية غير متكررة بدون علامات الترقيم	• كلمات من ٦ مقاطع أو أكثر (بدون حساب حركات الإعراب) • أفعال/أسماء معتلة الآخر	• الفعل الماضي المثنى •الفعل المضارع المثنى • فعل الأمر المفرد • جمع التكسير • واو القسم (والله)	• مفعول فيه (ظروف زمان ومكان) • حال • أداة الاستفهام هل	• مفردات فصيحة شائعة - سامر ٢	• بعض الرمزية أو عدم التصريح المباشر بكل المقصود في الجملة	
بيروت في يوليو ١٩٦٦	4	ح (صف 3)	8-ha	١١ هو أعلى عدد كلمات مطبعية غير متكررة بدون علامات الترقيم		• فعل الأمر الجمع • نون النسوة في الأسماء والأفعال (انتظرنَ دورهنّ) • سوابق أخرى: سين الاستقبال ، واو الاستئناف، فاء العطف • (ثم ، حتى ، أو ، أم ، لكن ، أمّا)	• المفعول المطلق • المفعول لأجله • المفعول معه • جملة فعلية تتعدى إلى مفعولين	• مفردات فصيحة - سامر ١ و سامر ٢ • أحرف النفي • الأرقام (العربية أو الهندية) 1,000,000-1,001	• بعض الرمزية يحتاج معها القارئ إلى مساعدة من يشرح له المقصود من الفكرة	
كتابةُ خطَّةٍ لمشروعِ الوحدةِ	4	ك (صف 4)	11-kaf	٢٠ هو أعلى عدد كلمات مطبعية غير متكررة بدون علامات الترقيم		• المشتقات على أنواعها (نركز على المشتقات العاملة لاسيما اسم الفاعل واسم المفعول)	• جملة أسمية خبرها جملة أسمية (فيها مبتدآن) • إضافة خيالية (لفظية) طويل القامة	• أسماء الوصل المثنى والجمع • متلازمات لفظية مثل شارد الذهن، وارف الظلال	• هناك درجة من الرمزية وحاجة للمعرفة السابقة كي يُفهم المقصود من الجملة	
اجْتَمَعَ الأَهْلُ في الْعيدِ.	4	و (صف 2)	6-waw	٩ هو أعلى عدد كلمات مطبعية غير متكررة بدون علامات الترقيم	• كلمات من ٥ مقاطع (بدون حساب حركات الإعراب)	• الفعل الماضي المفرد والجمع • جمع مذكر سالم	• جملة فيها فعلين (مثلا جملة فعلية مفعولها أن المصدرية)	• مفردات فصيحة - سامر ١	• المحتوى من حياة القارئ. • لا رمزية في النص.	
وَلا يُخَالِطُنا عَجْزٌ وَلا خَورُ	4	ل (صف 5)	12-lam	لا حد لعدد الكلمات المطبعية		• التصغير	• جمل اعتراضية (تفسير - دعاء...) • استثناء • حصر • البدل (غير حالات ما بعد اسم الإشارة) • تمييز	• مفردات فصيحة - سامر ٣ • اسم الفعل : إيهِ - صَهْ - آمين - حَيَّ - هَاؤُم - هاكَ - هَيَّا - هيتَ - هَلُمَّ إلى - مَهْ - رويدَكَ - • الأرقام (العربية أو الهندية < 1,000,000 • ذو • (بل - بلى - أجل)	• هناك درجة من الرمزية وحاجة للمعرفة السابقة كي يُفهم المقصود من الجملة	

This is a screenshot of the Google Sheet interface used for annotation. The first two columns on the left are the sentence and its word count. The third column is the readability level which is selected by drop down menus. The fourth yellow column and the first yellow row are not part of the interface, we added them for the purpose of explaining the structure to readers of this paper who do not know Arabic. The next 6 columns automatically display the text features from the annotation guidelines to help the annotators confirm their choices. The last column is for extra notes such as flagging problematic sentences.

A.4 Annotation Team

	$A0^P$	A1	A2	A3	A4	$A5^L$
Native Language	Arabic	Arabic	Arabic	Arabic	Arabic	Arabic
Other Language	En, Fr	En	En, Fr	En, Fr	En, Fr	En, Fr
Nationality	Syrian	Lebanese	Lebanese	Lebanese	Lebanese	Lebanese
Residence	USA	Lebanon	Lebanon	Lebanon	UAE	Lebanon
Gender	Female	Female	Female	Female	Female	Female
Background	Muslim	Muslim	Muslim	Muslim	Christian	Muslim
Degree	MA	BA	BA	MA	MA	B MA
Major	Applied Ling.	Arabic Lit.	Geography	Arabic Lit.	Arabic Lit.	Arabic Lit.
Experience	CT, LA, RA	PT, LA	PT, LA	CT, LA	CT, LA	CT, LA, RA
School	Private	-	-	Public&Private	Private	Public
Level	University	Elementary	Elementary	Secondary	Secondary	Secondary
Students	L2	L1	L1	L1	L1	L1
Years	16	16	22	22	8	25

Table 10: Annotator background information. All have extensive linguistic annotation experience. Certified Teacher (CT), Private Tutor (PT), Linguistic Annotator (LA), Research Assistant (RA). $\mathbf{A0}^P$ is the preprocessing and segmentation lead; and $\mathbf{A5}^L$ is the readability annotation lead.

A.5 Inter-Annotator Agreement between Annotator Labels and Unified Labels

	Acc^{19}	± 1 Acc^{19}	Dist	QWK	Acc^{7}	Acc^{5}	Acc^{3}
A1	78.4%	89.0%	0.42	93.4%	85.3%	87.0%	89.7%
A2	65.1%	76.4%	0.87	82.2%	71.6%	73.6%	79.3%
A3	66.4%	78.4%	0.78	86.0%	73.7%	75.8%	79.0%
A4	63.7%	76.6%	0.86	83.8%	71.8%	74.2%	79.5%
A5	85.1%	91.2%	0.31	94.8%	89.2%	90.3%	92.9%
Avg	71.7%	82.3%	0.65	88.1%	78.4%	80.2%	84.1%

Table 11: Inter-Annotator Agreement (IAA) results comparing initial annotations by A1-A5 to unified labels (UL).

B BAREC Corpus Level Distributions Across Splits

Level	All	%	Train	%	Dev	%	Test	%
1-alif	409	1%	333	1%	44	1%	32	0%
2-ba	437	1%	333	1%	68	1%	36	0%
3-jim	1,462	2%	1,139	2%	182	2%	141	2%
4-dal	751	1%	587	1%	78	1%	86	1%
5-ha	3,443	5%	2,646	5%	417	6%	380	5%
6-waw	1,534	2%	1,206	2%	189	3%	139	2%
7-zay	5,438	8%	4,152	8%	701	10%	585	8%
8-ḫa	5,683	8%	4,529	8%	613	8%	541	7%
9-ṯa	2,023	3%	1,597	3%	236	3%	190	3%
10-ya	9,763	14%	7,741	14%	1,012	14%	1,010	14%
11-kaf	4,914	7%	4,041	7%	409	6%	464	6%
12-lam	14,471	21%	11,318	21%	1,491	20%	1,662	23%
13-mim	4,039	6%	3,252	6%	349	5%	438	6%
14-nun	10,687	15%	8,573	16%	1,072	15%	1,042	14%
15-sin	2,547	4%	2,016	4%	258	4%	273	4%
16-ayn	1,141	2%	866	2%	114	2%	161	2%
17-fa	480	1%	364	1%	49	1%	67	1%
18-sad	103	0%	67	0%	13	0%	23	0%
19-qaf	116	0%	85	0%	15	0%	16	0%
Total	69,441	100%	54,845	100%	7,310	100%	7,286	100%

Table 12: Distribution of sentence counts and percentages across readability levels and data splits.

C BAREC Corpus Sources

We present the corpus sources in groups of their general intended purpose.

Some datasets are chosen because they already have annotations available for other tasks. We list them independently of other collections they may be part of. For example, dependency treebank annotations exist (Habash et al., 2022) for the texts we included from the Arabian Nights, Quran and Hadith, Old and New Testament, Suspended Odes Odes, and Sara (which comes from Hindawi Foundation).

C.1 Education

Emarati Curriculum The first five units of the UAE curriculum textbooks for the 12 grades in three subjects: Arabic language, social studies, Islamic studies (Khalil et al., 2018).

ArabicMMLU 6,205 question and answer pairs from the ArabicMMLU benchmark dataset (Koto et al., 2024).

Zayed Arabic-English Bilingual Undergraduate Corpus (ZAEBUC) 100 student-written articles from the Zayed University Arabic-English Bilingual Undergraduate Corpus (Habash and Palfreyman, 2022).

Arabic Learner Corpus (ALC) 16 L2 articles from the Arabic Learner Corpus (Alfaifi, 2015).

Basic Travel Expressions Corpus (BTEC) 20 documents from the MSA translation of the Basic Traveling Expression Corpus (Eck and Hori, 2005; Takezawa et al., 2007; Bouamor et al., 2018).

Collection of Children poems Example of the included poems: My language sings (لغتي تغني), and Poetry and news (أشعار وأخبار) (Al-Safadi, 2005; Taha-Thomure, 2007).

ChatGPT To add more children's materials, we ask Chatgpt to generate 200 sentences ranging from 2 to 4 words per sentence, 150 sentences ranging from 5 to 7 words per sentence and 100 sentences ranging from 8 to 10 words per sentence.[6] Not all sentences generated by ChatGPT were correct. We discarded some sentences that were flagged by the annotators. Table 13 shows the prompts and the percentage of discarded sentences for each prompt.

[6] https://chatgpt.com/

C.2 Literature

Hindawi A subset of 264 books extracted from the Hindawi Foundation website across different different genres.[7]

Kalima The first 500 words of 62 books from Kalima project.[8]

Green Library 58 manually typed books from the Green Library.[9]

Arabian Nights The openings and endings of the opening narrative and the first eight nights from the Arabian Nights (Unknown, 12th century). We extracted the text from an online forum.[10]

Hayy ibn Yaqdhan A subset of the philosophical novel and allegorical tale written by Ibn Tufail (Tufail, 1150). We extracted the text from the Hindawi Foundation website.[11]

Sara The first 1000 words of *Sara*, a novel by Al-Akkad first published in 1938 (Al-Akkad, 1938). We extracted the text from the Hindawi Foundation website.[12]

The Suspended Odes (Odes) The ten most celebrated poems from Pre-Islamic Arabia (المعلقات Mu'allaqat). All texts were extracted from Wikipedia.[13]

C.3 Media

Majed 10 manually typed editions of Majed magazine for children from 1983 to 2019.[14]

ReadMe++ The Arabic split of the ReadMe++ dataset (Naous et al., 2024).

Spacetoon Songs The opening songs of 53 animated children series from Spacetoon channel.

Subtitles A subset of the Arabic side of the OpenSubtitles dataset (Lison and Tiedemann, 2016).

WikiNews 62 Arabic WikiNews articles covering politics, economics, health, science and technology, sports, arts, and culture (Abdelali et al., 2016).

[7] https://www.hindawi.org/books/categories/
[8] https://alc.ae/publications/kalima/
[9] https://archive.org/details/201409_201409
[10] http://al-nada.eb2a.com/1000lela&lela/
[11] https://www.hindawi.org/books/90463596/
[12] https://www.hindawi.org/books/72707304/
[13] https://ar.wikipedia.org/wiki/المعلقات
[14] https://archive.org/details/majid_magazine

Prompt	Targeted #Words per Sentence	Prompt Text	% Discarded
Prompt 1	2-4	I am creating a children's textbook to practice reading in Arabic. I need short sentences containing 2 to 4 words that are limited to children's vocabulary. Give me 200 sentences in Standard Arabic -- no need to include English.	1.5%
	Examples	الشمس مشرقة. البنت تأكل الفاكهة.	
Prompt 2	5-7	I am creating a children's textbook to practice reading in Arabic. I need 5-word, 6-word, and 7-word sentences that are limited to children's vocabulary. Give me 150 sentences in Standard Arabic -- no need to include English.	1.3%
	Examples	الأسد ينام تحت شجرة كبيرة. الأطفال يلعبون في الملعب ويضحكون بسعادة كبيرة.	
Prompt 3	8-10	I am creating a children's textbook to practice reading in Arabic. I need long sentences (8-word, 9-word, and 10-word sentences) that are limited to children's vocabulary. Give me 100 sentences in Standard Arabic -- no need to include English.	1.0%
	Examples	الأرنب يقفز فوق العشب الأخضر في الصباح الباكر. القرد يتسلق الأشجار بسرعة ويقفز ببراعة من فرع إلى فرع.	

Table 13: ChatGPT Prompts. % Discarded is the percentage of discarded sentences due to grammatical errors.

C.4 References

Wikipedia A subset of 168 Arabic wikipedia articles covering Culture, Figures, Geography, History, Mathematics, Sciences, Society, Philosophy, Religions and Technologies.[15]

Constitutions The first 2000 words of the Arabic constitutions from 16 Arabic speaking countries, collected from MCWC dataset (El-Haj and Ezzini, 2024).

UN The Arabic translation of the Universal Declaration of Human Rights.[16]

C.5 Religion

Old Testament The first 20 chapters of the Book of Genesis (Smith and Van Dyck, 1865).[17]

New Testament The first 16 chapters of the Book of Matthew (Smith and Van Dyck, 1860).[17]

Quran The first three Surahs and the last 14 Surahs from the Holy Quran. We selected the text from the Quran Corpus Project (Dukes et al., 2013).[18]

Hadith The first 75 Hadiths from Sahih Bukhari (al Bukhari, 846). We selected the text from the LK Hadith Corpus[19] (Altammami et al., 2019).

[15] https://ar.wikipedia.org/

[16] https://www.un.org/ar/about-us/universal-declaration-of-human-rights

[17] https://www.arabicbible.com/

[18] https://corpus.quran.com/

[19] https://github.com/ShathaTm/LK-Hadith-Corpus

Author Index